POLITICAL WILL

Those who cannot remember the past
are condemned to repeat it.
GEORGE SANTAYANA
~

Each time history repeats itself, the price goes up
AUTHOR UNKNOWN
~

History is who we are
and why we are the way we are.
DAVID MCCULLOUGH
~

POLITICAL WILL

Dominating Force in American History

by Bill Loughrey

Scholarly & Specialized Publishing

CHARLOTTESVILLE, VIRGINIA

Scholarly & Specialized Publishing
1745 Gravel Hill Road
Dillwyn, Virginia
www.scholarlypub.com
©2009 by Bill Loughrey
First Edition
All rights reserved.
Printed in the United States of America.
Library of Congress Control Number: 2008944370
ISBN 978-0-9821057-0-2

COVER ART: BARNRAISING, CIRCA 1900

To

Phoebe, Elsbeth, and Schuyler Loughrey

Carol S. Lawson, Susanna L. Buschmann,

and Wickham Skinner and Alice B. Skinner

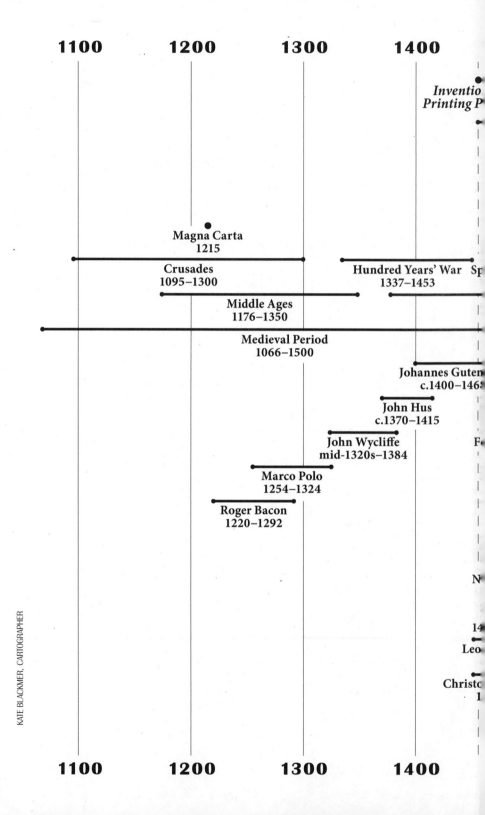

1100	1200	1300	1400

*Inventio
Printing P*

Magna Carta
1215

Crusades
1095–1300

Hundred Years' War Sp
1337–1453

Middle Ages
1176–1350

Medieval Period
1066–1500

Johannes Guten
c.1400–146

John Hus
c.1370–1415

F

John Wycliffe
mid-1320s–1384

Marco Polo
1254–1324

Roger Bacon
1220–1292

N

14

Leo

Christo
1

1100	1200	1300	1400

KATE BLACKMER, CARTOGRAPHER

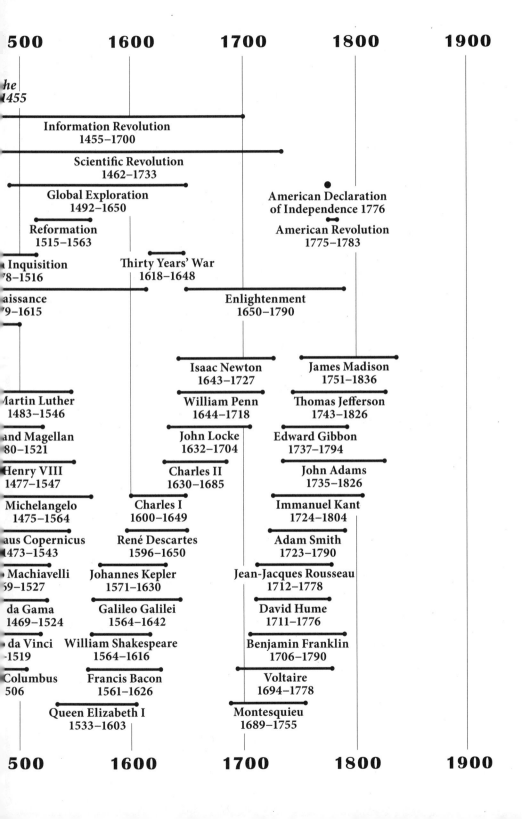

he
1455

Information Revolution
1455–1700

Scientific Revolution
1462–1733

Global Exploration
1492–1650

**American Declaration
of Independence 1776**

Reformation
1515–1563

American Revolution
1775–1783

Inquisition
'8–1516

Thirty Years' War
1618–1648

aissance
'9–1615

Enlightenment
1650–1790

Isaac Newton
1643–1727

James Madison
1751–1836

Martin Luther
1483–1546

William Penn
1644–1718

Thomas Jefferson
1743–1826

and Magellan
80–1521

John Locke
1632–1704

Edward Gibbon
1737–1794

Henry VIII
1477–1547

Charles II
1630–1685

John Adams
1735–1826

Michelangelo
1475–1564

Charles I
1600–1649

Immanuel Kant
1724–1804

aus Copernicus
1473–1543

René Descartes
1596–1650

Adam Smith
1723–1790

Machiavelli
59–1527

Johannes Kepler
1571–1630

Jean-Jacques Rousseau
1712–1778

da Gama
1469–1524

Galileo Galilei
1564–1642

David Hume
1711–1776

da Vinci
-1519

William Shakespeare
1564–1616

Benjamin Franklin
1706–1790

Columbus
506

Francis Bacon
1561–1626

Voltaire
1694–1778

Queen Elizabeth I
1533–1603

Montesquieu
1689–1755

contents

preface

AMERICA'S REVOLUTIONARY GENERATION radically transformed the human chronicle far more than is recognized by most historians. To understand the remarkable successes of America's founding fathers, imagine an index of human activity or, measured in more contemporary terms, economic growth throughout millennia: until 1800, this gauge realistically would be a straight line, reflecting that progress has been slow for almost all human existence. Since then, the line would curve rapidly upward, almost at an exponential rate of increase. Such a chart would look like this:

| 1000 BC | 0 | 1000 AD | 1500 | 1800 | 2000 |

The rate and scope of change that had to occur to alter the direction of that straight line so that it became almost perpendicular to its original course is absolutely phenomenal. During this period, Americans agreed upon a series of totally innovative changes explored in the first few chapters of this book: the original revolutionary era, Thomas Jefferson's democracy, Andrew Jackson's egalitarianism, and an agrarian revolution based upon John Marshall's ability to legally define and delineate the transformations in agriculture and transportation then in progress.

This radical tradition continued long past the early 1800s, exemplified by Lincoln's strong leadership in the Civil War. After this most difficult period, new innovations were allowed to sweep the nation: Edison's invention factory and the industrial revolution, the progressive era, the broadcasting revolution, Deming and Drucker's redirection of business management, and most recently, the information revolution, into which the United States led the entire world. The steady stream of innovations has been crucial to making progress. Their common denominator has been the political will insisting on personal freedom and liberty. "Rules preclude initiative. Regimentation precludes evolution. Letting accidents happen, mistakes be made, results in new ideas. Trial and error is the key to all progress."[1] America has been relatively free of restraints such as monarchy, hierarchical structures, bureaucratic organizations, and stratified social relationships.

It would be hard to overstate the level of individual change that was required to overcome the relative inertia of virtually all of human history. As one of the leading historians of the revolutionary period, Gordon Wood, noted: "If we measure the radicalism by the amount of social change that actually took place—by the transformations in the relationships that bound people to each other—then the American Revolution was not conservative at all; on the contrary: it was as radical and as revolutionary as any in history. . . . In fact, it was one of the greatest revolutions the world has known, a momentous upheaval that not only fundamentally altered the character of American society but decisively affected the course of subsequent history."[2]

The changes were not limited to government and war, but encompassed the culture, customs, habits, social relationships, and the basic conceptuality of the individual. In the modern world, common wisdom claims that social, government, and political change come slower than economic and technological change. Yet, the reverse was closer to the truth in the revolutionary era—social and governmental change often preceded and exceeded economic and technological change.

The founding fathers operated under the most difficult conditions imaginable, threatened by disease, wars, the frontier, and a life expectancy half of what it is today. The mere act of child-bearing was courageous—many women were unable to survive a half-dozen births, about average for the times. Wars and famine were twin plagues affecting society. There were few, if any cures or vaccinations for even the most common of deadly diseases.

At the core of the American Revolution was a will to innovate. That determination goes on today sweeping the globe and creating historically unprecedented economic wealth. For over a century between 1860 and 1970, for example, America led the world in the supplying energy and in manufacturing prowess. The most powerful force in American history, this spirit is responsible for the modern material world: the dozens of devices in automobiles, the hundreds of innovations in the typical house, and the thousands of inventions that guide everyday life. This common will created an expanding economic pie based on rapid economic growth and was responsible for American victories in three critical twentieth-century wars: World War I, World War II, and the Cold War.

In this book, we explore the history of this consistent culture of innovation, describe its foundations, and suggest how it is crucial to successfully handling the problems confronting America today.

1

George Washington
at the crossroads

GEORGE WASHINGTON (1732–1799) had far more in common with
Julius Caesar (100–44 BC) who lived almost eighteen centuries earlier,
than he would have had with Americans living today. From the time of
Julius Caesar to the time of Washington's presidency, technological,
social, and political changes were limited. But Washington's lifetime
and leadership encompassed the start-up of so many of these changes,
they became a major turning point in U.S. and, indeed, in world history. Not the most educated of our founding fathers, he was nonetheless
one of the most important leaders in the creation of the modern world
as we know it today. In the Revolutionary era, he was the only indispensable man.

Like commanders of the Roman armies, General Washington's
method of travel was by horse, covering a few miles an hour.
Washington and Caesar each headed armies held together by couriers,
and both relied on pontoons and boats to cross rivers and lakes. With
such primitive communications, an entire armada or a division might
well become completely out of touch with its commander.

As for Julius Caesar, information in General Washington's day traveled as fast as a horse. Both Washington and Caesar wrote mostly on parchment with quill pens. Almost the only way to speed up communications was to set up relays to pass information along on the battlefield or between local towns. News about the battle at Lexington and Concord, "The Shot Heard Round the World," took days to reach New York, weeks to reach the southern-most colonies, and well over a month to reach London, the seat of British power.

Today, Americans see news across the globe in real time and travel across our continent or to Europe in a day. A typical American routinely drives twenty miles a day just to get to and from work. Modern military soldiers travel in fast-moving tanks, pilots participate in dogfights well in excess of the speed of sound, rockets circle the globe in an hour, and naval vessels are modern cities several football fields in length.

The average income for the typical individual inched higher in fits and spurts from about $400 per year in the days of Julius Caesar to about $800 annually in General Washington's time in inflation-adjusted dollars. In between, there were periods when it declined significantly. By contrast, the average income in the United States in a year is now more than $30,000.

World population increased from 250 million during the Roman Empire to 800 million in colonial times when it began to explode. It has now reached well over 6 billion.

Infant mortality was extremely high and often understated. Actual life expectancy was mired in the 30s and 40s until the time of Washington. It then increased rapidly and is today in the 70s in developed countries. The increase in life expectancy of the past two centuries is greater than the total increase during all the rest of human history. Well-to-do American colonialists rode in carriages to avoid the necessity of stepping in sewage, human excrement, and garbage. By today's standards, public sanitation then was nonexistent. Improvements in public sanitation and vaccinations are the two most important factors contributing to the increase in life expectancy.

These illustrations, however, only begin to dramatize enormous changes. While no formal or structured stock markets existed until the past few centuries, if we assume Julius Caesar invested a few coins from the money changers, his investments would have been worth only a dollar or two in Washington's time, but would then have skyrocketed to between a quarter of a million and a million dollars today.

The World Gross Domestic Product, by rough estimates, increased fivefold from around $100 billion in the time of Julius Caesar to about $500 billion in colonial times. Then it soared by a factor of over a hundred times, to more than $50 trillion today.

Slavery had been a common practice throughout human history until colonial days, evident in some form in all major civilizations. Today, it is limited to a few primitive cultures and to criminal enterprises.

Until the American Republic, monarchy, tribalism, anarchy, and feudalism had been the predominant forms of governance, with monarchy generally preferred. Freedom and democracy flourished briefly in classical civilized cultures in Greece and Rome, for slightly longer periods in small communities in Switzerland, Italy, and Scandinavia, and were struggling to be established in England and Holland at the time America was being settled. Today, freedom and democracy is the preferred and most common form of governance.

Until colonial times, the concept of progress or continuous technological improvement was unknown. Water systems with aqueducts, for example, were arguably more advanced in ancient Rome, and Roman roads were better built than those in eighteenth-century America and Europe. Medical advances over the previous centuries were halting at best. In fact, in Western culture, medicine went backwards, losing key knowledge, in the feudal period and in the dark ages. George Washington was bled to death by his physicians, who believed that this treatment would heal him. The quality of eighteenth-century life was drastically different from our own. Nights were endured without electric lights, and household work was performed without the myriad of today's electric appliances.

For over a million years, from the first fires in caves, until candles were widely used (around 1800), the cost of lighting or illuminating a room changed glacially, improving by only a hundredfold. By contrast, Americans today can purchase 45,000 times more lighting for an hour of work than could the workers of just two centuries ago.

From Caesar to Washington, technological advances were few. The major advance from 500 to 1500 AD was arguably the stirrup to facilitate riding horses. Little of what we experience in our daily lives would make any sense to George Washington. Nevertheless he was the midwife for the birth of the New World. He had a unique instinct for understanding the big picture and making the right decisions. His personal skills and the decisions he made—more than anything or anyone else—created the modern world.

A New World was being created. Civilization was being transformed from an agricultural to an industrial basis. Americans experienced the enormous challenges of settling and conquering the frontier and were forced to address important issues of security—their vulnerability to nature, the Indians, and European nations. Washington stood at the crucial crossroads of human history.

2

The Transformation
from thirteen colonies
to one nation

It may be doubted whether so small a number of men ever employed so short a space of time with greater and more lasting results upon the history of the world.[1]

—SIR GEORGE OTTO TREVELYAN

THE BRITISH MARKSMAN CAPTAIN PATRICK FERGUSON, who invented the first breech-loading rifle, had George Washington in his sight—but impressed by Washington's indifference to death—did not pull the trigger. Washington, whose life was frequently in peril, believed his survival was pre-ordained. He was subject to clandestine plots by Tories and others who understood his inestimable value. "At the Monongahela, then in the battles at Trenton, Princeton, and Yorktown during the War of Independence, bullets and shrapnel seemed to veer away from his body as if he were surrounded by an electromagnetic field of invulnerability."[2] Leading his men forward at the Battle of Princeton, Washington ordered them not to fire until he gave the signal. Within less than thirty yards of the enemy he gave the command. His aide covered his eyes to avoid seeing him killed. When the smoke cleared Washington was sitting calmly in his saddle, unhurt. He waved his men forward, and the British broke and ran.

Today the American model is taken for granted, but in colonial times the paradigm was problematic, the general assumption being that democracy or a republican form of government could only work with a small number of people in a confined territory. The American Revolutionary cause was tenuous, mostly hanging by a thread. Some colonists feared the uprising would fail and believed the British would destroy the patriot armies. Yet, with the strength of many average citizens' faith and belief, the Revolution was carried out, consistent with the prophetic verse in Shakespeare: "There is nothing either good or bad, but thinking makes it so."[3]

Throughout the Revolutionary War period, colonists had a sense of being under the protection and guidance of divine providence. A litany of seemingly supernatural occurrences shaped the events that created the United States. From the beginning, America's founding fathers announced to the world they were establishing a revolutionary new order. Pictured on the Great Seal of the United States is the Eye of Providence and the closing section of the Declaration of Independence cites "a firm reliance on the protection of divine providence." A century later, German Chancellor Bismarck would complain: "God has a special providence for fools, drunks, and the United States of America."[4] The following are examples:

It is hard to believe, but for four seemingly isolated events, the British would not have been forced to withdraw from Boston at the outset of the war: if Henry Knox had not moved the huge cannon 250 miles from Fort Ticonderoga; if John Stark had not seized a key beach position at the outset of fighting; if a British admiral had had a chart of the Mystic River; and if a major snowstorm had not intervened to stop General Washington's assault on an impregnable position.

Early in the war, Washington faced a huge force of British troops on Long Island with the British fleet at his back. A fierce northeaster, which prevented the British fleet from attacking him, miraculously stopped when Washington retreated over the East River during a dark night and under the cover of a mysteriously appearing thick fog that protected his escape at dawn. When the fog lifted, the British were astonished to find that the Americans had vanished.

At the end of 1776, if Benedict Arnold, whose name is synonymous with treason, had not built a makeshift fleet to prevent the British from penetrating deep into New York territory, the patriots might never have had the opportunity to fight the battle of Saratoga, the turning point of the American Revolution. If Benedict Arnold had not successfully led his forces at the subsequent battle, the colonials may not have been able to force Burgoyne to surrender, and France may not have entered the war on the American side.

George Washington believed his restless army could not make the march to Yorktown and wanted to attack New York, but the city had too many British soldiers and was too well fortified. The French general Rochambeau persuaded him by pointing out the French fleet was en route to the Chesapeake and could trap Cornwallis on the Yorktown peninsula. Washington feared the fleet would be routed, but the French were able to score their only major win over the British at sea in history. When the British tried to sail from New York to rescue Cornwallis, the winds prevented their departure for days. When Cornwallis tried to leave the peninsula in the dead of night a violent thunderstorm thwarted his escape.[5]

George Washington frequently spoke of the important role of divine providence in the colonial triumph, even noting with chagrin that it "has done more for us than we were disposed to do for ourselves." At his first inaugural, Washington swore on the Bible and noted: "[I]t would be peculiarly improper to omit in this first official act my fervent supplications to that Almighty Being who rules over the universe, who presides in the councils of nations, and whose providential aids can supply every human defect . . . No people can be bound to acknowledge and adore the Invisible Hand which conducts the affairs of men more than those of the United States."

The Revolutionary War Leadership

The sense of being under the Eye of Providence helped to transform the patriot cause into a transcendent force with effective political leadership on three levels: *visionary,* *"the comforter,"* and the *executive.* Ubiquitous in both the Revolutionary War and the founding of the republic, this political leadership was essential to the success of the colonists, reflecting their strong reliance on individualism and the principle that the individual can make a difference in history. "Great events in history are determined by all kinds of factors, but the most important single one is always the quality of the people in charge; and never was this principle more convincingly demonstrated than in the struggle for American independence."[6] American leaders were not just superior, they were placed in their right roles: George Washington leading the army, John Adams running the War Board, Thomas Jefferson writing the Declaration of Independence, Benjamin Franklin responsible for international affairs and the peace treaty, James Madison writing the first draft of the Constitution, and Alexander Hamilton starting up the executive branch of government. In recent years, these revolutionary leaders have been much criticized for remaining as slaveholders despite their expressed desires for freedom for all humankind. For discussion of this issue, please see chapters 3, 6, and 7.

To exert leadership at the visionary level, an individual needs to be real and authentic, to be able to "see around corners," and to project a vision of the future. Washington's strength was the sheer force and character of his persona, as if he were divinely guided by the "Invisible Hand."[7]

> His very presence was eloquent. . . . Even shrewd Abigail Adams was swoony after meeting him. . . . Part of the charm was unquestionably physical. He was tall and red-haired, like Thomas Jefferson—each was two or three inches above six feet. But Washington *inhabited* his height, seemed tall to those who thought Jefferson rather collapsible, all wrists and elbow. In an era where horsemanship was often men's touchiest point of pride, Jefferson had to admit he

never saw Washington's lack of gait and control in the saddle. . . .

It is hard to exaggerate his impact on others, even before his great deeds were accomplished. . . . In the shadow of his mystery, other men's opinions grew. He was always wooden to vast designs because he was so rarely won. There was a sense that once set in motion toward any goal, he would be undeflectible—and so it proved. His powers exercised some weird attraction by their suspension as if they grew in secret. When he left Mt. Vernon (to go to Philadelphia), Martha is reported to have said (to Patrick Henry and Pendleton), "I hope you will stand firm. I know George will."

It was impossible to think there could be another man than Washington at the helm of the Constitutional Convention or of the first administration. Washington was Cincinnatus, the world hero as famous for his surrender of power as for his achievement of it. He took the lead at each crucial moment, in the war, in the framing and passage of the Constitution, in the governing of the country through its precarious first experiments—without Napoleonic excess, yet without weakness or pettiness.[8]

Washington cultivated his image of character and virtue. He was a self-made man who developed 110 conventions of civility which people knew about and tried to live up to. George Washington was the only indispensable man. "Benjamin Franklin was wiser than Washington; Alexander Hamilton was more brilliant; John Adams was better read; Thomas Jefferson was more intellectually sophisticated; James Madison was more politically astute. Yet each and all of these prominent figures acknowledged that Washington was their unquestioned superior."[9]

Thomas Jefferson's Declaration of Independence provided a crucial unifying vision for the colonists and a statement to the rest of the world of the principles upon which the United States was founded. It was circulated in dozens of papers, posted in public buildings in hundreds of towns, and printed in thousands of copies. Jefferson wrote the greatest statement on freedom and one of the most eloquent justifications for revolution: "We hold these truths to be self-evident; that all men are created equal; that they are endowed by their creator with certain inalienable rights; that among these are life, liberty, and the pursuit of happiness; that to secure these rights, governments are instituted among men, deriving their just powers from the consent of the governed." Jefferson was a poor public speaker, but these words from the Declaration of Independence became the creed of the American dream.

The Declaration was by no means assured—half a dozen of the middle colonies were initially under instruction not to vote for independence. A decisive factor in the outcome was a pamphlet by Thomas Paine, *Common Sense,* which clearly set forth the arguments against monarchy and British rule. Paine was the most powerful and radical writer of the founding fathers. As a result, he is often wrongfully marginalized by historians. He cogently set out the case for independence: "We have it in our power to begin the world over again."[10] John Adams made the crucial, moving, and powerful speech on July 1 that overcame the remaining opposition. Only on July 2 did it become clear that every colony would vote for Independence. Half of the signers, who by this very act were committing treason punishable by death, suffered personal consequences, such as having their homes burned or in being taken prisoner. Five signers of the Declaration of Independence were captured by the British. Richard Stockton never recovered from the torture during his captivity and died in 1781.

The Declaration was the culmination of a long struggle against the English authorities. In Virginia, the youthful Patrick Henry took the lead in opposing the Stamp Act, seeking to take the power of taxation away from Parliament and England. His eloquent speeches moved the Virginia House of Burgesses and secured passage of the Virginia resolves. Even during the ongoing recession, trade with America was much greater than Parliament and Britain had assumed. The colonists were unified and able to force repeal of the law and other restrictive measures, except for the duty against tea, left as a symbol of the supremacy of Parliament. At the Boston Tea Party, the colonialists dumped forty-five tons of tea into the harbor—enough to litter the beaches for miles and depress the company's profits for years. The British reaction was to pass the Intolerable Acts, closing the Port of Boston, stripping colonists of the right to elect members of the Upper House of their assembly, allowing royal officials to quarter soldiers in colonists homes at their expense, and enabling Royal officers indicted for murder to be tried in London. The southern border of Quebec was extended south to the Ohio River, barring expansion of colonies to the west. The first Continental Congress declared the Intolerable Acts null and void. In England, William Pitt and Edmund Burke tried to persuade Parliament to be conciliatory, but without success. For a year between Bunker Hill and the Declaration of Independence, the British made nothing significant in the way of conciliatory gestures. Patrick Henry issued his famous plea. Rising up from his seat, yanking apart imagined manacles and raising aloft an imaginary dagger, he shouted "Give me liberty or give me death." He plunged the dagger into his heart, falling back into his seat.

Benjamin Franklin was one of the founding fathers with enough vision to "see around corners." Historians have spent decades and volumes debating the crucial juncture in the metamorphosis to the modern world: the Battle of Saratoga (1777), the Declaration of Independence (1776), the life of Leonardo da Vinci (1452–1519), Martin Luther (1483–1546) refusing to recant, or a time frame like the decade of the 1520s. While the Reformation, Renaissance, and events in Europe had an important impact, the American Revolution was almost certainly the decisive development in the transformation to the modern world. The pivotal movement likely occurred in the presence of Benjamin Franklin in *The Cockpit* (a London debating auditorium formerly used for cockfights).

In 1774, everything had come to a head a few weeks after the Boston Tea Party. British solicitor general Alexander Wedderburn declared dumping the tea an act of treason. The London atmosphere was electric. In *The Cockpit,* Wedderburn sought to blame Franklin, sully his reputation, and even to put his life in peril.

At the time, London was the center of European intellectual and cultural life. The best of England had opened its doors to Franklin, consulted him, awarded him honorary degrees, and (as did the British Royal Society) gave him their highest accolades. Franklin loved London. He considered it his home, and would have become a permanent resident if he could have persuaded his wife to leave Philadelphia. Traveling throughout England and Scotland, Franklin received a jubilant welcome. He considered himself a Royalist and a true-blue Englishman and expounded on the glorious future of the British in North America. Originally, he believed the monarchy to be wiser and superior to the parliament. During the decade following the successful conclusion of the French and Indian War, both king and parliament began to assert their authority over the colonies, mostly in frustration over the huge war debts incurred. Franklin tried to conciliate, risking his good standing in the colonies.

But then came the critical moment in *The Cockpit.* Instead of debating the philosophical, legal, and constitutional issues raised by the colonists, the British indicted and vilified Franklin, who had been a loyal subject. He was called a traitor, an incendiary, a Judas, and was fired from his postmaster position. Franklin entered the auditorium a British subject and left it an American. Britain had lost its most important bridge to the colonies, probably the only person who could have reconciled the conflict.

Franklin sailed for home and took his place as one of the leaders of the opposition to British rule, working to ensure England's defeat and American independence. A full year before Congress declared independence, Franklin believed it was inevitable. He helped to prepare the colonists by proposing the Articles of Confederation to provide for national defense, security, and general welfare. He became a passionate advocate of revolution and helped to draft the Declaration of Independence, accurately predicting the American independence to be "the greatest revolution the world ever saw."[11]

The "comforter" or second level of leadership requires individuals who can connect with and comfort the people as well as become a leader of a community. "Washington was more than a general, he was the embodiment of all that was noblest and best in the American people."[12] He recruited top-flight talent. "In tough times in particular, a leader needs to surround himself with people who are smarter than he is, and they must have the grit to disagree with him and each other . . . A great leader has the courage to put together a team of people who sometimes make him look like the dumbest person in the room!"[13] Washington knew how to pick the best men for the key appointments, such as Henry Knox, Nathanael Greene, and Alexander Hamilton.

Washington was the commander-in-chief for the longest declared war in American history, an odyssey that kept him away from his Mount Vernon estate for eight years. He was at his best during times of greatest distress, such as at Trenton and Valley Forge. Washington subordinated himself and his army to civilian institutions and elected representatives and leaders. The outcome of the American Revolution was by no means inevitable. Arguably, time was on the side of the British with their almost limitless resources and technological superiority to wage war or as Washington aptly put it: "it will not be believed that such a force as Great Britain has employed for eight years in Country could be baffled . . . by numbers infinitely less, composed of Men oftentimes half starved; always in Rags, without pay, and experiencing, at times, every species of distress which human nature is capable of undergoing."[14]

The war would be won by the perseverance of the men of the Continental Army whose suffering would never be fully appreciated. More than anyone else, Washington understood the enormous sacrifices, including the gruesome winter at Valley Forge with the stench of 3,000 dying men and countless dead horses filling the air. Valley Forge was the center of both a rich agricultural area and the diffuse deployment of Washington's armies, extending for miles in each direction. The conditions were made horrendous by the collapse of the colonial supply system. In a brutally cold winter, most of his troops were without clothes, shoes, or blankets, some being without all three. The failure of the Congress to provide for the army at that critical time nearly ended the Revolution. The continued competition and foraging for food among the populace outside of Philadelphia helped Washington and his officers understand that the outcome of the war hinged on the battle for the hearts and minds of the American people. General Nathanael Greene, who had spent the winter foraging food around Valley Forge and much of his service time reading military history, understood the difficulties facing an army of occupation no matter how formidable its military prowess and the importance of winning popular sentiment and exercising political will.

Washington saw the Continental Congress as far too weak, supporting the army insufficiently, and failing to prosecute war profiteers. Congress never could keep commitments—it promised veterans half-pay for life and then full pay for five years. Troops went without pay for extended periods of time. Without a strong federal government, it was not possible to execute a war effectively.

Knowledge, information, and connections to the community were paramount. Washington was his own intelligence chief and operated many spy networks. Several were coordinated by Alexander Hamilton, providing precise, up-to-date information on the movement of the British army. At the siege of Boston, Washington had superior intelligence. If the British had known of the dire straits of the colonial force, particularly their lack of gunpowder, they might have scored a quick victory. When the British tried to knock out the French expeditionary force in Newport, Rhode Island, Washington's spies got wind of the plan. Unable to communicate with the French, Washington planted a packet of papers and had them captured by the British who, reading the "captured" American war plans, thought an attack on New York was imminent. They raced back to New York. By the time they figured out they were duped, the French had fortified Newport.

Washington won by keeping a standing army in the war. The annual desertion rate was 20 percent. He was always short on provisions. In the early battles, Washington lost every engagement and close to 90 percent of his army. At the end of the war, Washington quashed efforts at military coups, resigned his office, and went back to Mount Vernon, an almost unprecedented abandonment of power. "Washington's ultimate success as the American commander in chief, however, never stemmed from his military abilities. . . . [I]t was his character and political talent and judgment that mattered most. His stoicism, dignity, and perseverance in the face of seemingly impossible odds came to symbolize the entire Revolutionary cause."[15]

The third level of leadership is the ability to manage or execute. "*Did He get Back on the Horse?* Every leader makes mistakes, every leader stumbles and falls. The question is, does he learn from his mistakes, regroup, and then get going again with renewed speed, conviction, and confidence?"[16]

As an executive, Washington operated on two models: the Frontier and the Estate. Colonel George Washington's skirmish in the wilderness near Pittsburgh was the beginning of the French and Indian War, a worldwide conflict. He and many other colonials gained invaluable experience and knowledge from that war. They witnessed all of the horrors of fighting in the wilderness—Washington saw a brutal scalping in his very first battle where the Indians took off the skull as well and pulled out the brains. They learned the Indians were not particularly interested in victory or strategy, only scalps and tribute, occasionally engaging in the savage ritual of eating prisoners. Washington nearly lost his life several times: when an Indian in his party turned on him, when his guide fired his pistol at him without warning and missed, and when he was pitched from a raft into the freezing Allegheny River.

Washington gained considerable administrative experience in managing his Mount Vernon estate, a vast and elaborate enterprise having more employees than did the federal government during his presidency. After the French and Indian War, Washington cultivated grains rather than tobacco and reorganized his plantation. He discovered a new method for wheat farming and rotated crops. He was among the first to use mules, because they were smarter than the donkey, tougher than the horse. Washington struggled to pay off debts from failed tobacco crops and time spent fighting wars. He also built a large flour mill to grind enough for his neighbors, purchased a schooner for fishing and coastal trade, and hired a master weaver to provide clothes for the plantation and trade. In effect, he became a quartermaster and an expert in supply chain management.

Virtually overnight, Washington had been called on to develop a chaotic insurgency into an effective fighting force against the most professional military men in the world. He was virtually an amateur who had never commanded more than a regiment in battle. Washington was a disciplinarian, giving up to a thousand lashes to those found guilty of drunkenness and hanging deserters, even those who returned voluntarily.

> Washington spent the entire war in the field with the Continental army. He was not, by any standard, a military genius. He lost more battles than he won; indeed, he lost more battles than any victorious general in modern history. Moreover, his defeats were frequently a function of his own overconfident and aggressive personality, especially during the early stages of the war, when he escaped to fight another day only because the British generals opposing him seemed choked with the kind of caution that, given his resources, Washington should have adopted as his own strategy. But in addition to being fortunate in his adversaries, he was blessed with personal qualities that counted most in a protracted war. He was composed, indefatigable, and able to learn from his mistakes. He was convinced that he was on the side of destiny—or, in more arrogant moments, sure that destiny was on his side. Even his critics acknowledged that he could not be bribed, corrupted, or compromised.[17]

The scope and depth of leadership throughout the war was monumental. No one exemplified the personal strength and energy present at the founding of America more than Alexander Hamilton. French Prime Minister Talleyrand said the three greatest men of the epoch were Napoleon, Pitt, and Hamilton, but Hamilton was the greatest.[18] British historian Paul Johnson termed Hamilton the "archetypal self-made man of American mythology . . . Hamilton was a genius—the only one of the Founding Fathers fully entitled to that accolade."[19] Theodore Roosevelt said Hamilton was "the most brilliant statesman who ever lived, possessing the loftiest and keenest intellect of his time."

Hamilton's early life with his brother James was tragic and his rise unprecedented. An orphan on St. Croix in the Caribbean, he came to America as a young man, and rose to become George Washington's chief of staff at the early age of 22. Hamilton rarely spoke much about his gruesome past—some of which has been uncovered only during the past century.

> Tally the grim catalog of disasters that had befallen these two boys between 1765 and 1769: their father had vanished, their mother had died, their cousin and supposed protector had committed bloody suicide, and their aunt, uncle and grandmother had all died. James, sixteen, and Alexander, fourteen, were now left alone, largely friendless and penniless. At every step in their rootless, topsy-turvy existence, they had been surrounded by failed, broken, embittered people. Their short lives had been shadowed by a stupefying sequence of bankruptcies, marital separations, deaths, scandals, and disinheritance.[20]

After coming to America from St. Croix, Hamilton was mentored by New York educators and mercantilists who believed him to be a child prodigy. As a student, he became radicalized, joined the continental army, and (as an immigrant and illegitimate child who had seen the abyss) was comfortable playing a key role in extricating the continental army from a desperate situation.

After terrible defeats on Long Island and Manhattan, Hamilton helped to ensure a successful evacuation, coming to the attention of General Washington. With many enlistments expiring at the end of the year, the colonials faced the prospect they had lost the war or that one more defeat would mean the end of the American cause. On Christmas night, Washington crossed the Delaware with his most toughened veterans, many of whom were to be future leaders of the republic—Henry Knox, Nathanael Green, James Monroe, John Sullivan, and Alexander Hamilton. Crossing in the brutal cold on a journey where the footprints to the river were bloodied from the feet of men with broken shoes, Hamilton and his gun crew marched all night, cutting down the Hessians with murderous fire at Trenton where no American died in battle, although two froze to death. Later, Hamilton's crew helped to surround the British at Princeton, where three years earlier he had unsuccessfully sought admission. Legend has it that one of his cannon balls sailed into a campus building and beheaded a portrait of King George II.[21] Being an astute judge of talent, Washington made Hamilton a key advisor, considering him one of the best executives in the army. Because of his political, historical, and legal expertise, Hamilton then played a critical role. Like Washington, his service was marked by a recklessness, a bravado, and a valor that exhibited an indifference toward death. He became omnipresent in his role as Washington's chief of staff, convinced of the certainty of America's ulti-mate triumph.

John Adams, the only founding father to predict a long and costly war, helped to recruit Jefferson to write the Declaration and Washington to be commander-in-chief. He ran the War Office astutely with a War Board of five Members of Congress, courageously working to grant Washington the authority to act. Serving in effect as a Secretary of War, Adams was responsible for overseeing and processing the requisitions for supplies and equipment, the appointments and recruitment, and the myriad other details of running the army that were all constantly under-funded by the Congress. The Office and Board also oversaw and coordi-nated various financial currency functions and issues.[22]

In a surprise guerrilla attack, Benedict Arnold, Ethan Allen, and the Green Mountain boys achieved the first significant victory of the war, taking Fort Ticonderoga situated at the northern end of Lake George and regarded by some as the Gibraltar of North America. The 120,000 pounds of cannons and ammunition from the fort were then moved more than 200 miles in the dead of winter over the treacherous, snowbound Berkshire mountains to Boston where they were used to dislodge the British, a feat that was unimaginable except to Henry Knox, the Boston bookseller who led the expedition. The abandon-ment of Boston by the largest fleet ever seen in America and the strongest military force on the planet, forced by an army of amateurs, sent shock waves throughout the globe and was, according to Abigail Adams, "the work of the Lord."

The turning point of the American Revolution occurred on the same Upstate New York terrain. The British planned to capture New York in a three-pronged attack, dividing the colonies and forcing them into submission. General Howe was scheduled to march from New York City to Albany as part of the pincer movement, but instead, for reasons unknown even today, moved to attack General Washington at Philadelphia. Major General Leger marched down the Mohawk Valley along the future route of the Erie Canal, but was defeated at Fort Schuyler by reinforcements led by Benedict Arnold. General Burgoyne marched a large army from Montreal with the goal of capturing Albany and cutting off the New England colonies. The patriots used guerrilla tactics, such as cutting down nearly every tree along road arteries, destroying key bridges, rolling rocks into brooks to stop supply wagons, digging trenches to turn dry land into swamps, burning crops, and sweeping the country clean of livestock. Ethan Allen and his Green Mountain boys harassed British detachments and scavenging units. Burgoyne eventually traversed the terrain between the waters of Lake Champlain and the Hudson River but this crossing, which should have taken days, ended up taking weeks.

"Gentleman Johnny" Burgoyne, a misfit on the American frontier, exemplified why British armies would not survive this campaign. Through the impenetrable wilderness, he traipsed with thirty wagons containing his personal wardrobe, wine, and champagne, full tea service, the accoutrements of civilized European society, and even his mistress accompanied by other women with their wardrobes.

In the early, critical battle at Bennington, the colonials were particularly assisted by the fortuitous (or providential) presence of the New Hampshire militia, which enabled them to secure the critical supplies and materials that helped to decide the outcome of the final battle at Saratoga. When mercenary Indians working for the British scalped a young woman and Burgoyne refused to punish the Indians responsible, thousands of New England shopkeepers and farmers massed at Saratoga. Benedict Arnold performed heroically in commanding his troops at the battle. Daniel Morgan and his famous riflemen played a key role. Morgan had fought with Washington in the

French and Indian War, never forgiving the British for disciplining him with 500 lashes across his back.

The long campaign of attrition and pitched battle at Saratoga forced Burgoyne to surrender his entire army, which had totaled 10,000 men. When they surrendered, British soldiers were astonished at the rag-tag condition of the Americans, but impressed by their discipline. The victory, during the darkest days of the American Revolution, lifted the spirits of the colonialists, showed they were capable of defeating the British, and enticed the French into the war. Saratoga is regarded by many historians as one of the most decisive battles in world history.

George Rogers Clark laid the basis for America's claim to the entire Northwest Territory (Ohio, Indiana, Michigan, Illinois, Wisconsin, and Minnesota). The British and their Indian Allies killed and tortured thousands of colonials on the Frontier. The State of Virginia sent Clark and 130 men across the Ohio River to engage British Colonel Henry Hamilton, known as "hair buyer" for paying Indians to bring in colonial scalps. The Indians would torture prisoners, run them through the gauntlet, and then burn them at the stake. When a humane citizen cut the bounds to the stake, Hamilton threatened to imprison him. Clark and his men marched through neck-deep water in the bitter cold of midwinter to the British Fort Sackville at Vincennes in Indiana. Legend has it that Clark marched his troops back and forth in front of the British encampment, making it appear there were thousands of soldiers. He captured five Indians with scalps on their belts, tomahawking them to death in front of the fort. Hamilton then surrendered.

While the majority of colonials supported the war in 1775 and 1776, the colonials' political will declined as the war continued. For three years, Washington had focused his efforts on a strategy of capturing New York, believing the British would not abandon the conflict unless they suffered another loss as catastrophic as at Saratoga. In the summer of 1781, the colonial treasury was depleted, the army was disintegrating, and, in the absence of any decisive outcome, a negotiated settlement was likely the following year. Congress subsequently appointed the wealthiest man in the colonies, Robert Morris, to handle the colonial finances. The army became better paid, clothed, fed, and able to fight.

Washington maneuvered Lafayette south of Cornwallis to prevent a British escape from the Yorktown peninsula into the Carolinas. From New York, Washington dashed south to trap Cornwallis, personally managing every aspect of the march and its provisioning and transport, with emergency funding provided by Robert Morris. Washington made the British believe he would attack New York from Staten Island, but instead besieged Cornwallis at Yorktown. The French fleet under Admiral de Grasse was bound for Chesapeake to counter the British advantage at sea. In one of the most daring moves of the war, Admiral de Grasse brought his entire fleet from the West Indies, risking court-martial and being stripped of his command. The British did not realize he had 24 battleships. When the British sailed to the Chesapeake, de Grasse had not arrived, so they went to New York and returned without a full complement of ships. De Grasse's *Ville de Paris* was the most powerful warship on the seas, with 110 guns. He defeated the British and sealed shut the trap of Cornwallis, who found it inconceivable the British navy could lose control of the sea.[23] American and French artillery gradually and brutally wore the British troops down and forced their surrender.

Yorktown was "one of the most brilliantly conceived and smoothly executed operations in the history of warfare" involving the coordinated movements of disparate forces—two American armies, two French fleets, and a French army.[24] Surveying the field of action at Yorktown to ascertain his position and that of the enemy, Washington stood on a parapet for long stretches during an artillery barrage, despite pleas for him to step down. These requests were well-founded, because, by defeating the British, Washington was becoming the most famous man in the world.

The American Revolution was an international conflict, and the patriots operated globally, outmaneuvering the far more experienced British. Partly through instinct and partly by learning from William Pitt's brilliant global strategy in the French and Indian War, the founding fathers knew the importance of foreign alliances and international politics. Despite all insufficiencies, throughout the war and the early years of the republic, key leaders were sent to Europe to execute American strategy and represent the new nation. Benjamin Franklin arranged to have documents, such as the Declaration of Independence, translated, published, and circulated throughout Europe where there was so much tyranny and war that Franklin was convinced that "all Europe is for us" as a haven for liberty. Upon receiving information early in the war on the surrender of General Burgoyne, Franklin spread the news among influential French leaders. The British tried to negotiate a settlement, but Franklin skillfully prodded the French into entering the war on the American side. Spain and Russia came to the aid of the French, and the British were thus isolated diplomatically.

John Paul Jones, with the *Bonhomme Richard,* engaged the larger English ship *Serapis.* With the battle going poorly, the captain of the British vessel offered Jones the chance to strike his colors. According to legend, Jones replied: "I have not yet begun to fight." He rammed the British ship and in fierce man-to-man combat the French and American crew vanquished the British. Jones attacked the seaside town of Whitehaven, less than a hundred miles from London, making the British seem vulnerable and raising the morale of Americans.

With communications and travel being so difficult, the peace was negotiated by a revolving door of diplomats, the main actors being John Jay, Benjamin Franklin, and John Adams. Franklin was well positioned in Paris and the architect of the Peace of Paris. To the French, Franklin embodied America. Only he could have negotiated a continuous stream of loans from a nearly bankrupt French government. Congress would often overdraw the loans he negotiated, risking the country's public credit. At the end of the war, Franklin negotiated a separate peace with the British and then had to apologize to his French friends. The treaty with Britain was not finalized until a peace treaty could be negotiated with France. The United States skillfully manipulated the mutual fears of European powers to its advantage, gaining the respect of all Europe in what is regarded as "the greatest achievement in the history of American diplomacy."[25] As a result of the Treaty, the colonies doubled in size, becoming greater than Britain, France,

Germany, Spain, and Italy combined. John Adams predicted that the colonies would in time "form the greatest empire in the world."

On December 4, 1783, Washington gave a formal, final farewell to his troops at Fraunces Tavern, tearfully ending the gathering by proclaiming "I most devoutly wish that your latter days will be as prosperous and happy as your former ones have been glorious and honorable." Shortly thereafter, he made the following prediction: "The Citizens of America, placed in the most enviable condition, as the sole Lords and Proprietors of a vast Tract of Continent, comprehending all the various soil and climates of the World, and abounding with all the necessities and conveniences of life, are now by the late satisfactory pacification, acknowledged to be possessed of absolute freedom and Independency; They are, from this period, to be considered as the Actors on a most conspicuous Theatre, which seems to be peculiarly designated by Providence for the display of human greatness and felicity."[26]

The American Republic

The war for independence became the American Revolution, which in turn became a political movement to replace monarchy and aristocracy with republicanism and democracy.[27] America again had political leadership competent on the three key levels: visionary, the "comforter," and the executive. The Constitution was a visionary document that established a new government. The original Articles of Confederation provided for a weak central government. It took four years for the states to ratify. With its authority based in the states and not the people, the Confederation Congress did adopt the Land Ordinance of 1785 and Northwest Ordinance of 1787, which became the models for western expansion.

Initially, informal governments grew up around royal institutions. Many of the colonists decided that the granting of any authority required an act of the people to be given permanence by a written charter. Man's basic rights, however, were guaranteed, not granted, because they were inalienable.[28] During the war, more than a dozen state constitutions were adopted. After the war, the patriots developed and refined the concept of constitutionalism, a radical theory that demarcated, limited, and set boundaries for legislators' and government powers. As the colonists developed their own constitutions, the nature and location of ultimate power in each state was clearly delineated. The legal sphere and scope of laws was narrowly circumscribed with habit, custom, and tradition being considered the primary basis for values and standards rather than legal and administrative fiat, focusing authority in civil society rather than government.

The states became laboratories for the new republican form of government. Benjamin Franklin was instrumental in developing the Pennsylvania constitution. Madison and Jefferson played key roles in developing the Virginia constitution. While Jefferson was writing the Declaration of Independence, he was also preparing a draft constitution for the State of Virginia. Over three years, Jefferson drafted for approval 126 laws establishing the Commonwealth of Virginia. Jefferson's efforts basically overthrew the English legal system.[29] His legislation, for example, abolished entail (all land must be kept in the name of the family) and primogeniture (eldest son receives the entire inheritance). Subsequently, Jefferson worked for ten years to secure passage of his Virginia Statute on Religious Freedom, which provided for the separation of church and state.

Initially, the states tried to keep legislatures and the judiciary free of executive influence, given the problems with colonial governors and executive influence over Parliament, but more laws were enacted in the decade after the Revolution than in all of the colonial period. There were many conflicting, confusing, and overlapping statutes. Under the Articles of Confederation:

> [the] states were oppressing American citizens under a burden of taxation and regulation greater than any they had ever experienced, greater than any that had been coveted by the wickedest minister who had ever advised the British Crown. The level of taxes during the 1780s was ten to twenty times prewar norms. . . . Legislation was enacted to regulate what people could produce and sell and what they could charge for it; to interfere systematically with private com-

mercial transactions and suspend the obligations of private contracts; to prohibit the purchase of luxuries, prescribe what people could eat and drink, and govern what they could wear; to regulate private morality, indoctrinate the citizens with official dogmas, and suppress contrary opinions; to inflate the currency deliberately to pay for the ever-mounting costs of government.[30]

State legislatures became more feared than the executive, which led to granting back more authority to the executive. Constitutions were strengthened since they were generally immune from legislative encroachment.

Most European nations viewed the thirteen colonies as separate entities and deemed them not creditworthy. After the war, a major recession or depression was caused by poor credit, loss of European financing, withdrawal of the French and British armies, unemployment due to the disbanding of the continental army, and rampant land speculation. State efforts to counteract these economic forces failed, and the Articles of Confederation were in desperate straits. Some colonists claimed the Revolution was a failure, and monarchy, as the Europeans had firmly believed all along, was the superior form of government.

Under the Articles of Confederation, the new nation could not tax, pay its bills, nor provide for national defense. The states refused to honor obligations from the war and to fund veterans pensions. They wouldn't stand up to mercantilist European powers. Barbary pirates were seizing ships and selling the sailors into slavery. The Spanish staked out claims in the south and plotted to break away parts of the present-day Alabama and Mississippi. The states refused to pay debts owed to British creditors, so Great Britain continued to hold posts in the Northwest Territories. The states blocked efforts to facilitate interstate trade and the Confederation Congress couldn't even get a quorum to conduct business. The final straw was Shays' Rebellion in Western Massachusetts against tax and debt collections, which threatened the spread of anarchy. In 1787, there was consensus about the need for changes in the Articles of Confederation, but few expected a new constitution.

THE FOUNDING FATHERS' LEADERSHIP

Philadelphia, the site of the Constitutional Convention, was literally and figuratively a hothouse of activity, suffering from unbearable heat compounded by swarms of flies from the horse dung on the streets which required the windows to be kept closed. The Constitutional Convention was probably the greatest collection of political thinkers and philosophers ever assembled, including Roger Sherman, Oliver Ellsworth, John Dickinson, George Read, William Patterson, Robert Morris, James Wilson, George Mason, and John Rutledge. Patrick Henry refused to attend, because he "smelled a rat." Gouverneur Morris was the author of large sections of the Constitution, including the famous pre-amble: "We the People of the United States, in order to form a more perfect union. . . ."

The appointment of Virginian George Washington to head the convention was engineered by John Adams and James Madison, in part as an effort to alleviate southern concerns that New Englanders were too fanatical. Washington was reluctant to even attend. Upon his resignation as Commander-in-Chief of the continental army, he had made a pledge not to become involved in public affairs, an act which had gained him and the country unprecedented respect throughout the world. Washington was a minority in his belief the Confederation Congress was inept and the Articles of Confederation fatally flawed, an opinion he expressed when asked. He was concerned about the legacy the American Revolution would leave: the perception America was just another failed experiment in democracy and that his efforts in the war had been for naught. Washington also had to be deeply affected by the ongoing economic decline, which decimated his personal wealth by a half. He was forced to evict many tenants and squatters, including some who were his own former troops. In his correspondence with Madison he concluded, "We are fast verging on anarchy and confusion."[31] Madison believed the Constitutional Convention would likely initiate radical reforms, because most of the defenders of the status quo had decided to remain at home. The country was at a critical juncture and only Washington could supply the needed steadying influence. He understood the United States would have a major role to play in the world in the long-term and needed an effective government. Washington agreed to attend the Constitutional Convention when Madison apprised him a majority of the delegates favored radical reform.

As a youth, Madison was so weak and sickly his Princeton classmates worried that his superb intellectual powers would not come to full fruition because he would never reach his prime. He outlived all his classmates and upon his death in 1836 was considered "The Last of the Founders."[32] Frustrations with the Articles of Confederation and Virginia legislature drove Madison to study history and develop a model for a much more effective government, the Virginia Plan. Jefferson was in Paris, but sent his friend a large number of books on history, government, and politics. Madison wanted a national government with a veto over state laws as a means of reducing the overlapping, conflicting, and harmful powers of the state governments. In particular, he was concerned that state legislatures were vastly expanding the scope of government in the colonies.

Without George Washington and Benjamin Franklin, the Convention would not have been taken seriously, and the Constitution would have been dismissed. Some people supported the Constitution on the assumption that George Washington would be president. The nature and the powers of the office are loosely described, because the authors trusted Washington to define the office during his expected tenure as president. Franklin was a key player in brokering the final compromises. He made a powerful argument at the conclusion of the convention.

John Adams also made a valuable contribution. He wrote A *Defence of the Constitutions of Government of the United States of America,* a history of the republics that had so far existed in the Western world.

Madison's Virginia Plan was countered by the New Jersey Plan that gave states equal and additional rights and was supported by the smaller states. The Connecticut or Great Compromise determined that the House would be elected based on population, the Senate would be based on two members from each state, and a powerful presidency would be selected by electors. Both Madison and Washington thought the "Great Compromise" was a defeat for their concept of a national government, but they supported the final product. Madison also lost on the issue of federal veto of state laws. Given the narrow margin by which the Constitution passed in New York and Virginia, the entire plan may have failed if these original proposals had survived.

The provision for a standing army was probably the most controversial issue, but it was strongly supported by Washington and members of the Continental Army and the War Board. The anti-Federalists attacked it harshly. Another major criticism of the Constitution was that the president would be like the British king. Hamilton emphasized the accountability built into the office: election to a four-year term; the possibility of impeachment; no absolute veto; and, unlike the king, the president couldn't dissolve Congress and confer titles of nobility, nor appoint a church office.

Extraordinary ratification procedures were inserted into the Constitution. As the Articles of Confederation had taken four years to ratify, the members of the Constitutional Convention understood the urgency of ratification and the precarious situation in which the Articles had placed the republic. These procedures allowed citizens to express their opinions rather than state legislatures who would be inclined out of self-interest to oppose the Constitution.

In the conventions to ratify the Constitution, four states directly elected delegates, one (Rhode Island) held a direct referendum, and the remainder were appointed by the state legislature or executive authority. The *Federalist Papers* were one of at least two dozen series of essays, as well as commentary in most newspapers, sermons, letters, and thousands of other documents the 1,500 delegates at the ratifying conventions were exposed to. The *Federalist Papers* were, however, drafted by key participants in the Convention process, particularly Madison and Hamilton. "The great achievement of the authors of the *Federalist Papers* is not merely that they replied in detail to specific dangers that critics saw in the Constitution and explained in detail how the new government should, and would, work, but that they did so without repudiating the past, without rejecting the basic ideology of the Revolution."[33]

Madison was able to secure Virginia's support over Patrick Henry and George Mason who were far more effective speakers, because of his knowledge of the Constitution. John Marshall watched these debates and the Virginia ratification process was the beginning of his study of the Constitution that consumed his adult life. One of the keys to rapid ratification was the communications network set up by Alexander Hamilton to develop and distribute the *Federalist Papers* and then to use the latest information to secure ratification. He was the first to receive information on the ratification by New Hampshire and Virginia, using this knowledge to leverage ratification by New York, leaving only North Carolina and Rhode Island as holdouts.

> Madison is called the father of the Constitution. It is a title deeply deserved, on many counts. In the amazing time that stretched from the Annapolis Convention (September 1786) to the Virginia ratification (June 1788)—from his own thirty-fifth year to his thirty-seventh—he defended the Annapolis call to the Constitutional Convention in Congress, helped persuade Washington to attend it, did his research into the nature of the confederacies, drafted the Virginia Plan, played a key role in transforming that plan into the finished draft, defended that draft in Congress and in *The Federalist*, and then returned to Richmond where he defeated [Patrick] Henry and won his state's ratification.[34]

Madison drafted and secured passage of amendments as the Bill of Rights, ten of which were passed by the states. The Bill of Rights was patterned after protections in British law that ensured individual rights and liberty. The final two amendments were the capstones. The Ninth Amendment recognized that the rights in the Constitution were not the only ones enjoyed by the people. The Tenth stipulated that any powers not granted to the federal government were retained by the states or the people. Washington reviewed the amendments and didn't change a word. In three major states, ratification had been very narrow and supporters had won in several states only by promising changes. Madison steered the amendments through Congress, stopping many others proposed by opponents, and in the course of this process broadening popular support for the Constitution.

The Constitution was a major advance in the process of addressing the previously insoluble problem of how freedom, republicanism, and democracy could be implemented on a mass basis or as Lincoln put the question later "whether any nation so conceived and so dedicated can long endure." As a matter of common sense and efficiency, the founding fathers wanted a central government, not the chaos of thirteen sovereign state governments. When Washington assumed the presidency, governance was still chaotic. John Adams and others had serious doubts whether the new government would last the first full term in office.

The founding fathers did not want a big government, establishing a federal government miniscule by today's standards with only a half-dozen departments. In Washington's first term, Henry Knox had only a dozen civilian employees at the War Department and Jefferson had only six at the State Department. During his presidency, Washington had fewer employees in the entire federal government than he had managed on his Mount Vernon estate. By taking powers away from thirteen states and giving them to one federal government, the founding fathers were, in some respects, reducing the role of government. The conflicting and confusing nature of multiple different state statutes was crippling commerce and paralyzing the ability of the country to conduct international and military affairs. While the Federalists established a small government, the Jeffersonian Republicans believed in a tiny government. Under Jefferson, the federal government had only 130 employees and spent less than $10 million on operations, most of which went to pay down the national debt.

Although it was important for government to be small, it was essential for it to be effective and entrepreneurial. Benjamin Stoddert was designated by President Adams to head the Navy Department. From his service on the War Board and in Europe, where the Barbary pirates had used their control of the seas to blackmail and extract tribute from entire nations, including the United States, Adams believed naval power to be the critical factor in military power. When Stoddert took the helm in mid-June 1798, there was but one ship at sea. By the time he left three years later, the fleet had expanded to fifty-four. He accomplished this feat working in a suite of two rooms with just four or five clerks. The Navy had no professional staff and recruited mainly from the merchant marines, who had no recent experience on armed vessels, although some had fought in the Revolution. Rebuilding the navy was part of the Federalist effort to expand the defense establishment, including a gradual increase of the peacetime army from less than 1,000 men in 1789 to over 5,000 by 1800.

Previously, Washington and Secretary of War Henry Knox had obtained the services of ship designer Joshua Humphreys who strongly believed any ship built should be stronger, faster, heavier, and more efficient than any other of its class possessed by a foreign nation. In the crisis atmosphere during the aftermath of the "XYZ affair" with the French, Stoddert obtained authority to procure additional ships. He delegated authority to agents who had broad responsibility for the procurement of materials, expediting construction, and recruitment of crews.

Stoddert's team developed manufacturing capabilities, such as native production of a superior short-range gun and rolling copper sheaths required for protecting ship bottoms from barnacles and sea worms. Improvements in hemp and canvas manufacture, effective recruitment policies, and other advances were far-reaching legacies of Stoddert's tenure. His entrepreneurial and inventive efforts played an important role in securing foreign commerce for American industry and in protecting American shores during a time of acute vulnerability.

At the time, French privateers were seizing 330 American ships a year, exports and imports had dropped dramatically, and insurance rates had more than quintupled from 6 percent up to 30 or 40 percent of the value of the freight. French ships hovered in American coastal waters, and the entire American shoreline was basically defenseless. Rumors of foreign invasion and takeover began circulating in official circles. The French declared that any vessel loaded even in part with English goods would be subject to seizure, thus threatening about a third of American commerce. Stoddert's job was to protect the merchant marine, not just in coastal waters, but in a two-thousand-mile arc between America and the Caribbean. Humphreys' classy American frigates outmatched any French ship, and, when carefully deployed, were an extremely effective force. The most difficult aspect of the strategy was supplying the ships at vast distances from home bases where the United States had no supply or repair facilities. The system Stoddert developed functioned efficiently and the seizures dropped dramatically in 1798 and the following year. The Navy more than paid for itself with eight months of this effort.

The greatest moment came in February 1799 when the ship *Constellation* saw and gave chase to the French ship *L'Insurgente*, which was said to be the fastest ship in the French navy and had recently recaptured the *Retaliation*—a French privateer captured by Stephen Decatur. She had eluded the *Constitution* for three weeks as well as all the British ships that had pursued her. Cruising out of Guadeloupe, her speed and skill were insufficient and she was out maneuvered into ship-to-ship combat. "Within an hour and a quarter *l'Insurgente* became a valuable addition to the United States Navy. There was great exultation in America and [Captain] Truxtun and his crew were cheered at patriotic celebrations across the country. One Fourth of July toast was to 'Captain Truxtun: our popular Envoy to the French, who was accredited at the first interview.'"[35]

President Jefferson sent a large American fleet to the Mediterranean to protect United States commerce from raids by the Barbary pirates. U.S. warships provided convoy escorts for American merchant vessels and interdicted enemy ships. Commodore Edward Preble and Stephen Decatur fought the Barbary pirates in their own harbor, set afire the *Philadelphia* which had been captured by the pirates, and secured the release of American prisoners of war in an act Lord Nelson of the British Admiralty labeled "the most bold and daring act of the age."[36] American consul William Eaton marched a group of men 500 miles across the Libyan dessert and coordinated a successful attack with three American warships on the "shores of Tripoli."

Besides the vision of the Constitution and lean government, Washington served as the comforter to the new American community. Almost every act of the new government established a precedent. Never had there been a republican government exercising control over as large a population—and that fact alone led to a supposition in Europe of failure. Washington was the first president with executive powers, a cabinet, a foreign policy, appointments, and a legislative agenda. Washington basically invented the Cabinet, surrounding "himself with the most intellectually sophisticated collection of statesmen in American presidential history."[37] His first administration included the presidents for the next thirty-six years (Washington, Adams, Jefferson, Madison, and Monroe), Alexander Hamilton, Henry Knox as Secretary of War, John Jay as Chief Justice, and Edmund Randolph as Attorney General. Washington was effective at delegating authority. Adams praised Washington, "He seeks information from all quarters and judges more independently than any man I ever saw."[38]

Washington frequently toured the country to promote national unity, sometimes being out of contact with the seat of power for weeks at a time. Innkeepers would be stunned to see the greatest man in their world pulling up to their establishment. Washington assured the Jewish community of Newport, Rhode Island, that America was an enlightened country where "everyone shall sit in safety under his own vine and fig tree, and there shall be none to make him afraid."[39] He and Martha arranged sixteen marriages, including the most famous couple of his times—James and Dolly Madison.

Washington was a Federalist and opposed anti-government ideology, because the lack of a strong central government prolonged the Revolutionary War and had nearly destroyed his army. He served as a bridge between being governed by a monarchy or king and a president, providing patriarchal leadership while establishing an elected republican president. While Washington had brilliant advisors and cabinet members, he ensured that his executive branch spoke with one voice. Washington's lasting contribution to the presidency was his decision to limit his service to two terms, not life—as many people of his time assumed he would serve. "He was an extraordinary man who made it possible for ordinary men to rule. There has been no president quite like him, and we can be sure that we shall not see his like again."[40] Washington succeeded at governing in a way that no one else in history had governed and made the successful founding of the American republic seem inevitable.

"If Washington was the father of the country and Madison the father of the Constitution, then Hamilton was the father of the American government."[41] If George Washington was chairman of the board, then Hamilton was the chief executive officer, providing leadership at the management level. More than any other founding father, he understood banks, manufacturing, credit, and capital markets. As a young clerk in the Caribbean before his arrival in America, he had obtained a good grasp of international markets and finance. He structured the executive branch, personally writing many of the most important documents of Washington's presidency, including the papers on public debt, a national bank, and the industrialization of America. Hamilton believed the Congress was not structured to exert energy or act with decisiveness, qualities that needed to be exhibited by the executive branch. Washington treated other cabinet officers as advisors, while Hamilton was the individual who actually executed. "Hamilton set out to do for America what early-eighteenth century English governments had done in establishing Great Britain as the greatest power in the world. . . . That this small island on the northern edge of Europe with a third of the population of continental France was able to build the greatest empire since the fall of Rome was the miracle of the age."[42] Hamilton had a strong will and broad agenda, resulting in his being demonized not just by his Republican opponents, such as Jefferson and Madison, but by John Adams and his supposed Federalist allies.

The first Congress was the most productive in history. Taxes were raised through tariffs on imported goods. Funds totaling just $2.1 million over two years were provided to run the government, including salaries for officers. Bills to create executive branch agencies were enacted, including the State, Treasury, and War Departments. The Judiciary Act of 1789 created a court system, only the Supreme Court having been provided for in the Constitution. James Madison introduced and secured passage of the Bill of Rights. The first session of the first Congress was marked by a great deal of collegiality and little partisanship.

Congress was soon torn by division over the issues of public debt and slavery with "increasing talk about dissolving the Union and starting over." Southerners were disturbed about the Quaker petitions to abolish the slave trade and northerners resented the refusal of southerners to resolve the public debt issue.[43] Eventually, the first Congress also fixed the permanent residence of the nation's capital, guaranteed payment of the national debt, created a national bank, commissioned a regular census, and admitted Kentucky and Vermont as states. Washington was given authority to supervise the details for the design and construction of the nation's capitol, to be named Washington, D.C.

At the end of his first term, both Hamilton and Jefferson believed the country would split apart without Washington as President. Hamilton, in particular, played a crucial role in convincing Washington to serve a second term by noting: "North and South will hang together if they have you to hang on." There were vituperative attacks and mudslinging that even Washington could not stop, but which he could temporize to prevent the country from being torn apart. As was the case when asked to preside over the Constitutional Convention and serve his first term, Washington had substantial reservations. By the end of the first term, Washington's energy was flagging, and he had a number of maladies. With dentistry being primitive, he had only one or two teeth left and had been in constant pain since he had begun losing teeth in his twenties (legend has it that he lost two in the brutally cold crossing of the Delaware). He had a long history of illness and almost died twice during his first term. Heavy partisanship and bitter fights presented Washington with a very difficult task in recruiting for high-caliber appointments. He was deeply wounded by the harsh criticism of his presidency by partisans. "He found himself in the ironic position of being the indispensable man in a political world that regarded all leaders as disposable. Without him to center it, the political experiment in republicanism might very well have failed. With him, and in great part because of him, it succeeded; but in so doing it rendered the nonpartisan values he embodied anachronistic."[44]

Almost the entirety of Washington's presidency and Alexander Hamilton's tenure at the Department of the Treasury was devoted to the economic security of the new nation. Washington was trying to run a government like managing the Mount Vernon estate—based on good management and execution. His key asset was his pragmatic mind "uncluttered with sophisticated intellectual preconceptions."[45] He did not have a detailed knowledge of the mechanics and workings of economics. Fortunately, he relied on Hamilton who did.

"More than anyone else, Hamilton engineered the transition to a postwar political culture that valued sound and efficient government as the most reliable custodian of liberty."[46] When confirmed as Secretary of the Treasury, he hit the ground running, arranging loans from major banks in the first few days. Few of the founding fathers had any expertise in economics. Hamilton not only acquired the requisite knowledge, he had the determination to implement the right policies. There were only three members of Washington's executive council or cabinet and Hamilton became involved in most decisions. Hamilton had by far the broadest agenda and was the most effective individual in Washington's administration. In this role, Hamilton invented the concept of Chief Executive Officer or CEO, designed first for government and then transferred to the private sector for use to manage banks and then corporations. No other culture has invented the same concept or even a counterpart. Historically, it is uniquely American.

One of Hamilton's first acts was to raise revenues through tariffs—a source of contention throughout early American history. A duty of 6 cents a ton was placed on American flagged ships—50 cents on foreign ships. This protectionist differential provided a large boost to the American shipbuilding industry.

Shortly thereafter, Hamilton began to write his report on the public debt. The Revolutionary War was financed mostly by the printing press, but also from confiscation of property and foreign and domestic loans or public debt. The Articles of Confederation made interest payments by issuing more debt. The country bordered on insolvency. Washington asked for the records of the Confederation government, but was unable to decipher the finances, so he handed them over to Hamilton. Hamilton solved the problem by submitting a report to Congress to recognize the debt and assume responsibility for state debts, the total debt being close to $80 million. Hamilton knew this fiscal reform was a costly proposal, but recognized the importance of establishing credit and trust in the new government. Under the Articles of Confederation, interstate commerce was severely impeded, because each state had its own currency which was virtually worthless in any other state. The Hamilton proposal created a bond market by purchasing these debts, enabling the bearer to borrow money and facilitating interstate commerce. His report reminded Americans about the importance of the debt in carrying out the war and securing independence. He modeled his proposal after England's expansion of debt in the 1700s that resulted in increased public trust and a top-notch navy that led to a worldwide commercial empire and the beginning of the industrial revolution. The British public debt liquefied its national wealth, enabling it to pursue an expansionist foreign policy, wage war, and, with its small population, hire foreign soldiers (like the Hessians in the American Revolution) to fight its battles.[47]

Jefferson believed Hamilton's proposal would centralize political power and economic influence in the hands of a privileged few. He argued that many of the original holders of the debt (i.e., impoverished veterans) had sold their bonds to speculators who would profit. Hamilton believed assumption of the public debt would reduce speculation by giving investors certainty they would be paid off in full. Those who sold their bonds had exhibited a lack of confidence in the nation's future and it would be impossible to determine who originally owned much of the debt. Hamilton won the debate, in substantial part by winning enough votes in the Congress in agreeing to locate the nation's capital in Washington, D.C. Until the War of 1812, half of all federal expenditures were for debt payments. The debt fell rapidly and when the government needed funds for the Louisiana Purchase, it had good credit. The debt assumption gave bond holders a stake in the country. Hamilton's plan gave creditors various options for payment: full payment at lower interest rates, partial payment at higher rates, and the option of receiving government land in the West. Hamilton developed a short-term plan to fund his program through international loans and import duties.

Using his intuition and personal knowledge of banking, finance, and credit, Hamilton successfully countered the Panic of 1792. William Duer, a New York businessman, started a bank to corner the market on government six-percent bonds or "Sixes." Hamilton watched with trepidation as the price of Sixes rose rapidly for months until the bubble burst with the price dropping 25 percent in two weeks. Without any direct financial or government precedent to rely on, Hamilton devised an innovative approach, directing the Federal Treasury to borrow money from the banks which was then used to buy government bonds and lift the market price. He also told the banks to accept the bonds as collateral for loans, backing up his directive with government guarantees of the collateral. Within a month, the American financial system was stabilized and not a single bank failed until 1809, a tribute to Hamilton's engineering and improvisation.

Hamilton opposed a perpetual public debt and proposed a sinking fund to help prevent this from happening, an idea with important implications. The trading of Hamilton's government bonds led to the establishment of the New York Stock Exchange. Using these bonds as backing for bank notes, banks established a money supply and multiplied in number from three in 1790 to 29 in 1800.[48] United States credit went from practically nothing in the middle 1780s to the highest rating in the world by the turn of the century.[49]

Being well-versed in European financial institutions and a co-founder of the Bank of New York, Hamilton also proposed a national central bank, modeled after the Bank of England in the 1690s and successes in Germany, Holland, Spain, and France. Hamilton recognized the urgent need to develop a uniform currency, expand the money supply, handle foreign exchange, and develop a depository for government funds. His national bank was closely coordinated with his public debt proposal, with three-quarters of the bank financing being government securities.[50] The capitalization of the new bank was five times the capital of all existing banks in the United States.

Even though no Member of Congress had any banking experience, Hamilton shepherded his proposal through the Congress, but the three Virginian politicians closest to Washington opposed it. They viewed bankers as speculators and paper shufflers who obtained illicit profits. In fact, the legislation split the North and South, the latter being opposed. Working in a frenzy night and day, Hamilton pleaded successfully for a liberal interpretation of the necessary and proper clause. He wisely observed that rejecting a bank charter could severely limit other forms of charters, such as corporations which could be crucial to America's development. A national bank could manage the money supply, debt, and foreign exchange. Hamilton understood how banks could leverage America's wealth and prevent the country from becoming subservient to European mercantilists. After Hamilton's fifteen-thousand word rebuttal, Washington signed the legislation. Upon enactment, Hamilton went to work establishing an American currency. Previously, nine foreign currencies were accepted, but the United States did not have a viable one. He had to build a mint and coin money to establish an American currency. In developing the capability to mint coins, he relied on the calibrations of Isaac Newton for the British Treasury Board.

Hamilton proposed that the federal government promote the industrialization of America. He developed his *Report on Manufactures* that provided a blueprint for developing industry, but Congress took no action on it. As part of this national effort, the states issued charters to dozens of companies. Washington reluctantly backed Hamilton's policy, because he understood the importance of obtaining the most advanced weapons and for military self-sufficiency. Hamilton wanted to encourage entrepreneurs.

Some American historians regard Hamilton as the founder of American capitalism. Hamilton understood the importance of inventions that were being created at the time—steam engines, the cotton gin, and the use of interchangeable parts. Britain was using these inventions to exert world leadership and would, if left uncontested, dominate manufacturing. America had revolted against the British in part due to restrictions on its trading, financial, and manufacturing capabilities. Hamilton actively encouraged development of a textile industry. He believed agriculture and manufacturing had different economic cycles and could counterbalance one another. He understood the productivity increases that could be achieved through manufacturing. His writings foresaw the need for government involvement in infrastructure and regulation of the private sector. Jefferson and Madison were agrarian, opposed Hamilton, and had disdain for manufacturing. The conflict between Hamilton and Jefferson on this and other issues led to the development of political parties.

The extent of Washington's devotion to the economic security of the new nation was illustrated by his most difficult crisis—the Jay Treaty with England aligning America with British commercial interests. The treaty was a bet that England would be the power of the future, which proved to be correct. It also reflected America's dependence on the British Empire—for half of its exports and the overwhelming majority of its imports. The treaty was, however, highly unpopular—American sentiment was with the French for their support during the War. "No international treaty was ever more passionately denounced in the United States."[51] Jay said that he was burned in effigy in so many cities that he could walk the length of America at night lighted by the glow of his own figure. Only Washington's prestige enabled it to pass. English control of the seas helped to secure American trade, which roughly tripled in the seven-year period after the signing of the Treaty. This surge came notwithstanding the French efforts to unleash warships and privateers on American commerce. Despite the public criticism, Washington persevered, because it furthered the country's long-term economic and political interests.

Washington believed the events in Europe, such as the French Revolution, were only a sideshow and the critical issue for America was settling the frontier. He even served as commander-in-chief of the army to put down the Whiskey Rebellion. During his first term, Washington spent as much time on Indian affairs as on any other issue. When he personally brought his first treaties with the Indians before the Senate, a shouting match over procedural issues ensued, and he felt obliged to leave, ending the very brief role of the Senate as a full partner in these deliberations. He sought accommodation with the Native Americans and attempted to secure Indian sanctuaries, but his efforts failed.

Washington's farewell address was written jointly with Hamilton. The thrust of the statement was how to sustain national unity. His address never used the term "entangling alliances." It was not isolationist, favoring neutrality abroad and unity at home. Washington wanted America to stay out of war for twenty years to establish itself economically, a particularly wise policy given that Europe was engulfed in wars during this period. In significant part due to its distance from Europe and Asia, America was able to avoid war and conflicts except for minor skirmishes. Washington asserted America was a government based on moral standards. He believed slaves could be emancipated and lead productive lives. In his last will and testament, he ensured his slaves would be freed, selling off parts of Mount Vernon to provide for them. Washington was the most prominent Virginian to free his slaves. He was eulogized by Henry Lee as "First in war, first in peace, and first in the hearts of his countrymen," and widely recognized as the only one who could have performed these tasks in the founding of the American republic. "In effect, there were two distinct creative moments in the American founding, the winning of independence and the invention of nationhood, and Washington was the central figure in both creations."[52]

John Adams had a tough act to follow. He was principled, apolitical, and contemptuous of what was merely popular. Undiplomatic and impolitic, he was what one biographer referred to as "a party of one."[53] He retained much of Washington's cabinet which, unfortunately for him, maintained its loyalty to Hamilton as well as to the first president. This reinforced one of Adams' worst traits—he was inclined to make decisions alone without extensive consultation.

Adams did not support, but nonetheless signed, the Alien and Sedition Acts, which provided for the expulsion of aliens and imprisonment of anyone who uttered seditious statements, in effect abridging freedom of speech and press. He wisely avoided conflict with France, adhering to Washington's warning that a war would severely undermine the new nation's fledgling economy. With a change of only several hundred votes in New York City, he would have been re-elected.[54] Adams negotiated peace with France, but too late to affect the presidential election. The treaty let America out of her $20 million in obligations due the French for their assistance in the Revolutionary War. This diplomatic success also made possible the sale of the Louisiana Purchase just three years later.

Adams and Jefferson were enemies and opponents, which became the basis for forming two major political parties. They subsequently reconciled and died on the same day, July 4, 1826. In that era of primitive communications, Adams erroneously noted "Thomas Jefferson survives," but among his last words were the proclamation "Independence Forever!"[55] The first man to have slept in the White House, Adams wrote to his wife Abigail, "I pray Heaven to bestow the best of Blessings on this House and all that shall hereafter inhabit it. May none but honest and wise Men ever rule under this roof."[56]

The revolutionary generation proved extremely adept at making decisions to ensure the transformation of America from a tiny English colony into what became the greatest nation on earth. They felt guided by divine providence or the Invisible Hand. They were not infallible or necessarily geniuses; in fact, they made many mistakes. Washington engaged the British army in the open, early in the war, trying to strike a knock-out punch and nearly destroyed his own army. The Articles of Confederation were a failure and almost resulted in anarchy. Initial efforts to deal with the debts incurred from the war failed. After making a mistake, our early leaders were usually quick to admit error, take stock, find an alternative, and take another course. In one sense, they were fortunate to be blazing paths in a new world and facing a clean slate. If they went down the wrong road, they had the flexibility to quickly double back and take another route. They used this liberty to achieve three phenomenal objectives: independence, history's largest republic, and an American nation or union. By any reasonable standard, founding fathers were the best and smartest collection of public servants in history.

3

Origins and Nature
the american revolution

AN AMERICAN SCOUT EXPLAINS TO A BRITISH OFFICER that he is not going to Fort William Henry (in upstate New York) and the scout very nonchalantly says, "I'm going to "Ken-tuck-kee." The British officer, with a tone of incredulity says, "How can you go to Kentucky?" The scout replies matter of factly, "Well, you face north, turn left, and walk." Figuratively speaking, that is the history of America.

The founding fathers initiated radical reforms in an era awakening from centuries of little progress. The Old World, of course, played a role in developing the changes that took place in America, but much of Europe's own progress had been thwarted by war and adherence to traditional values and customs by monarchy and hierarchical structures.

The founding and formation of America was different. Our frontier and the civilization that moved westward represented a huge discontinuity in human history, a gap even greater than the oceans separating North America from Europe and from Asia. Anyone observing the history of the human race before the American Revolution might see little or no connection between what was happening worldwide and how mankind arrived at modernity. The outlines of today's world, however, could be seen in the colonies of the Revolutionary War period. Imagine an outside observer who, instead of viewing the entire world, was merely looking at that tiny outpost of western civilization, colonial America, and

- saw how many diverse settlements became one nation, the United States of America. The Puritans of New England, Dutch in New York, Quakers in Pennsylvania, Catholics in Maryland, and British and Germans in Virginia were the genesis of the words on the Great Seal of the United States—*E pluribus unum* (i.e., out of many, one).
- witnessed average American citizens becoming great military leaders in the Revolution by defeating the strongest military power in the world—typical Americans, like: Henry Knox, a bookseller from Boston; Nathanael Greene, a self-educated Quaker military strategist, merchant, and industrialist from Rhode Island; Francis Marion, a shy South Carolina planter; and John Sullivan a lawyer from New Hampshire.
- saw how the continental army utilized the skills of adventuresome military men from all over Europe, including Marquis de Lafayette from France, Casimir Pulaski and Thaddeus Kosciusko from Poland, and Baron von Steuben from Prussia who wrote the military bible for the Revolutionary Army.
- looked at the portraits of the wagon trains and the pioneer family willing to go to a new place to give the children a better future or saw the frontiersman and the great procession of the lone rifleman trekking west.
- saw how generation after generation of Americans gave their children a future—hopeful and better.

The outside observer who witnessed these phenomena could then understand how America and mankind arrived at today's world.

Many of us today have an idyllic, romantic version of the Revolutionary generation as conservative, established figures equivalent to the best of today's community leaders. We like to picture the founding fathers as "gentlemen, even stuffy or stodgy in powdered hair or wigs and knee breeches."[1] Some Americans view them as reactionaries for their role in slavery, the treatment of native Indians, the belief in Manifest Destiny, and the failure to grant women equal rights. Many other Americans have simply forgotten how radical the American dream was, how bold the founders of our democracy really were, and how the framers challenged the aristocratic assumptions and top-heavy power structures of Western civilization. The founding fathers were radical, even extremists by current standards. In terms of effectiveness and actual accomplishments, they were far more revolutionary than were the French later in the eighteenth century, the abolitionists of the nineteenth century, or the communists in the twentieth century. They were possessed by an unquenchable revolutionary spirit.

A leading historian of the Revolutionary period, Gordon Wood, emphasizes that this revolution was transcending, unprecedented, and radical:

> The colonists knew they were freer, more equal, more prosperous, and less burdened with cumbersome feudal and monarchical restraints than any other part of mankind in the eighteenth century. Such a situation, however, does not mean that colonial society was not susceptible to revolution. . . .
>
> If we measure the radicalism of revolutions by the degree of social misery or economic deprivation suffered, or by the number of people killed or manor houses burned, then this conventional emphasis on the conservatism of the American Revolution becomes true enough. But if we measure the radicalism by the amount of social change that actually took place—by transformations in the relationships that bound people to each other—then the American Revolution was not conservative at all; on the contrary: it was as radical and as revolutionary as any in history. Of course, the American Revolution was very different from other Revolutions. But it was no less radical and no less social for being different. In fact, it was one of the greatest revolutions the world has known, a momentous upheaval

that not only fundamentally altered the character of American society but decisively affected the course of subsequent history. . . .

By the early years of the nineteenth century the Revolution had created a society fundamentally different from the colonial society of the eighteenth century. It was in fact a new society unlike any that had ever existed anywhere in the world. . . . Americans had become, almost overnight, the most liberal, the most democratic, the most commercially minded, and the most modern people in the world.[2]

America's early settlers believed they were not only creating the New World, but bringing forth light and knowledge and pushing back darkness and ignorance. They saw the frontier as the edge of enlightenment forcing out barbarianism. Farmers were inventing new forms of agriculture and cultivation, improving their understanding of nature. Respect for God was spreading everywhere and was freely exercised. Personal relationships were more benevolent and less paternalistic. America's founding fathers were fighting battles for freedom and liberty against tyranny, establishing a republic to replace a monarchy and, whether they knew it or not, establishing a whole new civilization.

The Origins

Benjamin Franklin (1706–1790) was probably the archetypical founding father, known for his homely aphorisms and pragmatism. Self-made, optimistic, industrious, and frugal, he retired from business to spend the rest of his life in public service. With his business, science, political, and social acumen, Franklin, probably more than any other individual, understood what was happening at the time of the Revolution.

THE POWER OF THE PRINTING PRESS

While the quality of life and standard of living were dramatically different, the crucial issues confronting Franklin's generation have remarkable parallels to today's major problems. Franklin started as one of the first printers in America, a lowly artisan. Yet, no event had more to do with the initial success of America than did the fifteenth-century invention of the printing press. Franklin and later Americans were most effective at using it, establishing a distinguishing trait of American civilization: innovation and public information.

Originally invented in China, development of the printing press was severely constrained by the language and the culture—there were about 50,000 Chinese characters and its social organization was ultra-bureaucratic. For the goldsmith Johannes Gutenberg (1400–1468), the 26 letters of the alphabet were well adapted for the new movable type technology. His background in working with gold enabled him to develop a system for shaping large numbers of tiny pieces of metal through the use of punches and molds that formed the basis for movable type. Gutenberg then had to invent a method for composing the type into sheets that were reduced to pages, which in turn were folded and stitched into books.[3] His first book took almost twenty years to produce, appearing in 1455. His efforts were advanced by improvement in paper manufacture, better ink, progress in metallurgy, and experienced printers. In the next fifty years, more books were produced than in the previous thousand years. Large medieval libraries often contained only 100 to 300 books. Soon 40,000 editions of all kinds of works had been issued; 9 million volumes from over 100 presses. Prior to Gutenberg, a monk could copy 4 pages a day, 25 pages during a 6-day week, and 1,250 pages annually; a sixteenth century printer could produce 2.5 million pages a year. In an era characterized by a slow pace of change, the impact of one device, the printing press, is almost unfathomable, overnight delivering more than a thousand times more productivity as part of an algorithmic upward curve.

Franklin was known for publishing *Poor Richard's Almanac* with maxims and pithy statements such as "Three may keep a secret if two of them are dead." Almanacs, in fact, outsold all other books in eighteenth-century America. As printer and publisher, Franklin understood the importance of content and distribution and how to *mobilize* public opinion. He also knew how to avoid arguments and controversy, propounding his most important political treatises anonymously. Franklin, one of the ablest American writers, produced newspapers, pamphlets, and magazines. When a competitor became the postmaster and refused to distribute his newspaper, he turned the tables by wheedling the position for himself and eventually returning the favor. Four sets of world changes were triggered by the invention of the printing press: (1) The Age of Enlightenment; (2) global exploration and the scientific revolution, (3) Europe's failures and efforts to reform politically; and (4) the rise and fall of world civilizations and the Renaissance.

THE AGE OF ENLIGHTENMENT

Books made possible the unfolding of the Enlightenment between 1550 and the American Revolution in the late 1700s. The printing press developed a market for philosophical and scientific manuscripts. Authors, such as Copernicus (1473–1543), Francis Bacon (1561–1626), and Descartes (1596–1650), spread new scientific ideas, while powerful philosophers, such as Voltaire (1694–1778), Locke (1632–1704), and Rousseau (1712–1778) established a new worldview, which in turn resulted in new economic, political, and social revolutions.

> The West saw the emergence of a newly self-conscious and autonomous human being—curious about the world, confident in his own judgments, skeptical of orthodoxies, rebellious against authority, responsible for his own beliefs and actions, enamored of the classical past but even more committed to a greater future, proud of his humanity, conscious of his distinctness from nature, aware of his artistic powers as individual creator, assured of his intellectual capacity to comprehend and control nature and altogether less dependent on an omnipotent God.[4]

The Enlightenment fathered probably the greatest collection of distinguished philosophers whose ideas, philosophies, and views provided unique perspectives to challenge and stimulate the founding fathers in their efforts to establish a different civilization. Americans embraced moderate Enlightenment figures, such as John Locke and Isaac Newton, but were less enthusiastic about skeptics such as Voltaire and radical philosophers such as Rousseau. For the first time, the printing press ensured the widespread dissemination of these great intellects, not just among each other, but to a rapidly expanding literate population

Montesquieu (1689–1755), the writer most quoted by the founding fathers, wrote the first comparative study of civilizations, *Spirit of Laws.* He discussed the importance of the relationships between various spheres—economy, polity, religion, and society or culture, a concept that provided the basis for structuring American civilization. For liberty to flourish, he suggested a separation from and balance between each of these spheres to be necessary. Montesquieu originated the concept of separation of powers: the legislature should make the laws but not administer them; the executive should supervise their implementation, but not make them; the judiciary should limit itself to interpreting the law.

For Americans, John Locke (1632–1704) became a most influential philosopher of the Enlightenment. For Locke, knowledge of the world rested on man's experience. In essence, he was the "anti-philosopher," arguing that man should cease disputes over what could not be proved, such as metaphysical and religious doctrine. This would reduce the need for war and heated disputes over opinions and religious differences, focusing man's efforts on certain or practical knowledge such as that needed for improving human well-being and for global exploration. Locke wrote the treatises on government that guided the Constitutional Convention. He was the epitome of the traditional liberal, believing in the limited role of government and the importance of private property. Essentially his philosophy reflected the English system with its reliance on capitalism and the Parliament, which was at the time the most successful system in the world.

Other philosophers pioneered new ideas and concepts. These European thinkers and philosophers were widely read by and communicated with John Adams (1735–1826), Thomas Jefferson (1743–1826), James Madison (1751–1836), and Benjamin Franklin.

GLOBAL EXPLORATION AND THE SCIENTIFIC REVOLUTION

Global exploration had been spurred by the Crusades (1095–1300), which expanded Europe's horizon in the medieval era. Overland routes to Asia, such as those popularized by Marco Polo (1254–1324) in his *Book of Various Experiences,* stimulated demand for spices and other Asian products. The development of the magnetic compass helped to make ocean travel more reliable. The discovery of magnetic lodestone had been made in China, but it took several hundred years before the compass was developed to assist navigation. Europe began to build large, full-rigged ships. These improvements led to a decline in the costs of sea transport, which made imports much cheaper and increased demand. European legend told of an Atlantis waiting to be discovered beyond the the known horizon. The creation of joint stock companies enabled organizations that could bear the risk for expensive explorations by limiting the liability for individual investors.

Global exploration had subsequently been accelerated by European pluralism and competition—at least a half dozen countries had been racing to claim the New World. Two innovations spurred development of large ocean-going vessels: side oars that had been used for steering were replaced with the sternpost rudder, which required only one steersman instead of many; and the magnetic compass, which allowed the navigator to determine and maintain the ship's bearing even in the most inclement weather. Using these advances, Venetians had devised the great galley, which vastly extended shipping capabilities. Printing presses and books became articles of trade and spurred exploration efforts, some of which led to the discovery of the American continents. Books and pamphlets described probes of the explorers and made possible the creation of reliable maps. Exploration led to a new consciousness recognizing that most of earth was water not land. The world was no longer inward looking with limited horizons where people stayed close to home. Natives paid attention to what was happening beyond their villages; their perspectives became more global.

New discoveries had produced the Scientific Revolution. Scientists, such as Galileo (1564–1650) and Johannes Kepler (1571–1630), stressed the importance of the printing press and public information in unleashing the scientific method. Inventors and scholars were able to build on the work of distant colleagues. Published information enabled inventors and manufacturers to see the rapid adoption of their ideas and products in the marketplace. Printing changed the economics of processing technical information. Previously, it was more economical to keep such information secret or proprietary, but publishing created profits from the sale of books and an entire new market for making information public.

Based on previous Chinese and Arabia know-how, Roger Bacon (1214–1294) developed gunpowder. Formerly, in a siege, defenders had the advantages (catapults and battering rams being ineffective against fortress walls), but now the attackers gained the edge. In fact, few things have altered an activity more than gunpowder in revolutionizing war. Combat was no longer man-to-man—it was done at a distance. Bullets, cannons, and detonating devices blew up walls, buildings, and obstacles, radically changing war strategy. Monarchies became more and more absolute as the fief declined and power could be centralized. War became more destructive. European soldiers armed with guns could disburse large numbers of American natives and had a major advantage in their efforts at exploration and colonization. Military technology continued to advance. Mechanical locks made firing easier, rifling of the barrels ensured a true projectile, and breech-loading mechanisms made loading more rapid.

Benjamin Franklin was America's ambassador-at-large, chief scientist, and a citizen of the world. His reputation, experiments with electricity, and the Franklin stove were world renowned. Popular fascination with electricity made him an international celebrity, Immanuel Kant (1724–1804) calling him the modern Prometheus who stole fire from the heavens. He invented the bifocal lens and lightning rod. Franklin also mapped the Gulf Stream, saving countless lives and expediting commerce. His many positive attributes enabled him to overcome the European stereotypic image of America as a primitive and backward nation, enabling him to be a highly effective ambassador. His scientific background combined with extensive travel overseas made him one of the first global leaders.

Ben Franklin's worldview, his presence in Europe, and his practical bent helped to bring a sense of the rapidly expanding world to America. The powerful synergies between the information revolution, the scientific revolution, and global exploration brought enormous changes to Europe and initiated a search for a fresh paradigm for the New World.

EUROPE'S FAILURES AND EFFORTS TO REFORM

Europe had failed to make progress on crucial problems. For hundreds of years, the European continent was continuously torn by war: constant strife cast doubt on the ability of organized Christianity to foster peace and security, undermined Europe's ability to sustain any lasting economic growth, and stimulated people to migrate to the New World.

Europe and its monarchies suffered from a breakdown in morality. In most courts, gifts were required to get charters, patents, monopolies, and offices. Thomas Jefferson wrote that "no American should come to Europe under thirty years of age." Violators of this maxim would find themselves ensnared by female intrigue or worse by whores and "learn to consider fidelity to the marriage bed as an ungentlemanly practice and inconsistent with happiness."[5] Benjamin Franklin noted the "prevailing corruption and degeneracy of your [i.e., British] people."[6] After Charles II of England was betrothed to Catherine of Portugal, he claimed to be happily married. When Lady Castlemaine gave birth to his boy a few weeks later, Charles publicly embraced her, humiliating his wife. His many other dalliances were excused by the explanation that adultery is a royal privilege. When one of his mistresses was mistaken for another from Catholic France she said to the disapproving audience, "Be silent, good people; I am the Protestant whore."

Religious intolerance and suppression were omnipresent. The Catholic Pope banned many editions of the Bible, enforcing his edict with book burnings. Copernicus, Kepler, and Galileo faced persecution from religious authorities. Men were burned at the stake and broken on the wheel for unorthodox religious views. The Protestant English Parliament passed laws barring Catholics from practicing medicine or law, preventing them from serving as executors or guardians, forbidding them from traveling more than five miles from their homes, and requiring them to sign oaths of loyalty to the Protestant form of government. Priests were summarily executed for refusing to sign these oaths.

Religious intolerance and suppression in Europe led to the Reformation (1515–1563). The printing press ended the virtual monopoly the Catholic Church had held over information dissemination. Religious works were translated from Latin and printed in French, German, and English. The monarchy and the Church tried to control this emerging freedom of information through taxation, censorship, and licensing. Monks and copiers protested that their jobs would be eliminated. Library owners feared the value of their collections would be diminished. The clergy, quite correctly, feared the printing press would be a vehicle for subversive ideas.

On October 31, 1517, Martin Luther posted 95 theses in Latin at Wittenberg. The religious reformation might have foundered had it not been for the printing press. John Wycliffe (1330–1384) in England and Jan Hus in Bohemia (1370–1415) had previously initiated popular revolts, but they had to rely on word of mouth and made little progress. Luther, however, used the printing press effectively, issuing books, pamphlets, and private letters to disseminate his message. Within a decade of the beginning of the Reformation, the number of books rose six fold and four-fifths of these publications favored the Reformation, including many bestsellers. Books on orthodox Christianity were a hard sell. Luther's books outsold almost everything else and appeared in most languages. The printing and widespread dissemination of the New Testament in languages other than Latin revealed the Catholic Church to be out of step with public demand: increasing numbers of people could read the text themselves and find out, for example, how Christ showed sympathy for the poor. In contrast, the Church leaders lived profligately and cared more about catering to the wealthy than evidencing charity to the poor. Books were powerful tools of the Reformation and the printing press was linked to the revolt against the hierarchical Catholic Church.

For over a century after the Reformation, Europe was embroiled in war. Europeans realized these disputes could not be resolved on the battlefield. Judeo-Christian values and doctrine continued to play a major role, but with the war between religions unresolved, religious beliefs began to lose their hold over man. Science became the preeminent intellectual authority and human reason began to replace theological doctrine and the scriptures.

THE RISE AND FALL OF WORLD CIVILIZATIONS

The founding fathers were acutely aware of the importance of escaping the fate of classical civilization and were extremely anxious about this risk. "For the history of antiquity did not teach the inevitability of progress. It taught the perishability of republics, the transience of glory, the mutability of human affairs."[7] Brief periods of republicanism and democracy had been extinguished by barbarians and absolutism. There were extremely limited precedents—in some of the Greek city-states, the short period of the Roman Republic, in some Swiss cantons and Italian city-states, and, very briefly, in Denmark. All of these efforts failed or were relatively insignificant. In Greece, Rome, and contemporary experiments in Europe, citizenship had been limited, never exceeding in the thousands. Greece and Rome were fundamentally flawed, because the economy was based on slavery.[8] Much of the rest of history had been dominated by war, famine, disease, slavery, religious intolerance, and monarchy.

The discovery of the New World led to a debate about what causes the rise and fall of civilizations. During the war for independence, Edward Gibbon's (1737–1794) classic, *The Decline and Fall of the Roman Empire*, was published.

American settlers believed themselves at a crucial crossroads of history. Religion was the driving force for many of the members of the Revolutionary generation. Being well versed in the Bible and religious history, many compared their adventure to the story in Exodus, a biblical analogy of powerful symbolism. For many European settlers, America became the Promised Land. Despite the many obstacles, colonialists were optimistic about their prospects, believing they were "present at the creation." John Adams expressed his exasperation with the precarious nature of the American experiment when he pleaded, "The lawmakers of antiquity legislated for single cities. Who can legislate for 20 or 30 states, each of which is larger than Greece or Rome?"

The classical Greeks, however, had provided Americans with insight on how a tiny group of people could make a huge impact on human history. Greek strength was built on sea power and the Athenian fleet opened up ports to Greek trade, using superior technology and finances to dominate the Mediterranean. The Greeks developed coins, a cornerstone of modern commerce. Burgeoning trade gave the Greeks contact with other cultures, enabling them to improve their own society.

Rome itself served as a vessel for Greek civilization and later for Christianity. The American colonists frequently referred to and cited Cicero's Roman Senate. Christianity addressed a crisis of spirituality, a vacuum not filled by the Romans. As Christianity spread, the Roman Catholic Church evolved, becoming increasingly centralized. Emperor Constantine converted and instead of being its persecutor, Rome thus became Christianity's defender. "As the Roman Empire became Christian, Christianity became Roman."[9]

In addition to internal decay, attacks on Rome by the barbarians were critical to its decline. Rome had opportunities to push back the barbarians. Early in the first century of the Christian era, Roman legions attempted to pacify and civilize the region beyond the Rhine. In the Teutomburg Forest, tribesmen led by Arminius surprised and annihilated three Roman legions of 15,000 men. Subsequently, Caesar Augustus confined the empire to the existing natural frontier. Rome never secured the area above the Rhine, which then became a safe haven for the barbarians who eventually overran the Roman Empire and were assimilated or converted to Christianity. The barbarians were often family-oriented, egalitarian, and in many ways democratic. Greek and Roman culture was thus mostly extinguished with the Church playing a vital role in sustaining civilization. The role of barbarians in the decline of Rome and in extinguishing much of classical culture until the Renaissance (1379–1615) led to the colonists concerns that Indians and savages could snuff out American culture and civilization.

After the barbarian invasions, Europe was weak and decentralized. In this vacuum, the knight provided protection and became an almost invincible fighting machine. The invention of the stirrup enabled the knight to effectively use armor, swords, and lances while riding on horseback, which, in turn, led to seizure of church land and the establishment of feudalism. Beyond agriculture, most of a village's energy was devoted to supporting a knight, including attendants, squires, and dozens of peasant families, resulting in the creation of small, commercial enterprises. The knight controlled a fiefdom, a decentralized power base that encouraged other elements of medieval society to become autonomous, thus beginning a pluralistic society in which small groups obtained more authority and power.[10]

> This phase of 'feudal' civilization, the five or so centuries between the eighth and thirteenth centuries, provided the possible gateway to a kind of civilization never before envisaged in the world. A large, diverse, agrarian civilization was broken into small, competing quasi-states, unified under Christianity, yet preserving their differences. The system was based on contractual ties and not birth differences, on achievement rather than ascription. There was an antagonism, yet balance between the growing power of the Church and the State, but neither was dominant and they had not yet formed a close alliance. Most of whatever power kinship had once held had been destroyed. Commerce and towns were encouraged, as was technological innovation in the saving of labor in the difficult and population-scarce environment. Thought and recovered knowledge were relatively free of the jealousies of a powerful clergy.[11]

The four separate, distinct building blocks of modern pluralism were established: from Rome came government; from Christianity and Greece came culture; from barbarians came a focus on family and individual responsibility; and from Rome and the barbarians came the beginnings of capitalist economy with an emphasis on property rights. In Europe, this system spurred the use of gunpowder, printing, and other technologies, as composed to Asia where a single authority usually had monopoly powers, which brought stagnation. This technology advantage proved crucial at sea where cannon on ships ensured European dominance of most of the world. In contrast to the monolithic Chinese civilization, seven European states (Spain, Portugal, England, France, Holland, Sweden, and Denmark) exercised the naval power needed for planting colonies.

During the past few centuries, the bedrock of freedom and democracy has been the free flow of information, encouraged by a virtuous cycle in printing. The printing press continuously expanded the availability of publications—classical writings, music scores, philosophical treatises, and literary works. Until Gutenberg, only a tiny percentage of the population could read and few had access to books. Before printing, libraries were few with little access to even basic writings such as the Bible. Literacy became an important skill that revolutionized and eliminated many social structures. Entrepreneurial printers brought new products to market. This created a potent cycle— more and more people read the increasingly wide range of books available, spurring printers to produce more titles and more editions. New books and a devotion to study of the Scriptures resulted in nearly universal literacy among adult males in some communities.

Educated Americans learned much about the rise and fall of civilization from studying books and writings on China, Spain, and England. In 1500, Islamic, Chinese, and other Asian cultures were more advanced than Europe's. Africa was considered to be a continent of wealth. In the period between the thirteenth and sixteenth centuries, the Chinese might have become the dominant world civilization. The country produced silk, used high-tech weaving machines, and manufactured iron in dozens of foundries, consuming as much iron in the eleventh century as Europe consumed in the eighteenth century. The Chinese developed a primitive compass centuries before its use in Western Europe. China invented paper, printing, gunpowder, and water-powered machinery and may have been the first country to use paper money. When Vasco de Gama (1460–1524) reached East Africa, he found the natives surprised by the small size of his ships (the Chinese ships which had visited there previously were up to ten times the size) and by the limited and shoddy nature of his trading goods. Worldwide, Chinese culture was the most advanced intellectually, technologically, culturally, and socially.

The Chinese civilization was comparable to that of the Romans and had declined for reasons similar to the fall of the Empire—its over-centralization, being overrun by barbarians, and the lack of dynastic succession. Amazingly, the Chinese would limit foreign trade, fearing self-reliant ship captains. They did not use their superior technology and avoided creating an autonomous power beyond the central government control. The Chinese rid themselves of mechanical clocks, stopped development of water-driven spinning machines, and generally retreated from their own industrial and mechanical advances. China had no real concept of progress or improvement; Chinese authorities were isolationist, centralized, and bureaucratic. Chinese civilization did not develop clear lines between religion, politics, civil society, family, and government; it had a monolithic culture. China's failure to develop a pluralistic society and to effectively deal with the forces of globalization led to its slow decline.

After Columbus discovered the New World, Spain possessed the largest empire on earth, as well as the biggest navy. In the sixteenth century, its empire was arguably twenty times greater than had been the Roman empire; Spain spanned across the entire globe. Yet, England eventually emerged as Europe's global powerhouse.

Native Americans had no experience with European civilization and technology. Gunpowder enabled the more civilized societies to avoid the historical pattern of defeat at the hands of the less civilized forces. A few dozen European horsemen with guns could conquer thousands of Native Americans. In one such battle 168 Spaniards routed over 80,000 natives, killing thousands without themselves suffering one casualty. The American natives' isolated and illiterate cultures collapsed, because they failed to understand history, human invaders, or the superiority and effectiveness of the Europeans. Advanced levels of plant and animal domestication gave the Europeans major advantages. The horse, for example, provided an enormous military edge. The higher level of domestication had given the Europeans far more exposure to diseases (many human plagues develop as a result of interaction with other animal species) and built up immunities in the European population. The isolated Native American culture had experienced little or no exposure to smallpox and other European epidemics. As much as 95 percent of the native populations was wiped out by disease, with the remainder becoming demoralized by it. The more diverse and global European civilization had the advantage of metal tools (bronze and iron), mechanized power sources, the wheel, superior sea transport, and a pluralistic and literate culture.[12]

England's emergence as the leading global power was due to four main factors:

1. *An open, pluralist structure.* England did not have an absolutist and centralized political structure, but was relatively open. Church and state were separate. England gradually developed distinct separations between economic, political, social, and cultural spheres. Its social order was not rigid or caste-like. England never experienced feudalism to the extent that did continental Europe but was a society of small landowners who became businessmen in an established middle class. Private ownership provided individuals with a stake in society and in the community. In other empires, as wealth grew and defense became more expensive, taxes were raised, driving the poor into misery. In England, the wealthier middle class could afford to pay the higher taxes

2. *A constitutional government.* In England, the people had a constitution and government balanced by two houses. The Magna Charta (1215), through which the feudal barons had forced the monarchy to liberalize, provided concessions to the Catholic Church and commercial activities, and it granted individuals certain liberties and elections. English precedent, set in 1322, required the consent of a national assembly to establish the validity of any law. This series of events was critical to the

establishment of a genuine rule of law to which everyone and every institution was subject, one of the most crucial advances of the past millennium.

3. *Status as an insular island.* England's ascendancy was protected by its geographical separation from the European continent and its wars. In other countries, warfare led to large armies and heavy taxes, stifling economic growth.

4. *Commitment to capitalism, free markets, and free trade.* New forms of commerce and technological advances created wealth and furthered economic growth. The English modeled their ascendancy after the Dutch commercial successes of the 1600s. Dutch vessels carried three-fourths of the European sea trade and 10 percent of its adult males were sailors. England developed three of the critical components of capitalism: ownership, individual liberties, and enforceable contracts. Like other European countries, England was an empire, but its objective was to find customers for its goods rather than to extract wealth (which, on the Continent, was often squandered in war). This kind of trade and commerce led to manufacturing and the expansion of the middle class. Capitalism began in the home: father, mother, son, and daughter each played an entrepreneurial role, and many homes were miniature factories. By the mid-seventeenth century, England's capitalistic economy included: aluminum, brass, and paper factories; cannon foundries; and deep mines for coal, copper, tin, iron, and lead extraction.

The English also had a tradition of radical reform, including the Glorious Revolution, sometimes referred to as America's first revolution. Similar to the motivations of the American colonists, the British sought to secure personal liberties, republican government, common-law rights, capitalism, taxation limited to the extent of representation, and the rights of the people to conduct their international relations free of foreign influence. The British secretly invited Protestant Prince William of Orange from Holland to overthrow their out-of-touch Catholic monarch, King James II. This political revolution advanced representative government, created a Bill of Rights, and established the Bank of England as well as mechanisms for funding government debt.[13]

Monarchy was the predominant form of government throughout Europe. Even Montesquieu thought monarchy to be better than democracy, fearing despotism and rule by the mob or tribe. He was concerned about the fragility of liberty, that it had only flourished briefly in Greece and Rome, and that republics and democracies could not last very long. Monarchy was simpler to establish since it relied on force and power, while democratic forms of government required constant effort, management, and planning. Monarchy could deal effectively with the two most important functions of government at the time: mobilization for war and procurement of food during times of shortage. It was believed that free republican states could succeed only when they were small and that large republics would splinter into anarchy without the coercive power of the monarch. Monarchy provided its subjects with a security blanket, a set station and place in life that obviated the need to deal with the uncertainties of liberty and freedom.

The English monarchy, however, was charitable to the American colonies. Under King George II, Britain exercised strong leadership in the French and Indian War, which was the first real global war and which led directly to the American Revolution and helped to ensure its outcome. From the British, the colonists learned the importance of strategy and a global perspective. William Pitt developed the brilliant strategy that contained France in Europe, utilized British naval sea power to defeat the French in the Americas, and treated colonials as allies not subjects. Pitt had British forces seize French outposts in Africa, the Caribbean, and India, disrupting trade and commerce. The British leadership edge extended up and down the chain of command and into the civilian sector as well. The war created the desire for revenge by the badly vanquished French. Europe, particularly Prussia, ended the war exhausted. By contrast, America built a sense of identity that led eventually to independence. North Americans were joyful for the conclusion of the French and Indian war. Unlike Europe where the struggle was confined largely to men in arms, the American conflict was civily brutal, with Indians savagely preying on women and children in the most gruesome manner imaginable.[14]

In the Revolutionary War, the lackluster British commanders appointed by King George III provided a stark contrast to America's gifted leaders. Lacking leadership, the British no longer had a coherent strategy or global perspective. When George Washington was presented with a proposal to capture a leading British general, Alexander Hamilton dissuaded him from proceeding, because it was likely that King George would appoint someone more competent.

The Nature
of the American Revolution

America's leaders instituted radical changes in government, but also in religion, civil society, social custom, military strategy, the private marketplace, and the individual's relationship to the world. The Revolutionary War generation overthrew customs, habits, and traditions that had gone unaltered and often unchallenged for centuries, revolutionizing the way humans live and fundamentally altering subsequent history. The monumental and breathtaking changes that have occurred over the past two centuries are a direct result of the decisions and reforms made by this generation.

America's natural advantages included the extraordinary courage of its immigrants and the fecundity of its land and population. European turmoil and failures, along with conditions throughout the globe, encouraged migration to America. Never had man's prognosis looked so bleak as when the future proved so fulfilling and prosperous in the New World. China had stagnated. India was dissembling. Islam was in retreat. Japan was in limbo. South American and African civilizations had been destroyed. European countries such as Spain and Portugal were in decline—only Holland and England were progressing. Settlers coming to America faced starvation, disease, and a life-threatening voyage so as to set foot on what initially appeared to be an unpromising wilderness.

EARLY IMMIGRANTS

Americans were exceptional and unique. If European failures had provided the sole or major motivation for immigrating, millions of additional people would have broken away and come to America. "[T]here was something in the spirit of the men and women who voluntarily made the break and migrated, a force of character not simply determined by economic, political, or religious conditions—a force that made them different from their neighbors who remained in the turmoil and poverty of the Old World. That something was a quality of energy, enterprise, daring, or aspiration that was to be a power in the course of American history, immediately and by transmission through coming generations."[15]

The first set of European settlements in America failed; the second set barely survived. Walter Raleigh's initial "lost colony" in Roanoke and the Jamestown colony settled twenty years later were subject to calamitous droughts that may have been the worst of the past millennium. The Jamestown settlers survived only through innovating and adopting to the new environment, the leadership of Captain John Smith, and the fortuitous arrival of a relief party from Europe. The slightest miscalculation or misfortune could mean death, starvation, or dire poverty for a settler's family. On average, 5 to 10 percent of the immigrants perished on the voyage to the New World, and a comparable percentage died within a few months of arrival, from disease or by being severely weakened by the passage. Some of the new arrivals were criminals, outcasts, and slaves, but the very fact of their survival during the difficult or brutal crossing provided them with a special character.

Many of the immigrants were Puritans, who at first were only a small percentage of the immigrants, but at one point were 80 percent of the population in the North, 20 percent in the South. Eventually, however, Puritans were only a small percent.

Despite this environment, the population of the colonies exploded and their economies grew at a phenomenal pace. In 1700, the colonial economy was about a twentieth the size of Britain's; by 1775 it was two-fifths. The population doubled every generation. In 1700, America had been only a twentieth of the British and Irish population combined; by 1770 it had climbed to a fifth. At the end of the eighteenth century, people were being forced out from the East Coast by over-crowding and soil depletion. In one generation, North Carolina grew six fold and Georgia ten fold. Benjamin Franklin accurately predicted the number of Americans would exceed the British population within a century

In Europe, land was expensive and wages cheap, forcing people to delay having children. In America, land was cheap and labor was scarce, encouraging people to have children. Americans married at double the rate of Europeans and had twice as many children. Plentiful food produced healthier individuals. The per capita caloric intake of Americans was, on average, much higher than in Europe.

For settlers coming to the New World not only was there undis-covered land, there was also a new way of life and almost limitless opportunity. America was always reinventing, starting again, and indeed becoming a New World. The social structure let everyone start anew each generation. The seemingly endless space provided ample room for dissent, diversification, and the creation of enormous wealth. There was a hopeful sense of fecundity to the land, ethos, and people.

RELIGION

A crucial factor was the spirit and religious fervor that infused politics, the economy, the culture, and society. Most colonists possessed the ultimate safety net—their own faith. Blown far off course from their intended destination of the Hudson River, the Pilgrims ended up off the coast of Cape Cod. Since a new settlement could be viewed as an act of defiance, they decided to pledge their allegiance to King James and called their new colony Plymouth. Governor William Bradford, an eyewitness, reported that when the *Mayflower* passengers landed on the American shore in November 1620: "They fell upon their knees and blessed the God of Heaven who had brought them over the vast and furious ocean and, delivered them from all the perils and miseries [of Europe]." Religion was often the only anchor the immigrant could rely on for security. During the first winter, half of the passengers who made the voyage would die of starvation and disease, but no one would make the return trip on the *Mayflower* the next spring.

Religious persecution forced many Europeans to migrate to America and most settlers had a strong set of religious convictions. The long crossings and inspirational sightings of land became analogous to the trip through the wilderness, the passage across the Red Sea, and the entrance to the Promised Land. Rarely were a people more certain they were on the right track. "The Puritans surely were theology-minded. The doctrines of the Fall of Man, of Sin, of Salvation, Predestination, Election, and Conversion were their meat and drink. Yet what really distinguished them in their day was that they were less interested in theology itself, than in the application of theology to everyday life, and especially to society." As they were confronted with the difficulties of the frontier and the New World, their interests were practical. "They conceived that by going out into the Wilderness, they were reliving the story of Exodus and not merely obeying an explicit command to go into the wilderness. For them the Bible was less a body of legislation than a set of binding precedents."[16] Christianity provided the colonists with a crucial core value—moral fortitude.

They brought their religion from Europe, but also religious intolerance. For the mere failure to comply with dogma, houses were burned and inhabitants sent back to Europe. There were whippings, ears cut off, banishment, and the famous Salem witch hunt where those who admitted guilt were freed, while those who refused to confess were judged guilty. Efforts to institute formal state-sponsored religion spawned a paranoia that such efforts were going on in secret.

America was a big country with plenty of room for dissent. Roger Williams was to be sent back to England by the Massachusetts Bay Colony, but escaped through the woods during a harsh winter to Rhode Island, establishing a colony welcoming dissidents. Williams, who believed his family's survival was due to divine providence, appropriately named his settlement Providence. William Penn's father left him a fortune, including a huge claim against the British crown, which Penn subsequently persuaded the king to cancel in return for the large tract of land now known as Pennsylvania. His colony became the closest to any place in the British Empire in being free and democratic. Penn's colony thought big from the beginning—two dozen ships were in the first voyage to the New World. Philadelphia's design was much like London. Over time, religious intolerance declined, because there were many places in America where an individual could be religious and free.

In the first part of the eighteenth century, the Great Awakening changed colonial culture in profound ways. Spread by word of mouth, it urged a rebirth of faith, a New Man. From a religious perspective, it created an ethic of benevolence and loosened the Calvinist doctrine of predestination (that only those designated before birth by God could be saved). "God was perceived less often as transcendent and self-contained, more often as immanent and relational. Divine revelation was equated more simply with the Bible alone than with the Scripture embedded in a self-conscious ecclesiastical tradition. The physical world created by God was more likely to be regarded as understandable, progressing, and malleable than as mysterious, inimical, and fixed."[17] The leading movement figure, Jonathan Edwards, believed in a demanding, intense religious experience, a conversion of the heart. Oratorical sermons replaced written lectures. Edwards inspired unprecedented religious fervor and caused a huge upsurge in church membership and personal religious development.

George Whitefield delivered powerful, inflammatory, and enthusiastic sermons. When rejected by the established religious authorities, Whitefield persuaded Benjamin Franklin to arrange a hall to be rebuilt to accommodate his preachings, which were heard by as many as 20,000 people at once.

The Great Awakening emphasized a more spiritual version of the church, which resulted in a decline of the institution, but a transfer of its religious fervor to the nation or culture at-large. The Great Awakening was amorphous, without a beginning or end, without set ideology, hierarchical leadership, or formal religious doctrine. A formative event in American history, it gave religion an American flavor. The Great Awakening fostered the idea of equality, encouraged democratic feelings, and transformed Puritans into Yankees. It led to the

American Revolution. As John Adams noted, "The Revolution was effected before the War commenced. The Revolution was in the mind and hearts of the people: change in their religious sentiments, of their duties and obligations. This radical change in the principles, opinions, sentiments and affectations of the people was the real American Revolution."[18] The strength of the Revolutionary War generation was directly related to the spiritual strength of the Great Awakening, the belief in standing up for what was considered right.

This religious transformation and merging of religion and republicanism happened only in America. In the rest of the world, it was assumed that the concept of republican government contradicted the principles of traditional religion. In America, people became so accustomed to the unity of these two value systems, it "dulled the awareness of how strikingly original the new nation's 'Christian republicanism' actually was." They merged in a manner found nowhere else on earth. The French and Indian War against the papist France helped to drive this transformation. The Revolutionary War against the British discouraged adherence to traditional, orthodox Protestantism. This was in turn tempered by the excesses of the zealots of the French Revolution. "[T]he essential difference between the American Revolution and the French Revolution is that the American Revolution . . . was a religious event, whereas the French Revolution was an anti-religious event."[20]

PUBLIC VIRTUE

Out of this religious fervor came an intense desire to create a society based on virtue, an effort at a moral and social reformation. Classical republicanism encouraged public virtue and public service. The founding fathers believed they had a civic duty to lead the nation, build consensus, and serve the government, which should act in the public interest. By this they "meant that they would become the special kind of simple, austere, egalitarian and virtuous people that history and enlightened social science said was essential for the sustenance of a republic. The moral quality of their society thus became a measure of the success of their Revolution."[21] In the Puritan tradition there is a driving force that permeates American society to this day to improve things, to live up to one's duty, to do what is right, and to stand for everything that is right. These immigrants reacted with revulsion against the sexual promiscuity and immorality of European monarchs and royalty. This intense dislike was reinforced by the strong belief that that Europe was on the wrong track because of its immorality.

CIVIC INVOLVEMENT

A civil society evolved out of these austere values. From America's religiosity, countless charitable societies were created, and civil society expanded to take care of the poor. Benjamin Franklin was an architect of colonial civil society: he started libraries and volunteer fire companies, advised people on the dangers of fire, and worked to promote inoculation against smallpox. To make streets safe, he organized night watchmen. He started a hospital for the poor by using the concept of matching grants. To deal with smoke and cold indoors, he invented the Franklin stove, but turned down a patent in order to make the stove widely available. One of the voluntary associations begun by Franklin was the militia, predecessor of the continental army.

CULTURAL VALUES AND EQUALITY

The religious, spiritual, and ethical drive of the colonists spurred radical transformation of their cultural values. In the beginning, colonial America was a monarchical society which meant that each individual was subordinate to the king, not as an employee or soldier, but more as would be a child—dependent, "weak and inferior, without autonomy or independence, easily cowed by the pageantry and trappings of a patriarchal king." Monarchy was based on dependence from the king on down to bonded laborers and slaves at the bottom, but every one had their assigned role. "In such a society it was inconceivable, unnatural, for inequality not to exist.... The hierarchy of a monarchical society was part of the natural order of things, part of that great chain of existence that orders the entire universe."[22] Social ranks were designated, titles assigned, and detailed customs specified on how to deal with people above and below one's rank.

America had no rigid class structure. There was never a nobility and no permanently impoverished class (other than slaves). American society was rooted in English customs, which were more egalitarian than those of Europe. Nevertheless, there was, initially, contempt by the aristocracy for lower classes. As the Revolution progressed, titles and indentured servitude disappeared, as did some of the distinctions between gentlemen and commoners. Instead of appointing only gentlemen as officers, the continental army promoted based on merit and enlisted men were rewarded for exemplary service, a reform initiated by Alexander Hamilton that was a break with European custom.

Over time, traditional symbols of rank and social hierarchy were gradually barred or discouraged. The Constitution provided that "no title of nobility shall be granted by the United States; and no person holding any office of profit or trust under them, shall, without the consent of the Congress, accept of any present, emolument, office, or title, of any kind whatsoever, from any king, prince or foreign state." Titles and rank became offensive. People were to rise and fall on their own merits. Mobility was based on natural talent and not inheritance or governmental privilege or status. In an era dominated by monarchy, this was a radical concept.

In early colonial life, most relationships were paternalistic, based on a master/servant hierarchy. Women had no independent existence, but were referred to as "wife of" and "daughter of." They were often treated as children. They could not buy and sell property, make contracts, or exercise other legal rights. Children were often beaten and lived in fear of their fathers. Family relationships were crucial because the family was the basic unit of colonial America, the source of the overwhelming majority of economic, social, and cultural activity. In Europe, legal devices such as primogeniture (the oldest son is sole heir) and entail (all land kept in the family name) were used to maintain social class and gentility. Benjamin Franklin was the youngest son of the youngest son for several generations back. Franklin's will stated, in a note of bitterness, that the obligation to pass on something to posterity, "does not lie on me, who never inherited a shilling from any ancestor or relation."

Cultural changes, the Revolution, and rapid increases in the population broke apart paternal relationships. People moved away from the East Coast and the frontier gave them a radically different perspective. Relationships became less paternalistic, based increasingly on friendship. Affection became more important than dependency. The war undermined the power of the hierarchical family and hereditary privilege. Women assumed more responsibility for running the farms and homesteads. Their ability to own and dispose of property was expanded. Widows could own property and pass on land to children of second marriages. The colonies ended English patterns of inheritance; primogeniture was not used in New England. The colonists had vast expanses of land and desired to spread the wealth, fearing the eldest son might squander the family estate. Women were accorded the right to divorce and fathers no longer controlled whom their sons and daughters would marry. Family relations were more relaxed and intimate under democracy than monarchy. Women were more independent and admirable. Child raising practices were altered and the family become egalitarian. Overall, people were more civil and everyday manners became more important. Conversations were polite with fewer interruptions. Civility meant *being* a gentleman, which was no longer a class distinction.

Changes in social status were so rapid even some of the most perceptive Founding Fathers could not keep pace. Washington spoke of "the grazing multitude." He was harshly criticized for his leadership role in the Society of Cincinnati in which membership was hereditary. After the first inauguration, the House of Representatives directed that the president be addressed as "George Washington, President of the United States." John Adams and the Senate sought to "bring dignity and respect" to the federal government by using a title such as "His Excellency" or "His Highness the President of the United States and Protector of the Right of the Same" or "His Majesty the President." Adams pressed the issue, but was pilloried and ridiculed. There was no popular support for this idea. For the rest of his life, some people suspected Adams to be a monarchist.

MILITARY STRATEGY

The frontier and wilderness radically altered military strategy and tactics. Fighting the French and Indian War taught the colonials the strengths and vulnerabilities of the European warfare methods. The British were valiant, disciplined, and effective, but their regimentation was a fault in the wilderness. The British rules of engagement were more medieval than modern. Campaigns, for example, were not launched in the winter; men did not lie prone when the enemy was about to fire a volley. The colonials understood the inability of the leadership faraway in Britain to really know what was going on, particularly with the primitive communication systems then in existence. George Washington and groups such as Rogers' Rangers learned effective guerrilla and hit-and-run tactics, which enabled small forces to defeat large European military forces not trained for such operations. From one wilderness battle, Washington could remember vividly the screams of his wounded soldiers as they were being scalped on those parts of the battlefield controlled by the Indians. He joined with Daniel Boone to rally troops against the French outside Pittsburgh, allegedly having two horses shot out from under him and multiple bullet holes in his coat and pants.

The need to hunt for food and fight Indians resulted in the invention of the Kentucky rifle, which was longer, had a smaller bore, used a smaller ball, and was more accurate. It enabled Americans to develop a quicker and less strenuous means of loading. American gunsmiths made rifles of better quality than those from Europe. Great quantities of game and the early familiarity of boys with hunting made Americans probably the best marksmen in the world. Reports of the superiority of the American marksmen spread among the British regulars, who expected every American to be a sharpshooter—a potent form of psychological warfare that helped to convince the British that subduing the American populace would be a hopeless task. "The *Virginia Gazette* reported an exhibition by riflemen bound for Boston: while one man held between his knees a small board with a bull's-eye the size of a dollar, a rifleman at sixty yards put eight successive bullets through the bull's-eye. Washington arranged a similar exhibition on

Cambridge Common in August 1775, hoping that spies would carry the frightening word back to the British troops. At this very time the British musket was so crude that the official army manual did not even contain the command 'aim' for its musketeers."[24]

THE ECONOMY

Religion and the colonial spirit infused an energy and fervor into the economy. The rise of the American nation was wrapped in an entrepreneurial spirit: the early farmers who learned to plant and harvest indigo, tobacco, and rice; the pioneers who developed the hunting and fishing industries; and the craftsmen who developed the shipbuilding, iron, and flour milling industries.

The agricultural climate in eastern America was among the best in the world and almost anything would grow. Settlers ate far better than they had in Europe where starvation was present and the average diet was barely subsistence. In the Revolutionary War, European troops were amazed by the abundance in America, which probably had the highest standard of living in the world, and believed the colonials had become rich at the expense of the British.

The colonies became the granary of Europe. Indian corn provided great yields and nuts were plentiful. Rice was grown extensively in the Carolina lowlands, facilitated by dikes. Between 1700 and 1750, rice exports soared by a hundredfold. Thomas Paine deadpanned that America "will always have a market while eating is the custom of Europe." Indigo, used as dye in the textile business, was produced in large quantities. Tobacco was the most economical crop to grow, particularly in the South, yielding several times more profit than any other crop, but could only be planted for a few years on the same acreage. Land was most plentiful in the South and the climate was warmer. The only missing ingredient was cheap labor, the solution being slavery. These large, export cash crops led to the development of the plantation economy.[25]

Most of New England could not grow tobacco, forcing people there to work harder to earn a living. Fishing, game, and timber dominated the New England economy. Wood and fish were two of the largest American exports. Big game and fish provided food and smaller animals yielded fur and warmth. New England fisherman led a hard life and their endeavors carried them to difficult places—to the deepest recesses of Hudson Bay, Africa, and the coast of Brazil.

Whaling became one of America's first major industries, providing a plethora of products—almost every part of the whale had some utility. Initially, whaling was limited to those that washed up on the shores, but, with shipbuilding improvements pursuit of the whales on the open seas became feasible. Developing the capability to render the whale at sea enabled American whalers to hunt around the world. The industry was devastated by the American Revolution and the prohibitive tariffs England imposed following the war.

Fishing, whaling, and the availability of wood led to New England becoming one of the great shipbuilding regions of the world. Though scarce in Europe, wood was found in almost limitless quantities in America, making shipbuilding much cheaper. Ship construction required a wide range and large number of skilled workers in iron, sails, rope, and wood milling. New Englanders traveled all around the globe; their income from trading built well-to-do communities and grand houses of the most stylish architecture. The rough Atlantic Ocean toughened the Americans. Ships built to withstand Atlantic gales were superior to those built in the rest of the world—not only bigger and heavier, but faster and more mobile. In war, they were more effective battleships. In peacetime, they could carry larger cargoes at lower costs.

The colonists' economic relationship with England was ambivalent. The use of joint-stock companies and proprietorships facilitated the development of the colonies and established a tradition of venture capitalism in the New World. The colonial economy, however, had few of the commercial and industrial institutions that supported the English system, such as stock exchanges, banks, trading companies, and centers of capital. British law sought to protect its domestic industry, barring shipment of wool, hats, and finished iron from the colonies. Money, or the lack thereof, was a major problem. British law benefited

England by ensuring money (particularly in the form of gold and silver) would flow into England with ease to pay for high-value manufactured goods, but would flow out with difficulty for payment of low-value raw materials. British law, for example, prohibited establishment of banks in the colonies, the export of coinage to the colonies, and the use of paper money as legal tender. Without money, barter was often required, a cumbersome process particularly in difficult economic times. English laws stunted colonial growth.

In early colonial days, most economic relationships were that of patron and client; the rich controlled the wealth and the economy. The lack of paper money and financial institutions increased reliance on the wealthy to provide funds and resulted in dependence on benevolence. Labor and work were regarded as demeaning. Idleness was considered a favorable trait of gentlemen whose status was based on reputation and honor. The development of a paper currency and financial mechanisms such as credit reduced reliance on the wealthy. Perhaps the biggest change was a new attitude that labor was good and hard work increased wealth, prosperity, and productivity—an almost radical idea for the times. Work was no longer considered a symptom of poverty and idleness no longer symbolized entry into gentility, but was a sin. Wealth was actually less equally distributed, but people felt more equal.

Land speculation was a crucial source of wealth. A key difference between the colonies and the mother country was that most American farmers who were not slaves (i.e., two-thirds of the white colonial population) owned their own land, whereas in England landlords and the gentry owned a much greater portion of the land. This made the American economy more egalitarian.

WOMEN AND THE WAR

The colonial economy and the Revolutionary War radically changed the role of women. Wives and children created goods for the local market—spinning cloth and dressing skins for clothes, distilling liquor, and making whatever might sell locally. "No event in the eighteenth century accelerated the capitalistic development of America more than did the Revolutionary War. It brought new producers and consumers into the market economy, it aroused latent acquisitive instincts everywhere, and it stimulated inland trade as never before."[26] Supporting the British, French, and patriot armies created all sorts of demands and needs for blankets, shoes, food, wagons, and arms, that produced new markets, manufacturing facilities, and entrepreneurial interests. American woman were required to perform double duty in the fields and at home. "In various phases of war production and financing, as well as in revolutionary pamphleteering, in spying, in making bullets and other munitions, and in direct aid to fighters at the front, patriotic women were active in all the states." When husbands, fathers, and sons were away under arms, feminine responsibilities were wide-ranging. "When drives were made to raise money for the war, they organized committees to help, subscribed themselves and contributed their gold and silver objects to the common treasury." The English took notice. "Complained a writer connected with the British army in South Carolina, 'An officer told Lord Cornwallis not long ago that he believed if he had destroyed all the men in North America, we should have enough to do to conquer the women.'"[27]

In the war economy, many Americans led frugal lives and then donated their savings to pay for the patriot cause. Another source of revolutionary war funds and supplies came from privateers who commandeered hundreds of ships and millions of pounds of contraband used by the colonials. Trade with Europe was disrupted, which necessitated the development of an indigenous manufacturing sector. When trade recovered after the war, there was an acknowledgement of the importance of maintaining this capability, and war entrepreneurs became the basis for developing a permanent manufacturing sector.

By issuing hundreds of millions of dollars worth of paper currency or continentals, the Congress was somehow able to keep the country solvent, but at the cost of high inflation—prices doubled every year. Congress could continue the war only by issuing more and more currency. Foreign governments and individuals had no obligation to honor the American currency and were amazed and perplexed at how Americans financed the war by paper with no backing and no mechanism for redeeming it. When this system finally did come unglued, the collapse of markets and a drastically reduced monetary supply caused a severe economic downturn. This in turn led to calls for easy money, particularly by those in the interior of the country. These problems contributed significantly to the failure of the Articles of Confederation and the development of the Constitution. In the 1780s, Jefferson successfully negotiated a free-trade agreement with Prussia and labored to develop the "brilliantly uncomplicated system of coinage" for the country.[28]

ECONOMIC GROWTH

American values and religious focus led naturally to the concepts of private property and free markets and to perhaps the most radical notion of all—economic growth. A distinguishing characteristic of the revolutionary period was the ability of private enterprises to create new wealth and expand the economic pie.

Wealth—which was at the center of English mercantilist thinking before the American Revolution—was a static notion. The wealth of the world, measured primarily in gold and silver treasure, was supposed to be a fixed quantity, a pie that could be sliced one way or another. But the size of the pie could not be substantially increased. A bigger slice for Great Britain meant a smaller slice for France or Spain or somebody else, and one nation's gain was another's loss.

Our New World changed that way of thinking. People have come here not for wealth but for a better "way of life." America blurred the boundary between the material and the spiritual. All this was reinforced by the spectacular progress of our technology, exploiting the resources of a rich, little-known and sparsely populated continent.

The American Revolution then was, among other things, a struggle between the time-honored idea of "wealth" and a New World idea of "standard of living." This characteristically American idea appears to have entered our language only at the beginning of [the past] century. It could hardly have been conceived in an Old World burdened with the legacy of feudal "rights," landed aristocracies, royal courts, sacrosanct guild monopolies and ancestral cemeteries. Wealth is what someone possesses, but a standard of living can only be publicly enjoyed. For it is the level of goods, housing, services, health, comfort and education agreed to be appropriate.[29]

The American concept of growth signified that hard work and labor were not just mindless routines: they increased income, productivity, and wealth. The economy was not a zero sum game, but could create enormous new wealth and opportunity and a much improved quality of life.

SLAVERY

The American Revolution effectively ended the cultural climate that had allowed slavery to go basically unchallenged for centuries. Common in ancient times, slavery was present in major civilizations throughout history, and nearly universal in societies able to afford it. Aristotle, Thomas Aquinas, and John Locke agreed that slavery was an acceptable part of the social order. Few thinkers even challenged its immorality. African-American scholar Orlando Patterson noted that most non-Western cultures had no comparable word for "freedom;" it was generally equivalent to "licentiousness."[30] Prior to the Revolutionary era, as much as half the American population was slave and slavery initially was accepted as part of the social hierarchy, the lowest status. In the 1760s, slavery was viewed as a necessary and progressive institution in major cities such as Boston and New York, a view which would change drastically over the next two generations.[31] The First Great Awakening began a transformation in colonial thinking about slavery. By the time of the Revolutionary War, Americans began attacking slavery with a vehemence that was inconceivable earlier.[32]

Three phenomena were at work: the generic issue of slavery, indentured servitude, and the slave trade in human beings with Africa. Scholars have documented a wide range of different types of slavery serving a multitude of purposes encompassing warriors, wives, concubines, eunuchs, and government officials. In colonial America, slavery was broadly defined to include the power to tax without consent or as a force where man is obliged to act or not act. People living in a monarchy or despotic government were considered glorified slaves. Slavery was equated with dependency. By this definition, everyone in America was a slave, a position held by the Revolutionary leaders from John Dickinson to Alexander Hamilton to John Adams. By establishing the largest republican government ever, the founding fathers believed they had eliminated this form of slavery.

In the colonies, as well as slaves, there were tens of thousands of indentured servants, as well as apprentices bound to masters. As many as a half to two-thirds of immigrants came to America as indentured servants, some for life. Two of the signers of the Declaration of Independence, Matthew Thornton and George Taylor, had begun life in America as indentured servants. Colonial servants had many of the disadvantages of slavery. Laws controlled their movement and prevented runaways. Indentured servants were under the complete authority of their masters and could be sold, severely punished, and forbidden to marry. They had few if any legal rights and were often treated more harshly than were servants in England. For the laborer, however, servitude held out the attraction of escaping poverty, prison, or political turmoil. The major difference between slaves and indentured servants was that slaves served involuntarily. The Philadelphia population in servitude declined from between 40 to 50 percent in the middle of the eighteenth century, to 10 percent during the Revolutionary War, and to 2 percent at the end of the century

In ancient civilizations, slavery was usually local. It consisted of criminals and debtors, children abandoned by their parents, misfits, and malcontents who sold themselves and frequently their offspring into bondage. Slavery had become such a part of custom and tradition, it included no sense of moral wrong, just an attitude that the slave had experienced misfortune. Before 1500, most slaves were not Africans. By 1700, as a result of the slave trade, the majority of slaves were African.

The slave trade had expanded by being spurred by Islam, which paradoxically stated the natural condition of mankind to be free. Muslims could not be enslaved, only infidels captured in war. Since there were not enough Muslim conquests, a trade in slaves began, first with Europe, then Eurasia, and finally and most lastingly with Africa,[33] although Europeans seldom participated in the dangerous raids into the interior. The exportation of slaves had been profitable for centuries and native African dealers were able to offer a sufficient supply at cheap prices. Slave traders expected a high return on investment for a few months of work transporting the slaves. Out of the 10 million slaves exported to the Western hemisphere (in addition to the millions more who died in transit), an estimated 3.8 million went to the Caribbean, 3.6 million went to Brazil, 1.6 million went to Spanish colonies, and 600,000 went to British North America. Most American slaves were off-spring of those who made the brutal passage. In the rest of the western hemisphere slave populations declined, but in the United States the number increased rapidly, most probably due to better diet, increased fertility, and less harsh working conditions.

Under British common law, slavery was legal in the United States prior to the Declaration of Independence. One out of every five Boston families owned slaves. Slaves constituted 12 percent of the Rhode Island population and a quarter of the New York City workforce. While initially barred from participating by the Council of War, African Americans eventually comprised between 6 and 12 percent of the fighting force in the Revolution, the most integrated army until the Korean War.[34] The number of slaves in Virginia doubled between 1755 and 1783 and tens of thousands more were imported into America between 1783 and 1807, the legal end of the slave trade

The leading abolitionists were Quakers, who had little credibility, being pacifists during the Revolutionary War. Americans would have remained subjects of the British Empire if the Quakers had their way. In 1775, one of the first anti-slavery societies in the world was organized in Philadelphia. By the middle 1780s, Benjamin Franklin, convinced that the slave trade and the condition of slavery must be eradicated, had enlisted in a Quaker abolitionist group. He was particularly disturbed by reports that a third of the hundred thousand slaves being shipped from Africa each year died in passage. (Mere survival on a ship was difficult—the mortality rate for some European immigrants was as high as that reported for slave passengers and for patriot prisoners of war held in ships in New York harbor was even higher.) Franklin had accepted the provision on slavery in the Constitution, because the southern states would not otherwise ratify it. James Madison believed slavery to be the most important division in the Constitutional Convention. At the time, Madison thought it "dishonorable to the American character" that it wasn't abolished immediately. Even Alexander Hamilton did not publicly advocate abolition, because he recognized it would split the country. Jefferson, a slave owner as were Washington and Madison, was an outspoken opponent of slavery. He unsuccessfully sought to have it abolished in his native Virginia. His anti-slavery language in the draft of the Declaration of Independence, placing responsibility for the slave trade with the British King, was deleted at the insistence of Georgia and South Carolina. His effort to prohibit slavery in the new territories failed by just a single vote when only one other southerner voted for his initiative. The vast majority of delegates to the Constitutional Convention believed slavery to be morally wrong. But if slavery had been abolished, at least Georgia and South Carolina would have refused to join the United States and would have had no laws restricting the importation of slaves.

The Northwest Ordinance barred the future entry of slaves into the areas north of the Ohio River. The American Constitution allowed the abolition of the slave trade in 1808, which Jefferson helped achieve through legislation he initiated as president. The compromise did count slaves as three-fifths of a person, providing an incentive for states to free slaves to increase their representation. The Constitution, however, also compelled the return of fugitive slaves, requiring the national government to subsidize enforcement of the slave system. During the three decades after the beginning of the Revolutionary War, every Northern state initiated complete slave emancipation. President Jefferson's statement upon passage of the law prohibiting the slave trade at the earliest possible date under the Constitution was the strongest official condemnation of slavery until the presidency of

Abraham Lincoln, urging an end to "those violations of human rights which have been so long continued on the unoffending inhabitants of Africa."[35] James Wilson, probably the most learned lawyer and framer of the Constitution, supported the slave-trade clause "as laying the foundation for banishing slavery out of this country; and though the period is more distant than I could wish, yet it will produce the same kind of gradual change which was pursued in Pennsylvania."[36]

If the Constitution had attempted to abolish slavery, there might be no United States of America as we know it. The North did not have the economic strength to win a war with the South until well into the nineteenth century. There would likely be at least two nations, if not a fractured group of countries. History and the world today would be very different. America's founding fathers staked out a strong anti-slavery position but were forced to compromise on the slave trade by the southern states, which would have refused to join the union.

POLITICS AND GOVERNMENT

The religious beliefs of the Puritans in the seventeenth century had a long-ranging impact on the political and legal system of the colonies. The Puritans tried to reform both England and America, but their English effort failed and resulted in the restoration of the monarchy. John Winthrop and his Puritan colleagues viewed efforts in the colonies as an experiment or a pilot project not only to create a radically improved New World, but as a model to save and revitalize the Old World

The Puritans' first act in America was *The Mayflower Compact*, a revolutionary contract to resolve dissension on their voyage based on the original covenant between God, Moses, and the Israelites. Unlike previous contracts between individuals in a hierarchy (such as monarch and subject, or master and servant), this contract was signed by the head of each family unit. Though the original Jamestown settlers were motivated by economic gain and a desire to improve their social standing, the *Mayflower* men and women were religious idealists seeking the Promised Land, establishing a Kingdom of Heaven on earth.

They were not a group of unattached individuals—in Virginia a ship of single women was sent and men could select their brides by paying the cost of shipping. The Puritans were a community, the first group traveling as families. Gradually, greater numbers of Puritans immigrated to America, in some years totaling thousands on dozens of ships.

The colonies established lean governments. Massachusetts, with a population of 300,000, ran its government on $100,000 a year.

> The provincial governments were Lilliputian by modern standards. They were not impersonal bureaucracies, but familiar persons whose numbers could usually be counted on one's hands. Prominent colonialists knew personally the governors, justices, customs collectors, naval officers and other leading magistrates with whom they dealt. They drank and dined with them, played cards or the violin with them, and sometimes went to church with them. Even the provincial assemblies were miniscule. New Hampshire's assembly had thirty-five members; New York's twenty-eight; New Jersey's twenty; Maryland's sixty. Massachusetts's house of representatives was extraordinarily large at 117. The combined membership of the New York colonial assembly and council was even smaller than a committee in today's House of Representatives. Gentlemen in such tiny political worlds were necessarily familiar with one another.[37]

The colonials jettisoned the overregulation found in most European countries, in particular the intrusive customs process. Governments relied on edicts to the private sector to perform most services and issued sanctions against those who did not perform their duties.

In the early 1700s, the lower house of the legislature in every colony increased its powers, sometimes even usurping executive functions. These legislative bodies closely reflected the political will of the colonists. Tax rates were kept low, and the citizen legislators became accustomed to making crucial decisions. Record growth was directly related to the fact that Americans could spend virtually all of their income, sending almost nothing on to the government. America was ideally suited for a republican form of government—it had no established church, no titles or nobility, no distinctions of wealth, and no underclass except slaves. It did have experience with self-governance.

The Revolutionary era changed the colonists' status from subject to citizen. Even prior to the war, colonial republican governments were a step away from monarchy and this gap widened to a chasm as these governments and their citizens became radicalized. The colonists recognized that republican governments require people to sacrifice their self-interest and can be more difficult to maintain and susceptible to corruption. Hence, the moral character of the citizenry and their leaders was crucial to good government and the protection of liberty.

Patronage, a major source of employment, was considered the lifeblood of monarchy and created obligations and dependencies that became the basis for political authority and control. Many colonists considered the power of appointment to be evil. Its abuse was a critical source of revolutionary ardor, a primary cause of the war. The Crown sought to appoint Royalists, not people of merit. The Revolution raised the issue of who was to be sovereign and which set of leaders was to have the political authority. The existence of the monarchy, the taxation without representation, and the local presence of officials appointed by the Crown gave the colonists a deep fear of a widespread conspiracy against liberty, a danger that drove their desire for revolutionary change.[38]

An informed citizenry was at the heart of colonial government. The quest for knowledge had a powerful effect on the colonists. In early America where citizens faced the daily pressure of survival, the frontier, and making or farming most of what they consumed, reading and history were nevertheless important pursuits. There were public libraries, reading clubs, lectures, and debating societies. "The extensive sale of books, pamphlets, almanacs, magazines, and newspapers was one indication that there was a wide reading public in all parts of America. Foreign travelers in the eighteenth century were deeply impressed by the amount of reading that was done in homes and in taverns 'on the house,' and they contrasted this mental alertness with the stolidity of the ignorant masses in their own countries." The colonists cited passages from a wide range of periods in history, particularly classical civilization. "Books, pamphlets and tracts that passed from reader to reader, formal instruction in schools, the dissemination of learning by fathers and mothers, training at home by private tutors, formed only a part of the process by which Americans were equipped with knowledge and ideas for dealing with affairs private and public."[39] In the early eighteenth century, newspapers added instruction on current issues to the colonial college curricula.

The colonists quoted frequently from the thinkers of the Enlightenment, English common law, the Puritans, and English radicals, the latter having a particularly forceful effect by their testimonies to the corrupting and enslaving nature of the English system. About half the books in colonial America were religious and many of the rest were schoolbooks. The Bible was by far the most widely read title, but political publications such as John Locke's *Treatise of Government*, Montesquieu's *Spirit of Laws*, and Adam Ferguson's *An Essay on the History of Civil Society* were read, discussed, and written about so frequently their contents became common knowledge in the colonies. From the classics and English writers such as Blackstone, Americans derived their understanding of history. Indeed, ideas and history, "permeated the very air Americans breathed."[40] They were present at the theater and oratory performances, which were sources of popular entertainment. The Revolutionaries exploited every available means of communication, linking together their networks by energetic letter writing. Jefferson designed an instrument with five yoked pens for writing multiple copies of his letters. New ideas were spread through pamphlets, weekly newspapers, broadsides, almanacs, and sermons.

Training in the arts of self-government was widespread. There were bookshops and coffeehouses. There were thirty-eight American newspapers at the time of the Revolutionary War, and each one was full of letters, speeches, and documents on the issue of independence. Philadelphia had twenty-three printing establishments and seven newspapers, more than in London. Countless pamphlets reflected a myriad of views about independence, the war, and the relationship with Britain. Over 1500 were produced by the end of the war and more than any other form they are the distinctive literature of the period and describe the meaning of this transforming event.

KNOWLEDGE

The revolutionary generation relied on readings from history in developing the Declaration of Independence and the Constitution. George Washington began his presidency by reading extensively, including *Debates in the House of Commons,* to help develop his plan of government, much as he had based the scientific management of his plantation on readings on agriculture. Noah Webster noted the contrast with Europe: "Let Englishman take notice that when I speak of the American yeomanry the latter are not to be compared to the illiterate peasantry of their own country. The yeomanry of this country . . . have considerable education. They not only learn to read newspapers every week, and besides the Bible, which is found in all families, they read the best English sermons and treatises on religion, ethics, geography and history."[41] The colonists took their quest for knowledge seriously. When John Peter Zenger, the publisher of the *New York Weekly Journal,* was prosecuted for criticizing the colony's governor, the jury defied the judge and acquitted him.

> The most fertile novelty of the New World was not its climates, its plants, it animals, or its minerals, but its new concept of knowledge. The wealth of the new-found land could enable men to live well by Old World standards, but the realization that knowledge itself might be different from what men had before believed—this opened up realms never before dreamed of. Men in the New World found unsuspected possibilities in life everywhere. No American invention has influenced the world so powerfully as the concept of knowledge which sprang from American experience. . . .
>
> When has a culture owed so little to its few "great" minds or its few hereditarily fortunate men and women?

One of the contrasts between the culture of Europe and that of the United States is that the older culture traditionally depended on the monumental accomplishments of the few, while the newer culture—diffused, elusive, process-oriented—depended more on the novel, accreting ways of the many.[42]

THE ROLE OF THE INDIVIDUAL

The net effect of the revolutionary changes was to radically transform the individual's relationship to the world. Individualism is at the core of the American model, giving unprecedented weight to each person's choices, interests, and claims. The colonial view was that individuals are unique, endowed by their creator with certain inalienable rights, which belong to every man, woman, and child. The political system must be built around these rights. Instead of a chain from God to king to duke to knight to serf as in the medieval and the European world, Americans believed in their direct link to God. Individuals can voluntarily loan their rights to the state. The Constitution says "we the people, in order to perform a more perfect union," which reflects the fact that the people have voluntarily loaned power to the government.

This individualism was very different from prior historical experience. By the late eighteenth century, most Americans shared both their mistrust of intellectual authorities inherited from previous generations and their belief that true knowledge arose from the use of one's own senses—whether the external senses for information about nature and society or the moral sense for ethical and aesthetic judgments. Most Americans were united in the conviction that people had to think for themselves in order to know science, morality, economics, politics, and especially theology. These changes provided the individual with the genuine capacity to exercise free will. In turn, communities of freely associating individuals acquired the capability to assert more effectively their political will. The colonists created an American civilization before they created an American nation. They had become Americans.

The printing press played a crucial role in each of the major transformations in the colonial era and facilitated the development of freedom, democracy, and the free enterprise system. The founding fathers skillfully picked and chose the best aspects of previous civilizations and what was happening in Europe; they incorporated those features into American civilization. The American Revolution was a success because it was radical. It drastically changed the model of civilization that had been in place for thousands of years. The founding fathers destroyed monarchy, eradicated social distinctions, abolished privileges, and obliterated social hierarchies. There was not just a Revolutionary War; there was a revolutionary culture. Fundamental alterations of society, culture, and social relationships transformed America into the most liberal, democratic, and advanced civilization in the world.

4

Jefferson's
authentic democracy

WHEN PRESIDENT KENNEDY honored forty-nine Western Hemisphere Nobel Prize winners, he proclaimed it, "the most extraordinary collection of talent, of human knowledge, that has ever been gathered in the White House, with the possible exception of when Thomas Jefferson dined alone."

Jefferson (1743–1826)—a politician, diplomat, president, architect, draftsman, connoisseur of painting and wine, anthropologist, author, bibliophile, classicist, musician, lawyer, educator, estate manager, agronomist, theologian, and well-versed in almost every branch of science from astronomy to zoology—was a true renaissance man. He corresponded with English scientists and Scottish philosophers; he advised those who began the French Revolution. Jefferson suffered deeply from losing four of his six children in their youth, the death of a child in her twenties, and the premature death of his wife. Jefferson's era, nevertheless, and his presidency created an intensely new political focus in Western history.

Jefferson was exhilarated by the prospect of perpetual change, expressing the hope that every generation would have creative energy to renew society and concluding that all laws and constitutions should naturally expire after nineteen years or the span of a generation. Following the death of Washington and the radicalism of the revolutionary era, Jefferson initiated and unleashed another wave of enormous change. Great authorities, established theories, and the world of metropolitan sophistication were jettisoned in favor of fresh thought and the wisdom of local experience. Faithful to their provincial lives, convinced of the rightness of their principles that they wished to make real, the American people, as James Madison wrote, "accomplished a revolution which has no parallel in the annals of human society."[1] The Revolutionary War replaced the British monarchy with a republic, then the Jeffersonians superceded classical republicanism with democratic values and even greater civil equality. "By the early nineteenth century, America had already emerged as the most egalitarian, most materialistic, most individualistic—and most evangelical Christian—society in Western history. . . . Perhaps no country in the Western world has ever undergone such massive changes in such a short period of time. The Revolution resembled the breaking of a dam, releasing thousands upon thousands of pent-up pressures."[2]

Believing that the Federalists had betrayed the true principles of the American Revolution, Jefferson carried out a second revolution to inculcate the force of American political will which has been described as "the rise of ordinary people into dominance."[3] Until the American Revolution, the very term "democracy" had been used in a pejorative sense throughout history. Even in Jefferson's times, few persons belonging to the Revolutionary generation used the term "democracy"—it was still the scourge of the ruling classes and not a word deemed to be flattering. John Adams linked democracy to mobocracy and vile populism. Other founding fathers continued to believe it to be synonymous with anarchy, atheism, and evil. French aristocrats, Tories, and even Edmund Burke all denounced democracy.

The changes were so fast, furious, and radical that many of the founding fathers lost faith in their revolution and judged it harshly. In moments of depression, Jefferson felt despair. George Washington, towards the end of his life, expressed concerns and reservations.

The founding fathers were unsettled and fearful not because the American Revolution had failed but because it had succeeded and succeeded only too well. What had happened in America in the decades following the Declaration of Independence was after all only an extension of all that the revolutionary leaders had advocated. White males had taken only too seriously the belief that they were free and equal with the right to pursue their happiness. Indeed, the principles of their achievement made possible the eventual strivings of others—black slaves and women—for their own freedom, independence and prosperity.

The very fulfillment of these revolutionary ideals—the very success of the Revolution—made it difficult for those who benefited from that success, for ordinary people and their new democratic spokesmen, to understand the apprehensions of the founding fathers. The people looked back in awe and wonder at the revolutionary generation and saw in them leaders the likes of which they knew they would never see again in America. But they knew that they now lived in a different world, a democratic world, that required new thoughts and new behavior. . . .

A new generation of democratic Americans was no longer interested in the revolutionaries' dream of building a classical republic of elitist virtue out of the inherited materials of the Old World. America, they said, would find its greatness not by emulating the states of classical antiquity, not by copying the fiscal-military powers of modern Europe, and not by producing a few notable geniuses and great-souled men. Instead, it would discover its greatness by creating a prosperous free society belonging to obscure people with their workaday concerns and their pecuniary pursuits of happiness—common people with their common interests in making money and getting ahead. No doubt the cost that America paid for this democracy was high—with its vulgarity, its materialism, its rootlessness, its anti-intellectualism. But there is no denying the wonder of it and the really earthly benefits it brought to the hitherto neglected and despised masses of common laboring people. The American Revolution created this democracy, and we are living with its consequences still.[4]

There were four aspects of Jefferson's revolution—the Second Great Awakening, equality, democratic governance, and the flourishing of civil society.

The Second Great Awakening

Beginning in the 1790s, the Second Great Awakening encouraged broad-based, mass-based participatory religion—free of rituals, symbols, and form. There were huge revivals and ministers were employed by the congregation not the church hierarchy, as people took over their churches in the same manner as they were taking over their governments. Evangelical churches developed effective outreach and had the greatest increase in membership. The message was personal empowerment, an inner motivation that promoted resentment against traditional political and social authority and institutions. As previously described, the First Great Awakening occurred prior to the Revolutionary War and was a major force in establishing American independence. The Third Great Awakening is considered to have occurred in the late 1800s, while the Fourth Great Awakening is generally regarded as commencing in the 1960s and 1970s.

From its inception, American religion was based more on English tradition and tended to be free of constraints, ritual, and hierarchical institutions. Churches were searching for a revolutionary theology to accompany the on-going political and social changes that were rooted in religion and divine providence. During the revolutionary era, the churches were nation-building agents and facilitated the development of the founding fathers' ideology. They played an important role in ending aristocratic privilege. The importance of religion grew, but with an absence of a dominant religious authority. Religion was separated from politics, church separated from state. Freed of traditional restraints, the church and religion needed to help provide an alternative structure and ensure the development of personal inner resources to survive. Common sense and intuition became the foundations for theological thought and the survivors of the Revolutionary assault on inherited privilege and hierarchical institutions. Human consciousness became the authority and surest mechanism for grasping the ways of God.[5]

Jefferson was supportive of this movement; he wrote the Virginia Statute for Establishing Religious Freedom and worked to eliminate statutes that granted religious institutions abusive powers. His Virginia law banned the raising of any tithe or the establishment of any religious tests. He worked hard to undermine autocratic churches, particularly the established church in Virginia, the Episcopal Church. The Quakers, who had left England to escape religious persecution, were not part of the established religion in Virginia, making the members subject to prosecution and arrest. Their meetings were prohibited, and it was a crime even to bring a Quaker into the state on a vessel. This inequality left a deep impression on Jefferson in his steadfast support for religious freedom. Jefferson understood the proper separation and distinctions, attending religious services in the Capitol when there was not a suitable church available in the early days of the nation's capital.

Throughout the nineteenth century, new American religions blossomed, such as Mormonism and Christian Science. Joseph Smith, the founder of Mormonism, was brutally murdered. Brigham Young assumed leadership of the group and moved it to Utah, a state settled almost entirely by members of this faith. Mormonism is today one of the world's fastest growing religions. Mary Baker Eddy revived the ancient Christian tradition of spiritual healing. Her church established over 3,000 branches in dozens of countries. She founded *The Christian Science Monitor.*

The Second Great Awakening formed the basis for the abolition-of-slavery movement, which was a religious movement until northern, mainly Republican, politicians developed an antislavery coalition. The eventual fruits of the Second Great Awakening included every constitutional amendment between the Civil War and the Great Depression, particularly those ending slavery and extending suffrage. It played a key role in rights for indigenous Americans, women's rights, temperance, and the educational reform movement.

Alexis de Tocqueville described the force of religion in American society and the influence religion extended over people's lives. Religion's role was vast and extended to morals, customs, and family life. Tocqueville wrote that "the religious atmosphere of the country was the first thing that struck me on arrival in the United States. . . . It must never be forgotten that religion gave birth to Anglo-American society. In the United States, religion is therefore mingled with all the habits of the nation and all the feelings of patriotism, whence it derives a peculiar force. . . . Liberty regards religion as its companion in all its battles and its triumphs—as the cradle of its infancy, and the divine source of its claims. It considers religion as the safeguard of morality, and morality as the best security of law, and the surest pledge of the duration of freedom."[6] Tocqueville noted that whereas in France the spirits of religion and freedom were diametrically opposed, in America they were complementary and reinforcing.

Tocqueville understood the connection between religious spirit and the strength of capitalism. In Jefferson's time, prosperity replaced austerity as the guiding economic principle. Entrepreneurialism permeated the culture, and commerce became linked to every aspect of society. Mercantilists became trusted instead of despised. America was changing centuries of Western commercial tradition. It was a bustling, expanding civilization with no one and no thing in charge. Yet, order seemed to grow out of the chaos.

Equality

Tocqueville opened his influential *Democracy in America* with the following passage:

> Amongst the novel objects that attracted my attention during my stay in the United States, nothing struck me

more forcibly than the general equality of conditions. I readily discovered the prodigious influence which this primary fact exercises on the whole course of society by giving a certain direction to public opinion and a peculiar tenor to the laws; by imparting new maxims to the governing authorities, and peculiar habits to the governed.

I soon perceived that the influence of this fact extends far beyond the political character and the laws of the country, and that this is no less empire over civil society than over the government; it creates opinions, gives birth to new sentiments, founds novel customs, and modifies whatever it does not produce. The more I advanced in the study of American society, the more I perceived that this equality of condition is the fundamental fact from which all others seem to be derived, and the central point at which all my observations constantly terminated.[7]

Equality was the key to the new American civilization, the most powerful force unleashed by the Revolution.

In the decades following the Revolution, American society was transformed. By every measure there was a sudden bursting forth, an explosion—not only of geographical movement but of entrepreneurial energy, of religious passion, and of pecuniary desires. . . . There had been seepages and flows before the Revolution, but suddenly it was as if the whole traditional structure, enfeebled and brittle to begin with, broke apart, and people and their energies were set loose in an unprecedented outburst.

Nothing contributed more to this explosion of energy than did the idea of equality. Equality was in fact the most radical and most powerful ideological force let loose in the Revolution. Its appeal was far more potent than any of the revolutionaries realized. Once invoked, the idea of equality could not be stopped, and it tore through American society and culture with awesome power.[8]

American culture with its open-class structure was much closer to England than to France or to the rest of Europe, which had a caste-like structure. Over time, merit became the basis for social status and achievement, not birth, the basis for advancement. The family was no longer patriarchal, it was egalitarian. American women were accorded high status—able to think for themselves, speak freely, and act on their own volition. While men and women worked in different spheres, each were recognized for their prowess in their respective worlds. There was equal regard for both and each were considered of equal worth.[9]

> If equality had meant only equality of opportunity or a rough equality of property-holding, it could never have become, as it has, the most powerful and radical ideological force in all of American history. Equality became so potent for Americans because it came to mean that everyone was really the same as everyone else, not just at birth, not in talent or wealth, and not just in some transcendental religious sense of the equality of all souls. Ordinary Americans came to believe that no one in a basic down-to-earth and day-in-and-day-out manner was really better than anyone else. That was equality as no other nation has ever quite had it.[10]

The commitment to and feeling of equality was omnipresent, even though inequality was a fact of life. Landholdings, for example, became roughly as concentrated in the United States as in England. Yet, Americans did not feel poor, because there was so much land that many more people were property owners, their standard of living was much higher than in Europe, and there was a genuine feeling of equal opportunity.

Tocqueville found America already very homogeneous. Unlike work in Europe, work in America was a "necessary, natural, and honest condition of all men.... Not only is no dishonor associated with work, but among such peoples it is regarded as positively honorable; the prejudice is for, not against it."[11] This was in sharp contrast to the European situation where a gentleman was expected to be idle and work therefore was devalued. The American passion for work was particularly strong among the American middle class, which became the dominant social group.

During Jefferson's era, aristocracy, gentry, and the notion that idleness was a sign of gentility were attacked, met with a scathing criticism of everything those concepts stood for. The claims of absentee landlords became subservient to the claims of those who worked the land. In the North, support for the concept of work and disparagement of idleness made the Southern plantation and its aristocratic governance seem out of place. The value of hard labor was extended to include intellectual work, business management, and other cerebral efforts, so that it was not only the common laborer, but also the manager, the lawyer, and other professionals who were hard workers.

The Federalists were routed from power in significant part due to their aristocratic tradition, attempts to stratify America, and, in particular, their anti-immigrant, nativist bent. Jefferson aligned himself and his party with new immigrants, who could become naturalized and full-fledged citizens after only five years. New England Federalists attempted to deny immigrants the right to hold office and to vote and tried to impose a tax on naturalization. Jeffersonians let Federalist laws like the Alien and Sedition Act expire and repealed the Naturalization Act, which had raised the residence requirement for citizenship from five to fourteen years. He released from imprisonment those who had been convicted under those laws. Jefferson and the Democratic Party became the special friend of immigrants, a constituency that sustained the party in difficult times and helped it eventually to extinguish the Federalists.

Jefferson banished protocol and had a simplicity of manner. He would answer the front door of the White House if he happened to be walking by (sometimes even in his bathrobe). He rode horseback unaccompanied by servants. He jettisoned dueling and obsession with honor. He tried to free men from constricting institutions. "He saw ordinary folk as so many Gullivers tied down by a hundred strings of custom and command."[12] Jefferson believed that by releasing these restraints people would flourish, as opposed to the prevailing view that they were weak and needed structure and guidance. He was generally optimistic, creating within his inner circle of advisors a camaraderie and sense of vision and purpose.

Equality focused America on the future: "Aristocracy naturally leads the mind back to the past and fixes it in the contemplation thereof. But democracy engenders a sort of instinctive distaste for what is old. . . . There is not a country in the world where man more confidently takes charge of the future, or where he feels with more pride that he can fashion the universe to please himself."[13]

Democratic Governance

Jefferson observed that America's new democracy was a radical break with the past and had rendered useless almost everything written before on the structure of government. He dramatically shrank the size of government, yielding an annual surplus; he had a compassionate and trusting governing style. Jefferson had the most stable administration for a two-term president—only one Cabinet office changed hands. Jefferson favored an open government and himself was transparent, baring his soul in his correspondence. Jefferson was open, candid, informal, counting himself as one vote in Cabinet deliberations—although most decisions were made by consensus. His party dominated the Congress resulting in a good relationship, never vetoing a single piece of legislation. Jefferson believed laws should be made for the people and not the state. If people make them and can repeal them, there is greater respect for the law. Extraordinary changes were occurring, yet not all of them positive:

> Everything seemed to be coming apart, and murder, suicide, theft, and mobbing became increasingly common responses to the burdens that liberty and the expectation of gain were placing on people. . . . American grain farmers, particularly those in western Pennsylvania, Kentucky, and Tennessee, found it easier and more profitable to distill, ship, and sell whiskey than to try and sell the perishable grain itself. Consequently, things got to the point where

almost everyone or his cousin had a distillery. The number of distilleries increased rapidly after the 1780s, reaching a peak of 20,000 by 1830. In 1815 even the little town of Peachem, Vermont, had thirty distilleries. Distilling whiskey was good business because, to the astonishment of foreigners, nearly all Americans drank—men, women, children, and sometimes even babies—everywhere and anywhere, all day long. Washington, who himself had a distillery, thought as early as 1789 that distilled spirits were "the ruin of half the workmen in this Country." John Adams was mortified that his countrymen were more intemperate than any other people in the world. . . .

By 1800 Americans were already known for pushing and shoving another in public and for their aversion to ceremony. And in succeeding years' there were frequent complaints over "the violation of decorum, the want of etiquette, the rusticity of manners in this generation." Violence was perhaps no more common that it had been earlier, but now it seemed more bizarre. During the forty-five years between 1780 and 1825 there occurred ten of the twelve multiple family murders that were reported or written about in America from the seventeenth century through 1900. It was as if all restraints were falling away. Fist fighting even broke out repeatedly in the Congress and the state legislatures.

Urban rioting became more prevalent and destructive than it had been. Street, tavern, and theater rowdiness, labor strikes, racial and ethnic conflicts—all increased greatly after 1800. These eruptions of mob violence occurred in the early Republic were uncontrolled and sometimes murderous.[14]

A key trait of the new American democracy was the absence of government, which undoubtedly contributed to this disorder. "What is most striking to everyone who travels in this country, whether or not one bothers to reflect, is the spectacle of a society marching along all alone, without guide or support, by the sole fact of the cooperation of individual wills. In spite of anxiously searching for the government, one can find it nowhere, and the truth is that it does not, so to speak, exist at all."[15]

Jefferson believed the source of energy in society was not government, but the public or political will or consent of the governed. He believed that energy increased as the government decreased. Public opinion is a common space "in which people who never meet understand themselves to be engaged in discussion, and capable of reaching a common mind."[16] This public sphere emerged in the eighteenth and early nineteenth centuries through printed publications such as books, pamphlets, and newspapers and in conjunction with face-to-face gatherings in salons, saloons, drawing rooms, coffee houses, town meetings, and legislative bodies. Increasingly, public opinion became the governing authority for America.

Jefferson was a masterful communicator, conducting voluminous correspondence with opinion leaders and making known his positions on key issues. He originally opposed many of Hamilton's proposals such as a national bank and the assumption of public debt. His Treasury Secretary, Albert Gallatin, however, who did favor cutting taxes and spending and his general approach, told Jefferson that Hamilton's machinery was "the most perfect system ever formed."[17] Jefferson worked long and hard to fashion a consensus message, reassuring the defeated Federalists on their important issues such as the national bank and retaining certain government appointments while adhering to the basic principles of his victorious Democratic-Republicans. He solicited viewpoints far and wide and communicated his message through verbal and nonverbal means. Jefferson answered much of his own mail personally and occasionally granted audiences to unexpected guests. He often bared his soul in correspondence, leaving him prey to critics. He routed incoming correspondence to the heads of his departments and required them to furnish responses for his review in order to be apprised of what was happening in his administration. When he encountered opposition, he exerted his personal charm, John Adams exclaiming one "can never be an hour in this man's company's without something of the marvelous."[18]

Jefferson's presidency was low-key, almost invisible, to reflect his commitment to minimalist government. He never vetoed a bill, but surreptitiously interjected himself into the legislative process by having his ideas introduced by his supporters and carefully monitoring their progress through the legislature. Jefferson eliminated taxes raised by the Federalists and relied only on tariffs, land sales, and surpluses from the post office. For many Americans, their only contact with the government was through the delivery of the mail.

As part of this new way of doing things, suffrage was extended and property and religious qualifications for voting and holding office were eliminated. Rotation in office was initiated (Jefferson turned down a third term and firmly established the two-term precedent) and victors in an election were allowed to take over the political jobs held by their predecessors—the spoils of office. This latter reform eliminated the jobs of men of old and rich families who had served for generations without threat of removal. The method of selection of presidential electors was changed. Originally, most were chosen by the state legislatures with only five states establishing popular elections. By 1828 all but two of the twenty-four states had popular election. The national nominating convention became the method for political parties to select presidential candidates, instead of party caucuses.

American democracy worked as a result of its dynamism. It was "a system that shifted with the growth and movement of the population and in which representatives were bound to constituent wishes."[19]

Civil Society

The radical transformation triggered by the American Revolution greatly strengthened civil society. Americans joined a broad range of voluntary associations that guided much of America. A decade after the Revolution these associations began to appear even though they were not specified in the Constitution, the Bill of Rights, or any law.

> [N]ewly independent American men and women
> came together to form hundreds and thousands of new vol-

untary associations expressive of a wide array of benevolent goals. . . . People cut loose from traditional social relationships, it was observed as early as 1789, were "necessarily thrown at a considerable distance from each other, and into a very diffused state of society." The various voluntary associations and institutions enabled them to come together in new ways and to combine their mites for charity most effectively. By the 1820s in Massachusetts alone these associations of like-minded men and women were forming at the rate of eighty-five a year.[20]

When Tocqueville arrived in America he found voluntary associations were one of the distinguishing characteristics of the culture.

Americans of all ages, all conditions, and all dispositions, constantly form associations. They have not only commercial and manufacturing companies, in which all take part, but associations of a thousand other kinds—religious, moral, serious, futile, general or restricted, enormous or diminutive. The Americans make associations to give entertainments, to found seminaries, to build inns, to construct churches, to diffuse books, to send missionaries to the antipodes; they found in this manner hospitals, prisons, and schools. If it be proposed to inculcate some truth, or to foster some feeling by the encouragement of a great example, they form a society. Wherever, at the head of some new undertaking, you see the government in France, or a man of rank in England, in the United States you will be sure to find an association.[21]

A logical outgrowth of the Revolution, associations helped to fill a void between citizens and government that otherwise would have been filled by government itself. These associations, as de Tocqueville noted, were commercial, religious, and moral. They built churches, distributed books, opened hospitals, built prisons, and started schools. They also initiated country and county fairs, established asylums, provided for orphans, and attempted to suppress vice and immorality.

Local fraternal societies, for example, would contract with local doctors by competitive bid for their services and members would pay a small fee to be part of the network. The catalyst for the formation of these associations has been fairly widely debated, but Tocqueville had perhaps the best explanation. In a society moving toward individualism (and away from the ties of monarchy) citizens are independent and powerless unless they learn to voluntarily help one another. "There was nothing in the Western world quite like these hundreds of thousands of people assembling annually in their different voluntary associations and debating about everything. . . . So prevalent did these social organizations become that eventually some people . . . came to fear that the social principles of these organizations were threatening that 'individuality of character' that was so important to Americans and the real goal of all social action."[22]

While in other countries the state was relied on to solve social problems, private associations took the place of government in early nineteenth-century America. The Second Great Awakening provided the moral foundation for the associations and their efforts to improve the nature of society. Gradually, instead of relieving the suffering or treating the symptoms, these associations attempted to change human behavior, whether alcohol, drug, or gambling addictions, or eliminating corruption.

> The temperance movement had the most far-reaching effects. In the decades leading up to the 1830s, the consumption of alcohol rose sharply. By one estimate the annual per capita consumption of alcohol was 10 gallons in 1829, up from 2.5 gallons in 1790. Respectable Americans were appalled by the results: rowdy urban streets, saloons on every corner, young men showing up for work drunk. . . .
>
> The effect of this effort was dramatic. Between 1830 and 1850 annual per capita alcohol consumption for persons aged fifteen and older fell from 7.1 gallons to 1.8 gallons. What effect this had on behavior, especially criminal behavior, is impossible to say, but most people at the time believed that it made a difference for the better. And in ret-

rospect we know that crime rates declined far faster than one would have predicted by knowing only the aging of the population. . . . Whatever effect these associational activities had, it was as much from the routine moral training and social pressure they produced as from the religious convictions they imparted.[23]

Jefferson's Presidency

Thomas Jefferson was involved in two of the most important transfers of power in history. He narrowly lost to John Adams in the first contested presidential election in America, but beat him in the rematch. The succession of power from George Washington to John Adams to Thomas Jefferson represented the greatest peaceful transfer of authority in human history up until that time, the first was between two different men of the same political persuasion, the second was the initial outside takeover of the government—the Federalists had controlled the federal establishment since 1789.

The campaign that ended John Adams' presidency after a single term was one of the nastiest in America history. Adams, following the customs of his time, did not campaign, but his supporters called Jefferson an atheist, anarchist, demagogue, and worse. Jefferson and his supporters were as venomous. It was alleged that President Adams sent his vice-presidential running-mate Charles Pinckney to England to procure four pretty girls as mistresses, two for himself and two for Adams. "I do declare upon my honor," proclaimed Adams, "if this be true General Pinckney has kept them all for himself and cheated me out of my two."[24] The method of operation of the Electoral College stipulated that each elector cast two votes and meant that, while Jefferson won the popular vote, he was tied with his vice presidential running mate Aaron Burr in the electoral college and the race was thrown into the House of Representatives. With the old Congress responsible for the balloting, the Federalists were determined to deny Jefferson the presidency. Finally, several Federalists in the House, led by James Bayard, Delaware's sole representative, cast blank ballots to make

Jefferson president, ratifying the popular vote on the 36th ballot of the House. The Twelfth Amendment to the Constitution provided for separate balloting for president and vice president.

The Louisiana Purchase, the acquisition of half a continent, symbolized Jefferson's vision for America's future and his contribution to the strength of the Union. Louisiana's cost was three cents an acre, because Napoleon needed funds for war with the British and feared its superior sea power would enable capture of the Louisiana Territory. He had already attempted to sell the land to Spain. The military expedition of his brother-in-law to quash the slave revolt in Haiti proved to be a catastrophic defeat, convincing him to change course and sell to America. Afraid that Napoleon might renege on his offer while Congress and the states debated what authority was necessary and whether a constitutional amendment was required to complete the transaction, Jefferson plunged ahead arguing that "to lose our country by a scrupulous adherence to written laws, would be to lose the law itself."[25] Like Washington, Jefferson recognized the importance of the West as frontier to America's future, thinking of it as "almost endlessly renewable and boundlessly prolific."[26] He overcame concerns that (like the British acquisitions after the French and Indian War that led to the Revolutionary War) the purchase would create insurmountable problems that might eventually lead to the fragmentation or balkanization of America.

Jefferson believed the Louisiana Purchase to be a legacy for generations. With this acquisition, the United States became sixteen times larger than the British Isles. Jefferson expected that it would be a thousand years before the frontier reached the Pacific Ocean. He authorized and supervised the Lewis and Clark expedition, which captured the imagination of the entire country and helped him to develop an expansive interpretation of the land covered by the Purchase.

The Jefferson Era

America tried to avoid becoming embroiled in European wars. Britain, however, claimed a right to search neutral ships and impress sailors on

U.S. ships whom they believed to be British citizens. About a quarter of the seamen on American ships were indeed English citizens, many seeking to escape their obligation or duty to fight with the British navy. When the ship *Chesapeake* refused a demand to be inspected, the British fired broadsides, killing three men and then boarded and impressed four more. Jefferson passed up an opportunity to resolve these issues by accommodation when he declined to submit a treaty to the Senate negotiated by James Monroe and William Pinckney.

In response, Jefferson and his Secretary of State James Madison initiated an embargo, closing American ports to foreign trade, hoping to avoid war and force England and France to alter their policies. Jefferson and Madison believed the embargo would work, even though over three-quarters of American trade was with Great Britain, while less than 10 percent of British trade was with the United States. The majority of American revenues came from customs duties on trade with the British. Not surprisingly, this departure from Jefferson's minimalist approach to government did not achieve its intended objective, undermined the American economy, and lowered America's credibility as a trading partner. Between 1807 and 1808, federal revenue was cut in half, exports fell by well over half, and the economy plunged into a deep recession.[27] Smuggling became so rampant along the Canadian border that Jefferson declared Lake Champlain to be in a state of insurrection. As governor of Virginia during the Revolutionary War, Jefferson had failed to effectively defend his colony against British incursions, was almost captured by the enemy, and had his actions reviewed by an inquest. When combined with his lack of military service and some of his actions as president, serious questions have been raised about his judgment on national security matters. Unfortunately, Jefferson refused to recognize the Haiti government comprised of former slaves who had achieved independence from European imperialism, defeated the French, and made possible the Louisiana Purchase. Jefferson continued to play a role in the regimes of his two successors—James Madison and James Monroe, helping to ensure his political dominance and a basically continuous government approach for twenty-four years.

President Madison wanted to blunt domestic opposition to Jefferson's embargo by repealing and replacing it with a law applying only to trade with France and Britain. Smugglers easily circumvented this policy. Congress then passed legislation to remove all trade restrictions against the two belligerents, but declared that if one revoked its edicts, it would re-impose sanctions against the other. Napoleon duped Madison into believing he would take such action, whereupon it was announced that the United States would reopen trade with France and embargo trade with Great Britain. The British renewed their blockade and increased their impressments of American seamen.

Madison was brilliant, a genius at academic and intellectual exercises such as drafting the Constitution, writing *The Federalist Papers*, and establishing a Bill of Rights. But he was not as effective as president. He actively worked to bring on the War of 1812, which was subsequently labeled Madison's War, but did little to prepare for it. Neither he nor Jefferson provided financial support for the military, refusing even to fit and man the advanced frigates built by the Federalists. Like Jefferson, Madison had no military experience and miscalculated the difficulty in defeating the British. They both believed themselves to be following Washington's advice to keep out of foreign wars.

Madison's hand-picked successor, James Monroe, was easily elected and had a strong cabinet—John Calhoun as secretary of war, future presidential candidate William Crawford as secretary of the treasury, and John Quincy Adams who was perhaps the greatest secretary of state with his formulation of the Monroe Doctrine. Monroe had impeccable integrity, could not hold a grudge; he made a good will tour of the Northeast, initiating the "Era of Good Feeling."

The War of 1812

The vote for the War of 1812 passed narrowly, in the House by 79 to 49 and in the Senate 19 to 13. The British attempted to avoid the conflict by making concessions, but with the communications lag it took weeks for this information to reach American shores and Madison had already declared war; he would have withheld the declaration if he had been aware of the British actions. Being tied to England by commercial interests, New England basically sat out the war, still furious about the Jefferson and Madison embargoes. During the war, the on-again off-again embargoes instituted by Madison stiffened New England opposition. As a rule, the farther away someone went from New England, the stronger the opposition to British policies which were thwarting American expansion west and south. The lust to conquer Canada was an important motivating factor for the war as well.

The weak military posture of the Jeffersonian Democratic-Republicans decimated the army. At the start of the war, the military was inexperienced, more closely resembling a rabble. American attacks on three fronts to capture Canada were abysmal failures. At sea, the new nation fared much better, particularly due to the privateers who seized British ships, Captain McDonough's victory on Lake Champlain, and Admiral Perry's famous victory on Lake Erie ("We have met the enemy and they are ours"), which secured that militarily strategic body of water. Admiral Perry's victory was the only surrender of a complete squadron in British naval history. American success at sea was directly attributable to the high quality of the ships, more effective leadership, and better training in the use of the guns on each vessel. The Americans utilized the frigates designed by Joshua Humphreys which were still among the most advanced in the world.

After the 1814 triumph over Napoleon, the British had control over more than 40 colonies, a quarter of the world's population, and most of its sea lanes. The British would have been able to direct additional forces at the colonies. While they were obsessed with defeating Napoleon, they had at best lukewarm interest in fighting America. Nevertheless, the British invaded and pillaged Washington, burning the White House, the Capitol, and the Library of Congress. The lack of preparations by Madison and the military in defending Washington were appalling, but the government was so small and weak the loss had little military significance. The British next attempted to level Baltimore, but local forces held. During this battle, Francis Scott Key was inspired by the fighting to write the national anthem, "The Star-Spangled Banner."

The Treaty of Ghent to end the War of 1812 was negotiated by a high-powered team supervised by Secretary of State James Monroe, which included John Quincy Adams, Secretary of the Treasury Albert Gallatin, House Speaker Henry Clay, and James Bayard, a retired Congressman. Although the importance of the negotiations is reflected by the caliber of the delegation, the results were meager with boundaries remaining the same as at the beginning of the conflict. The peace treaty was signed, but again slow communications meant the word did not travel fast enough to stop Andrew Jackson's victory at The Battle of New Orleans, an event that ratified the legitimacy of the Louisiana Purchase, bolstered American confidence, and helped to justify what was otherwise a fruitless war. The negotiators did conclude a treaty abolishing all discriminatory duties and provided Most-Favored-Nation treatment for both British and American products, substantially remedying the problems that had been created by the embargo.

The War of 1812 cost over $150 million and increased the national debt from $47 million to $127 million. The conflict forced America to rely less on international trade and develop an indigenous manufacturing sector, facilitating adoption of the factory system. Five future presidents served in the war's military support: James Monroe, Andrew Jackson, William Henry Harrison, John Tyler, and Zachary Taylor.

Trade was an important vehicle for holding nations together and avoiding war. Madison and Jefferson advocated trade sanctions and embargoes as an alternative to the use of military force. They opposed a standing army and building up the navy, because they believed it would lead to a monarchical type of government. Theoretically, it was better in their mind to have the country invaded and its capital burned than to surrender the principles of republican government. Historians view the war as accomplishing or settling nothing, but it validated the revolutionary experiment in limited republican government. America withstood the most powerful nation in the world and widespread domestic opposition "without one trial for treason or even one prosecution for libel."[28] In 1817, John Adams told Jefferson that Madison's administration had "acquired more glory, and established more Union than all his three Predecessors, Washington, Adams, Jefferson, put together." This was a sentiment shared by Henry Clay, Daniel Webster, and the American public. Madison and his party remained in power for 40 of the next forty-four years.[29]

President Kennedy understood the power of Thomas Jefferson's intellect and thought as he dined alone in the White House. As one of the greatest revolutionaries of any era, Jefferson was able to establish democratic principles throughout American civilization. He was probably the most effective combination of revolutionary and national leader in human history.

5

Jackson's egalitarianism

DECISIVE AND EFFECTIVE—whether fighting the British, Indians, Congress, or the Bank of the United States—Andrew Jackson got the job done. Prone to violence and rage, he was physically unwell, racked by disorders exacerbated by wounds from duels and military battles. Yet, when a would-be assassin pulled the triggers of two pistols at point blank range in the Capitol and both shots miraculously misfired, President Jackson, instead of ducking, attacked the assailant.

Jackson (1767–1845) was the most popular president of his time, even rivaling George Washington. Political pundits and elected officials underestimated the strength of the popular sentiment or political will that had created his presidency. Jackson's national appeal started with his victory at the Battle of New Orleans, which electrified the country; it was one of the most one-sided contests in American history and came on the heels of his capture of Pensacola and Mobile. For America, the War of 1812 had largely been one military defeat and one disaster after another until in that battle Jackson inflicted 2,000 casualties on the British invaders while suffering a mere dozen American fatalities. His victory restored public confidence and made him a national hero.

A source of inspiration to Lincoln on the eve of the Civil War, revered by Theodore and Franklin Roosevelt, and hailed by Harry Truman as one of the four greatest presidents—along with Washington, Jefferson, and Lincoln—Jackson expanded the powers of the presidency in ways that none of his six predecessors had. He was the first president to come from the common people, not from an educated elite, and he never ceased to see himself as their champion. He was the first to build what we would recognize as a political party. He was the first to maintain a large circle of private advisors—what was called his Kitchen Cabinet—to help make policy. And he was the first to insist on the deference he thought due the chief executive as the only official elected by all the people. It was a distinction he believed made the White House, not Capitol Hill, the center of national power and national action.[1]

In the first half of the nineteenth-century, the dominant political figures in the Republic were Thomas Jefferson and Andrew Jackson. Both shared a commitment to equality and democracy, distaste for privilege and moneyed power, but the two individuals were very different: Jefferson—an intellectual, Jackson—a man of action. Jefferson was a civilian, Jackson a war hero. Jefferson was born an aristocrat; Jackson was a self-made man. Jefferson dominated the presidency between 1800 and 1825, and the Jackson era extended from 1829 to 1860. Jackson is considered the first president without direct links to the founding fathers, although two of his brothers were killed in the Revolutionary War and, as a young child, he was captured, held prisoner, his forehead slashed with a saber by the British. It is probable that neither Jefferson nor Jackson would have been elected president without the nonvoting slaves that gave the South more votes in the Electoral College.

Just as Jefferson's election precipitated a crisis of succession, the election of 1824 also threatened to unravel America's constitutional structure. Andrew Jackson outpolled John Quincy Adams by a decisive 4-to-3 margin, but did not have an electoral majority. Jackson's heroism and independence appealed to the general public and all three of his three major opponents were connected to what had become a discredited incumbent administration (i.e., the Washington establishment). John Quincy Adams received the smallest share of the popular vote in history for anyone elected to the presidency. Turnout was only 25 percent due to the limited sectional appeal of the candidates. A fourth of the electors were chosen by state legislatures and not by voters at the polls. The election was decided in the House of Representatives where each state's delegation had one vote.

In the 1824 election, Henry Clay (1777–1852) would have been elected president by the House of Representatives, but he came in fourth against "a political flyweight, a military chieftain, and a physical wreck."[2] Only the first three candidates were eligible. Most members of the House of Representatives aspire to become Speaker during careers spanning years and often decades. Henry Clay was elected to the post on his first day in the House, because of being a respected and effective leader of a youthful group of War Hawks. Known as the Great Compromiser, he is generally considered to be the greatest Speaker in the history of the House.

Clay suffered a hard life. He was one of only two out of nine brothers and sisters that survived childhood; this caused his mother to be permanently embittered. Clay's own children gave him nothing but anguish and trouble: of his eleven children, all six of his daughters died early in life, one son was a chronic alcoholic, two sons were committed to lunatic asylums, and one was killed in the Mexican War. James Madison, the last surviving founding father, desired that Clay be president. Clay was almost certainly the greatest politician to never become president, coining the phrase "I had rather be right than be President." He ran for election five times, losing the nomination fight twice and the general election three times.

Henry Clay manipulated the vote in John Quincy Adams' favor on the understanding that he be named secretary of state, which at the time was presumed to be the stepping stone to the presidency. The decision haunted the rest of Clay's public career, which spanned almost three decades as Speaker, member of the Senate, foreign ambassador, and four more unsuccessful runs for the presidency. Never having served in the military himself, Clay had already gained the unending enmity of Andrew Jackson by having had the audacity to attack his war record. While Adams was the most qualified candidate (his long distinguished career in foreign affairs began when he was fourteen), his presidency never achieved credibility. The failure of the Constitution to provide for a democratic succession in effect destroyed Adams' presidency. As leaders of the National Republican, or Whig, party, Adams and Clay proposed aid for domestic improvements and other programs to expand the role of the federal government, but were able to achieve very little due to the lack of political will to energize their proposed programs. While Adams had impeccable personal integrity and was one of the smartest presidents, he was out of touch with the public. By his own admission, he had little political sense.

The election was denounced as a "corrupt bargain." Jackson's name was almost immediately put forth for the next presidential election, launching a three-and-a-half-year campaign that was one of the ugliest in American history. Adams was labeled a monarchist and harshly criticized. Jackson was called a murderer, a drunken and ignorant farmer unqualified for office. His mother was called a prostitute, his wife an adulterer and bigamist. Jackson's wife died soon after the election and he believed her death was caused by these attacks and the stress of the campaign. The "corrupt bargain" was the single, central event that shaped Jackson's philosophy of government. He constantly fought corruption and special interests and supported rule by the majority and the general public. Jackson was the first president from beyond the seaboard states and his election moved political geography toward the West. He ran on a reform ticket with the most politically sophisticated operation of any presidential campaign up until that time. Jackson and his teeming public support launched another revolution; the common man became the ruling authority. Radical economics leveled monopolies and eliminated privileges. Western expansion reached across the continent.

Jacksonian Democracy

Because the settlers had access to land and a relatively high standard of living, more men voted in America than anyplace else. Property class restrictions limited the franchise to the wealthy 15 percent in England, but permitted more than half the adult men in the colonies to vote, making America a good laboratory for democracy. Between 1800 and 1850, the property tax requirements for voting were gradually eliminated, in some cases by state constitutional conventions. America became more egalitarian. The common man gradually became involved in all facets of government. The House of Representatives was transformed from a small body of well-off, well-educated men to a heterogeneous mass of several hundred men from a diverse group of social, economic, and cultural classes, organized along political party lines. A more diverse, democratic House of Representatives was created by a federal law that required individual congressional districts instead of statewide or citywide at-large districts. The parties ended the practice of choosing their presidential candidates in the congressional party caucuses and began staging party conventions.

President Andrew Jackson took the concept even further, granting no tenure and appointing common men to office. Jackson tried to reform the government and patronage by encouraging rotation in office. Contrary to common belief, he was not a strong supporter of the spoils system, but used patronage to implement rotation in office. From his perspective, this initiative reformed a political establishment that was unresponsive and had conspired to deny him the presidency in the 1924 campaign. When Martin Van Buren fired Solomon van Rensselaer, a postmaster from the other party who had been injured by the British, Jackson overruled him, saying, "That man has taken British lead in his body. I will not remove him."[3]

Jackson's first inauguration was remarkable—it was open-house, not invitation-only, and resulted in a near riot with uncouth backwoodsmen making a shambles of the elegant White House. It marked the beginning of an even more populist, democratic form of government in America. Jackson was a strong supporter of openness in government and encouraging the full disclosure of the executive branch proceedings. Jackson supported a strong presidency but believed the role of government should be strictly limited. He worried particularly about the potential impact of moneyed interests and moved to reform and overhaul every government agency. As the economy expanded, however, so did the government. The number of federal employees almost doubled during Jackson's eight years; civil service opportunities were opened up to more people. His appointments, however, were at best marginally effective, and included a couple of outright crooks who undermined his reform efforts.

Through his recognition of the expansion of the rights of individuals, the changing relationships among the classes, and the move toward egalitarianism, Jackson became enormously popular. He was affectionately called the Hero or the Great Captain as he responded to the needs and demands of the people, not merely workers but entrepreneurs as well. His opponents, by contrast, were more concerned about maintaining the status quo and complained that the Republic had degenerated into a democracy, referring to the negative connotation the latter term held for many people. Jackson moved quickly to pay off the national debt, a goal he achieved early in his second term, which made him even more popular. To pay down the federal debt, Jackson opposed many funding initiatives in the Congress. When pressed to approve of these spending programs, he threatened to increase taxes, which the proponents of largesse agreed was worse than a veto.

By 1835 America was clearly different and the foreign visitor, Alexis de Tocqueville, developed the basis for the concept of "American exceptionalism." Historians argue about the extent to which this term connotes goodness, greatness, or imperialism, but it is clear that Tocqueville was describing a New World that was indeed very different from the Old World: "The great advantage of Americans is, that they have arrived at a state of democracy without having to endure a democratic revolution and that they are born equal, instead of becoming so." By democratic revolution, Tocqueville was referring to the bloody failure experienced by the French. Americans experienced their own quiet, bloodless democratic revolution after John Adams' presidency.

The outlines of modern American society were clearly present: democracy, individualism, the role of private property, the absence of rank, the importance of education, and equality (except for slaves). The transition from a republic was not easy, with that form of government being viewed positively as administered by the most worthy and enlightened men. Democracy was viewed by many as mobocracy or government by the unwashed masses, possibly the worst form, even worse than monarchy. Indeed, the form of democracy that was at stake applied only to white males, less than half of the population. Yet, the transition was revolutionary:

> Democracy appears when some large number of previously excluded, ordinary persons—what the eighteenth century called "the many"—secure the power not simply to select their governors but to oversee the institutions of government, as officeholders and as citizens free to assemble and criticize those in office. Democracy is never a gift bestowed by benevolent, farseeing rulers who seek to reinforce their own legitimacy. It must always be fought for, by political coalitions that cut across distinctions of wealth, power, and interest. It succeeds and survives only when it is rooted in the lives and expectations of its citizens, and continually reinvigorated in each generation. Democratic successes are never irreversible.[4]

Radical Economics: Leveling Monopoly and Eliminating Privilege

Andrew Jackson rode a wave of popular sentiment for revolutionary economic reform from fast-growing and wealth-creating regions such as the frontier and New York State, home of the radical Locofocos.

> Taking up his presidential duties, Jackson thought the country was suffering from a crisis of corruption. If virtue was central to the well-being of the nation, then corruption

and selfishness were corrosive, and could be fatal. By corruption, Jackson did not mean only scandal and mismanagement. He meant it in a broader sense; in the marshaling of power and influence by a few institutions and interests that sought to profit at the expense of the whole. He was not against competition in the marketplace of goods and ideas. Like the Founders, he believed in vigorous debate, and like Adam Smith, he put his faith in the capacity of free individuals to work out their destinies. But he was very much against the special deal or the selfish purpose, and he was very much in favor of his own role as defender of the many and protector of the nation. In Washington, he was intent on dismantling the kind of permanent federal establishment that created a climate in which, in his view, insiders such as John Quincy Adams and Henry Clay could thrive no matter what the people beyond Washington wanted.[5]

Jackson waged that war against privilege and monopoly. The Charles River Bridge, for example, which collected monopoly tolls from the people of Boston, was owned by various privileged interests who leveraged the cash flow to create considerable wealth. After a popular outcry, the state chartered a new bridge a few hundred feet away from the old. Authorized to collect tolls only until it recovered the cost of construction, the bridge became toll-free. The owners of the Charles River Bridge sued, claiming their private rights had been violated. The Jackson appointees to the Supreme Court found in favor of the defendants, recognizing the claims of the larger community against a private monopoly. "Regardless of its apparent anticorporate sentiments, the decision actually aided the growth of industry by denying monopolistic claims of older companies whose charters implied or were believed to have granted exclusive privileges. The decision reflected the direction the nation was taking in its rise toward a fully developed industrial society and the on going evolution of Jacksonian Democracy."[6]

A symbol of class and privilege was the Bank of United States, run by the Philadelphia patrician Nicholas Biddle. As part of his fight against wealth and privilege, Jackson made war against the bank. The first national bank had been enacted over the objections of Jefferson and Madison. After the country faced bankruptcy by the War of 1812, the second national bank was passed with the authority to issue bank notes, enabling it to automatically expand or contract the supply of currency, which was an effective way to control the economy. The bank was extraordinarily powerful, not politically responsive, and often made loans for political purposes. Subsequently, it was found that the bank had engaged in fraudulent activities and at the end of his life Biddle spent much time in litigation over criminal activity at the bank. Jackson's veto of the bill renewing the bank was only the tenth veto in Congressional history and established the then revolutionary principle that a president could stop a bill from becoming law on policy grounds as long as he could sustain the veto. Jackson's veto greatly expanded presidential prerogatives, created an uproar, but was sustained. His veto message sparked a popular uprising that helped him win a near landslide election in 1832 over bank proponent Henry Clay, who misread popular sentiment.

The first six presidents vetoed a total of nine bills; Jackson alone vetoed a dozen. Previous presidents signed bills that they were opposed to but thought constitutional. Jackson vetoed bills he opposed, vastly expanding the concept of presidential power. "Jackson's vision of himself as the embodiment of the people standing against entrenched interests, combined with his appetite for control and for power, led him to see the veto as more than an occasional tool. Congress should consult with the president in advance of sending legislation down Pennsylvania Avenue, Jackson said—a novel notion in 1830."[7]

In his second term, Jackson touched off another furor when he fired his secretary of treasury for refusing to remove funds from the bank, establishing the right of the president to fire cabinet officers. The dismissal action earned him an unprecedented censure from the U.S. Senate. In the midst of the fight over the bank, Biddle drastically curtailed loans and credit with the intent to produce panic. When Jackson succeeded in killing the Second Bank of the United States, state legislatures chartered 200 new banks, which issued so much paper money that speculation became even more rampant. Funds withdrawn from the national bank were deposited in state banks, which in turn increased the amount of currency or bank notes in circulation. The increase in money supply invariably led to inflation and, speculation.

Jackson implemented a hard money policy to replace Hamilton's system and to "prevent periodic depressions . . . the rise within the state of independent powers not responsible to the people . . . and the rule of a moneyed aristocracy systematically exploiting [the common man]."[8] Workers had often been paid in depreciated paper currency and felt they were regularly cheated by paper money, which led to speculation, inflation, and then to depression. The valuation of gold was increased from 15 to 16 to one, resulting in more gold being coined in one year than in the first sixteen years of the mint's existence. Speculation continued, particularly in land, causing Jackson to require purchases to be in gold or silver. Jackson stuck to his hard-money principles the remainder of his term. His actions eventually burst the speculative bubble, but led to a severe economic downturn.

In the 1830s, five-sixths of the people in jail in New England and the Mid-Atlantic states were debtors. When a farmer or other citizen couldn't pay his bills, he could go to jail. When a bank couldn't pay its bills, it just suspended payment and continued in business. This was offensive to the average American and a federal law was passed to prevent imprisonment for debt.

Jackson transformed the office of president into a pulpit for national leadership, radically altering public perception of the office by claiming the presidency and not the Congress was the direct representative of the American people, a revolutionary proposition for the times. He viewed himself as the head of the government executing the popular will, responsive to and a servant of the public. Jackson characterized his actions as battling against corruption, waste, and dishonest politicians, thus establishing an even stronger bond between himself and ordinary people. All of these actions created controversy and earned him considerable enmity in some circles and strong opposition, including censure, in the Senate from Henry Clay, Daniel Webster, and John Calhoun. His conduct sometimes bordered on the authoritarian as he nursed long-time prejudices and resentments.

Jackson had a reputation for being rough-hewn, vulgar, low-class, and a firebrand. An hour before an interview with British royalty, James Buchanan found the president in "old clothes, feet on the desk, enjoying his corncob pipe." Buchanan was horrified and reminded the president of the high rank of his guest. Jackson told him to mind his own business and a dread overcame Buchanan as a meeting with Queen Victoria approached. "What was his surprise when Jackson descended to the coach in person, faultlessly arrayed, escorted the distinguished visitor to the House, and entertained her for an hour with such grace and courtesy that she declared she had never met a more elegant gentleman in all her travels."[9]

Martin Van Buren (1782–1862) succeeded John Calhoun as Jackson's vice president when Calhoun gained Jackson's enmity by voting to break a tie in the Senate and to kill Van Buren's nomination as minister to Great Britain. Van Buren had built a political organization in New York that was one of the first statewide political machines, running the political business of the state from Washington. Van Buren opposed a strong central government, but his role as head of the New York political machine hardly fit the mold of a man of the people.

As Jackson's successor, Van Buren was overwhelmed by the depressed economy throughout his term. Within weeks of his inauguration, there was a major financial crash; the Panic of 1837, part of a worldwide depression. Faced with a drain on gold and silver reserves, the Bank of England raised rates and curtailed credit, forcing many British merchants to do the same with their American clients. This caused a reduction in manufacturing and commerce and a rapid decline in cotton prices, which in turn caused defaults on loans to U.S. banks. The defaults reduced reserves and forced the banks to suspend redemption of their bank notes with gold and silver, which meant these notes were no longer accepted as payment. Between 1836 and 1840, the U.S. money supply dropped by a third. Without a national bank, Van Buren had no flexibility to expand the money supply. The depression caused federal revenues to fall by half and almost 90 percent of manufacturing plants to close. Van Buren was decisively beaten by former general, William Henry Harrison, the first of two times the Whigs won the presidency with a war hero when the Democrats failed to manage the economy. The Whig party ran a popular general four out of the five times they had a serious presidential contender.

Western Expansion

Prior to the Jackson era, Americans were largely packed in between the Appalachian Mountains and the Atlantic Ocean. Many people never ventured more than fifty or a hundred miles from home. There was, however, a sense of optimism and adventure and a belief that a bright future lay ahead. Jackson's era was a breakout time when the country stretched ocean to ocean, a go-go period referred to as *go ahead* or what might later be called "progress." The force of the great American culture swept away anything in its path—the last resistance of the British Empire, the Spanish, and the Indians. The people were driven to make money, work, and improve their conditions. They expected their children to do even better, many of them by exploring and settling the great frontier. Family, church, and community ties were weakened by industrialization. By moving from place to place, some individuals lost their tightly knit communities and their feeling of belonging, leaving a void that was filled by work, money, and the drive to get ahead. This drive was not just materialistic, it was reform-oriented, developing the basis for women's rights, temperance, concern for the poor, and education reform, as well as utopianism.

In his early years, Jackson didn't subscribe to diplomatic solutions or limited wars, he simply wanted victory. He was famous for his efforts in the Indian wars. In his *The Winning of the West*, Theodore Roosevelt described "the spread of the English-speaking peoples over the world's western space" as "the most striking feature of the world's history." Only "a warped, perverse, and silly morality" would condemn America's conquest of the west.[10] Often, the Indians were not the peaceful people as they are depicted. They were continually fighting and raiding against other tribes. The European settlers were just other sets of tribes to raid and fight. The Indians were nondiscriminatory in their savagery, killing missionaries, women, and children as well as armed militia and soldiers. These acts extended not only to scalping, but other forms of torture as well. Today we might call them terrorists. In one incident, a young Indian attacking a wagon train slipped into a wagon of terrorized children and killed twelve of them, "slicing their heads from their bodies in a fury of bloodlust."[11]

The Indian tribes chose sides in the French and Indian War and were known as savages by the enemy. Indians were largely neutral in the Revolutionary War, due in part to Washington's able emissaries to the Iroquois. Those who did fight were mostly on the side of the British, particularly later in the war. Many Indians once again sided with the British in the War of 1812, thus demonstrating their cultural and political incompatibility with Americans. Consequently, a great deal of fear and mistrust existed between the Indians and settlers. The founding fathers and colonialists were concerned about the vulnerability of the American frontier and civilization to the Indians. Barbarian invasions had precipitated the fall of the Roman Empire, extinguishing civilization for centuries. In the early days of the Pennsylvania colony, the Quakers unsuccessfully attempted a peaceful, conciliatory approach towards the Indians. They were ousted from their leadership role by the populace.

George Washington and Secretary of War Henry Knox attempted to develop a conciliatory policy towards the Indians, but were significantly out of touch with popular sentiment. As part of his intense focus on the frontier as America's future, Washington made conciliatory Indian policy as one of his top priorities, but it was one of the very few times as president he did not get his way, because too many settlers had been treated brutally by violent Indians. Washington believed Indians were involved in a holding action, eventually to be displaced by a wave of white settlers.

When the Indians resisted ceding their land, the settlers pursued a policy of purchasing it. Washington and Jefferson attempted to encourage assimilation and integration, but the population exploded and the country expanded too rapidly to make that humane and civilized policy possible. The weak American government made settlers vulnerable to the fierce and warlike tribes on the frontier. Treaties were used as temporary expedients, but the settlers did not intend to honor them. This mistrust fed a rapidly deteriorating situation as huge waves of migrants moved to the frontier with insatiable appetites for land.

In pursuit of the Seminole Indians, who had repeatedly raided across the border into Georgia, Jackson invaded and captured the state of Florida without obtaining any prior authorization or approval, a daring action which raised eyebrows from many in Washington who feared he was running for president and others who viewed his campaign as in direct conflict with the Constitution. John Quincy Adams was one of the few people to defend Jackson's actions and persuaded the Spanish it was in their best interest to relinquish the territory to the United States. Jackson then served as the first governor of the Florida territory.

Jackson adopted a ten-month-old Indian boy, Lyncoya, whose mother died in one of Jackson's victorious battles. He treated the boy as his son. When he ran for president, Jackson did not lose a single state where Indian warfare was a major concern. Indian uprisings occurred periodically. As president in the 1830s, Jackson had extensive knowledge of Indian affairs and as a strong leader could take advantage of situations where he had strong support from a populace that feared and mistrusted the Indians. He secured passage of the Indian Removal Act, which enabled the president to exchange unorganized public lands in the west for Indian land in the East. The removal policy was considered the best option for preserving Indian culture and safety, perhaps saving the tribes from extinction. The Indians were to be compensated for their improvements, be given perpetual title to the new land, have all costs reimbursed, and be given one-year subsistence pay. Jackson showed genuine concern for the welfare of Native Americans and many chiefs regarded him as their friend. His efforts to move the Indians forced both sides to face the inevitable, that the American settlers would force the Indians out of the coveted land. If they stayed, they would be subject to state and local laws and a culture in which they could not survive. Jackson acquired an enormous amount of territory from the Indians—more than the combined states of Massachusetts, New Hampshire, Vermont, Connecticut, Rhode Island, New Jersey, and

Delaware. Over 70 treaties were signed for 100 million acres of land in the East, at a cost of $68 million and considerable loss of life.

The heavy-handed American policy destroyed the Indian culture and heritage, resulting in the needless deaths of thousands of innocent victims. The cruel removal of the Cherokees and their eight-hundred mile Trail of Tears, for example, cost well over 4,000 lives out of the 18,000 evicted. While Jackson has been condemned for his role in removing the Indians, Chief Justice John Marshall, in his five-volume biography of George Washington, described the Indians as constantly engaged in duplicitous and brutal acts of savagery, particularly against women and children.[12]

Jackson's one notable foreign policy failure was his inability to acquire Texas. Davy Crockett, Jim Bowie, and over 180 defenders were massacred and the movement for Texas independence used *"Remember the Alamo"* as its battle cry. Sam Houston, a friend of Andrew Jackson and former governor of Jackson's home state of Tennessee, led the army of volunteers who eventually captured Santa Anna, the perpetrator of the Alamo, forcing him to recognize Texas independence. In 1836, Jackson hesitated to annex Texas and jeopardize the election of his hand-picked successor, Martin van Buren, who in turn rebuffed these overtures throughout his presidency to avoid the controversy over whether to create another slave state. Van Buren's successor, William Henry Harrison, died after only one month as president, but after John Tyler assumed the office, he submitted a treaty to annex Texas in 1844 near the end of his term. The treaty was disapproved because of opposition from the anti-slavery north.

In the 1844 election, Henry Clay and Van Buren misread the political will on the Texas annexation issue and both came out in opposition, whereas, to obtain Jackson's support for the nomination over Van Buren and then win the general election, James Polk supported annexation. With a switch of 5,000 votes in New York, Clay would have won. Texas annexation was approved by a joint resolution (requiring a majority vote instead of two-thirds) just after Polk's election. The fear of a rivalry with the newly independent Texas state, as well as its alliance with Britain, drove the annexation debate.

The energy and strength of the American society and economy of the era after Jackson was personified by James Polk (1795–1849), one of the more effective yet obscure presidents, who presided over the acquisition of more territory than any other American president. Yet he was dour and disliked by many. Polk took office in an era of extremely limited government—the entire federal bureaucracy consisted of only several hundred employees, and the annual federal budget was less than $100 million. He successfully focused on a few key issues while working 18-hour days.

Polk first settled the issue of the Oregon territory, acquiring the territory, including Puget Sound, in a compromise with Great Britain. Mexico, an early banana republic, had repudiated its debts, launched forays into Texas, and pillaged foreigners during its periodic civil wars. When Texas was annexed by the U.S., Mexico severed diplomatic relations. President Polk offered to purchase California for $25 million and New Mexico for an additional $5 million, but was rebuffed. When Mexican troops raided across the disputed border, Polk declared war. While the war was one-sided, it still sparked much internal dissent. Henry David Thoreau refused to pay war taxes and his *Essay on Civil Disobedience* became an American classic. General Zachary Taylor defeated Santa Anna at Monterey and Buena Vista. General Winfield Scott won at Vera Cruz, and took Mexico City. Polk rotated his generals, trying to prevent them from becoming too famous and possible candidates for the opposing party in 1848. He failed, Taylor won the presidency.

The Treaty of Guadalupe Hidalgo ended the Mexican war, but was negotiated without the authorization of President Polk who felt he had no choice but to submit it for ratification. Polk wanted to acquire part of northern Mexico, but the negotiators, including General Scott, ignored his wishes. The U.S. paid $20 million for the rest of Texas, New Mexico, Arizona, California, Colorado, Utah, and Nevada. Although he achieved his objectives, Polk left the presidency a controversial figure, often using intrigue and secrecy to achieve his ends.

Exploration of the West caught the imagination of the nation. John Fremont covered a greater expanse of the West than any other explorer. His expedition reports, written by his beautiful wife, the daughter of Missouri Senator Thomas Hart Benton, made him a national figure. Partnering with Kit Carson on three expeditions, he mapped much of the area from the Great Plains to the Pacific and focused national interest on the Rockies, eventually resulting in this terrain becoming part of the United States. During the Mexican War, Fremont was exploring California. Brigadier General Stephen Kearny marched from Kansas to California, meeting up with him to declare that territory's independence from Mexico. Fremont was the first Republican Party candidate for president and came surprisingly close to winning the election.

In 1848, gold was discovered near Sacramento. The California gold rush set off mass hysteria and westward migration. Gold was the standard used by the Bank of England, the world's de facto central bank. World currencies were pegged to gold, and most trade was conducted in gold. By the early 1850s California was producing almost half of the world's gold, facilitating a true gold standard, and accelerating the development of America's capital markets. Speculation ran rampant. The volume of activity in the markets increased by a factor of ten. When a steamer with $1.6 million in California gold sank in a hurricane, panic hit the Wall Street market, spreading to Europe.

California became a state in only three years—over 90 percent of its residents were men, a result of the rigors of the frontier. It took six months to get to California either by the land route or around Cape Horn. This remoteness led to the development of the clipper ship, which reduced the trip time in half and led to the expansion of the New York and Boston shipyards, which were a critical factor in enabling the North to blockade the South in the Civil War. Trekking across the Panama isthmus could reduce the trip distance in half. When a railroad was built across Panama, serviced by steamships on the Pacific, the advantage of the clipper ship ended and its use declined.[13]

Andrew Jackson and his successors (Van Buren, Tyler, and Polk) had a far-reaching positive impact on the frontier and our democracy.

> Jackson has inspired some of the greatest men who
> have followed him in the White House—presidents who

have sought to emulate his courage, to match his strength, and to wage and win the kinds of battles he waged and won. Running at the head of a national party, fighting for a mandate from the people to govern in particular ways on particular issues, depending on a circle of insiders and advisers, mastering the media of the age to transmit a consistent message at a constant pace, and using the veto as a political, not just constitutional, weapon, in a Washington that is at once political and personally charged are all features of the modern presidency that flowered in Jackson's White House.[14]

The scuttling of the national bank, however, resulted in over a century of ineffective economic and monetary policy. The Jacksonians completed an egalitarian revolution that transformed America, but not enough to avert a Civil War over slavery. President Jackson had a strong vision for America, although his vision was somewhat flawed. His method of leadership or mechanism for comforting the nation was to inspire it and provide effective executive decision making.

6

John Marshall
defines the agrarian transformation

JOHN MARSHALL'S LIFE (1755–1835) paralleled the course of early American history. He served in George Washington's army and was at Valley Forge. He gained fame for standing up to the French in an infamous affair, refusing a bribe offered by Talleyrand. He served in Congress and as secretary of state, basically acting as president for several months during the end of John Adams presidency. As the leading disciple of Washington, he wrote a five-volume biography of Washington and a history of the American people that was the authoritative source for thirty years.

When Marshall became Chief Justice in 1801, the role of the court in constitutional law was uncertain and the Court had little prestige or authority.[1] Nominations to the Supreme Court were almost routinely declined. The attorney general was not a full-time employee, but a private lawyer on presidential retainer who didn't even live in Washington. Marshall relied on the work of some of the leading legal theoreticians such as William Blackstone and James Wilson, one of the original justices to the Supreme Court. Wilson believed the founding fathers had acted on revolutionary principles in successfully establishing a new nation, and, because the revolution represented a significant break with the past, those values should be inculcated in future generations. Wilson noted that U.S. laws would be based on the consent of the people whose obedience they require in contrast to English law which began with the concept of a sovereign issuing commands. Marshall built on William Blackstone's *Commentaries,* which used reasoning to apply broad principles to individual cases. This method of analysis was more cohesive and less bound to a hodge-podge of precedents. Marshall was a strong believer in Montesquieu's separate and independent spheres of government. He was not particularly in favor of big government and corporations, but rather of federal over state power to reduce conflicting and confusing statutes, to protect rights of associations such as corporations, and to protect free enterprise from intrusive government.

Under English tradition, the British Constitution was construed by the Parliament. The U.S. Constitution did not clearly give judicial review to the Supreme Court. Alexander Hamilton, who humorously referred to his law practice as "the art of fleecing neighbors," was responsible for establishing the concept of judicial review.[2] The framers of the Constitution had only vaguely discussed the notion that the courts could overturn federal laws. Hamilton's writings in *The Federalist Papers* were the basis for judicial review, establishing the principle that the U.S. Constitution is the paramount law, subject to the jurisdiction and interpretation of the Supreme Court. In one of Marshall's early cases, the Supreme Court was interjected into a highly partisan fight between the Federalists and the Jeffersonian Democratic-Republicans, specifically being asked to issue a command to Jefferson's secretary of state to carry out President Adams' appointment of a justice of the peace. The Court held that, although the justice of the peace was entitled to such a written order, the Congress had violated the Constitution in expanding the grounds for issuing it. The decision made it clear the Constitution was a paramount or supreme law that cannot be altered by an act of the legislature. The courts have the authority to interpret the laws and resolve conflicts. "The authority of the Supreme Court to declare an act of Congress unconstitutional was now the law of the land."[3] There was little public criticism of this decision and general praise from the press for avoiding a constitutional confrontation. Seven years later, the Court struck down a state law as being in conflict with the U.S. Constitution.[4]

Banks provided financing for the entrepreneurial revolution then in its infancy and played a crucial role in economic growth. In America, the first bank was established in 1781, and twenty-five more were opened by 1800, sixty more by 1810, and over 300 by 1820. Banks provided both short- and long-term credit for farmers, merchants, artisans, craftsmen, and others. Initially, England was ahead economically, in part because it had severely limited banking in colonial America, but the United States caught up quickly. John Marshall empowered the corporation and the financial system by his decision in *McCulloch v. Maryland,* often regarded as the most important decision in the history of the Supreme Court. At stake was the authority of the state of Maryland to tax the Bank of the United States.

Many of the founding fathers were suspicious of banks, John Adams even claiming that "Every dollar of a bank bill that is issued beyond the quantity of gold and silver in the vaults represents nothing and therefore is a cheat upon somebody." Fortunately, others such as Hamilton understood the functioning and importance of banks. Besides Hamilton's central bank, there were state banks that required a charter and an act of the legislature, which made banking a political football and the source of much corruption as politicians sought to secure charter banks for their personal benefit or to favor their friends.

The controversy between the Federalists and the Republicans in creating the Bank of the United States in 1791 led Republicans in the Congress to block renewal when its charter expired in 1811. James Madison supported renewing the bank, but was so ineffective that his own vice president, George Clinton, cast the decisive vote to kill it in the Senate. When the Congress declared the War of 1812, it had no way to provide for the war's financing other than public subscriptions to sell bonds. Most of the wealthy people with liquid funds lived in the

Northeast, which was neutral or opposed to the war. State banks expanded to fill the void, but their growth was based mostly on their license to print money. Gold and hard assets flowed into the areas where banks were most secure such as in New England. Notes from other states were often not honored and had little or no backing. Almost every bank beyond New England did not have gold or silver on hand to redeem the paper money submitted by customers. The U.S. government teetered on the verge of bankruptcy. The British spurned Russian offers to mediate, believing they could win the war by virtue of their superior financial position. Treasury Secretary Gallatin persuaded the wealthiest man in America, Stephen Girard, whose credit rating was far superior to the government's, to subscribe to the loans necessary to continue the war effort. Madison continued to press for chartering a second Bank of the United States, but the political context had radically changed. The South and West, in need of capital, supported the bank while the Northeast, with its manufacturing prowess, had little or no need of funds. Congress re-chartered the Bank as an alternative to the state chartered banks then in existence.

With the country growing rapidly, the second national bank did not have the same power, leverage, or authority as the first bank. Initially, the bank stimulated an economic boom, but when an economic contraction set in, the bank called in loans, resulting in the insolvency of many businesses and state banks. Maryland expressed its outrage by placing a stamp tax on all banks not chartered by a state legislature. James McCulloch was a Baltimore branch manager who refused to pay the tax.[5]

The case was argued over nine days by some of the great legal minds of the time. Marshall concluded that Congress had the constitutional authority to create the bank, relying on Hamilton's memorandum to Washington to define the necessary and proper clause to mean appropriate rather than indispensable. With respect to the authority of Maryland to tax the bank, Marshall issued his famous proclamation: "the power to tax involves the power to destroy." He determined that "the states have no power, by taxation or otherwise, to retard, impede, burden, or in any manner control, the operations of the constitutional laws enacted by the Congress." The decision was a firm endorsement of national supremacy. Marshall's opinion strengthened the notion that economic transactions were part of the private or voluntary realm and were protected from legislative intervention. Contracts were immune from tampering by state legislators. This decision did not expand the authority of the federal government as much as it restricted state sovereignty and limited forces which were undermining and threatening the Union.

Marshall believed in capitalism and its importance to America's future. His decisions, for example, severely limited state interference with the right to acquire private property. Georgia's legislature corruptly benefited from the sale of land, was thrown out in the next election, and its legal authority was revoked by an enactment of the newly elected legislature. Some investors had already sold their interests, claiming ignorance of the fraud. The Marshall court ruled that the rescinding act of the new legislature was in violation of the contract clause of the federal constitution, thus limiting the power of the legislature over the lives, property, and fortunes of individuals. Marshall upheld the principles of limited government and the unalienable rights to private property.

The corporate veil was upheld as well when the Court determined that a corporation charter was a private contract protected from interference by a state legislature and the trustees of Dartmouth College could not be sued individually. Early in his career, Marshall argued a similar case before Edmund Pendleton, who served in many respects as his mentor and taught him the importance of the Court speaking with one voice through its chief justice. Marshall argued and Pendleton upheld his view that a college's charter gave it broad authority and a professor is not entitled to an order restoring him to his position.[6]

Dartmouth College was chartered as a private educational institution and its self-perpetuating board of directors was dominated by the Federalists. The Jeffersonian-Republicans enacted legislation to establish a board of overseers to be appointed by the governor and to change the school from a college to a university. Daniel Webster, a Dartmouth alumnus, secured his reputation as one of the great orators by his argument in the case. Marshall ruled the Dartmouth charter to be a contract beyond control of the legislature. By granting the corporation many of the same protections as an individual, Marshall made it an important vehicle for private investment. By upholding the corporate veil, he enabled corporations to attract investors and directors that might participate in risk-taking ventures.

Before the Dartmouth College case, corporations were generally restricted to religious, educational, or political purposes. Shortly thereafter, many different types of corporations were established, particularly for turnpikes and transportation projects. Soon the corporate structure encompassed insurance companies, manufacturing concerns, canals, and ferries. Many more corporate charters were granted in America than in Europe. The pressure to create corporations became so great that general incorporation laws were enacted. Without a specific act of the legislature required, the powers of government to review corporations were diminished and incorporation was no longer granted only to friends of the powerful. New York State provided the privilege of incorporation first to religious associations, then to manufacturers, and later to banks and other entrepreneurial activities.

First enacted in New York, the limited liability corporation, which protected stockholders from liability, had a major impact; it enabled investors to decide how much they could invest, limiting their losses. This in turn freed up enormous amounts of capital from safe investments to those more risky, such as railroads and telegraph companies. The increased availability of capital led to the rapid expansion of stock exchanges. The New York Stock Exchange was formed in 1817, twenty-five years after the first exchanges in Philadelphia and New York City. By the end of the century, New York would overtake London as the world's leading financial center (British law did not provide limited liability until 1854).

The principles established by Marshall's legal approach had a positive and far-reaching effect on America's colonial economy. Increasingly, the courts became involved in adjudicating between the public sphere and private rights, removing these decisions from politics and the state legislatures. By focusing power at the federal level,

Marshall forestalled and largely pre-empted conflicting, duplicative, and confusing state statutes. He prevented the private sector from becoming subject to the whim and caprice of political winds blowing in the Congress or the executive branch of government. This gave a stability to the American legislative and regulatory regime that proved a huge boost to the capitalist economy and helped to establish the entire country as a common market. Political and legislative uncertainty undermines risk-taking and the creation of wealth. In fact, Marshall's principles and decisions may have provided too much stability, with the Supreme Court overturning many of the reform efforts of the next hundred years.

At John Marshall's funeral, the Liberty Bell cracked as it tolled, a fitting tribute to the man who, more than any other person, defined America: Marshall established the principles of judicial review, played a key role in developing constitutional law, asserted federal supremacy over the states, and imbedded capitalism and market principles into jurisprudence. Oliver Wendell Holmes proclaimed that "if American law were to be represented by a single figure, skeptic and worshipper alike would agree that the figure could be one alone, and that one, John Marshall."

> His tenure spanned the terms of five presidents: Jefferson, Madison, Monroe, John Quincy Adams, and Andrew Jackson. Under his leadership, the Supreme Court became a dominant force in American life. The broad powers of the federal government, the authoritative role of the Court, and a legal environment conducive to the growth of the American economy stem from decisions that flowed from Marshall's pen.
>
> More important, the Marshall Court established the ground rules of American government. The Constitution reflected the will of the people, not the states, said Marshall, and the people made it supreme.[7]

The Role of Technology and Individualism

The initiatives of the founding fathers laid the groundwork for technological and industrial growth, overhauling ancient methods of agricultural and goods production. For thousands of years, people moved no faster than by horse and farmed using the same basic power: muscle, wind, or water. As far as most people were concerned, these were the given parameters and basic facts of life that would never change. Yet, in the early nineteenth century, America was in the process of transforming everything—socially, culturally, and politically. Soon, everything would change economically and technologically, as well.

> In application the thousands of inventions, major and minor, made between 1790 and 1850, utterly transformed methods that had been employed almost unchanged for hundreds of years in manufacturing, transportation, mining, communications, and agriculture. Considered in its largest terms, the revolution meant releasing the production and transport of goods from the limitations of human hands and strength, supplemented by animal, wind, and water power. No longer was the amount of goods produced to be determined by the number of human beings employed in the process. Henceforward production could be expanded indefinitely by the substitution of mechanical fingers for human fingers and mechanical power for human power. For the first time in the history of the human race the possibility of an abundant production, freed from the leash of mere human energy, loomed on the horizon of people's capable of developing the Industrial Revolution toward the goal set by the potentials of technology.[8]

Besides Marshall's groundbreaking legal framework, the founding fathers provided the philosophical underpinnings for a revolutionary culture of individualism rooted in the forces unleashed by the invention of the printing press. This individualism played a crucial role in transforming the United States. Democracy meant freedom for the individual, who became powerful in America—individual power, culminating in universal suffrage, widespread innovation, and entrepreneurialism. As we now know, individual freedom correlates closely with economic growth. "Americans were well-positioned for economy-building by virtue of their sense of self-worth and their ability to pursue their dreams relatively free of unwanted masters. The 'rugged individualists' among them didn't stop at clearing land and farming, but went on to form joint-stock companies to build railroads and factories and to exploit the inventions of creative minds."[9]

Continuous and sustained economic growth became possible through technological advances, perhaps the most revolutionary transformation in this period of change. Previously, there had been no real concept or understanding that technology could be used for sustained progress and economic growth. With America's limited number of people, the need for inventions, ingenuity, and innovation to exploit its vast resources was a powerful spur to the use of science for practical purposes. John Marshall in particular understood that innovation or putting ideas into action had far more potential to create wealth than the simple possession of gold or land. Instead of dominance being determined by the ability to wage war, it was increasingly determined by technology and economic vitality. Through technology, man gained increasing control over his environment. In the two-hundred years after 1800, the world population increased seven times over what it had been previously—through much lower infant mortality rates, vaccinations that wiped out disease, and advances that greatly lengthened life expectancy. New inventions greatly improved agricultural productivity. Transportation advances drastically lowered costs, expanded agricultural production, and enabled settling in the American interior. Employment in the manufacturing sector exploded. In 1824, two million people worked in American manufacturing, ten times the number just five years earlier.[10]

Adam Smith's *The Wealth of Nations* was published in 1776, the year the steam engine was introduced and the year of America's Declaration of Independence, in what may be called the first year of capitalism. Smith never used the term *laissez-faire*, was not considered an individualist, embraced strong government, and believed society transforms people into moral beings.[11] His *Wealth of Nations* advocated free trade with other nations and unfettered commerce at home. In international trade, the U.S. had inherent advantages including its natural wealth, high-tech shipbuilding, and the lack of any monopolies to dismantle. Alexander Hamilton in effect put the American dollar on the gold standard, which helped thwart inflation and encouraged long-term growth. During Washington's and Hamilton's tenure, trade commenced with China. New England goods, such as furs, went to Oregon and China, and tea, silks, porcelain, and other luxury goods came back to New England.

Adam Smith also used the metaphor of the machine. He saw society as a vast machine with an invisible hand guiding it. The wealth of a nation was not tied to gold or silver, but to people with their labor, services, skills, and goods. He introduced the principle of the division of labor, a key concept of the industrial era that led to huge increases in productivity. This was due to three factors: "first to the increase of dexterity in every particular workman; second, to the saving of the time which is commonly lost in passing from one type of work to another; and lastly, to the invention of a great number of machines which facilitate and abridge labor, and enable one man to do the work of many."[12]

The division of labor and invention of new machines led to the factory system. This process of industrialization generated surpluses, which encouraged exchanges and trade. Adam Smith recognized the rapid economic growth in North America as compared to the tepid growth in Europe and to stagnation in China. While Smith accurately outlined the changes leading to the industrial revolution, he failed to predict the huge increase in wealth and wages and the stunning transformation of culture and society under the dynamic, fast-changing model in America.

The industrial revolution changed the basic economic structure of England; in America, however, it created an entirely new economy. Economic growth never averaged more than 3 percent annually in England, but it averaged 5 percent in America. In a few decades, production methods in agriculture, manufacturing, and transportation changed more than in the previous two thousand years. Small farms were gradually replaced by large tracts of land professionally managed with machinery and with chemicals to greatly improve yield. Raw materials were discovered and mined to produce new industrial goods. Better communication and transportation transformed agriculture and made possible big corporations and governments. These changes furthered democracy by developing a large middle class and fostering upward mobility. Overall, the standard of living and quality of life significantly improved, despite cyclical declines and pockets of poverty.

The American System

Individual inventions made major contributions to progress in the industrial revolution, but the American system of manufacturing and production was even more critical. Absent local and regional preferences, standardization occurred and the scarcity of labor drove further mechanization of production. The process of building houses, for example, changed from carpentry to millwork, enabling the structure to be quickly put together. Doors and windows were manufactured in volume and assembled in standard sizes. A French ship carrying windows that were not standard had to give away much of its cargo. The balloon-framed house eliminated the need for heavy beams, special joints, and masonry walls. Instead, precut 2 by 4s were nailed together for the frame, drastically reducing costs and using an abundant local material. Power machines such as lathes, saws, and planers were developed that made the process even faster and more efficient. The balloon-frame system facilitated the expansion of villages into cities. This system was applied to many other areas—textiles, gun manufacture, meat slaughtering, flour milling, and petroleum refining. Shops that built machinery for textile plants created machines for other industries. Engines and machine tools created for special purposes had applications for many industries. In this New World, there was little resistance to these innovations and less commitment to old ways.

After developing the cotton gin, Eli Whitney turned his energies to creating a system of interchangeable parts that helped to revolutionize manufacturing, particularly in the North and eventually making that region economically dominant. He played an important role in thrusting America into the forefront of the industrial revolution. While the South had a close relationship with Britain by virtue of its cotton trade, the North was an industrial power rivaled only by Britain itself. Whitney developed muskets with parts so uniform they were "interchangeable." His exhibit of this technology is celebrated as the beginning of the American system of manufacturing. History has revealed, unfortunately, that the demonstration was rigged and the parts, while uniform, were not interchangeable. Nevertheless, Whitney's idea became part of the evolution in manufacturing towards precision and interchangeability. His vision became the standard for the development of manufacturing over the next decades.

LAND

Abundant land facilitated the concept of private property and ownership. The greatest source of wealth and money was government land sales. Federal offices were set up, pricing land at $2 an acre. The minimum purchase started at 640 acres, subsequently reduced to 320. Only 25 percent had to be paid upfront, the rest over four years. Even this figure was halved, so that a large farm could be purchased for $160 cash. Millions of acres were sold and success stories abounded. There were half a million farms in 1800; by 1850 this number had grown to one and a half million. In a few decades, the entire Mississippi Valley was settled, an area of well over a million square miles, the size of Western Europe. The fertility of the soil yielded surpluses, creating need for a marketplace to dispose of them. The large supply of land led to a complete changeover in agriculture encompassing cotton and textiles, timber and housing, ice, and food. This revolution was facilitated by new farm machinery and assisted by the Smithsonian Institution and university research, which provided weather forecasts, high quality maps, and experimental farming methods.

TEXTILES

Phenomenal advances in the textile industry were the major driver of this agrarian-industrial revolution. Decades of trial and error in England in the early and middle eighteenth century developed new technology that replicated the methods and gestures of hand spinners and mechanized weaving, resulting in the development of a spinning jenny or wheel, weaving eighty threads at a time. The mechanization of spinning cotton and wool into yarn came initially, reducing costs and increasing demand. Development of Richard Arkwright's cotton spinning-machine, John Kay's flying shuttle, and James Hargreaves' spinning jenny streamlined the processing of cotton into yarn. Samuel Crompton combined aspects of these machines to develop the mule which could be made into massive machines, sometimes with more than a thousand spindles.[13] Whereas in 1765 half a million pounds of cotton were spun in England, all by hand, by 1784 there were 12 million pounds produced, all spun by machines. Hand spinners, many of whom worked at home, lost their jobs, but some shifted their production to weaving. The increased production of yarn led to greater demand for weavers.

At the same time, advances in steam-driven technology evolved gradually over a period of decades with the assistance of numerous scientists and inventors. James Watt built his first complete steam engine in 1765, introduced it commercially in 1776, and spent twenty-five years perfecting it. In 1785, Edmund Cartwright developed a power loom driven by Watt's steam engine, basically ending the role of hand weavers. This brought ruin to a large number of practitioners of this craft and they tried to destroy the new machine. The steam engine initially used wood for fuel, but the invention of a safety lamp for coal miners vastly expanded the sources of coal. Precision gauging, fixed settings, the substitution of rotary for reciprocating motion, and the invention of machines that built factory machines such as mills and jennys, all improved the production process. The steam engine, new sources of capital, and the development of factories made possible the mass production of clothing and other textiles. Developments in chemistry furthered this revolution, particularly research on the use of dyes and chlorine to bleach cloth. Textile factories employed thousands of women and children in slave-like conditions, who worked from before dawn to after dusk with little food, many becoming crippled for life.[14] Wages gradually declined and the working environment deteriorated until living conditions were worse than anything previously known in England.

When Eli Whitney invented the cotton gin, he helped to transform the South into one of the wealthiest economies in the world. Whitney was introduced to the southern cotton farmer by the widow of revolutionary war hero Nathanael Greene. Farming and slavery were at the time on a deep decline. Cotton grew fast, but could not be harvested without a great deal of labor. Whitney's cotton gin provided a fairly simple mechanism for solving this problem. Instead of separating the cotton seeds from the fibers, his device separated the fibers from the seed. He made relatively little profit for his invention, because as a Yankee transplant in the South, he could not successfully enforce the patent and his device could be easily duplicated. Whitney inflexibly demanded a portion of each farmer's crop in return for supplying the cotton gin, a model the southerners rejected, which gave them an excuse to use pirate gins. He was also handicapped by his manufacturing facility in New Haven, which had to be closed due to scarlet and yellow fever epidemics, lost twenty machines in a fire, and couldn't produce enough to meet demand. Whitney sent a letter to Robert Fulton noting "I had great difficulty to prove that the machine had been used in Georgia and at the same moment there were three separate sets of this machinery in motion within fifty yards of the building in which the court sat and all so near that the rattling was distinctly heard on the steps of the courthouse." When Whitney attempted to seek redress from the South Carolina legislature, the planters tried to arrest him to put him in prison. Eventually, South Carolina and other states provided him over $100,000 for his efforts, but these sums barely covered his legal and developmental expenses.

Before the cotton gin, a slave took one day to pull one pound of cotton lint. Whitney's cotton gin separated out 50 pounds in a day. In an era measuring productivity improvements in small increments, a fifty times increase was revolutionary. The South proved to be the best place in the world to grow cotton at that time. Exports tripled the first year of Whitney's invention and increased by well over a hundredfold in 25 years. By 1850 exports increased 15,000 times to 2 billion pounds. Between 1790 and 1860, Georgia's per capita production rose by 50 times, including 10 times in only a decade. By 1830 America was producing over half the world's cotton and output continued to double each decade, its share of the world market reaching 70 percent by 1850.[15] Between the American Revolution and the War of 1812, the price of cotton yarn fell 90 percent and continued to plunge until the Civil War when it was only 1 percent of what it had been in the Revolution, one of the most rapid declines in history.[16]

Growing and harvesting cotton continued to be labor intensive, requiring an increasing number of slaves. Picking cotton became the bottleneck in the revolutionary changes transforming the textile industry. While fewer than 5 percent of white southerners owned slaves and well under 1 percent owned more than 100 slaves, cotton and similar commodities were a large portion of the southern economy. Andrew Jackson's effort to relocate Indian tribes opened up vast amounts of land for use in producing cotton in Mississippi, Alabama, and Louisiana. Slaves became increasingly valuable assets, making it harder to convince southerners to abolish slavery. It took 10 to 20 slaves to farm 100 acres of cotton and the price rose from $300 per slave to $1,000 and even to $2,000. Some older tobacco plantations made most of their money from slave-breeding. The founding fathers, most of whom opposed slavery, believed it would slowly die out or be abolished, but the cotton gin and the spread of cotton farming ended such hopes. Cotton created enormous wealth—Natchez, Mississippi, had the highest number of millionaires per capita in the world and they built numerous fancy mansions. Cotton producing states were the first to secede from the Union.

British textile manufacturing was initially the most advanced, and for its mills Britain became enormously dependent on cotton from the South. Yankee ingenuity found a way of overcoming the British advantage in manufacturing. The United States stole the technology, which was extremely difficult to do, because the British barred anyone working in a textile manufacturing facility from leaving the country. In America, Francis Cabot Lowell used his photographic memory to steal the schematics for spinning machines and power looms; he built them from scratch in Massachusetts. Samuel Slater worked in an English mill, surreptitiously came to America and used his memory to start a cotton yarn factory. Along the Merrimack River huge factories were built to mill the cotton into clothes. Lowell wisely rejected many of the inhumane conditions he had found in British cities. In his factories, young women were forced to work fourteen hours a day in clean but highly regimented conditions. Church was mandatory and many of the women workers became teachers and social reformers. Lowell built his highly complex, capital-intensive factory for a cotton-clothes market that barely existed. He built the first fully integrated plant beginning with cotton and turning it into finished cloth with dye. This effort was modeled on Oliver Evans' integrated flour mill, which converted grain directly into flour in one process. Lowell secured protection from Congress, in the form of tariffs over 80 percent, to thwart competition from British mills. Demand for the cloth exploded and soon a steam locomotive railroad line was needed to bring the cotton from the Boston harbor and transport the finished cotton cloth back. The mills brought enormous wealth to New England, particularly to the Boston area.

The machinery was increasingly mechanized and sophisticated, making textiles America's most advanced industry. America went from using the pre-industrial jenny around 1790 to having 100,000 powered cotton spindles by 1810. This figure more than tripled in each of the next two decades so that there were 1.2 million spindles and 33,500 looms by 1831. In only a couple of decades, America leapfrogged the British. American workers had better conditions, were better motivated, and were sustained by the concept that they were living the American dream. These advances created a huge demand for cotton, diminishing the roles for wool and linen. In a century, the percentage of clothes made from cotton went from just 4 percent to approximately 75 percent.[17]

SHOES

Advances in manufacturing made Boston the largest boot and shoe market in the world. Until the 1850s, most of the production was done by manual labor. In 1858, a machine was invented to sew the soles of the shoes to the upper part; thus speeding up the process a hundred-fold and making mass production possible. The industry boomed.

WOOD

Harvesting wood became another major industry. Clearing was a precondition for agriculture, yielding much of the productive farmland in the Midwest. Without concern for the natural environment, entire states were deforested, the wood used for fuel, to build houses and commercial structures, and for shipbuilding. Wood provided not only home and factory heat, but was the major fuel in steamboats and railroads. Wood was a crucial link between the agricultural and industrial ages. The wood or timber industry powered the industrial revolution and its harvest provided fields for corn, wheat, and a plethora of other agricultural products. Corn production provided feed for cattle and led to the rapid development of the meat-packing industry.[18]

The plentiful wood supply led to the development of the furniture industry. A single plant in Cincinnati produced 125,000 chairs a year. Another facility produced thousands of bedsteads a week. Workers were in great demand to plane, paint, and varnish the manufactured products.

ICE

New England was ridiculed for having no cash crop, only ice and rocks. Yet, the region's resourcefulness was incredible and an ice industry was developed. Very little ice was consumed until early in the nineteenth century when in a few years consumption increased more than in the millennium before. Between 1820 and the Civil War, consumption of ice in New Orleans, for example, went up seventy fold.

Frederic Tudor is perhaps the best known ice entrepreneur. Referred to as the "Ice King," he started in the business at age thirteen, built it up by personal flamboyance and vicious competition, and sought a monopoly. In the early 1800s, he was derided for his idea of shipping ice to the Caribbean. He tried to educate the public on the uses for ice and encouraged people to like cold drinks by charging the same for chilled and unchilled drinks. Tudor would sell his ice at a penny per pound until his competitors' stock melted, then raised prices to make his profit. His breakthrough came when he designed an economical and efficient ice house, reducing melting loss from 60 to 8 percent. He also co-developed a special bit to mass produce uniform blocks from natural ice and established a monopoly over the use of such devices. Both Tudor and his co-inventor, Nathaniel Wyeth, passed up Harvard to go into business, much like the later-day Bill Gates. Wyeth designed an ice scraper to clean surfaces for a more uniform product and discovered that sawdust could be used to prevent blocks from melting together, creating demand for what up until then had been a useless byproduct of New England lumber mills. Initial efforts to ship ice failed. When a shipload was sent to Martinique, there was no ice house for storage and the natives who had never used ice didn't know what to do with it.

> [Tudor's] adventuring energies were never confined. In his early years he had traded in pimento, nutmeg, flour, sugar, tea, candles, cotton, silk, and claret. Later he dug for coal on Martha's Vineyard; he invented a siphon for pumping water from the holds of vessels; he made a new design for the hull of a ship; . . . he operated a graphite mine; he made paper from white pine; and he experimented with the raising of cotton and tobacco at Nahant. He brought to New England the first steam locomotive, an engine of one-half horsepower which ran on the sidewalk at four miles an hour pulling a car for one passenger. He set up what was probably the first amusement park in America. And he even tried raising salt-water fish in Fresh Pond.

Tudor's miscellaneous speculations from time to time plunged him deeply into debt, even after he had put the ice trade on a profitable basis. For example, his speculations in coffee involved him to the extent of $200,000 before the end of 1834, but this drove him to redouble his efforts in the ice trade, out of which he managed to repay the coffee debt in the next fifteen years.

Tudor had now decided to ship his ice halfway around the world—to the East Indies. In May, 1833, in the most spectacular experiment of his career, Tudor sent his ship *Tuscany* with 180 tons of ice to Calcutta. To reach India from Boston, the *Tuscany* had to cross the equator twice, preserving its cargo unmelted for four months. Tudor reminded his captain the ice had never been carried so far south; this was a "discovery ship." The *Tuscany* reached its destination, bringing the combined delights of a new toy and a new candy. The first shipment sold profitably, Tudor's reputation soared, and before long the ice trade flourished between Boston and the Far East. Using experience gained in the Caribbean, Tudor built a large Calcutta ice depot and encouraged Anglo-Indians to buy household refrigerators and water coolers; he tried to change their eating habits by his well-preserved shipments of apples, butter and cheese.

Soon ice was being shipped from Boston to all parts. By 1846, sixty-five thousand tons were shipped; only ten years later more than twice that amount went in nearly four hundred different shipments to over fifty different destinations in the United States, the Caribbean, South America, the East Indies, China, the Philippines and Australia. Ice had become a major commodity, a New England staple for the world market.[19]

FOOD PROCESSING

In addition to developing a world market for ice, the process for canning foods was established. A German immigrant, H.J. Heinz, started in the canning business. A manufacturing process was developed for tin cans. In the decade of the 1860s, the processing of containers of canned food rose from five to thirty million annually. Refrigeration and canning meant people could enjoy good food year-round. Ice and canning improved the delivery of food, expanded the time for work, and increased mobility significantly. Gail Borden experimented for ten years to develop condensed and evaporated milk which helped provisioning in the Civil War and made his name a synonym for milk. In 1837, candle-maker William Proctor joined with soap manufacturer James Gamble to form Proctor & Gamble to make and market household goods, mostly from industrial wastes such as hides, bones, and bristles.

FARM IMPLEMENTS

New mechanical inventions and processes changed the methods of production and improved productivity. In 1797, Charles Newbold patented the first cast-iron plow which was a single, solid unit. James Wood designed a plow using cast iron with interchangeable parts to facilitate repairs, but it worked poorly in the Middle West where soil would not turn over but instead fell back into place once the plow passed. John Deere designed a plow using a circular steel blade to solve this problem. A diligent farmer who worked the seed in by hand could not plant more than ten acres per season. Moses and Samuel Pennock invented a drill to sow in furrows a controlled volume of seed from a tube. George Brown developed a double-row seed drill pulled by a horse.[20] By the 1830s, tens of thousands of these plows and other farm implements were being manufactured annually.

Farmers cannot grow more than they can reap and thresh, and thus the harvest became a bottleneck. Cyrus McCormick's reaper, invented in 1833, eventually opened up vast acreages of land to agriculture. McCormick's background paralleled Eli Whitney's. Their fathers were mechanics and both were tinkerers. Harvesting had been the limiting factor in wheat production—there was a limited time after wheat ripened when it could be taken in. A man could only cut about an acre of wheat per day by wielding a scythe, the implement used to harvest food for thousands of years. In 1832, McCormick broke the harvesting process into components and invented the first mechanical reaper, which included the six key features for all future reapers. He worked hard to perfect this machine, not selling them for years even though they enabled a man to harvest 8 acres in a day. When the British harvest failed in 1845, forcing repeal of British laws that protected farmers from international competition, McCormick built a plant in Chicago to mass-produce harvesters, selling 5,000 in 5 years. In 1839 only 8 bushels of wheat were shipped out of Chicago, 10 years later 2 million shipped. Automated threshing machines were developed to complete the last link in the harvesting process. In contrast to the textile industry where cotton-picking remained a bottleneck and caused the rapid expansion of slavery, wheat production was almost fully mechanized. By the late 1840s, giant combines could harvest as much as 25 acres a day.

ARMAMENTS

E.I. du Pont began manufacturing gunpowder and other explosives, placing a premium on invention but barely surviving his early years when the du Pont mill blew up several times. Sam Colt designed and built a repeating pistol that eliminated the need to reload and radically altered the war against the Indians. His invention was not widely accepted at first and his initial factory was forced to shut down. The Colt pistol was so effective in battle, however, that eventually there was a huge demand; he became one of the wealthiest men in America. His adoption of the principle of interchangeability in a steam powered factory enabled him to take advantage of volume production. While Colt guns still had to be hand-fitted, they cost about a third as much as the competition. These new manufacturing processes and efforts at forging, boring, and uniformly cutting metal placed the English in the embarrassing position of being surpassed by the American system.

THE MIRACLE OF MACHINES

The increased reliance on manufacturing changed the dynamics of the marketplace, enabling unprecedented expansion, because there was no real limit on how much could be produced by machines. They could be located almost anywhere and there were no human limitations on the length of operation or strength of the machine. Manufacturing, however, was susceptible to panic followed by industrial collapse. A farmer would always have the means to produce something even in desperate times, but an unemployed factory worker could become virtually destitute. Severe downturns occurred in 1819, 1829, 1837, 1847, and 1857, but the economy still averaged 5 percent growth annually.

TRANSPORTATION

The transportation revolution was instrumental to the development of agriculture—bringing settlers to America and to the frontier and taking products to market. Continuing improvements in transportation facilitated the division of labor and manufacturing, taking production from the home and moving it to factories. During the eighteenth century, overland transportation in the colonies was formidable, if not impossible. The great transportation revolution involved improvements in sail power, roads, turnpikes, canals, railroads, and steamboats. Where modes and links intersected, new towns grew up—Cincinnati, St. Louis, Chicago, Atlanta, New York, Philadelphia, Boston, and Baltimore. The time of travel for people was cut from weeks to days and from days to hours, while the cost of carrying freight was reduced from dollars to cents per ton-mile.

Faster sailboats and reductions in the costs of ocean transportation opened up immigration, increasing America's population and supply of labor, but also lowering American wages which were high by European standards. Prior to 1810, the voyage took 30 days. About 5 to 10 percent of the ships' passengers died during the crossing with another 5 to 10 percent dying of disease or conditions contracted during the voyage. The cost was equivalent to a year's wage. By 1860, the time of the journey was reduced by a fourth, mortality declined by 90 percent, and the cost went down by 90 percent as well. American ship-pers were particularly aggressive on the high seas, taking frequent risks and more often shipwrecking, but also making better time and sailing at much less expense. Instead of ships randomly determining the time of their crossing, regularly scheduled passenger sailings were imple-mented, greatly improving service. The British paid subsidies to American shipbuilders, who produced a third of British vessels engaged in Atlantic trade.

The United States dominated the whaling industry, outfitting over 700 of the 900 whaling ships in the world. Whaling became the fifth largest industry in the country. Capital investment was in the tens of millions of dollars and employment totaled in the tens of thou-sands of people. In a good year, the industry would catch thousands of whales and produce hundreds of thousands of barrels of oil used mostly in lighting.[21] New Bedford, Massachusetts, became the center for half of the whaling industry and one of the wealthiest cities in America. Whaling put the United States at the forefront of global exploration and efforts to open world markets. During the middle of the century, however, the industry declined rapidly from over-fishing, naval conflict during the Civil War, and competition from natural gas, kerosene, and oil.

The building of a road system was crucial to development of the country and agriculture. The first national road was opened from Cumberland, Maryland, to Wheeling, West Virginia, where settlers could then travel down the Ohio River. Many other roads followed, as money was set aside from the sale of land and other proceeds. Both the quality of construction and methods of financing gradually improved. The quality and strength of wagons also progressed and some men made their living by driving horse-drawn wagons. Turnpikes were built to bring farm products to market. Philadelphia had a turnpike built to Lancaster to siphon off as much trade as possible from the Susquehanna River and the Chesapeake Bay water routes that benefited Baltimore. The road was built to a uniform width with layers of crushed stone and gravel and a rounded surface to allow water to drain off quickly. Good roads significantly improved travel times in the North, but the southern road system remained primitive, holding back the region's economic development. Henry Clay proposed the "American system" whereby state and federal governments would build roads, canals, and harbors to aid industrialization. He had a difficult time securing passage of his ideas, because, as a result of his controversial election, John Quincy Adams was an ineffective president and Andrew Jackson was committed to paying off the national debt and vetoed spending bills.

Technology for canal building had progressed slowly in Europe, even though the lock had been developed in the fifteenth century. In America, several dozen canal companies were chartered in a number of states, but few canals were actually built due to the high capital costs and lack of engineering expertise. The Erie Canal, however, "succeeded far beyond anyone's dreams" and was "the most consequential public works project in American history."[22] The cost of the canal was prohibitive—three-quarters of the entire federal budget at the time or a third of all the banking and insurance capital in the state. New York Governor Dewitt Clinton was the force behind the canal, but its building was considered impractical, being labeled "Clinton's ditch." The canal required the removal of three times more dirt than the Great Pyramid, mostly by hand. When pressed for federal funds, Thomas Jefferson wrote Governor Clinton, noting that George Washington couldn't obtain $200,000 for a thirty-mile canal "and you talk of making a canal *three hundred and fifty miles through the wilderness! It is a splendid project, and may be executed a century hence. It is little short of madness to think of it at this day.*" President James Madison vetoed a bill that would have provided funding.

The Erie Canal was built, owned, and operated by the State of New York. As many as 50,000 workers were employed to dig the canal. Building it required 8 years, but in its first year the Erie Canal carried 221,000 barrels of flour, 435,000 gallons of whiskey, 562,000 bushels of wheat, and 335,000 tons of freight. In less than a decade the debt was paid off and feeder canals were being built. It ensured New York's status as "The Empire State" and the largest state economically for decades and made New York City the most important commercial city in the world.[23] Before the canal, shipping a ton of flour cost four times what it took to produce. Once the canal was completed the cost of shipping declined by 95 percent and was completed in a third the time. Other commodities benefited similarly.[24]

At the end of the War of 1812 there were less than a hundred miles of canals. Twenty-five years later, there were 3,000 miles of canals, although none were as successful as the Erie Canal, which linked the Atlantic Ocean with the Great Lakes. During the 1837 crash, canals in six states repudiated their debts, sparking protests from European investors. As a result, infrastructure investment was gradually turned over to the public sector. The completion of the Erie Canal, however, had opened up the Midwest and created enormous demand for transportation.

The development of the railroad followed canals and was far more productive. Railroads developed by piecing together a series of improvements: numerous inventions were needed, including many changes in locomotives, the "T" rail, the spike, link and pin couplings, timetables, roadbeds of crushed stone, and the Standard Gauge or uniform width. Even today, rail is the most economical method of moving freight over land; rail can go many places that canals and steamboats cannot, and it can move freight during all seasons. The Erie Canal spurred the development of the Baltimore & Ohio railroad as another route to the west. Charles Carroll, the last living signer of the Declaration of Independence turned the first shovel for the railroad, an act he thought might be even more important than the signing. Railroad opponents proclaimed long-term biological dangers to persons going twenty to thirty miles an hour and that noisy engines would sicken cattle and poison milk and meat. Others argued that communities would be inundated with unwanted commodities.

Nineteenth-century technology for building rail systems was more advanced in Europe, but more mileage and railroads were built in the United States than in all of Europe. By 1840, 3,000 miles had been constructed. In the interior of the country, agriculture became increasingly based on rail and canal transport. The railroad penetrated to areas with large amounts of manufacturing and agricultural exports. By the Civil War, the United States was outbuilding Europe by a considerable margin—9,000 miles were built by 1850 and 31,000 by 1860, two-thirds in the North. American rail lines cost a quarter of the European continental lines and one-seventh of those built in Britain due to cheaper land, more effective capital markets, and better technology. The Europeans frequently over-built and over-designed their locomotives, track, bridges, and other structures, while economic considerations drove the American market.

While the rail and locomotives were originally imported from Britain, the United States gradually developed its own capabilities, mostly from textile manufacturing systems. Locomotives were built in machine shops near the textile complex at Lowell, Massachusetts, and were developed out of machines used for textiles and printing in Philadelphia. Improvements were made to the European technology, such as using four engine wheels in front instead of two to enable greater traction. Rail manufacturing in Pennsylvania used blast furnaces and an abundant local source of anthracite coal. In 1832, Matthias Baldwin began to manufacture locomotives, producing over 1500 including some for export. Between 1837 and 1855, the manufacture of locomotives increased ten fold.[25]

Journeys that formerly took weeks were reduced to mere days by rail. In 1800 it took six weeks to reach St. Louis from New York, but by 1860 it took just three days by rail. Telegraph lines laid along the tracks became the basis for dispatching trains. The railroad built the world market by interconnecting thousands of local markets for passenger traffic, commodity shipments, and communications by telegraph.

The steam engine and its offspring, the steamboat, made major contributions to transportation. The steam engine was a product of close coordination between industry and science. Several philosophers and scientists suggested the basic principle for the steam engine. Several inventors contributed important innovations in its evolution. Thomas Newcomen, an iron worker and blacksmith, experimented with primitive steam engines. James Watt actually got the idea for his particular steam engine while repairing a model of Newcomen's engine, which had been invented 57 years earlier in 1712, and of which over a hundred had been manufactured in England by the time of

Watt's repair work. Newcomen's engine, in turn, followed the steam engine that the Englishman Thomas Savery patented in 1698, which followed the steam engine that the Frenchman Denis Paper designed (but did not build) about 1680, which in turn had precursors in the ideas of the Dutch scientist Christian Huygens and others.[26] Watt's steam engine was unveiled in 1776 and was four times more fuel efficient than previous versions, increasing its possible uses and applications. Watt then developed a rotary engine that converted the reciprocal up-and-down motion into a rotary motion, further expanding economical uses. The steam engine was a radical invention because previous power sources were severely limited—water power to where water was present, and men and animals to the extent of their physical endurance. The steam engine could go almost anywhere and be used for extended periods of time.

Patent protection for the steam engine thwarted the development of the steamboat in Britain, but had no such effect in America. The steamboat became the wedge for the industrial revolution in the Midwest. Steamboat tonnage rose from 1,000 in 1810 to 17,000 in 1820, to 64,000 in 1830, and 202,000 in 1840.[27] John Fitch, an entrepreneur, developed the first steamboat and William Symington advanced the technical design. Robert Fulton, however, built a better boat using an engine from James Watt's firm, incorporating parts of Fitch's and Symington's design. He had more capital and money as a result of a relationship with the powerful Robert Livingston. He initiated regular steamboat service up and down the Hudson River with a monopoly secured by Livingston. Fulton was granted a similar monopoly on the lower Mississippi by the state of Louisiana. He gradually built a steamboat empire, having developed the only feasible way to consistently move cargo and people upstream against powerful river currents. The British were sufficiently worried about his entrepreneurial ingenuities that they tried to kill or capture him during the War of 1812.

Other inventors contributed to development of this steam power. Oliver Evans built the first high-pressure steam engine for factories, significantly increasing the power of the steam engine. Evans even designed and developed an amphibious vehicle for his engine and was responsible for other important inventions such as an automated production technique for milling, as well as a machine gun and a gas lighting system. Henry Shreve used Evans' invention to build the first steamboat with a high pressure engine that cost half as much to build, took up less space, and weighed a fraction of a low-pressure condensing engine. Unfortunately for Shreve, the boilers exploded on his first trip, killing fourteen people. Shreve took on the Fulton steamboat monopoly on the Mississippi. Travel time upriver was halved and then halved again and profits increased by double digits. Shreve also invented the snag boat that removed the thousands of stumps and obstacles under the water that were responsible for the majority of all steamboat accidents. His boat had giant claws, cranes, a pulley and windlass system, and a battering ram. Trunks as large as six feet wide were hauled up and fed into a sawmill on deck. Shreve cleared the river in six years, reducing passage by days and saving many lives. Shreve also cleared the Red River which was so "snagged" that hunters and settlers crossed it unaware of the stream underneath. Congress cut off the funding for his work, forcing him to obtain a private bank loan to complete it.[28]

Thomas Gibbons, who hired Cornelius Vanderbilt as a captain, challenged the New York monopoly by openly sailing his boat in and out of the city's harbor, knowing that seizure would be reciprocated by the State of New Jersey which strongly opposed the monopoly. New York authorities even tried to board and arrest Vanderbilt, but he hid out in a secret compartment while a sweet, innocent female passenger was placed at the wheel and passengers denounced the police. The Supreme Court read the Commerce Clause as giving Congress comprehensive powers to regulate interstate commerce and concluded that a state legislature had no right to create a steamboat monopoly. With Chief Justice Marshall authoring the opinion, the Court ruled states could not regulate and provide for steamboat monopolies and that by having a coasting license provided by the federal government, Gibbons had the right to sail anywhere in the United States. Daniel Webster argued the case for Gibbons and claimed credit for the victory. The court ruling was widely praised, particularly in the press. This decision opened up competition with the number of ships in New York waters, which increased from 8 to 46 in nine months with fares therefore declining rapidly. The decision was called the emancipation proclamation of American commerce. It stopped the granting of other monopolies as well and eliminated other barriers to interstate commerce.[29] The decision thus helped to integrate the American people into a single nation or common market woven together through unfettered interstate commerce. A trip from New York to New Orleans that took four weeks by sailing vessel in 1800, took only five days by steamboat at the time of the Civil War. Politicians and tradesmen could congregate in national conventions and associations and truly national movements could be launched very quickly. By 1850, steamboats could travel across the Atlantic Ocean and subsequent development of steel hulls and better steam engines further improved maritime steam transport.

NEWSPAPERS

The steam engine revolutionized other delivery mechanisms. Rotary presses driven by steam engines could print more copies of a newspaper in an hour than could be printed by a hand press in a week. New machines reduced the costs for making and cutting paper. Newspapers nationalized their coverage and used their vastly expanded circulation to pay for the additional expense.

The newspaper became a major force in shaping American life. The number of newspapers grew from fewer than 100 in 1790 to over 230 in 1800. By 1810, Americans were buying more than 20 million copies of 376 newspapers annually, the largest circulation in the world. Between the 1820s and 1840s, the cost of a daily fell from a nickel to a penny. From 1800 to 1840, the number of newspapers mailed through the postal service increased by almost a hundredfold to almost 150 million per year. Rates were far cheaper than for other mail. If newspapers had paid the same rates, their mailing costs would have been 700 times higher.[30] The newspaper helped transform public opinion into the vital principle and guardian underlying American politics, government, and culture. "It became the resolving force not only of political truth but of all truth, from disputes among religious denominations to controversies over artistic taste. Nothing is more important in explaining and clarifying the democratization of American culture in the early 1800s than the new conception of public opinion. In the end it became America's nineteenth-century popular substitute for the elitist intellectual leadership of the revolutionary generation."[31]

MEDICAL TECHNOLOGY AND PUBLIC HEALTH

Major medical advances were occurring as well. More accurate diagnoses and descriptions of human physical disorders were developed. New surgical procedures and operations were attempted and some successfully performed on a routine basis. More precise knowledge of the composition of drugs and chemicals enabled the development of new cures. Crawford Long, William T.G. Morton, and physicians at the Massachusetts General Hospital developed anesthetics to lessen pain and permit new surgery. As these techniques were implemented, they had a huge impact on medicine. Medical education was expanded, standards improved, and participation opened up to women.

The major advance in public health was not medical, but public sanitation and community water supplies. Unbeknownst to the colonials, sewage and waste from outhouses and chamber pots emptying into the street were contaminating the water and leading to epidemics of cholera and yellow fever. Philadelphia, chronically plagued by yellow fever epidemics that decimated the population and forced the nation's early government to disband or flee to the countryside when its leadership met there, developed the first modern water supply and built domestic bathrooms. In the bathroom, sanitation improved with the upgrading of the bath, toilet, and water closet, as well as with the extensive use of porcelain. It was believed that disease could be prevented by flushing the streets daily (it would be decades before the connections were made between disease and bacteria, mosquitoes and viruses).

Benjamin Latrobe (who built the first section of the U.S. Capitol) developed the plan for the Philadelphia system based on the use of steam engines at the pumping stations. He met with much opposition, particularly from citizens who had heard about the explosions of these engines on western riverboats. It was much later in the nineteenth century before public water supply and sewage systems were widely provided by local municipalities. The biggest setback was the dearth of people who would pay for the water. Although people were initially reluctant to pay for water they could get for free, once installed, running water for the house became a major labor saving device with an almost limitless number of uses and a middle-class necessity. New ways to use water seemed almost endless and supply shortages became prevalent until meters were deployed. The development of cement pipes and large sewer systems moved disease-creating waste away from populated areas. The improvement in the quality of water and the removal of waste eliminated or drastically reduced whole categories of disease, vastly improved the quality of life, and helped to increase life expectancy.

AMERICA'S ENTREPRENEURIAL SPIRIT

In the early 1800s, U.S. technological advances were augmented by an explosion of the entrepreneurial spirit. An estimated 80 percent of Americans were self-employed. "There was more peddling and shop keeping than existed anywhere else in the world. In the 1820s Americans first used the term 'businessman' to express more concisely what so many of them were doing. Americans everywhere in the country were obsessed with commerce. 'It's a passion as unconquerable as any which nature has endowed us,' said young Henry Clay to the House of Representatives in 1812. 'You may attempt to regulate it—you cannot destroy it.'"[32] The transition from agricultural work where men were their own bosses to manufacturing where they worked for someone else was difficult.

The new technologies and entrepreneurialism opened up vast horizons. The population continued to explode, doubling in almost every generation. Approximately 70 percent of the population was under the age of twenty-five. Frontier states, in particular, experienced explosive growth, some of them becoming among the most populous in a single generation. Industrialization greatly increased the percentage of city dwellers. Between 1800 and 1900, New York City grew by sixty fold to become the world's second largest metropolis after London. Chicago, which didn't even exist as a city in 1800, ranked fifth in the world with a population of 1.7 million by 1900. The city built the largest railroad station on earth, too big by far said Eastern railroaders, but outgrew it in only a decade. Chicago became the world's greatest grain market, the chief marketplace for the vast herds of cattle that arrived by rail from the prairies, and the world's number-one lumber-market.

The industrialization of the cities threatened the social order (through increases in crime, disease, and moral decay) and popular democracy (by nurturing disorderly mobs). Life expectancy in the North declined by a quarter and even more than that in large cities; life expectancy in New York and Philadelphia at one point was six years less than that of Southern slaves. "The big cities of the 1840s and 1850s were not only incubators of crime and vice but also destroyers of the cultural vision of the founding fathers."[33]

America's entrepreneurial spirit was based on three principles. First, new experiences forced Americans to rethink old rules. The U.S. was innately more entrepreneurial than Europe, because European rules no longer applied when people migrated to America. When faced with the great forests of the East, the Appalachian Mountains, the Great Plains, and the Great American Desert, people were forced to rethink many of life's aspects. When settlers arrived in America with all of the highfalutin European rules and entered the great forest of the North American continent, knowing how to use an ax was more important than knowing how to read the classics. The wilderness taught Americans that learning what works is more important than knowing what somebody who studies things says.

Secondly, free markets are more productive than markets within bureaucratic systems and hierarchical structures, because bureaucracies try to force new experiences into old structures or rules, limiting the possibilities for change. By contrast, entrepreneurs demonstrate thirst for new knowledge and determine how to change to meet challenges. With the scope of nineteenth- century government so small, the power of the market was greater and people repeatedly did what worked. Even Alexander Hamilton strongly favored marketplace solutions over bureaucratic programs. When by prior agreement the entire federal government moved from Philadelphia to the new capital in Washington, D.C., the move went relatively quickly and smoothly, because only 130 officers and clerks had to be transported. A shortage of labor also impelled the early Americans to innovate and develop new inventions to obtain improvements to daily living and to the workplace.

Thirdly, technological innovation can precede scientific understanding. If something cannot be explained yet it works, then the response is to do it. American know-how is at its best when it is practical, when it is oriented toward achieving technical breakthroughs. European science was ahead of American science, but Americans excelled at the practical, at what worked, at using scientific knowledge to develop technology. American ingenuity built an American economy that overwhelmed the European economy by the twentieth century. Specifically, the American interest in knowledge and the practical resulted in a plethora of new inventions.

> Before the early nineteenth century; even among the notoriously peripatetic population of the United States, people seldom ventured more than fifty miles from where they had been born, or, if they did, never saw their birthplace again. Now, in less than a lifetime, it had become possible to travel a hundred miles in a day, receive instant word from someone a thousand miles away, and read of events that were taking place, right then, halfway around the world. It was possible to have hot water run out of a tap, be warm on the coldest night, read a book at night without eyestrain.
>
> These miracles of daily life that piled one upon the other in the first decades of the nineteenth century—railroads, telegraph, newspapers, heating, lighting, running water—induced a mood of optimism and a belief in progress that had not been known before.[34]

In the first half of the nineteenth century, the United States grew at a rate unparalleled in history. Its land area more than tripled, its population quadrupled, and its economy expanded by seven fold. Between 1820 and 1860, international trade increased by almost tenfold and national wealth as valued by taxable property increased 400 percent.[35] Chief Justice John Marshall had defined an historic revolution.

7

Lincoln
civil rights lost, renewed, then cast adrift

ABRAHAM LINCOLN (1809–1865) towered over the Civil War era as he guided America through its most devastating experience. Not only were U.S. slaves emancipated, Lincoln and his generation were instrumental in instituting the reforms and the programs that prepared America for the industrial age. Even beyond freeing the slaves, Lincoln played a critical role in establishing the institutions that eventually freed humanity from the bondage of totalitarian regimes. His aide John Hay, who later served as Theodore Roosevelt's secretary of state and worked for three presidents who were to be assassinated, observed: "There is no man in the country, so wise so gentle and so firm. I believe the hand of God placed him where he is."[1]

Slavery: The Defining Issue

Abraham Lincoln, far better than his contemporaries, understood the founding fathers' basis for the concept of America—— not blood ties, racial homogeneity, or nationality. In 1857, he laid out this basic foundation: "I think the authors [of the Declaration of Independence] intended to include all men, but they did not intend to declare all men equal in all respects. They did not mean to say all were equal in color, size, intellect, moral development, or social capacity. They defined with tolerable distinctness, in what respects they did consider all men equal—equal in certain inalienable rights, among which are life, liberty and the pursuit of happiness."[2] The founding fathers had banned the spread of slavery to the Northwest Territories and did not envision its spread to the West. They had planned for its extinction as part of a national bargain. But, instead of implementing the desire and hope of the founding fathers to end slavery in the new nation, the political culture of Lincoln's era was expanding the scope and reach of slavery. Since the revolutionary era, the condition of African Americans in the United States had deteriorated sharply and their "ultimate destiny had never appeared so hopeless."[3] As the Marquis de Lafayette emphasized at a commemoration ceremony in Boston: "I never would have drawn my sword in the cause of America if I could have conceived that thereby I was helping to found a nation of slaves."[4]

The principle and concept of union, or The Union, was not based on a firm foundation prior to the Civil War, just as democracy and the republican form of government had been on precarious footing during the Revolutionary War era. The North and South were two different cultures, two different economies, and two different societies. Slavery, however, was the one issue that more than any other defined the differences between the North and South, constantly simmering under the surface, a situation one observer called a sleeping serpent.

The three greatest leaders of the period—Henry Clay, Andrew Jackson, and Daniel Webster—all gained stature by their advocacy of The Union, providing the framework and philosophy for Lincoln's effort to save it. Orations by the Great Expounder of the Constitution, Daniel Webster, were so powerful, they were widely viewed as "Godlike Daniel."[5] Webster suffered through the death of two of his five children in their infancy. He then experienced the death of his son from typhoid fever while fighting in the Mexican War and of his daughter from tuberculosis, both in the same year. Webster formulated the key doctrine for arguing that only The Union could safeguard freedom and democracy.

Henry Clay brokered the Missouri Compromise, as well as two other compromises in 1833 and 1850, postponing southern secession from the 1820s until almost forty years later. Only Clay had the position, leadership ability, authority, and sheer determination to execute these negotiations, earning the title the Great Compromiser. Clay owned slaves throughout his life but nevertheless believed slavery to be a great evil.

Pressured by northern industrialists to keep tariffs rising, Congress eventually resorted to the "Tariff of Abominations" which significantly increased tariffs. The 1829 recession soon followed. The protectionism of the manufacturing sector and the Republican Party would result in high tariffs for most of the next hundred years. During this period, tariffs were the major source of government revenue. Yet, high tariffs represented a heavy government intrusion into the free market system, harmed the consumer, and ultimately undermined America's ability to lead in the world.

Andrew Jackson played a critical role in preserving The Union, believing that abolitionists would destroy it, because the South would never agree to give up the practice of slavery. Nullification was the greatest crisis of Jackson's presidency and his finest hour. John Calhoun and South Carolina so strongly opposed the "Tariff of Abominations" that they claimed the state had a right to declare the law null and void and withdraw from the Union. The real issue was not the tariff, but the threat to slavery, which made the threat to the Union even greater. Jackson moved to isolate South Carolina by supporting Georgia in its efforts to remove the Cherokees. Daniel Webster attacked the states' rights position with outstanding oratory proclaiming, "Liberty and Union, now and forever, one and inseparable!" His speech dominated the national news for weeks. Jackson became the first American president to advocate The Union as a perpetual entity, intuitively and instinctively understanding its importance. He pledged to enforce the law and Constitution and do everything possible to preserve it, including using force if necessary. To meet the threat of secession in 1861,

Lincoln based his words and actions on Jackson's leadership during this crisis.

The high point of the founding fathers fight against slavery occurred during John Adams' Administration after hundreds of thousands of slaves had been freed by the Revolutionary War, Washington had emancipated his own slaves, and President Adams had provided supplies and naval assistance to aid the Haitian revolution against slavery. From a modern perspective, the debate over slavery is an open-and-shut case, but in terms of early nineteenth-century America it was a close call. While the revolutionary fathers had set the country on a path toward the elimination of slavery, the Constitution sanctioned it and did not provide for its repeal or eventual prohibition. While ending slavery was the most radical proposal of the Second Great Awakening, southern religion was passive and class-stratified, emphasizing social stability and embracing the notion that slavery was a republican bulwark against tyranny. Northerners, on the other hand, embraced a religion of market values and a future of rapid change aided by science and commerce.

> Common sense moral reasoning perceived directly and intuitively the propriety of the slave system and perceived with equal force its impropriety. Republican principles contradicted slavery and affirmed slavery. Most damagingly, Reformed, literal approaches to the Bible could sanction slavery and also condemn it. The potent tools with which evangelicals had constructed the nation lost their potency when they turned to address this issue. . . . An oft-quoted observation from Abraham Lincoln's Second Inaugural Address highlighted the theological conundrum of the Civil War. Both North and South, he said, "read the same Bible."[6]

The Bible had recognized and accepted the institution of slavery as a given fact of life, the position of most southern and many northern theologians. Christians and the Bible accepted the legitimacy of slavery as an institution that had been present for thousands of years. Abolitionist sentiment, however, sought to argue that God abhorred slavery and the Bible didn't justify slavery as it existed in the United States: the letter of the Bible sanctioned the holding of slaves, but the spirit of Christianity opposed the institution. Theologically, many American religions relied on the Bible alone, distancing their practices from the institutional, ecclesiastic, and denominational factors present in Europe. Thus, the proslavery argument was formidable

> All who wished to use the Bible in antebellum America for arguing in any way against slavery faced a double burden of staggering dimensions. It was the same whether they held that the letter of the Bible should give way to its spirit, or if they claimed that what the Bible seemed to teach it did not really teach, or if they suggested that what the Bible taught did not apply to the American situation and its system of slavery.[7]

In pre-Civil War America, the Bible was accorded reverence and deference. The issues of slavery and race, however, became inextricably interconnected, even though they were two separate problems. The Bible did not endorse the conviction of many Americans that among the peoples of the earth only Africans or African Americans were to live in chattel bondage.

South Carolina re-opened the slave trade between 1803 and 1808, importing tens of thousands of slaves, mostly for work on cotton plantations. As Thomas Jefferson grew older, he observed that the emancipation sentiment was not spreading among the next generation. At the end of his life, he identified increasingly with the Southern rights position, making his famous observation that "We have the wolf by the ears and we can neither hold him, nor safely let him go." By 1820, both Madison and Jefferson had reversed their positions and favored extending slavery into the territories, as did the overwhelming majority of southern legislators.

Yet, in many places throughout the planet, slavery was being eliminated. The anti-slavery movement had become a global force, part of the worldwide struggle for democracy. Great Britain outlawed the slave trade in 1801 and abolished it in 1807. It then emancipated its slaves in

1834, providing compensation to slave owners of 20 million pounds sterling. There was a four-year period of uncompensated apprenticeship, making the effective date 1838. British Quakers and religious activists had great sway over the British government, whereas most slave owners lived in distant colonies and had little political clout. Another decisive factor in the British action was the well-known diagram of a ship loaded with hundreds of slaves, lined up in rows and squashed together. Hundreds of posters of this image exposed the horrors of the passage across the ocean. All Latin America emancipated its slaves, except for Cuba, Puerto Rico, and Brazil. In the first half of the nineteenth century, in fact, more than two dozen countries and territories in the Western Hemisphere abolished slavery. The British Navy, the biggest sea power and only institution that could enforce abolition throughout the world, even seized slave ships and freed slaves. The famous slaves on the ship *Amistad* won their freedom because the slave trade had been outlawed in Spain and they had been illegally kidnapped. In Russia, the Czar enlisted the ablest men in his land to emancipate the serfs and set them free on the day before Lincoln's inauguration.

America Regresses on Slavery

Isolationism in the United States blinded the nation to what was happening in the rest of the world. The South, in particular, was insular, if not outright isolationist. In 1816, John Calhoun had introduced and secured passage of legislation providing for internal infrastructure improvements, but the bill was vetoed by President James Madison. Henry Clay and John Quincy Adams tried unsuccessfully to pass aid for internal development. Instead of a national infrastructure, the northern states built their own improvements while the South's dependency on slavery and a primitive economic system relegated it to second-class economically. The South had few telegraph lines and the rail lines it built basically connected cotton plantations with seaports for export. By mid-century the North was interconnected by railroads and telegraph lines. The North encompassed almost all of the canals that had been built as well as the vast majority of roads. The South's insular culture bred paranoia; plantation owners claimed the massive slave revolts in the Caribbean were caused by the British abolitionists and that abolitionism in America would spark similar revolts in the South. President James Buchanan's Administration took only lukewarm actions to stop efforts to circumvent the prohibition on the slave trade, even giving a frosty reception to British requests for assistance. The South, in this period, became one of chattel slavery's last bastions.

Increasingly mired in its slavery system, the South went to extremes to defend it. Slavery in the South increased from 700,000 slaves in 1790 to over 1 million in 1810 to 4 million in 1860. The propagation of slaves was directly related to the need to harvest cotton in the Deep South. John Calhoun was a fervent nationalist until his home state of South Carolina became overwhelmingly dependent on the cotton crop. During the first half of the nineteenth century, the South regressed and established a caste slavery system. Slavery became a symbol of the possession of wealth and indicated a gentleman of leisure who was above labor in the European tradition. Southerners, for the most part, believed slaves were better off in the South than in Africa, noting most slaves were treated humanely and were taken care of better than in their homeland. They claimed the North was hypocritical as it brought the slaves into the country and then profited from its manufacture of southern cotton. As time went on, slave owners accepted the defense of the slave system as their duty and responsibility. By the 1840s, the South had converted the debate over slavery from an argument about a necessary evil to whether it was a positive good.

To reconcile slavery with the national commitment to equality, race became the justification, because it was an easily distinguishable difference. The argument was made that African Americans were an innately inferior race. In this context, southerners argued there was a right to own slaves and anyone infringing on that right was violating the liberties of the slave owners.

Southern states responded to the slightest insurrections or threats by extending controls over free blacks and even to whites. Private manumissions declined as southern states prevented whites from emancipating their chattel slaves except by legislative permission. Southern courts even overturned wills that freed slaves. Most southern states considered, and several passed, legislation requiring African Americans to either submit to slavery or leave the state. Migration of free African Americans from other states was often barred.[8] Free African Americans had their rights abrogated and were often persecuted or re-enslaved. Southern mobs seized anti-slavery tracts and whipped and killed individuals with anti-slavery sympathies. The South passed laws providing long prison terms for exercising free speech and empowered officials to confiscate objectionable materials. Postal officials routinely intercepted abolitionist and northern publications that appeared in the southern mail. Southern states even barred slaves from being taught reading and writing. The South became a closed society, where advocating abolition was a felony and bounties were placed on abolitionists. By the late 1850s, the measures extending slavery had become so extreme, there was little room for compromise once Lincoln was elected.

Any action in the North either for or against slavery and African Americans became justification for extreme anti-slavery actions in the South. Beginning in the 1820s, abolitionist sentiment began to sweep across the North. By the 1830s, William Lloyd Garrison, his disciple Frederick Douglass, and other abolitionists began a concerted movement to end slavery. Within two years of its inception, the American Anti-Slavery Society grew to 400 local chapters and by 1838 to more than 1,000. The abolitionists, nevertheless, were strongly opposed by most people in the North, many of whom hated African Americans. When asked why the local regiment of the militia was not called out to protect Garrison as he was dragged by a rope, it was pointed out that most of the regiment was in the crowd. Anti-abolitionist acts of terror occurred throughout the North, including riots in Boston and New York. In 1837, the Reverend Elijah Lovejoy, famous for his denunciations of slavery, was shot and killed by a mob; the death of a white man over the issue of African-American slavery cast a pall over every American's right to speak his mind on the subject. The South claimed that abolitionists were causing insurrections, thereby justifying the harsh treatment of slaves.

Bigotry in the North was used as an argument to make southern slavery acceptable. Before the Revolutionary War, the North had tens of thousands of slaves, slave revolts, and criminal conviction rates for African Americans of 100 percent. New York had one of the largest populations of slaves in colonial America and Connecticut didn't outlaw slavery until 1848. Northerners allowed free African Americans to be abducted into slavery, often under the auspices of the fugitive slave laws.[9] Alexis de Tocqueville observed that "race prejudice seems stronger in those states that have abolished slavery than in those where it still exists, and nowhere is it more intolerant than in those states where slavery was never known."[10] Many people in the North wanted to prevent slave labor from becoming competition for free labor. African Americans were not allowed to serve on juries, and only the New England states gave them the same voting rights as whites. Most localities in the North had laws mandating discrimination. Even among northerners who supported equality, most placed their support of the Union over any opposition to slavery. Northern scientists claimed to offer proof African Americans were an inferior race.

In 1857, the anti-slavery forces were further inflamed by the infamous Supreme Court decision on *Dred Scott,* a slave who had sued for his freedom based on several years of residence on free soil. The Supreme Court had a pro-slavery record, particularly Chief Justice Roger Taney (who was in office so long he swore in seven presidents). Taney's opinion held that African Americans were not citizens and had no rights under the Constitution, regardless of whether free or slave. Taney wrote that African Americans are "beings of an inferior order" and had "no rights which any white man was bound to respect." The Court ruled they could not be considered American citizens and, since the Constitution allowed slavery, Congress had no power to exclude it from the territories. The Court even ruled the already repealed Missouri Compromise was unconstitutional—the first time an important federal law had been struck down. The court adopted the southern position on slavery. Taney erroneously believed that a forceful court decision would end the conflict between North and South.

The decision had a far-reaching impact. The federal government, which previously had been ambivalent, began denying African

Americans all privileges associated with citizenship. The states passed discriminatory legislation. Arkansas, for example, passed a proposal to enslave all free African Americans who did not leave the state within a year. In the North, state laws enabling African-American suffrage were imperiled. The *Dred Scott* decision bitterly divided the nation and led directly to the election of a Republican president, Abraham Lincoln.

> Slaveholders felt both physically threatened and morally degraded by the antislavery crusade. What they sought with increasing passion was not only security for their social system but vindication of their social respectability and personal honor. The defense of slavery accordingly lost its earlier strain of ambivalence and became more emphatic, with elaborate appeals to history, the scriptures and racial theory. More and more, the South came to resemble a fortress under siege, expelling or silencing its own critics of slavery and barricading itself against abolitionist oratory and literature. Southerners in Congress closed ranks against even mild antislavery proposals, such as a termination of slave trading in the District of Columbia. They argued that any concession to the spirit of abolitionism would denigrate the South and serve as an entering wedge for further attacks on the slaveholding system. During the final stages of the sectional controversy, many southern leaders compromised their own states' rights principles by demanding a Federal policy unreservedly protective of slavery. Some of them even insisted that all northern criticism of the institution must cease or be suppressed by the states in which it originated. One consequence of these and other proslavery excesses was the enlistment in the antislavery movement of a good many northerners who felt little sympathy for the slave but had developed a strong aversion to the "slave power."[11]

Lincoln understood what was at stake—not just the future of the Union, but man's great experiment with freedom and democracy as well. He wrote to a widow who had lost her five sons on the battlefield:

I feel how weak and fruitless must be any words of mine which should attempt to beguile you from the grief of a loss so overwhelming. But I cannot refrain from tendering to you the consolation that may be found in the thanks of the Republic they died to save.

I pray that our Heavenly Father may assuage the anguish of your bereavement, and leave you only the cherished memory of the loved and lost, and the solemn pride that must be yours, to have laid so costly a sacrifice upon the altar of freedom.

Why Slavery Expanded

The government and political system failed to surmount the economic condition that provided incentives to expand slavery. Regression on the slavery issue was in part due to inertia and the inherent association of blackness with death, danger, evil, and grief. The major rationale, however, was the rapid technological advance in the textile industry, in particular the development of the cotton gin. A sharp increase in demand for cotton caused a bottleneck in the hand picking of cotton, and slavery expanded rapidly. Southern soil was the best land in the world to grow cotton, and the cotton gin and other advances in the textile industry were among the greatest technological changes in history. Rapid technological advances are often difficult for cultures to cope with. The advances in technology, the much greater demand for cotton, and the resulting Southern wealth became a pretext to continue and expand the institution of slavery.

Slavery in the South was lucrative and decentralized. Half of the southern slaveholders owned fewer than five slaves and over 70 percent owned fewer than 10. Most larger plantations were run by African-American drivers and managers. During the decade and a half prior to the Civil War, the value of slaves rose rapidly, the average price rising from $200 to $800; prime field hands were worth $1,500.

The South dominated the federal political system for the first seventy-two years. Southerners represented 24 of the 36 Speakers of the

House, 25 of the 36 presidents pro tem of the Senate, and 20 out of 35 Supreme Court justices. During 49 of these 72 years, the president of the United States had been a southerner and a slave holder. In the Congress, southern Democrats used their power to dominate the key posts and committee chairmanships.

By the end of the 1850s, however, the South was losing its political power and dwindling to a minority. With a much larger population, the North controlled the U.S. House of Representatives by a wide margin. The number of free states exceeded the number of slave states for the first time, giving the North an advantage in the Senate as well. Republicans gained seats in Congress in each election of the 1850s. What had long been a Democratic bastion was on the verge of Republican control. Southern politics continued to be dominated by the planters, whose chief interest was maintenance and expansion of slavery. This single-minded motivation and interest proved successful and revealed a fundamental flaw in the American system, one that has never been fixed: a determined minority can impose its will on a less interested majority.

There were other flaws in the political system as well, including "Americans' failure between the administrations of Jackson and Abraham Lincoln to elevate great statesmen like Clay, Webster, or Calhoun to the presidency. Instead, the parties nominated 'available' men—politicians and especially non-politicians without stature, experience, or past records and the enemies such records produced."[12] Webster was urged to become vice president on William Henry Harrison's ticket and brushed off the offer. At the time, the vice presidency was regarded as irrelevant, a useless office. It was perhaps Webster's biggest mistake—Harrison died after serving only one month.

In contrast to the founding fathers, the presidents of the pre-Civil War period did not provide appropriate leadership at the visionary, Comforter or executive levels and the stature of the holders of this crucial office was much lower during the generation before the war. A critical failing of the popular democracy was to elect the president based on likeability and electability instead of merit. In the 1836 election, John

Quincy Adams noted "the remarkable character of this election is that all the candidates are at most third-rate men."[13] In 1848, Zachary Taylor, a political novice, had never voted in a presidential election. He was slow in starting up his administration and, didn't have effective advocacy before the Congress.

Franklin Pierce was the nation's youngest president (1853–1857). When strong leadership was needed, he became one of the weakest presidents because of his inexperience. All three of his children died, the last before his eyes in a railway accident just before he assumed office. His wife disliked politics and public appearances and lived in a state of depression due to the deaths of her children. Although Pierce was from New Hampshire, he pandered to the South with most of his appointments. He was also expansionist—agreeing to the Gadsden Purchase to facilitate a southern route for the transcontinental railroad and attempting to purchase Cuba, an action that resulted in a diplomatic fiasco.

On paper, James Buchanan (1857–1861) was among the most qualified individuals to become president, serving a decade in the House, a decade in the Senate, five years as minister to Russia and Britain, and four years as secretary of state. Yet, his presidency was one of the weakest and most corrupt in the pre-Civil War period. Defense contracts were awarded to political contributors without competitive bidding. Postmasters siphoned off public funds into the Democratic Party. Judges were bribed to naturalize immigrants so they could vote.

The authors of the Constitution had set up a system of checks and balances to limit the scope and extent of government action and, in a small republic, this system worked well, but in a rapidly expanding nation it could create problems. Between 1840 and 1860, the only productive session of Congress was the first session of the first Congress of a president's term. The remaining sessions were either too short or were marred with partisan conflicts. Absent strong executive leadership, the country was adrift. In 1849, 1855, and 1859, Congressional inaction was compounded by prolonged fights over the Speaker of the House lasting for weeks. Between 1835 and 1844, the House of Representatives instituted a gag rule that barred consideration and even discussion of slavery issues. It was repealed only after extensive protests by John Quincy Adams and other northerners.

The first third of the nineteenth century witnessed the Missouri Compromise, the effort to preserve the Union in the debate over the Tariff of Abominations, and Andrew Jackson's success in transforming the presidency into a pulpit for national leadership. It might be expected that presidential campaigns would become forums for national debates over the major issue of slavery, but the campaigns were largely devoid of substance and even excitement. In the six elections between 1836 and 1856, major presidential candidates did not personally campaign. The 1840 campaign between William Harrison ("Tippecanoe and Tyler Too") and Martin van Buren did have hoopla, songs, and slogans, such as "Log Cabin and Hard Cider Democracy." In the long term, its major contribution to American civilization was the term "booze," named for the most sought after item of the campaign, a miniature log cabin filled with Old Cabin Whiskey bottled by the E.B.C. Booz Distillery. Harrison ran an active campaign but it lacked any real substance. His opponent Martin Van Buren had a set of policy and position papers and lost, in large part due to the on-going Depression. James Polk didn't even make any tours and published only one letter. Franklin Pierce remained silent and stayed at home. The Republicans joked that James Buchanan was dead from lockjaw, because he said virtually nothing during his campaign.

Even Abraham Lincoln was somewhat of a fluke, winning the nomination over two better-known opponents who were viewed as not being as electable and winning the general election over a fractured and divided opposition. Lincoln understood the failures of this system and was a big fan of Henry Clay who probably would have seriously addressed the issue of slavery if he had been elected president and might have averted a Civil War.

Lincoln's Compassion and Election

Lincoln was revered for his compassion and ability to comfort and heal the divided and decimated American community. Growing up on the frontier as his family moved from place to place, he was self-taught. Lincoln's father was listless and suffered from watching a Shawnee raiding party murder his own father when he was six years old. Lincoln's mother died early in his life and his barely literate father remarried, leaving the children at home alone at an early age while he looked for a new wife. Lincoln became very close to his stepmother who was instrumental in his personal growth. His connection with the frontier and log cabins became so legendary that a Congressman once proclaimed: "It is indeed fitting that we gather here today to pay tribute to Abraham Lincoln, who was born in a log cabin he built with his own hands."

Lincoln was lanky, rough-hewn, and awkward, but he was also brilliant and had a photographic memory, learning the classics as well as the writings of the founding fathers. He spent time in the South and learned the arguments of pro-slavery advocates. His first love, Ann Rutledge, died of typhoid fever. His sister died in childbirth. He married Mary Todd, who had turned down Stephen Douglas, perhaps figuring Lincoln to be better presidential timber.

Lincoln served three terms in the Illinois House of Representatives and one term in the U.S. House of Representatives, where his service as a Whig was regarded as less than successful, because he didn't support the highly popular Mexican War. Driven to re-enter national politics after his term in the House, he sensed a downward moral drift in the country. Prior to becoming president, Lincoln was not religious in the traditional sense, but rather viewed spirit and God as providence. He never joined a church, but became more religious in the presidency, using the Bible as the basis for many of his most famous statements.

The Compromise of 1850 was the swan song for the three Great Debaters: Daniel Webster made his last speech in opposition to slavery; John Calhoun was on his death-bed in his last stand in support of slavery; and Henry Clay, in his seventies, was once again acting in the role of the Great Compromiser. Clay's compromise gave the Union ten more years to gain the strength it would need to defeat the South and find the nation's greatest leader, Abraham Lincoln. A tougher Fugitive Slave Law was enacted and created a class of court officials to seize runaways without due process, making it difficult for abolitionists and northerners to refuse to return slaves to their owners. The impact of the fugitive slave law was to inflame many people in the North, particularly since the law could be used to recover slaves who had run away long in the past. Also, it was abused so as to kidnap people who had never been slaves, but now had little or no legal recourse. In one case, a man was torn from his wife and children and delivered to someone who claimed the man to have been a slave nineteen years before. Fugitive slave Margaret Garner tried to kill her four children to prevent their return to slavery. Harriet Beecher Stowe's novel *Uncle Tom's Cabin* became a bestseller, creating enormous sympathy for slaves. Northern mobs began attacking slave catchers instead of abolitionists. When these groups were prosecuted, northern juries refused to convict them.

After the three great debaters left the Senate, Stephen Douglas forged another compromise—the 1854 Kansas-Nebraska Act. The purpose of the law was to provide a route for the transcontinental railroad through America's heartland by opening the lands for settlement and statehood. To gain southern support for passing the bill, Senator Douglas included a provision allowing slavery by popular vote in what had been considered since the Missouri Compromise to be free territories, such as Kansas where the border with Missouri was teeming with agriculture based on slavery. This was viewed as a betrayal by much of the North, placing America at direct odds with the rest of the world— expanding slavery in an era when it was on the decline. A leading journalist noted that passage of this legislation had created more abolitionists in two months than William Lloyd Garrison had created in twenty years. The result was extreme violence, "bleeding Kansas," and many northern legislatures passing statutes making it difficult to enforce fugitive slave laws, albeit most of these state laws were subsequently determined to be unconstitutional by the Supreme Court.

The 1854 election was the beginning of a series of elections that saw a major realignment in voting patterns. Northern Democrats who supported the Kansas-Nebraska Act were swept out, the nativist and anti-immigrant Know-Nothing Party emerged, and the anti-slavery Republican Party surged. The United States experienced one of the heaviest influxes of immigrants in percentage terms in its history, amounting to one-seventh of the total 1845 U.S. population. Throughout the 1830s and 1840s, anti-catholic and ethnic riots occurred in northeastern cities. Nativists started up the American Republican Party in the 1840s and the Know-Nothing Party in the 1850s, both of which became significant forces.

James Buchanan won the presidential election of 1856 because, despite being from Pennsylvania, he represented the southern Democratic Party, which competed against two regional parties—the Republicans in the North and Whig remnants in the South. Buchanan then tried to ram through legislation to make Kansas a slave state to counter the entry of Minnesota and Oregon as free states.

In 1858, Lincoln became a national figure by virtue of his famous debates with Stephen Douglas. The era before the Civil War was "an age when speech-making prowess was central to political success, when the spoken word filled the air from sun-up til sun-down."[14] Lincoln ran for the Senate against Douglas as the Republican nominee, when senators were still selected by state legislatures. Lincoln's nomination by the Republican Party was one of the first occasions that a political party formally selected a nominee for the Senate.

Douglas was "the nation's most likely choice for president in 1860. His struggle with Lincoln for re-election to the Senate in 1858 therefore commanded national attention. Making full use of newly constructed railroads, the two candidates traveled nearly ten thousand miles in four months. They crisscrossed Illinois, their tireless voices intermingling with the sound of bands, parades, fireworks, cannon, and cheering crowds. Each community tried to outdo its rivals in pageantry and in winning the greatest turnout from the countryside."[15] Thousands of people came from miles around to listen to the debates. They voted for their state legislators who eventually re-selected Douglas. While Republican candidates for state legislature outpolled the Democrats, northern Illinois was underrepresented in the legislature and the Democrats took the majority of seats, then elected Douglas.

By telegraph, newspaper reporters relayed the verbal jousts to the rest of the nation as the debates were of general interest throughout the country. This war of words focused America on the evils of slavery and on the nation's future being at stake. Engaging in a pre-emptive strike in his first campaign speech, Lincoln charged that the federal government claimed its policy was to reduce dissension over slavery, but it had worsened agitation over the issue until, "in my opinion, it will not cease until a crisis shall have been reached and passed. 'A house divided against itself cannot stand.' I believe this government cannot endure permanently half slave and half free."

Douglas, a polished performer, tried to be on both sides and never took a clear position, protesting that "The Almighty himself has drawn across this continent a line on one side of which the earth must be for ever tilled by slave labor, whereas on the other side of that line labor is free." Throwing Lincoln on the defensive for his refusal to accept the Court's *Dred Scott* Scott decision, Douglas charged that Lincoln wanted equality and citizenship for the negro. Douglas tried to cast his rival as a radical and a supporter of equality, certain that no such candidate could win in a state with Black Laws that barred African Americans from voting, holding political office, giving testimony against whites, sitting on juries, and coming across state lines to become residents. Lincoln turned this criticism around by pressing Douglas on whether he would accept the logical extension of the *Dred Scott* decision that Illinois and other free states could not prohibit slavery within their own boundaries. Lincoln charged that Douglas and the Democrats not only wanted to abandon the fight to end slavery, but that they wanted to make it permanent throughout the nation, striking at the heart of freedom and equality in America. Lincoln was most disturbed by Chief Justice Taney's gratuitous assertion that neither the Declaration of Independence nor the Constitution was ever intended to include African Americans. So gross seemed this distortion of the founding fathers' intent that Lincoln's previous faith in the judiciary was shattered and never again would he give deference to the rulings of the Court.

The slavery debates played into Lincoln's strength—he could emphasize how indefensible and evil that institution was. Lincoln exhibited exceptional knowledge of American history, often quoting Henry Clay, his Whig hero. Lincoln had clear convictions on what he viewed as the paramount issue of the times—slavery. While he came across as homespun and awkward, he could at times be possessed, focusing the nation's attention on the fact that all Americans, from both North and South, knew in their hearts slavery was wrong. Even Robert E. Lee acknowledged, "slavery as an institution is a moral and political evil."[16]

Lincoln thus demonstrated himself as leader of the anti-slavery movement, creating a crucial distinction from Stephen Douglas. Lincoln focused on every man's common human bond, whether African American or white. The Douglas argument was that slaves were just property. Lincoln made slavery a big issue by humanizing it and putting it into personal terms. Because African Americans were human, slavery was immoral and "founded in the selfishness of man's nature. No man is good enough to govern another man, *without that other's consent.*" Lincoln also believed that slavery must be viewed from a global perspective, keeping America a beacon of freedom for the rest of the world. In terms of the role of democracy and republicanism throughout the globe, "the world's best hope depended on the continued Union of these States."[17]

Although Lincoln opposed slavery in the debates, he didn't support racial equality. He was not, "in favor of making voters of the negroes, or jurors, or qualifying them to hold office, or having them to marry with white people . . . (T)here is a physical difference between the white and black races, which I suppose, will forever forbid the two races living together on terms of social and political equality." Still, Lincoln was ahead of his times and played an essential role in blazing the trail of human equality. He concluded the debates by stating the conflict is "on the part of one class that looks upon the institution of slavery *as a wrong,* and of another class that *does not* look upon it as a wrong. . . . It is the eternal struggle between these two principles—right and wrong— throughout the world. They are the two principles that have stood face to face from the beginning of time; and will ever continue to struggle. The one is the common right of humanity and the other the divine right of kings."[18]

Democrats lost so many seats in the 1858 election, there was an expectation of a Republican victory in the presidential election of 1860.

Southern Democrats continued to demand orthodoxy and ideological purity from northern colleagues, bolstering the Republican Party and sealing the Democrats' fate in the 1860 election. In Kansas, John Brown hacked to death several pro-slavery men as their terrified wives pleaded for their lives. After these murderous exploits, John Brown in 1859 led a tiny army into the village of Harpers Ferry in Virginia, and seized the arsenal. Brown thought an invasion of the South could stir an uprising and free the slaves and believed his venture would make a huge impact even if it failed. No slaves joined Brown; his vision of a mass of slaves being liberated was illusory. The southern slave system was too decentralized and entrenched. Colonel Robert E. Lee and his army unit recaptured the post, capturing Brown and killing ten of his men. When he was hanged for his actions at Harper's Ferry, one Kansas widow wrote that her son was desirous to be present at his execution.

Brown's revolt further raised tensions in the South, spreading fear of slave insurrections and northern dominance. Historians and academicians have dismissed Brown as a misfit and insane. Brown's actions, however, had a powerful effect. Even his Virginian captors had admiration for the way he handled himself after capture. His hanging brought mourning in the North. His actions legitimized and gave credibility to moderate men like Lincoln. Brown's attack and hanging reinforced the northern dismay over slavery and crystallized public sentiment against the institution. Brown's attack stirred up fear in the South, causing politics in that region to go awry. Abolitionist efforts to foster insurrection stirred up the most deep-seated fears of southern planters over their ability to keep African Americans subordinate and maintain the slave system. Brown's hanging made him a martyr. By the end of the Civil War, the tune *John Brown's Body* was the most popular song in the North.

Between the end of the Revolutionary War and the onset of the Civil War, America's territory had tripled, the population had increased eight fold, and the economy skyrocketed eighteen fold.[19] In 1800 the population was evenly distributed between North and South, but by the middle of the century only a third lived below the Mason-Dixon line. The population explosion altered the balance between North and

South. New York and Pennsylvania both outstripped Virginia, which had the largest population during the Revolutionary War and provided four out of the first five presidents. Philadelphia and New York became huge cities of half a million and a million people, respectively, while only ten percent of the South lived in cities at all. The odds were against a southern victory with 20 million people in the North and only about 5 million in the South, not counting slaves. White males of fighting age totaled four million in the North, barely over a million in the South. The North was open to immigration and received many men from Germany, Ireland, and the South itself, which supplied 200,000 men for the northern cause. This demographic shift led to parallel changes in politics—the election of Lincoln as president and eventually a Republican majority in the Congress.

Not yet fifty-two, Lincoln was one of the youngest men ever to serve as president, literally coming out of nowhere to win the election. In 1860, he won the Republican nomination over the strongly favored William Henry Seward, former governor and senator from New York, and Salmon Chase, immediate past governor and senator from Ohio. Lincoln benefited from his role in the battleground state of Illinois, out-worked his opponents, and ran a much shrewder campaign. The Republican Party platform was engineered for wider appeal, endorsing a protective tariff to appeal to industrialists in the North and larger free homesteads to appeal to the West. These new positions broadened the base of the party and were crucial to the eventual outcome—one of the more effective uses of the party platform in history.

With the rapid population growth in the industrial North, just three states (New York, Pennsylvania and Ohio) had as many electoral votes as the eleven states in the South that seceded. The precise catalyst of the conflict is unclear—northerners did not vote for Lincoln to pre-cipitate southern secession and the Republican Party position on slav-ery was quite moderate. Lincoln was less radical on the slavery issue than the other two leading Republican candidates. Lincoln would almost certainly have won the election even if the Democrats had been united. He carried fifteen of his eighteen states with a popular majority, enough to give him an electoral majority. Lincoln received the second smallest share of the popular vote on record after John Quincy Adams (less than 40 percent). In most southern states, Lincoln was not even on the ballot and his supporters didn't campaign, leaving southerners to suspect the worst. He did not get a single recorded vote in five southern states nor carry any of the fifteen southern states.

The Causes of the Civil War

The grim determination of two different cultures was the root cause of the clash. The Civil War, as the name suggests, was an epic conflict between two strong and very different civil societies over an internal contradiction in one of the principles of American democracy—slavery in a political system with a basic creed that every man is free and created equal. While many in the South even today call it the War Between the States, it was a civil war between two great civil societies, pitting American against American, state against state, neighbor against neighbor, father against son, and brother against brother. In Texas, Confederates captured Galveston, shelling and seizing the USS Harriet Lane. Major A.M. Lea boarded the vessel and found dying on the deck his son. Captain John L. Englins, an Englishman with the Confederacy, led his Florida company on a valiant charge, overran the federal guns, and accepted the surrender of their commander, his brother.[20] The male relatives of Jefferson Davis' wife were all in the Union army. Mary Todd Lincoln had brothers and many relatives in the Confederate Army, several of whom were killed. Rumors circulated that Mary was a Confederate spy.

The intensity and absolutism of both cultures led to a clash between two sides with no room for compromise. Both sides presumed to act with divine guidance or God's favor with an unyielding rigidity that led to the cataclysmic conflict.

> No one could have predicted the magnitude of the explosion that rocked America following that opening shot. . . . Yet most of what America was before the Civil War went into sparking that explosion, and most of what the nation

became resulted from it. Entirely unimaginable before it began, the war was the most defining and shaping event in American history—so much so that it is now impossible to imagine what we would have been like without it.[21]

Each side approached the conflict as a family argument. Neither side thought it would last very long and, at the beginning of the war, General Sherman was judged to be insane for making predictions about large numbers of casualties. His estimates proved to be too low. The war produced as many American casualties as all the other wars combined from the Revolutionary War through the Iraq war. Shelby Foote, a great Civil War historian, noted that the war started "because we failed to do the thing we really have a genius for which is compromise. Americans like to think of themselves as uncompromising. But our true genius is for compromise. Our whole government's founded on it. And it failed."[22] Nevertheless, even today it is hard to fathom what that compromise would have been. Four of the most capable United States Senators worked on a compromise for over forty years—Henry Clay, John Calhoun, Daniel Webster, and Stephen Douglas. They didn't find one that worked over the long term. In 1860, there were four million slaves, one out of every seven Americans. Without the Civil War, slavery would not have been abolished—at least by legal action. A constitutional amendment would have been required with two-thirds in Congress needed to pass it and three-quarters of the states necessary to ratify it. As an economic system, slavery might have ended without a civil war. If there had been secession without a war, slaves could have escaped much more easily to the North, particularly with the Fugitive Slave Act repealed. But this would have been a long and tortuous process. Few slaves, perhaps only a thousand a year, were able to use the Underground Railroad that ferried escapees to freedom before the war. On the other hand, the invention of a machine to revolutionize cotton picking, as International Harvester did in 1946, might have caused the system to collapse.

By southern standards, Lincoln was too radical, but not for the public in the North. His election enraged the South, which previously had some form of control over all three branches of government. The election triggered a drastic reaction from the pro-slavery forces—South Carolina seceded on December 20, 1860, Mississippi on January 9, followed by Florida, Alabama, Georgia, Louisiana, and Texas. By Lincoln's inauguration in March, the thirty-three states of the Union had been reduced to twenty-seven (Kansas having joined while the seven were seceding). The vote to secede was very close in some states, particularly Georgia. The turnout in the elections and referendum was generally much lower than in the presidential election. The upper south opposed secession and even Virginia at least initially refused to go along. Once the outcome of the presidential contest was known, the secession events occurred at great speed—Jefferson Davis being inaugurated two weeks before Lincoln.

The South had a few limited advantages. The North faced the difficult task of conquering and occupying the South and its determined army, while the South only had to achieve the more limited objective of fending off the North and inflicting enough damage to force the North to give up. The South was bigger than all of Western Europe today. If the Confederates won, they had a bright future. If they were defeated, they would lose everything. Southerners saw themselves as carrying the mantle of the American revolutionary tradition. As the hot bed of revolt, the South believed it was fighting for its principles against tyranny, waging a second American Revolution. The South was led by Robert E. Lee, who Winston Churchill later described as "one of the greatest captains known to the annals of war" and Teddy Roosevelt thought "without any exception the very greatest of all the great captains that the English-speaking people have brought forth."

The South believed that Lincoln's election marked the beginning of governance by Black Republicanism. Even though Republicans controlled neither house of Congress or the Supreme Court, southerners felt slavery would be doomed under a Lincoln presidency, that they had nothing to lose. The South, in effect, refused to accept the outcome of a fair election. Secession was a catharsis and sparked outpourings of joy. The southerners believed they were the true revolutionaries. Secession united the North, because almost everyone agreed that the Union was not a voluntary association of states. Many southerners erroneously believed the North would accept secession or that they could win an armed conflict. They did not expect the North to fight. Some southerners assumed that all of the southern states would secede. The seven states that seceded at first represented only a third of the free population of the South. Four other states later joined their cause, but the Border States never really became part of the confederate effort. Southerners also assumed the British would intervene on their behalf to keep the cotton flowing and the French would sympathize with the southern aristocratic culture. Working people in Europe, however, strongly opposed slavery and any assistance for the South.

Even though he served as president during the critical four-month period between the November election and March inauguration, Buchanan was a lame duck president and could do little to prevent southern secession. He was passive, vacillating, running scared. Privately, he proclaimed he was the last president of the United States. Buchanan might have embraced the precedents set by Andrew Jackson in the fight over Nullification, but he failed to use them. The leading Republican newspaper, the *New York Tribune,* which was edited by Horace Greeley, concluded the South should be allowed to secede. Many abolitionists were happy to have the South secede, so they could live in a country free of all of the vestiges of slavery. Others initially blamed the abolitionists for the secession of the South. If Lincoln could have assumed the presidency immediately, war might have been avoided or the course of the conflict significantly altered, but in this period he was powerless to prevent the disintegration of the Union. Throughout the four months prior to inauguration, he said nothing, hoping to avoid any further alienation of the southern states. Instinctively, Lincoln understood the best way to unify the rest of the country was to wait for the first act of southern aggression.

Some modern historians have classified Lincoln as a chronic depressive. Early in his life, he did have periods of depression; these are understandable as he was brought up in dire poverty and forced to watch helplessly as three of the women he was closest to died from disease—his mother, sister, and sweetheart Ann Rutledge. As President, he was not chronically depressed, although he was melancholic.

Melancholy was part of his nature and served as a source of empathy, creativity, and achievement. Later in life, two of his sons died early. When Lincoln's dearest son Willie died and he was feeling the burdens of the presidency, he turned to religion for solace, praising "the Providence of God who has never deserted us."[23] Medical practice was primitive, and little could be done to help the sick. Yet, those deaths proved valuable experience for the bloodbath that Lincoln was to go through as President when much of Washington became in effect a hospital ward. After the death of her son while in the White House, Mary Todd Lincoln would visit nearby military hospitals with hundreds of young men who endured ghastly wounds, suffered from amputations without anesthesia, and often died without any friends or family present.

Lincoln's Technological Genius

Lincoln's understanding and use of technology were decisive. He viewed the history of the human race as a history of improvements, inventions, and progress, with patent laws the apex of this process.[24] When Lincoln had run for the state legislature at age twenty-three, he advocated building a railroad to the west, noting, "no other improvement . . . can equal in utility the railroad."[25] Throughout his life, he was a leading advocate for railroads. Understanding the importance of new technology and how to use it, Lincoln is the only president to hold a patent and handled many legal cases involving complex scientific issues. When, for example, the ship companies sued the railroads after a collision with an abutment, arguing bridges posed a safety challenge, Lincoln won the suit, understanding that a loss would have meant railroads could not cross rivers and streams without putting the train on a ferry. Lincoln patented a device for floating stranded boats off river shoals. He incorporated the National Academy of Sciences.

Lincoln would wait for news at the telegraph office and make instantaneous decisions that often made the difference in winning battles and saving lives. Lincoln asked many businessmen and inventors to visit the White House, and he personally attended technical demonstrations. With his background in inventions, he was able to determine what weapons were effective and get them delivered as soon as possible. He even brought an inventor to a cabinet meeting to demonstrate a new weapon. Because he had personally fired them and understood they would make a major difference in the war, Lincoln overruled the War Department and directed it to order breech-loading rifles. Repeating and breech-loading rifles enabled soldiers in assaults to fire many more rounds of ammunition. Introduction of the weaponry was limited by the lack of standardization and the difficulty ordnance supply officers experienced in procuring multiple forms of ammunition. Lincoln was involved in the development of the *Monitor,* one of the great breakthroughs in naval technology.[26]

The North's Advantages

The most decisive factors in the Civil War were the North's technological and manufacturing edge coupled with the political leadership of Lincoln and the military leadership of Grant, both of whom understood how to use this edge to advantage. The North's superior transportation system had reduced the cost of shipping by between 80 and 90 percent, spurring agricultural production and flooding northern cities with well-to-do workers who had the disposable income to spend on manufactured goods.[27] The North had twice as many miles of railroad tracks and almost all of the national capacity for producing locomotives and rolling stock. The southern railways were used to get cotton to market and were almost useless for war; few lines moved interstate trade, and there were at least three different gauges of track.[28] During the war, the confederate army was often short of food, even though it was available on the farms, because the railroads that ran from the interior to the coast, did not interconnect, and were below standard.

New York, Pennsylvania, and Massachusetts each produced more manufactured goods than the entire South. During the decade of the 1850s, capital investment in manufacturing doubled from half a billion to over a billion dollars, much of this increase made possible by the expanded money supply as a result of the discovery of gold in

California.[29] The industrial North out-produced the South by eight to ten times. The corridor between New York and Wilmington, Delaware, was the world's fastest growing industrial area. The Confederacy produced less than 50 thousand tons annually of pig iron, while Pennsylvania alone produced over a half million tons. The self-sufficient Cambria iron works in Johnstown, Pennsylvania, embracing 25,000 acres with iron ore, coal, limestone, and firebrick clay, all locally abundant, produced over 1500 tons of pig-iron and railroad iron a week.

Firearms production in the North exceeded output in the Confederacy by 32 to 1. A single county in Connecticut had nine firearms factories, it manufactured guns worth ten times the value of the entire production in the South. In ship tonnage, the North had a 25–1 advantage.

In wheat production, the North held a virtual monopoly. The North had invested in scientific agriculture and crop diversification, whereas the South was wedded to the single-crop cotton, which depleted its soil.

The tradition-bound South lacked a strong work ethic, and was far behind in innovation and entrepreneurial activity. Approximately 90 percent of U.S. businessmen and inventors were from the North. The forward-looking northerners invented or improved the steamboat, clipper ship, telegraph, revolver, steel plow, mechanical reaper, and many other devices. The North grew more and more wealthy, while the South was economically stuck in the ways of the past.

Not all the North's technological and industrial strength was useful for war, but portions were almost certainly decisive. In New England, ice and fishing industries drove the shipbuilding business, which stimulated the requisite craftsmen to continue to improve ship technology. New England had easy access to critical materials: timber, tar, chains, rope, anchors, nails, and other commodities. The South had no machine shop to build marine engines, whereas the North had a number of such shops. The North had nurtured one of the largest shipbuilding industries in the world and many historians believe the success of the naval blockade was decisive in the outcome of the war. The

North's maritime advantage was probably the critical factor in winning the war in the West. Early in the war, the South had some success staving off the Union navy using raiders and guerrilla tactics, but in time the Union's maritime strength gradually tightened the noose around the entire South.

The Use of Technology

Civil War needs stimulated major technological advances or "firsts": railroad artillery, successful submarine, periscope for trench warfare, submarine battle, land-mines, flame throwers, naval torpedoes, aerial reconnaissance, aircraft (balloon) carrier, antiaircraft fire, machine guns, steel ships, revolving gun turrets, battle photography, and electrically exploded bombs and torpedoes. Railroads played a decisive role in the war's first battle, transporting troops for the first time, and delivering the reinforcements that gave the Confederacy victory at Bull Run.

As America's industrial and technological ingenuity produced more effective weapons, however, military leaders did not keep pace: they did not develop suitable tactics. Infantry assaults became increasingly brutal as earthworks and entrenchments became virtually impregnable. The rifled musket barrel and better ammunition extended the range and efficiency of the infantry's basic weapon; thus a charging man could be killed or maimed at fives times the previous distance. The Union artillery was significantly superior, with rifled cannon that were more accurate, and with better powder and fuses. Military leaders were slow to recognize these technological advances and continued to mass their men to make charges, exposing their forces to enormous casualties. Thousands of men would die in the murderous assaults prescribed by martial tradition.

Lincoln the Communicator

Lincoln had an unassailable power to persuade. He was a master of the English language. He was also readily accessible, frequently riding a horse on the streets of Washington, being shot at on more than one occasion, and being the only president to come under fire in a military conflict. Lincoln always sought other people's views for what he termed his "public opinion baths." Virtually anyone could get to see him.

Lincoln and the North exploited their advantage of being electronically connected through the telegraph. During the war, Andrew Carnegie helped to extend it across the Potomac into rebel territory. Lincoln utilized the telegraph to communicate with his military leaders in the field, exerting control over military decisions and strategy. For the first time, a national leader could communicate from afar and instantaneously with his field commanders. America had always maintained a separation between civilian and military leadership, but this separation was significantly altered by the telegraph. Many of the nation's other leaders failed to comprehend the importance of the technology. The bill authorizing the use of the telegraph barely passed the House of Representatives, 89 to 83, with the margin being provided by northern members of Congress. One southern representative mockingly proposed using the money for mesmerism.[30]

The North accrued additional advantages from its industrialization. Literacy was somewhat higher than in the South, much higher if slaves were taken into account. The United States had approximately a third of all the newspapers in the world, mainly concentrated in the North. New York had twice as many newspapers as all the major southern states combined, while Ohio, still very much a frontier state, had as many newspapers as all of the South. Better education and information channels improved the North's chances for consensus against slavery.

With full journalistic coverage, the Civil War was the first war waged in the eyes of the world. President Lincoln and the North used their very effective communications systems, particularly telegraph, to mobilize and drive public opinion. The South had built only two telegraph lines, one along the coast and the other down the Mississippi, while the North had created a spider-web network of lines connecting major cities. With the telegraph, newspapers were no longer merely a source of local news: they covered breaking events from afar. Daily newspapers spent huge sums on news coverage, and correspondents were present on all fronts. It was expensive to keep reporters in the field and the costs of transmitting a telegraph were high (e.g., five cents a word between New York and Washington). Consequently, six New York newspapers pooled resources and formed the New York Associated Press to share these expenses. This cooperative delivered news throughout the nation for a fee. Even this mechanism didn't quench the public's news thirst; local papers raised their rates to expand their newsgathering, including over 300 war correspondents traveling with the troops. The *New York Herald* had a correspondent with every division of the army. The war was the most important story in American history, deciding the future of the country. News coverage became more and more extensive, containing pages of electronically delivered reports. Lincoln did not hesitate to seize a newspaper or a journalists' writings if the content or coverage were imperiling the war effort.

Some of the coverage opposed the war effort, discouraged volunteering, and even published misleading information about the war. The news media created public celebrities and determined important individuals' public persona. Journalistic treatment of military generals was erratic, with some of the least effective receiving effusive coverage, while some of the best, such as Sherman and Grant, were routinely panned. General George Gordon Meade became the commander of the Army of the Potomac as a virtual unknown because of a conspiracy by reporters not to mention his name as a result of the poor treatment he customarily accorded the press. While much of the press was anti-Lincoln, the president was effective at dealing with journalists, particularly in the use of open letters sent to editors. Lincoln understood the importance of this medium, "public sentiment in this country is everything. With public sentiment, nothing can fail; without it nothing can succeed."[31]

Lincoln's Centralized Power

Utilizing the North's superior economic base, President Lincoln and the Republicans gradually developed the beginnings of modern centralized government and the financial infrastructure that made a large, industrial economy possible. Banking and other economic institutions provided the North with additional advantages. In the 1850s, Wall Street became a world financial center with large amounts of securities being sold to Europeans. The South had no comparable source of money supply and little banking. The South had 30 percent of the country's assets (mostly land), but only 12 percent of the circulating money and 21 percent of the banking assets. It had little indigenous gold or silver, no reserves, and little capability to raise funds—the northern blockade drastically reduced tariffs as a source of revenue, and the southern economy gradually shrank during the war.

Lincoln worked to establish a new banking system with a uniform national currency based on public credit that included nationally chartered banks with the capability of purchasing government securities as backing for their bank notes. These national banks were required to have minimum amounts of capital investment and government bonds as backing for bank notes in circulation. A 10 percent tax was placed on notes issued by private or state banks. By the 1870s, a new banking system was in place that included more than 1600 national banks.

Lincoln vastly expanded national government. Before the war, federal spending was less than 2 percent of the economy. The average citizen had little or no contact with the government—even the post office delivered only a fraction of the mail, particularly in urban areas. Federal spending suddenly shot up from under $200,000 to $2 million a day. Before the war, the federal government had never spent more than $75 million a year. After the war, it never spent less than $230 million.[32] National debt increased 42 fold to a then-staggering $2.8 billion.

Prior to the Civil War, the only major tax was the tariff. The North advocated high tariffs, but the South strongly favored low tariffs. As soon as the South seceded, the North passed higher tariffs. Congress expanded the products that were covered and raised average duties from 20 percent in 1860 to almost 50 percent by 1864. Republicans kept them high for the next seventy years. During the war, imports dropped significantly as a percentage of goods sold even though there was more economic activity. High tariffs jeopardized British neutrality in the Civil War, because not only were the cotton states major customers, the northern states used protectionist tariffs to keep out British manufactured goods. During the decade of the Civil War, the number of manufacturing firms almost doubled as did most measures of manufacturing activity. The resources and capabilities developed in the Civil War were converted to civilian uses after the war, making the United States (i.e., the North) an industrial powerhouse.

In the North, revenues from traditional sources declined—no taxes or tariffs could be collected from the Confederacy and the Homestead Act passed in the early part of the war gave settlers free title after working the land for five years. Secretary of the Treasury Salmon Chase raised enormous amounts of funds from Wall Street and through a Philadelphia banker, Jay Cooke, who issued bonds for as little as $50 to the public and waged a bond drive. Before the war, less than 1 percent of Americans owned securities. With war bonds, the figure reached 5 percent in northern states. Largely through Cooke's efforts, the government raised money as fast as it needed the funds, reaching the level of $2 million a day in 1864. Two-thirds of the North's needs were supplied by selling bonds with per-capita sales increasing from under $1 before the war to $75 at the end. The Confederacy could raise only 40 percent of its much lower level of funding.

To raise more revenue, everything in the North was taxed: income over $600 ($12,000 in year 2000 dollars) at 3 percent; income over $10,000 at 5 percent then 10 percent; stamp taxes on legal documents; a real-estate tax; a tax on almost every form of professional license; excise taxes on commodities and livestock; and tolls and receipts for railroads and most forms of transportation. Lincoln and the Republicans even created the first Internal Revenue Service to ensure collection. The income tax was based on the British income tax that financed the Napoleonic Wars and was collected through withholding. The North raised 21 percent of its revenue by taxes: the South raised 6 percent. By the end of the war, taxes in the North were higher than in any other nation. The South was a tax haven with widespread tax evasion.

Both sides funded most of the balance through the printing press—the North raised 11 percent of its money: the South raised over half. This introduced inflation into the markets—prices rose 10 percent annually in the North, and even higher at the end of the war. Inflation was so rampant in the South, in the triple digits, that the well-known term was coined "not worth a confederate dollar." Rampant inflation resulted in a feeling of desperation throughout the entire South, with people making speculators and merchants the scapegoats.

As a financial center, New York City profited enormously, setting up a gold exchange to meet the requirement that tariffs be paid in gold, developing bond trading to finance the war debt, and supplying stocks and capital to the firms profiting from war expenditures. New exchanges opened up to handle all of the business. Much of the money raised went into industrial corporations. Capital for these firms was raised on Wall Street, and profits were reinvested to meet additional capital needs. Wall Street financiers experienced an unprecedented boom and luxuriated in great wealth, a stark contrast to the many who were fighting and dying on the battlefield.[33] In 1865, Wall Street as a financial center was second only to London, reaching $6 billion in transactions.

Freed of opposition from states-rights southerners, Lincoln presided over what is arguably the greatest transfer of power from the states to the federal government, with the possible exception of Franklin Roosevelt's presidency. Besides the broad economic powers used to fund and carry out the war, Lincoln and his Civil War government established a system of land-grant colleges, encouraged immigration, and gave away vast tracts of frontier land to settlers and for the transcontinental railroad. A veterans' pension program was started; funding for the pensions increased from 2 percent of federal spending during the war to 29 percent by 1884. Farmers were granted a bigger voice in government by creation of a cabinet-level Department of Agriculture. A Department of Education was established, albeit not until 1867. Washington, D.C., tripled in size during the war, and civilian employment increased four fold. The large military force that was established served the nation for several generations, eventually being used to fight Indians and break strikes. An economic infrastructure was developed, including banks, markets, and railroads, providing the foundation to further the Industrial Revolution after the war.

Lincoln's Leadership

During the war, Lincoln and his cabinet provided strong, visionary leadership. While in the White House, Lincoln took no vacation, spending almost every waking hour dealing with the problems of the country. As president, Lincoln spent much of his time among the troops and was extremely popular among the military. He practiced what is now known as "management by wandering around," meeting with generals and officers in their homes and offices and in the field. He visited the sick and wounded in the hospitals. He gained access to key information and was always aware of the big picture.

During the time between his election and inauguration, Lincoln quietly "made the unprecedented decision to incorporate his eminent rivals into his political family, the cabinet . . . evidence of a profound self-confidence and a first indication of what would prove to others a most unexpected greatness." His three major nomination opponents became cabinet officers as did three leaders of the Democratic Party— the strongest men from every major faction. "Every member of this administration was better known, better educated, and more experienced in public life than Lincoln."[34] His competitors became his colleagues, guiding the country through its darkest days.

Over the long term, Lincoln had one of the strongest cabinets, although not all of his choices were stellar. Simon Cameron, his first secretary of war, paid high prices for tainted food, shoddy knapsacks and uniforms, and weapons that blew thumbs off the soldiers who fired them. Cameron pocketed kickbacks for no-bid contracts, proclaiming "An honest politician is one who, when he is bought, will stay bought." While Lincoln fired him for the scandals and violating his express orders, Cameron continued to have a successful political career. When Thaddeus Stevens complained that Cameron would steal anything except a red-hot stove, Lincoln demanded a retraction. Stevens replied, "Mr. President, I now take that back. He would steal a red-hot stove."

Like Lincoln, most of his cabinet led tragic lives. Salomon Chase almost incomprehensibly lost three wives at very young ages, but allowed his beautiful, ambitious, daughter Kate help him to become one of the most lavish hosts in Washington. Edward Stanton saw his young daughter, younger brother, and wife of twenty-nine die of fevers. He wrote his young son a letter of over one hundred pages, so that he would have memories of his mother. At a young age, he was ebullient with a soft and tender personality, but became toughened and an intimidating trial lawyer. Throughout the war, Lincoln and the cabinet faced the outbreak of life-threatening diseases that afflicted their families.

As soon as he was inaugurated, Lincoln became pro-active, even though he had no real previous administrative experience and extremely limited elective experience. If the South were allowed to secede, he believed, it would soon be seeking to add parts of the West and Border States to its slave empire. Without authorization, Lincoln's Secretary of State Seward assured the Confederacy that Fort Sumter, off Charleston, South Carolina, would be abandoned. When five of seven of his cabinet recommended that he do nothing to help Fort Sumter, Lincoln nevertheless sent a naval expedition with food and supplies to relieve it. When the commanding officer Major Robert Anderson did not yield, the fort was fired upon and captured. The decision to attack Fort Sumter by Jefferson Davis and his cabinet was made four years to the day before Lee's surrender at Appomattox. After the fort surrendered, Lincoln immediately asked for 75,000 volunteers. This precipitated a terrible blow to the Union, which was the secession of Virginia, the seat of Revolutionary power. West Virginia then broke off from Virginia and formed a state loyal to the Union. Perhaps most importantly, Virginia's secession resulted in General Robert E. Lee declining Lincoln's offer to become commander-in-chief of the Union forces, resigning his commission, and taking up a command in the rebel forces. The attack on Sumter transformed the North and resulted in a surge of nationalism and anti-southern hatred. Volunteer quotas for troops on both sides were exceeded. The build-up was one of the most rapid and effective ever, roughly five times as fast as World War I. Lincoln acted authoritatively yet cautiously in the early days after Sumter to successfully retain the support of the Border States. He did lose states in the upper South— Virginia, North Carolina, Tennessee, and Arkansas. Lincoln didn't raise the issue of slavery early in his term; fearing he would alienate the Border States, where public sentiment had not matured.

After the surrender of Fort Sumter, the city of Washington was almost deserted and the residents feared Confederate troops would capture it. From the White House, Lincoln could see Confederate flags hanging from buildings across the river in Virginia. Lincoln delayed the convening of Congress for three months and in the interim greatly expanded the armed forces, detained people suspected of disloyal activities, suspended *habeas corpus,* spent funds not appropriated, suspended publication of newspaper stories, and undertook a range of actions that were popular, but exceeded what were generally regarded as presidential powers. No other president, however, had been faced with the dissolution of the Union. In order to keep Maryland in the Union, Lincoln suspended the writ of *habeas corpus,* refused to obey a decision of Chief Justice Taney declaring his actions invalid, jailed thirty-one state legislators, installed federal marshals at the polls to prevent disunionists from voting, and gave Marylanders in the Army three-day furloughs to vote. Lincoln worked to oust the Missouri state government, but heavy-handed tactics resulted in Union troops killing 28 civilians, which converted many Union supporters into secessionists. He placed the state under martial law. Thousands of civilians were imprisoned without procedural safeguards. Lincoln tried these people in military courts or held them without trials. Hundreds of newspapers were suspended for varying lengths of time.[35] Lincoln authorized raids on every telegraph office in the nation, seizing all telegrams sent or received for the previous year or two. Using this information plus that of informers, men were taken from their homes in the dead of night, thrown into jail, and held without communication with the outside world. Republicans were increasingly unpopular and nearly lost control of Congress in 1862 despite the absence of southern Democrats.

The Role of Naval Power

The South's Achilles heel was its maritime inferiority. Few navy officers defected from the Union. The Confederacy started the war with few commercial or war ships. It attempted to build ironclads and other warships overseas, most of which were never delivered because of State

Department intervention and agreements with other nations. Precipitating a long decline in the nation's merchant marine, American ship owners re-flagged their vessels with British colors to make them immune to capture. In 1860, the country's merchant marine shipped over 70 percent of the tonnage clearing American ports, a figure which fell to less than half in 1865 and under a quarter by 1890. One of America's original great industries became a casualty of the war.[36]

The confederacy had 3,500 miles of coastline, 10 major ports, and well over 100 other inlets. The North had only a few war ships and two bases in the South. In the first year of the war, the North was successful in capturing a number of southern ports: Hatteras Inlet in North Carolina, Ship Island in Mississippi, and Port Royal in South Carolina. The North developed innovative tactics to fight battles. Instead of remaining stationary, the ships would steam back and forth past forts in an oval pattern, becoming moving targets. Gradually, the Union navy gained a reputation for invincibility; this demoralized the South. The Rebels, however, did develop sophisticated methods for circumventing the blockade, such as sailing only on moonless nights, burning smoke-less anthracite coal, and using channels without navigation marks to escape by using coded lights to guide the pilots. Gradually, the blockade became more effective: the North seized only one out of ten ships at the beginning of the war, but one out of two by the end. The blockade crippled the southern economy and helped keep France and England out of the war.

Naval power was crucial in the battle for the West. Louisiana and Texas combined had a population and wealth comparable to Virginia's. Mississippi was richer and more populous than South Carolina. General Grant used the transportation revolution to profoundly alter the nature of war. He put 15,000 men on water transports accompanied by gunboats and within 3 days captured Fort Henry. He then forced Fort Donelson to surrender, a crucial battle because it ended the aura of invincibility of the Confederate troops and prevented Great Britain from seriously considering support of the Confederacy.

The North built almost all of America's steamboats and had facilities for repair and maintenance. During the war, the North doubled its production of the merchant marine to a level not exceeded until the twentieth century. A thousand large state-of-the-art steamboats were available to take the Union army deep into the Confederacy by using navigable rivers. The North built a fleet of gunboats, launching the first one in 45 days after it was commissioned. All of the canals, channels, and efforts to eliminate snags became improvements enabling the movement of troops during war. The rivers were more effective transports than the rails—they could not be cut. Twice as much military freight was moved by water as by rail. In the West, northern river power overwhelmed the southern forces.[37] Using the Union's near monopoly on sea power, David Farragut captured New Orleans, the South's greatest city. He ran his fleet past two forts and a gauntlet of barges, rafts, and fire barges on the Mississippi River, forcing the city to surrender and sealing the blockade of the entire South. While leading a fleet into Mobile Bay after a mine had sunk an iron-side ship, Farragut climbed the mast of his ship, the *U.S.S. Hartford,* to see over the smoke and shouted "Damn the torpedoes, full speed ahead!" Several thuds were heard as the ship sailed through the minefield, but none exploded.

The South attempted to defeat the blockade by deploying mines, underwater craft, and ironclad ships like the *Merrimack* (traditionally spelled *Merrimac*), which destroyed 3 ships and killed 250 Union sailors in its first day of terror at sea, precipitating panic in the North. When the Federals evacuated the Norfolk navy yard in the spring of 1861, they left the disabled *Merrimack* behind and did not completely destroy it. The Union only belatedly recognized this threat, but the commissioned ship *Monitor* fortuitously arrived the day after the *Merrimack*'s first engagement. Lincoln himself appears to have made the decision to build the iron-side with its unconventional design by the Swedish engineer John Ericsson. "The *Monitor* was unlike any ship ever built, for Ericsson intentionally made it as innovative as possible; it was said that it contained at least fifty 'patentable inventions.' In form it really was more submarine than ship, with the only thing protruding above the water being its pilothouse and steam-powered gun turret, with twin eleven-inch Dahlgren guns, the most advanced in the U.S. Navy. The twenty-one-foot diameter turret was round to deflect shots off its eight-inch-thick armor plate."[38] The key innovative feature of the *Monitor* was the turret system of mounting guns that could reach every point of the compass and enabled the armor to be concentrated and harder to pierce. The one day battle between these two ships was one of the most momentous in history, rendering current navies of the world obsolete. The Union soon produced a whole fleet of these ironclad ships.

Emancipation and Turning Point

Lincoln believed emancipation could be achieved through gradualism and compensation to slave owners. His opposition to slavery came within the bounds of the Constitution, which sanctioned it, whereas the abolitionists were purists. The radicalism of the abolitionists, however, was an essential ingredient in ending slavery. Lincoln was able to harness this energy by first favoring the Union. Once convinced the Union would be preserved, he then moved to free the slaves. His Emancipation Proclamation, issued five days after the victory at Antietam, was the most revolutionary document since the Declaration of Independence. It became effective January 1, 1863. The Emancipation Proclamation did not liberate any slaves in the Border States or areas the Union had already conquered. It did offer freedom to those who fled to Union lines. The Proclamation had a strong positive impact on world opinion and helped keep European nations from assisting the South. It was not helpful, however, to the Republicans running for Congress in November. The 1862 elections went against the prosecution of the war and enlistments dropped to almost nothing, forcing the use of the contentious draft. During the war, many slaves resisted their owner by engaging in what amounted to a general strike and many northerners were radicalized against slavery. The Emancipation Proclamation recognized what had already been achieved on the battlefield. The Union generals clearly saw that the war had, for all practical purposes, already ended slavery, General Grant noting, "Slavery is already dead and cannot be resurrected" and Sherman concluding, "All the powers of earth cannot restore them their slaves any more than their dead grandfathers."[39]

The turning point of the war was the battle at Gettysburg, the inspiration for Lincoln's famous address. Lee invaded the North in an effort to score a knockout blow. Only three days earlier, General George Meade had taken control of the 97,000-man Union Army. The bloodiest battle of the war and possibly the most desperate fight that had ever taken place: Gettysburg's casualties totaled more than 50,000 men.

On November 19, 1863, Lincoln traveled to Gettysburg to dedicate the new Union cemetery. The featured speaker was Edward Everett of Massachusetts, a diplomat, clergyman, and celebrated orator. The president was invited to offer a few remarks. Everett spoke for not quite two hours. Then Lincoln rose. Presuming the president could be counted on to go on for a while, a local photographer took his time focusing, but Lincoln spoke just 269 words. He started off by reminding his audience that just eighty-seven years had passed since the founding of the nation, and then went on to embolden the Union cause with some of the most stirring words ever spoken. Lincoln was heading back to his seat before the photographer could open the shutter.

Lincoln understood there had been no successful democracy in the history of the world on the scale of the United States. No large democracy had ever extended voting rights to the extent America had by 1860. The French Revolution and the major democratic uprisings in the first half of the nineteenth century had failed or been suppressed. Lincoln was wrestling with what he saw as a truly fragile experiment, which, if it failed would take with it the hopes of every common, ordinary person on the planet. He struggled with the question of whether there is some fatal flaw in popular, democratic government that dooms it to failure. He had that sense he was an extension of the original settlers and the Declaration of Independence. Like John Adams, he understood that the American Revolution occurred in the hearts and minds of American colonials long before the Revolutionary War.

> Lincoln repeatedly made a similar argument in his great speeches from 1857 on. America was a nation built on political ideals, set forth notably in the Declaration. This explains why he saw in slavery such an enormous threat. It was more than an odious institution which wreaked great

harm on those subject to it. National acceptance of the ideas underlying slavery, of the sort Chief Justice Roger Taney urged in his majority opinion in *Scott v. Sanford*—would entirely destroy the nation founded on the Declaration's ideals. American nationality was primarily a moral idea, not the result of a legal writ.[40]

Lincoln believed the establishment of America to be a radical break with the past, a new civilization based on ideas and principles, not on ancestry. Lincoln recognized America as an experiment in the concept that each individual person is as important as a king. He understood that America is about the survival of the idea that free men and women have every right to govern themselves and this is the heart, the crux of whether the entire human race would revert back to monarchy and aristocracies with common people being dictated to, or would, in fact, prove that freedom can work.

Lincoln's Gettysburg address and the image of thousands of troops in Gettysburg graves resulted in a spiritual awakening. While not a firm believer in or member of an institutional church, Lincoln read the Bible almost daily and understood its hold over the imagination of the American people. He concluded that the Almighty had placed him in the presidency as a humble instrument of God's will. His evolving faith in God was developed with the assistance of Quakers, enabling him to not just "save" the Union but recreate it as a much stronger, more cohesive Union than before.[41] Many references in the Gettysburg Address are biblical and represent a description of America then at its most important turning point. Lincoln provided transcendent meaning and force to democracy, helping to ensure its triumph.

Grant's Leadership

During the Gettysburg campaign, Ulysses S. Grant was finishing off his western campaign with victories at Vicksburg and Chattanooga. His risky, brilliant strategy to besiege Vicksburg, which even Sherman believed was close to lunacy, was also a turning point. The back-to-back victories at Vicksburg and Gettysburg ensured that European nations would not intervene on behalf of the Confederacy. On July 4, news of those victories swept across the North. General George Thomas also distinguished himself in the West, becoming the only Union general to drive the Confederates from a fortified position in a complete rout and doing this twice at Nashville and Chattanooga, earning the name "Rock of Chickamauga." By capturing Chattanooga, Generals Grant and Thomas destroyed the Confederates east-west communications system.

Grant then moved east to command the Army of the Potomac to eventual victory. His philosophy of combat was reflected in his nickname gained from his courageous siege of Fort Donelson, Unconditional Surrender. He believed that, "the art of war is simple enough. . . . Find out where your enemy is, get at him as soon as you can, and strike him as hard as you can, and keep moving on." Grant failed in his battle with alcohol, as a farmer, an engineer, a clerk, and even as a debt-collector. At the start of the war, he was in debt, a drunk, yet responsible for a wife and four children. The war liberated Grant and changed his life. Although a failure as a civilian, he had a great organizational and military mind. When informed about Grant's weakness for alcohol, Lincoln is rumored to have said: "If I knew his brand, I'd send a barrel or so to some other generals."

> He was not impressive to look at. He was a small man on a big horse, with an ill-kept, scrappy beard, a cigar clamped between his teeth, a slough hat, an ordinary soldier's overcoat. But there was nothing slovenly about his work. He thought hard. He planned. He gave clear orders and saw to it they were obeyed, and followed up. His handling of movements and supplies was always meticulous. His Vicksburg campaign, though daring, was a model of careful planning, beautifully executed. But he was also a killer. A nice man, he gave no mercy in war until the battle was won. Lincoln loved him, and his letters to Grant are marvels of sincerity, sense, brevity, fatherly wisdom, and support. In October 1863, Lincoln gave Grant supreme command in the West, and in March 1864 he put him in charge of the main

front, with the title of General-in-Chief of the Union army and the rank of lieutenant-general, held by no one since Washington and specially revived in Grant's favor by a delighted Congress.[42]

Grant's communications skills were one of his more underrated traits. Not only was he a clear and concise writer, he was in constant contact with his troops and almost invariably knew more than anyone else about what was happening on a battlefield. He was one of the best riders in the army and would sometimes scurry around a battlefield on horseback to glean the best intelligence. He set a pace no staff officer could match, riding as if he and the horse were one, leaving trailers many yards behind. When he rode the lines, men would gape in awe. Grant created a communications network linking each military unit with his headquarters. Later in the war, he would string telegraph wires to his forward positions on the battlefield, keeping in constant contact with the latest fighting. Grant used aerial reconnaissance by combining the balloon with the telegraph. Reels of wire were mounted on mules and a wagon was provided with a telegraph operator, battery, and telegraph instruments for each unit. Wagons were loaded with light poles and iron spikes to string the telegraph. As soon as a military unit went into camp, it would put up the wires. By communicating clearly and knowing more than anyone else, Grant could command the battlefield.

Grant did not merely rely on technology and his equestrian skills, he built a phenomenal intelligence network. General Phil Sheridan, who single-handedly turned around the battle of Cedar Creek in the most exemplary case of battlefield leadership in the war, created an entire organization of scouts, sometimes dressed as Confederate officers, other times pretending to be displaced farmers or roving horse doctors. They routinely rode through Confederate lines, even speaking the same dialects, gleaning information about troop strength, position, provisions, and where the enemy was headed. They were a wild, reckless crew, but gave the Union superb intelligence.[43]

By contrast, General George McClellan, whom Lincoln eventually relieved of his command, always found an excuse not to attack or move his army, because he believed he was greatly outnumbered. His intelligence reports came by and large from Allan Pinkerton who reported detail down to the last digit but whose reports were almost always wrong. The entire officers corps believed the Confederates had a huge advantage in numbers and this belief became the basis for extreme caution. The Union officers could have conducted their own reconnaissance, but did not. A Washington quartermaster scanned the Richmond newspapers and made a more accurate estimate, but he was ignored.[44]

Until appointing Grant, Lincoln had tried unsuccessfully to imbue a number of Union generals with the leadership skills to command the Army of the Potomac, but they all failed. By contrast, the South had superb leadership in Generals Lee and Stonewall Jackson. Lee was skillful at appointing generals with great personal strengths and at effectively utilizing those strengths. "[A] story about General Robert E. Lee illustrates the meaning of making strength productive. One of his generals, the story goes, had disregarded orders and had thereby completely upset Lee's plans—and not for the first time either. Lee, who normally controlled his temper, blew up in a towering rage. When he had simmered down, one of his aides asked respectfully, 'Why don't you relieve him of his command?' Lee, it is said, turned around in complete amazement, looked at the aide, and said, 'What an absurd question—he performs.'"[45] Stonewall Jackson may have been an even better leader than Lee but was killed during battle at Chancellorsville. The South won only one major battle after his death. Jackson gave his men a feeling of invincibility and was able to get the extra mile out of them. Nobody could get their men to march greater distances and when they arrived at the battlefield, Jackson would often immediately hurl them into combat until every effort had been made to gain victory. He gave all of the credit to God and Providence, attempting to avoid fighting on Sunday at all costs. He was eccentric, a loner, but he had a great sense of strategy, and his forces made some of the greatest marches in human history. He was not infallible, having fought poorly at the Seven Days Battle in the Peninsula campaign. Nobody in the war was more feared by the enemy or treated with a greater sense of awe by his own men.

Colonel John Mosby was one of the most feared of all the Confederate cavalry leaders. His guerrilla raids behind Union lines caused him to be so hated that any of his men who were captured were shot. On a night-raid, he allegedly discovered union General Edwin Stoughton in an illicit relationship and woke him up, causing the general to demand "Do you know who I am, sir?" To which Mosby replied "Do you know Mosby, General?" Stoughton queried, "Yes! Have you got the rascal?" Mosby replied: "No, but he has got you."[46]

Confederate General Nathan Bedford Forrest had twenty-nine or thirty horses shot from under him and killed over thirty men in hand-to-hand combat. He is regarded as an authentic military genius, a born soldier, probably the most feared cavalry commander of the war and a master of the lightning strike. The only time during the conflict he was surprised in battle, by a rear attack, he rallied his men to charge in both directions. Sherman called him the most remarkable man the Civil War produced on either side. George Barnhart Zimplemen of the Texas Rangers went through more than four hundred battles and skirmishes.

The war also produced many of the nation's future leaders. In a June 1864 battle near Lynchburg, Virginia, a former vice-president of the United States, Confederate General John C. Breckinridge, faced two of the six future presidents in Union uniform—General Rutherford B. Hayes and Major William McKinley (the four other future presidents were U.S. Grant, Chester Arthur, James Garfield, and Benjamin Harrison). Seven future members of the Supreme Court fought, four for the Union (including Oliver Wendell Holmes) and three for the Confederacy.

Throughout most of the war, there was a general lack of leadership in the Army of the Potomac, which arrived late to almost every key battle. In the military, generals are rarely disciplined for being just a little late. In the first major battle, the Union Army initially routed the Confederates, but reached Bull Run so late there was sufficient time for enemy reinforcements to arrive by rail. During the peninsula campaign, McClellan was at the gates of Richmond but hesitated to attack and, by the time he did, Stonewall Jackson's corps had arrived to reinforce Lee's army. General Burnside outmaneuvered Lee and was ready to cut him off by crossing the Rappahannock, but the pontoons he had ordered to cross at Fredericksburg didn't arrive in time because someone neglected to tell the supply command their provision was urgent. Burnsides' pontoons were six days late in getting started because a supply officer put the order in the mail instead of relaying the request by telegraph. By the time the pontoons arrived, Lee was well-entrenched and the ensuing battle was a disastrous defeat for the northern forces. Lee's army was twice allowed to escape southwards after decisive defeats at Antietam and Gettysburg. Grant's big attack at Cold Harbor was to take place at dawn when the Confederates were off balance but never occurred until they were well-entrenched the next morning. If the Union troops had moved rapidly on Petersburg instead of hesitating when confronted with Confederate works that looked formidable but were devoid of soldiers, the siege would have been averted and the war might have been six months shorter.

A glaring example of this non-leadership occurred during the Petersburg siege. Pennsylvania coal miners came up with the scheme of tunneling under the Confederate earthworks. A lengthy tunnel was dug and a huge powder keg prepared. At the last minute, the Union generals changed the original plan of sending in African-American troops without combat experience, because the undertaking was risky and it could subsequently be argued that they had been callously sacrificed. Instead, the most under-strength division was sent in first with a lackluster general and the weakest brigade put in front. The explosion was enormous, but occurred two hours late. The entire hillside—cannon, men, and earthworks—flew up into the troops waiting to attack, causing them to scatter. By the time the Union troops were re-organized, the Confederates began to recover. One of the federal generals in charge was drunk and the other stayed far from the scene of the battle. The federal units ran in a state of confusion into the gargantuan hole that had been created, where they became sitting ducks for the Confederate gunnery. Even though General Grant had ordered the men back to their positions, the Union generals continued to send in troops, including the African-American unit, long after the huge gap in the Confederate line was closed, resulting in huge numbers of casualties. Grant called it the "saddest affair I have witnessed in the war. Such an opportunity for carrying fortifications I have never seen and do not expect again to have."[47] At one point, Lincoln, Stanton, and Chase became so disgusted with their military leaders, they took matters in their own hands and directed the capture of Norfolk by circumventing the chain of command.

Grant adopted a two-pronged strategy. General Sherman would march through Georgia destroying the economic links of the Deep South and east-west communications. Thousands of white southerners and slaves joined Sherman's march to sea. Sherman's efforts would have been much more difficult, if southern strategy and conscription had not removed most military-age males from the Deep South. Sherman did not have to fear unconventional or irregular warfare and destroyed over $100 million in property and freed 40,000 slaves. Despite his reputation for being ruthless, Sherman suffered nominal casualties and killed few southerners. Both Grant and Lee suffered far higher losses, but didn't receive the same stigma. Sherman had a firm grasp of the relationship between the industrial economy and the ability to make war, thoroughly sacking cities such as Atlanta and Meridian, Mississippi. Almost as much as Grant, he was responsible for bringing an end to the war. In Sherman's march through South Carolina, Confederate General Joe Johnston watched his "progress, unbelieving; and when he saw Sherman's army bridging rivers, building roads across swamps, and wading through flooded backwaters making just as much time as it had made on the dry roads of Georgia, he wrote that 'I made up my mind that there had been no such army in existence since the days of Julius Caesar.'"[48]

As the second part of his strategy, Grant would move forward clearing the Wilderness region west of Fredericksburg in preparation for an assault on Richmond and Lee's army. His goal was not only to capture Richmond, but to fight Lee's army until it had no fight left. Grant pushed forward at The Battle of the Wilderness, Spotsylvania, and Cold Harbor, taking 50,000 casualties, but costing Lee 20,000, a precursor of the trench warfare in World War I. During the fighting at Spotsylvania, Grant proclaimed, "I propose to fight it out on this line if it takes all summer." He was considered a butcher, but his casualties were a smaller percentage than Lee's at Gettysburg. At key junctures, he relied on Sheridan, the hard-charging cavalry general, to ensure that the Army of the Potomac did not continue to show up late for key engagements. Grant's leadership was crucial in inspiring troops to re-enlist in early 1864 when they were entitled to go home. Even though his army sustained horrifying casualties, he made the difficult decision to keep pressing on, refusing to admit defeat. He laid siege to Petersburg, freed Richmond, and secured Lee's surrender at Appomattox.

The End of the War

With his unique perspective and perseverance, Lincoln was successful in leading America from a slave-owning society to one of free citizens, even though society remained bound by human prejudice. The outcome of the war was in doubt as late as the 1864 election, a referendum on whether the North should continue fighting the war to unconditional victory. After three years of war:

> What had the North to show for this staggering carnage? Stalemate at Petersburg; stalemate in the West; a small Confederate army under Jubal Early rampaging through Maryland to the very outskirts of Washington; even in Georgia, Sherman's war of maneuver seemed to have bogged down in the steamy trenches before Atlanta. "Who shall revive the withered hopes that bloomed at the opening of Grant's campaign?" asked the leading Democratic newspaper, *The New York World.* "STOP THE WAR!" shouted Democratic headlines. "All are tired of this damnable tragedy. . . . If nothing else would impress upon the people the absolute necessity of stopping this war, its utter failure to accomplish any results would be sufficient." Republicans joined the chorus of despair. "Our bleeding, bankrupt, almost dying country . . . longs for peace," Horace Greeley told Lincoln, "shudders at the prospect of . . . further wholesale devastations of new rivers of human blood." The veteran Republican leader Thurlow Weed observed in August that

"the people are wild for peace. . . . Lincoln's reelection is an impossibility."[49]

The entire southern war strategy was geared toward securing a Democratic victory in the November election and the Confederate secret service undertook a concerted effort to sway northern opinion. Although Lincoln was re-nominated almost unanimously in June, by August some Republicans wanted to dump him.

> Lincoln was well aware of his probable fate in November. "I am going to be beaten," he told a friend in August, "and unless some great change takes place, *badly* beaten." On August 23, the President wrote his famous "blind memorandum" and asked his cabinet members to endorse it sight unseen: "This morning, as for some days past, it seems exceedingly probable that this Administration will not be re-elected. Then it will be my duty to so cooperate with the President elect, as to save the Union between the election and the inauguration; as he will have secured his election on such ground that he can not possibly save it afterwards."[50]

Lincoln's race against former Army General George McClellan was one of the nastiest in American history. It had been over three decades since a president had been re-elected. Some Americans believed a two-term presidency was a step backwards toward monarchy and away from true republicanism and democratic values. Lincoln was regarded by parts of the news media as a joke and a mere rail-splitter. During the campaign, he was called just about every possible bad name, a tactic which the Republicans reciprocated. Two reporters for the *New York World* issued a pamphlet claiming that Lincoln advocated miscegenation and other racial mixing. Divine Providence once again intervened. Sherman captured Atlanta; Sheridan scored a series of spectacular victories over Jubal Early in the Shenandoah; and Grant advanced on Richmond.

Lincoln's second Inaugural Address may have been his greatest speech, as he urged the nation to finish the struggle. When he appeared on the platform to begin the speech, the sun, which had been hidden all day, suddenly burst forth. At this juncture, Lincoln towered over the American scene, an almost complete turnaround in six months. His moral stature and intellectual strength were without peer: he acted on principle, always trying to do the right thing.

Whatever opinion Southerners held about the sinfulness of slavery, President Lincoln certainly felt that the bloody Civil War was the nation's atonement. His second inaugural address in early 1865 was filled with Biblical imagery. "Fondly do we hope, fervently do we pray, that this mighty scourge of war may speedily pass away," said the President. "Yet, if God will that it continue until all the wealth piled by the bondsman's two hundred and fifty years of unrequited toil shall be sunk, and until every drop of blood drawn with the lash shall be paid by another drawn with the sword, as it was said three thousand years ago, so still it must be said, "the judgments of the Lord are true and righteous altogether."

But Lincoln's inaugural also held out the promise of lenient terms for the defeated South. "With malice toward none, with charity for all, with firmness in the right as God gives us to see the nation's right, let us strive on to finish the work we are in, to bind up the nation's wounds, to care for him who shall have borne the battle and for his widow and his orphan, to do all which may achieve and cherish a just and lasting peace among ourselves and with all nations."[51]

Lincoln was magnanimous in what seemed then almost certain victory. He did not presume that the moral high ground belonged only to the North. Lincoln believed that God ruled over all events, but that the United States or the North might not be a uniquely chosen nation and universal standards of justice were of greater consequence. The ways of God or providence might not be immediately clear and might even be ultimately obscure. A stark contrast could be drawn between Lincoln and the religious theologians:

Abraham Lincoln, a layman with no standing in a church and no formal training as a theologian, propounded a thick, complex view of God's rule over the world and a morally nuanced picture of America's destiny. The country's best theologians, by contrast, presented a thin, simple view of God's providence and a morally juvenile view of the nation and its fate.

The theologians talked as if God had accomplished all that had been done, yet they assumed that humans could control their own destinies. Lincoln urged his fellow citizens to seize the opportunities of the moment but did not assume that they could control their own fate. For the theologians there was little mystery in how God dealt with the world; for Lincoln there was awesome mystery. For the theologians, God's power remained securely tethered to the interests of the United States, however differently that interest was perceived. But for Lincoln, God's power was controlled by no one but God.[52]

The Civil War, arguably, was without parallel for human suffering. There were more than 600,000 deaths. Confederate prisons were themselves a death sentence. Civil War hospitals were bloodier than the battlefield. The majority of surgeries were amputations, some of them unnecessary. Walt Whitman, whose poetry described the devastation of the Civil War, visited 600 hospitals and more than 100,000 men. One temporary hospital housed 70,000 casualties. The estimated cost of the Civil War ran into the billions of dollars, far exceeding the worth all of the slave property in the entire country and many times the value of all slaves. Including pensions, the cost of approximately $10 billion far exceeded the amount that would have been necessary to buy the freedom of the 4 million slaves of the census of 1860. The equivalent loss of life and property in today's terms would be more than 10 million dead and a cost of several trillion dollars. Yet, few wars have had as revolutionary an outcome as the Civil War—the liberation of 4 million slaves.

Lincoln visited Grant while the siege of Petersburg was being broken. He visited Richmond shortly after it fell. African-American workmen recognized him, hailed him as the Messiah, fell on their knees, and kissed his feet. Lincoln quickly retorted "Don't kneel to me. That is not right. You must kneel to God only, and thank him for the liberty you will hereafter enjoy." Throngs of former slaves soon surrounded him.[53]

Grant gracefully accepted Lee's surrender, allowing southern officers to keep their side arms and horses. Grant traveled to Washington to give his account, but Lincoln was gone, assassinated. John Wilkes Booth plotted to kill not only Lincoln, but Vice President Andrew Johnson and several cabinet officers. Lincoln was assassinated on Good Friday and thousands of African Americans from far away journeyed days to Illinois for the Springfield funeral, knowing "that their greatest friend was passing to his rest and the future seemed dark to their vision."[54] When Lincoln died, Stanton famously observed that he now belonged to the ages. The Russian writer Leo Tolstoy concluded that although Lincoln was not a great general like Washington, he "was a humanitarian as broad as the world. He was bigger than his country—bigger than all the Presidents together."[55]

> The American Civil War was the first great conflict of the industrial age. Indeed it was the greatest military event of the hundred years that came between the fall of Napoleon and World War I, fought on a scale previously unimaginable and foreshadowing the desperate global struggles of the early twentieth century.[56]

The North achieved an historic victory, conquering a territory greater than all of Western Europe against fierce opposition.

Reconstruction

One of the tragic outcomes of the Civil War was the extent to which the war destroyed or weakened civil society in both the North and the South. Powerful forces had been unleashed. Families were shattered by the divisions caused by the war and the many deaths, both military and civilian. Many community and neighborhood organizations simply ceased functioning. The war, nevertheless, greatly strengthened industrial institutions such as the large corporation, the factory system, and the private entrepreneur. These institutions encroached upon the weakened civil society. The focus of work moved out of the family into the factory and into private businesses. New industries and corporations required employees to work long hours, reducing the time that might have been spent to bolster the institutions of civil society. Increasing concentrations of industrial workers created slums, crime-infested neighborhoods, and corrupt cities. The real victors were capitalism and the industrialists who profited from the war or were able to leverage their wealth in the explosive economic growth that followed in the North and West. The defeat of the South and the ensuing industrialization resulted in a less diverse and more homogeneous society. The loss of diversity was tragic, but the sense of unity was a plus. Before the war, people would say "the United States are;" after the war, they would say "the United States is."

> The war had changed America profoundly. "The contest touches everything and leaves nothing as it found it," as a New York Times editorial saw it in October 1867. "Great rights, great interests, great systems of habit and of thought disappear during its progress. It leaves us a different people in everything." Two years later Professor George Ticknor of Harvard observed that the Civil War had opened a "great gulf between what happened before in our century and what has happened since, or what is likely to happen hereafter. It does not seem to be as if I were living in the country in which I was born."[57]

Before his death, Lincoln had already provided for liberal pardons, procedures for the establishment of new governments in the South, and the end of slavery in Border States and fugitive slave laws. Lincoln supported the Thirteenth Amendment prohibiting slavery, but he did not live to see the states ratify it. Originally, the amendment failed to garner the required two-thirds vote in the House of Representatives due to unanimous opposition from the Democrats. In the November 1864 elections, Republicans gained enough seats to pass the amendment and Lincoln undertook a massive effort to lobby swing Democrats to pass it before the new Congress convened. The Supreme Court and many Senators watched the historic vote. Lincoln favored clemency for the South, the most lenient position. He had issued a proclamation restoring suffrage to everyone who had taken an oath of loyalty and provided for statehood when 10 percent of the voters had taken the oath.

The South was in ruins, although reports of damage from the fighting were somewhat exaggerated. The agricultural economy was devastated by the loss of slave labor and many men absent during the war, which resulted in land and machinery being neglected. Most of the social and economic systems in the South were destroyed. The financial institutions that had provided farm credit were gone. The average wealth of farm operators fell by over 90 percent and the value of land by over 50 percent. Within a decade, cotton production returned to pre-war levels, but the world market price declined, particularly because of larger crops of cotton from Egypt and India. Southern farmers failed to adjust by planting other crops.[58] Until the middle of the twentieth century, the South didn't fully recover.

President Andrew Johnson did not have the authority Lincoln had enjoyed nor an electoral mandate. He was also from the South. During the war, Johnson was the only Senator from the South to remain in the Senate and was the Union's wartime governor of Tennessee between 1862 and 1864. He initially favored lenient Reconstruction policies, including emancipation, restoration of property rights, and amnesty and pardon for those who took an oath to the Union. His policies were, however, erratic. He failed to give the South the needed assurances and he alienated the Radical Republicans, who controlled Congress.

Johnson tried to prosecute Jefferson Davis, Robert E. Lee, and others for war crimes, but Grant had made a commitment to leniency and threatened to resign after a federal grand jury indicted them. Johnson was eventually forced into proclaiming an unconditional amnesty. While Johnson was more magnanimous than the Radical Republicans, he believed African Americans were not capable of self-government, whites alone must rule in the South, and Radical Republicans were traitors. Johnson even implied that Lincoln's assassination had been part of God's plan to make him president.

President Johnson flip-flopped on an earlier commitment to govern the seceded states like conquered states. Under his protection, the initial southern state governments were almost indistinguishable from their Confederate predecessors. Nearly all the congressmen elected by those governments were ex-Confederates. Refusing to admit members from southern states who were mostly holdovers from a South dominated by slavery, the Radical Republicans kept control of Congress and appointed their own committee to oversee Reconstruction and prevent moderate Republicans and Democrats from watering down their revolutionary proposals.

People in the southern states were not willing to treat African Americans as equals, even though most of them had been loyal to their masters during the war. Southerners gave in to emancipation, but would not accept equality, because they assumed that free Negroes would be an inferior caste, which is how they were actually treated in most parts of the North. Even the Radical Republicans did not support social equality; legal equality was as far as they would go.

Southerners attempted to enact "black codes" severely curtailing the rights of African Americans. Southern states passed harsh laws reducing free slaves to a state of "slaves without masters;" this included: limiting their freedom of movement; forbidding their association with some classes of people; subjecting them to discipline and surveillance; abolishing their legal rights; requiring them to work certain jobs; and submitting them to penal labor almost without cause. African Americans were arrested for vagrancy, required to pay a large fine, and then forced to work until the fine and court costs were paid. They were usually not allowed to hold office or vote. Freed slaves clamored for more schools, teachers, and books, but they were taught in inferior schools or sometimes not at all. Education was actually discouraged and literacy rates for whites and African Americans declined. Slave owners would claim children that couldn't be cared for by making them indentured servants. In Mississippi, African Americans were paid only once a year, but could be fired just before they were to be compensated. In Virginia and Louisiana, African Americans who refused any offer of work could be flogged and hired out in chain-gangs. In Alabama, they could be forcibly hired out for six months at a time.[59] The federal government banned imprisonment or enslavement for debts, but the southern governments prosecuted African Americans for attempting to defraud creditors. The plight of African Americans in many southern jurisdictions was little better than under slavery.

Under laws enacted specifically to intimidate former slaves, tens of thousands of African Americans were arbitrarily arrested, hit with high fines, and charged for the costs of their own arrests. These court costs constituted much of the income for southern law enforcement officials running these kangaroo court systems. With no means to pay these ostensible debts, prisoners were sold as forced laborers to coal mines, lumber camps, railroads, quarries, brickyards, and farm plantations. These prisoners were

> subject to the whip for failure to dig the requisite amount [of coal], at risk of physical torture for disobedience, and vulnerable to the sexual predations of other miners—many of whom already had passed years or decades in their own chthonian confinement. The lightless catacombs of black rock, packed with hundreds of desperate men slick with sweat and coated with pulverized coal, must have exceeded any vision of a hell a boy born in the countryside of Alabama—even a child of slaves—could have ever imagined.[60]

Operating as an American Gulag, African Americans would simply disappear into the system, never to be heard of again. The intimidation spread sheer terror through the African-American community. A loved one could simply be snatched in broad daylight or the middle of the night and never be heard from again. This system was, in some respects, worst than slavery, because the white southerners had no financial interest in their captives and no incentive to prevent their death or disability. Hundreds died without any record of their deaths. Thousands of African Americans were simply seized by southern landowners and compelled into years of involuntary servitude. Government officials leased falsely imprisoned African Americans to small-town businessmen, provincial farmers, and major corporations. Armies of these African Americans were repeatedly bought and sold, and were forced through beatings and physical torture to do the bidding of white masters for decades after the official abolition of American slavery, even as late as World War II. Efforts by the federal government to bring an end to this system were met with a fierce opposition reminiscent of the violent attitude toward abolition prior to the Civil War.[61]

White resistance to African-American voting and reconstruction of the South resulted in violence and formation of secret, hostile, organizations such as the Ku Klux Klan. Confederates channeled their energies into paramilitary groups such as the Klan, Knights of the White Camellia, the White Brotherhood, and other militant organizations. With the blessing of General Robert E. Lee, Confederate General Nathan Bedford Forrest was chosen as the Grand Wizard of the Klan. As an agent of the Democratic Party, the Klan would assassinate and intimidate southern Republicans. The Klan, for example, followed up an attack on a Republican Party meeting in Louisiana with the murder of hundreds of African Americans in the area. Atrocities were routinely committed against African Americans, including mutilation and mass hangings. Lynchings reached record levels in the years immediately following the Civil War. Between 1877 and 1966, only one white man was found guilty in Georgia of killing an African-American man despite dozens of lynchings and hundreds of unexplained deaths.[62] Over 100 African Americans were killed in one incident in Louisiana, but no one went to jail for the crime. The Supreme Court overturned the verdicts of the only three who were convicted. The Klan initiated a reign of terror throughout much of the South, murdering more than 150 African Americans in one year in a single Florida county, killing hundreds in the area surrounding New Orleans, and precipitating race riots in Mississippi and Arkansas.

America gave free land to immigrants in the West, but the land available in the South for African Americans was often not suitable for agriculture. Instead of breaking up the plantations as proposed by the Radical Republicans, African Americans were forced to become sharecroppers, in effect being bound as if they were serfs. After overwhelmingly defeating the efforts of the Radical Republicans to provide freed-men land from plantations and estates, Congress passed a bill to enlarge the Freedmen's Bureau to protect former slaves from discrimination. President Johnson vetoed even this mild reform and his veto was sustained. Congress then passed a civil rights bill which spelled out rights to be enjoyed equally without regard to race, including making contracts, bringing lawsuits, and "enjoying security of person and property." It applied not only to the South, but also to the North where discriminatory laws were still in force. Johnson vetoed this bill as well, but was overridden, the first major legislation in American history enacted over the objections of the president.[63]

The Radical Republicans continued to press Johnson and secured a veto-proof Congress with sweeping victories at the polls in 1866. The Fourteenth Amendment to the Constitution, the equal protection clause, provided the eventual basis for desegregation. The South refused to ratify the Fourteenth Amendment, bringing on an impasse and driving the moderate Republicans towards the position of the radicals. The Fourteenth Amendment prohibited states from abridging "the privileges or immunities of citizens" or depriving "any person of life, liberty or property, without due process of law." The amendment voided all Confederate war debts and claims for compensation for emancipated slaves. The Congress enacted the Reconstruction Act and several related measures, all over Johnson's veto. The Reconstruction Act divided the South into five military districts and required each state to ratify the Fourteenth Amendment and establish a constitution providing for rights for slaves in order to regain self-rule and congressional representation.

The radicals passed many forms of far-reaching legislation, stripping the Supreme Court of jurisdiction over *habeas corpus* cases and severely limiting the president's ability to remove officers. When President Johnson tried to replace his secretary of war and most of the military commanders in charge of Reconstruction in the South, he was impeached and only survived by one vote in the trial in the Senate. The fallout from impeachment shifted the balance of power from the presidency to the Congress for the remainder of the nineteenth century.

By the time of Grant's election in 1868, six Southern states had been readmitted and had ratified the Fourteenth Amendment, making it part of the Constitution. President Grant played a key role in securing passage of the Fifteenth Amendment, guaranteeing the right of African Americans to vote. Grant believed Reconstruction was the most important issue and was a moral force on equal rights for African Americans. His role in Reconstruction paralleled the role of Washington in founding the country. Grant was widely consulted on Reconstruction legislation and he was extremely fearful of seeing his military gains sacrificed on the altar of political expediency.[64] To facilitate enforcement of the civil rights laws, legislation was created to establish a Department of Justice and to consolidate federal legal authority under the attorney general. Grant proposed and secured passage of legislation to prevent violence against African Americans in the South, particularly by the Ku Klux Klan. Grant then sent troops to enforce the law, occupying parts of the South and suppressing much of the violence. Grant sought to annex Santo Domingo as a haven where African Americans could govern themselves and migrate if they desired, an effort he was harshly criticized for by the press. In his second term, he fought hard for a civil rights law that prohibited racial discrimination in public transportation and accommodations and in jury selection. He was vigorously supported by seven African-American members of congress. As Grant acknowledged, his military intervention in the South was widely criticized, but continued in order to secure equal rights for African Americans and preserve the gains made during the Civil War. He was arguably a more steadfast supporter than any other president over the next eighty years of African Americans and their newly gained rights. He also spoke out and worked hard to gain rights for American Indians.

The effort at Reconstruction is sometimes characterized as a failure or a form of rogue government, but during this period significant progress was actually being made toward equality for African Americans. The Radical Republicans in the Congress had provided the legislative framework to provide equal rights to African Americans, including three constitutional amendments, a number of reconstruction laws, and several civil rights statutes. Southerners used violence, social ostracism, and economic pressure to limit African-American gains and oust "scalawags" (i.e. Southern Republicans) and "carpetbaggers" (i.e. Northerners seeking to take advantage of Reconstruction in the South). African Americans claimed popular majorities in three states and many higher offices including two U.S. Senate seats, but never gained representation in proportion to their numbers. Allied with the "carpetbaggers" and "scalawags," they passed legislation in several states expanding democracy and eliminating archaic features of state laws and constitutions. No significant amount of funding was provided for Reconstruction. At the time, Americans did not believe it was the role of government to tax people and then give the money to someone else for their personal use.

Proponents of Reconstruction became disillusioned as the results fell far short of expectations. "By the 1870s, perception of tragedy, failure, and missed opportunities was ubiquitous."[65] This feeling was most intense among free slaves and abolitionists. Three major factors in the retreat from Reconstruction allowed segregationists to re-establish their supremacy in the South.

First, progress on civil rights legislation was reversed by the courts. An activist Supreme Court repeatedly declared acts of the Reconstruction-era unconstitutional. In five rulings between 1876 and 1906, the Court struck down provisions of congressional statutes designed to guarantee civil rights to African Americans. In the *Civil Rights Cases,* the Court declared unconstitutional the provisions of the Civil Rights Act of 1875 that made it a crime to deny anyone equal access to public accommodations. The Court overturned an anti-conspiracy statute intended to protect blacks from retaliation by the Ku Klux Klan and lynch mobs. The Court also overturned a provision of the Civil Rights Act of 1866 which would have punished state officials for obstructing African Americans from voting. In 1898, the Court upheld literacy tests and poll taxes designed to disenfranchise African Americans. In 1903, the Court refused to intervene in a case involving a blatant denial of the right to vote on racial grounds. The Court struck down a provision of the 1870 Civil Rights Act that gave African

Americans the same right to make and enforce contracts as enjoyed by white citizens.[66] The effect of these decisions was to cripple federal enforcement and help bring an end to Reconstruction.

Homer Plessy was one-eighth black, appeared white, and could have passed as such in most social circumstances. He was arrested boarding a train to challenge a Louisiana law requiring railroads to assign African Americans separate carriages as a violation of the Fourteenth Amendment. The law under which Plessy was prosecuted was absurd, making the railroad conductor the final authority on whether a traveler was white or African American, his eyes being the measure of racial purity. The Supreme Court had already severely curbed the effectiveness of the Civil Rights Act of 1875 by limiting its scope and allowing private individuals to discriminate if they owned restaurants, inns, or theaters. In *Plessy v. Ferguson*, the Court ruled, with only one dissent, that separate but equal public accommodations were constitutional, setting back civil rights for decades. John Harlan, the lone dissenter and a former slave owner, proclaimed, "The destinies of the two races are indissolubly linked together, and the interests of both require that common government of all shall not permit the seeds of race hate to be planted under the sanction of the law." The day the Court decided the *Plessy* case, more than fifty decisions were handed down. Three other decisions were reported on the front page of *The New York Times*. The *Plessy* decision was relegated to page three under railroad news.[67]

In 1890, Mississippi adopted a constitution with a series of tests and qualifications designed specifically to exclude African Americans from voting. In 1894, Congress repealed the statute requiring federal oversight of elections in the South. In a case involving an Alabama law, the Supreme Court upheld restrictions designed to prevent African Americans from voting. The opinion was written by Oliver Wendell Holmes, who was from Massachusetts.

The major impact of the Supreme Court decisions was to encourage segregation to take hold in the South and to end participation of African Americans in southern politics and government. In 1896, McKinley lost at least three southern states as a result of failure to enforce the Fifteenth Amendment. Over 130,000 African Americans did vote in Louisiana in 1900, a figure which plunged over 90 percent by 1904. Little attention was paid to this regression—the northern press barely even covered this issue.[68]

Secondly, the Depression of 1873, which lasted for years, caused the focus of the North to turn from Reconstruction and equal rights for African Americans to economic issues

Thirdly, the election of 1876 effectively ended Reconstruction. New York Governor Samuel Tilden won the popular vote and lost the Electoral College by one vote in a presidential election that arguably was stolen. Rutherford B. Hayes went to bed a defeated candidate and even the headlines the next day declared Tilden the winner. John C. Reid, the managing editor of *The New York Times*, convinced Republican national chairman Zach Chandler that Hayes could win if he swept all the electoral votes in three southern states still occupied by the North—South Carolina, Florida, and Louisiana. The other states had already obtained self-rule—all voted for Tilden. However, almost no African-Americans were allowed to vote in the states where there was controversy and Hayes would have almost certainly won all three states if they had been granted the right of suffrage. The Republican National Committee claimed victory, a boast it stuck to unwaveringly. An Electoral Commission was appointed with fifteen members, but only one member was not closely wedded to the Republican or Democratic parties. He accepted an appointment to the U.S. Senate and his replacement voted to accept all of the Hayes electors and not one committed to Tilden. In order to avoid having the election overturned in the U.S. House of Representatives, Hayes agreed to withdraw occupying troops from the last three southern states, invest in the South's economic development, and bring a "return to normalcy" which was really a euphemism for abrogating African-American rights. Subsequently realizing the effect this had in the South, Hayes devoted much of his time, energy, and money after he left the White House to education for southern African Americans.

Southerners refused to accept the changes in Reconstruction laws and dared the federal government to enforce them. Ultimately, the

South won. By the 1890s, harsh laws were passed and rigid customs imposed. Jim Crow laws were passed in the southern states, initially applying to transportation, because it involved close contact with passengers, frequently overnight and often involving women. Before long, African Americans couldn't do anything without facing some form of government-imposed color bar.

> There were Jim Crow schools, Jim Crow restaurants, Jim Crow water fountains, and Jim Crow customs—blacks were expected to tip their hats when they walked past whites, but whites did not have to remove their hats even when they entered a black family's home. Whites were to be called 'sir' and 'ma'am' by blacks who in turn were called by their first names by whites. People with white skin were to be given a wide berth on the sidewalk; blacks were expected to step aside meekly.[69]

"An uninformed observer of the South in 1910 might well be pardoned if he or she concluded that the Confederates had won the Civil War."[70] A window of opportunity was missed to consummate Lincoln's revolution that would not present itself for another several generations.

8

Edison's
invention factory

EARNING MORE THAN 1,000 U.S. PATENTS, fruit of his innovative inventions, Thomas Edison (1847–1931) personified the entire American industrial revolution, that occurred in the nineteenth and early twentieth centuries. Edison produced more patents than the number that had been issued by the U.S. Patent Office through 1834, that included the cotton gin, steam engine, and all of Benjamin Franklin's many technical projects. By the time he died, Edison's inventions were generating 12 percent of our Gross Domestic Product, and 1 in 8 U.S. jobs were based on his ideas, accounting for the livelihood of 10 million or more Americans. In effect, Edison created an economy greater than the size of California, France, or Italy—collectively twice the size of all federal, state, and local government budgets at the time. More than any other individual, he was responsible for America becoming the world leader in manufacturing by the end of the nineteenth century.

Edison's long, prolific life spanned most of the industrial revolution in America. Born on February 11, 1847, in Milan, Ohio, Edison became a school dropout and at an early age worked for Western Union where he learned to be a telegraphic expert. By developing an invention to double telegraphic capacity, Edison saved Western Union millions of dollars.

No one worked harder—Edison studied books and experimented at all hours of the day and night. His slogan was, "Invention is 1 percent inspiration and 99 percent perspiration." He rarely slept—taking cat naps in a rocking chair while holding iron balls; when he dozed off, just before he reached deep sleep, the balls would crash to the floor, waking him up refreshed. He worked his assistants around the clock. When asked about pay and hours, he would bark out, "We don't pay anything, and we work all the time!"

Henry Ford, his friend and neighbor, called Edison the world's greatest inventor and worst businessman. Edison was taken advantage of in numerous business transactions largely because his focus remained permanently on the next invention. He was hard-of-hearing, but, because of that limitation, he produced a device to brace his mouth on his phonograph invention so that he could feel its vibrations through his teeth and "hear."

Earning the title Wizard of Menlo Park (where he worked in New Jersey), Edison developed the concept of the industrial laboratory. Most early inventors were sole practitioners, but Edison saw the advantage of a more systematic approach. He viewed discoveries as accidents or luck and wanted to emphasize inventions as products of purpose. His goal was to produce a modest invention every ten days and a major one every six months. Edison tried hard to assemble the most competent men and state-of-the-art equipment so as to produce startling new products. By making innovation a systematic process, Edison's work resulted in new industries and he thus produced more national wealth than created by any individual before or since.

"Edison consistently sought technological solutions to business problems. He saw continued innovation as the best means of defeating the competition."[1] His research laboratory or invention factory learned to focus on commercially viable products. He industrialized American ingenuity. Not only did he develop patentable products, but Edison envisioned how to translate them into commercial applications, including their financing and marketing plans. When he and J.P. Morgan worked on forming General Electric in 1892, they established a laboratory in New York State. The Schenectady facility soon became an example for many other corporations—Alexander Graham Bell and George Westinghouse, for example, modeled their research operations after Edison's laboratories.

Edison's success was built on the American nineteenth-century culture that valued manufacturing, entrepreneurship, and innovation. His era was free of the rules, prohibitions, and litigation that have often frustrated present-day inventors and entrepreneurs. By the beginning of the twentieth century, the American manufacturing system was setting standards for the rest of the industrial world. Important new methods had been developed to improve the manufacture of guns, for example. The federal government set up an experimental factory in Harpers Ferry, Virginia, that developed *interchangeable* parts using sophisticated machine tools; this revolutionized gun production. Assembling guns was much faster; damaged parts could be replaced from stock. Each advance became a stepping stone for other new manufacturing technologies. Soon, sewing machines, typewriters, harvesters, reapers, and bicycles were made using interchangeable parts. Creating precision machine tools was an essential part of this process. The importance that society placed on these skills enabled Edison to recruit the people, to develop the processes, and to gain the recognition needed to sell his products and ideas in the marketplace.

The invention that gave Edison the most difficulty was the storage battery, a device perplexing inventors even today—the need to improve battery power is still a critical bottleneck in many industries. After 9,000 experiments, all failures, his assistants tried to discourage him. "Those are not failures," he responded, "Those are 9,000 things we've learned that don't work." After 41,000 more experiments, Edison gave the world the nickel alkaline storage battery, which for more than seventy-five years was used in everything from buses to Navy submarines.

Edison's 1877 invention of the phonograph became a national sensation, making it possible to reproduce a musical presentation. When developing the device, however, Edison believed it would be used to record the last words of dying people, to teach spelling, and to announce clock time—reproduction of music was barely considered. In fact, he declared the product had no commercial value, but then launched an office dictation business, and also, at first, Edison objected to the jukebox as a debasement of his device, detracting from its use in the office. A German immigrant, Emile Berliner, who had already invented a telephone transmitter superior to that of Alexander Graham Bell, developed a method for mass producing phonographic records. Eventually, the phonograph became Edison's personal favorite, because it offered music in every home, and he felt that music, next to religion, truly elevated man more than anything else.

By his invention of the kinetoscope (movie projector), kineto-graph (camera), and kinetophone (a phonograph to capture sound), Thomas Edison gave birth to the motion picture industry. The concept for movies originated with Peter Mark Roget (of thesaurus fame), who had authored a paper in 1824, noting that visual images linger in the eye after a scene changes. If a person were to observe a series of rapidly changing pictures, the lasting image of one picture will form a bridge to the next, creating the sense of continuity and motion. Louis Daguerre had developed the first practical photographs, predecessor of cine-matography and television, changing people's perception of the world and of themselves. He used silver iodide to capture an image on a lens and developed a process to fix the image on a copper plate. Edison was a good friend of George Eastman, who brought revolutionary change to the photography business, developing the handheld camera, simplifying film processing, and supplying Edison with film for his motion picture inventions. Eastman's revolutionary camera enabled anyone to take pic-tures, not just photographers who knew chemistry and could develop film. Peter Juley, a German immigrant, was a pioneer in the develop-ment of color. Photography changed the recording of history and gives future generations perspective on the past.

Edison himself saw little future in motion pictures—his devices could only be viewed by one person at a time. The business took off, however, when Auguste Lumiere converted these devices into both a camera and projector and assembled thirty-three people in a 100-seat theater to view some one-minute video clips. Edwin Porter developed a movie studio and after eleven years released his epic *The Great Train Robbery*. The result was a new form of entertainment astounding audiences throughout the globe. Attendance skyrocketed when families went to the movies once a week even during the Great Depression. There were more movie theaters than banks, twice as many as there were hotels, and three times as many as department stores. Censorship and family viewing limited movie content to what today would be considered the equivalent of a rating of GP.

These inventions by Edison and his colleagues caused changes in daily life exceeding anything ever witnessed by mankind, even over periods of thousands of years. Edison's genius gave Americans numerous new devices that have become indispensable elements of contemporary life, including simple conveniences such as waxed paper and the gummed envelopes in which millions of letters are mailed every day. Other major contributions include the automatic telegraph system, fluorescent lights, Portland cement, and the fluoroscope (which he chose not to patent because of its widespread application to surgery and medicine). Among Edison's inventions are the first embossing machine, an electric pen, the mimeograph machine, the carbon transmitter that made the telephone audible and commercially viable, and the Ediphone, a version of the telephone.

Edison developed the entire concept of the electrical grid and power system, from the light bulb to the power plant. Jump-starting metropolitan use of electricity was development of the "dynamo" by Siemens and Halske in Germany, which consisted of coils of wire in which a magnetic field would develop when the generator began to rotate. Edison had extensive knowledge about gas lighting and electric arc lighting—electrical current flowing between the points of two rods of carbon produced a white light as it burned that was 500 times more powerful than a gas light. Prior to Edison's work, applications of electricity were limited to those such as telegraph which used only small and intermittent electrical currents. Edison's insight and vision brought lighting and electricity to thousands of residences and offices and enabled the home and workplace to be transformed by hundreds of other devices. Edison established the Edison Electric Light Company, subsequently reorganized into the General Electric Company. The major advantage of the light bulb was that it could be easily and instantaneously turned on and off. Edison installed his first electrical plant on a steel ship that left port at Chester, Pennsylvania, and sailed around Cape Horn to California, where, after a two-month voyage, all 115 lamps still worked.

In 1882, Edison secured the rights from New York City to build the first power grid, which included much of the Wall Street financial neighborhood. Using six of the world's largest dynamos, he built the first power plant. Working at night to avoid worsening traffic congestion, he wired neighborhoods and hooked up owners of houses and stores who were willing to subscribe to the new service. Edison had to solve many logistical problems to make the system work, including: building a central power station, designing and manufacturing his own dynamos economically (to convert steam power into electricity), ensuring an even flow of current, connecting miles of underground wiring, insulating the wiring against moisture and accidental discharges, installing safety devices against fire, designing commercially efficient motors to use electricity in elevators and other devices, designing and installing meters to measure individual consumption, and inventing and manufacturing a plethora of switches and other devices. Edison had to finance most of the cost himself, but he had generated sufficient wealth to do this from his telegraph and telephone patents.[2] Electricity remained expensive and public use was low, because most middle income Americans could not afford the service. For many Americans, nevertheless, Edison's electrical grid had turned night into day. [3]

When George Westinghouse set up his own research lab, he developed the concept of alternating current or AC as contrasted with Edison's direct current or DC. He hired an individual from Edison's lab, Nikola Tesla. Tesla designed an AC motor, held hundreds of patents himself, and developed an entire electric power grid for the AC system. Westinghouse's electrical grid was far more efficient with its alternating high and low voltages. Edison tried to label AC a safety hazard, claiming the high voltages were extremely dangerous and encouraging its use in the electric chair. Being more efficient, AC was better suited for long-distance transmission, and Westinghouse won contracts such as the electrical-generating facilities at Niagara Falls. Edison's marketing efforts succeeded for a short period, but eventually the more efficient and effective AC standard and system prevailed.

Samuel Insull worked with Edison on his early efforts to commercialize electricity, but then struck out on his own to establish Chicago Edison, taking two initiatives to radically bring down costs. Commercial and retail facilities had their own generators to keep costs down, leaving individual customers to share the very expensive generating capacity. Insull consolidated facilities and switched to AC to reduce costs. On a trip to England, he observed the turbine stream engine that was much more efficient than the reciprocating engines with crank shafts then in use. He persuaded General Electric to produce them and his own company to install the revolutionary new technology, but only by personally assuming the risk should the technology fail. Second, electricity could not be stored and usage peaked during certain periods. Insull found an inventor in England who had developed a meter that not only measured how much was consumed (which many types of meters already did), but kept track of when it was used. This allowed Insull to develop load management, charging more during peak periods and shifting use towards off-peak periods, significantly lowering capital costs by reducing the overall capacity needed to supply his customers. In the first year the meter was used in Chicago, electrical rates fell 32 percent while overall demand soared.

Electricity transformed the California economy. In 1924, only 35 percent of homes nationally were wired for electricity. In California, the figure was 83 percent. The cost per kilowatt hour was $1.42 versus a national average of $2.17.[4] Ezra Scattergood masterfully negotiated with seven states to form a coalition to harness the Colorado River by building the vast Boulder Dam to create the world's largest municipal power system, which provided California with even cheaper power.

Electric power revolutionized the factory system. Steam engines were more efficient the larger they were built, but small electrical engines were almost as efficient as big steam engines. The larger engines constrained the placement of tools in factories and the pace at which they functioned. Electrical engines gave manufacturing plants much more flexibility and productivity. This changeover, as well as the entire process of converting homes and applications to electricity, took time. In 1899, only 3 percent of American factories used electric motors. In the early 1920s the figure reached a third and by the end of that decade, it was over a half.[5] In 1869, steam engines delivered 1.2 million horse-power, but electrical engines delivered 45 million horsepower in 1939, forty times more. Electricity powered the vast majority of the new labor saving appliances, such as refrigerators, vacuum cleaners, washing machines, hair dryers, clothes dryers, radios, and televisions. In comparison to Europe, the United States suffered from a labor shortage, which provided incentives to deploy labor-saving devices that improved productivity. Electricity was the spark for the internal combustion engine, but was much safer than oil-burning lamps and drastically reduced fires, the scourge of cities for centuries. The full effects of the use of electricity were not felt until decades after the initial invention. Finally, in the 1920s, worker productivity soared, increasing at several times the previous rate, and manufacturing production doubled. Electricity was responsible for half this improvement.[6] In the first two decades of the twentieth century, the volume of electrical power produced increased by twenty fold.

The Great Era of Innovation

The century after the Civil War was to be an Age of Revolution—of countless, little-noticed revolutions, which occurred not in the halls of legislatures or on battlefields or on the barricades but in homes and farms and factories and schools and stores, across the landscape and in the air—so little noticed because they came so swiftly, because they touched Americans everywhere and every day. Not merely the continent but human experience itself, the very meaning of community, of time and space, of present and future, was being revised again and again; a new democratic world was being invented and was being discovered by Americans wherever they lived.[7]

After the Civil War, the development of new technologies played a key role in the growth and development of America. The victory of the North liberated American technology, which would have been stifled under the rigid, hierarchical southern system. Patents issued annually in the U.S. increased from 3,500 in the early 1860s to 24,000 by the end of the century and the tens of thousands by the time of the Great Depression. In the year Edison was born (1847), only 495 inventors won patents; in the year of his fortieth birthday, more than 20,000 individuals obtained patents.[8] The U.S. courts developed the most effective patent system in the world, "rewarding not only novelty but social utility and not only inventions but their prompt delivery to the marketplace, while encouraging free use by all of imported techniques."[9]

Whatever else might be said of the Civil War, it was hospitable to the science underlying technological changes that had given it power. For only technology could master the needed domain for these rulers: strip the forests, open the land, build the railroads, pick the cotton, thrash the wheat, harness the energy. In Europe the business class had to fight an unremitting struggle for centuries against the political rulers and social aristocracy: only in England and Germany did it win; especially in Germany, where Bismarck built a technological welfare state in alliance with the army. In America the sway of the business class was undisputed. It lavished its gifts on science (although not always wisely) through research funds and big laboratories, because science in turn opened a cornucopia of profits. It whipped technology on because every discovery of new techniques and processes meant the cutting of costs, the opening of new areas of investment, the reaching of new heights of productivity. America became the Enormous Laboratory.[10]

During and after the Civil War, phenomenal levels of growth continued—the U.S. population reached 30 million in 1860, 40 million in 1870, 50 million in 1880, 63 million in 1890, 75 million in 1900, and 100 million by the start of World War I. Despite a slight increase in restrictions on immigration, a million immigrants entered each year.

The longest expansion in America prior to World War II occurred during the Civil War. The net effect of the war was probably to retard economic growth in the industrial sector and stimulate agricultural growth outside the South. The rate of capital formation experienced a considerable jump.[11] After the war, industrial production increased rapidly. At the time of the Revolutionary War, the United States had only a tenth of one percent of the world's manufacturing output. At the beginning of the twentieth century, its share had skyrocketed to 23.6 percent of a much larger world manufacturing sector, and it was, by far, the leading manufacturing nation in the world.[12] Between 1859 and 1914, manufacturing output increased eighteen fold. By 1917, after mobilization for World War I, it had risen thirty-three fold.[13]

America's rate of economic growth exceeded that of any other country in world history up until that time. From a tiny sliver of the world's economy, the United States grew into the world's economic superpower by 1900 and in the 1920s produced almost half of the world's manufactured goods. By the middle of the 1920s, the U.S. produced over half of the world's iron, timber, and cotton, as well as over 60 percent of the world's petroleum, lead, steel, and sulfur. Sometime about 1890, the U.S. economy became the largest in the world, even though America's population was half that of Russia and a fifth of China's. Between the Civil War and World War I, the U.S. grew faster than any major economy, even on a per-capita basis. European leaders continued to believe Europe was the focal point of the world and the center of Western power whereas in the real world these accolades belonged to America.

The founding fathers had not anticipated this highly centralized industrial economy for their new nation. The industrial revolution largely consisted of the mass production of countless inventions, enabling humanity to escape its physical limitations through the use of machines. Power became more centralized in industrial corporations and the nation's capital. In the twentieth century, this trend continued and even accelerated, only reversed recently by the information revolution. While these centralized, hierarchical institutions were in conflict with the original model conceived by the American revolutionaries, many of these institutions became positive forces by reviving the pluralist tradition. The new business enterprise was followed by the labor union, the civil service, the hospital, and the modern university. Each of these new institutions became autonomous power centers assuming new functions and preventing the culture from becoming dominated by the sovereign state or large, multinational enterprises.[14]

The conversion to the factory system led to a change in the workforce. The middle class made up 6 percent of labor force in 1870, rising to 25 percent by 1940. The proportion of self-employed Americans plummeted from four-fifths in the early 1800s to a third in 1870 and to only a fifth by the 1940s. The United States, like other industrial countries, saw a rapid increase in the urban population. In 1850, only one city (New York) had more than 250,000 people. In 1890, three cities exceeded one million people and eight more surpassed 250,000. The population explosion in major cities resulted in overcrowded tenement housing. New York City blocks of 200 by 1,000 feet were often home to 2,500 families or more, as high as any concentration in the Western world. These structures were made mostly of wood. Fires ravaged many cities, because the buildings were basically kindling, particularly in the absence of any fire codes. American democracy flourished when it consisted of farmers, small cities, and self-employed workers. By the 1890s, however, this idyllic world was besieged. Economies of scale in manufacturing bankrupted many smaller businesses, ruined some middle-class families, and undermined belief in entrepreneurial capitalism. Farmers were hard pressed with falling prices and rising debts. Between 1870 and 1910, farm prices fell by about 40 percent and, in the 1920s, plunged again. The frontier was closing, cheap land was disappearing, and workers and farmers depended on incorporated groups and businesses for jobs. Employees at large corporations worked long hours at low pay with little job security.

Enormous abundance was being created: national wealth increased an estimated four fold between 1870 and 1910. Wealthy families set up foundations for research in science and for improving the condition of mankind; these included organizations such as the Carnegie Corporation, the Rockefeller Foundation, and the Ford Foundation. In 1848 John Jacob Astor died as America's richest man and was worth $25 million. Less than thirty years later, Cornelius Vanderbilt left $105 million. Andrew Carnegie was worth about half a billion when he sold his steel business in 1901 and then donated the wealth for libraries, universities, education, and other public purposes. John D. Rockefeller was worth close to a billion dollars and spent his later life giving away much of his wealth.

After the Civil War, there was no global economy as we know it today. Yet, the period between 1860 and 1913 was one of increasing globalization and new markets. Admiral Matthew Perry visited Japan, breaking that country's tradition of isolation from the outside world and gradually opening it up to the West. Railroads and steamships greatly reduced shipping costs, and thus facilitated rapid expansion of world trade. In the United States, a protectionist policy of high tariffs, introduced via the political ascendancy of the Republicans, accrued trade surpluses. The freedom of interstate commerce, guaranteed by the Supreme Court and the Constitution, made America by far the largest free-trading area in the world. In 1900, Americans bought 97 percent of their manufactured goods from domestic producers.[15] America's share of the world export market doubled, because of its rapid growth. As a result of protectionist trade policies, exports rose more than seven fold between the Civil War and World War I, while imports increased only five fold. Manufactured goods increased from about a fifth to almost a third of all exports; certain advanced manufacturing products surged even faster. Prior to the Civil War, the United States exported only about $6 million worth of iron and steel products. By the turn of the century, this figure reached over $120 million, and included locomotives, rails, electrical machinery, sewing machines, and typewriters.[16]

Protected from the need to make large military expenditures due to its distance from Europe, the U.S. government actually shrank in size while European governments were expanding. Government outlays declined steadily until the middle 1880s and then remained steady at a low level until World War I. Public debt declined by over 80 percent.

Incorporated organizations played a central role in America's industrialization and served to help create the enormous new wealth. The corporate structure had been ratified by John Marshall and the Supreme Court and was initially limited to public purpose activities such as for building canals, railroads and turnpikes. Over time, the impediments to the use of the corporation in other areas were removed. By the end of World War I, corporations employed six-sevenths of the U.S. workforce and produced seven-eights of its total measurable output.[17] Gradually, the corporate structure evolved to form trusts and holding companies. Lack of an adequate labor supply and the effectiveness of the corporate structure and financial markets led to a re-balancing of the relationships between capital, labor, and production. Between 1850 and 1910, the average manufacturing plant in leading industries multiplied its capital by 39, its wage-earners by 7, and its output by more than 19.

After the Civil War, the Supreme Court flip-flopped on the application of federal laws to corporations. Initially, notwithstanding the passage of the Fourteenth Amendment, the Court held that states could define property and determine the limits on its use, including the power to charter corporations and control management. The Fourteenth Amendment was applied only to the rights of the newly emancipated slaves. Business corporations were subject to the conflicting and varied laws of the states, stifling development of national industry and markets. Eventually, the Court held that a corporation was a person and could not be deprived of basic rights without due process of the law. Soon the laws and actions of the state authorities were superseded by those of the federal government. Countless laws, policies, and decrees of the states and local government were voided, providing a major boon to centralization and economic expansion. America also had strong patent laws that provided incentives for inventors and industry and greatly encouraged development of new technology. Frequent patent wars, however, frustrated the development of new businesses.

Financial accounting systems were crucial to developing the modern corporation and made major contributions to the revolution in manufacturing. Historically, most corporations had kept their finances secret or released misleading information. Stockholders, brokers, and bankers increasingly demanded expanded information on the workings of businesses so they could ascertain the true value of a corporation and whether to invest funds in it. Over time, a full balance sheet was required, including revenues, expenses, and earnings. Public companies began issuing quarterly and annual reports. These reports are routine today, but were revolutionary in their time and gave investors the information to make better investment decisions. Independent auditors certified and audited these books and reports. The cash register was invented by James Ritty, a saloon owner in Dayton, Ohio; it became utilized nationwide to accurately tabulate business income and receipts. Major Wall Street banks and the New York Stock Exchange forced companies that wanted bank financing or to be listed on the exchange to comply with generally accepted accounting procedures (often referred to as GAAP). Associations were set up to audit and verify the credentials for accountants. New York State passed legislation establishing a legal basis for the profession and developed the concept of the *certified public accountant.* This legislation was soon adopted by all fifty states.[18]

In terms of taxation, the development of financial accounting practices was a two-edged sword. Both the income and corporate taxes became more enforceable. A "cottage" industry developed, however, to allow investors not to be taxed at all instead of being taxed twice (i.e., on dividends and income).[19] Loopholes, tax lawyers, and tax accountants became as American as apple pie.

Statistics were developed for a wide range of uses—in weights and measures, quality control, and machine tooling. While the numbers improved productivity and fostered economic growth, they also reduced the role of craftsmanship, ensured products would not be any better than the norm, and minimized the importance of things and trends that could not be counted.

The growth in manufacturing resulted in complex networks of suppliers, creditors, and purchasers. It was often hard to sort out who was dealing with whom and who could be trusted. The concept of credit became essential. Lewis Tappan developed the credit reporting business, handing it over to his son-in-law, Robert Dun of Dun & Bradstreet. Credit reporting was critical for the measurement of risk and the development of a uniform American market.

Marketing and advertising became far more systematic and sophisticated, changing the marketplace and the way consumers bought products. Retailers John Wannamaker, Montgomery Ward, Charles Walgreen, F.W. Woolworth, R.H. Macy, and Marshall Fields pioneered in the use of mass advertising and merchandising. Goods and services that previously were only for the rich were brought to the masses. Mail-order catalogues reached all America, particularly housewives who were often isolated in their daily toils. Warren Sears began with the sale of watches and expanded his business until it became Sears, Roebuck, and Co., selling through the postal service instead of through stores. Sales of large volumes of products by mail enabled the firm and others to receive huge discounts from manufacturers and to drastically reduce prices. Sewing machines, which were $50 to $100 in the local stores, for example, sold for under $20. Many in the middle class could afford what had previously been regarded as luxuries. This form of marketing radically altered entire industries in unforeseen ways. The cream-separator became standard in the dairy business when Sears cut the price in half. Price reductions on bicycles and buggies had a similar impact in the transportation sector.[20]

In response, local stores improved their bargaining power with suppliers by consolidating into chains. The James Butler Grocery Company, founded by a foreign-born Irish Catholic, at one point had 1,350 grocery stores. A&P was formed to bring down the price of foreign-produced tea and coffee, opening up 7,500 stores during World War I and over 15,000 stores by 1936 when it ran into the antitrust statutes. Paradoxically, the antitrust laws probably did more damage to the independent retailers by denying them the ability to form trade associations to effectively compete against the larger chains, such as A&P.

AGRICULTURE AND THE WILD WEST

The growth and industrialization of the American agricultural sector created revolutionary changes in human behavior. Eating habits were radically altered by the bountiful supply of food, by new methods for preservation, and by phenomenal improvements in productivity. The ancient scourge of famine was basically eliminated. After the Civil War, agriculture continued to be the leading field of employment and industrialization of this sector played a major role in the overall economic expansion. Through the middle of the 1880s, half of the U.S. population was dependent on farming. Land sales continued to fuel the agricultural boom. During and after the Civil War, settlers could claim large tracts of land and, by fulfilling the residency requirements, they could get much of it for free. The Homestead Act of 1862, signed by President Lincoln, enabled any head of a household to claim 160 acres, make certain improvements, occupy it for five years, and then claim full possession without any payment. Subsequent federal statutes allowed for the free acquisition of up to 1120 acres (half of which was desert land). Hundreds of millions of acres were transferred into private hands, totalling an area much larger than the state of California. Tens of millions of Americans became descendants of homesteaders.

Improved methods of raising cattle made cattle ranching possible on the high plains. Cattle towns grew up around these ranches. Cattle drives and trails created enormous wealth but entailed incredible risks. Cattle herding became almost an art form, under the leadership of experienced hands such as John Wesley Iliff and Charles Goodnight. Weeks on the trail could make men more jumpy than the cattle, resulting in stampedes. Cattle stampedes in the dead of night could result in the loss of the entire herd because cowhands could not see precipices, gullies, and prairie dog holes that would have been difficult to navigate even during daylight. In the early 1880s, the invention of barbed wire by Joseph Glidden and Jacob Haish helped to provide lines of demarcation to establish property rights and opened up huge tracts of land in the West for farming. H.W. Putnam developed machines that produced hundreds of miles of wire per day at a fraction of the original cost. A prolonged fight ensued over the patent rights. The invention also created fierce conflicts. Farmers and settlers claimed the same land for farming and ranching, enforcing their claim with barbed wire fences. Herders, who claimed the entire West as their birthright, were incensed by its use. Vigilantes fought over the placement and stringing of the wire, but eventually the loss of the open range meant the end of the giant cattle drives and the demise of the herders. Huge industrial corporations began to farm and process food. Trusts were formed in a range of agricultural commodities, such as sugar, linseed oil, cottonseed oil, and whisky.

The West came to epitomize American freedom and individualism. Water was critical to farming in the West. A system of water rights was developed and westerners drilled shafts with metal cylinders powered by windmills. A settler could obtain 650 acres of land if it was irrigated in three years. Realistically, however, in the dry West, only farms of 2500 or more acres were viable. This led to great hostility by the westerners towards government and the East. Breech-loading guns, Colt revolvers, and repeaters provided the settlers with the technology they needed to settle the West and stave off Indian attacks. Wanton killing of the buffalo, however, led to their virtual extinction. Stagecoaches were the common carriers of the day, transporting mail, freight, and people.

The West became a mining powerhouse, outputting not only gold and silver, but other metals as well. Montana, for example, produced about a quarter of the world's copper. Mining operations expanded rapidly—more coal was extracted in the period 1897 to 1907 and more iron ore was mined between 1890 and 1910 than in all the nation's previous history.

The logging business was revolutionized by the introduction of the railroad, which made it possible to cut forests far from navigable rivers. The capital-intensive nature of the industry resulted in entrepreneurs being replaced by large timber and paper companies such as Weyerhaeuser, International Paper, and Kimberly-Clark. The economics and incentives of the business encouraged reforestation and large firms often planted more than they consumed. In 1914, Weyerhaeuser built the world's largest sawmill in Everett, Washington.

As the West expanded its production, New England continued to pioneer in ice manufacture and distribution, refrigeration became crucial in the vast expansion of agricultural products available for use in the home. Between the Civil War and the turn of the century, ice consumption skyrocketed by from five to ten times. In warm winters and summers, there were major shortages, so that the number of ice plants soared, particularly in the South. By 1910 there were over 2,000 plants using coal-fired steam engines to make ice. Sears, Roebuck introduced cheap refrigerators and ice boxes for the home, but these devices still required frequent deliveries by the iceman. In 1875, Gustavus Swift invented the refrigerator freight car, which greatly extended agricultural markets. In 1918, the Kelvinator Company developed a home refrigerator that automatically controlled the temperature and eliminated the need for an ice man. General Motors bought the product and marketed it as Frigidaire, selling just 10,000 units in 1920. The market exploded to 560,000 units in 1928. During the 1930s, prices continued to decline and hundreds of thousands of units were sold.

In the Midwest, the Germans secured a virtual monopoly over the manufacture of beer, including brewers like Frederick Pabst, Joseph Schlitz, Frederick Miller, and the Anheuser-Busch family. Frank Ball developed new advances in the canning business and Ball Corporation became a huge company that gradually changed America's eating habits by preventing spoilage in preserved foods. Clarence Birdseye founded the company bearing his name and developed a method for flash-freezing food to preserve taste as well as product.

Until World War I, the slaughtering and meatpacking industry was America's largest employer, in significant part due to the advances in refrigeration and canning. Swift and Philip Armour organized meat production by breaking down the slaughtering of cattle and hogs into numerous single operations—America's original assembly line. They developed uses for discarded parts in marketable animal products such as brushes, margarine, glue, pharmaceuticals, and fertilizer.

Advances in food production led to differentiation in consumer diet, and the concept of healthy nutrition. Until after the Civil War, food groups were generally considered to have the same nutritional value. In some periods, fresh fruits and vegetables were considered hazardous to a person's health. Gradually, however, America moved towards democratizing its diet, improving its tastes, and increasing the variety and quality of food.[21]

Building on earlier efforts to manufacture textiles and to improve clothing production, Elias Howe invented the sewing machine, which Isaac Singer redesigned to improve reliability and versatility. The new machine drastically lowered the cost of ready-made clothes—a shirt that had once taken fourteen hours to make could now be produced in a little over one hour. This led to the concept of "size" in clothing manufacturing, enabling people to purchase and think of themselves as belonging to a numerical size when buying shoes and clothes. Though textile workers feared for their livelihoods, the increased demand made up for the reduction in labor and fall in prices.

Cotton mills moved from New England to the South, expanding by fifteen fold in the period between the Civil War and the end of the century. Cotton itself, however, was not nearly as lucrative. Most mills were now powered by steam rather than water. Technological change, including steam-power, made machinery in cotton mills far more sophisticated. The South became the center for cotton exchanges and manufacturing.

Southern agriculture began to change, diversifying away from cotton and expanding to grow apples, peaches, oranges, lemons, peanuts, watermelon, and vegetables. The railroad refrigerator car was particularly important in getting those foods to market. Southern lumber mills expanded rapidly until their number exceeded mills in the Great Lakes region in production.

The use of farm machinery extended into all aspects of agriculture, causing the percentage of workers in agriculture to decline as productivity rose rapidly.[22] For example, John Deere mass-produced plows, the Armour brothers developed meat packing plants, Thomas Lynch became a well-known distiller of spirits, Adolphus Busch developed beer breweries, and Cyrus McCormick led the effort to develop mechanical agriculture equipment, selling not just reapers, but mowers, harvesters, and harvester binders.[23] Millions of people had always labored to harvest grain using tools that had changed little in thousands of years—the sickle and the scythe. The reaper radically and quickly changed this system and improved productivity several fold. After his initial efforts to market the reaper faltered, McCormick developed a financing mechanism that enabled farmers to purchase the invention and to use it. By selling more and more reapers, by 1877 McCormick had driven the price down from $120 to $18 and was revolutionizing agriculture. Even as 90 percent of America's farms were without electricity, the low price of power in California resulted in the rapid deployment of electrical machinery to milk cows, to irrigate, and to perform a range of agricultural functions. California agriculture became the most productive in the world. By 1905, the basic design for the gasoline-powered tractor had emerged. Within a decade, there were about 25,000 tractors on farms, within two decades half a million tractors, and by the middle 1930s there were over one million. New methods, crops, and breeds made similar contributions to improved productivity and efficiency.[24]

THE HOME

Vast improvements in homebuilding and technology used in the home increased the standard of living and greatly reduced reliance on human servitude and low-wage workers. Glass windows were taxed as a luxury in Europe, but were mass produced for the general market in America, as the ancient art of glass blowing was replaced with new technologies to make flat or sheet glass. After World War I plate glass could be produced in a continuous flow.[25]

Household devices proliferated. America led the world in labor-saving devices, particularly in the kitchen. House-cleaning and laundry appliances became available and common, eliminating drudgery only the rich could escape previously. Interior illumination and public libraries spurred reading, boosted sales of books, magazines, and newspapers, and altered the economic model of publishing. Central heating radically enhanced home activities.

MEDICINE

Medical treatment made consistent, steady progress throughout the century after the Civil War. In 1867, Joseph Lister developed antiseptics and disinfectants that improved sanitation and the ability to perform surgery, though too late to help with those wounded in the Civil War. Scientists discovered how to purify water through filtration, chlorination, and aeration technologies, reducing public-health disorders and extending life spans. Robert Wood Johnson developed antiseptic dressings and promoted the theory of airborne germs, starting Johnson & Johnson, which founded a bacteriological laboratory that invented sterilized gauze and the Band-Aid.

COMMUNICATIONS AND TRANSPORTATION

Communication and transportation networks, especially the railroad system, greatly expanded urban and export markets; this, in turn, drove the deployment of new technology and economic growth.

The postal service was the backbone of national and international communications. Postal rates were based on how far the mail had to go, but the department was not always efficient. The price of sending a three-page letter from New Orleans to St. Louis was four times the cost of shipping a barrel of flour. Letters were sent COD (collect on delivery) so that many letters went undelivered. In 1848, when Zachary Taylor won the Whig nomination, he did not know of his success for weeks because he refused to pay the COD on several official notifications that ended up in the dead letter office. Private mail companies sprang up and delivered half the mail at rates that were as much as 80 percent lower than the government rates. They instituted innovations, such as the adhesive postage stamp, prepaid delivery, mailboxes, and home delivery. With the federal post service threatened with insolvency, President Tyler's Postmaster General Charles Wickliffe responded by instituting many of the private companies' practices.[26] Fast postal service gave Eastern merchants the advantage in trade because they knew more than people in remote areas about the conditions of the market. Until the 1870s, the Post Office was the biggest organization in America.

Communications barriers were a fact of life in colonial America—information traveled at about the speed of a horse. It had long been known that electric current could be transmitted distances via a wire, which could be manipulated to convey information. In the early nineteenth century, new mining and manufacturing capabilities made wire much cheaper and advances in electronics were occurring with regularity. An electric arc light was developed by Humphrey Davy in 1808; electromagnetism was observed by Hams Christian Oersted in 1820; Michael Faraday made the first electric motor in 1821 and the first primitive dynamo in 1831. The telegraph was used in the Napoleonic wars to inform the British Admiralty of an invasion, but afterwards its use was discontinued.

There were many experiments with electric telegraphs, but Samuel Morse developed the first commercial system. He only invented the Morse code: his initial system was built with the help of the scientist, Joseph Henry. Morse tried to make the code visible so it could be read, but soon realized it could be intercepted by ear and compromised. Morse had ample assistance from the government. A congressional appropriations built the line between Baltimore and Washington for the initial demonstration. The first effort to bury the wire failed. The second effort by Ezra Cornell, founder of Cornell University, developed a way to string the wires down the railroad line to complete the project on time. Morse tapped out his famous words "What hath God wrought!" Within years, every major American city had a line, most of them using pathways from the fast spreading railways. The first practical application was to wire ahead to law enforcement authorities to catch criminals, which received wide publicity. Edison's invention that enabled multiple messages to be sent down a telegraph line provided Edison with the funds to set up his invention lab in Menlo Park.

The first transatlantic cable was a failure, but pioneers, such as Cyrus Field, learned from mistakes and the second effort in 1866 was a success, ending the isolation of America from the rest of the Western world. Messages could be sent within hours that before had gone by ship and had taken months.[27] Previously, for example, it took four weeks to carry news from New York to London and an additional week to Berlin. In 1870, the telegraph made the world truly global when Japan, China, India, and Australia were linked together by cable with the rest of the world. By 1874, there were over 650,000 miles of wire and 30,000 miles of submarine cable, connecting tens of thousands of cities. Wall Street benefited greatly as it used the telegraph to help it to become the world's biggest marketplace—the largest market generally having the best prices. Western Union offices grew to over 2,000 in 1866, more than 6,500 in 1875, and almost 10,000 in 1880. Growth was over 10 percent a year, the number of messages increasing five fold to 30 million annually.[28]

The telegraph spurred development of the newspaper, which previously contained mostly local news and political advocacy being published by one political faction or another. The high speed rotary press facilitated development of news journalism by turning out thousands of newspapers nightly at much lower prices. James Gordon Bennett founded the *New York Herald* as a paper for a mass audience that emphasized the news, including business coverage and stock prices. He established a presence in Washington, D.C., breaking the grip of the local papers and establishing the press corps. He coined the term "leak" and used the telegraph to report on the Mexican War, often scooping the official reports by days. By the Civil War, his was the largest and most influential newspaper in the country, its circulation being greater than the total circulation of all newspapers fifty years earlier. Bennett developed the model for the modern newspaper and established the concept that news keeps people informed and connected.[29] Daily newspaper circulation exploded from a million in 1870 to 15 million by 1900 to 42 million in 1929. Prices fell and the size increased with cartoons, gossip columns, and expanded editorials. The linotype machine, color printing, and photoengraving all contributed to the inventions spurring newspaper publishing.

The telegraph was somewhat limited, because it required skilled operators at each end. In 1876 Alexander Graham Bell's invention of the telephone again changed the nature of communications forever. As a speech therapist and teacher of the deaf, he had discovered how sound waves could be converted into electric current. Many advances were required, including loading coils, automatic switchboards, carrier currents, and solving the problem of indistinct and muffled sounds (Edison again stepping into the breach). Bell designed a combination of electromagnets, diaphragms, and resistors that allowed him to transmit an array of frequencies, including speech.[30] His patent became one of the most valuable in history. Subsequent investigation determined that Bell stole the crucial technological breakthrough from Elisha Gray.[31]

The applications of Bell's patent were not readily apparent and Western Union turned down his offer to sell the technology. Within a decade over a quarter of a million telephones were in use throughout the world and, by 1891, one in ten American homes had a phone. Bell's company, AT&T, used its patent of the telephone to develop a monopoly on phone service, giving it a seventeen-year head start to penetrate the best markets and making it the largest private business in the world. When the patents expired, independent phone carriers sprang up everywhere. Theodore Vail understood the unique nature of the telephone system and made customer service a top priority, unheard of at the time. He made it a primary task of his regional telephone companies to ensure regulatory bodies were strong, setting rates, and protecting the public (and making it more difficult for competitors to enter his markets). Vail set up Bell Laboratories, which developed technology to make North America one network and new technologies for the transmission of data and video (i.e., television and computerized information).

Further advances occurred in transportation systems. Telegraphs, telephones, steamships, and railroads replaced horses, couriers, and sailing vessels. Previously, only light or expensive goods could be economically traded, such as precious metals, luxury textiles, cotton, and tobacco because it cost as much to ship products like wheat and iron as it did to produce them. New technologies caused shipping costs to plummet 60 to 95 percent, enabling a much wider range of goods to be transported and leading to a twenty-fold increase in world shipping capacity.[32]

THE PANAMA CANAL

Just as the Erie Canal jump-started economic growth in the early nineteenth century, the Panama Canal made a similar contribution in the early twentieth century. Construction was made possible by the Hay-Pauncefote Treaty granting the U.S. broad authority to build the Canal in return for charging everyone the same fares. The French builder of the Suez Canal had tried to dig the Panama Canal for seven years, but lost tens of millions of dollars and thousands of men to disease and failed, precipitating a scandal shaking France to the core. Workers on the Panama Canal had to survive ticks, chiggers, spiders, ants, tarantula, puma, jaguar, some of the most poisonous snakes in the world, and rainfall measured in feet, not inches. The basic tools for clearing were the ax and machete, although advanced dredges and earth removing equipment made the excavation much easier. Searing tropical heat made Panama "hell on earth" with malaria and yellow fever rampant. European technology and lifestyles were particularly ill-suited for this terrain. An American contractor was the only major participant to complete its mission. While the French ignored the advice of their professional engineers, America eventually embraced and acted on the recommendations of its own technical experts.

After the battleship, the *Maine,* had blown up in Havana harbor, the Battleship *Oregon* was forced to steam 12,000 miles around Cape Horn, instead of the 4,000 miles that would have been required if the French had been able to complete the Panama Canal; this event made its eventual construction imperative at least in the mind of President Theodore Roosevelt. Without the Canal, San Francisco was closer by boat to London than to New York. Considerable sentiment developed for the route through Nicaragua, but, when the French dropped the asking price for buying their failed effort, the Panama route was clearly superior.

Panama was far removed from the rest of Columbia; it took fifteen days for a letter to get to the capital of Columbia, if it got there at all. Since the 1840s, there had been at least fifty insurrections, civil disturbances, and riots in Panama. On at least ten occasions, the United States had been required to intervene in the country's affairs.[33]

Theodore Roosevelt helped to support a revolution of local Panama residents concerned over the rejection of the Canal treaty with Washington by their Columbian legislators. This revolt established

Panama's independence from Columbia and ensured that the Canal would be built across the isthmus. Walter Reed helped to make construction possible by demonstrating that yellow fever was caused by a mosquito bite, a connection many had sought to establish but could not prove. Only by drawing blood in the first three days of infection, taking twelve to twenty days for incubation, could the fever be transmitted. Yet, Reed's findings and the efforts of the medical community were only begrudgingly accepted. The initial American effort also flopped as a result of excessive bureaucracy and control from Washington, plus the panic engendered by the spread of tropical disease due to the failure to take precautions recommended by the U.S. medical community.

Mainly due to the insistence of the chief engineer of the Canal, John Stevens, the U.S. Army's William Crawford Gorgas designed and managed a campaign against the disease-carrying mosquitoes of the isthmian jungles that finally made area inhabitants safe from tropical disease and enabled the Canal to be built. Stevens had been the chief engineer for the Great Northern Railroad, the only transcontinental rail route built without government subsidies. Initially, he suspended much of the work on the Canal until the basic infrastructure was put in place to successfully execute the project. The Canal Zone became a miniature American civilization with many of the amenities of North America, including the YMCA, dances, and band concerts. Stevens procured huge American railcars and locomotives for the extensive excavation.

George Goethals was responsible for the eventual construction of the Canal, perhaps the greatest engineering feat of the ages. Modern explosives, the largest mechanized earth movers ever built, a dam that created the largest manmade body of water yet formed, and locks that dwarfed anything ever attempted before were all combined in a construction project that took a decade to complete. American steam shovels moved ten times more dirt than had the French in their best month. The amount of dirt removed was the equivalent of the size of 63 Great Pyramids, a Great Wall of China between New York and San Francisco, or of a train of railcars circling the globe four times at the equator. In many years, over a thousand miles of railroad track had to be built. During some years, removal of massive rock and mud slides devoured over a third of the workdays. The Canal consumed more than 60 million pounds of dynamite, more explosive power than had been expended in all the nation's wars until that time.[34] Each of the 6 locks had 2 chambers and was among the largest structures in the world, 1,000 by 100 feet and 60 feet deep, requiring a total of 5 million sacks and barrels of cement. The eventual total cost was $350 million and 25,000 lives. The tolls were approximately a tenth the cost of sailing around South America, saving American and world shippers tens of millions of dollars annually.

President Roosevelt's visit to the Canal during construction was the first time a president had been outside of the country while in office, which made the Canal a popular success. William Howard Taft hired the chief engineer who turned around the project, recruited the subsequent chief engineer who ensured its success, and visited the Canal seven times, twice as president. When Taft was inaugurated the Canal was only half complete; it was finished during Woodrow Wilson's presidency. The Canal opened less than fifteen years into the twentieth century. No other construction project was to surpass it in combined scale and strategic significance.

AIR FLIGHT

The most spectacular advance in transportation was air flight. Samuel Langley had the support of the U.S. financial community, as well as that of the U.S. government, and effected several successful unmanned flights. In his attempt to become the first man to fly, he catapulted over the Potomac, crashed, and failed. The distinction went instead to two bicycle repairmen—Wilbur and Orville Wright. Langley had spent $50,000 of government funds in his failed attempts, whereas Wilbur and Orville spent $1,000 of their own hard-earned money. The Wright brothers interest in flight had begun well before they were teenagers; their parents were well-educated and encouraged their curiosity. Wilbur was a superb athlete, who had suffered a major hockey accident, and was thus unable to continue high school or to attend the Yale Divinity School as expected. The Wright brothers succeeded where so many others failed by relying on previous innovators and their own intuitions. Sir George Cayley (1773–1857) established the principles for heavier-than-air flight, including lift, drag, and fixed and arched wings. The German Otto Lilienthal had applied these theories to the construction of many gliders and made more than 2,000 flights, but died from injuries suffered in a crash in 1896. His efforts and death hooked the Wright Brothers on flight. American inventor Hiram Maxim (1840–1916) launched a four-ton machine several inches from the ground with a steam engine generating 300 horsepower, demonstrating the importance of generating power to gain flight. Octave Chanute (1832–1910) collected and compiled a wealth of information on flying that advised the Wright brothers who adopted their biplane design from one of his gliders.

In 1893, Wilbur and Orville opened a bicycle repair shop in Dayton, Ohio, to help fund their research and experimentation. Dayton was an entrepreneurial haven with countless little workshops or "factories" and more patents per capita than any other city. The Wright Brothers developed several prototypes before they eventually were able to fly. For three years, they visited Kitty Hawk in North Carolina each summer to improve their glider. Wilbur understood, unlike previous inventors, the need to control and the interrelationship between the three axes of motion—pitch (nose up or down), balance or roll (lateral roll) and yaw (left and right movement). Their plane was built to be flown as a cyclist rides a bicycle—by being responsive instantly to motions of the air and object.[35] The brothers had more knowledge than anyone else in the world about flying. They developed the most efficient glider in the world and flew it over 600 feet in 1902 at Kitty Hawk, considered among the best places in the world to try to fly an object, with its long beaches and sea breezes for lift. Wilbur developed a moveable rudder, making it possible to precisely balance the glider in flight. The brothers then had to develop their own engine, because automobile and other vehicle manufacturers saw no commercial application for light-weight engines. Similarly, the maritime industry had no design for propellers that could cope with aerodynamic forces instead of with liquid water. The Wright Brothers argued incessantly over the propeller design, sometimes even adopting the other brother's key points in the previous argument. They worked well into the winter season, braving bad weather and numerous mechanical problems. In 1903, the flights with an engine went as far as 800 feet and lasted almost a minute. After four successful flights, a huge gust of wind turned their plane upside down, causing it to cartwheel down the beach and crushing its wings and engine, ending their flying for the year.[36] The brothers succeeded through a disciplined process of design, testing, innovation, and refinement of each new device.

Orville and Wilbur returned to Dayton and tried to replicate their efforts the next year. The much heavier and more humid air in Dayton made flight much less successful. Even so, by the end of the year, they had flown five-minute flights and circled up to four times. The achievements of the Wright Brothers were widely disregarded by governments at home and in Europe, the French in particular dismissing the possibility that mere bicycle repairmen could have solved the almost mythical problem that had eluded man for thousands of years—how to fly. Orville and Wilbur finally received a patent in May 1906, just as eminent scientist Simon Newcomb proclaimed it was demonstrable "as complete as is possible for the demonstration of any fact to be" that "no possible combination of known substances, known forms of machine, and known forms of force can be united in a practicable machine by which men shall fly through long distance in the air."[37] For three years, the Wright Brothers did not fly, waiting for a contract to deliver an airplane. After successfully delivering planes in the United States and Europe, they then fought extensive patent battles, which completely exhausted Wilbur, leading to his premature death in 1912.[38] Airplane technology developed rapidly during World War I, leading to air-to-air combat, followed after the war by trans-Atlantic flight in 1919 and the first around-the-world flight in 1924, which took 175 days. Air travel reduced the time for delivering mail between the coasts from three months in 1850 to just one and a half days by 1924.

America didn't dominate all forms of transportation. New England had been the world's largest builder of sailing vessels, but with the shift to steam and the change-over to foreign-flagged ships in the

Civil War, there was a dramatic decline in domestic shipbuilding. By 1900, only about 10 percent of U.S. foreign trade was transported on U.S. ships. J. P. Morgan was not inclined to get involved in such a risky business, but when the shipbuilding industry earned record profits in 1900, he helped finance a combination of U.S. firms which in turn took over two of the largest British companies in the business. Morgan expected Congress to help subsidize a U.S.-based merchant marine. The subsidy was never forthcoming, and the shipbuilding industry went into a depression, but Morgan went ahead with the venture that controlled a fifth of the North Atlantic trade. The deal necessitated a side agreement with the German government allocating the shipping trade across the Atlantic. The British were shocked to lose these strategic assets, but its government reluctantly acceded to the combination.

RAILROADS

The railroad played a central role in America's industrial revolution; the transcontinental railroad was the instrument through which Americans gained control of their entire continent. Prior to the transcontinental railroad, lines were built to connect areas with robust economic activity, enabling them to be largely privately financed. Great bridges over the Ohio, Mississippi, and Missouri rivers significantly expanded the reach of the railroad. The transcontinental railroad was based not merely on economics, but symbolized that the Union would persevere in the Civil War, and that it would connect the East and West Coasts, uniting all of the states in one seamless transportation network. Federal and state government involvement was crucial to its development. Lincoln's administration resurrected the old Henry Clay and Whig proposals for internal improvements such as railroads, claiming they were necessary for war purposes. Enormous subsidies were provided to complete the project. The federal government, with Lincoln's support, initially loaned $65 million to the first transcontinental railroad companies and provided hundreds of thousands of acres in land as a direct subsidy. Many of the states gave the railroads additional acreage and tens of millions of dollars in added subsidies and loans. The railroads received close to

250,000 square miles, including a quarter of the states of Minnesota and Washington, a fifth of Wisconsin, Iowa, Kansas, North Dakota, and Montana, and an eighth of California. This constituted an area larger than Germany or France. The size and scope of the project, however, was so gargantuan that the total value of the land was only a fraction of the $4 billion construction cost. The railroads also had the right of eminent domain, special charters, exemptions from taxation, and monopoly protections. The Lincoln Administration secured passage of legislation that established uniform rates and subsidized the standardization of tracks, rail connections and financial acquisitions. [40]

In 1862, with the onset of the Civil War and southern members absent due to secession, it was easier to pass legislation. The Pacific Railroad legislation specifically provided for two companies to benefit from building and operating the railroad between the Missouri River and Sacramento: the Central Pacific from the west and the Union Pacific from the east. These railroads were provided: 200 feet of right-of-way when crossing public land, title to 6400 acres of land for each mile of track, and government loans—$16,000 for every mile on flat land, $32,000 for the foothills, and $48,000 in the mountains. The loans were 30-year bonds, which the rail companies would have to sell, but the government would pay the interest. If the railroad was not finished by July 1, 1876, the companies would forfeit the property. The law was changed in 1864 to increase the land grants to 12,800 acres per mile and allow the railroads to sell mortgage bonds using the government bonds as collateral.[41] By the time of the final settlement at the end of the century, the U.S. government was paid back over $60 million in principal and $100 million in interest.[42]

Building the transcontinental railroad was an extraordinarily difficult task, particularly across the Sierra Nevada mountains. Theodore Judah had provided the bold vision to start up the Central Pacific Railroad and was the individual most responsible for passing the Pacific Railroad bill. He raised money from several wealthy donors who then took over the company. (One of these donors, Leland Stanford, bequeathed the money to establish Stanford University on his 900-acre horse farm in Palo Alto.) The terrain and climate on the Sierra Nevadas were terrible. Winter lasted for much of the year and tunnels had to be built through miles of rock and trestles constructed over miles of valleys. The turnover of men because of the weather and accidents from explosives was so severe that the railroad largely relied on Chinese workers, who lived on little food, were impervious to the heat and the cold, stayed sober, and worked endless hours. Much of the digging and building had to be done by hand, because most modern construction machinery had not been invented and steel had only limited uses in building structures. The most difficult stretch was built along cliffs by hand with Chinese workers suspending themselves from waist-high baskets woven from reed. In tunnels, they chipped away rock at the rate of eight inches a day. They didn't merely need to tunnel through rock, but also through 40-foot snow drifts as well. Explosions of black powder to tunnel through rock caused snow avalanches, burying individuals and entire camps. Some were not found until spring, upright in the snow with their work implements still in hand. The logistics were monumental—most of the rails and engines were made in the East and shipped to San Francisco around Cape Horn—an 18,000 mile voyage.

The Union Pacific was built west from Iowa under the supervision of General Granville Dodge, who was ideally suited to command the major construction job. The role included fighting off Indians unhappy with the invasion of their homeland and hunting ground. The railroad was constantly subject to Indian raiding parties. A band of Cheyenne cut the telegraph line, pulled up railroad spikes, bent the rails, and watched a train derail, killing a half dozen passengers. Another freight train crashed into the wreck and overturned. The Indians burned the trains and cars, killed and scalped at least seven people, and threw the bodies into the flames.[43]

The competition between the two railroads to lay track spurred the work. At the beginning, three miles of track was a good day, a figure which increased to six, then seven, and then seven and a half. In 1869, on a bet the Central Pacific laid ten miles in one day, near the final juncture of the two roads in Ogden, Utah. At Dale Creek, the Union Pacific erected a 700-foot mammoth bridge of wood over a 130-foot gorge, one of the great engineering feats of the nineteenth century.

The expansion of the railroads was used by governments to stake claims on land. Canada rushed to complete its transcontinental railroad to prevent the United States, for example, from staking claims in its Pacific Northwest territory. The Canadian transcontinental railroad, however, took 20 years to complete and the Russian Trans-Siberian Railroad took forty years. Within twenty years, there were four additional transcontinental railroads in the United States.

The success of the project was unprecedented. Newspapers carried headlines about the progress of the transcontinental railroad at least weekly and sometimes daily, even in Europe.

> Americans were a people such as the world had never before known. No one before them, no matter where or how they lived, had had such optimism or determination. It was thanks to those two qualities that the Americans set out to build what had never before been done. . . .
>
> How hard they worked is an astonishment to us in the twenty-first century. . . . Their hands were tough enough for any job—one never sees gloves in the photographs—which included pickax handling, shoveling, wielding sledgehammers, picking up iron rails, and using other equipment that required hands like iron. . . . They were men who could move things, hammer things in, swing things, whatever was required, in rain or snow or high winds or burning sun and scorching temperature, all day, every day. Nebraska can be hotter than hell, colder than the South Pole. They kept on working. They didn't whine, they didn't complain, they didn't quit, they just kept working.[44]

No railroad anywhere had crossed a continent stretching across some of the more treacherous and desolate terrain in the world. It was sheer audacity to propose a railroad over and through the Sierra Nevadas. Nothing like it had even been tried; nobody had ever tunneled through granite, the composition of this majestic mountain range. Almost a century later, when aerial surveys determined the best route for the interstate highway system, it paralleled the original route for the transcontinental railroad. It had taken America over two hundred years to expand over the Alleghenies and into the Ohio Valley, but the expansion across the rest of the West, expected to take another two hundred or even a thousand years, was completed in a few decades by the greatest building project of the nineteenth century.

Commodore Cornelius Vanderbilt built up the New York Central Railroad, leaving the largest personal fortune up until that time and becoming the second wealthiest American in history after John D. Rockefeller. Physically imposing, at the age of 50 he beat senseless one of the best New York boxers of his day.[45] As a child, Vanderbilt began work ferrying passengers between Staten Island and Manhattan, earning a reputation for being tough and reliable and repaying his mother's $100 loan plus an additional $1,000 in his first season. Vanderbilt worked in the steamboat business with Thomas Gibbons, the litigant who won a famous Supreme Court case *(Gibbons v. Ogden)*. He left the steamboat business, which had high fixed costs, for the railroad business, which also had high fixed costs, but had fixed lines as well. As a steamboat owner, he was among the first to be accused of being a "robber baron," named after medieval extortionists who purportedly lived along the Rhine and charged boats a fee to pass their castles unmolested. Vanderbilt's improbity was to accept payments to stop competing on a particular line or river. He simply moved his boats to someplace else where they could float and accept passengers and freight. His business philosophy was to operate as efficiently as possible and cut prices until the competitors sold out or went bankrupt. These were hardly the type of business practices that penalized consumers. In fact, his presence almost invariably led to lower fares and prices.[46]

The evolution of the railroad entailed development of a vast system of improvements and a plethora of inventions. Henry Pullman built the sleeping car that is his namesake; he also founded an entire town comprised of his workers' dwelling places. His car became famous when Mrs. Lincoln asked that it be part of the President's funeral train. To ensure a market for his cars, Pullman had to lobby hard for differing railroad track gauges to be replaced by a single national standard. Railroads were built along stockyards and shipped the cattle to slaughterhouses. Philip Armour and Gustavus Swift developed special refrigerator cars. Automatic couplers by Eli Hamilton Janney and air-brakes by George Westinghouse greatly improved railroad safety. Stopping a train had been very difficult—each car's brakes had to be set individually; derailments were frequent. Westinghouse's air brake enabled the train operator to brake all cars at once. These improvements added costs and the railroads were slow in implementing them until forced to by the efforts of Lorenzo Coffin. He worked for years to require use of the air brake through the railroad safety appliance law. Oil burning locomotives replaced coal- and wood-burning engines. The telegraph provided the mechanism for coordinating railroad traffic, particularly where there was only one line. By World War I, the railroad had 77 percent of intercity freight traffic and 98 percent of the passenger traffic.

The railroads became so powerful they literally controlled time. The building of national railroad networks created havoc with scheduling. Every locality was responsible for setting its own time. Generally, time was adjusted about one minute for every eleven miles traveled east or west. Some states had dozens of time zones. Railroad scheduling was chaotic, if not impossible. Congress was afraid of offending farmers and rural people by adopting standard time zones, but the railroads were forced to as the means of developing orderly schedules. In 1883 the railroads began operating on four standard time zones.

The railroad was originally built mainly to haul freight. Freight costs declined one percent a year in the first half of the nineteenth century and by one and a half percent a year in the second half. The railroad was so fast it became ideal for passenger traffic. By 1870, a rail ticket could get an individual across the entire continent in a few days—a trip that took Lewis and Clark (who traveled over only two-thirds of the continent—from St. Louis to the Pacific) over a year and a half less than seventy years earlier. The railroad integrated many communities and markets. Previously, this integration had occurred only at ocean and sea ports and towns with access to canals.

The railroads were an engineering marvel, but railroad owners soon became monopolists, as they over-charged farmers, consumers, and miners. Many branch lines were *de facto* monopolies and states tried to set up commissions and regulatory authorities to oversee rates. The Supreme Court ruled that the states did not have the power to regulate railroads moving goods across state lines. Congress then established the Interstate Commerce Commission (ICC) with legislation barring rebates and price fixing practices. In 1894 the Supreme Court ruled the ICC did not have authority to set actual rates, but in 1906 Congress provided the agency with that power. The Court upheld the amendment to allow the ICC to set and adjust rates and the agency became the model for other federal regulatory schemes.

Railroads were a capital-intensive industry, requiring far more capital than did textile plants or even canals. Total new investment in railroad equipment and track during the peak year of the 1880s exceeded all investment in the United States up until 1850. Railroad track mileage increased from 30,000 miles in 1860 to 166,000 in 1890 to 240,000 at the turn of the century. In the 1870s and 1880s, railroads, despite their risky nature and huge fixed costs, were the major market for capital. Their market value or capitalization was greater than all other industrial corporations combined, the latter being considered even riskier investments. Manufacturing powerhouses such as Standard Oil and Carnegie Steel generated sufficient income that they rarely tapped capital markets.

Many railroads were poorly run, were not structured for profitability, and contributed to financial panics of the period. The railroads were the first businesses widely managed by people who had little or no ownership interest. At the time, the law did not require them to act in the interest of the stockholders. Managers would often act in their individual interests at the expense of stockholders and customers. J. P. Morgan's intervention was frequently required; he became the most powerful force in the railroad industry by reorganizing the various companies into a mature business by the end of the nineteenth century and he exerted control to stop firms from reverting to bad practices by appointing colleagues to many company boards.[47] During the panic of 1873, Morgan had imposed order on the railroads—he controlled the largest number of them. He developed trusts to coordinate activities and avoid ruinous competition, such as the Sugar Trust and various railroad trusts. The Sherman antitrust law was passed to regulate these trusts, which were agreements where stockholders provided a board of trustees, controlling a portion of their stock, in return for a trust certificate. When the trusts failed to work as planned in the recession of 1893, holding companies were created, most of which were set up under New Jersey law. Morgan believed in trusts and holding companies as a way of establishing order and responsibility, provided they were done honestly and protected the consumer. As a financier, Morgan tried to prevent railroads from operating unprofitably. He leaned on major railroads to stop their plans to overbuild each other in order to ensure their long-term financial viability. He stopped the New York Central Railroad from overbuilding the Pennsylvania Railroad through the Allegheny Mountains. Decades later, the tunnels that had to be abandoned were used for the Pennsylvania Turnpike.

The railroads required huge initial investments and had high fixed costs, so they needed large volumes of traffic or high prices to make a profit. On competing lines, usually between cities, railroads couldn't charge enough to achieve profitability, so they tried to make up for the lost profits by raising rates on short-haul routes, enraging farmers and small businessmen. Rapid economic growth, however, eventually ensured the financial viability of the railroads. Total rail mileage went up seven fold and the value of manufactured goods shipped expanded seventeen fold, but the financial prospects for the industry were secured by a thirty-five fold increase in the freight-hauls shipped annually.[48] Railroads shared this financial windfall with their customers. Passenger rates declined 50 percent in the second half of the nineteenth century, while freight rates went down well over half in the last three decades of that century and by as much as 90 percent between the Civil War and World War I.

INVESTMENT BANKING

The explosive growth in the industrial and railroad sectors required a huge expansion of the capital markets. The Wall Street stock market and its most important banker, J.P. Morgan (1837–1913), became the financial center of the nation. Morgan's grandfather was a founder of the Aetna Fire Insurance Company and had major investments in Hartford, Connecticut. J. P. Morgan's father, Junius Morgan (1813–1890), and mentor started one of the first global investment banking firms, rivaled only by Barings and Rothschild. Morgan spent a great deal of his childhood in Europe, particularly London, the financial center of the world at the time, where his father familiarized him with international banking and investment, foreign cultures, and foreign languages.

Morgan worked hard to ensure capital requirements were met. The boom-and-bust cycle in stock markets and speculative excesses made Americans reluctant to invest in Wall Street ventures. Morgan instilled confidence in the markets, believing that "character determines credit." His life was built on trust and respect. In a country with a weak financial system, Morgan's word moved markets. He believed concentration of wealth was inevitable and in the public interest.

In its early years, America was dependent on foreign capital. Morgan coordinated the transfer of an enormous amount of wealth from Europe to the United States and acted as the nation's central banker. Morgan was born in the year Andrew Jackson let the national bank expire; he died the year the Federal Reserve System was created by legislation. He played a leading role throughout the critical decades of the late nineteenth and early twentieth centuries in providing stability to a marketplace that loathed uncertainty. Morgan was the first major stock promoter and investment banker. By 1912, he held seventy-two directorships in forty-seven companies. He became the subject of enormous public scrutiny and antitrust lawsuits. In the end, the pressures of congressional hearings and public criticism drove him to deep depression and insanity.

J. P. Morgan provided warranties and other investment options to attract capital to the industrial sector. One of his first investments was Edison Electric, which his father criticized at the time for being particularly risky. He recognized that Edison was not the one to run the business and installed a professional to manage what became General Electric (GE), which remained the major player in the electrical industry until after World War II.[49] GE was the only company on the original Dow Jones Industrial Average that remained there one hundred years later.

At the turn of the century, steel overtook railroads as the nation's most important business and Morgan worked also to consolidate that industry by addressing many of the same problems of overcapacity, cut-throat pricing, and speculation. In 1901, he bought out Andrew Carnegie for $480 million and combined Carnegie's firm with a number of smaller ones to create the world's largest industrial corporation. Morgan capitalized the company at the then unheard of figure of $1.4 billion, equivalent to 7 percent of the U.S. Gross National Product. The firm was an integrated company that controlled everything from coke and coal to steel mills to railroads. It controlled over half the nation's steelmaking capacity and was appropriately named U.S. Steel. The joke soon making the rounds told of a teacher asking his student about the origin of the world who replied—"God made the world in 4000 B.C., and in 1901 it was reorganized by J.P. Morgan."

OIL AND ENERGY

New inventions and technologies created entire new markets and enormous wealth. For almost all of human history, man's chief source of energy had been wood. The use of coal as an energy source was a key factor in the British industrial revolution in the nineteenth century. Oil was originally used for medicinal purposes. George Bissell launched a crusade to use it as an illuminant, recruiting the first professor of chemistry at Yale University, Benjamin Silliman, to endorse his approach (Yale then being the scientific capital of America). America's industrial revolution was creating a huge demand for artificial illumination, the main source of supply being whale oil, which was expensive. The other alternatives were ineffective or inaccessible. While oil, particularly in the form of kerosene, had been used for centuries for illumination in the Middle East, knowledge of these applications in the West had been lost.[50] Oil in the Middle East would bubble right up to the surface, while in the United States it was largely found well below ground level. In America, the major barriers to the use of kerosene were two fold: the lack of supply due to a non-existence of drilling capability; and the absence of a cheap lamp well-suited for interior uses that would overcome the problems of smell and smoke. The second problem was solved by importing an Austrian lamp with a glass chimney produced in Vienna. The Chinese had developed salt boring or drilling techniques fifteen hundred years earlier that found their way to Europe by the 1830s and then to America where in 1856 George Bissell saw a picture of a drilling rig on Broadway in New York. Edward Drake was dispatched by Bissell to Titusville, Pennsylvania, and became obsessed with the idea of drilling for oil. In 1859, after a year and a half of effort, he had no results. All the investors had lost belief in the project and Drake was ordered to close the mine. His salt-boring-drill struck oil at sixty-nine feet just as the shut down order arrived. Drake had no mechanism for storing the oil, so he used whiskey barrels. Soon, there was a huge surplus of oil, the price plummeted, and the whiskey barrels cost more than the oil itself.[51] One caught fire and the entire supply area suddenly exploded.

Within a decade of Drake's discovery, American oil production soared from 2,000 barrels a year to 4.25 million, and then to 60 million barrels by the turn of the century. The price was volatile, ranging from 10 cents a barrel to $13.75.[52] Due to the huge capital requirements, supply began to lag behind demand after the initial surge in production caused prices to plummet. Drilling at deep levels was enormously expensive and efficient refineries were even more costly.

John D. Rockefeller developed the modern oil industry, understanding better than anyone the technology, capital, and transport requirements. Rockefeller thus showed great foresight and leadership; he grasped the new drilling techniques, the use of pipeline networks, new oil storage techniques, rapidly advancing refinery technology, and the delivery system for refined products. He invested the proceeds from his drilling and transport business into oil refineries. Rockefeller gradually consolidated American refining capacity that was under his control by purchasing small competitors when the cost of entry was scarcely more than that of opening a store. He introduced economies of scale such as large refineries and more efficient transport, driving costs far below those of competitors. During an economic depression in the 1870s, Rockefeller bought out competitors, kept costs down, improved the quality of his products, and began to vertically integrate into oil and ore lands and distribution systems such as tank cars, ships, and storage facilities. Rockefeller controlled the overwhelming majority of oil production and exports, in effect exercising monopoly power and using predatory pricing to keep his market share. He required meticulous accounting and exerted fierce oversight of the finances and operations, for example, by reducing the number of beads of solder used to seal his five-gallon kerosene cans from forty to thirty-nine. Many competitors sold out to Rockefeller in return for a block of stock and a seat on one of his corporate boards. He wanted everyone involved in his enterprises to profit and thrive and, after his initial years, had good employee relations with no strikes.

> So highly did Rockefeller value personnel that during the first years of Standard Oil he personally attended to routine hiring matters. . . . Taking for granted the growth of his empire, he hired talented people as found not as needed.
>
> Far more than a technocrat, Rockefeller was an inspirational leader who exerted a magnetic power over workers and especially prized executives with social skills. . . .
>
> Employees were invited to send complaints or suggestions directly to him and he always took an interest in their affairs. His correspondence is replete with inquiries about sick or retired employees. Reasonably generous in wages, salaries, and pensions, he paid somewhat above the industry wage.[53]

His Standard Oil company "was the biggest and richest, the most feared and admired business organization in the world."[54]

Rockefeller was raised by his mother, a devout, stern Baptist who instilled in him the virtues of order, frugality, and prudence. He would wear the same suits until they had to be replaced. Rockefeller's children had only one tricycle, forcing them to learn to share. His namesake son walked to school and worked on the Rockefeller estate for laborers' wages. When his family's spending was too high, he would ask rhetorically, "who do you think we are, Vanderbilts?" Rockefeller concealed from his children the magnitude of his wealth. His daughter Bessie at Vassar

> went on a shopping expedition with some classmates to purchase a Christmas present for a favorite teacher. At a Manhattan store, they found the perfect gift: a $100 desk. Since Bessie and her companions had only $75, they asked the merchant if he could wait a few days for the remaining $25. He agreed to do so if a New York businessman would vouch for them. "My father is in business," Bessie offered meekly. "He will vouch for us," "Who is your father?" asked the man. "His name is Mr. Rockefeller," she said, "John D. Rockefeller; he is in the oil business." The man gasped. "John D. Rockefeller your father!" When he agreed to ship the furniture, Bessie imagined he had merely changed his mind to please them.[55]

Rockefeller was extremely religious and abstemious, refraining from tobacco, alcohol, caffeine, and, based on available evidence, extramarital sex. His father was dishonest, flamboyant, and a bigamist, moving in and out of his life so he could be with his second family. Rockefeller kept this part of his life a secret, as he did most of his dealings at Standard Oil. After retiring from Standard Oil, he gave more than $475 million to charity, started up and endowed the Rockefeller Foundation, and became a model for future philanthropy, having always tithed to his church. Rockefeller was strongly committed to education for African Americans; Spelman College in Atlanta bears his wife's maiden name.

Rockefeller was fortunate to be in the oil business during a time of rapid economic growth and vast expansion of markets. While electricity did supplant oil for internal lighting, the internal combustion engine was developed and used in cars, trains, and factories. Internal combustion engines used on ships, for example, were far more efficient and freed up space for additional cargo. Many electrical power plants used petroleum. About 1880 Rockefeller controlled 80 to 90 percent of the oil industry. When small producers secretly built a pipeline to circumvent his control, Rockefeller bought into the business and soon controlled the pipelines as well. He generally tried to become the low-cost producer. His investments and energy drove down the price of oil and oil products by well over half, spurring new uses, and benefiting the consumer.[56]

In the late 1890s, Russia became the largest crude oil producer in the world, surpassing the United States. This competitive advantage did not last for long. With Russian production suspended by war and revolution, American oil played a critical role in World War I. U.S. production rose to 67 percent of the world output in 1917. In contrast to the trust-busting at the beginning of that decade, government worked with business to allocate supplies to the Allies and the most important needs for the war. Shortages of both coal and oil forced some difficult decisions in allocating supplies, compounded by the fact that automobile ownership doubled between 1916 and 1918. Between 1911 and 1919, gasoline supply and demand rose from 7 million to 350 million gallons in substantial part due to the explosive growth of the automobile industry. Technology developed in World War I furthered oil exploration and production. Surface geology had yielded an ample supply of oil, but geophysics, such as the seismograph, provided new ways of "seeing" into the ground. Aerial photography, better drilling techniques for deeper wells, and microscopic analysis of fossils all helped lead to record discoveries of new oil deposits in the 1920s.[57] In the years after World War I, new discoveries by chemists in the oil refining sector permitted the introduction of a wide range of new products and the industry experienced record growth.

America had an abundance and variety of energy sources—oil, water-power, steam-power, coal, and electricity. Turbines were, for example, deployed at Niagara Falls to generate power. Energy use increased twenty fold between the end of the Civil War and the beginning of the Great Depression in the late 1920s. America produced and distributed energy more effectively and cheaply than did any other country.[58]

STEEL

Andrew Carnegie (1835–1919) not only built the nation's steel industry but also many of its public libraries. For over a century, beginning shortly after the Civil War, steel production was the measure of a nation's industrial power. Iron and steel production had been around for hundreds of years. What Carnegie did was to radically drive down costs and thereby expand applications. Steel, in lieu of stone, for example, became used in building skeletons: the nation saw skyscrapers dominate the skyline. Cheaper steel made the manufacture of automobiles increasingly profitable and the building of expansive bridges possible.

Carnegie's father was a skilled weaver in Scotland whose cottage work was eliminated by the industrial revolution in Great Britain. His sister, who had moved to America earlier, and his mother encouraged Carnegie's father and family to move to the United States. Andrew was twelve when they immigrated to Pennsylvania and shortly thereafter started to work in a variety of odd jobs and industries—as a bobbin boy and a telegraph messenger. Eventually, he made money in the telegraph and railroad businesses. He purposely picked steel as his industry, because of its prospects. There were cheap anthracite coal deposits in Pennsylvania, iron ore in Minnesota, and cheap transport on the Great Lakes, making Pittsburgh a logical capital for steel. One of Carnegie's early moves was to buy Henry Clay Frick's company that produced coke, a derivative of coal. Sir Henry Bessemer developed a steel-making process which was used simultaneously in Britain and the United States, enabling large amounts of very strong steel to be produced very cheaply. The Bessemer process was dependent on phosphorus-free iron ore, which fortuitously was found in great quantities in the Upper Peninsula of Michigan. New rail and canal lines were built to transport ore to Carnegie's Pittsburgh mills.

The open-hearth steel-making process, also imported from Europe, allowed manufacturing that was even cheaper and with ores previously unusable. Knowing savings would rapidly offset costs when high volumes were being manufactured, Carnegie quickly switched to the open-hearth process even though he had just completed major investments in the previous generation of technology. The U.S. produced very little steel at the time of the Civil War. With Carnegie's energetic management, steel production increased from 100,000 tons annually in 1870, to over a million tons in 1880, and 10 million tons by the turn of the century when Carnegie's company produced more steel than did all of Britain. Pittsburgh quintupled in size and became host to more industrial firms than all but a handful of cities in the world, including headquarters for Westinghouse Electric, Gulf Oil, Alcoa, Heinz Foods, and Mellon Bank.

Carnegie was zealous about inserting both accounting and accountability into the manufacturing process. Investing heavily in the latest equipment and technology, he used unit costs and productivity to cut prices to increase market share. Carnegie acquired many patents and was acutely aware of the importance of intellectual property in developing new business methods and generating profits. Steel was vital to many other industrial products. By keeping the price of steel down, many other products could be sold cheaply and the standard of living significantly increased. Carnegie understood the economic cycle and the importance of making the most of bad times, retaining as much in profits as he could in the good times to take advantage of opportunities in the down cycles. He sought out the best managers and paid them the highest wages. In one of the great labor-management confrontations in history, Carnegie broke the union at his Homestead plant. He liked to think of himself as a champion of the working man, but cheaper labor improved his profitability, a more important goal.[59]

Carnegie's mills were several times more efficient than the most technologically modern in Europe and drove down the price of steel by as much as 90 percent during the two decades before the turn of the century. This productivity improvement had a phenomenal impact on the U.S. standard of living: it also made Carnegie the richest man in the world.[60] Carnegie found new uses for steel in bridges, railroads, mass transit systems, military applications, and in new building technology. Carnegie's control of his huge empire was unusual, because most founders could not keep up with the capital needs of their firms. Carnegie reinvested his profits instead of paying them out to investors as dividends. Eventually, he sold the Carnegie steel corporation for

$480 million and spent the rest of his life giving away his money to projects useful to the public.

The steel industry spawned whole new industries and inventions. Carnegie ran one of the first companies to build iron railroad bridges to replace the wooden structures that so often broke down, disrupting rail traffic. New steel bridges dominated the New York City skyline. When it was completed, the Brooklyn Bridge was the world's longest span. The Hell Grate Bridge over the East River demonstrated the potential of the steel arch. When it opened, the George Washington Bridge over the Hudson River was twice as long as any suspension bridge. The use of the steel arch was extended by the Bayonne Bridge connecting Staten Island and New Jersey. The Verrazano-Narrows Bridge between Staten Island and Brooklyn was the world's longest for many years.

Along with the architectural design work of Louis Sullivan, Daniel Burnham, and John Root, steel made possible the skyscraper, which required elevators. There are today well over a million Otis elevators throughout the globe not only in office buildings, but in malls, apartment houses, silos, and museums. Elisha Otis was a tinkerer. Hoists had been around since the time of Rome, but Otis improved the concept by developing an automatic safety system. His business didn't take off until he used it in a publicity stunt at the 1853 New York World's Fair, riding one of the cars to the top of the shaft and cutting the cable with his own hand to demonstrate the effectiveness of the safety system. Otis died still in debt, but his sons built the business, buying out thirty competitors on their way to becoming the world leader in the elevator industry. Steam powered hoists moved only about fifty feet per minute, slower than many people could walk. Electrical motors radically changed the business, increasing the speed to 600 feet per minute. Electricity also moved air and water through the skyscrapers, making central heating and cooling possible. Portland cement was used throughout these structures to provide fire protection. With these innovations, building size increased by a dozen floors a decade and the highest concentration was in New York City where higher rents could be charged. The Roaring Twenties saw the construction of the Empire State and Chrysler buildings and Rockefeller Center. The Empire State Building rose on the site of the old Waldorf Astoria in just 14 months, with over 350,000 tons of glass, steel, limestone, and brick. A monument to the irrepressible optimism of America, it was built in the midst of the Depression at half of the projected cost, profiting from the decline in prices. It was the tallest skyscraper in New York for forty years. Surviving a crash by a 10-ton B-25 bomber in 1945 at 200 piles per hour that started a fire engulfing eleven floors, the building was open in 2 days for business as usual.

ALUMINUM

Andrew Mellon (1855–1937) made fortunes investing in various components of the industrial revolution and was considered a man of integrity. Mellon created the Mellon Institute, an early version of the think tank, which resulted in 600 patents and dozens of new companies. He backed Charles Hall the inventor of the process that greatly expanded the use of aluminum and helped him to found the Alcoa company. Aluminum was abundantly present but just a curiosity and more expensive than gold until Hall developed his process, which used huge amounts of electricity to convert the ore into a lightweight metal with limitless uses. Most investors could not see how this new metal could be exploited, but Mellon understood instinctively. Rapid declines in the cost of electricity further drove down costs for this metal, and it replaced steel in many products.

RUBBER AND PLASTICS

Charles Goodyear (1800-1860) spent most of his life heavily in debt, trying to develop vulcanized rubber. Rubber came to America about the time of Alexis de Tocqueville in the 1830s. Its debut was less than auspicious—it was belatedly found to be susceptible to radical changes—hardening to the consistency and brittleness of china in winter, melting into a bubble-gum-like substance in summer, and emitting a terrible odor when placed in contact with oil or acid. Vulcanized rubber is found in many products used today. Obvious applications are tires, shoes, floors, raincoats, and rubber bands. It is also found in countless places that are not so obvious—elevators, televisions, computers, refrigerators, motor bearings, transmission belts, and printed circuit boards. Rubber is a critical insulating material for electrical power, telephones, and plumbing. Powered flight would not be possible without rubber. Virtually every piece of machinery contains crucial components made of rubber. Being heavily in debt, Goodyear's family lived in misery, frequently having its belongings pawned off, and constantly having its meager living accommodations doubling as a laboratory to develop his latest improvements for rubber. Goodyear failed to secure intellectual property rights for his invention in Great Britain and fought a seemingly never-ending patent battle, being represented by Daniel Webster. Hundreds of inventors and businessman worked on the problem, but Goodyear's persistence yielded the final result. His eventual solution was to heat rubber with sulfur, lead, and a couple of other minor elements to make it vulcanized.[61]

Plastics were invented by an immigrant from Belgium, Leo Baekeland (1863–1944), who mixed chemicals in his garage, hoping to find a substitute for shellac, then in short supply, the only source being a beetle found in India and Burma. Baekeland directed one of several teams working on a substitute—all of them met with repeated failures. He eventually made the first synthetic substance that would not conduct electricity, would not melt or break, and was quick and cheap to make. His product, originally called Bakelite, was invented at a time there were many devices being developed with interchangeable parts and plastics soon had almost limitless possibilities. It was used on most household appliances, in many weapons systems, and in countless applications for automobiles—in the starter or ignition, couplings, timing gears, steering wheels, door handles, instrument panels, gearshift knobs, and engine caps. Baekeland tried to license his invention, but most manufacturers could not replicate his success. He was forced to start his own manufacturing company, eventually selling it to Union Carbide. In the late 1920s Du Pont Company chemists developed polymers, the next generation of plastics.

American Civilization in 1900

The turn of the century was a critical time for America. Henry Adams, the great grandson of John Adams, wrote: "measured by any standard known to science—by horsepower, calories, volts, mass in any shape—the tension and vibration and volume and so-called progression of society were fully a thousand times greater in 1900 than in 1800." His 1854 Harvard education he thought was useless, probably nearer in thought to the year 1 than to that of the year 1900.[62] In the previous decade, America had become the largest economy on earth. The country had made enormous advances in agriculture and manufacturing and was leading the world in both fields. Imagine attending a class on American civilization in 1900—the median age of an American was only twenty-three years old. There would be few cars and little electricity, which was largely restricted to big cities and factories. The class would probably have met by gas light. There were very few phones, which were used sparingly due to the high costs of making a call (four dollars a minute across the country). There was no radio, except on ships. Many of the clothes worn today didn't exist, because synthetic fabric hadn't been invented. Contact lenses hadn't been developed. Writing was done with a different kind of pen, because ball-point and gel pens didn't yet exist. A third of the class seats would be empty, representing the people who would have died of diseases cured since 1900—life expectancy was just forty-seven years. This scenario doesn't even include some of the really big changes, such as television, the atomic bomb, spacecraft, and numerous advances in medical technology.

The year 1903 was a landmark with three major achievements—the Wright brothers flight at Kitty Hawk, Henry Ford producing his first automobile, and the first motion picture, *The Great Train Robbery.* Compare these early twentieth century changes with the advances of the last one hundreds years—the landing on the moon, the discovery of DNA, the development of the computer chip. Today, a traveler gets in a computerized car that has air conditioning, is sealed against road noise even though roads are paved, has tires that work an extraordinary number of miles without breaking, puts in a CD, drives to the airport, gets aboard a 747 to go to Paris or London or Tokyo. The airline shows a color movie and feeds passengers on the plane. No one gets off and says, ""What a miracle!" They normally say something like, "I've already seen the movie and the food wasn't very good." Many things are taken for granted, just become part of life.

The normal way of viewing change and technology is to conclude "we know the past changed and now we're modern. We live in the modern era." It is human nature to think, "I am now living in the modern era." A far more accurate view of technology and change is that we are in the middle or perhaps just past the beginning of a huge wave of change. If you think "we are smart, look how far we have come," that represents a kind of arrogance. Instead, we should look at the process as part of a long, exciting journey. Then we begin to get the sense of the scale of change and how much there is to live through and how much will become different. An outstanding example of this progressive concept is the American automobile.

The Automobile Changes Everything

In the early twentieth century, the railroad was the transport mechanism of choice for goods. The automobile became the personal transport device by the 1920s, although early in the century, the idea that the automobile would replace the horse was satirized: cars would often break down and were less reliable. Financial markets balked at investing in the new industry. The automobile was considered a device of the mechanically inclined and a luxury suitable for the well-to-do. Yet, the 5000-year reign of the horse as the prime mover of man was soon over. For New York City alone, this meant 2.5 million less pounds of manure in the streets and 60,000 gallons less urine everyday; and 15,000 fewer dead horses every year.

Actually, America was relatively slow to develop the automobile: Germany and France initially led the way. Industrial entrepreneurs Gottlieb Daimler and Carl Benz built the first cars powered by internal combustion engines. The Duryea brothers, Charles and Frank, built a gasoline engine motor vehicle in 1893 and made thirteen "motor wagons" in 1896. Like the Wright brothers, they were bicycle builders and repairmen, fashioning the first steering wheel, a tiller based on bicycle handlebars. All early cars were built by hand craftsmen, so the car would work as a unit, but if the owner took a part off the car and tried to fix a neighbor's car made by the same craftsmen, he could not repair it. This was the centuries-old process used for carriages.

The U.S. was, however, an incubator for industry and manufacturing. By observing the meat-packing industry and other manufacturers, Henry Ford (1863-1947) developed interchangeable parts and the mass production methods for the automobile. The ice industry in New England led to refrigeration, which, in turn, built the meat-packing and slaughtering industry into the nation's largest employer; this system provided the basis for the automobile assembly line. By mastering the concept of mass production, Ford created the ability to take parts from any box, put them together, and make a car, which had a level of precision unheard of at the time. To do this, every part had to be precisely machined. Ford put all of these parts together in an assembly line. Ford engineers utilized machine tools to drastically reduce the labor and materials required for various stages of molding, stamping, planing, and drilling. The assembly line became not just a method of manufacturing, but a philosophy of economic life.[63]

The genius of Edison's invention factory energized a strong foundation for the many inventions and innovations required to produce a vehicle. With the availability of cheap oil, Ford could use the internal combustion engine to revolutionize transportation. American predominance in a wide variety of industries such as steel, rubber, and plastics gave Ford the materials and capability to develop a world-class car. He built upon the know-how of countless revolutions that had already made America a great industrial nation. Ford's mass production techniques became one of the central organizing principles of American industry for much of the twentieth century.

Henry Ford's relentless drive to lower costs resulted in the Ford Model T, one of the amazing economic success stories in world history. Earlier versions of the automobile were built for the rich; Ford sought to develop a car for the multitude, and Thomas Edison gave him early encouragement. After establishing two companies that failed and numerous prototype models, Ford developed a car that was safer, more reliable, stronger, and easier to drive than other automobiles. He started out selling thousands of Model T's at $850 each and within a decade he was selling hundreds of thousands a year at half the price. The Model T was assembled in an hour and a half. As the volume and popularity ramped up, the cost went down to $360 in 1916 when over 700,000 were sold and then to $265 after World War I, even with the inflationary pressures caused by that conflict.

Ford enticed workers to his production lines, and then into buying cars, by offering an unheard-of $5 a day in wages for those on the job more than 6 months. His motivation was several fold: to provide workers with sufficient funds to buy his product, reduce employee turnover, and improve morale. Even with these high wages, labor costs were being reduced by over 7 percent a year.[64] Ford developed the purchasing plan for the consumer, enabling monthly payments until enough funds had been accumulated to purchase a Ford.

Ford's innovations on the assembly line doubled production almost every year. By the end of another decade when he discontinued the Model T, he had sold a total of 15 million and had more than $700 million in undistributed profits. Ford became a billionaire. His mass-produced automobile fueled egalitarianism and enabled the masses to gain freedom of movement. Ford built his cars so the owners could perform repairs with a set of tools included with the car. He drove down the costs of his cars by manufacturing his own engines, brakes, gears, and axles instead of buying them from subcontractors. The U.S. Patent Office and the courts gave George Selden a patent on the internal combustion engine. Ford spent years in court, so he could produce a car with his own more efficient engine without being forced to pay royalties. Ford developed a lightweight steel to make his cars lighter and faster, as well as cheaper to run. The time for assembly was drastically reduced by improving productivity on the assembly line. In 1914, he produced half of America's cars with only one-sixth of the workers in the automobile industry.[65] In 1920 Ford was producing half the cars built in the world. The success of the Model T caused the entire automobile industry to take off. From 4,000 cars in 1900, the country produced 187,000 in 1910. By 1920 some 1.9 million cars rolled off assembly lines, and 8.1 million vehicles were registered. By 1929 production was up to 4.5 million cars, and 23.1 million had been registered.[66]

The automobile is in many ways an American phenomenon, symbol of U.S. industrial dominance. Early pioneers in the industry included: Ransom Olds, who was the first mass-producer of gasoline automobiles in the world and founder of Oldsmobile; William Durant, founder of General Motors (GM); Frederic and Charles Fisher, who founded Fisher Body; John and Horace Dodge, who initially owned a bicycle company and became a major parts supplier; David Buick, who built the world's most powerful engine that became the basis for GM cars; and Walter Chrysler, who founded the Chrysler Corporation. Bicycle manufacturers made enormous progress in developing the metal forming techniques used to make automobile bodies. By 1908, an estimated 485 different manufacturers were building cars in the United States. Employment grew nearly a hundredfold during the first decade of the twentieth century. Just prior to World War I, Americans owned well over two-thirds of the more than one and a half million automobiles on the planet, and had 75 percent of the world production. By the middle of the century, American ownership actually increased to 80 percent or 40 out of 50 million cars then in the world. In the early seventies, U.S. manufacturers had dropped to below half of the world production, but Americans still owned over 100 million of the 220 million cars on the planet. The automobile was in many ways the culmination of the industrial revolution—a mass produced method of transportation involving the assemblage of countless industrial inventions and improvements in manufacturing.

Until the 1920s, Ford Motor Company was on a run—producing more and more cars. If someone had asked in 1921 "What will be the dominant automobile company?", almost everyone would have said, "Ford Motor Company." In 1922, however, Alfred Sloan took over GM when it was near bankruptcy and began to reinvent it. GM had been a collection of companies bought by Sloan's predecessor and the founder, William Durant. Most of these businesses were bought from their entrepreneurial founders and consisted of parts and components manufacturers or car assemblers. Sloan changed the nature of the auto industry so that when he retired in 1956 the General Motors Company had become the largest industrial company in the world.

Over time Sloan implemented at least five major reforms. First, he invented the annual production change so that new models were turned out every year, because the consumer wanted a status symbol and proof of being up to date. Ford allowed the Model T to be produced just one way to drive down costs. Sloan came along after World War I and said, "Gee, people are getting richer. They already have a Model T. I'll bet they want something new and some variety. Not only that, they are going to want to show off their social status to their neighbors. We'll charge slightly more for them and our advertising will emphasize that if you get a promotion, you ought to trade in the Ford for a Chevrolet." He made the consumer feel he needed the 1925 Chevrolet and not an old 1924 Ford. Ford despised the annual model change, because it drove up costs. But there was a new generation that was willing to pay for the social value—the customer was defining a new market. The consumer already had basic transportation. Customers then defined the value of status, comfort, and looking good to their friends.

Second, Sloan developed a plan to enable the customer to pay on the installment plan. Previously, the customer would pay for the car in cash or by special loan agreement. Over time, installment credit exceeded other types of consumer credit and became the normal and accepted method of buying a car.

Third, he created the used-car market. Sloan left his job for one week every quarter and sold cars on a lot somewhere in America. He went all the way down what has been described as the "directed telescope." He is at the head of GM in Detroit and went all the way down to the front line of the corporation. He stood out there, in a different part of the country every quarter, listening to customer questions. Sloan found that if his great strategy were to work, buying a 1925 Chevrolet to replace the 1924 Ford or Chevrolet, the customer had a problem—getting rid of the old car. Sloan invented the used-car market, because if he couldn't find a way to get rid of the old car or to use the old car as a form of down payment, he couldn't get the customer to buy a new one.

Fourth, Sloan made a number of technological advances, including the closed body, automatic transmission, turn signals, power steering, hydraulic brakes, power brakes, and air conditioning.

Fifth, he developed the modern personnel system, including the labor contract, stock options, and incentives.

Sloan used innovation and invention to develop what was the greatest industrial corporation in the world. He believed he was not as smart as Henry Ford, but that a collection of smart people working in a committee could beat a genius working solo. Sloan was famous for never making a personnel decision the first time it came up. Only when it came up with the same name two or three times in a row was he willing to proceed. Peter Drucker cited him for exemplary employee and human relations.

GM outmoded Ford. Henry Ford refused to alter his basic model, because he thought cheaper was better and viewed the car as just a form of transportation. He even refused to put an electrical starter in his Model T because of the weight added by the addition of a battery. Many customers had a great deal of difficulty cranking their cars to start. Alfred Sloan saw cars were far more than that: status symbols and, for many people, a statement about their personalities. GM provided an entire range of models to customers. In 1927 in the midst of the boom, Henry Ford was forced to shut down his product line for eighteen months to produce a new Model A.[67]

The invention of the automobile changed American society in fundamental ways. Automobile production had a huge impact on the economy, using 20 percent of the steel produced in the country, 80 percent of the rubber, and 75 percent of the plate glass. In the 1920s, the explosive demand for cars helped fuel an unprecedented boom—Gross National Product (GNP) increased 59 percent between 1921 and 1929, with GNP per capita up 42 percent and personal income by 38 percent. The mileage for paved roads increased from almost nothing in 1900 to 369,000 miles in 1920 to 662,000 miles by 1929. The new roads stimulated the local economies, including the establishment of countless gasoline stations and motels.[68] The average annual miles driven per car increased from 4500 in 1919 to 7500 in 1929. During this decade, the drive-in service station became popular, along with hot-dog stands and roadside restaurants. At the beginning of the 1920s almost all of the 100,000 establishments selling gasoline were general stores, grocery stores, and hardware stores. By the end of the decade, the 300,000 establishments selling gasoline were almost all gas stations or garages. Brand advertising became important. The tradition of providing road maps for free started. Price fluctuations generated public outcries and congressional hearings. The modern automobile industry was rapidly maturing.[69]

The automobile shifted the balance of power from centralized hierarchies back towards the individual. The automobile outmoded rail transit—the last transcontinental railroad was built in 1904. As electricity and telephones had done, cars encouraged decentralized metropolitan areas. These three inventions gave every individual throughout a region access to the same power, communications, and mobility, as long as each was hooked into the electrical grid, telephone network and road network, respectively.[70] The automobile helped to end the isolation of farms and rural areas and allowed development of suburbs beyond railroad lines. Farms became more accessible; farm machinery became more mechanized and cheaper (tractors and other equipment were being more efficiently built with mass production).

People could more readily commute to work and had more job flexibility. The automobile industry created millions of jobs. For the last half of the twentieth century, 1 in every 6 or 7 jobs in America was related to the automobile. Many of those jobs were with suppliers, others were with service stations, or repair shops.

The automobile had far more impact in the United States than anywhere else. In the 1960s, approximately 4 out of every 5 cars in the world were registered in America. There were 5 people for every car in the United States, 30 in England, 33 in France, 100 in Germany, 702 in Japan and 6,130 in the Soviet Union. Gasoline became a major share of U.S. oil and energy consumption.[71]

The financial system was significantly altered, as more and more people went into personal debt to buy cars. Installment loans and other techniques for selling cars spawned a new financial industry.

Previously, most shopping was done at the general store and by catalogue, but now shopping centers and the mall became shoppers' magnets. Consumers had more options for banking, and rural banks began failing even in the prosperous 1920s, a trend that escalated in the Great Depression.

The automobile made possible the fast-food industry. In an increasingly fast-paced society, more and more meals were eaten inside cars. The automobile brought other cultural changes. It became a top status symbol, often the primary determinant of social standing in the community. Teenagers early priority became obtaining a driver's license, which perhaps became the vehicle for their first sexual experience. Often, the car rather than the family became an introduction to sex.

Unfortunately, the car became the major cause of death for people between the ages of 15 and 45, as well as a major crime accessory.[72]

> The automobile was essential to the day-to-day operations of the well-organized criminals on urban frontiers. Gangsters were often better equipped than the law-enforcing agencies that had to operate within limited budgets and had to persuade public bodies of the reasonableness of their requests. The automobile gave the Prohibition gangsters the "getaway car" in which they could elude the police, dispose of their enemies and quickly move to another jurisdiction where the pursuing police had no authority. The automobile also made their customers more mobile, and this enabled them to disperse their illegal activities into roadhouses far out in the countryside, or when more convenient to concentrate their gambling resorts, houses of prostitution and speakeasies in suburbs like Chicago's Cicero. It is hard to imagine how bootleggers of beer and liquor could have prospered by relying on the slow-moving horse and wagon or on the inflexible routs of the railroads.[73]

By the end of the 1920s the U.S. was the leading economy, manufacturer, and exporter in the world. Quite a run for a country that started out only one hundred fifty years earlier as a sliver of the East coast with a tiny percentage of the world's population.

Looking back over the twentieth century just past, many individuals and forces have been credited with the fall of fascism and communism. Edison, perhaps more than any other individual, contributed to the demise of totalitarian regimes. He totally turned Marx's concepts and thoughts on their head. Edison's invention factory freed the middle class and the ordinary individual from many ancient everyday drudgeries; it democratized access to new technologies and the latest products; it let everyman live life in the style of a king. Edison helped to make America into an industrial powerhouse with the economic and military strength to bring an end to these two political systems. When he died at age 85, the Statute of Liberty's illuminated torch was extinguished in tribute.

9

Theodore Roosevelt
and the not so progressive era

AT A STOP IN MILWAUKEE during his 1912 campaign for the presidency on the Bull Moose ticket, a deranged man shot Theodore Roosevelt (1858–1919) at point blank range. After righting himself from the shock, Roosevelt instructed the crowd not to harm his would-be assassin, waived off doctors urging him to seek medical treatment, and proceeded to the auditorium to speak as scheduled. Even though the bullet fractured a rib and lodged near his lung, he delivered the hour-and-a-half speech, gaining strength as he proceeded even as he bled profusely. The crowd reached a near frenzy as he concluded his speech with charismatic flourish. He then admitted himself to a hospital.

Though born into wealth and privilege, Theodore Roosevelt had major obstacles to surmount. Weak from asthma and other maladies, he survived childhood through a regime of rigorous exercise. Roosevelt also worked hard to meet his commitments to his revered father, including abstaining from sexual intercourse until marriage. In his youth, doctors informed him that he must lead a limited life because of a weak heart, but he nevertheless became an athletic boxer and outdoorsman and married one of the most beautiful and socially well-placed girls in

Boston, Alice Hathaway Lee. An avid mountain climber, Roosevelt scaled the Matterhorn less than twenty years after it was first conquered. As a New York Assemblyman, he raced home from Albany upon the birth of his first child, only to find both his young wife and own mother terminally ill. The diary for that date, Valentine's Day 1884, reads only, "the light has gone out of my life." The terrible Midwest winter of 1885–1886 wiped out Roosevelt's inheritance tied up in thousands of cattle, but caused him to return East, to become a full-time writer, and to re-enter politics and national life.[1]

An avid speed reader who could consume two or three books daily, Roosevelt wrote at least 8 million words in 3 dozen books, hundreds of magazine articles, and 150,000 letters. Fluid in several languages, he would accommodate guests by switching to their native language. Roosevelt had no speechwriter or press agent, but had much to say on almost any topic.

President Hayes attempted to appoint Theodore Roosevelt's father to replace Chester Arthur as Collector of Customs for the Port of New York. Senator Roscoe Conkling opposed the nomination, a stressful ordeal that led to the father's death and turned Theodore into a committed reformer. As a man of action, Roosevelt brought a high level of energy to every job he held—New York Assemblyman, City Police Commissioner, Civil Service Commissioner, Assistant Secretary of the Navy, Governor of New York, and leader of the famous Rough Riders. Under heavy fire at Kettle and San Juan Hills during the Spanish-American War, Roosevelt took heroic action to secure a victory that eventually catapulted him into the presidency.

The ascension of Roosevelt to the presidency in 1901 gave the progressive movement an energetic and enthusiastic national leader who embodied its spirit. President Grover Cleveland regarded him as "one of the ablest men yet produced in human history." Roosevelt selected highly qualified individuals, delegating authority and responsibility to them with the expectation that they would exercise their independent judgment. His administration was staffed by top-flight people such as Henry Stimson as U.S. Attorney, John Hay as Secretary of State, and William Howard Taft and Elihu Root who each served as Secretary of War.

Roosevelt understood and seized upon America's expanding role in the world. For mediating the Russo-Japanese War, he received the Nobel Peace Prize, an irony considering his militarism and reputation for "speaking softly and carrying a big stick." Roosevelt dealt effectively with public revulsion over the allegations of widespread use of water torture by American troops against guerrillas in the Philippines. Advocating military preparedness, he dispatched the naval fleet on a voyage around the globe. The sixteen battleships became a symbol of America's new-found greatness, and countries around the world begged to have the fleet call at their ports

Roosevelt doubled the number of national parks, declared over fifty wild-bird refuges, and set aside 150 million acres of timberland, including Muir Woods, Mount Olympus, and the Grand Canyon. When Congress passed a provision in an omnibus appropriations bill to stop the designation of any more forest reserves in six states, Roosevelt spent night and day proclaiming national forests in those very states before signing the required legislation. More than any other president, he understood the importance of conservation and man's role in preserving the earth.

The Progressive Movement and the Big Corporation

Genesis of the progressive movement was the great industrial and cultural revolution of the nineteenth century that brought rapid change, crime, poverty, and unsafe working conditions as well as uneven improvements in health, education, nutrition, and longevity. Around the turn of the century, there was a prevailing mood of irritation among Americans. "The average American in great numbers had the feeling he was being 'put upon' by something he couldn't see or get his fingers on; that somebody was 'riding him'; that some force or other was 'cowing' him. . . . This unseen enemy he tried to personify. He called it Invisible Government, the Money Interests, the Gold Bugs, Wall Street, the Trusts."[2] This mood was caused by industrialization, plus the end of the

U.S. frontier and its free land, the new income tax, the rise of trusts and monopolies, the boom-and-bust economy, and perhaps elements of American life that suddenly had enlarged including the new concept of the U.S. as a world power.

Industrialization resulted in a movement away from family farms, small businesses, and entrepreneurial activity. The rise in agricultural productivity diminished the role of the small family farm. Large farms could profit more effectively from mass production techniques and new technology. Thomas Jefferson's ideal of the yeoman farmer disappeared as agricultural corporations expanded their market share and took advantage of protective tariffs. To help offset these effects, farmers did organize into cooperatives, such as the Grange. Increased productivity and larger farms enabled the U.S. to maintain a competitive advantage and to lead the world in producing agricultural products. Many of America's entrepreneurial farmers became factory workers, losing their independence.

Increasing percentages of workers became employed in the manufacturing sector, moving to the cities and becoming more vulnerable during recessions. In 1850, 15 percent of the American population or 3.5 million people lived in cities of more than 2500 inhabitants; by 1900 it was almost 40 percent or 30 million people. In *How the Other Half Lives,* Jacob Riis described the dire poverty and suffering of Americans in New York tenements. The majority of New Yorkers lived in squalid structures four- to six-stories high with several families squeezed into each floor. Children survived by peddling newspapers, blacking boots, begging, and stealing, often missing meals and school. Over 90 percent of family spending went to food, clothing, and shelter. Women often worked 16-hour days at wages of 60 cents a day.[3] The poverty brought on by the industrial revolution went against the grain of the American Revolution and national sensibilities. Protest movements mushroomed; there was an air of unease.

The driving forces of the progressive movement were the Second and Third Great Awakenings, which overlapped considerably and were responsible for abolitionist and temperance movements, efforts to eliminate graft in government, educational and civil service reform, child labor laws, and women's suffrage. During the progressive era, social reform replaced personal reform and religious conversion as the thrust of the religious reform movement. As a result of death and service in the Civil War, many fathers were absent from the home and women were more responsible for child rearing. This more nurturing and caring environment produced a more progressive and reform worldview; expansion of the franchise was probably its most significant achievement. The Fifteenth Amendment to the Constitution guaranteed African Americans the right to vote, the Seventeenth Amendment provided for the direct election of Senators, and the Nineteenth Amendment provided for women's suffrage after a long struggle by advocates such as Elizabeth Cady Stanton and Susan B. Anthony. The secret ballot became the accepted method for voting in lieu of individuals casting votes publicly.

The progressive movement had other successes as well. In the 1880s and early 1890s after President Garfield's assassination by a disgruntled federal jobseeker, Theodore Roosevelt headed the Civil Service Commission that sought to implement the reforms to make federal government employment opportunities available to all American citizens, to allow only the meritorious to be appointed, and to ensure that public servants not be penalized for expressing their political beliefs.[4] State and local governments made some tentative efforts to improve worker safety, to limit child labor, and to improve health care and welfare. During Roosevelt's administration, muckrakers and publications such as Sinclair Lewis's *The Jungle* led to improved food safety and inspection laws. Roosevelt proposed and secured passage of legislation prohibiting corporate contributions in federal elections. Women were granted property rights and given control over their income.[5] Many other ideas for social improvement originated in this era, including popular initiative via the ballot, pensions, and workers' insurance.

The Triangle Shirtwaist fire in New York killed forty-six women, many of them forced to jump to their deaths. The tallest fire ladder reached only to the sixth floor, the factory being on floors eight through ten. The fire led to passage of dozens of reform bills, including strengthened fire and safety codes, workers' compensation, a 54-hour workweek for women and children, and a ban on night factory work for women. The proponents of reform included future Democratic presidential nominee Al Smith, and Franklin Delano Roosevelt, then a state Senator.

The progressive era, however, was not everything the name implied or that historians made it out to be. The Civil War had destroyed much of civil society in the South and weakened it in the North; but instead of restoring it, the nation became transfixed in a state of suspense over the effects from the war and industrialization. The Congress, the executive branch of government, and political system reacted slowly to industrial concentration and the enormous changes that were occurring after the Civil War. Pragmatism was emphasized over commitment to principle and doing what is right. The Progressive Era attempted to address abuses such as child labor, corruption, pitiful working conditions, and impoverished neighborhoods. Many of these initiatives had mixed results and left the institutions of civil society in a demoralized condition. Only very limited legislation was passed before the end of the century, as action was frustrated by government corruption and powerful industrial corporations.

Worse still, this so-called "progressive era" witnessed regression in critical areas. After the Civil War, which had given America its most wrenching experience, the courts and the South turned the clock back on civil rights, relegating African Americans to a status only somewhat better than slavery. As the role of government expanded, so did the level of corruption. Progressives did act to stem that venality, but these efforts met only with mixed success. Overall, government operated more on patronage and less on principle, emphasizing spoils more than issues. While the levels of immigration continued to soar, legislation was passed limiting the free influx of people, beginning a slow process of turning inward and closing the borders. American industry continued to penalize the consumer and live in fear of competition by supporting high tariffs and trade barriers, leading to a virulent form of protectionism. Sterilization was legalized. Civil society and the private sector were forming new pluralist models, such as the labor union, public trusts, public library systems, and hospitals, but the political culture and government often thwarted these initiatives.

When President McKinley (1843–1901) was assassinated in Buffalo in 1901, Theodore Roosevelt assumed the presidency and decided to put an end to unchecked expansion and consolidation by big business. The single greatest change of the industrial era was almost undoubtedly the rise of the entrepreneur, capitalist, "titan," or "tycoon." In the Industrial Age, America became defined, more than any other civilization in history, by Andrew Carnegie, J.P. Morgan, John D. Rockefeller, Henry Ford, and other businessmen, who had more impact on America than had any president, philosopher, or celebrity from that era. Increasingly, the wealthy formed tight social cliques that might turn into combinations in restraint of trade. During the 1890s, the hundred largest corporations grew by several fold and controlled as much as forty percent of the economy. At the start of the twentieth century, 4,000 families controlled 20 percent of the nation's wealth. Rockefeller was the richest man in the history of the republic. Carnegie, Morgan, and others were not far behind. The Vanderbilts and other wealthy families owned numerous million-dollar mansions.

In *America as a Civilization,* Max Lerner described the traits of these giants and the differences in their styles:

> Where other civilization types have pursued wisdom, beauty, sanctity, military glory, predacity, asceticism, the businessman pursues the magnitudes of profit with a similar single-minded drive. . . . The survivors in the fierce competitive struggle were those who most clearly embodied the businessman's single-mindedness of purpose. . . .
>
> There is one division which cuts across most of the Titans of the earlier prewar era of America—the split between the Puritan and the magnifico. J. Pierpont Morgan, the greatest of all the Titans, was a magnifico in the sense that he operated on a scale of magnificence. . . . There was a lustiness and a grandeur of scope in their private as in their business lives. They bet and gambled, lived conspicuously, gave parties, sailed yachts, were seen in the European capitals; there were legends of the stables of women they kept; they built palatial homes and crammed them with art treas-

ures rifled from the museums and collections of Europe. There was a native optimism in them: in business as in private life they were "bullish"; their motto was Morgan's "never sell America short"; their fortunes were made on the upward arc of an expanding economy. They saw far enough ahead to see the expansion and contributed to it their boldness and measure of vision.

There was another strain, however, represented by Daniel Drew, the Rockefellers, Henry Ford: not the strain of magnificence but of taut Puritan qualities. These men came out of the small towns and remained at home in small-town America. They were abstemious, church-going, taught Sunday-School classes. They spent little on themselves, and what they did they spent quietly. Like Rockefeller, they handed out shiny dimes; like Ford, they plowed everything back into the business. They had the eccentricities in which men can indulge when they sit on top of a pyramid of power. They were apt to be gloomy men and presented a stern visage to the world, at once unsmiling and unrelenting. Yet, they were probably closer than the magnificos to the theological roots of capitalism: the demonstration of virtue through success, the doctrine of calling, the gospel of work and thrift.[6]

Rockefeller, Carnegie, Morgan, and other business leaders were moving rapidly to create the modern corporation and an entire new economy. Outdated laws made it difficult for corporations to operate nationally, much less globally. State incorporation laws often limited economic activities to just one state. These industrialists were often acting as the radical reformers, inventing new corporate structures and types of organization to implement what seemed to them to be to the benefit of the country, the consumer, and their business and industry. Their journalist and muckraking opponents were often actually the conservatives, opposing change. The practices of these businessmen or "robber barons" were sometimes brutal but usually legal. The slow political process and weak government could barely monitor what was happening much less take action to enact legislation and ensure enforcement of the rules.

Rockefeller used the corporate structure to build his business and developed the trust to manage and hold his investments. When the trust was limited, he formed a holding company that dominated the industry and eventually enabled Standard Oil to pay large annual dividends. Rockefeller extorted money from railroads, even securing secret rebates on oil shipped by his competitors, in effect levying a tax on his competition. While such activities were often not illegal when they occurred, they raised substantial questions about the concentration of wealth.

Increasingly, states enacted antitrust and anti-monopoly legislation. These state laws were often conflicting and overlapping and usually had little effect; state courts frequently took decades to sort out the legal issues and the Supreme Court ruled states cannot regulate commerce originating or ending out of state even if there is no alternative form of federal regulation. In 1890, the federal government enacted the Sherman antitrust law, which was vague but generally targeted at the extraction of railroad rebates by Standard Oil, cartel agreements, and monopolistic horizontal mergers. In 1903, railroad rebates were specifically prohibited by law. Initially, enforcement was haphazard and resisted by the courts. In the 1890s, Supreme Court decisions condoned many monopolistic practices and made them hard to prosecute at the federal level. The Interstate Commerce Commission was established and eventually granted authority to limit the rates set by railroads and, in later decades, trucking firms and water carriers.

Mergers jumped from 69 in 1897 to over 1200 in 1899, but President McKinley did not interpose any antitrust obstacles.[7] When his successor Theodore Roosevelt asserted the jurisdiction of the federal government over these trusts and corporations, the government's power to control them was questionable. Large integrated corporations had over 100,000 employees and a market value in the hundreds of millions of dollars, and, in the case of U.S. Steel, well over a billion dollars. Roosevelt feared the possibility of social unrest and initially relied on the use of publicity to rein in corporate behavior.[8] As part of his antitrust effort, Roosevelt proposed and Congress passed a bill establishing a Department of Commerce and Labor, including a Bureau of Corporation that monitored and investigated concentrations of wealth and potential violations of antitrust laws. A law was passed expediting the processing of antitrust suits in the courts.

J. P. Morgan's Northern Securities Company merged the Great Northern, the Northern Pacific, and the Chicago, Burlington and Quincy railroads into a single northwestern company with considerable power over rates. President Roosevelt invigorated the antitrust movement by directing Attorney General Knox to prosecute Northern Securities trust, which controlled rail traffic between the Great Lakes and the Pacific Coast. The suit was in part an effort to boost the Roosevelt Administration's popularity and relations with the press. Morgan was stunned, because his lawyers had put together the trust with careful attention to antitrust laws. Morgan was particularly upset that this action came without any prior warning, jeopardizing huge amounts of funds that had been invested in the market. He went to Washington to confer with the president and attorney general, pleading for their understanding and urging them to fix the problem. Roosevelt said that would not be possible and Knox was blunter, "we don't want to fix it up, we want to stop it."[9] Roosevelt's change of course pummeled the stock market. Both Morgan and Roosevelt believed trusts to be the inevitable outgrowth of economic development, but Roosevelt thought there needed to be a countervailing force and Morgan feared robust competition because the market value of monopoly businesses was much higher and more stable. The government only narrowly won its case when the Supreme Court, in a surprise 5-4 ruling, switched gears and put some teeth into the Sherman Act by reversing earlier decisions.

At the turn of the century, newspapers began to hire college graduates to work on their stories and editorials. Increasing competition between and among newspapers and magazines for subscriptions stimulated sensational news stories. Newspaper circulation exploded, reaching its height in terms of numbers of papers sold in 1910. Roosevelt was among the first to use the term "muckraker," believing the journalists had gone overboard in raking up gossipy reports. Henry Demarest Lloyd made antipathy toward "monopoly" popular by writing some of the first muckraking stories. Independent and muckraking newspapers became an important check on the industrial corporation and corporate wrongdoing.

Muckrakers also used the power of the book to put forward their ideas. Henry George produced *Progress and Poverty,* which sold over two million copies, in which he argued that land ownership was the basis for the gulf between rich and poor, and advocated a tax on land, the forerunner of proposals to tax investments and investment income, which dominated political debate in the twentieth century. George urged land owners to have a social conscience because if they did not, the alternative was socialism.

Rockefeller and the Standard Oil Company were the subject of scathing books and editorials. In 1881, in the *Atlantic Monthly,* Lloyd exposed the monopoly and its practices. Characterizing the company as a ruthless monopoly consuming everything as it went and driving competitors out of business, Ida Tarbell became famous for her *History of Standard Oil Company,* a series on Rockefeller that first appeared in *McClure's* magazine and then as a two-volume book. Both Tarbell's father and brother were victims of Standard Oil competition; her father warning that Rockefeller would ruin her magazine. Tarbell's investigations documented deceit and ruthless tactics, providing evidence for the antitrust suit against Standard Oil. Her writings became the talk of the nation and created outcries for reform.

Publicly, after being denounced for their ruthless business practices, Rockefeller and Standard Oil appeared impervious to the criticism, believing they were building the world's greatest corporation and protecting the market from the forces of unbridled competition. Privately, Rockefeller, his wife, his son, and two out of three of his daughters were afflicted by serious medical disorders after publication of Ida Tarbell's series. A man with generally open and democratic tastes, Rockefeller was forced to wall off his estates and hire detectives to protect against assassination threats. Even Mark Twain, author of *The Gilded Age,* "recoiled at the sanctimonious tone the press often adopted."[10]

Many Americans were alarmed by the rapid transformation from their eighteenth-century economy based on small businessmen and yeoman farmers to the new system based on industrial combinations or trusts. Because of its size and closed, secretive, culture, Standard Oil was particularly susceptible to public criticism. Many of its critics expected some action to reign in the abuses. Half a dozen states instituted various actions to curb the company, but Standard Oil viewed these efforts as just a craze. Rockefeller believed strongly in his persuasive powers and that he could convert just about anyone to his position, pointing to the many former competitors on his board and in his company as proof of his influence.

Increasingly, American politics became divided between the muckraking, populist viewpoint and the capitalist class and its beneficiaries. Muckrakers, historians, and journalists alike blamed large corporations for much of the public's anger, ennui, and alienation during this period, attributing much of the bad feelings and monopolistic activities to the "robber barons," "titans," and "tycoons." This analysis was arguably simplistic. The industrial revolution favored mass production, which necessitated much larger organizations. The victory of the North in the Civil War created a climate hospitable to new technologies. Large corporations were best positioned to develop and deploy new products and services. The world's economy became more global with the opening of Japan in the 1850s, contacts made with Europe during the Civil War, and the rapidly expanding international financial markets resulting from better communications and faster travel. Globalization favored large enterprises that could rapidly penetrate international markets with new products and technologies. Even enterprises as large as Standard Oil had difficulties competing internationally, Rockefeller thus losing much of the European and Asian markets to international competitors such as Shell Oil.

Most of what the government, the muckrakers, and the progressives did to reform the economy merely, in retrospect, seemed to have exacerbated the situation. Academicians and historians chronicle the boom-and-bust economy between the Civil War and World War I, but that too may be an oversimplification. During this period, America grew rapidly, eventually supporting the largest economy in the world: it was far more boom than bust. Large enterprises had the capital and scope to profit more effectively in extended booms. Rapid cyclical downturns, however, resulted in consolidations of entire industries; this also benefited large businesses with lots of cash. Both Carnegie and Rockefeller were masters at hoarding cash and wealth during upswings and using the proceeds during recessions to buy up the competition at bargain-basement prices. The primary reason for these wild swings was the absence of any central or national bank, which had been repealed by Andrew Jackson, who tapped into popular sentiment against the bankers. Government had no way to regulate the cycles. The populists and muckrakers opposed large concentrations of wealth and the gold standard. The effect of this populist sentiment was to lessen the faith of Europeans and other investors in America's financial markets, causing wider and more frequent swings and counterproductive panics. Businessmen like Rockefeller and Carnegie who successfully navigated the downturns, felt trapped by these disruptions. The havoc and uncertainty threatened their ability to build lasting financial systems. This spurred them to rapidly consolidate their industries and buy out their competition.

Efforts to regulate the large corporations had unintended consequences. The Sherman Antitrust Act exemplifies compromise legislation enacted after an extensive debate between the progressives (who opposed the new trusts, monopoly prices, and ruthless efficiency) and pro-industry legislators (who touted the benefits of mass production, rapid economic expansion, the revolutions in communications and transportation, and improvements in productivity). The legislation split across party lines—Sherman was a Republican. The law was written very generally, leaving interpretation to the courts. Contrary to the intentions of its authors, the law was initially applied more to labor unions than business corporations; the antitrust laws were used most effectively against labor boycotts and strikes. Then, to the extent antitrust laws were used against labor unions, they weakened the ability of workers to stop the concentration of economic power in large corporations. To the extent antitrust laws were used against corporations, they ruled out price-fixing agreements and encouraged more consolidations and bigger mergers, exacerbating the problems labor was experiencing with big corporations. Small companies could not collude to raise prices, but large companies could consolidate their industries and use their market power to set prices.[11]

Even more importantly, industrialists like Rockefeller, Carnegie, and Mellon were creating the institutions the society so badly needed to counter-balance the impact of the industrial corporation and the lasting effects of Civil War on society. John D. Rockefeller funded and helped to establish Colonial Williamsburg, the Museum of Modern Art, the University of Chicago, Rockefeller Center, and private-public partnerships for social change. He established the Rockefeller Institute of Medical Research, home of numerous Nobel laureates, life-saving medical advances, and the world's most advanced institution for medical research. Of the 400 Nobel prizes awarded during the twentieth century in physics, chemistry, medicine, and economics, over 60 were received by individuals associated at one time or another with the University of Chicago. When Rockefeller sought a federal charter with an independent board for his charitable trust, the federal government declined to act. Instead, he received a charter from the State of New York, but the governance mechanism for the Rockefeller Foundation was dominated by the family and "mocked the idea that it was a public trust."[12] Andrew Carnegie provided extensive funding for educational institutions and the nation's system of public libraries. Andrew Mellon donated his art collection and the funding to build the National Gallery of Art. He started up the first think-tank, the Mellon Institute, that provided seed money for scientific research and many business ventures.

In his 1904 presidential election campaign, Roosevelt accepted contributions from Standard Oil executives, railroad magnates, major bankers, and a wide range of industry executives, prompting outcries from the Democrats. Many of these businessmen regretted their donations because they had little or no impact on Roosevelt's decisions. The Standard Oil board regarded its contributions as among its worst investments. One donor bemoaned, "we bought him and he didn't stay bought."

In autumn 1906, the federal government filed an antitrust suit against Standard Oil. Theodore Roosevelt spoke out strongly against the company for its abusive and monopolistic practices. Standard Oil also had to contest twenty state antitrust suits. As these cases progressed, the company's share of the market for crude oil dropped from 32 to 14 percent, and its share of refining dropped from 86 to 70 percent. In 1909, after Roosevelt left office, the lower federal court ruled against the company and ordered its dissolution. Due to the death of two judges, the Supreme Court heard the case twice. In 1911, a decision was finally issued, and the Court ruled unanimously that Standard Oil was a combination in restraint of trade. The company was given six months to dissolve itself.

By the time of the Supreme Court decision, many of Standard Oil's violations and illegal practices were decades old. Even prior to the break-up, Standard Oil was vulnerable to foreign competition, losing much of the European market to Shell Oil and the Asian market during the 1890s when Russia became the world's largest supplier of crude oil, and foreign competitors built huge storage facilities in Asia and gained access to the Suez Canal. Major oil finds in Texas and Oklahoma opened up the domestic market, encouraging the formation of new companies such as Gulf Oil and providing new sources for foreign competitors. The break-up did broaden competition and development of new technology in the oil industry. Standard Oil of Indiana, for example, developed a breakthrough in refining to help support the nascent automobile industry, enabling the extraction of more gasoline per barrel of oil. This innovation came just as the demand for gasoline exploded, exceeding the need for kerosene for the first time in 1910.

The Supreme Court decision had no effect on Rockefeller's wealth. which more than doubled after Standard Oil was dissolved, making him the first billionaire (or close to it—he and his children claim he was never actually worth over a billion—only well over $900 million). The decision split the company into new companies that became Exxon-Mobil, Chevron, Amoco, Arco, and Conoco. The stock in the new companies was distributed pro rata to the stockholders in Standard Oil. The parts were worth more than the whole.[13] A century later, Rockefeller's descendants were the only members of the Fortune 400 wealthiest

Americans from the turn-of-the-century, except for the Hearsts.

It is tempting to conclude that Roosevelt's antitrust policies failed or backfired. J.P. Morgan queried "How the hell is any court going to compel a man to compete with himself?" Morgan became even more powerful, as the government became more dependent on his ability to keep the markets liquid in economic downturns. Rockefeller's leading biographer concluded "It was certainly not their intention, but the trustbusters helped to preserve Rockefeller's legacy for posterity and unquestionably made him the world's richest man."[14] Even Roosevelt retrospectively denounced the decision for driving up the price of the stock and Rockefeller's fortune. Rockefeller's increase in wealth, however, had less to do with the antitrust decision than with the rise of the automobile, which was just beginning to make unprecedented demands on the petroleum industry. The enforcement of antitrust laws eventually resulted in American capitalism becoming more oligopolistic, while European countries such as Britain and Germany tended to be monopolistic. The American system proved to be superior. Government sanctioned monopolies have been resistant to innovation and often unable to compete effectively in the free marketplace.

New industries, technologies, and wealth were created through the leadership of Rockefeller, Carnegie, Edison, Morgan, Mellon, and others. They were responsible for the United States supporting the largest economy on the planet in their day and after. Powerful forces were tapped by these industrial and financial geniuses. Vilifying them, as the muckrakers and critics did, devalued their effective harnessing of the forces that helped to create America's economic strength.

Roosevelt was a strong executive, but experienced no major challenges to his presidency, such as a domestic or international crisis. He did leave a progressive legacy with his strong antitrust and preservation policies and the U.S. role in clearing the way for the Panama Canal. Roosevelt had a strong foreign policy with a global perspective. In contrast to the materialistic tycoons and titans that dominated the era, he still represents the heroic, fighting virtues of the soldier or national leader.

The Progressive Era and Corruption

Theodore Roosevelt was the personification of the progressive movement, but the actual era of social reform spans the period between the administrations of presidents Grant and Coolidge (1868–1928). Ulysses S. Grant (1822–1885) inherited greater burdens and more difficult problems than any other president, except perhaps Abraham Lincoln or Franklin Roosevelt.[15] Grant governed as he believed Lincoln would have governed: magnanimous in victory and protective of the rights of former slaves. In the aftermath of the Civil War, Grant played a major role in downsizing the federal government, drastically reducing taxes and government spending, eliminating a fifth of the national debt, and reversing the balance of trade from a $130 million deficit to a $120 million surplus.[16] Grant had the vision and foresight to send seven expeditions to Central America to develop a route for the Panama Canal.[17] He was the only president in eighty years to serve two full terms. Yet, from the perspective of some historians, he is seen as a drunk and butcher. Hounded after Shiloh and Cold Harbor and at other times during his career by whispering campaigns, Grant delivered in the clutch and was widely revered. While his administration is considered by most historians to be riddled with incompetence and corruption, he won re-election by a record vote and was seriously considered for a third term, even though no president except Lincoln had won a second term in forty years. Grant named Hamilton Fish as Secretary of State, and Fish was one of the most effective international ambassadors in the history of the republic, very much in the tradition of John Quincy Adams.

Grant is often considered to have been among the worst presidents because of the scandals in his administration, yet Grant was honest to a fault and not directly involved in the scandals. Like Washington, he tried to remain above partisanship and factionalism. In Grant's era, government had become much larger and with more opportunity for corruption. On several occasions, Grant acted naively and failed to dismiss corrupt and incompetent subordinates, but he had no personal involvement. Criticized by reformers for patronage practices that had been in place for generations, he was the first president to advocate civil service reform.

The Credit Mobilier scandal, considered to be the worst case of corruption in the nineteenth century, did not involve Grant's Administration directly, but did involve Members of Congress who accepted gifts or bribes in the form of stock. In fact, most of these inducements occurred prior to Grant's presidency. Root of this scandal was the enormous largesse the Congress and the states had bestowed on the companies building the transcontinental railroad. Credit Mobilier was a creative financing mechanism established by the owners of the Union Pacific transcontinental railroad. Since operation of the railroad was unlikely to generate any profits soon, both companies building the transcontinental railroad set up separate corporations to fund the initial construction that would generate enormous profits and wealth quickly. These construction companies took exorbitant fees from the railroads, becoming giant launderers for funds from the federal government to the railroads to the construction companies to the greedy individual owners of the railroads. The company used the inflated stock to bribe or buy off members of Congress. Credit Mobilier issued 300 percent annual dividends to its owners, but could not pay its bills.

A group of distillers who bribed government officials to avoid the whiskey tax, the infamous Whiskey Ring, was formed during the administration of Andrew Johnson and only overlapped with the Grant presidency. Grant's administration secured 350 indictments of people involved in this scheme. Grant is accused of appointing corrupt officials to key positions, but only one of his twenty-five cabinet officers was convicted of corruption. Several were falsely accused.[18]

Jay Gould and Jim Fisk attempted to corner the U.S. gold market, enlisting the president's brother-in-law to act as a go-between to prevent intervention by the federal treasury. They met with Grant, persuading him to appoint an acquaintance to oversee federal gold sales and providing him with private transportation on several occasions (which was perfectly legal). Once Grant became aware of the scheme, he directed his brother-in-law to quickly end the speculation. It was a measure of the public perception of corruption in government that most people on Wall Street believed Fisk and Gould when they claimed to have the cooperation of the federal treasury. Grant took prompt action to release gold to stop Gould and Fisk from cornering the market. While historians have criticized Grant for being naïve in this matter, he actually was perceptive and took aggressive action to foil the speculators. The use of the telegraph and the development of the stock ticker increasingly riveted the public's attention to the Wall Street market. Unlike any previous financial event, the effort to corner gold mesmerized people across the country and thousands thronged in the streets of lower Manhattan, their every breathe hanging on the latest rumor about the price of gold.[19]

Corruption was widespread at the state and local level as well. City governments tended to be corrupt, particularly as they grew in size. More often than not, big-city governments, often referred to as political machines, were controlled by the Democrats. The growth of the Republican Party in many cities and outlying suburbs was a direct reaction to corruption in the cities. Republicans became the opposition reform party. Perhaps the most well-known boss was George Washington Plunkitt who was immortalized in the book that contained his political philosophy, *Plunkitt of Tammany Hall,* as told to William Riordan, a reporter for the *New York Evening Post.* He made the distinction between "honest graft" and "dishonest graft":

> There's all the difference in the world between the two. Yes, many of our men have grown rich in politics. I have myself. I've made a big fortune out of the game, and I'm getting richer every day. But I've not gone in for dishonest graft—blackmailing gamblers, saloonkeepers, disorderly people, etc.—and neither has any of the men who have made big fortunes in politics.
>
> There's honest graft, and I'm an example of how it works. I might sum up the whole thing by saying: 'I seen my opportunities and I took "em." Just let me explain by examples. My party's in power in the city, and it's going to undertake a lot of public improvements. Well, I'm tipped off, say, that they're going to lay out a new park at a certain place. I see my opportunity and I take it. I go to that place and I buy up all the land I can in the neighborhood. Then the board of

this or that makes its plan public, and there is a rush to get the land, which nobody particularly cared for before. Ain't it perfectly honest to charge a good price and make a profit on my investment and foresight? Of course it is. Well, that's honest graft.[20]

Plunkitt claimed he used the same methods when bridges and roads were built. Perhaps the funniest escapade involved the sale of old granite blocks. Plunkitt found that his enemies at Tammany Hall had conspired to bid up the price for these bricks at a public auction. Plunkitt, knowing each of the bid riggers personally, went to them and offered each one the number of stones they wanted absolutely free. When the auctioneer opened the bidding, "How much am I bid for these 250,000 fine paving stones?", the only bid he got was "Two dollars and fifty cents." Plunkitt had once again seen his opportunity and had taken it. The final bill for the New York county courthouse, scheduled to cost $250,000, was nearly $14 million. The bill for carpeting the courthouse was high enough to carpet most of the city. Carpenters were paid $2 million for $30,000 of work. One contractor bid $60,000 for fire alarms and when asked if he would kick back $225,000 agreed to a $450,000 contract. Boss Tweed bought and sold judges, elected officials, and even journalists. He ultimately died in prison.[21]

Muckrakers like Lincoln Steffens exposed corruption in books, such as *The Shame of the Cities*. Because the cities in total spent more money than the federal government, big-city bosses became the target of progressive reformers, with much more being at stake. The progressive era is often characterized as a struggle between reformers and corrupt industrialists. Yet, many businessmen believed the government so corrupt that it was part of the problem of regulating the marketplace effectively, not a solution. Businessmen learned to rely more on their private efforts than on an avaricious government. Many critical fights involved citizen reform groups and journalists against both the corrupt government and rapacious industrialists.

Perhaps the best example of corruption was the epic struggle over the Erie Railroad. Cornelius Vanderbilt became president of the New York Central Railroad and merged it with his Hudson River Railroad, forming a line from New York to Buffalo. Established in the 1830s to compete with the Erie Canal, the Erie Railroad connected Lake Erie to New York. Vanderbilt tried to takeover the Erie Railroad to control all railroad commerce on the route, which was legally permissible at the time. Daniel Drew was treasurer of the Erie Railroad and known to simply manufacture or print up additional certificates to manipulate the stock price and control of the corporation. Vanderbilt obtained an order from a "friendly" judge (i.e., one that was personally beholden to him) preventing any such watering down of the stock. Drew ignored the order and obtained a ruling from a "friendly" judge upstate removing Vanderbilt's ally from the Board and another order from a "friendly" judge in Brooklyn directing him to continue his activities.

Vanderbilt obtained a further ruling from his judge enforcing the original order along with a police officer to arrest the offending parties, causing Drew and his allies to flee to New Jersey. Drew's Erie directors lined the pockets of the New Jersey legislature to "persuade" them to grant a New Jersey charter for their railroad, but were thwarted when Vanderbilt's lobbyists bribed enough legislators to defeat the bill. The New York legislature had already passed a bill in effect legalizing bribery. A bill was submitted to that body ratifying the actions of the Erie board, designed to draw bribes from both sides. One legislator reportedly received $100,000 from one side to influence the bill and $70,000 from the other to leave town. Public sentiment against Vanderbilt owning both lines forced him to compromise. Legislators scurried to make last-minute deals with Vanderbilt and his opponents. Drew and his partners Jay Gould and Jim Fisk continued to manipulate Erie securities, in part to compensate Vanderbilt for his watered down stock. Investors were widely upset by the tactics of Drew, Gould, and Fisk, because they diluted the investments of other shareholders and put investors in the position of having little or no ability to determine how much stock was outstanding. After the legislatures refused to take action to end such a lucrative source of bribes, the stock exchanges required companies to list and register all securities. Drew, Fisk, and Gould declined to comply and Erie was thrown off the major exchanges.[22]

The Boom and Bust Cycle

Unemployment was a problem created by the nature of the industrial economy. In the agricultural economy, the farmer generally produced at least something of value when the economy was in a down cycle. In the industrial era, workers were often left unemployed in a downturn, had no income, and produced virtually nothing when they were laid off. Monetary policy is the most effective tool of the government for regulating these down cycles in an industrial economy, a strategy not widely recognized by economists until after the Great Depression. Without a national bank or a consensus on gold or silver, federal monetary policy failed to prevent recessions, and the private sector eventually had to assume responsibility for overseeing the economy. Grant's entire second term was dominated by the 1873 Depression. Still, with the average citizen believing there was little that a president could do to stop or address a recession, he left office a popular president. The depression was precipitated by the unexpected bankruptcy of Jay Cooke & Co., the firm that had led the bond drives in the Civil War. The telegraph and transatlantic cable spread the panic, with the stock market closing for ten days. In the 1874 election, in the midst of the depression, Republicans lost in a record landslide—a total of 90 seats in the House of Representatives, which was the biggest rout in history.

In 1893, panic again swept the Wall Street markets and, by the end of the year, 15,000 companies and 500 banks failed. The economy shrank by 12 percent and unemployment rose from 3 percent in 1892 to 18.2 percent two years later.[23] In most industries, the key factor contributing to the depression was overcapacity. Without a central bank to curb the expansion, runaway growth eventually triggered a deep downturn, the worst until the Great Depression of the 1930s. The country had been running on a dual currency system: reverting to the gold standard in 1879, which enabled greenbacks to be converted to gold; and a second system based on silver, the value of which was pegged at 16 silver to 1 gold. Discovery of additional silver deposits depressed the price until the market value was 20 to 1, even though Congress stuck to the original ratio. With this imbalance, people did the logical thing and spent the silver and kept or saved the gold. Demand for gold increased and there was a run on gold reserves, as people sought a safe haven. The two metal system—gold and silver—caused Europeans to fear their American debts would not be honored, which had happened in the 1830s recession when many bond issuers became insolvent and nine states defaulted on their debts. In 1893, J. P. Morgan pressured the government to abandon the bi-metal system and revert to gold, whereas agrarian and populist interests demanded that the country go off the gold standard so they could repay their debts in cheaper money, causing a run on the country's gold stock.

In 1894, two bond issues for $50 million each restored the gold reserves, but only temporarily. Congress refused to permit another government bond issue to buy more gold to replenish the reserve, because popular sentiment was running against gold and Wall Street and in favor of silver. The anti-gold fever worsened the depression by triggering a run on gold and stocks. As a result, European and American investor confidence in the government and the gold standard plummeted. The government came within hours of running out of gold. To maintain public confidence in the gold standard, the Department of Treasury needed to maintain $100 million in reserve, but the fund balance was below $50 million and falling by the millions every hour.

President Cleveland understood J. P. Morgan was the only person with the resources and public confidence to end the panic. Afraid he would appear to be pandering to Wall Street interests, President Cleveland initially refused to see Morgan when he took a train to Washington. With the situation deteriorating by the minute and faced with a government default that afternoon, Cleveland and his economic team finally negotiated with Morgan and Morgan's advisors.

Morgan offered to raise $100 million from his investor allies and to ensure the gold would not flow back to Europe, as it had been since the onset of the depression. The United States was, at the time, the world's largest debtor nation. Morgan's lawyers found an obscure Civil War statute that would allow the floating of government bonds without further congressional action. Morgan developed a syndicate to market U.S. securities for bullion to replace the depleted gold stocks. In one transaction, he purchased over 3 million ounces of gold in exchange for bonds worth over $60 million. Morgan was publicly criticized for making money off the bonds when he purchased them from the government and then resold them in the private market. He never revealed the amount of his profit in this transaction. He single-handedly saved both the federal government and the gold standard, widely embraced by investors as a foil against inflation. Morgan was attacked repeatedly in the United States; his participation with the Rothschilds in Europe provoked a public display of anti-Semitism.[24]

The lessons learned from the 1870s and 1890s enabled J. P. Morgan to effectively navigate the panic of 1907 without an ensuing recession.[25] America had gone back to a gold standard in 1900 after a discovery of vast new deposits, and after two mining engineers developed a process for extracting gold from low-grade ore. Gold stocks were nevertheless failing to keep pace with industrial expansion, and no one was in charge of the banking system, which was near collapse. There were over twenty-thousand banks and no common reserves or coordination, which was particularly critical in the fall when rural banks withdrew funds to meet the demands of the agricultural harvest. Many of these small state and local banks issued notes or paper with promises to repay in gold, promises that could not be met during a run on the banks. Government attacks on big business and convulsions in foreign markets triggered a crash.

Morgan assembled leading bankers and financiers. Under his leadership, this team provided the liquidity necessary, in the places where it could be used most effectively, to save the entire financial system from banks to the stock exchanges, albeit a number of concerns were allowed to fail. John D. Rockefeller made half his fortune available to bail out the stock market, publicly stating that the nation's credit was sound. He worked with Morgan to keep the stock markets open and the credit markets liquid. Other wealthy men also pitched in. By force of individual will, Morgan stopped the stock exchange from closing, even though the interest rates for margin calls exceeded 100 percent. He personally threatened to take action against anyone who tried to short the market to take advantage of the panic.[26] On Friday night, he even called in religious leaders and urged them to preach calm on Sunday. His actions were widely praised at the time, particularly by President Roosevelt. Ironically, some of his solutions to the liquidity problem also required agreement and waivers from Washington for what would have been violations of the antitrust laws. Subsequently, there was considerable public acrimony and debate over these exemptions that were made to prevent further panic. Morgan's effort provided the basis for establishing the Federal Reserve Bank seven years later.

Grover Cleveland

Grover Cleveland (1837–1908) was the only president to serve two terms non-consecutively and the first president to be wed in the White House, where he married the 21-year-old Frances Folsom. Prior to his election, it was alleged he had an illegitimate child with a department store employee. While unsure of the child's paternity, Cleveland paid support, but at one point had to institutionalize the mother for alcoholism and to put the child in an orphanage. His honesty about the affair contrasted with the shady dealings of his Republican opponent James Blaine and helped propel him to the presidency.

As president, Cleveland was a man of integrity and an extraordinarily hard worker. He was unpretentious and "tried to steward the nation's resources as he stewarded his own."[27] Cleveland fought against enlarging pensions, high tariffs, and other expansions of government power. Manufacturers and Republicans fought hard for the protectionist tariffs raised during the Civil War. These tariffs had yielded government surpluses for twenty-eight years between 1866 and 1894 and a reduction of government debt from 50 percent of the Gross Domestic Product to well under 10 percent. In his re-election effort, Cleveland lost in part because he had signed legislation lowering tariffs. Republicans raised substantial sums of money from corporations seeking higher tariffs and other government support, followed by scare tactics such as claiming tariff reductions would lead to wage cuts and job losses.

Originally, Civil War pensions were only provided to those veterans too disabled to work. Many veterans, however, obtained pensions

fraudulently, including deserters. Others obtained special pension legislation from their Senator or Representative and no president ever dared
to veto one—until Cleveland, who rejected over 100 such bills. The
number of pensions almost doubled at the very time they should have
been declining as veterans grew older and passed on. The Republican
newspapers accused Cleveland of being mean-spirited, even though he
cited specific reasons for each of his vetoes.

To show Cleveland's mean-spiritedness, some newspapers gave examples of pension bills he had vetoed. One of
the press favorites was the pension of Sallie Ann Bradley, an
Ohio woman who said her husband had died as a result of
wounds suffered during the war. Furthermore, she claimed,
two of her four sons had been slain in battle, and of the two
who survived, an exploding shell had ripped off the arm of
one, and the other had lost an eye in battle. They could not
earn enough to sustain their aged mother. And President
Cleveland, the brute, would not allow Mrs. Bradley to have a
pension.

As the post-veto furor raged, a Wilmington, Ohio,
newspaper investigated the claim. It found that Mr. Bradley
had not died from Civil War wounds. He had 'choked to
death on a piece of beef when gorging himself while on a
drunken spree.' Two of the sons indeed were dead, but one
had died during an epidemic after the war and the other had
committed suicide while drunk. None of the arms of the two
surviving sons had been torn off by a shell. One son, a shoe-
maker, had lost an eye, but he lost it 'while working at his
trade from a piece of heel nail striking it when repairing a
pair of boots.' The two surviving sons were able to support
their mother, if they wished to do so.[28]

Congress then passed a general pension reform bill ostensibly limiting eligibility but actually expanding it. Cleveland vetoed this bill as
well, claiming that to extend eligibility beyond disabilities would make
the plan a welfare program. Cleveland believed that churches and com-

munity organizations and not the federal government should be responsible for those individuals who had claims beyond disability. *The Washington Post* supported the veto and Congress sustained it. Cleveland also opposed veterans' preference, except when the applicants were equally qualified. Cleveland vetoed twice as many bills as all his predecessors combined. He even vetoed drought relief, arguing the people, not the government, should provide this support and raising private funds to provide the relief.

The Spanish-American War

Drooling over their likelihood of recapturing the presidency, Republicans relished their prospects for the 1896 elections. Thomas Reed, one of the most effective Speakers of the House in history, was the favorite. Henry Cabot Lodge said there had never existed "a more perfectly equipped leader in any parliamentary body at any period." Reed ended the practice that allowed a minority of the House to block action by refusing to respond to quorum calls, earning the title Czar Reed. The Democrats carried the fight all the way to the Supreme Court, which ruled the Speaker could count as present those who were physically present but who refused to respond when their name was called on the roll. While William McKinley was notorious for his 1890 tariff bill that resulted in many Republicans being swept out of office, he was selected as the Republican candidate because of his more amiable personality. Reed's sharp tongue and biting intellect preceded him, as did his undisciplined three-hundred-pound hulk. When a Member of Congress propounded that he would rather be right than be president, Reed demurred that he needn't worry, he wouldn't be either. When asked what to write in an obituary about a Democratic colleague, he deadpanned, "anything but the truth."[29] He famously defined a statesman as a dead politician.

McKinley saw two of his infant daughters die and his wife was an invalid. He attempted to lift her spirits through attendance at state dinners and other official functions. McKinley ran a "front-porch" campaign, which was the first modern election effort. Mark Hanna raised millions of dollars for McKinley from well-heeled special-interest groups, twice what his Republican predecessor Benjamin Harrison had generated. Hanna used these funds to run the first real publicity campaign with posters, pamphlets, banners, and buttons. Hanna jokingly would say, "There are two things that are important in politics. The first is money, and I can't remember what the second one is." He applied business methods to political campaigns and, for example, had Teddy Roosevelt shadow William Jennings Bryan's campaign as he traveled across the Midwest. Pro-McKinley railroads offered voters cheap fares to travel to McKinley's front porch, turning his yard into a sea of mud when it rained. Hanna was famous as a businessman who made the most of his money with help from government, developing an expertise in manipulating the levers of power though lobbying and influence-peddling.

Hanna's effort to elect McKinley was made easier by his populist opposition, William Jennings Bryan, who united the conservative establishments from both parties against his campaign. Bryan ran exclusively on the silver issue, to the relief of Republicans. He was such a rabid ideologue that one observer concluded: "Probably no man in civil life has succeeded in inspiring so much terror, without taking life." The McKinley election marked the beginning of four decades of Republican control of the federal government, interrupted by only one Democratic President, Woodrow Wilson, who won with less than 50 percent of the vote both times. During this forty-year period, the Republicans lost control of the Senate for just six years and the House of Representatives for only eight years. This historic realignment was caused in significant part by the depression during Cleveland's presidency.

Spain suppressed a Cuban insurrection, arousing American attention. New changes in printing technology enabled American newspapers to become more profitable through expanded circulation to attract advertising. To draw new readership, the newspapers inflamed the situation in Cuba by exaggerating the repression and embellishing the stories concocted by Cuban nationalists. Joseph Pulitzer and William Randolph Hearst were the leading purveyors of these tactics, which became known as yellow journalism.

This was an era when news correspondents doubled as adventurers and heroes. Henry Stanley had tracked David Livingstone through the jungles of Africa for the *New York Herald;* cub reporter Winston Churchill was about to start writing dispatches on the Boer War, getting himself captured in the process and then making a dramatic escape, which he wrote up in breathless detail. In the case of Cuba, Hearst's paper received a published report about a young Cuban woman named Evangelina Cisneros who had been abused and jailed by Spanish soldiers. The story sparked a tremendous outcry in the United States. At Hearst's instigation, thousands of Americans signed petitions demanding that [she] be released. After these failed efforts to secure her freedom, an enterprising Hearst reporter in Cuba slipped into the Havana prison where she was being held, sawed through the bars in her cell, disguised her as a boy, and made off with her to freedom.[30]

McKinley was skillful in the execution of his war strategy. Hesitant to enter at first, he made sure that America was prepared for the conflict. McKinley sent the *USS Maine* to Havana in a show of force. The ship blew up. Americans considered it an act of war, triggering the Spanish-American conflict. Theodore Roosevelt wrote "The *Maine* was sunk by an act of treachery on the part of the Spaniards." The American press echoed this sentiment and sensationalistic journalism made war imperative. It was not a mine that caused the ship to explode, but a fire in a coal bunker that ignited the forward magazines. The real cause was not known until confirmed in a study by Admiral Hyman Rickover in 1976. Theodore Roosevelt, commanding the Rough Riders, became a national legend. A bigger hero was George Dewey who led his small naval expedition into Manila Bay and destroyed the Spanish fleet without a single American being killed. Manila Bay was the first major battle the United States fought overseas and Dewey was accorded a hero's welcome when he came back home. Spain was in the last throes of its empire and lost 50,000 men, mostly to disease, whereas the U.S. suffered only 385 battle deaths and 2,000 lost to disease. In the treaty to end the war, the United States annexed Puerto Rico, the Philippines, and the island of Guam from Spain.

While the expansionist policy that led to the Spanish-American War has been discredited by modern historians as Manifest Destiny and imperialism, the policy had widespread popular support at the time. Manifest Destiny spawned a series of abuses and land grabs, but the overall policy was effective. In 1815, there were only two completely independent nations in the New World—the United States and Haiti. The rest of the Western Hemisphere was dominated by European colonies. Manifest Destiny provided a free, democratic alternative to imperial colonization. The Monroe Doctrine, which barred foreign intervention in the Western Hemisphere, was the tool used to implement this policy. During the decade in the middle eighteenth century when Texas was independent, it made a number of overtures to Great Britain, causing far more controversy over annexation than surrounded the acquisition of other territories. Cuba is an example in which Manifest Destiny didn't succeed. America tried to acquire the island but failed. A Cuban rebellion broke out in 1868 and continued for a decade. American support for the insurgents nearly caused a war between the U.S. and Spain. At the end of the nineteenth century, chaos and turmoil in Cuba precipitated the Spanish-American War. In the twentieth century, Cuba became a victim of totalitarian dictators and communist governance, putting the world on the verge of nuclear annihilation in the 1960s missile crisis while becoming mired in some of the worst poverty and economic mismanagement in the Western Hemisphere.

President Polk tried, but failed to acquire much of Mexico. During the U.S. Civil War, Mexicans accepted the Archduke of Austria as a puppet government protected by the French troops of Napoleon III. In World War I, the Germans sought allegiance with Mexico to thwart the United States alliance with France and Great Britain. Instead of a balkanized continent of nations allying with different countries in Europe and constantly at war, there was one United States of America and only one major war—the Civil War. While historians have blamed Manifest Destiny and imperialism for the Spanish-American War and the acquisition of territory that caused the controversies that led to the American

Civil War, without this policy European nations would have almost certainly been involved in constant wars, intrigue, and alliances in the Western Hemisphere.

The political culture in this so-called era of reform (1870–1914) was hardly one that could be called progressive. Campaigns for president were largely vacuous and often won by the candidate who did less campaigning. Grant won both of his elections by saying virtually nothing while his opponents campaigned. Rutherford B. Hayes had a very limited track record besides his war experience and stayed at home in what turned out to be the most disputed and fraudulent presidential election in history. When all of the disputed electoral votes were given to Hayes, Tilden observed, "I shall receive from posterity the credit of having been elected to the highest position as a gift of the people, without any of the cares and responsibilities of the office." James Garfield was a campaigner and did prevail over the demur Winfield Hancock, but his election was considered one of the most boring and inconsequential in American history. In one of the nastier elections, Grover Cleveland made only two appearances but prevailed over his ethically-challenged, active opponent James Blaine. Benjamin Harrison ran a stay-at-home front porch campaign, but was able to defeat Grover Cleveland who made only one appearance. In the re-match, Cleveland did campaign on the issues and won. William McKinley stayed at home in his two elections, but won both of them against his barnstorming opponent William Jennings Bryan, who made a record 36 speeches in one day.[31] Although Theodore Roosevelt thought Secretary of State Elihu Root the best candidate to succeed him as president, he couldn't even seriously consider him because he was a corporate lawyer. William Howard Taft became his candidate instead. Besides Roosevelt's leadership, much of what happened during this era was hardly progressive or favorable for reformers.

Presidents Taft and Wilson

Roosevelt's hand-picked successor, William Howard Taft (1857–1930), generally governed as a progressive. While not popular due to his lack of charisma and 300-pound girth, Taft vigorously supported enforcement of the antitrust laws, helped to secure adoption of the income tax , and supported direct election of United States Senators. Theodore Roosevelt and the progressives took exception to Taft's tepid effort to reform the tariff structure and his lack of conservation programs, and they opposed Taft for re-election. Roosevelt broke with Taft when he sued U.S. Steel on antitrust grounds. Roosevelt had promised J. P. Morgan that the government would not file suit after his efforts in 1907 to rescue the economy. Roosevelt won the most primaries, but Taft took the convention with the most votes from the party bosses. Roosevelt split from the Republican Party and set up the Bull Moose Party.

Woodrow Wilson (1856–1924) won over the divided opposition and the Democrats carried the Senate and House of Representatives as well. For his defiance of the party bosses upon his election as governor of New Jersey, Wilson had a reputation for progressivism and reform. He combined populist and evangelical appeals with policies previously identified with the Republican reform agenda. Wilson was without religious prejudice; he was quoted as firmly believing in divine providence and he secured the confirmation of the first Jewish Supreme Court judge, Louis Brandeis. Wilson was, however, an overt racist and white supremacist who segregated the federal government. His first appointment to the Supreme Court was James McReynolds, regarded as a bigoted reactionary. In his *A History of American People*, Wilson stated: "At last there had sprung into existence a great Ku Klux Klan, a veritable empire of the South, to protect the Southern country."

Wilson largely accomplished his first-term goals, which he called the New Freedom. He was the first president to offer a legislative program for Congress to pass. Wilson pushed through tariff reductions, a bill establishing the Federal Reserve System, a prohibition on the sale of products made by children under the age of sixteen, and the Clayton Antitrust Act, which more specifically defined business practices prohibited by antitrust laws and provided an exemption for lawful labor activities.

Increases in veterans' pensions and payment of Civil War debts necessitated huge increases in tariffs and excise taxes, which led to a revolt by farmers and westerners who wanted income and corporate taxes. By 1872, the Civil War income tax had been phased out. The 1893 depression caused a precipitous drop in revenues resulting in the enactment of another income tax that applied only to the wealthiest Americans, well under 1 percent of all households. In a decision that generated intense interest, the Supreme Court originally split four to four on the constitutionality of the tax. When the case was re-argued, it was assumed the sick judge would vote to uphold the tax, but one of the other judges switched his vote, and the statute was struck down five to four, a decision that drew strong popular opposition. Some legislators were determined to pass the tax a second time, but President Taft felt this might precipitate a crisis between the Court and the two popularly elected branches of government. He attempted to defuse the controversy by supporting a congressional effort to submit a constitutional amendment permitting an income tax to the states and accepting a corporate income tax. The income tax was passed and ratified on the basis that few if any people would have to pay it, mostly wealthy people on the East Coast. In today's dollars, a taxpayer would pay no tax on the first $250,000 in income and then only 1 percent. The top rate of 7 percent kicked in only for those making more than the equivalent of $6 million a year.[32] The constitutional amendment passed just before Wilson's inauguration and the income tax was one of the first laws to be passed in his administration. The corporate and income taxes were never reconciled. Dividends were taxed twice, while interest payments were not taxed at all, providing a huge incentive for corporate debt in lieu of equity.

World War I

In Europe, World War I erupted unexpectedly; it precipitated a panic on world markets. Most markets closed for much of the war; it took months before the New York Stock Exchange could fully re-open. American exports of agricultural goods skyrocketed, replacing Russian exports embargoed by the German and Turkish Black Sea blockade. During the war, the United States greatly improved its competitive position in the world. Farm income more than doubled. America's manufacturing exports also expanded, first to markets in Latin America and Asia which opened to U.S. firms as a result of the war, and then to Europe for steel, arms, vehicles, and railroad stock with which to fight the war. Du Pont alone supplied 40 percent of allied munitions; its military business increased by a factor of 276 and its annual revenues by a factor of 25. Germany forfeited domination of the chemical industry to Du Pont when it lost export markets due to the British blockade. The American economy grew strongly throughout the war and the Dow Jones Industrial average had its largest percentage gain in history in 1915. The shortage of labor and certain materials speeded the deployment of labor-saving technological advances. Because they were needed in the war, the price of horses became so high that tractors replaced horses on many farms.

Wilson's initial neutrality policy helped the Allies. The British blockade reduced American trade with Germany to a fraction of what it had been before the war, while trade with the Allies multiplied. At the start of the war, the Allies had ten times more trade with the United States than did the Central Powers, a multiple which quickly reached the hundreds. America became the Allies' supplier and banker. American machine tools and know-how were vital to the Allies who were finally able to match German industrial strength toward the end of the war. The German U-boats had no real historic precedent and the Allies underestimated their strategic impact. Previously, ships were seized, but not sunk unless they resisted. Passengers would be removed from the ships if they were captured. Submarines, however, had no space to take on the passengers or crew of a captured ship. Submarine warfare was complicated by the British blockade that aimed to starve Germany. The *Lusitania* was sunk, killing 1198 people, including 128 Americans. The sinking of the *Lusitania* could have been considered grounds for U.S. entry into the war. Wilson demanded and obtained a reversal of German policy, providing that passenger liners would not be sunk without warning and evacuation. Investigators, however, subsequently discovered the *Lusitania*'s manifest was fraudulent and much of its cargo was indeed armaments.

Eventually, U-boat damage caused America to declare war on the Germans in 1917. Wilson delayed the declaration to try to preserve his role as negotiator or referee, but then decided the United States must "make the world safe for democracy." Initially, the Germans sank ships at three times the rate they could be built. The Allies formed convoys, which were an enormous success: only 600 troops drowned of over a million troops that crossed the ocean. In the early part of the war, America built very few ships, because the Civil War caused merchant marine vessels to be chartered under the flags of other countries and lower wages abroad made American production cost-prohibitive. The U.S. built the largest shipyard in the world on an island in the Delaware River with over 350 buildings and 80 miles of railroad tracks. On July 4, 1918, ninety-five ships were launched from American shipyards, including seventeen ships from San Francisco.

America had the world's largest economy, much of which was converted to war purposes. Ironically, the failure of the progressive movement to rein in big business eventually helped American industry to provide the war effort necessary to achieve victory in Europe. Woodrow Wilson recruited Wall Street financier Bernard Baruch to head the government war effort, appointing him to head the War Industries Board. Baruch was given virtual dictatorial powers over the economy, even setting prices and forcing manufacturers to produce certain goods. When America formally entered the war, it used many of the methods that had worked for the North in the Civil War. The army was quickly mobilized, increasing from 200 thousand to 4 million men, half of whom were drafted.

The sums required for World War I dwarfed what had been needed even for the Civil War, which had been fought primarily with cannon, rifles, and a few ships. World War I was fought with expensive artillery, tanks, large ships, and airplanes. The size of the armed forces was much larger, and transatlantic deployment of troops and equipment was far more expensive and complicated. In the end, the federal government spent $32 billion in winning World War I, ten times more than it had spent for the Civil War and more than twice the total operating budget of the federal government since its inception in 1789.[33]

Federal spending skyrocketed from hundreds of millions of dollars annually into the billions of dollars, never falling below three billion dollars annually after the war.

Bond drives were used to raise funds for the war. With $10 billion in war loans, the U.S. financed a large portion of the military expenditures of its allies. The government generated almost $2 billion in funds by issuing War Savings Certificates for as little as $5 and war stamps for 25 cents, which could be pasted in books and, when 20 stamps had been accumulated, exchanged for $5 certificates. Many Americans borrowed from their banks to buy war bonds. Debt financing totaled more than $20 billion, creating a credit bubble that burst after the war. As a developing country, the U.S. had been a debtor nation, owing approximately $3.5 billion at the start of the war. By its end, foreign governments, principally France and Britain, owed the U.S. almost $10 billion and the nation was a net creditor by over $12 billion.

To help pay for World War I, Congress passed an inheritance tax, an excess profits tax, an excise tax on corporate stock, and an increased income tax, expanding it to include the middle class. The top tax rate was increased from 10 to 67 percent and then to 77 percent. Tax payments skyrocketed, with the corporate income tax receipts more than tripling between 1916 and 1920 while personal income taxes more than quintupled, totaling over $1 billion. Total revenues increased from $761 million in 1916 to $6.6 billion in 1920. Still, the federal deficit increased from $1.2 billion in 1916 to $25 billion in 1920.

American troops, armaments, and supplies were decisive in determining the outcome of the conflict, ensuring victory for the Allies. Russian withdrawal from the war made possible the concentration of much greater numbers of German troops along the western front. Thus, in 1918, American aid and troops were crucial to stemming this German tide. While all of the major countries in Europe were drained by the war, America emerged strengthened and the leading world power. World War I caused the loss of 9 million combatants and 5 million civilians and between $250 and $400 billion in damages. The level of devastation was unprecedented. Worldwide farm production declined by a third, manufacturing dropped by a fifth, and in Russia by seven-eighths. During the 1910s, United States manufacturing rose from about a fifth to a third of the world production, the country having been spared the ravages of the war.[34] The burden of German reparations was set at $32 billion, about a tenth of the total cost of the war.

Wilson changed the basis for American foreign policy to more idealistic, internationalist, and humanitarian concepts. His policy was not based on narrow constructs of self-interest, but on altruism and the belief in the moral supremacy of democracy. Wilson tried to break down traditional diplomacy and to replace it with more democratic processes. Rejecting the balance of power, he sought to place America on a higher moral plane.[35] Wilson set up a committee of academicians to prepare the U.S. for the peacemaking process, but his famous Fourteen-Point Plan was put together hurriedly without consultation with Allies.[36]

Wilson's League of Nations was based on several prior initiatives. John Hay, McKinley's secretary of state, had hoped to bring the world's great nations together in a combine of states. Theodore Roosevelt sought to channel America's nationalism into a responsible internationalism with an idealistic vision. Senator Henry Cabot Lodge thought the United States needed to act in concert with other great powers as a necessary step towards peace. In 1915, William Howard Taft was a co-founder of the League to Enforce Peace. Wilson's initiatives were in many respects utopian and sought to replace nationalism with a new internationalism.[37]

America won the war, but lost the peace when Wilson was unable to secure U.S. approval of the Treaty of Versailles and U.S. participation in the League of Nations. Wilson's initial decision to attend the Paris peace conference in person was controversial when it was made. In hindsight, it was a mistake. He achieved only a few of his goals at the conference, giving away most of his positions to obtain a provision for a League of Nations. He was never able to obtain popular and opposition Republican support for his peace program. He attacked the Republicans in the election of 1918 and, after they won a decisive victory, made little effort to work with them.[38] At the very point when America was poised to assume global leadership, Wilson's initiatives would have diminished the ability of the nation to assume these powers and control its future by placing its fate in the hands of an ineffective international agency. Many Americans were reluctant to accept his arguments that more foreign trade would result and that the well-being of mankind would be advanced. Wilson was re-elected in 1916 on the premise that "he kept us out of war," a commitment even he admitted probably could not be kept. His credibility was less than stellar when he barnstormed the country and asked people to support the League of Nations. During treaty negotiations, Wilson inserted a number of provisions that made the success of the League less likely.

Congressional resistance to approving the treaty was based on the conclusion that the Constitution preserved to Congress the sole power to declare war and belief the treaty was unfair to Germany, a conclusion borne out by subsequent history and a concern that, if addressed, might have stopped the rise of Nazism and Adolf Hitler. The Armistice and the Versailles Treaty spared Germany geographically from much of the ravages of the actual fighting of the war. Americans were amazed by the contrast between the ruins of northern France and the prosperity of Germany. As a result, many Germans believed they had not been defeated in battle, but had been surrendered by their own political leadership.

Even though Wilson had previously suffered strokes, he took his case to the people, traveling to all but four states in the West. Wilson suffered another stroke, plus a nervous breakdown. The failure to satisfactorily resolve U.S. participation in the peace process was undoubtedly due in significant part to the fact Wilson had become gravely ill. Vice President Marshall was unqualified for the presidency and did not want the job. Wilson's wife Edith acted as president for seventeen months. She attempted to keep his condition a secret and few people had access to him. Even important strategy memos on the League of Nations were left unopened. Mrs. Wilson's efforts to conceal the president's true condition from the American public impaired the nation's governance. Wilson refused to accept Henry Cabot Lodge's reservations, instructing his allies in Congress to vote against them and ensuring the defeat of the Treaty. With Wilson incapacitated and the White House isolated, a bleakness and sense of frustration permeated Washington. When the

Democrats were trounced in the 1920 election, Europeans viewed the results as a repudiation of Wilson's internationalism. Wilson lacked the political skills, connections, and the willingness to compromise needed to put his ideas into action. Wilson's vision went unimplemented.

The war had the effect of vastly increasing the size and scope of government. Particularly in those countries known for military imperialism—Russia, Japan, and Germany—the state became dominant. As was the case during the Civil War, the power of the American government expanded enormously: the level of taxation skyrocketed, a Fuel Administration enforced gasless Sundays, a War Labor Policies Board intervened in industrial disputes, and a Food Administration under Herbert Hoover fixed prices for commodities.

In the end, America had little to show for hundreds of thousands of casualties and spending tens of billions of dollars, other than a large war debt the Europeans felt little obligation to pay. A large portion of the loans to the Allies were incurred after the close of hostilities, but little was obtained in the way of leverage for peace or commitments for repayment. Theodore Roosevelt was a strong supporter of the war and his popularity and that of the progressive movement suffered as a result. Americans fought an expensive and brutal war for European empires that not only ignored but also exploited Wilson's foreign policy.

Harding and Coolidge

In the United States, the rapid economic expansion to meet the needs of the war had resulted in high rates of inflation with prices rising 2.5 times in only 7 years, albeit far less than in Europe where they were rising 3 times in Britain, 5 times in France, 6 times in Italy, and 20 times in Germany.[39] In the United States, inflation from the war created demands for higher worker pay. In 1919 there were thousands of labor strikes. Returning soldiers spread influenza among themselves and the American public; more people died in the 1919 flu epidemic than in the war itself. In some cities as in Chicago and Omaha, for example, race riots occurred.

Immediately after the war, the Federal Reserve System (the Fed) failed in its first major test. It had kept interest rates low to facilitate war measures. In response to the rampant inflation, the Fed raised the discount rate from 4 to 7 percent and held it there for a year. Money supply contracted by 9 percent and unemployment shot up from 4 to 12 percent. A recession set in and wholesale prices declined by 40 percent.[40]

Social unrest and inflation followed by deflation and high unemployment was a recipe for political disaster that enabled the Republicans to dominate the U.S. political process in the 1920s, controlling the White House, Senate, and House for the entire decade. While the 1920s are often referred to as the Roaring Twenties and sometimes known as the decade of Prohibition, the period was characterized by unprecedented economic growth and stability—real output rose at an annual rate of 4.7 percent, the unemployment rate averaged only 3.7 percent, and consumer prices rose only three-tenths of 1 percent annually. During the period between World War I and the Depression, the nation's wealth doubled. Between 1921 and 1929, the gross national product rose by a half. Over the course of the decade, investment in plant and equipment doubled. In 1920, only 35 percent of U.S. households had electricity, a figure which reached 68 percent by the end of the decade. Prohibition became an example of the excesses of reform and is the only constitutional amendment to have been repealed, which bred disrespect for the law.

During the early 1920s, the central thrust of government was to reduce spending and taxation. Taking over from the incapacitated Woodrow Wilson, President Harding assumed office during one of the sharpest recessions in American history. Harding moved rapidly to create a central agency to oversee the budget and institute spending reforms. He brought about massive cuts in government spending, as much as 40 percent, through careful management and a deliberate plan. Soon, the economy was booming again.[41]

Andrew Mellon, appointed by Harding, was probably the most powerful secretary of the treasury since Alexander Hamilton, so dominating that senators jokingly said three presidents served under him: Harding, Coolidge, and Hoover. In the early years of his tenure, Mellon cut federal spending by over 50 percent and the national debt by well over a third. He utilized "trickle down economics," cutting taxes on the rich to increase capital and investment, which in turn stimulated economic growth. When Congress cut personal income taxes three times, revenues did not fall, they rose, and the wealthy taxpayers paid an even higher percentage of the total taxes.[42]

Perhaps the most important characteristic of the age was the minimalist government.

> Federal government spending amounted to only 3% of the gross national product, federal revenues to 4%, and most of that went to pay for past wars. Of the federal government's $3.3 billion in outlays in 1930, 22% went to national security, split between the Army and Navy. Another 25% went to veterans' services and benefits, and 21% to interest on the national debt, almost all of it incurred in World War I (though cut in half through the surpluses and deflation of the 1920s). That left only about one-quarter of the budget, well under $1 billion for all other government functions. Federal taxes did not impinge noticeably on the lives of most citizens. The individual income tax produced a slightly smaller share (28%) of federal revenues in 1929 and 1930 than the corporate income tax—about $1 billion each. Only a small minority of Americans—4 million in 1929 and 3.7 million in 1930, in a nation of 30 million households—paid income tax in these years. The bite of the tax had been vastly reduced by Treasury Secretary Andrew Mellow cuts in the high wartime tax rates; the cuts reduced rates most sharply on the rich but took half the taxpayers off the rolls and left rates low enough so that those with incomes as high as $10,000—enough to live in a comfortable house with servants—paid a derisory $90 in 1929 and $154 in 1930.

> Nor were the state and local governments vastly bigger or more intrusive. Spending by all governments totaled only 12% of the gross national product in 1927, with more than

half of that accounted for by local governments. Effectively, if inarticulately, the different levels of government divided major revenue sources among themselves. The individual and corporate income taxes belonged to the federal government, the sales and gasoline and motor vehicle taxes to the states, and the property tax almost entirely to local governments, who relied on that plus charges, fees and a little state aid for virtually all their revenues. Spending was also neatly arranged. Local governments spent over 90% of their money on schools. State spending was more varied, with the largest amounts spent on highways (25%), higher education (10%), hospitals (7%), and natural resources (5%). Altogether, all units of government in the prosperous year of 1927 spent some $11 billion in an economy of $90 to $100 billion. The burden of government sat very lightly indeed upon the nation.[43]

Reductions in government spending were not indiscriminant. Perhaps the most important single development of the era was the growth and spread of education. The number of high schools skyrocketed from 800 in 1880 to 2500 in 1890 to over 6,000 in 1900 to more than 10,000 in 1910. Between 1910 and 1930 spending on education rose five fold, from $426 million to $2.3 billion. Illiteracy rates fell sharply. The Twenties was the age of the Book-of-the-Month-Club and the Literary Guild. A record number of books were published with a particular interest in the classics.[44] It was a lively decade, and its spirit is captured by the syncopated Jazz Age beat.

President Warren Harding (1865–1923) looked like a president, being handsome with blue eyes. He had at least two extramarital affairs, one with Carrie Fulton Phillips, the wife of a friend, and another with Nan Britton who claimed he fathered her child. Historians have used these affairs, his drinking, and lack of intellectual capacity as a basis for classifying Harding as one of the worst presidents. Actually, the Harding Administration was effective and his presidency marked a "return to normalcy."

Harding believed that America's matchless society was the creation of volunteerism and that only government could spoil it. If he could plant a Rotary Club in every city and hamlet, he said, he would "rest assured that our ideals of freedom would be safe and civilization would progress." That was a general view. "There is only one first-class civilization in the world" wrote the *Ladies Home Journal.* "It is right here in the United States." That was also the view of most American intellectuals, to judge not by their subsequent rationalizations in the Thirties but by what they actually wrote at the time. . . .

Harding believed this cultural supremacy would arise inevitably provided the government allowed the wheels of free enterprise to turn. Far from selecting cronies from "the buck-eye state" (as later alleged), he formed a cabinet of strong men: Charles Evans Hughes as Secretary of State, Andrew Mellon at the Treasury, Hoover at Commerce. . . . The cabinet was a cross-section of successful America: a car manufacturer, two bankers, a hotel director, a farm-journal editor, an international lawyer, a rancher, an engineer and only two professional politicians. . . .

Harding's regime was agreeably liberal. Against the advice of his cabinet and his wife he insisted on releasing the Socialist leader Eugene Debs, whom Wilson had imprisoned. . . . He freed twenty-three other political prisoners the same day, commuted death-sentences on the "Wobblies" (Industrial Workers of the World) and before the end of his presidency had virtually cleared the jails of political offenders.

There is no evidence that Harding was ever anything other than a generous and unsuspicious man. But Harding made two errors of judgment: appointing the florid Senator Fall, who turned out to be a scoundrel, and believing that his Ohio campaign-manager Harry Daugherty, whom he made Attorney-General, would screen and protect him from the influence peddlers.[45]

A series of scandals erupted. Harding acted diligently, forcing the director of the veterans' bureau Charles Forbes to leave because of his role in accepting kickbacks for overpriced hospitals. Forbes was subsequently convicted and sentenced to two years in jail. Secretary of Interior Albert Fall was convicted for accepting bribes in the leasing of the Teapot Dome and Elk Hills oil preserves. Fall not only tricked Harding: he hoodwinked the entire Senate as well. When his name was submitted for confirmation, the Senate resorted to the procedure of approving his appointment by acclamation and with accolades. Fall's acceptance of bribery was uncovered years later, long after Harding had left office; there was no evidence of any personal involvement of the president. Fall was the first Cabinet officer to be convicted and imprisoned for a felony committed while in office.

Shortly after the scandals broke, Harding died of a cerebral hemorrhage on a trip to the West Coast; his wife died only a few months later. While historians have attributed his death to the scandals, it is more probable that he was simply overwhelmed by the responsibilities of the office. He occasionally spoke of being in over his head. Soon after his death, the press and the muckrakers began a campaign against Harding's administration, characterizing it as the most corrupt in American history. It was believed that Harding's wife had destroyed most of his papers, which was considered evidence of guilty secrets. When his papers were opened in 1964, there was no evidence to support the accusations. Besides the booming economy, Harding had other accomplishments, including famine relief in the Soviet Union, which was only begrudgingly accepted by the Communist government. Ironically, he may have prevented the Communists from being consumed by angry Russian mobs.

When Harding died, Calvin Coolidge (1872–1933) was at his father's house in a remote Vermont hamlet. Awakened at midnight, he was sworn in by his father, who was a notary public, in a ceremony illuminated by a kerosene lamp. Born on a Fourth of July, Coolidge was close to his mother and sister whose deaths were only five years apart, casting a pall over his youth. Coolidge became nationally known for breaking the Boston police strike, which he thought would end his political career. He succinctly described the public sentiment: "There is no right to strike against the public safety by anybody, anywhere, anytime." Coolidge was religious, but not in a pious or fundamentalist fashion. He noted, "Our government rests upon religion. It is from that source that we derive our reverence for trust and justice, for equality and liberty, and for the rights of mankind." His "rectitude comforted Americans in a time of shifting values."[46] By dealing effectively with Harding's scandals, he turned a liability into an asset.

No public man carried into modern times more comprehensively the founding principles of Americanism: hard work, frugality, freedom of conscience, freedom from government, respect for serious culture (he went to Amherst, and was exceptionally well-read in classical and foreign literature and in history). . . .

It suited Coolidge, in fact, to mislead people into believing he was less sophisticated and active than he was. . . . In fact few men have been better prepared for the presidency, moving up every rung of the public ladder: parish councilor, assemblyman, mayor, State Representative, State Senator, President of the State Senate, Lieutenant-Governor, Governor, Vice-President. At every stage he insisted that government should do as little as was necessary ("He didn't do anything", remarked the political comic Will Rogers, "but that's what people wanted done."). But he also insisted that, when it did act, it should be absolutely decisive. . . . He articulated a generally held belief that the function of government is primarily to create a climate in which agriculture, manufacturing and commerce can seize the opportunities which God and nature provide. . . .

The press liked his dependability, flavored by eccentric habits. . . . Journalists also sensed he was wholly uncorrupted by power. On August 2, 1927, he summoned thirty of them, told them, "The line forms on the left," and handed each a two-by-nine-inch slip of paper in which he had typed: "I do not choose to run for President in 1928." . . .

When the decade was over, and the prosperity had been, for the moment, wholly eclipsed, it was seen retrospectively, especially by writers and intellectuals as grossly materialistic, febrile, philistine, and at the same time insubstantial and ephemeral, unmerited by any solid human accomplishment. . . .

But the view that the 1920s was a drunken spree destructive of civilized values can be substantiated only by the systematic distortion or denial of the historical record. The prosperity was very widespread and very solid. It was not universal: in the farming community particularly it was patchy, and it largely excluded certain older industrial communities, such as the textile trade of New England. But it was more widely distributed than had been possible in any community of this size before, and it involved the acquisition, by tens of millions, of the elements of economic security which had hitherto been denied them throughout the whole of history. The growth was spectacular.[47]

Prosperity was the hallmark of the Coolidge era. He kept federal spending constant, cut taxes, reduced the deficit by a quarter, and favored a light regulatory approach. Across-the-board reductions were made in the income tax. The 1925 tax law eliminated a third of those who paid taxes from the rolls and provided a personal exemption greater for individuals who were married than those who were not. The highest tax bracket was reduced from 70 percent during the war years to 50 percent, then 40 percent, and eventually to 20 percent. The estate tax was halved and the gift tax zeroed out. Coolidge worked hard to cut spending, but Congress overrode a veto of the veterans' pension bill, forced him to accept funding for the cataclysmic Mississippi River flood, and made other spending ad-ons. Media coverage of the worst natural disaster in the nation's history until that time, the Mississippi River floods, forced Coolidge to set the precedent of the federal government paying for relief. Nevertheless, in the 1920s, the American economy grew faster than in the more widely heralded booms of the 1960s, 1980s, and 1990s.[48]

American capital and financial markets now dominated the world. The United States became the world's banker, with over a billion dollars a year in loans gushing out of New York. But these markets were somewhat cautious, the American people and the business community felt burned and taken advantage of as a result of the billions of dollars that had been lent to successfully bring an end to World War I, little of which was being repaid. The allies' inability or refusal to honor their debts contributed to the growing sentiment towards isolationism in the most powerful nation on earth. This in turn was a factor in events spinning out of control. European governments tried to force Germany to pay reparations so they could repay their loans to the United States. As America's focus became internal, trade barriers and tariffs continued to be imposed by U.S. businesses, making it more difficult for Europe nations to earn money to pay off their debts.[49] After Wilson vetoed a bill raising tariffs on his last full day in office, Harding promptly signed an identical bill, failing to grasp that Germany's ability to pay reparations was contingent on rapidly increasing exports and in turn England and France were expecting to use German reparations to repay their debts.[50] America's great wealth and economic prowess sparked a consumer-led boom.

The heart of the consumer boom was in personal transport, which in a vast country, where some of the new cities were already thirty miles across, was not a luxury. [The U.S. was manufacturing] five-sixths of the world production and one car for every five people in the country. This gives some idea of America's global industrial dominance. In 1924 the four leading European car producers turned out only 11 per cent of the vehicles manufactured in the U.S.A. . . . . The meaning of these figures was that the working class as a whole was acquiring the individual freedom of medium- and long-distance movement hitherto limited to a section of the middle class. . . . [A]ir passengers rose from 49,713 in 1928 to 417,505 in 1930 (by 1940 the figure was 3,185,278 and nearly 8 million by 1945). What the Twenties demonstrates was the relative speed with which industrial productivity could transform luxuries into necessities and spread them down the class pyramid.

Indeed, to a growing extent it was a dissolvent of class and other barriers. Next to cars, its was the new electrical industry which fueled Twenties prosperity. . . . First the mass radio audience, signaled by the new phenomenon of "fan mail" in autumn 1923, then regular attendance, especially by young people, at the movies (from 1927 talkies) brought about the Americanization of immigrant communities and a new classlessness in dress, speech and attitudes. . . .

The Twenties in America marked the biggest advances for women of any decade, before or since. By 1930 there were 10,546,000 women "gainfully employed" outside of the home: the largest number, as before, were in domestic/personal service (3,483,000) but there were now nearly 2 million in clerical work, 1,860,000 in manufacturing and, most encouraging of all, 1,226,000 in the professions. Equally significant, and culturally more important, were the liberated housewives, the "Blondies," to whom their appliances, cars and husbands' high wages had brought leisure. . . .

In 1929 the United States had achieved a position of paramouncy in total world production ever hitherto attained during a period of prosperity by any single state: 34.4 percent of the whole, compared with Britain's 10.4, Germany's 10.3, Russia's 9.9, France's 5.0, Japan's 4.0, 2.5 for Italy, 2.2 for Canada and 1.7 for Poland. The likelihood that the European continent would lean towards America's "original social structure," as Siegfried termed it, increased with every year the world economy remained buoyant. Granted another decade of prosperity on this scale our account of modern times would have been vastly different and immeasurably happier.[51]

Notwithstanding his frugality and innate suspicion of government, Coolidge pursued a fairly progressive agenda, seeking anti-lynching legislation, an expanded minimum wage to include women, and a ban on child labor. He implemented a truly progressive federal income tax—98 percent of Americans paid no tax at all and 93 percent of taxes were paid by the wealthiest Americans.

Coolidge was a laconic New Englander, but his temperament seemed appropriate for his times. Coolidge's voice and temperament were well-suited for radio. He held 500 press conferences, more than any other president before or since.[52] During his 1924 campaign for president, he employed public relations experts to help with his image. Coolidge effectively used the newsreel in movie theaters and the radio. He was effective at reaching unprecedented numbers of people with new technologies. Coolidge could reach tens of millions of people with a single speech. By contrast, Teddy Roosevelt reached only 13 million people with the thousands of speeches he gave throughout his lifetime.

Coolidge was alleged to have said "the business of America is business." What he actually said just once in a speech to journalists was "the chief business of the American people is business." His philosophy was: "People are not created for the benefit of industry, but industry is created for the benefit of people." The wealthy were disproportionately well-off. America's income and wealth were more highly concentrated than at any other stage of its history. The top tenth of 1 percent had as much income as the bottom 40 percent. The prosperity of the 1920s was widening the gap. The top half of 1 percent controlled a third of the wealth, while 80 percent of Americans had virtually no savings.[53]

Coolidge restructured international debt to make European reparations payments more feasible. Charles Dawes, who eventually became Coolidge's vice president, won the Nobel Peace Prize for chairing a committee that temporarily defused the German reparations issue. Coolidge's foreign affairs team had mixed results in limiting naval armaments and efforts to outlaw international wars.

Coolidge is criticized for not preventing the Great Depression, but even after the fact economists could find no basis for the notion it could have been predicted. Like all human beings, Coolidge couldn't foresee unpredictable events. Furthermore, the basic cause of the Great Depression was the failed government policies that were adopted and implemented after Coolidge left the presidency.

H.L. Mencken considered him "an obscure and unimportant man" but later concluded upon his death "when Jefferson's warnings are heeded at last, and we reduce government to its simplest terms, it may very well happen that Cal's bones now resting inconspicuously in the Vermont granite will come to be as revered as those of a man who really did the nation some service." Coolidge's taciturn personality was in part his nature, but also a reaction to the death of his 16-year-old son in 1924, which caused him to fall into a melancholic state. "He was a different person after that," wrote one of his leading biographers.[54] But he was still a man of honesty, simplicity, intelligence, and common sense. When Coolidge left office, he was popular, and the nation was experiencing unprecedented prosperity and peace.

Republican presidents between the Civil War and the Great Depression have been criticized for scandals, their blind support of the business agenda, and failing to provide a government safety net, particularly when contrasted with the social legislation implemented in Europe. Much of this criticism may be unwarranted; most of it misses the mark. These presidencies' failures are more basic and more profound. America was becoming the most powerful and economically vibrant nation on the planet. Except for Theodore Roosevelt, the Republicans did not provide the strategic vision, leadership, and energy to enable America to fulfill its global role. Republicans failed to address issues such as cyclical unemployment, tariffs, and America's role as world leader. Washington "was a town and a government entirely unprepared to take on the global responsibilities."[55] As a result, even though the United States had the most efficient and productive manufacturing and agricultural sectors in the world, its world trade lagged behind other major industrial nations. America's per capita foreign trade was less than a quarter that of New Zealand and Australia, a third of Britain's, and less than that of Germany, Canada, and France. Protectionist policies, for example, triggered a trade war with its neighbor Canada, in which Canada retaliated by granting preferential trading status to Britain, Australia, and the British West Indies.[56] Republicans were protectionists when they should have been ardent free traders.

Republicans also did not comfort the American community.

While giving lip service to the concept of civil society, they did not rein-vigorate the institutions of civil society weakened and destroyed by the Civil War. While Democrats were hamstrung by their support from southern segregationists, Republicans did not address racism or the Jim Crow system in the South. They also supported a series of restrictions on immigration, eventually resulting in the closing of America's bor-ders. As conservatives, Republicans shied from expanding the role of civil society and setting a national agenda. Unlike the founding fathers and Lincoln, they viewed the role of the presidency as narrow. Industrialization compartmentalized society and Republicans went along with this fragmentation and had limited views of their role. Their conservatism became a repudiation or negation of America's revolu-tionary tradition.

Both Coolidge and Harding lacked vision and perception of tech-nology's amazing future. They failed to take actions to develop world-class institutions to address problems and fill the vacuum created by the refusal of the United States to join the League of Nations. Coolidge, for example, allowed Commerce Secretary Herbert Hoover to excessively regulate the radio broadcast spectrum; Coolidge did not use his cabinet for brainstorming or to develop an overarching strategy. He failed to deal with isolationism and xenophobia. Coolidge never traveled west of the Mississippi and had no interest in international travel. His only for-eign travels had been his one-week honeymoon to Montreal and a brief presidential visit to Havana.

In some respects, the 1920s were regressive. Coolidge supported and signed a bill placing caps on immigrants based on the 1890 census. The law severely limited immigration over the next four decades and helped consign many European Jews to death at the hands of the Nazis. In 1927, Oliver Wendell Holmes wrote the Supreme Court decision holding that an eighteen-year-old girl considered to be feebleminded could be sterilized. There was only one dissenting voice. Most state courts had ruled involuntary sterilization to be unconstitutional, so rel-atively few had been sterilized. Once the procedure was ruled constitu-tional, tens of thousands of men and women were forcibly sterilized.[57]

Conclusion

As the name implies, the progressive era was one of reform and moving forward in some areas. Yet, the progressive era was not as reform-oriented as the name suggests. The so-called robber barons or tycoons were actually the advocates and proponents of radical change; they were opposed by the muckrakers and so-called progressives, who did serve as a badly needed check on corporate influence and power.

After the Civil War, the Congress, the executive, and the political system reacted slowly to industrial concentration and the enormous changes occurring. Legislative action was frustrated by government corruption and the expanding economic power of business, particularly industrial corporations that used their wealth to purchase special favors, to control the two major political parties, and broker government deals. American industry continued to penalize the consumer and to live in fear of competition by supporting high tariffs and trade barriers.

Worst still, this so-called progressive era witnessed severe regression in some critical respects. The country went backwards on immigration and race, with African Americans assigned a status only slightly better than slavery.

As the role of government expanded, so did, unfortunately, the level of government corruption. While progressives did act to stem the corruption, their efforts met with only mixed success. The progressive era reforms did, mercifully, save the country from large bureaucracies and expensive government programs that, in a welfare state, would drive profligate spending. The progressive era left American civilization with a muscular private sector, an enfeebled civil society, and a lean but ineffective government.

10

World War II
ends the great depression

Hoover's Failed Presidency

IRONICALLY, HERBERT HOOVER(1874–1964) probably had more knowledge about economics than any other individual to hold the presidency. During his tenure in office, however, the prosperous, less-government era of the 1920s was brought to an end by the horrors of the Great Depression. Even the economics profession didn't anticipate the Depression, nor recognize the nation to be in one until after the fact, and then offered little in the way of solutions until Hoover left office. For most of Hoover's term, economists were optimistic the economy would turnaround. The leading economists at Harvard and Yale and the founder of *Forbes* magazine predicted recovery. In a 1988 article in the *American Economic Review*, economists analyzed the data available in the late 1920s and concluded the Depression could not have been forecast.[1]

Probably more than anyone else, President Herbert Hoover is inextricably linked with and blamed for the Great Depression. Yet, prior to his election to the presidency, Hoover was an American success as a production manager. An orphan from a rural background, he went on to make millions in mining. A highly successful businessman with international experience and Secretary of Commerce with an extensive government background, Hoover was an engineer whose businesses extended throughout the globe. His business success led him to conclude: "If a man has not made a million dollars by the time he is forty, he is not worth much."

In World War I, Franklin Roosevelt (1882–1945) or FDR served with him in the Wilson Administration and wrote, "I wish we could make him President of the United States. There could not be a better one." Hoover gained fame for his humanitarian efforts at worldwide famine relief for Belgium in World War I, Russia after the communist revolution, and Europe after World War II when he helped to feed millions of starving children. He was praised by John Maynard Keynes as the only man who emerged from the post-World War I peace process with an enhanced reputation.

Hoover did make a pair of major mistakes, probably two out of the three worst blunders in American history. Over the objections of numerous economists, he signed into law the Smoot-Hawley Tariffs, making American levees the highest and most restrictive in its history. America was saddled with extraordinarily high tariffs even though it was economically the most competitive nation on the planet. Secondly, Hoover stood idly by while America's monetary supply shriveled, dropping by 30 percent during his administration. The number of banks fell from 25,000 to 15,000, a reduction which caused the worst panic in American history.

Over the next few decades, it became clear that the Great Depression was not a failure of capitalism, but rather the result of failed government policies. The fallout from these twin errors, however, was enormous. Hoover's blunders made Karl Marx a prophet, almost ended faith in capitalism, and converted countless Americans and other people across the planet to communism and socialism. Even though academicians and intellectuals did not see the Depression coming, many of them moved sharply to the left, blaming what the Republicans had done in the 1920s (which they had not protested against at the time) and embracing FDR or politics even further to the left.

In Germany the depression helped Adolf Hitler rise to power, paving the way for World War II. In Japan it strengthened the military clique that was dedicated to creating a Greater East Asia co-prosperity sphere. In China it led to monetary changes that accelerated the final hyperinflation that sealed the doom of the Chiang Kai-shek regime and brought the communists to power.

In the realm of ideas, the depression persuaded the public that capitalism was an unstable system destined to suffer ever more serious crises. The public was converted to views that had already gained increasing acceptance among the intellectuals: government had to play a more active role; it had to intervene to offset the instability generated by an unregulated private enterprise; it had to serve as a balance wheel to promote stability and assure security. . . .

The depression also produced a far-reaching change in professional economic opinion. The economic collapse shattered the long-held belief, which had been strengthened during the 1920s, that monetary policy was a potent instrument for promoting economic stability. Opinion shifted almost to the opposite extreme, that "money does not matter." . . . The Keynesian revolution not only captured the economic profession, but also provided both an appealing justification and a prescription for extensive government intervention.[2]

Contrary to popular belief, and, as was previously stated, the 1920s was not a decade of speculation and loose money, but a period of powerful economic growth with strong gains in income, output, life expectancy, exports, and investment. By the end of that decade, investment reached levels not exceeded until the boom of the 1980s. Patent applications were higher than any period until the 1960s. Life expectancy increased by over five years. Output per person rose over 40 percent.[3] During the decade, the Federal Reserve Bank (the Fed) pursued a policy that was more deflationary than inflationary and the money supply increased less than in comparable periods of rapid expansion. The great stock market boom was compressed into the years 1927–1929 and was largely a Wall Street phenomenon, not experienced on other markets across the globe.

For most of the decade, the nation and the Fed were in a quandary over the farm economy which was in a period of decline even as the rest of the country was booming. Agricultural areas were reeling from the technological changes brought on by the industrial revolution. A third of cropland had been used to provide fodder for horses. As the automobile and tractor replaced draft animals, more land was used to produce food for humans resulting in large surpluses. The increasing mobility of farm and rural families caused rural banks and stores to lose business to competition in nearby towns and cities. In the 1920s, these enterprises began failing in increasing numbers.[4] Europeans erected trade barriers that limited foreign sales by the American farmer. America had a hundred-year history of high tariffs and could not credibly argue for free trade for farmers.

The strength of the American economy attracted gold from Europe. To help reduce this flow, the Fed in 1927 lowered interest rates in the United States, stimulating the economy, but causing speculators to believe they could borrow cheap, buy stocks on margin, and make a killing in the market, which is what they did do for two years. The Wall Street stock market relied increasingly on call money—funds used to buy stocks on margin. This worked well while the market was going up, but it accentuated the decline when the market's bubble burst. The stock market began to overheat, but consumer prices actually were stagnant, remaining in a deflationary cycle. In 1928, the Fed did raise the discount rate to curb the economy and speculative excesses. By the spring of 1929, an economic contraction had started months before the stock market crash.

On September 3, 1929, Roger Babson made one of his periodic warnings about the likelihood of a stock market crash, which was put out over the wire. This time, his remarks in Wellesley, Massachusetts, were taken seriously and in the last hour of trading and for the next seven weeks stocks plunged until they finally collapsed on Black Tuesday, October 29. The net result was a 40 percent decline, 23 percent in the last week, in significant part due to margin calls.[5] Some people had their entire assets wiped out overnight and others lost a substantial portion of their wealth. By the end of the 1920s, stocks were a higher percentage of America's assets than ever before, so the market crash had a more drastic impact than had previous panics. Yet, even at the end of the crash, market prices were still higher than they had been just a few years earlier.

Few banks failed in 1929, less than the average for the decade. The New York Federal Reserve Bank asked for authority to make additional increases in the discount rate when the stock market was surging in early 1929 and to reduce the rate when the market crashed to facilitate liquidity in the market. The Washington Federal Reserve Bank turned down both requests. After the stock market crash, the New York Federal Reserve Bank provided some liquidity and brokerage houses carried some accounts that were below margin requirements, preventing additional pressure to sell. When the president of the New York Federal Reserve Bank was criticized by the chairman of the Federal Reserve Board in Washington, however, other regional Federal Reserve Banks failed to provide additional liquidity. The Federal Reserve System also failed to perform its function as lender of last resort. Instead of extending loans to troubled commercial banks to avoid runs, it largely closed its discount window.[6] Still, the markets began to recover. In the beginning of 1930, *The New York Times* declared Admiral Byrd's flight over the South Pole to be the biggest news story of 1929.

In spring 1930, Hoover pronounced the depression over. The stock market had recovered half of its loses from the previous fall. He then signed the Smoot-Hawley bill, which instituted the highest tariffs in history and caused other countries to retaliate against American exports. Over a thousand economists urged him to veto the bill. As soon as he signed it, the market again began to slide and it continued on a downward path for two and a half years. The Fed kept rates high into 1930 causing a serious shortage in the money supply. The Bank of the United States failed at the end of 1930, the largest bank failure in history—sending shockwaves throughout the financial system.[7]

Still, in spring 1931, it looked as though recovery would begin and the bottom had been reached, but in Europe it was actually falling out. Numerous banks failed, including a number in Germany and Austria where American banks had placed funds to take advantage of high interest rates. Britain went off the gold standard and dozens of countries followed suit, shocking the global financial system. In the most disastrous decision of the period, the Fed tried to maintain the gold standard and raised rates resulting in severe contraction in money supply.[8] By the end of the year, bank failures were epidemic, mortgages were being foreclosed in record numbers, and people were withdrawing their money from banks in record amounts. Economic activity fell by 20 percent as car production plummeted, setting off huge layoffs in the economy's largest sector.

In 1932, the Fed stubbornly stuck with its restrictive monetary policy. Deflation set in. When people put up some of their own funds and borrow money to buy a house or business, deflation can quickly wipe out their equity and leave them only with debts which can exceed the value of the asset. Panic and the lack of public confidence caused customers to withdraw funds from the banking system. Needing cash to meet withdrawals, banks resisted making new loans and even called old loans. After four years of overly restrictive monetary supply, the financial system virtually collapsed at the end of 1932.

The very existence of the Fed lulled people to sleep in the belief that drastic measures were not necessary and the Fed would take care of the issue. In actuality, it was the worst banking crisis in history. There was nothing endemic in the capitalist system nor were there contradictions in the system, just a series of bad monetary decisions, each one exacerbating the previous one.[9]

Hoover has been criticized both for doing too little and for intervening excessively in the economy, prolonging and deepening what would have been a recession. He actually took both approaches or it may be said that he vacillated. Hoover was the first president to make a focused effort to counter a recession, a strategy Martin Van Buren, Ulysses S. Grant, Grover Cleveland, and Theodore Roosevelt didn't try. Previous presidents believed depressions and recessions were part of a natural cycle and pursued a hands-off policy, but that was not Hoover's temperament. He extracted promises from industrial leaders not to cut wages. He made a number of unfortunate and quotable pronouncements, such as: "We in America today are nearer to the final triumph over poverty than ever before in the history of any land. . . . We shall soon with the help of God be in sight of the day when poverty will be banished from this nation." In his 1932 re-election effort, he even repeated this statement almost verbatim

During Hoover's term, government revenues plunged and total expenditures by all governments rose to 20 percent of the shrinking economy, the largest increase in peacetime.[10] The Agricultural Marketing Act gave the farmers over $500 million. Hoover launched huge public works projects and urged governors to do the same, spending a record $700 million in 1931. More public works were started in Hoover's four years than in the previous thirty, including the Hoover or Boulder Dam and the San Francisco Bay Bridge.[11] After two years of deficit spending didn't work, there was an agreement with Congress in 1932 to bring the budget back into balance. Hoover decided to submit a huge tax increase to Congress, the largest in peacetime, and it passed by wide margins, jumping rates in the highest tax brackets to over 60 percent.

At times, Hoover was an activist. Decades later some members of the Roosevelt Administration credited him with being the originator of much of the New Deal.[12] He tried to pass a federal Home Loan Bank to free up capital from mortgages, but Congress was dilatory and raised the collateral requirements, limiting its effect. Hoover created a National Credit Corporation to deal with the problem of failing banks. The Corporation was provided with $500 million to lend to shaky banks. The bankers who ran it were reluctant to support the banks that needed it and the corporation languished. In 1932, the Reconstruction Finance Corporation was passed. The agency had capital of $500 million and authority to borrow an additional $1.5 billion, issued tax-exempt bonds, extended credit to banks and corporations, and provided liquidity to the economy. FDR expanded it. Hoover signed a Glass-Steagall Banking Act, as did FDR.[13] The first Glass-Steagall Act enabled the central and regional Federal Reserve Banks to use more financial instruments as collateral and to sell gold to meet the requirements for foreign withdrawals, but it was only effective for a year.[14] Hoover worked to form a Home Owners' Loan Corporation to make financing available to people in danger of losing their homes. Hoover greatly increased the number of and funding for public works; FDR created a Public Works Administration. Hoover originally suggested a bank holiday. When a bad drought hit the Midwest, he created a National Drought Relief Commission, with the federal government providing the know-how and expertise and the states providing the funding. The Red Cross and other charities were also expected to provide relief. The plan did not work, because of inadequate funding and private relief organizations were overwhelmed.

Most bankers and policy makers urged Hoover to do little or nothing, which is basically what he did during a crucial eighteen-month period when Americans gradually came to the conclusion the Depression was not going to end soon. Hoover's business career was in manufacturing and mining and he did not have a good grasp of finance. He understood the physical processes of production, but was suspicious about banking and demonized Wall Street. He failed to understand warnings from some economists that the money supply was too tight.[15] When the veterans marched on Washington demanding a promised war bonus (that was not due for another dozen years), Hoover ordered General Douglas MacArthur and Major George Patton to bring in troops but exercise restraint. They didn't obey orders to deal with the veterans peacefully and violently ousted the demonstrators. Hoover vetoed the veterans' bonus act (which was promptly enacted over his veto), and a bill which proposed the Tennessee Valley Authority. When citizens were becoming extremely concerned about the economy, Hoover appeared to be doing little or nothing to solve the problem, although one action did leave a lasting impression—the tear gassing and quelling of the veterans demonstration in Washington.[16]

By then, the damage was spreading rapidly—Gross National Product was down by almost half. Between mid-1929 and mid-1932, wholesale prices dropped by 40 percent. As revenues sagged, the government accrued the worst peacetime deficit in history. Over 5,000 banks failed and deposits plunged by half. Interest rates on Treasury bills were actually negative.[17] Between 1929 and 1932, stock prices crashed by almost 90 percent. Industrial production was down by over half. Public confidence was shattered by the economy and Hoover's lack of charisma and leadership. Hoover was an ineffective communicator and unable to gauge public opinion. As Secretary of Commerce, Hoover was the best source of news in Washington. The press greeted his election with enthusiasm, but Hoover then dismantled the public relations apparatus that got him elected. He dealt only with a select group of friendly correspondents. Personally, Hoover was cool and aloof. "Hoovervilles" sprang up everywhere—shantytowns of the homeless and unemployed. A "Hoover blanket" was a newspaper that served as a cover to keep a homeless person warm. A "Hoover wagon" was a car with no gas.

Many cities went bankrupt, median income dropped by 50 percent, 30 percent of farmers lost their homesteads, and the nation's birth rate declined by a record 15 percent. Unemployment soared from 3.2 to 25 percent and millions more were working at reduced wages. Most of the unemployed were without income and their families were in the same predicament. Many families were evicted or moved out of all or part of their homes to make them available for rent. In 1932, many schools were closed down and more than 300,000 children could not attend school due to a lack of funding. An estimated 1500 institutions of higher education went bankrupt and enrollments fell by 250,000. Books sales fell by half.

> The story of the Chicago schools was a great Depression epic. Rather than see 500,000 children remain on the streets, the teachers hitchhiked to work, endured "payless paydays"—by 1932 they had received checks in only five of the last thirteen months—and accepted city scrip to be redeemed after the Depression, even though Chicago bankers would not accept it. Somehow the city found money to invest in its forthcoming World's Fair of 1933, when Sally Rand would gross $6,000 a week, but it turned a deaf ear to the Board of Education. A thousand

teachers were dismissed outright. Those who remained taught on at immense personal sacrifice. Collectively the 1,400 teachers lost 759 homes. They borrowed $1,128,000 on their insurance policies and another $232,000 from loan sharks at annual interest rates of 42 percent, and although hungry themselves, they fed 11,000 pupils out of their thin pocketbooks. . . .

The New York City Health Department reported that over 20 percent of the pupils in the public schools were suffering from malnutrition. In the mining counties of Ohio, West Virginia, Illinois, Kentucky, and Pennsylvania, the secretary of the American Friends Service Committee told a congressional committee the ratio was sometimes over 90 percent, with deprived children afflicted by "drowsiness, lethargy, and sleepiness," and "mental retardation." A teacher suggested that one little girl go home and eat something; the child replied, "I can't. This is my sister's day to eat." Lillian Wald, a social worker, asked in anguish, "Have you ever seen the uncontrolled trembling of parents who have starved themselves for weeks so that their children might not go hungry?" . . .

"Nobody is actually starving," President Hoover told reporters. "The hoboes, for example, are better fed than they have ever been. One hobo in New York got ten meals in one day." In September 1932, *Fortune* flatly called the President a liar and suggested that twenty-five millions in want might be a fairer description of the nation's economic health.[18]

Hoover had not traveled much or toured the nation between his inauguration and the campaign of 1932. He was out of touch. Hoover's White House became an extremely depressing place, reflecting the personality of its occupant, which tended to be dour even in the best of times. Hoover tried several different strategies and did more than previous presidents had done, but new leadership was needed.

FDR: Rendezvous with Destiny

FDR's landslide election was a watershed event in American history, ending the seventy-year reign of the Republican Party and ushering in sixty years of rule by the Democratic Party. The Democrats gained firm control of the Congress. Americans were losing faith in the American dream and feared the future. FDR, who had suffered through the personal calamity of polio in 1921, had enormous personal strength and understood the need for reassurance. His strong will and personal victory over polio enabled him to stay upbeat throughout his entire presidency. His leadership was based on his self-confidence and the ability to fall back on his personal fortitude, transmitting his cheerful strength to others and providing assurances to a frightened nation. FDR's sonorous voice was ideal for radio, conveying energy, compassion, and confidence. Each radio address was the result of extensive preparation and many drafts, with careful attention paid to delivery and the sound of FDR's voice. "More than any other previous president, he studied public opinion: he read a variety of newspapers; he analyzed polls; he traveled the country when he could and dispatched his wife when he could not; he brought in people of clashing temperaments to secure different points of view; he probed visitors at dinner; he tried out his ideas on reporters. . . . He was able to sense what the people were thinking and feeling."[19] FDR personalized the presidency, giving people a feeling of intimacy with the office. He "was warm, personal, concrete, and impulsive . . . He had little regard for abstract principle, but a sharp intuitive knowledge of popular feeling. Because he was content in large measure to follow public opinion, he was able to give it that necessary additional impulse of leadership which can translate desires into policies."[20] FDR could muster the nation's political will and the presidency became the focus of governance, the decision-making authority, the initiator of action, and the spokesman for the national interest.

Between FDR's election in November and Hoover's departure in March, the economic situation deteriorated even further. Americans lived through probably their worst winter since Valley Forge. Production continued to plummet and tens of thousands of farms went through foreclosure. The Michigan banking system collapsed and the panic spread to other states. Bank holidays had been declared by the governors of seventeen states. Immediately prior to FDR's inauguration, the Fed's figures showed the week's gold loss to be $226 million and there wasn't enough money in the Federal Treasury to meet the federal payroll or to redeem the $700 million in short-term certificates that were due shortly. Even Hoover characterized the situation as "on the verge of financial panic and chaos." Part of this was due to uncertainty over FDR's presidency.

> The new nominee was lightly regarded by political commentators and some thought he had no chance to win. . . . "No one, in fact, really likes Roosevelt," H.L. Mencken wrote just after he was nominated, "not even his own ostensible friends, and no one quite trusts him." He "is in general far too feeble and wishy-washy a fellow to make a really effective fight." Mencken called him Roosevelt Minor. . . . He seemed to have no clear philosophy. He campaigned against budget deficits and for direct relief for the hungry. He astounded speechwriter Raymond Moley by replying when asked to choose between two contradictory arguments, "weave the two together."[21]

FDR had never advocated radical action. As financial panic hit the nation, however, there was a genuine emergency. The New York Stock Exchange and the Chicago Board of Trade were closed, the latter for the first time in eighty-five years. Banking in most states was suspended.

FDR rallied America during the depths of the Great Depression by speaking of America's rendezvous with destiny. He made another famous statement at his first inaugural: "the only thing we have to fear is fear itself." The radio networks carried his inaugural address to a nation yearning for action. Using the Trading with the Enemy Act, he initiated a "bank holiday" to suspend the nation's banking until emergency reform could be implemented and insolvent banks permanently closed. The entire money supply had practically ground to a halt and there was so little cash that state and local governments had taken to issuing scrip. FDR's Treasury Secretary stopped this practice and issued

currency backed by bank assets. FDR's inaugural address had an immediate uplifting effect, broadcast over radio throughout the country and
stimulating hundreds of thousands of positive letters. He turned the
banking system around in his first week, secured passage of emergency
banking legislation from Congress in one day, and restored the confidence and optimism of the American people in just a few days in office.

The key decision was to go off the gold standard, an initiative FDR
took 45 days after his inauguration. Government gold stocks backed
paper currency. Individuals, businesses, or other governments could
exchange paper money for gold at a fixed price. In the United States,
the price was one ounce of gold for $20.68 between 1879 and 1933.
Governments would go to great lengths to protect their gold stocks,
because without them, the foundations of public trust in money and
government would, it was thought, disintegrate. But this mentality
drove governments around the world to take actions that worsened the
Depression. Countries that left the gold standard recovered from the
Depression more quickly. [22] Once America jettisoned the gold standard, the economy began to recover.[23] After Roosevelt's actions, the
money supply increased rapidly in 1934, 1935, and 1936. In 1933, the
stock market went up more than 50 percent and 1935 was a strong year.

FDR used the media and every other tool at his disposal for a
most remarkable first hundred days, securing enactment of over a
dozen major laws. "When he came to power, the people had seen stagnation go dangerously far. They wanted experiment, activity, trial, and
error, anything that would convey a sense of movement and novelty. At
the very beginning of his candidacy Roosevelt, without heed for tradition or formality, flew to the 1932 nominating convention and
addressed it in person instead of waiting for weeks in the customary
pose of ceremonious ignorance."[24]

There was little overall strategic vision. As Eleanor Roosevelt
noted: "The President never thinks. He decides."[25]

> In the eye of the Hundred Days hurricane, from
> March 9, when the Emergency Banking Act was cheered
> into law, to the passage of the National Industrial Recovery
> Act (NIRA) on June 16—the new Chief Executive was con-

tinually revealing fresh reservoirs of imagination and energy. Before Congress adjourned in exhaustion he would have
delivered ten major speeches, given birth to a new foreign
policy, presided over press conferences and cabinet meetings twice a week, taken the country off of the gold standard, sent fifteen messages to the Capitol, and shepherded
through its chamber thirteen major pieces of legislation,
including insurance for all bank deposits, refinancing of
home mortgages, Wall Street reforms, authorization for
nearly four billion dollars in federal relief, legalization of
beer, and laws creating the Civilian Conservation Corps
(CCC), and Tennessee Valley Authority (TVA). . . . It was all
improvised. 'Take a method and try it,' he told his New
Dealers. 'If it fails, try another. But above all, try something.'
He interpreted his landslide victory as a mandate for
change, almost any change as long as it was quick.[26]

Actually, Roosevelt's efforts were more purposeful than that; they
were a compilation of many things that had been done or proposed
before. The National Recovery Administration, for example, was the
re-creation of the War Industries Board from Word War I. The
Tennessee Valley Authority predecessors were the Muscle Shoals power
plants built under the National Defense Act of 1916 and legislation that
had been vetoed by Presidents Coolidge and Hoover. The Agricultural
Adjustment Act was a renewed Food Administration from World War
I and an extension of the agriculture legislation passed in the 1920s
during the deep decline in the farming sector. The National Labor
Relations Board was a holdover of the War Labor Policies Board. Many
of FDR's other initiatives were extensions of policies started in Hoover's
presidency or had European counterparts from years earlier.

The aftermath of Roosevelt's first One Hundred Days was, finally, a bottoming out of the four-year decline in the economy and an up
tick. The stock market rose 60 percent (from almost an all-time low),
economic output recovered from its lowest levels since before World
War I—increasing 80 percent by 1937. Federal deposit insurance was
established, ending the run on federal banks by guaranteeing the

deposits of individuals up to $5,000 per account. For decades, there was never a run on a Federal Deposit Insurance Corporation insured bank. The money supply finally rose with emergency banking legislation and a new Federal Reserve Act. The Federal Reserve Board and the president took more control over the banking industry, Wall Street, and interest rates. For the first time in a century, the country had strong central banking.[27]

FDR's policies sometimes seemed erratic, following no coherent philosophy. During the first hundred days, he submitted $500 million in spending cuts to Congress and complained, "For three long years, the Federal Government has been on the road to bankruptcy." He cut disabled veterans pensions, called for reductions in teachers' salaries, and took other actions to support balanced budgets. Yet, FDR funded extensive public works projects—over 100,000 public buildings, tens of thousands of bridges, 300 new airports, and several hundred thousand miles of new roads (although no interstate highway system). When Secretary of State Cordell Hull tried to reverse the increased trade barriers created by Smoot-Hawley at the World Economic Conference in the spring of 1933, FDR put the damper on the conference. FDR used the IRS, the Secret Service, and the FBI to investigate his designated personal enemies, pursuing a personal vendetta against Andrew Mellon until his death.

FDR was urged to nationalize the banks, but instead placed them under closer federal supervision and extended credit to worthy banks. In late 1933, with the economy still stumbling, FDR seized control of the monetary process and set the price of gold. One day, in bed, he raised the price of gold 21 cents. When Henry Morgenthau, his future Treasury Secretary asked him why, FDR replied "it's a lucky number, because it's three times seven." Morgenthau subsequently wrote: "If anybody ever knew how we set the gold price . . . I think they would be frightened."[28] In January 1934, the Gold Reserve Act was passed and FDR established the price of the metal at $35 an ounce where it remained until 1971. With the economy still flat and farm prices depressed, FDR agreed to the Silver Purchase Act in June 1934. The government bought silver in large quantities until its holdings equaled a third of the value of the government's gold. Interest rates were lowered and terms lengthened, particularly for those who were able to offer security. The government became the biggest lender in the country.

Between 1929 and 1933, the Dow Jones average was down nearly 90 percent, trading volume was down over 60 percent, broker loans declined by 90 percent, and new issues of stock declined by over 95 percent. A series of new securities laws helped to bring more transparency to the stock market, providing the average shareholder with much more information and thus leveling the playing field. This encouraged middle class Americans to participate—which was good for their wealth and good for the markets, a win-win situation. The Securities Act of 1933 required disclosure of detailed information for new securities in a registration statement to be filed with a Securities and Exchange Commission (SEC) and certification of this information by an independent accountant. This information included detailed balance sheets, profit and loss statements, salaries and perquisites of officers and directors, commissions paid to underwriters, and over a couple dozen items of information previously seldom released by corporations. The Securities Exchange Act of 1934 required this information for existing securities, formally established the SEC, empowered it to change the rules of the exchanges, and prohibited stock manipulation and other practices. The Federal Reserve Board was given the authority to set minimum margin requirements for the purchase of stocks on credit. These margins, which had plunged to as low as 10 percent in the 1920s, ranged from 40 to 90 percent. Insider trading, short sales, and the permissible ratios of debt to capital were more closely regulated.

Requiring separation between banking and stock market transactions, the Glass-Steagall Act was passed because it was widely believed many banks had failed because they were trading in stocks. Even though the central Federal Reserve Bank had erroneously overruled the efforts of the New York Federal Reserve branch to prevent speculation and bring liquidity to the markets before and during the crash, authority was increasingly centralized in Washington. A double standard was created—private sector organizations would be held accountable, but government agencies would not. This legislation forced the break-up of the House of Morgan and resulted in compartmentalized commercial and investment banking. Subsequent analysis showed that banks with diverse businesses and interests were less likely to fail and the securities underwritten by commercial banks were not any more risky than those handled by investment banks. Most of the revelations presented at the congressional hearings were not supported by the evidence, only by an overzealous prosecutor. The majority of the banks failing in the Depression were one office banks in small towns that became insolvent when their traditional agricultural economies collapsed as part of the transition from an agricultural to an industrial society. Glass-Steagall actually increased risks in the banking industry by barring banks from lucrative areas of investment. This legislation would have been much more effective if it had been narrowly targeted at the real abuses, such as banks that had lists of preferred customers who were given special deals on stocks.

Banking and securities legislation and suspension of the gold standard addressed the critical issues of the Great Depression, but FDR and the Democrats believed there was a large vacuum to fill as a result of the failure of the Republican Party to revitalize civil society and to address social issues. They made a fateful determination to rely on government to address these issues. FDR and the Democrats embarked on a radical change in American politics by systematizing interest group politics to encompass union workers, consumers, senior citizens, farmers, and just about any trade association or public interest group. They changed the meaning of the term "liberal" to embrace groups rather than individuals. Theodore Lowi drew this distinction in his book, *The End of Liberalism,* by which he was referring to the traditional definition of the concept of liberalism. The prior definition assumed a clear distinction between the state and the remainder of society, placing clear limitations on government power. With the New Deal, this separation became blurred if not virtually meaningless. Interest groups expropriated government powers and funding for whatever claims they desired and could impose politically. Power came to be exercised by regulatory agencies and authorities, not just the traditional legislature and executive. Government became accountable to the interest groups rather than the people or individual citizens, a phenomenon Lowi labeled the Second Republic. The impact on the federal government was profound. By the end of FDR's first term, federal spending exceeded total spending for state and local governments for the first time during peacetime. The number of government agencies was proliferating and their authority rapidly expanding.

Besides the financial system, the most urgent problem was farming and the rural population. Many rural areas had been in rapid decline since World War I and were now in abject poverty. Agriculture had been in a recession throughout the 1920s and plunged into a deep depression. In 1932, farm income was only a third of the already-depressed 1929 level. The surplus in cotton, for example, was such that the world market could be satisfied in 1933 without harvesting a single plant.[29] The solution was to increase the price level for crops and to pay farmers to produce less. To further reduce supply, acreage was retired, what became labeled as a conservation policy. Licenses were required to be in the agriculture business. A tax was placed on food production to pay for these programs, which the Supreme Court later declared unconstitutional. Wealthy farmers took payments for their least productive land and cultivated their better acreage more intensively. At a time when many Americans were going hungry and unable to buy badly needed clothes, the Agricultural Adjustment Act was paying farmers not to produce cotton, sugar, and other commodities and to pare back cattle and pork production. These government support programs remained in effect seven decades later, making huge outlays in good times as well as bad times. While the United State was the biggest and most efficient producer in the world, little effort was made on behalf of free trade and opening up foreign markets. The Democrats were not willing to follow-through on their one hundred year opposition to tariffs, fearful of the fights with interest groups that had stymied earlier Republican presidents. During FDR's first term, the agricultural sector did make a major improvement with farm income up over 50 percent.

The unrelenting drought and dust bowl of the 1930s would, however, more directly solve the surplus problem. Just about everything that could go wrong did. The dust bowl was initially viewed as barren land and then used as a cattle range. The tractor made it possible to grow wheat in this terrain and the Turkish embargo of Russian wheat and World War I greatly expanded demand. When the wheat bubble burst, prices plunged and the farmers ploughed under even more grassland in a desperate effort to produce more grain to compensate for the lower rates. The expanded supply put even greater downward pressure on the price. Over 5 million additional acres were cultivated, the equivalent of over two Yellowstone Parks.

When a wet cycle turned to drought with extreme heat, the wheat would not grow and the prairie turned to dust and sand. Dust storms would blot out the sun and penetrate the thin particles into homes, cars, and buildings. Four-foot drifts of sand closed roads. The dust storms dumped 6,000 tons of dirt on Chicago in one night, reached New York City, and blanketed ships three hundred miles off the Atlantic Coast in brown. In a single afternoon, a storm carried twice as much dirt as was dug out in seven years of building the Panama Canal. In March and April of 1935, storms dumped five tons of dust per acre on western Kansas, enough to fill a line of trucks 96 miles long, hauling 10 loads a day for a year or 46 million truckloads. "Dust pneumonia" penetrated lungs and killed many people, particularly infants.

The dust bowl was the greatest single American environmental catastrophe of the century. As Washington debated whether to provide federal aid, a dust cloud darkened the city, the air turned a reddish color, and the sun vanished. Funds were approved the next day and eventually rain, tenacious people, and government soil conservation programs restored the land.[30]

In the area covered by the Tennessee River valley, income was half the national average and only two percent of farms had electricity. The Tennessee Valley Authority (TVA) became an engineering marvel, receiving widespread national and international coverage as an example of government that worked. Electricity rates were less than half the national average, which spurred economic growth and the establishment of whole new industries in the valley. While the traditional argument has been that the TVA was better than its private sector counterparts, it benefited from government subsidies in a capital intensive industry that a private company couldn't effectively compete with. FDR initiated the Rural Electrification Administration to bring similar benefits to other rural areas.

Some of the New Deal legislation was targeted to address social problems caused by Hoover's inaction. The Federal Emergency Relief Administration was funded with $500 million to provide aid to families without regular income. The Civilian Conservation Corps registered more than 2.5 million youths in camp, exposed them to some of the most scenic parts of America, and left monuments on the purification and preservation of land and water. The New Deal required the able-bodied to work with most of the programs administered through block grants to the states.

FDR and Congress created the Home Owners Loan Corp. to prevent foreclosures by purchasing defaulted mortgages from banks, then refinancing them at lower rates for fixed, fifteen-year terms. About one in ten Americans with nonfarm, owner-occupied houses secured aid from the agency. By the time its life ended in 1951, about 80 percent of the borrowers paid off their loans early or on time and the agency earned a small profit.

FDR also responded to the rapid decline in industrial production. He continued and expanded the Reconstruction Finance Corporation. The National Recovery Administration (NRA) was a key part of the New Deal, initiated in the Congress when the economy continued to decline in 1933. The NRA represented a vast expansion in the powers of government, setting employee wages and dictating what and how consumers could pick products in stores. Through industry codes, the NRA stipulated wages, hours, prices, and levels of production for each industry. The codes were usually the product of the largest companies in an industry and were used to create monopolies and raise and fix prices. The agency had licensing powers to coerce businesses into going along with the codes. In 1935, the Brookings Institution concluded that the NRA retarded the recovery. The Supreme Court unanimously declared the law unconstitutional.

Some of the new programs provided badly needed infrastructure, one of the few areas Hoover had effectively addressed. In spending approximately $6 billion, FDR's Public Works Administration (PWA) built the Bonneville dam, the Tri-borough Bridge, the hundred-mile causeway from Florida to Key West, and 70 percent of the new educational buildings constructed between 1933 and 1939. The PWA also improved 32 Army posts and built the carriers *Yorktown* and *Enterprise*, 4 cruisers, 4 destroyers, submarines, and fifty military airports. As an initiative of one of chief engineers of the Panama Canal, the Hoover or Boulder Dam was completed two years ahead of schedule, being the equivalent of a 102 story building and requiring three-and-a-half million square feet of concrete.

Labor became a core constituency of the New Deal and Democratic Party. Labor union unrest spread as the Depression continued. During Hoover's presidency, union membership declined to about where it had been at the beginning of the century—the United Mine Workers had fallen to less than 100,000 members and the AFL was losing thousands of members a week. The autoworkers initiated sit-down strikes, first carried out in Europe. The union targeted General Motors and brought the largest auto producer to its knees, winning a forty-hour week, time and a half for overtime, union recognition, seniority, and input on working conditions such as the speed of the assembly line. The union then went after Chrysler and other manufacturers, causing them to capitulate. Next, John Lewis and his union went after U.S. Steel, negotiating an agreement similar to that with General Motors. Soon, the union had 30,000 contracts and 3 million members. When Lewis' union struck Republic Steel, a police riot occurred which resulted in the killing and wounding of dozens of people, including women and children. The year 1937 was the most savage in history for labor violence and reached the high mark for strikes (more than 4,000). Over 80 percent of the strikes ended in settlements favorable to unions.[31]

In 1935, Congress passed the National Labor Relations Act that guaranteed the right of workers to join a union and to bargain collectively with employers. A National Labor Relations Board (NLRB) was set up to prevent a lengthy list of unfair labor practices and supervise union elections, vastly expanding the power and authority of the labor union movement. The social security bill established a federal-state system of unemployment compensation based on some experimental programs at the state level. In 1938, the Fair Labor Standards Act prohibited child labor, and established a minimum wage of 25 cents an hour and a maximum work week of forty-four hours. In the years after its passage and before World War II, union membership doubled and by the early 1950s unions represented 35 percent of the workforce, up from 6 percent at the beginning of the Depression.

The New Deal vastly expanded consumer protection and government regulation of the private sector by adding four additional regulatory agencies, more than had appeared in all the years before 1933. Besides the SEC and NLRB the Federal Communications Commission (FCC) replaced the old Federal Radio Commission and was given extensive powers over the radio, telephone, and telegraph industries (and later television and the Internet). The Motor Carrier Act of 1935 put the trucking industry under the jurisdiction of the Interstate Commerce Commission (ICC). In 1938, the Civil Aeronautics Board (CAB) was established to regulate the commercial aviation industry. James Landis pioneered in regulatory law by ensuring that the legislation was coordinated with the administrative and enforcement acts of the regulatory authorities to reduce the number and extent of unintended consequences.

Until 1937, medicines and drugs were largely unregulated. An antibacterial syrup killed over 75 people, including many children with ailments as minor as sore throats. No tests were conducted on the syrup and the company accepted no responsibility, paying just a small fine for misbranding the product. Stronger legislation was bottled up for years by the medical industry, aided by the press which received large amounts of advertising revenue from the drug companies and declined to cover congressional action on the legislation. The small, anemic Food and Drug Administration devoted its entire staff of agents to tracking down the drug, which would have killed 4,000 people if all of the product that was manufactured had been consumed. The Congress passed the Food, Drug and Cosmetic Act, requiring drug manufacturers, for the first time, to prove the safety of their products before putting them on the market.

Elderly citizens were particularly hard hit by the Great Depression. Social Security was probably Roosevelt's most popular initiative and important program, although the first check was not issued until 1941.

To fund all of these programs for interest groups, tax revenues were needed. In his first two years, however, FDR didn't have a legislative majority to increase taxes. When the Democrats achieved an unheard of landslide in the 1934 off-year elections, he had the votes to pass steep increases on the wealthy, including higher corporate, income, and inheritance taxes. Federal income taxes were ratcheted up throughout the 1930s, as top rates were increased from under 30 percent to over 70 percent, but, to the surprise of their proponents, these actions did little to fill the federal coffers. "[T]he rich reacted in an entirely predictable way—a way Andrew Mellon *had* predicted in 1924: They began to shelter income again. And by this time their lawyers, accountants, and lobbyists in Washington had mastered the art." The creation of the modern tax code greatly expanded the power of the government and accountants and lawyers. "Those faced with steeper and steeper income tax rates have developed ever newer and better ways to shelter income in the interstices of the conflicting tax laws. . . . The result has been an unending explosion in the size of the tax code and the number of people lobbying for changes in it.[32] During the Depression, highly publicized congressional hearings highlighted wealthy individuals, including a number of partners at J.P. Morgan, who paid no income taxes. Overlooked in the hysteria that followed these revelations was the fact that failed government policies had helped to create enormous losses in the stock market, which were used to offset income and eliminate tax liabilities.

By the end of FDR's first term, unemployment had declined by a third and panic had largely disappeared from the markets. In 1936, FDR and the Democrats scored the largest, most sweeping victory in history, controlling the House by 334 to 89 and the Senate by 75 to 17 and losing only Vermont and Maine in the Electoral College. FDR won by a wide margin in 1940 as well, establishing the dominance of the

Democratic Party for three generations and ensconcing Democratic machines in almost every major city throughout the country, eventually putting a product of one of their political organizations, Harry Truman, in the White House.

Since John Marshall's tenure in the early nineteenth century, the Supreme Court had been a source of stability and conservatism, often overturning reform initiatives and opposing efforts to regulate and tax the private sector. Between January 1935 and June 1936 the Court sparked a major controversy by ruling against FDR's New Deal in eight of ten major cases, basically concluding that the federal government did not have the authority to assume many national economic powers. The Court unanimously struck down the National Industrial Recovery Act as an unconstitutional delegation of legislative power to the executive branch and a usurpation of states rights. The Court threw out the revenue portions of the Agricultural Adjustment Act as an improper use of taxing power. The Court then moved to strike down the Securities and Exchange Act, the Guffey-Snyder Coal Act, and the Municipal Bankruptcy Act. Congress retaliated, overturning more of the Court's decisions on important measures than during any other period. The country was facing a constitutional crisis with the likelihood that the National Labor Relations Act, the Social Security Act, and most New Deal legislation would be held unconstitutional.

After his landslide re-election and considering several options, FDR responded with a "court-packing" plan aimed at changing the Court's philosophy by putting justices sympathetic to his position into new positions created on the bench. It was a major miscalculation, which failed in Congress and was highly unpopular. His proposal precipitated formation of a Republican-Southern Democratic alliance that played a major role in politics for the next sixty years, generally opposing activist and progressive initiatives supported by FDR, left-wing Democrats, and their allies. From 1937 to 1940, the Court did respond, largely through the efforts of Chief Justice Charles Evans Hughes, by sustaining all of the major New Deal legislation and reversing itself on minimum wage laws. By 1941, Roosevelt had seven of his own appointments to the Court and had named Harlan Stone as Chief Justice.

The Causes of the Great Depression

What caused one of history's most dramatic reversals of fortunes—the Great Depression? The key factor was the extraordinarily restrictive monetary policy. The Great Depression was "mainly a monetary event."[33] When compared to other major financial crashes (i.e., Japan's in the late 1980s and America's in the early 2000s) where central banks were able to keep markets liquid, the money supply in the 1930s was an incredible 50 percent below where it should have been. In actual dollars, the money supply shrank about 30 percent between 1929 and 1932.[34] Instead of providing liquidity for banks in trouble, the Federal Reserve's loans to commercial banks plummeted from over $1 billion in 1929 to only about $100 million in 1933. If the Federal Reserve (the Fed) had not existed, the banking system would have had over $1 billion more in reserve assets.[35] Between spring 1931 and the end of 1932, the effective real interest rate was 15 percent. The Federal Reserve Bank never really made monetary policy work well until after World War II. In the second half of the twentieth century, for, example, the economy was only a third as volatile as in the period 1919-1945, the early years of the Fed.

Wild swings in the economy continued until after World War II because the Fed didn't understand its role, the business cycle, nor how to effectively use the tools at its disposal. While economists and bankers observed the painful economic panics and collapses, they had very little sense or understanding of how money and the gold supply affected the economy. Some economists did not believe there was a connection between monetary policy and economic activity. Originally, the Fed had only a small portfolio and was expected to focus on the gold supply and not on employment or economic activity. Some members of the Fed erroneously believed that their actions constituted easy money and thought they had simply failed to revive the economy. Most members, the press, and much of the population believed deflation was the inevitable consequence of previous speculative excesses, which became a self-fulfilling prophecy.[36]

During the late nineteenth century, the private sector never developed formal mechanisms for dealing with boom and bust cycles, instead relying on the market to take its course. Even the most ardent supporters of the free market system knew this was not a good solution. J. P. Morgan, for example, gradually developed and honed the skill of knowing when to act and how much liquidity to supply to limit the damage. By the turn of the century, he was able to use his knowledge and reputation to dampen or avert a market crash or depression, as he clearly did in 1907. As a reward for this public service, however, he was pilloried by the press and the public and his integrity impugned by a congressional committee. Morgan believed that his word and integrity were all that really mattered in the financial markets—confidence was the key factor. These attacks undoubtedly precipitated his mental breakdown and subsequent death. Without him, there was no one in the private sector that could effectively help the government deal with the traumatic and deepening effects of the Great Depression. Indeed, the history of the Great Depression could very well be summed up in one question: *J.P. Morgan, where were you when we needed you?*

The lack of effective policies for dealing with specific industries, particularly critical ones such as automobiles, electronics, and agriculture, is a cause of the Great Depression that has generally been overlooked.

The automobile, the personification of the industrial revolution, was the primary force behind the 1920s boom. General Motors was the growth stock of the decade, increasing by over 40 times between the beginning and end of the decade. Once the stock market declined, high ticket, capital intensive manufacturing such as the automobile industry was particularly hard hit as people had little cash and liquidity to make purchases. American car sales plummeted by two-thirds from 4.6 million in 1929 to 1.5 million in 1932.

Two problems crippled the auto sector. People who were living close to the edge could just postpone the purchase of the next car. No policies were initiated to change this mindset. Secondly, the government didn't build the road network fast enough to accommodate the booming industry. The interstate highway system wasn't even started until the 1950s. Making the case for better long distance roads, Dwight Eisenhower and other luminaries had made a cross-country tour before the boom of the 1920s even began. Hitler was able to help turn around the German economy by building the Autobahn to connect the entire country.

Besides the automobile industry, electronics (i.e., radio), was the most important sector driving the 1920s' rapid growth. In 1928, RCA stock had gone from 85 to 420, but growth in this sector came to a screeching halt in the 1930s. RCA and the FCC stopped the next generation of technology in its tracks, preventing radio conversion from AM to FM.

In 1923 and 1926, the courts ruled that the federal government did not have the power to regulate the radio broadcasting spectrum. Herbert Hoover, then Secretary of Commerce, had predicted there would be chaos if the government was not allowed to allocate spectrum. The Congress then banned private ownership and authorized the FCC and its predecessor to not only regulate, but also to license and determine who had free speech rights. The Supreme Court upheld the Radio Act of 1927 with Justice Felix Frankfurter concluding that such regulation was compelled by the inherent nature of broadcasting. Thirty years later, Ronald Coase showed how this was not true, that by auctioning the spectrum it could be allocated to the highest value user—helping him to win a Nobel Prize. Coase was particularly concerned that lawyers and economists had imposed regulations without understanding the new technology.[37] In the interim, the economic damage had been done, including worsening the Great Depression. More recently, advances in technology have developed smart receivers that distinguish between signals in the same frequency, undermining whatever slim reed of logic might still be attached to the government allocation of spectrum.

Technological advances were revolutionizing agriculture, rapidly increasing world output. Farmers continued to produce at the level they had during the boom years of World War I and then European farms came back into production. Better farm machinery, new plant varieties, and potent new chemical fertilizers yielded much larger harvests. Between 1925 and 1929, the prices of most commodities declined and large surpluses accumulated. A number of economic dislocations also occurred: rayon reduced the need for cotton and wool; replacement of draft animals by farm machinery reduced the demand for oats and hay; and the amount of land devoted to farming continued to increase, further driving down prices. Government efforts to stabilize prices failed. Tariffs and domestic content requirements encouraged more local production which exacerbated the surplus.

Congress passed the Agricultural Adjustment Act to provide subsidies for farmers growing crops on allotted acreage. World-wide agreements were entered into for tea, rubber, and wheat production. Many different forms of government regulation were initiated, some of them nationalistic. A few of them actually worked fairly well, stabilizing and increasing prices.

Most analyses of the Great Depression have focused on the economic causes of the event. The generic definition of the term, however, implies an emotional state of dejection and a gloominess as well. There were social and political factors that contributed to the length and depth of the Great Depression. While populism generated many of the reforms of the progressive era, it also yielded a legacy of nationalism, protectionism, racism, isolationism, and nativism.

Protectionism was pandemic and a major factor contributing to the Great Depression. Since the inception of the republic, protectionism had ruled. While the model treaty at the end of the Revolutionary War submitted by the American peace commissioners laid out a plan for global free trade, one of the first bills passed by Congress set tariffs to raise revenue to pay for the new government. In 1816, the first protective tariffs were passed, establishing a 25 percent duty on woolen and cotton goods and 30 percent on iron products. Ratcheting up tariffs became a habitual fix and increases became almost routine, occurring in 1818, 1824, 1828, and 1832. Tariff rates increased steadily from the Morrill Act in 1861 to the Smoot-Hawley Tariffs in 1930, with a slight pause after the Civil War and during World War I. After 1850, foreign trade declined as a proportion of the economy. High tariffs were reciprocated by other major nations, shutting off international markets to American goods and services.

The Smoot-Hawley Tariffs raised U.S. duties to the highest level in American history during peacetime, causing international trade to plunge. The higher tariffs were supported by labor and business to keep out foreign competition. This was a particularly dubious policy given that the United States was a major exporter and the largest and most efficient agricultural and industrial power in the world, manufacturing almost half of the global output. The law precipitated retaliation by dozens of nations. Canada raised tariffs three times. The United Kingdom introduced the imperial preference and France, Japan, and the Netherlands followed with similar tactics. Between 1925 and 1931, average tariff levels for Belgium and Germany more than doubled, while for Italy they tripled, and for France and the United Kingdom they quadrupled.[38] Germany imposed quantitative restrictions on trade and foreign exchange, actions which were copied by France, Italy, the Netherlands, Eastern Europe, and Latin America. Governments that owed debts to the United States could not engage in the trade necessary to pay off those debts. By fall 1930 foreign trade was only 75 percent of 1929 levels; by the fall of 1931 it was 50 percent, and by the fall of 1932 it was just 35 percent. The volume of world trade fell at just about exactly the same rate as U.S. imports and exports. Exports did not reach the 1929 peak again until 1950, falling to levels lower than prior to 1914.[39] The rapid decline in exports had a severe impact on a domestic market where demand was also shrinking.

FDR downgraded American participation in the London Economic Conference which sought to reverse the Smoot-Hawley and other protectionist policies. He did initiate and obtain the approval of Congress for the reciprocal trade program to make tariffs and trade barriers dependent on the laws and treatment of the trading partner. This was largely an empty gesture, because it was barely implemented and had almost no effect. Smoot-Hawley basically remained the law of the land.

Nativist and restrictive immigration policies contributed to the severity of the Great Depression. Total immigration rose dramatically from the hundreds of thousands per decade in the early nineteenth century to the millions by the end of the century; by then most of the immigration came from Eastern Europe not Western Europe. The foreign born population increased from 4 million in 1860 to over 10 million by 1900 and there was at least a tacit understanding of the contributions immigrants made to economic growth. President Grant proposed legislation to restrict immigration. President Chester Arthur secured passage of legislation placing a head tax on entrants and excluding lunatics and idiots. The Quarantine Act of 1892 gave the president the authority to stop all immigration if there was danger of an epidemic. Congress excluded Chinese coolies, paupers, idiots, polygamists, anarchists, and other classes. It then attempted to bar illiterates, but Presidents Cleveland and Taft vetoed the bill and there were not enough votes to override. Wilson also vetoed it, but he was overridden. The new law also basically barred immigration from much of Asia. In 1905, discontent with America's treatment of Chinese immigrants and visitors led to a boycott against American goods and investment by China. Chinese were spoken of derisively as "celestials" and "coolies." They paid taxes but were denied citizenship, could not vote, and could not send their children to school. White laborers would assault and rob them and cut off their pigtails. Yet, more than any other group they were responsible for completing large constructions projects such as the transcontinental railroad.[40]

In 1907, Congress mandated that any American woman who married an ineligible alien (i.e., an immigrant who was not white) was to be stripped of her citizenship. The Courts spent the next decades trying to define race, often accepting applications from some countries as eligible whites, but rejecting others as nonwhite. In the early 1920s, the Supreme Court changed the definition twice in three months.[41]

Excessive nationalism from World War I and fear of communism as a result of the revolution in Russia drove popular sentiment to stem immigration. Americans were afraid millions would migrate to the U.S. to escape the destruction, debts, and devastation in Europe as a result of World War I. In 1921 Congress placed temporary numerical limits on immigration at 3 percent of the number of foreign-born persons of each nationality. In 1924 Congress placed an overall limit on immigration from Europe of 150,000 and set a limit of 2 per cent of the foreign-born persons from each country based on the 1890 census, a clear strike against southern and eastern Europe. The numerical limits were enforced by the use of visas. Basically, the United States reversed its open-door policy for immigrants and no longer continued its role as a refuge and asylum for those who were persecuted and in need. The open-door policy had exhibited a confidence in the soundness of American institutions; the ensuing nativism played on fear, racism, and jealousy. During the 1920s and 1930s, immigration plummeted and even many victims of Hitler's sadistic policies were turned away.[42] Immigration declined rapidly from its peak of nine million a decade around the turn of the century and almost stopped entirely in the 1930s. During the decade of the 1930s, population growth slowed to by far the slowest rate of the century.

After the demise of Reconstruction, racism and segregation relegated African Americans to second-class citizenship, resulting in the underutilization of a major pool of labor and leaving America still grappling with the most important principle of the American Revolution that "All men are created equal." From the Civil War to the end of the century not a single Democrat ever voted for any civil rights legislation.[43] When the Democrats gained control of the White House and the Congress, they repealed civil rights laws passed during Reconstruction. Gradually, many Confederate officeholders and military leaders were elected to the Congress as Democrats from the South.

When Theodore Roosevelt invited Booker T. Washington to the White House for dinner, a storm of protest swept the South, and South Carolina Senator Ben Tillman said that it would take another thousand lynchings or killings before the African American "will learn their place again." President Taft promoted a former Klansman to Chief Justice of the Supreme Court. Woodrow Wilson's racist and segregationist policies sparked a resurgence of the Ku Klux Klan, which soon had a million members. Wilson fired every African American working for the federal government in the South and did nothing about the many lynchings during his presidency, including one of a pregnant woman who was burned at the stake with the fetus being ripped alive out of the womb and stomped to death.

During World War I, more than 300,000 African Americans

served in the U.S. armed forces. American law forbade stationing African-American troops alongside white soldiers, so they had to fight beside French units. Having shared the burden for freedom and democracy, they returned home to segregation, discrimination, and "Jim Crow" laws. During the Wilson and Harding Administrations, about a hundred race riots occurred. In 1919, at least twenty riots occurred in what became known as "Red Summer." Sensational press accounts of an unidentified African-American man's assaults on white women in Washington, D.C., precipitated several days of rioting. In 1921 in Tulsa, Oklahoma, whites assembled a lynch mob for an African American accused of making advances towards a white women in an office building, starting a riot that destroyed most of the African-American neighborhood, reportedly including the dropping of dynamite from airplanes onto a ghetto, killing more than 75 people and destroying more than 1,000 homes. The disturbance was largely erased from history until a race riot commission was set up in 1997. In some towns in the West and Midwest, African Americans were threatened with death if they remained overnight. In the South, lynchings were even advertised ahead of time. Pictures were taken of some lynchings because participants knew they would not be convicted by a white jury. The basic definition of "lynching" was a public murder where the perpetrators were known but not punished. In Georgia, an African-American veteran of World War I who had the audacity to wear his decorated military uniform was lynched. In Omaha, a lynch mob tried to kill the mayor and sheriff and burn down the jail. The mob then shot prisoner William Brown hundreds of times, set him on fire, and dragged him through the street for hours before dangling his torso from a trolley pole. Lloyd Clay was accused of entering the bedroom of a nineteen-year-old white girl and attempting to violate her. The girl didn't positively identify him, but a local mob of more than a thousand people broke into the jail and captured him. As his flaming body was heisted up a tree, men, women, and children took turns firing bullets into him as if they were at a target range. Later it was revealed that the girl's visitor was a white man she didn't want her parents to know about.[44]

Ku Klux Klan membership soared to 4 or 5 million Americans, including 250,000 in Pennsylvania, before membership collapsed mainly from internal disputes. Historians of the time, such as Charles Beard, dismissed notions that the Civil War was fought over slavery, blaming the clash on the differences between the industrial North and the agricultural South. Another noted historian, Avery Craven, blamed the Civil War on moral agitators and concluded slavery was not worth fighting over.[45] In 1922 the Supreme Court ruled that Japanese could not qualify for citizenship. African Americans were disproportionately impacted by the Great Depression and experienced extremely high rates of unemployment. In 1937, anti-lynching legislation was filibustered in the Senate.

Anti-Semitism spread as a result of the increase in immigrants from Eastern Europe. Jews were excluded from clubs and elite spas such as Saratoga. Henry Ford in his later years preached anti-Semitism, as did the Catholic Father Charles E. Coughlin. Although Franklin Roosevelt was known for his anti-Semitic remarks, he recruited many Jews to his administration.

Throughout the 1930s, labor strife was widespread. Fearing erosion of southern support, even FDR was reluctant to support pro-union legislation. With the bottom falling out of most of the markets, corporations had little they could offer the unions. A commission on labor union violence concluded that the U.S. "has had the bloodiest and most violent labor history of any industrial nation in the world." Walter Reuther, for example, was beaten to a pulp by company goons armed with rubber hoses and blackjacks. Gunman later threatened his life. As President of the UAW, he was critically wounded by a hired killer firing a ten-gauge shotgun as he talked with his wife. While in the hospital, his brother Victor's right eye was shot out and the UAW headquarters dynamited.[46]

In 1937 and 1938, some of the steepest declines in industrial production, employment, and the stock market occurred. Unemployment rose to 20 percent, the Gross Domestic Product was down 18 percent, and industrial production dropped 32 percent. The severe recession cast serious doubt on the efficacy of FDR's New Deal and whether its economic program had any purpose other than social welfare. Once again, there was a severe contraction of the monetary supply. The Fed doubled the reserve requirements for private banks, drastically reducing their ability to extend credit. FDR and his administration appeared to have little inkling about what caused the recovery in 1933 and failed to act to reverse the tight credit.

There were other causes of this sharp downturn. In response to the threat that Sen. Huey Long would run for president on a third party ticket in 1936 and siphon off Democratic votes, FDR endorsed a "soak-the-rich" tax plan, additional protections for workers' rights, and legislation to break up utility holding companies as well as other anti-business initiatives. Long was assassinated, but FDR was already committed to the program and in 1937 many of these initiatives became law. New taxes on undistributed profits reduced the ability of corporations and businesses to make new investments and retain employees. The top tax rate was close to 70 percent, among the highest in the world. In addition, the Social Security tax was being collected, but benefits were not being distributed, placing an additional fiscal drag on the economy. Americans began to have a desperate sense of permanence about the Great Depression.

In 1939, almost 10 million Americans were unemployed, over 15 percent of the work force. The number of people employed in 1940 was the same as in 1929. When asked publicly in 1940 whether the New Deal was economically sound, one presidential advisor replied "I don't really know what the basic principle of the New Deal is. . . . I know from my experience in government that there are as many conflicting opinions among the people in Washington under this administration as we have in the country at large."[47] FDR's policies were no longer working and had it not been for the war, the economy would have continued to drift.[48] In 1938, Republicans, who had lost seats in the last four elections, gained 80 seats in the House, 8 seats in the Senate, and 11 governorships. Government spending, the New Deal, and other efforts to fire-up the economy did not work. It took World War II to finally end the Great Depression.

It would be difficult to conceive of a set of government policies that could do more to undermine job creation and economic growth than those pursued during the Great Depression: tight money, higher taxes, more regulation, and a protectionist trade policy. When these policies were combined with the racism, isolationism, and nativism rampant at the time, it is easy to comprehend why the era is characterized by the term "Great Depression."

The Great Depression was America's second biggest failure after the Civil War. It was caused by a lack of leadership in the private sector and an almost complete breakdown in government policymaking and regulating mechanisms. America had become an economic superpower, but it did not yet have the governing mechanisms, expertise, and leadership to become a true world leader.

World War II

World War II was the worst human catastrophe in history. The Axis powers nearly won the war and their victory may have plunged humanity into a second Dark Age. FDR's greatest triumph was overcoming the isolationism that swept the country in the 1930s and then rallying the nation to confront the Axis challenge. By the time America woke up, the German Reich and its protectorates had conquered more territory than Alexander the Great, Caesar, Genghis Khan, and Napoleon—everything from the Arctic Circle to the Sahara Desert and between the English Channel and Moscow. There were only four free countries in Europe—Britain, Ireland, Switzerland, and Sweden.

Theodore Roosevelt had been a strong opponent of isolationism and saw its dangers for America. Contrary to the view of some historians, the 1920s were not isolationist, as prosperity and fast ocean liners encouraged rapid increases in travel and international trade. The United States government did not play a sufficiently active role in world affairs given its economic stature, but this inertia reflected popular sentiment against Europe for the lack of effort to repay its World War I debts to the U.S. Many people believed the Depression originated in Europe and some even claimed it was intentionally inflicted on the American economy. The collapse of foreign trade and international economies in the early 1930s helped contribute to a surge of isolationism which was exacerbated by congressional hearings exposing widespread profiteering in World War I.

Isolationists revised the history of World War I to depict it as a creation of war profiteers, greedy bankers, and Woodrow Wilson's propagandists, blaming them for the death of American boys and the unpaid European war debts. Some scholars even tried to sell the theory that Europeans had tricked the country into World War I. In a Gallup Poll, 71 percent of the respondents agreed. Politicians gained support by decrying American entry into World War I and claiming nothing was accomplished by American participation. Congressional hearings fostered this isolationism and resulted in the passage of laws to prohibit loans and other assistance to belligerents, whatever the cause of the conflict, and imposing an arms embargo on all parties, regardless of who the victim was. Among college students, pacifism was trendy—39 percent of undergraduates said they would not participate in any war and another 33 percent said they would do so only if the United States were invaded. At Columbia and Berkeley, strongholds of pacifism, only 8 percent were willing to fight under any circumstance. Americans feared a second world war would mean their efforts in the first were for naught. Even the Veterans of Foreign War were paying little attention to events in Europe and demanding neutrality legislation. Republicans in particular continued to push hard for an isolationist foreign policy. America failed to understand the relationship between its physical safety and prosperity and the existence of a free world beyond its shores.[49]

The isolationism of the 1930s is perhaps not surprising given the distance of events—there were no regularly scheduled transoceanic airplane flights and oceanic vessels took a week to cross the Atlantic and two weeks to cross the Pacific, when conditions were just right. FDR understood the danger of the dictators in Europe and tried to educate Americans on the perils of the isolationist position, beginning in October 1937 with the Quarantine Speech, which was promptly attacked by the isolationists. He subsequently obtained congressional approval of the Vinson Naval Act for a billion-dollar two-ocean navy and authorization for a vast expansion of aircraft making capabilities.

FDR's effort was greatly aided by the initiation of transatlantic radio coverage of contemporary European events, which brought Hitler's demagoguery and aggression directly into the living rooms of Americans. The reports of Edward R. Murrow, the first live broadcasts from overseas, helped to drive home the importance of British resistance and of defeating Adolf Hitler. His reports captured America's imagination, radically altering the contemporaneous notions of distance and time. The nation was transfixed by the crisis in Czechoslovakia, for example, and the percentage of people who thought that the United States would be drawn into war in the not too distant future more than tripled to around 70 percent. In 1940, media coverage of the German invasion "described panzer thrusts far behind Allied lines, the slaughter of refugees by Stuka dive bombers, and endless lines of blond Aryan youths who had hurtled into the Lowlands and France shouting, 'Heil Hitler!'" Americans soon knew terms such as Blitzkrieg, Dunkirk, and the Battle of Britain. The German Luftwaffe began destroying British cities. As a means of terrorizing their opposition, the Nazis advertised their atrocities. This backfired in America and mobilized public opinion against Hitler's cause. While Americans overwhelmingly supported a military build-up, they were reluctant to enter the war, just as they had been in World War I.[50] America was economically the strongest nation on the planet, but it was ranked sixteenth militarily, behind Spain and Portugal. It had fewer troops than did the small nation of Yugoslavia.

FDR developed the lend-lease concept to prevent Great Britain from being knocked out of the war economically—the British economy was literally on its last legs. Roosevelt launched the program to provide the Allies with war goods. The British desperately needed escort vessels to protect convoys against U-boat attacks, and FDR's program transferred 50 destroyers to Great Britain in return for leases on bases in British possession. By June 1940, FDR was exhibiting strong leadership by abandoning formal neutrality and supporting Great Britain. He enabled Churchill to continue to fight alone on the Western front. With the German invasion of Russia in June 1941, FDR announced production targets; large-scale military production and weapons superiority was intended to reduce American casualties. Mobilization was spurred by tax legislation, which allowed defense contractors and manufacturers to write down their investment in plants and infrastructure in 5 years. Four months before Pearl Harbor, the draft was extended in the House of Representatives by just one vote. FDR's actions led the American people, step by step, into World War II.

> In less than three years, Roosevelt had taken his staunchly isolationist people into a global war. As late as May 1940, 64 percent of Americans had considered the preservation of peace more important than the defeat of the Nazis. Eighteen months later, in December 1941, just before the attack on Pearl Harbor, the proportions had been reversed—only 32 percent favored peace. . . .
>
> Roosevelt was not so much bent on war as on defeating the Nazis; it was simply that, as time passed, the Nazis could only be defeated if America entered the war. . . . Roosevelt sensed that the survival of his country and its values was at stake, and that history itself would hold him responsible for the results of his solitary initiatives. And, as was the case with Lincoln, it is a measure of the debt free peoples owe to Franklin Delano Roosevelt that the wisdom of his solitary passage is not, quite simply, taken for granted.[51]

The attack on Pearl Harbor in December 1941 came as a complete surprise, mainly due to America's isolationist perspective that led people to conclude that such an attack was not possible. Senior American officials, including the president, expected a Japanese attack, but they thought it would be in Southeast Asia and hadn't seriously considered the possibility it would come at Pearl Harbor, because they didn't believe Japan had the range to field aircraft carriers that could attack as far away as Hawaii. American intelligence lost track of the entire Japanese fleet. The absence of a reconnaissance mission to forewarn of the attack was inexcusable and resulted in the disciplining of the two commanders at Pearl Harbor. Radar picked up Japanese aircraft, but operators thought the blips were B-17s coming from

California. The level of incompetence was such that some Americans believed there had been a conspiracy to withhold information about the attack and that FDR was involved as a means of inflaming public opinion in order to make America enter the war. Even MacArthur failed to take proper precautions to prevent the destruction of his air force in the Philippines, which was thought to be the target of the Japanese fleet. He had lined his planes up wingtip-to-wingtip, believing them to be out of range of the Japanese aircraft. In a nutshell, America's isolationist bent was its own Pearl Harbor—making its policymakers unable to fathom the range and capabilities of the Japanese military.

Pearl Harbor enraged and inflamed American public opinion, FDR proclaiming December 7, "a date which will live in infamy." He expressed confidence and hope that Americans "in their righteous might" would prevail.[52] America quickly initiated the most extensive mobilization in history. Pearl Harbor galvanized America's free enterprise system into action with a sense of national purpose.[53] American commitment was needed, because the perception in Europe was that Hitler was close to knocking the Russians out of the war and that Great Britain might not be too far behind. The early part of America's entrance in the war was difficult, particularly due to the lack of preparedness. In the first few weeks of the war, the Japanese conquered almost a million square miles and one hundred million people. Even Singapore, a symbol of Western power, fell to the Japanese juggernaut. Lights along the East Coast silhouetted ships for German submarines to sink in full view of people on shore. Losses to German submarines bordered on the catastrophic. The Germans sunk over 2800 boats. The Allies reversed the heavy losses to the submarines by better tactics—interlocking convoys, the use of radar and other detection devices, breaking the German naval code, and use of long-range airplanes. American industry built ships faster than the Germans could sink them, producing 5600 merchant ships during the course of the war.

To effectively wage war, FDR needed a strong central government and large amounts of funds. In the 1930s, he had built a much stronger, centralized government that facilitated mobilization and he had learned how to raise taxes by "soaking-the-rich." The young were asked to sacrifice their lives. Like other conflicts, World War II vastly expanded the size and scope of government. Federal spending multiplied by tenfold and revenues by seven fold, with the remainder being financed by debt. During the period 1938–1944, America experienced explosive economic growth far greater than any other nation or region of the globe with Gross National Product rising from under $100 billion to well over $200 billion, the strongest surge in America history. Productivity continued to improve at a rapid pace, several times faster than at the turn of the century.

FDR believed World War I had relied too much on borrowing and too little on taxes, resulting in inflation. During World War I, 13 percent of Americans paid income taxes, a percentage that declined to 7 percent in subsequent years, but rose to 64 percent in World War II. During the war, there was a constant battle between those in Congress who favored broad-based taxes versus those that favored a highly progressive tax system, with FDR being in the latter camp and generally prevailing. He was particularly supportive of a progressive income tax, because excise taxes and tariffs were so regressive. In the largest tax increase in history as a portion of the total economy, congressional legislation raised income tax rates, the tax rolls by 30 percent, the corporate tax rate, and the excess profits tax. The personal income tax became imbedded into the American economy. The number of taxpayers soared by tenfold from 4 million to 40 million, the rates to as high as 94 percent, and the amount of revenues collected from $2 to $35 billion. Tax withholding was instituted, smoothing out the Treasury's cash flow. Previously, people paid taxes every year on the filing date, creating a considerable uncertainty every year about the level of federal revenue. As a result of high tax rates on the wealthy, the war deficit was not as great in percentage terms as either the Civil War or World War I.

FDR's administration ran fourteen straight deficits totaling more than $200 billion, 100 times what the deficit had been at the end of the Civil War, 17 times what it had been in 1930, and cumulatively the highest it had ever been as a percentage of the economy. Much of this debt was assumed by banks, insurance companies, and other financial institutions. Personal savings skyrocketed from $4 billion in 1940 (the same as 1929) to more than $135 billion.[54] Bond financing was basically the same as in World War I, with FDR rejecting proposals for forced savings. The bond drives were viewed as a mechanism for ridding the country of the last vestiges of isolationism and consistently exceeded their announced targets by several billion dollars.

After Pearl Harbor, Congress increased military spending from 6 percent of the economy to 38 percent, including 90 percent of the federal budget. Even though it produced more war materials than all the Axis nations combined, American spending on civilian goods still went up 20 percent over pre-war levels. With crop yields up 25 percent as a result of new fertilizers, high-yielding seeds, new insecticides, and new machinery, America became the breadbasket of the world. There were, however, major inconveniences. Many items were severely rationed or not available at all, including cars, gasoline, many foodstuffs, and whiskey. "[T]he mass production that provided the tools of war and the military forces that won the battles did not perform as smoothly as we remember more than half a century later. Contemporaries complained about one bottleneck after another in war production, one snafu after another in military operations. There were massive inefficiencies and wastes of manpower. War produces a command economy, and a command economy, as we have come to know, is inevitably much less efficient than a market economy."[55]

The Allied victory in World War II was directly related to America's economic power and manufacturing prowess. America became what Roosevelt labeled the "arsenal of democracy." "Although [America] was fighting a war on two fronts—every strategist's nightmare—she soon proved that she had the necessary financial, industrial and manpower resources, combined with the geographical security, to bring both to successful conclusions."[56] German and Japanese industry, efficiency, and ingenuity far exceeded anything in Europe and Asia, respectively, but were no match for America. The government issued over $100 billion in military contracts in the first six months of 1942, more than the entire Gross National Product in 1940.[57] The United States produced almost 300,000 planes, over 100,000 armored vehicles, almost 90,000 ships, 27 aircraft carriers, 370,000 artillery pieces, two and a half million trucks, 5 million tons of bombs, 20 million fire arms, and 44 billion rounds of ammunition. By contrast, the original blitzkrieg by the Nazis was achieved with just 2500 tanks, 3000 airplanes and 10,000 artillery pieces.[58] The U.S. Navy commissioned 18 fleet carriers, 9 light carriers, 77 escort carriers, 8 battleships (and repaired those damaged at Pearl Harbor), 46 cruisers, 349 destroyers, 420 destroyer escorts, and over 200 submarines. American shipyards turned out 16 ships for every one produced by Japan.[59] Historian Bruce Catton concluded: "The figures are all so astronomical that they cease to mean very much . . . the total is simply beyond the compass of one's understanding. Here was displayed a strength greater even than cocky Americans in the old days of unlimited self-confidence had supposed; strength to which nothing—literally nothing, in the physical sense—was any longer impossible." [60]

At the onset of America's entry into World War II, Germany and Japan had technologically advanced air forces with more than 50,000 planes apiece, while the Allies had fewer than 10,000 planes, many of them World War I vintage. Within a year, America's industrial ingenuity closed the gap and by the end of the war the U.S. was producing 100,000 planes a year, achieving such air superiority the Allies were able to cripple the enemy's ground capabilities. Even with this level of productivity, losses were catastrophic with two-thirds of the 12,000 B-17 bombers being destroyed and 100,000 U.S. casualties. Over 600,000 Americans were involved in the design, production, and flying of planes during the war.[61]

Supply logistics were monumental—American forces in Europe used 100 times more gasoline in World War II than World War I and half the tonnage shipped during the war was oil.[62] To carry out the offensive in France, the U.S. military had to provide its forces with 20,000 tons of supplies daily while they were advancing as much as 75 miles in a single day. Gasoline and fuel oil were brought to the front through flexible pipelines built under the English Channel. Even though the Allies experienced the worst storm in forty years two weeks after D-Day and the severest flooding in decades during the fall, they were able to keep supply lines open. In the German siege of American troops at Bastogne, over 800,000 pounds of supplies were delivered by air in five days.

The surge in manufacturing production overcame the slow mobilization effort caused by isolationist sentiment prior to the war. While this effort crushed Hitler, it did not come early enough to permit an Allied invasion of mainland Europe in 1943, which would have enabled the liberation of many of the Eastern Europe territories that ended up behind the Iron Curtain. Existing federal agencies were not up to the task of dealing with the upheavals the war would demand, and FDR created virtually an entirely new government of men from the private sector who worked at a dollar a year to supervise war production.

FDR made up with the J.P. Morgan Company and other important money managers who were essential to his war aims and had been victimized by the isolationist forces. He and the private sector were able to overcome their mutual hostility and join in the common cause to defeat the Axis powers. The ramp-up in production was achieved through central planning agencies, such as the War Production Board, the agency run by Don Nelson, who had handled procurement for Sears, Roebuck's 100,000 item catalogue and understood the scope of the American economy, as well as how to manage a huge inventory of products. The Board, which determined priorities for military weapons systems and procurement, eventually totaled over 25,000 employees.

Nelson addressed shortages such as rubber that largely came from plantations in Southeast Asia overrun by the Japanese. The government launched a program to end dependence on imports, including cutting through patents, marketing agreements, and shortages of materials. By the end of the war, more than 50 American rubber facilities were being operated by dozens of manufacturers. New sources were developed in the Amazon rain forest and by planting latex-producing plants that would grow in the United States. Eventually, private companies such as Du Pont developed synthetic rubber, but there was still not much available for civilian use—a particular problem for private automobiles with worn or flat tires. The new materials that were developed resulted in a wide range of new chemical products and markets.

American industry, particularly large corporations, played an expanded role. Economist Joseph Schumpeter concluded that the benefits of economies of scale exceed whatever evils associated with their large size. Large firms could produce more cheaply than small, competing firms. In 1940, 175,000 small firms manufactured 70 percent of the U.S. goods. By the middle of 1943, the ratio was reversed and 70 percent was produced by the 100 largest firms.[64]

The cumulative investment in U.S. manufacturing plants was $50 billion from the inception of the country through 1939, but $22 billion more was invested within three years. Annual industrial output went from $50 billion to $150 billion. While efforts were made to help small businesses, about 70 percent of the war contracts went to the one hundred largest businesses. While the U.S. effectively used mass production techniques, the Axis countries were not nearly as proficient. The German army had 150 different makes of both trucks and motor cycles. Mass production efforts lagged far behind in Germany and Japan.[65]

U.S. production reached the level for all three Axis countries and then doubled again. Japanese manufacturing capabilities increased just 2 percent during the early part of the war when U.S. capacity was increasing 35 percent. Nazi war production never reached full stride until 1943. Except for tank manufacture, Russian production lagged far behind.[66] The enormous advantage in manufacturing and the commitment to defeat a hated enemy were, more than any other single factor, responsible for America's greatest military triumph.

American delivery of supplies and materials to Europe was aided greatly by Hitler's irrational decision to hold many of his U-boats in reserve off the coast of Norway, overriding his military officers' insistence that they be deployed off the coast of America. Even with this decision, the Axis destroyed almost 8 million tons of shipping in 1942 alone. The U.S. merchant marine built less than 100 ships a year before the war and were tasked with building almost 3,000 right away. American shipping was aided greatly by the prodigious Henry Kaiser who was dubbed Sir Launchalot and by 1945 was producing more than a ship a day. Roosevelt, who visited his West Coast plants, was a friend of Kaiser.

In Vancouver he saw the launching of a ship whose keel had been laid ten days before—quite a contrast with the 180 days it had taken to build a ship in World War I and only one of Kaiser's many phenomenal achievements. Bald, stocky, born in upstate New York the same year as Roosevelt, Kaiser was a New Deal industrialist, one of the first American capitalists to build a big business on government contracts and government financing. . . . Kaiser had started in the road-paving business on the West Coast in 1914, just as governments were preparing to pay millions to put hard surfaces on the first tracks that made up most of the country's roadways. He started sand and gravel and cement businesses and got construction contracts for Boulder Dam, the San Francisco-Oakland Bay Bridge, Bonneville and Grand Coulee Dams, the Mare Island Shipyard, and the Los Angeles Breakwater. John Gunther lists eleven public projects totaling $148 million and during the war Kaiser built over 700 ships worth some $1.8 billion—phenomenal amounts at the time. He also got the government to finance his plants: five months before his ride in the back seat of Roosevelt's car in Vancouver, the RFC had agreed to lend him $110 million for his steel mill in Fontana, California, and four months after the ride it was completed.[67]

When told to produce ships faster, these war capitalists cut construction time from 196 to 27 days and by 1943 were turning out a ship every 10.3 hours. In 1942, General Electric alone raised its production of marine turbines from $1 million to $300 million.[68] The United States delivered hundreds of thousands of tons of military supplies and millions of tons of food to the Soviet Union through the Arctic ports of Murmansk and Archangel, the icy Pacific ports of Siberia, and through the Persian Gulf to the port of Basra. These shipments included tens of thousands of miles of telephone lines, 14,000 aircraft, 7,000 tanks, thousands of rail locomotives and cars, and entire factories to produce tires, aluminum, and pipes.[69]

General Motors increased defense production from $75 million in 1940 to $1.9 billion in 1942 and $3.7 billion in 1943, including tanks, tank destroyers, armored cars, aircraft, aircraft engines, machine guns, trucks, diesel engines, commercial trucks and many types of parts and components. The rapid rate of obsolescence of weapons posed a continual problem for manufacturers like GM who had to constantly change its product mix.[70] Dodge built a factory in Chicago for aircraft engines covering over six million square feet, about 50 percent of the automobile industry's capacity before the war. Ford built a new plant from scratch with the largest room in the world that produced bombers so rapidly they couldn't be parked or stored. They taxied out to a runway, made a test flight and flew off to combat. The company produced more war goods than the entire Italian economy. The Boeing plant in Seattle turned out more aircraft per square foot than any other plant in the United States. The Consolidated plant in Fort Worth, Texas, was the longest assembly line in the world. California accounted for a sixth of the war production and its manufacturing output more than tripled. California drew workers to its aircraft plants, shipyards, and ports.[71]

The U.S. success was in stark contrast to the failures of the Axis, whose military officers were accustomed to conflicts won on the battlefield and not in the factory. Materials shortages, particularly fuel shortages doomed the Nazi campaign in North Africa where Field Marshall Rommel had no gasoline to counterattack. Allied efforts to destroy Germany's capacity to make synthetic fuels led to a huge shortage of gasoline for aircraft, virtually grounding the Luftwaffe during the period after D-Day. Allied bombing continued to focus on petroleum facilities and fuel shortages doomed the surprise German counterattack in the Battle of the Bulge. Similarly, American submarine warfare in the Pacific targeted oil tankers and created severe shortages that prevented the Japanese from effectively waging war. As the shortages worsened, pilots were not even given any training—just instructed to follow their leaders to the targets. Some Japanese ships were converted back to coal, reducing speed and flexibility. At one stage of the war, Japanese planes had only enough fuel to fly two hours a month.[72] Kamikazes cut fuel requirements in half, helping to ensure that the missions would be carried out. In 1945, Germany produced the first experimental jet aircraft, but they had to be towed to the tarmac by oxen to save fuel.

D-DAY: DECISIVE TIME

The invasion of Normandy was probably the most complex single activity ever undertaken by human beings. The military logistics and requirements for D-Day alone were staggering—7,000 ships, 12,000 tons of supplies a day, requiring 2,500 vehicles to be unloaded. The effort necessitated the creation of portable harbors at landing places such as "Omaha Beach"—the nearby ports were too fortified or were destroyed by the time they were captured. It was one of the most important single days in the history of the human race. The Allied Supreme Commander, General Dwight D. Eisenhower had to make the final decision. The Allies had a three-day window to make the landing. If they had waited until the next opportunity, they would have faced the most severe summer storm in thirty years. It probably would have destroyed much of the invasion force. Eisenhower wrote in a very tight, succinct style, comparable to Lincoln, saying, "I have full confidence in your courage, devotion to duty, and skill in battle. We will accept nothing less than full victory. Good luck, and let all of us beseech the blessing of Almighty God upon this great and noble undertaking." He also gave the troops a letter imploring them to adhere to the highest standards of behavior. FDR's speech on D-Day was offered as a prayer, for "our sons, pride of our Nation. . . . Give strength to their arms, stoutness to their hearts, steadfastness in their faith"; and for people at home "to wait out the long travail, to bear sorrows that may come. . . . Give us Faith in Thee." He concluded: 'faith in our sons' faith in each other; faith in our united crusade."[73]

Eisenhower's message was in stark contrast to the military tradition of other conquerors and would-be conquerors of the continent. Eisenhower's life is a case study of how in America an individual may start out as a Kansas farm boy and launch 900,000 people on to the continent of Europe. During the 1920s and 1930s, Eisenhower had been a career military man of relatively low rank when America had a genuine peacetime military. There were no wars to fight and public sentiment and the Congress kept the U.S. out of the events in Europe. Eisenhower could have just sat around, spending time at the officer's club, socializing with the few other career military people who were basically getting paid to do little or nothing. Instead, Eisenhower spent his time studying logistics, American history, American battles, and the great battles of world history. He had a premonition or perhaps more accurately he intuited that this information and knowledge would one day be extremely important to him. In the late 1930s, when he was almost 50 years old, he was still a relatively obscure military man of low rank. World War II propelled him into a leadership role and he had prepared himself so well, learned the lessons of history so well, that he was eventually placed in charge of the Allied invasion. In this job, he was mastermind of the most complex operation in human history. Knowing the lessons of American and world history, Eisenhower shouldered the great moral burden and in the end was the man who said go or no go.

For the World War II generation, D-Day was the decisive moment of its lifetime. The men had the courage needed to free other people. The Allies secured their foothold at substantial cost of life. The beach-head soon expanded so that within 12 days 600,000 men and 90,000 vehicles were on the beaches massed for the drive inland. The Allies built a portable harbor at the seaside town of Arromanches, enclosing two square miles comprising 600,000 tons of concrete and one million yards of steel. It took 100,000 men to build and 20,000 men to operate. Two-and-a-half million men, half-a-million vehicles, and four million tons of supplies came ashore by that route.[74]

German defense efforts were hobbled by the rigid structure of its military that robbed its troops of the initiative to respond to the attack. The Allies spent considerable effort camouflaging the attack and the Nazis were fooled into believing for days after the landing that the Normandy operation was just a diversion. The Allied forces had a much more decentralized structure and they could improvise—which is exactly what they did when many things went wrong during the D-Day landings and throughout the war. The flexible command structure allowed them to reconstitute themselves after the landing and carry the day. The landing on Utah beach was missed by over 1,000 meters, but the commander on the scene made a decision to charge straight ahead to take the Nazi fortification. When hidden German machine guns and infantry picked off personnel operating bulldozers to clear the way for American advances, imaginative Americans converted Sherman tanks into bulldozers, which were impervious to these types of fire. Yankee ingenuity and resourcefulness overcame enormous obstacles. When the Germans were dug in on steep cliffs in Italy, the troops scaled mountains with their encumbered equipment, capturing the German headquarters where the commander exclaimed: "You can't be here. It is impossible to come up those rocks."[75] For the invasion of Europe, entrepreneurial Allied troops developed new tanks with amphibious capabilities and attachments such as saws to cut through hedge rows, flamethrowers to eliminate Germans in pillboxes, and rotating chains to clear mines.

The feat is all the more remarkable given that the United States launched another massive invasion only two weeks later half a world away—in Saipan, which was the staging area for much of the rest of the war against Japan, including the dropping of the two atomic bombs.

NEW TECHNOLOGY

American technology was in substantial part responsible for the vast expansion in manufacturing capacity and played a major role in other areas. By the end of the war, Americans had more effective fighter planes and bombers, stronger battleships, and submarines with greater range. Using radar transmitter technology originating in Great Britain, Americans developed radar systems for bombing through difficult weather and terrain, hunting German submarines, improving artillery accuracy, and pinpointing attacking airplanes before they reached their targets. FDR designated Dr. Vannevar Bush to head critical research and his technology group made advances in radar, sonar, rockets, penicillin, jets, pesticides, amphibious vehicles, and atomic fission.

Americans combined superior technology with entrepreneurial

spirit. At Guadalcanal, the troops took only a few days to build a crucial airbase the Japanese thought would take more than a month. The Americans had a vast array of bulldozers and construction equipment and the know-how to deliver it quickly to remote locations, while the Japanese only thought in terms of muscle-power.[76] The carrier Yorktown was repaired in only three months, just in time to be able to sink four enemy carriers at Midway when the Japanese planes were caught out of commission for refueling and rearming. Jimmy Doolittle developed a plan to launch B-25 bombers off Navy aircraft carriers to conduct air raids on Japan. American military officers were stunned to see his B-25 take off from the short flight deck. These raids caused panic among Japanese civilians who had been told by the government their nation would never be subject to attack.

Building on Britain's code-breaking efforts developed over fifty years, encryption and decryption capabilities enabled American intelligence to break German and Japanese codes. Both the Japanese and Germans believed their codes could not be broken, considerably aiding the Allied effort. The Germans even informed the Japanese their codes had been broken, but Tokyo didn't believe the Americans were capable of such a feat. Code-breaking enabled the Americans to track and sink the Japanese merchant marine and navy as well as the German U-boats and their supply ships, which were Hitler's most effective weapons. The famous German battleship Bismarck and dozens of U-boats went to their watery graves when their positions were given away by the breaking of the German code.

One of the first electronic computers was used to help break the code. Computers were also crucial to winning the air war over the Germans. Anti-aircraft technology used measurements of the altitude, azimuth, and slant range of enemy aircraft and continually recalculated the target's future position. In an era of vacuum tubes, these devices took truckloads of men and machinery to help accurately aim each gun.[77]

American code breakers enabled the military to achieve a decisive victory at Midway, the turning point of the Pacific war, where four of Japan's largest and fastest carriers were destroyed, as well as over 300 airplanes. After Midway, a U.S. submarine offensive against Japanese supply-ships, relying on code-breaking and communications technology, sank a substantial portion of the Japanese merchant marine. In the Atlantic, German submarine warfare crippled American efforts to supply Allied forces through the middle of 1943. At one point, the Germans were able to change their code procedures to prevent them from being read, while breaking the Allied ciphers. For months, essential supplies were denied Britain as much of the Allied shipping was destroyed. Until the spring of 1943, German submarines continued to sink record volumes of American ships, operating with impunity. Finally, the Allies broke the new German codes and secured their own ciphers, tipping the balance of the maritime conflict. Advances in radar and convoy operations helped the U.S. stop the German submarine campaign.[78]

Interception of Japanese diplomatic transmissions from Berlin provided the Allies with the best information on Hitler's intentions, as well as a detailed description of the terrain where the D-Day invasion was launched and critical strategic information that enabled Allied bombardments to keep mobile German units from annihilating the invaders. Fearful that Japanese officers schooled in the United States knew how to intercept military messages, American cryptographers employed Navajo Indians as radio operators and used their native language. Their code was one of the very few in history never to be broken.

THE ATOMIC BOMB

Culmination of American and Allied technological superiority was the atomic bomb, the product of phenomenal advances in physics during the first decades of the twentieth century. Madame and Pierre Curie discovered radioactivity in uranium, suggesting there were unseen reservoirs of energy to be tapped. Ernest Rutherford identified the atomic nucleus and his protégé James Chadwick discovered the neutron. German physicists Otto Hahn and Fritz Strassmann provided proof of fission, releasing findings showing that when they bombarded uranium with neutrons they produced some quantities of a different, lighter element. The concept of splitting the atom was an oxymoron—since the ancient Greeks atoms had been the basic element or unit of matter and literally meant "indivisible." The theory of atoms being that each element was truly elementary and the atom itself was the lowest common denominator of matter. An atom of one element could not be transformed into another element. Hungarian Leo Szilard's experiments demonstrated that along with energy, neutrons were released, creating the possibility of a nuclear chain reaction. This energy might be a source of industrial power or an explosive. In 1931, Ernest Lawrence at the University of California at Berkeley had invented the cyclotron, which facilitated research into the atom and radioactivity. At Princeton, Robert Van De Graaff developed a device for creating beams of subatomic particles.[79]

During World War I, Thomas Edison headed a panel of inventors entitled "How to Make War Impossible" that encouraged government to "produce instruments of death so terrible that presently all men and every nation would well know that war would mean the end of civilization."[80] The production of the bomb was much more difficult than planners originally thought and was made possible by a combination of European theory and American industrial technology, resources, and entrepreneurial attitude. As developments in nuclear physics proceeded at a rapid pace, most of the leading physicists, at least initially, didn't believe that an explosion could result. Most of the key concepts were publicly available. Scientists were left alone to exchange ideas and contemplate the consequences of the new technology, but few understood the ramifications of the theory. Scientists freely discussed the possibility of blowing up entire cities using nuclear devices, but even editors and newspaper reporters who were present failed to grasp the importance of what they were hearing. And the man on the street couldn't even pronounce the word "physicist." The American scientific community didn't know the Nazis were actually far behind their efforts. Published reports of German scientific activities were thought to represent a small part of the Nazi effort. The most important sources of uranium in the world were Czechoslovakia and the Belgian Congo, both readily accessible to the Germans. Nazi secrecy made Americans fear the worst.[81]

Perhaps the most frightening aspect of the reign of Adolf Hitler is that he was literally just one insight away from ruling the world. If he had understood the importance of the theory of relativity, physics, and nuclear fission, he probably would have developed the atomic bomb in advance of any other nation. In the 1930s, Germany had three times as many Nobel laureates as America. Hitler believed basic physics was Jewish physics and his reign of tyranny forced many of the most knowledgeable scientists to emigrate to Great Britain and the United States, including Albert Einstein, Klaus Fuchs, Enrico Fermi, and Neils Bohr. Having written off much of nuclear physics, Hitler concentrated his research resources elsewhere—rockets, jet aircraft, and snorkel submarines.

The nuclear field was in flux and even the leading scientists were unsure both of what they knew and what the ramifications were—Einstein even told *The New York Times* that nuclear fission could not result in an explosion. Scientists were considered impractical and eccentric—even private industry would not hire them. They were literally in their own world—freely allowed to talk to each other—even if they were from different countries at war with each other. Government officials and layman didn't understand them. Scientists were largely unconcerned about communicating their knowledge and discoveries to the general public. When the process of nuclear fission was discovered, no effort was made to keep it secret, but it was barely even mentioned in the press. The scientists were so removed from the rest of the world, they had no idea of how to present their case to President Roosevelt. At one point, they thought of warning FDR by having Einstein send a letter through his friend the Belgian queen mother, which could have been a disaster had it fallen into the hands of Hitler when he invaded that country the next spring. When Einstein's letter was read to FDR, he quickly understood the potential, noting to his first visitor "what you are after is to see that the Nazis don't blow us up." Neither Einstein nor Neils Bohr, the two leading physicists, was allowed to participate in the development of the atomic bomb, because both were considered security risks.

The Manhattan Project began haltingly. After calculating the feasibility of using uranium to develop a powerful bomb, leading scientists took months to inform superiors and the president of the finding. General Leslie Groves was put in charge of the Manhattan Project, having only recently completed work on the massive project to build the Pentagon. His management skills accelerated the project. When Groves took over the project, he provided the needed leadership and found the key scientist, J. Robert Oppenheimer. The effort was greatly strengthened by the waves of exiles from Axis countries who, even though brilliant, were not "racially pure," and therefore subject to execution by the Nazis, and forced to leave Europe.

FDR appointed Dr. Vannevar Bush, former dean at MIT, to oversee this effort, which eventually cost $2 billion and employed over 100,000 people. The Manhattan Project built some of the world's largest factories ever and marshaled a broad range of resources and new technologies. Improvements in uranium fabrication and enrichment paved the way to a nuclear chain reaction. The first reaction took place at the University of Chicago, under the direction of famous physicist Enrico Fermi. The leading laboratory, responsible for assembling the device, was located in remote Los Alamos to improve security. Groves insisted on installing J. Robert Oppenheimer as head of the Los Alamos laboratory, over the objections of Army security who didn't like the communist affiliations of his relatives. Los Alamos was a community created literally overnight out on the New Mexican desert. Another facility at Oak Ridge, Tennessee, was constructed to separate the fissionable uranium from natural uranium and was the world's largest factory under one roof. Construction of Oak Ridge required over 10,000 tons of silver worth $300 million. Uranium was then converted to plutonium for a bomb at the Hanford Site in the state of Washington. An explosives expert, George Kistiakwsky, made critical contributions to the development of a triggering device. The Americans compressed 30 years of science into 4.

Ironically, the totalitarian governments that drove America to develop the bomb failed to undertake efforts to manufacture their own. Unlike the United States which had the most formidable economy in the world, they did not have the industrial capacity to build a bomb. Neither the Germans, nor the Japanese, nor the Russians placed a high priority on the project. German efforts to build an atomic reactor were thwarted by the sabotage and destruction of heavy water from a Norwegian manufacturing facility. Much to the subsequent amazement of the Allies, Hitler had never committed to a full-scale production program for the atomic bomb, but this was not known until the end of 1944 when General Patton took Strasbourg and scientists were able to review the private papers of the key German physicists—revealing they were at least two years behind. Until that time, the Allies had assumed the Nazis had the lead by a wide margin.

The Soviets placed little priority on their own capability; their major thrust was to steal the American technology. The Soviets advanced their nuclear capability through an extensive espionage network thrown around Los Alamos through Anatoli Yakovlev who developed relationships with Julius and Ethel Rosenberg and, most importantly, Klaus Fuchs, the noted atomic physicist who worked on the testing part of the project. Fuchs provided detailed notes on the application of theoretical fission to the building of a bomb, because he thought he was working for peace by helping the Soviets. This data was supplemented by other spies including Morton Sobell and Alan Nunn May.[82] Despite pleas of innocence, Julius and Ethel Rosenberg went to the electrical chair. Soviet archives showed that at least Julius conspired to steal America's atomic secrets, although Ethel may not have been involved. Many of these spies thought their motives were pure and they were helping to balance world power. The subsequent revelation of these traitorous activities would have a particularly devastating impact on American society which, separated from much of the rest of the world by two vast oceans, had been a relatively open one. The recriminations from these treacherous events led to a deep sense of distrust in America and eventually spawned McCarthyism. By advancing the time the Soviet Union had the atomic bomb by at least several years, these spies probably helped to enslave Eastern Europe. If the United States had been the only country with the atomic bomb in the 1950s, President Eisenhower could have taken stronger action to help satellites of the Soviet Union when they revolted against communist oppression.

Truman's decision to drop the bomb on Japan has been challenged by later-day historians, although there was little controversy at the time. The Japanese routinely marched their prisoners of war to death or used them for construction projects such as those described in *The Bridge Over the River Kwai*. Allied prisoners in Japanese camps died in captivity at much higher rates than in German camps. The Japanese committed atrocities such as experiments in Manchuria involving plagues of anthrax and typhoid and the rape of Nanking, "perhaps the most appalling single episode of barbarism in a century replete with horrors."[83] The Japanese were determined foes, frequently engaging in suicide missions when faced with defeat. Even as late as the middle 1950s World War II Japanese soldiers hiding out on remote islands refused to give up.

American commanders expected a U.S. invasion of Japan to face suicide boats, human torpedoes, waves of kamikaze planes, and a Japanese slogan—"One hundred million people die proudly." The fight for Okinawa had cost America more than 10,000 killed and 35,000 wounded, as well as dozens of ships and over 700 airplanes. In an invasion of Japan, General Douglas MacArthur expected 50,000 casualties the first day and a campaign that would last years. American policy makers knew they could not depend on Soviet help unless that country was to profit directly. The total Japanese strength on the mainland would include 2.3 million troops, 4 million military employees, and 28 million members of the militia. Military planners believed that occupying Japan would take two huge invasions. MacArthur's chief surgeon thought the first of these invasions, to occupy the island of Kyushu, would result in 395,000 casualties in the first 120 days. Any invasion would require devastating air attacks. Fire bombings of Dresden, Germany, and Tokyo had already claimed the lives of hundreds of thousands of people. Japanese figures on the over 60 cites and areas fire-bombed by the B29s showed the destruction of over 2 million buildings, 9 million homeless, over 250,000 killed, and 400,000 injured.[84] Americans had just paid dearly for their occupation of Okinawa—more than 12,000 were killed. During the entire war, not a single Japanese unit had surrendered.[85] At the time of the decision on the bomb, the

Japanese were entering into secret negotiations with the Soviet Union to carve up Asia. Intelligence sources found that Japan's militaristic leaders were adamantly opposed to surrender to the Americans or British. Pleas to the Japanese to unconditional surrender were rejected.

> The evidence is crystal clear. The use of nuclear weapons to end World War II quickly and decisively averted the death or maiming of hundreds of thousands of American soldiers, sailors, marines, and airmen. It also saved the lives of some 400,000 Allied prisoners of war and civilian detainees in Japanese hands, all of whom were to be executed in the event of an invasion of Japan. Above all, it saved untold hundreds of thousands more Japanese—perhaps millions—from becoming casualties of pre-invasion bombing and shelling, followed by two invasions and forcible occupation.[86]

A former head of the Japanese Medical Association concluded, "When one considers the possibility that the Japanese military would have sacrificed the entire nation if it were not for the atomic bomb attack, then this bomb might be described as having saved Japan."[87]

Even after the dropping of two bombs, the Japanese were deadlocked over whether to surrender, with Emperor Hirohito being forced to break the stalemate. Truman held up preparations for delivery of a third atomic bomb until Japanese intentions were clear. Truman's original decision was made with wariness—he asked two teams of soldiers, civilians, and scientists to search for other choices—four scientists agreed unanimously with the plan that was carried out. After the initial test in the American desert, the committee of advisors concluded, "We can propose no technical demonstration likely to bring an end to the war. We can see no acceptable alternative to direct military use." Even as the *USS Missouri* was sailing into Tokyo Bay to accept surrender, Japanese kamikaze bombers were preparing to sink it, deterred only at the last moment by Emperor Hirohito's brother. What if, as was virtually certain, thousands and thousands of Americans had been killed when there had been a weapon available that could have ended the war?

America pursued a racist policy during the war—the evacuation and internment of Japanese Americans, which was directed by FDR and approved by the Supreme Court. There was little basis for this imprisonment, other than the fact the victims were Japanese. The Japanese were given just forty-eight hours to dispose of their homes, businesses, and possessions and were allowed only hand luggage in their settlements. They lost close to a billion dollars in wealth. They were forced to centers that were tiny apartments without running water or adequate cooking facilities and with public showers, baths, and latrines. Discrimination was widespread. Insurance companies canceled policies with people of Japanese descent. Retailers refused to serve them. California Attorney General Earl Warren froze their funds and attached them. Several governors warned Japanese to stay out of their states. A farmer who hired Japanese workers had his barn put to the torch and threats made upon the life of his youngest child. The press fanned the flames, particularly columnist Walter Lippmann. A significant number of these internees enlisted for duty in the European theater without a single desertion. One Japanese regiment was the most decorated unit in the entire army, but many of the honors on behalf of the fallen sons were accepted in relocation camps by parents denied the freedom for which their sons had died.

Like the Revolutionary War and the Civil War, World War II saw the emergence of great military leaders, such as Generals Marshall, Eisenhower, and Patton. George Marshall was named chief of staff even though he ranked below thirty-two other men. He oversaw the fastest and greatest mobilization in human history. Peter Drucker described the development of this leadership:

> Altogether General Marshall offers a good example how one makes strength productive. When he first reached a position of influence in the mid-thirties, there was no general officer in the U.S. Army still young enough for active duty. . . . The future generals of World War II were still junior officers with few hopes for promotion when Marshall began to select and train them. Eisenhower was one of the older ones and even he, in the mid-thirties, was only a

major. Yet by 1942, Marshall had developed the largest and clearly the ablest group of general officers in American history . . .

This—one of the greatest educational feats in military history—was done by a man who lacked all the normal trappings of "leadership," such as personal magnetism or the towering self-confidence of a Montgomery, a de Gaulle or a MacArthur . What Marshall had were principles. "What can this man do?" was his constant question. And if a man could do something, his lacks became secondary.

Marshall, for instance, again and again came to George Patton's rescue and made sure that this ambitious, vain, but powerful wartime commander would not be penalized for the absence of the qualities that make a good staff officer and a successful career soldier in peacetime. Yet Marshall himself personally loathed the dashing *beau sabreur* of Patton's type.

Marshall was only concerned with weaknesses when they limited the full development of a man's strength. These he tried to overcome through work and career opportunities.

The young Major Eisenhower, for instance, was quite deliberately put by Marshall into war-planning in the mid-thirties to help him acquire the systematic strategic under-standing which he apparently lacked. Eisenhower did not himself become a strategist as a result. But he acquired respect for strategy and an understanding of its importance and thereby removed a serious limitation on his great strength as a team builder and tactical planner.

Marshall always appointed the best qualified man no matter how badly he was needed where he was. "We owe this move to the job . . . we owe it to the man and we to it to the troops," was his reply when someone—usually some-one high up—pleaded with him not to pull out an "indis-pensable" man.[88]

Both Marshall and Eisenhower were effective at keeping the political decision-making process separate from the military execution. They did not fight battles, but were effective organizers, strategists, and among the original supply chain managers. George Marshall described Eisenhower's leadership: "You have completed your mission with the greatest victory in the history of warfare. You have commanded with outstanding success the most powerful military force that has ever been assembled. You have met and successfully disposed of every conceivable difficulty incident to varied national interests and international political problems of unprecedented complications. . . . He was the most successful general of the greatest war ever fought."[89] Admiral Ernie King and Chester Nimitz devised and implemented the successful carrier war in the Pacific, also decided by logistics and strategy more than on the battlefield. MacArthur fought intensely and effectively throughout his long land-sea route from Australia to Japan, accepting the formal surrender.

Heroic examples of leadership were numerous throughout the war including Brig. General Anthony McAuliffe, deputy commander of the 101st Airborne Division. When surrounded at Bastogne, Belgium, during the Battle of the Bulge, the Germans demanded his surrender. He sent a one-word reply—"Nuts!" and was later rescued.

With FDR in increasingly poor health, the end of the war resulted in one of his greatest failures. He bypassed normal diplomatic and legal channels, using Harry Hopkins to deal directly with Soviet leader Joseph Stalin. FDR misjudged Stalin's territorial ambitions. He was not alone—even Eisenhower failed to recognize that his troops' penetration into Europe would determine post-war political lines. Winston Churchill tried unsuccessfully to warn the Americans about the Soviets' intentions. At the crucial Yalta meeting, FDR blocked Churchill's efforts to coordinate in advance in order not to feed Soviet suspicions. FDR made concessions to obtain a Soviet declaration of war against Japan that proved unnecessary. The atomic bomb would end the Pacific War, but, at the time, it hadn't even been tested and no one knew for sure that it could even detonate much less how powerful it would be. FDR was a dying man. Even when Stalin failed to live up to his commitments in the immediate aftermath of Yalta, FDR never pressed Eisenhower to push his troops deeper into Europe.

FDR's death at the war's end left America shocked and afraid—there had been only rumors about the president's condition. People remember the place and time they heard of his death, just as they did John F. Kennedy's only two decades later. Millions of Americans traveled to see his funeral train and procession.

> That Saturday afternoon was probably the quietest of the war. Across the country department stores were draped in black. The Ringling Brothers Barnum & Bailey circus had canceled its matinee. Movie theaters—seven hundred in New York alone—were closed. Newspapers had finished their runs early, for they were carrying no advertisements this day. Even grocery stores were locked up from two-o'clock to five, and at four-o'clock, when services began in the East Room, America simply stopped. AP, UPI, and INS teletypes slowly tapped out : S I L E N C E. Buses and automobiles pulled over to curbstones. Trolley cars were motionless. Airplanes in the sky just circled overhead; those that had landed parked on their runways and did not approach terminals. Radios went dead. There was no phone service, not even a dial tone. In New York's subway tunnels, 505 trains halted where they were, and everywhere you saw men taking off their hats and women sinking to their knees. In that long moment the United States was as still as the two hundred worshippers gathered in the East Room of the Executive Mansion.[90]

FDR's was in tune with the national pulse and had a special relationship with the downtrodden, having helped them escape from the desperation of the Depression. Four years after his death, a poll found that 40 percent of Philadelphia residents listed FDR as their first choice as the greatest person in history. Only 10 percent listed Lincoln and 5 percent Washington.

FDR ran an activist government and led the country through two of its greatest crises. A White House clerk calculated that FDR made thirty-five or more decisions for every one Coolidge had made.[91] His willingness to listen to new ideas opened the floodgates to new policies and programs, revolutionary change not seen since the days of Presidents Jackson and Lincoln. FDR was able to concentrate the full power of the United States to the sole purpose of defeating the Axis powers. His administration had many pluses—broadening the base of people who participated in society, exuding confidence in the future, and fighting isolationism. "No personality has ever expressed the American popular temper so articulately or with such exclusiveness. In the Progressive era national reform leadership was divided among Theodore Roosevelt, Wilson, Bryan, and La Follette. In the age of the New Deal it was monopolized by one man, whose passing left American liberalism demoralized and all but helpless."[92]

In some respects, Harry Truman was as surprised as anyone to be president; most of his friends at least privately believed he would not be a great president and he is widely regarded as the worst-prepared president in history—an act of irresponsibility on Roosevelt's part. Yet, he had determination and a deep understanding of history.

> Arriving on the sidewalk that first Friday morning, he hailed an AP correspondent: "Hey, Tony, if you're going down to the White House, you may as well hop in with me." The Secret Service agents looked pained, and their displeasure turned to alarm when downtown, he insisted upon walking to his bank. They were unaccustomed to a President who walked anywhere. News that the new chief executive was a pedestrian swept adjacent blocks, creating the greatest traffic jam in memory, and Truman ruefully conceded that his bodyguards were right—Presidents couldn't go to banks; it had to be the other way around. He enjoyed the deference, but whenever his new duties were mentioned, he paled, "Boys, if newspapermen pray," he told the White House press corps, "pray for me now."
>
> In perspective his behavior seemed natural. The death of the great leader had unnerved everyone; yesterday

Truman had been sworn in—after a frantic search for a Bible—by a confused Chief Justice who thought the new President's middle name was Shippe, when in fact the S stood for nothing. Afterward Truman impulsively kissed the Bible. At the time he knew no more about prosecution of the war than the average reader of the *Washington Post*—which, in fact, had been his principal source of information. Roosevelt had told him nothing. Truman had never been in the White House war room. It is astonishing to reflect that during his first day in office he had never heard of an atomic bomb, while Joseph Stalin know almost everything about the Manhattan Project.[93]

Truman moved quickly to address the Congress and get up to speed on foreign and domestic issues that he had never even been briefed on. His service as a Senator gave him a bond of friendship with many in both the House and Senate and they wanted him to succeed.

The loss of World War II would have been cataclysmic—leaving most of the world to dictators who had been mass murderers. The exterminations in Europe and Asia would have been mere precedents for what would have occurred in Africa, Arabia, India, and what was left of China. It would have meant not just the end of Western Civilization, but of civilization as man had known it for several hundred years.

The war finally ended. Just three-and-a-half years after America's abrupt entry into it the Nazis were not merely checked or defeated—but rather annihilated in one of the most brutal and extraordinary military achievements in history. No one knows how many people perished in the madness—at least 48 million people and possibly as many as 60 million. These figures are greater than all of the deaths in all of the wars in the nineteen centuries after Christ and twice as many as in the Great War—World War I. The death toll included 24 million in the Soviet Union, 6 million in Poland, 4 million in China and Germany, and 2 million in Japan, as well as 1 million in Yugoslavia and the Philippines. By comparison, Britain's toll was 347,000 and the United States lost 298,000, but had total casualties of over one million. About

8 million Soviet troops died in the war and three-quarters of Hitler's soldiers who died did so on the Eastern Front. The Eastern Front was the central battlefield of World War II where the vast majority of German troops fought and where thirty million people died. The fight against Nazi Germany was what the great military historian John Erikson called "Stalin's war." Soviet losses in World War II included over 20 million people, hundreds of towns, thousands of villages, millions of homes, tens of thousands of industrial plants, and approximately 100,000 collective farms.[94] English-speaking troops killed 200,000 Germans, but the Soviet Union killed over 3 million. For many, the victory was hollow—forty five years of oppressive communist rule was to follow.

Socially, politically, economically, militarily, culturally, racially, sexually, demographically, even mythologically, World War II was the crucible that forged modern America. It was *the* transforming event that reshaped all who lived through it. Only the American Revolution that created the new nation and the Civil War that preserved the Union rank with it in importance.

For America, the energy unleashed by the war ended the lingering Great Depression of the 1930s and created an unmatched economic and technological colossus. It set in motion new laws that transformed the way we lived, bought homes, went to college. It changed the future for women and blacks at home, and produced both benevolence and arrogance abroad. It engendered decades of belief in authority and official assumptions about the rightness of our course, in contrast to the disturbing and more recent spawning of disbelief in government and institutions. It proved the triumph of democracy over fascism, yet left intact and even strengthened the power of Soviet communism, which then challenged the United States for world leadership over nearly the next half century.

Out of the war came a flow of inventions that enabled Americans to explore space, possess the power that could destroy civilization, share labor-saving gadgets that made possible greater leisure time, and enjoy the comforts of the most expansive consumer society in history. The war changed America's attitudes about itself, its leaders, its political system, its place in the world and in history, all in ways unimaginable.[95]

11

Truman and Eisenhower
end the cycle of war

There was never a country more fabulous than America. She sits bestride the world like a Colossus; no other power at any time in the world's history has possessed so varied or so great an influence on other nations. . . . Half of the wealth of the world, more than half of the productivity, nearly two-thirds of the world machines, are concentrated in American hands; the rest of the world lies in the shadow of American industry.
—ROBERT PAYNE, BRITISH HISTORIAN, WINTER 1948–1949

AMERICA'S DOMINANCE WAS BROADLY BASED at the end of World War II. Eighty percent of the world's gold was under U.S. control and the dollar was the world's currency, the basis for world trade. Three-fourths of the world's invested capital was in the United States. With seven percent of the world's population, America produced over half the oil and nearly half the electricity. Americans harvested half the grain and a third of the cotton grown on earth. U.S. production of all minerals was about four times larger than the second largest producer, the Soviet Union. The American consumer was by far the best-fed, best housed, and best-clothed civilian in the world. Americans owned 70 percent of the world's automobiles and 83 percent of the civilian aircraft.[1] "No country in history possessed such a preponderance of military and economic power."[2]

America was indeed the leading nation on the planet and, as a result, the world was a safer and more peaceful place. Spurred on by the specter of a nuclear holocaust, Presidents Truman (1884-1972) and Eisenhower (1890-1969) effectively used this American power and its influence to stop the endless cycle of war that had ravaged Europe for centuries. To its misfortune, the continent had been continuously embroiled in wars beginning with the Norman Conquest in 1066 through the end of World War II.[3] European nations would lead the world in scientific knowledge, research, and invention, but forfeited this advantage to the destruction caused by war. Nearly a hundred million people died in the global conflicts of the first half of the twentieth century, but only a few million died in the second half, in substantial part due to America's new role in the world. Throughout its history, America had tried to "serve as a model for the rest of the world while remaining apart from the rest of the world."[4] The attack on Pearl Harbor in December 1941 shattered the illusion that the United States could remain separate. The United States had to assume global responsibilities. Unlike the aftermath of World War I, Americans now accepted their world role as a global power while the country was going through seismic change.

American foreign policy had to overcome the failed federal government policies that caused the Great Depression, erroneously blamed on the capitalist system. These U.S. policies caused socialism and communism to surge throughout Europe, in countries as diverse as Belgium, Greece, Italy, and Czechoslovakia. The communists received over 20 percent of the vote in France, Italy, and Finland. In Eastern Europe, 20 to 50 percent of the population aligned with left-wing political parties. The Soviet Union touted the planned economy, which was seen as the wave of the future throughout the globe, not just in communist countries. After the Second World War, demobilization proceeded rapidly in America, but the Soviets maintained their level of defense spending and began to overtake the United States in a number of critical military areas.

Harry Truman may have been the most well-read president; he had an extraordinarily broad knowledge of history. Living in the White House, he intimated that he sometimes felt as if he was actually reliving history and the critical events that formed America. Although Truman had been a failure as a farmer, miner, oil promoter, and a merchant, in World War I, he served with distinction and was loved by his men. He remained a reserve officer until he became president. In the early 1930s, Truman failed to win the nomination for the governorship of Missouri and a member of Congress. He assumed his career was over, but in 1934 won a Senate seat. FDR opposed his re-election to the Senate, because of his close connection to political boss Tom Pendergast who had been indicted for fraud and income-tax evasion. Nevertheless, Truman won an improbable victory.

In the Senate, Truman chaired the special committee to oversee the defense build up and to ensure that it was done honestly and efficiently, learning concomitantly an enormous amount about the military and defense industry. He became a well-respected Senator and one of the most influential. His experience prepared him for the presidency, and he was not an accidental president, but rather a product of the American political system. Even though Truman had not been adequately prepared by FDR to assume the presidency, he was able to provide a fresh perspective to many of the crucial issues in the aftermath of World War II. In contrast to the failure of U.S. foreign policy after World War I, the Truman Administration established a wide range of successful international programs—containment of the Soviet Union, membership in the United Nations, development of the Marshall Plan, NATO, the occupation of Japan, recognition of Israel, the General Agreement on Tariffs and Trade (GATT), and creation of the modern national security organizational structure. Truman's presidency was most prolific in terms of action on foreign affairs and national security, with a level of energy that was literally breathtaking.

Truman was honest and known to say, "Three things ruin a man—power, money, and women. I never wanted power. I never had any money, and the only woman in my life is up at the house right now." He was measured against FDR, but was not as successful a public communicator, being drab and homespun at using the radio, therefore ineffective. But he was strongly committed to American tradition, religion, and principles of right and wrong, and this able character communicated itself to the American people.

After centuries of war in Europe, the U.S. took the lead in establishing the rule of law as a guide to world behavior. Previously, foreign countries could not rely on international law or legal relations with each other. Laws and agreements were frequently violated with little or no sanctions or consequences for the violator. In fact, the advantage generally accrued to the aggressor who could use the element of surprise without suffering any considerable dishonor or fear of legal action.

Truman appointed George Marshall as his secretary of state, the first career soldier to hold that post. It was one of the best and most important decisions of his presidency and provided him with critical international experience. Marshall's leadership in World War II enabled him to quickly discern what was important from the insignificant, which made him invaluable in America's new global responsibilities.

Truman and his advisor George Kennan formulated the policy of containment, which guided American foreign policy for the next forty years, eventually leading to the demise of the Soviet Union. In the summer of 1947, Kennan introduced the concept in the journal *Foreign Affairs*. The basic principle was to counter Soviet force wherever it appeared or encroached until it collapsed, stopped, or moderated. A network of worldwide bases and a system of foreign aid were established to implement the strategy. Kennan warned that any sign the United States is exhibiting "indecision, disunity, and internal disintegration" would have "an exhilarating effect on the whole Communist movement." He said the United States needed to create "among the people of the world generally the impression of a country which knows what it wants, which is coping successfully with the problems of its internal life and with the responsibilities of a World Power, and which has a spiritual vitality capable of holding its own among the major ideological currents of the time." His thinking was prophetic. Eight countries in Europe and two in Asia became communist between 1945 and 1949, but in the next twenty-five years from 1949 to 1974 only two—North Vietnam and Cuba—turned communist.

Dean Acheson worked with the president to secure aid from Congress for Greece, where the British were pulling out due a lack of funding and resources—England's economy was at a standstill. The resulting speech to Congress became known as the Truman Doctrine, making it United States policy to support free people resisting aggression and subjugation. This strategy was an historic departure from traditional American foreign policy and placed the U.S. squarely in the path of Soviet expansion.

Established in April 1949, the North Atlantic Treaty Organization (NATO) was the first U.S. peacetime military alliance made since the signing of the Constitution. This organization was formed to counter the Soviet threat to Western Europe.

After World War II, the League of Nations was regarded as ineffective in its role as an international governing body and failed to act as a prophylactic in the events leading to the war. In 1944 and 1945, conferences in Washington, D.C., and San Francisco developed a framework for establishing the United Nations (UN), focusing in particular on mechanisms for enforcing key international decisions. The second conference in San Francisco began shortly after FDR's death with the strong support of President Truman, who worked hard to ensure early Senate approval of the treaty establishing the UN, which was passed by an 89-2 vote. Truman supported the passage of the Universal Declaration of Human Rights and won Security Council approval of sanctions against North Korea.

The Great Depression, the Smoot-Hawley Tariffs, and the failure of the League of Nations spurred the major trading nations to create GATT in April 1947. By supporting GATT, the Truman Administration was reversing a century of American protectionism. FDR's Secretary of

State Cordell Hull emphasized that countries embracing free trade had been allies in the war. World trade did not begin to return to the level of the late 1920s until the completion of GATT. As tariff reductions were phased in during the 1950s, world trade grew explosively, encouraging the spread of democracy to Europe and parts of Asia. After the implementation of GATT, exports grew twice as fast as the world economy and the volume of world trade doubled every ten years.[5]

The success of GATT in the 1950s gave participants the confidence to make additional reductions in the Kennedy Round in the 1960s, the Tokyo Round in the 1970s, and the Uruguay Round in the late 1980s and early 1990s. In 1995, the World Trade Organization was established and world trade rules were extended to services, intellectual property, technology, and other new areas. By the end of the millennium, over 150 countries had joined this organization that so effectively had placed the world economy on a sound footing.

In 1944, the Bretton Woods accords established the rules for commercial and financial relations among the world's major industrial nations. The International Monetary Fund (IMF) was given authority over the major economic policies of member nations. The World Bank was provided with billions of dollars to lend governments around the globe. Bretton Woods instituted fixed, but adjustable exchange rates subject to IMF approval (a restriction that was never enforced). The world monetary system was pegged to the dollar, and became a flexible, gold-based system. American leadership of the Bretton Woods system delivered economic growth, low unemployment, and stable prices, with Japan being the most dramatic success story.[6]

In July 1947, Congress passed the National Security Act, placing control of the armed forces firmly in the civilian Department of Defense, setting up the Central Intelligence Agency, combining various intelligence functions, and creating the National Security Council to give the president expert advice on defense and foreign affairs. This law created the modern national security organizational structure. In a sharp break from the past, Truman insisted that a civilian agency, not the military, control the future development of the atomic bomb.

Basic to support for the Marshall Plan was fear that—without U.S.

aid and intervention—starvation, bloodshed, and chaos would occur in Europe. Industrial Europe was disintegrating and rural Europe could not sell its food, because there was nothing to buy in exchange. Economies of the European victors in the war shrunk by more than a fifth of what they had been before the war, while the losers declined by a half or more, regressing back to economic levels not seen since the turn of the century. Winter 1947 was one of the worst in memory; in the streets of Europe people were dying of starvation. There was fear of Soviet intervention if America came to Europe's aid. Marshall complained, "The patient is sinking while the doctors deliberate."

When Marshall announced his plan at a 1947 Harvard commencement, it received little notice by the press, but the British and French seized the opportunity and called a conference of European nations. Stalin prohibited the Soviet Union and satellite states such as Poland and Czechoslovakia from participating in the conference, or in the plan. In the United States, the left opposed the Marshall Plan as American imperialism. Conservatives opposed it as a government handout and foreign entanglement. The continued deterioration of the political situation in Europe, however, resulted in passage of the Marshall Plan by Congress almost a year later in April 1948. America lent or gave 2.4 percent of its Gross Domestic Product to Europe to carry out what is considered one of America's most effective foreign policy initiatives and greatest government successes.[7] Marshall Plan assistance was approximately 5 percent of most recipient's national incomes and the equivalent of hundreds of billions of dollars (in 2000 dollars). Much of the money sent to Europe was actually used to purchase industrial commodities and agricultural goods from the United States. Within six years, Western European economies surpassed the record of recovery during the entire period from the end of World War I through the Depression. The Marshall Plan was the "most daring and constructive venture in peacetime international relations the world has ever seen." European industrial production was up over 60 percent, steel production almost doubled, and aluminum and cement production were up over two-thirds from 1947. West Germany's transformation was described as an economic miracle.[8]

After World War II, Chinese Nationalist leader Chiang Kai-shek had been on the verge of eradicating communist Chinese forces in that country, but General George Marshall, sent to broker a peace, insisted that he halt his efforts at the end of 1945. At the time, even the Soviets recognized the Nationalists as the legitimate government of China. American popular opinion opposed risking another war to aid the Nationalist Chinese.[9] Chiang was not well-liked even though he was a staunch ally. Some American diplomats wanted to give the untried communists a shot at power. The State Department thought Chiang was a major obstacle to the peaceful settlement of differences between the two sides. Marshall obtained an agreement between the two parties, but the communists backed out at the last minute. Over time, the communists were able to re-group and mount a sustained offensive. Chiang was forced from the mainland and evacuated to the island of Taiwan, where he was protected by United States naval power. Mao Tse-tung's declaration of the People's Republic of China meant that communist control extended to a third of the world's population and a quarter of its land space. Americans soon accepted the doctrine that there was a worldwide communist conspiracy, a belief that would guide foreign policy over the next few decades and which failed to recognize the differences between the Soviet Union, China, North Korea, and North Vietnam. The Chinese Nationalist defeat was stunning and led to widespread recriminations in the United States: Who allowed Mao, the puppet of Stalin, to defeat Chiang Kai-shek and his Nationalists? Who "lost China"?

By contrast, the occupation of Japan was seen as an outstanding success. American aid and strategy may even have been too effective. The Japanese economic miracle that followed World War II resulted in high quality manufacturing products in the 1960s and 1970s. Under General Douglas MacArthur's stewardship, Japan emerged as a one-party democracy with a dynamic market economy. War crime trials led to the conviction of the country's war leaders. The education system was overhauled, religious liberties expanded, women empowered, trade unions introduced, secret police abolished, and a free press established.

Truman was a strong supporter of the establishment of the State of Israel, which became an extremely popular issue with the belated public exposure of the Nazis' Holocaust and with the long history of anti-Semitism in Europe. Arab groups and nations believed they were being forced to pay for the crimes of Hitler. The United Nations narrowly approved the partition of Palestine and the formation of a new country, but then Truman changed course and called for a trusteeship over Palestine. George Marshall and others strongly argued for a go-slow approach on the Israeli-Palestine issue. Nonetheless, as a result of Truman's personal commitment, the United States was the first to recognize the new Jewish state. For more than half a century, Israel was the only democracy in the Middle East.

The effort to deal with communist aggression dominated the last year of Truman's first term and his entire second term. The Berlin airlift began in 1948, followed by the Soviet Union's explosion of an atomic bomb in 1949 and the Korean War in 1950. To survive, Berlin needed 8,000 tons of supplies a day. The initial airlift only brought in slightly over 1,000 tons, but was ramped up to 5,000 tons by the end of the year and the necessary 8,000 tons by April 1949. Stalin would have blocked an effort at land relief, so Truman developed the appropriate air strategy: the airlift was a clear U.S. victory. On May 12, 1949, the blockade ended after 277,804 flights and the delivery of 2.3 billion pounds of food and supplies.

During his first term in office, the atomic bomb gave Truman a clear advantage in world diplomacy. Truman mistakenly thought the Soviets would be unable to build a bomb and others agreed. In September 1949, when the Americans discovered the first evidence the Soviets indeed had the bomb, it weakened Truman's hand and strengthened communism across the globe, leading to aggression in Korea and other places.

Considerable controversy surrounded building the hydrogen or "fusion" bomb. Most of the nuclear community was opposed to it, with the notable exception of the project's chief scientist, Edward Teller. Truman asked, "Can the Russians do it?" When told they could, he concluded, "In that case, we have no choice." From the perspective of history, it would have been a mistake to follow the nuclear community's opinion, because Andrei Sakharov, inventor of the Russian fusion bomb, later said that Stalin would have perceived U.S. failure to proceed as a deception or sign of weakness.

Truman also proposed an ambitious domestic agenda. Only days after the Japanese surrender, Truman sent his first postwar message to Congress calling for a 21-point domestic program, including expanded unemployment compensation, an increase in the minimum wage, tax reform, crop insurance for farmers, and federal aid to farmers. A coalition of southern Democrats and Republicans, however, stymied much of his agenda. Throughout Truman's tenure as president, there were union strikes and labor violence. The coal, rail, and steel unions all went on strike. Truman forced settlement of the railroad strike, threatening to draft the strikers. The actual settlement was reached as he was addressing the Congress urging drastic action, a dramatic event critics erroneously concluded was staged.

The rapid press of events seemed to overwhelm Truman. His popularity plummeted, a common joke being to discuss a policy initiated by FDR and then end with the punch line, "What would Truman do if he were alive?" A Truman beer was considered to be one with no head. In the 1946 election the Republicans swept and controlled the Congress for the first time since 1932. After the election, another coal strike occurred; Truman took action to have the union held in contempt, a decisive and popular action.

The epidemic of strikes led to the passage, over President Truman's veto, of the Taft-Hartley Act outlawing the closed shop and secondary boycotts, making unions liable for breach of contract, and curbing and requiring disclosure of their political activities. The president was given the power to interrupt a strike by calling for a "cooling off period." The legislation leveled the playing field and drastically reduced the work time lost to strikes.

Congress passed the Employment Act of 1946 which set full employment as a national goal and established the Council on Economic Advisors and the Joint Economic Committee of the Congress. For the first time, this law made it the responsibility of the government to deal with the business cycle and established full employment as a national goal. It was based on John Maynard Keynes' macroeconomic policies that encouraged government to seek full employment and described how supply and demand and the federal budget deficit affect the national economy. Under Keynes' theories, the government could increase employment through spending increases or tax cuts. Even though there was an almost universal expectation that the U.S. and the world would revert to the Depression-era economy, the 1950s and 1960s saw stable and rapid growth in the United States, Western Europe, and Japan, a phenomenon many economists deemed a vindication of Keynes theories.

During the 1930s and early 1940s, the enormous expansion of the federal government had begun to spawn a widening array of scandals. The Reconstruction Finance Corporation became a bastion of influence peddling. The Bureau of Internal Revenue, whose top officials were all patronage appointees, including the regional and deputy regional directors, became a hotbed of bribery for tax evasion. The scandals in the Truman Administration became a campaign issue. Truman was forced to fire his attorney general for obstructing Internal Revenue investigations.

At one point, Truman's popular support fell so far it was considered a national joke that "To err is Truman." The Democratic powerbrokers, particularly FDR's New Dealers, were going to dump him. At the Democratic convention, Truman called the Republican Congress back into session and, when not much legislation resulted, he denounced and ran against the "do nothing Congress." Truman waged his famous whistle stop campaign aboard the *Ferdinand Magellan,* the special presidential Pullman car, and traveled nearly 22,000 miles.

Based on FDR's previous efforts, pollsters and pundits concluded that the actual campaign was a mere ritual and the leader on Labor Day would win. The Republican nominee, Tom Dewey, was decisively ahead in all the September polls and many polling firms ceased questioning voters. George Gallup gave up polling the race, because he believed it was a waste of money. Huge crowds came to Truman's rallies and demanded, "Give 'em hell, Harry!" Later he would say, "I never gave anyone hell. I just told the truth and they thought it was hell." Dewey ran a positive, reform campaign, rarely criticizing Truman, running as if he had the election won. Some people expected Dewey to serve four terms like FDR, leaving in 1965. Newsweek ran a poll of the 50 leading political pundits and not one picked Truman, who saw the poll and proclaimed, "I know every one of these 50 fellows. There isn't one of them has enough sense to pound sand in a rat hole."

Almost all the biggest and most influential newspapers endorsed Dewey, including *The New York Times* and *The Wall Street Journal.* By running a mechanical, aloof, and issueless campaign, however, Dewey lost. Truman's victory was a heavy blow to the prestige of the polls and the news media. In one of the most famous photographs in American political history, the *Chicago Tribune* went to press on election night with the lead headline "Dewey Defeats Truman," which the newly elected president hoisted high the next day. Few of the big contributors believed Truman would win, so he had few obligations to pay off and appointed a stellar cabinet in his second term.

After his election as president, Congress obliged Truman by raising the minimum wage from 40 to 75 cents an hour, extending Social Security to 10 million new beneficiaries, passing a housing law for low-income families, expanding water-control, irrigation and hydroelectric facilities, and increasing support for farmers.[10]

During the Truman and Eisenhower administrations, federal debt as a percentage of the Gross National Product was more than cut in half.[11] Both presidents believed the biggest Cold War threat was that the communists would cause the nation to spend so much on defense that government expenditures would bankrupt the country or budget deficits would cause inflation, which would damage the nation's economy. Even the military feared high defense spending and budget deficits because the strength of the nation was so dependent on its industrial capacity. The military, on its own initiative, sought to hold spending to $13 billion in 1950. Conservative Republicans in Congress cut defense spending so much that the budget surplus reached 4 percent of the economy in 1948.

The Korean War dominated Truman's second term. Korea was a letdown for the American people, who expected the peace to be maintained. When war broke out, America was again caught unprepared and the war's execution rekindled the sense of betrayal that had arisen from Pearl Harbor, FDR's handling of Yalta, and communist aggression at the end of World War II. The attack by North Korea came almost as a complete surprise, but that should not have been the situation. The United States refused to supply the belligerent South Korean government with military aid; Mao-Tse-tung encouraged North Korea to attack South Korea in order to make it imperative for Stalin and the Soviet Union to give him and China advanced technology and military assistance.[12] Intelligence officers in Seoul picked up a number of reports of an imminent invasion. The U.S. military, however, did not react. The U.S. was able to secure UN support, because Stalin was boycotting to protest UN refusal to unseat the Nationalist Chinese government. North Korean tanks rolled into Seoul, the capital, and moved far south. At first, only a small number of American troops were available to fight in South Korea, most of them with no combat experience. General Douglas MacArthur quickly reversed the direction of the conflict and appeared to gain the upper hand, promising to get the troops home by Christmas. Opposed by the Pentagon, MacArthur's landing at Inchon was brilliant, in only two weeks Seoul was retaken and half of the North Korean army surrounded.

At MacArthur's urging, a decision was made to attack beyond the original 38th parallel. After the success at Inchon, Truman and the Joint Chiefs did little to curb MacArthur, who rapidly advanced to the Yalu River on the China border but then was attacked by tens of thousands of Chinese troops hiding in the hills and forests. After Thanksgiving, when the Chinese entered the war, the Americans were once again surprised, although MacArthur had been warned by intelligence operatives to expect a massive attack. As the Americans beat a speedy retreat under the weight of 300,000 Chinese (a force which MacArthur had erroneously estimated to be 30,000), the credibility of the government suffered another blow. The troops performed admirably, with part of the American force able to hold around the 38th Parallel, but the 1st Marine Division was cut off and surrounded. Eventually, they were able to break out, a legendary operation which resulted in two memorable quotes. When the Marines were forced back, General Oliver Smith proclaimed,

"Gentlemen, we're not retreating. We are just attacking in a different direction." Colonel Lewis Puller remarked: "The enemy is in front of us, behind us, to the left of us, and to the right of us. They won't escape *this* time."

MacArthur was in a difficult position—expected to fight a war as a limited engagement and not alienate the allies of the American effort. In effect, his hands were tied and his war strategy became ineffective. After the death of General Walker in a jeep accident, General Matthew Ridgway assumed command of the Eighth Army in Korea and restored its fighting spirit, turning around the war once again. Instead of being faced with an evacuation from all of Korea, the Eighth Army returned to the offensive. Truman wisely turned down MacArthur's pleas to use atomic weapons. MacArthur frequently interjected himself into foreign policy and troop morale suffered after the Chinese attack—it was Ridgway's efforts that turned the tide. On a number of occasions, MacArthur disobeyed instructions, which eventually resulted in his being fired by President Truman for insubordination. MacArthur disobeyed the order, for example, that only South Korean troops should approach the Chinese border; he bombed too close to Chinese territory; and he sent letters to Members of Congress opposing the president's policies. Truman's decision was unpopular and harshly criticized by Republicans, resulting in a public uproar. MacArthur came back to America to a delirious reception, addressed Congress, and then was treated to a ticker tape parade in New York by millions of people, estimated to be more than the number attending Eisenhower's parade after World War II. The Pentagon stayed behind Truman, and MacArthur's popularity waned, particularly as he toured the country attacking the president while wearing a military uniform. He tried to run for president, but his campaign never took hold. The Korean War continued, to undermine Truman's presidency, but Churchill returned as prime minister and praised Truman's tenure as president by saying, "you more than any other man have saved Western civilization." Only two other students ever surpassed MacArthur's academic and athletic achievements at West Point, one of them being Robert E. Lee. MacArthur and his father were the first father-son team to receive the Medal of Honor.

The Korean War severely weakened the Democrats. It was widely assumed that conservative Robert Taft would represent the Republicans, supplanting the Dewey, moderate wing of the party. Taft, who died a year after he lost the nomination, was an isolationist and many Republicans were looking for an internationalist such as General Dwight Eisenhower (1890–1969), as well as a likely winner. There was a defining moment on the floor of the convention, preparing the Republican Party for the ascendancy of the conservative west and south, ironically coming from the Midwestern Senator Everett Dirksen seeking to get the attention of "all our good friends from the Eastern seacoast." Looking directly at New York Governor Tom Dewey he defiantly proclaimed, "we followed you before and you took us down the path of defeat." His remarks would echo down the years to a younger generation of conservative Republicans. Tom Dewey was, however, instrumental in having conservative Senator Richard Nixon put on the ticket.

Eisenhower had done little for the rank-and-file Republican voter and his views on many issues were largely unknown. He had almost no political campaign experience and initially seemed a fish out of water. "Ike," however, quickly adapted his style to the political arena, and his competitive spirit and likeability proved extremely valuable. He conducted a barnstorming campaign traveling over 30,000 miles by air and 20,000 miles by rail, visiting 232 towns in 45 states. Eisenhower won by a wide margin, promising to go to Korea to try to end the conflict. He outraged Truman by refusing to defend Marshall against attacks by Joe McCarthy. The two had strained relationships after the exchange and subsequently never worked together.

Eisenhower concluded a truce in Korea despite intense objections from members of his own party, one of his greatest achievements. Starting out with a large deficit due to military commitments made by President Truman, including the Korean War, Eisenhower steered a tricky course between the insatiable demands of the military and a tax-cutting Congress. While many conservative Republicans demanded that he slash spending, congressional Democrats urged him to increase military spending, claiming a bomber gap and then a missile gap. Eisenhower responded, "The relationship between military and economic strength is intimate and indivisible." He prepared the nation for a Cold War of indefinite duration without running up a large deficit. He avoided exaggerating near-term threats and expensive domestic initiatives. After the Korean War, he and the Congress reduced taxes by ending temporary war levies. Eisenhower warned of the dangers of inflation and paid for high-priority military initiatives by eliminating low-priority programs and instituting economies in procurement. He expanded atomic weapons programs at the expense of conventional forces, for example, even when this policy precipitated the resignation of General Matthew Ridgway.

The last president to come out of the nineteenth century, Eisenhower had genuine rural, farm roots. His family was deeply religious and Mennonite. Yet, he had administered probably the most complex operation in human history—D-Day. He was a highly popular commander, generally opposed privilege and supported his troops, frequently visiting and personally encouraging them. As he had done during the war, he cultivated the press corps and held press conferences almost every other week (193 in all) where he used his position to command the headlines and the national debate, while at the same time downplaying issues he believed were unimportant. Eisenhower's was the last administration when traditional American values were almost universally revered, the family accorded deference, patriotism almost unanimously honored, religion highly valued, and business success emulated not envied.

As head of the Allied forces in World War II and mastermind of the D-Day invasion, Eisenhower demonstrated organizational brilliance: "Organization cannot make a genius out of an incompetent. On the other hand, disorganization can lead to disaster."[13] Eisenhower developed the modern organizational structure for the presidency, including a chief of staff, national security advisor, congressional liaison, and science advisor. It worked so well that some of his critics claimed that his tenure proved the nation could do fine without a president.[14]

During World War II, the news media were put under censorship. The Alien Registration Act enabled people to be arrested, not for what they said or did, but for membership in an association in which the avowed purpose was overthrow of the government or revolution. In this suspicious environment, the biggest story of the postwar era was that of the mean-spirited Senator Joseph McCarthy who, in a Lincoln's Day speech, claimed to have a list of 205 known communists in the State Department.

Transcripts of KGB cables and other materials released at the end of the Cold War revealed Soviet espionage to be far-reaching. There is no evidence, however, that McCarthy identified any new subversives or brought to light any spying activities not already known to American authorities. McCarthy's charges came long after the communist infiltration had done most of its damage and during a time when the communist party was in rapid decline.[15] McCarthy attacked war hero George Marshall and Secretary of State Dean Acheson. He traveled throughout the country making accusations which poisoned the political environment. The press corps aided his efforts by trumpeting his accusations, but not researching or even critically examining the allegations. As a result of television hearings, McCarthy became a celebrity. Broadcasters shied away from confronting him, because he encouraged supporters to contact sponsors and demanded that they drop broadcasters who opposed him.

Reasons for the influence of McCarthy are complex but probably tie back into Depression and World War II issues. The New Deal constituted the greatest expansion of government authority in American history during peacetime, circumscribing some of the freedoms and liberties (particularly property rights many Americans believed to be part of the original Constitution) and creating considerable resentment and bitterness. This was exhibited in the hatred and animosity towards FDR, particularly in the upper economic classes and among conservatives. Even until World War II, America was, relatively speaking, a free and open society and an island removed from the troubled, war-ridden European-Asian continents. Communist infiltration of American society definitely impacted the openness of American culture. The Soviet Union developed one of the most successful espionage webs in history involving key U.S. scientists and officials. When this infiltration resulted in compromising national secrets related to the atomic bomb, the effect was devastating.

Democrats were embittered that McCarthy was successful in branding them soft on communism, a tactic that Republicans resorted to often over the next several decades. Yet, the FDR and Truman Administrations had not heeded the warnings about subversives nor did they investigate with any vigor until it was too late. The spying and various leaks were among the most treacherous episodes in American history. Truman's loyalty program, which resulted in over 1,000 dismissals and 5,000 resignations, didn't take hold until 1947. Democrats claim they were reluctant to investigate due to the fear of endangering intelligence sources, but the Soviet Union was already aware that its communications and intelligence community were compromised.

Giving nuclear secrets to Stalin, as was done by Klaus Fuchs and Julius Rosenberg, was certainly the most catastrophic compromise of national security in American history, possibly ensuring the enslavement of a large part of Europe for decades. With nuclear parity, the United States was unable to take pre-emptive action to stop Soviet suppression of uprisings in Eastern Europe. It was fortuitous that Stalin, widely regarded as less than fully sane (a madman according to Nikita Khrushchev), did not resort to the use of this stolen weapon. The level of paranoia at the time is best illustrated by the tragic fate of a Japanese fishing vessel that inadvertently wandered too close to a H-bomb test and much of the crew was radiated and at least one man experienced a harrowing death. The episode was considered a Soviet plot to embarrass America. A special panel suspended the security clearance for the leading nuclear scientist, J. Robert Oppenheimer, destroying his career. Subsequently, little was discovered in the Soviet archives that would support this action, although he was arguably guilty of insubordination.

The use of the term McCarthyism became a tactic of left-wing politicians to deflect an inquiry or investigation, usually by conservatives. Investigative journalism was in short supply and many of McCarthy's reckless charges went without challenge. McCarthy was skillful at manipulating the press, visiting small towns to make his allegations where local reporters and journalists from the wires would not check the charges. Much deference was accorded him, because he was a senator. The press became an almost willing accessory, with few national reporters investigating the story. McCarthy tried to play the "good old boy," giving the press charges in time to make newspaper deadlines and supplying materials at slow times such as Sundays. McCarthy's momentum was derailed by Army special counsel Joseph Welch whose performance at the congressional hearings unraveled the Senator's position and led to his censure by the Senate. Edward R. Murrow produced a television show exposing McCarthy as a fraud, which was a major turning point. President Eisenhower also played an important role, but he believed that confronting McCarthy directly would only give him more publicity and credibility:

> With considerable cunning and in great secrecy he directed his friends in the Senate to censure McCarthy, while using his press chief Jim Haggerty, to orchestrate the publicity. The process culminated in December 1954 and is perhaps the best example of the "hidden hand" style of leadership which Eisenhower delights to employ and which research brought to light many years after his death.
>
> Eisenhower was the most successful of America's twentieth-century presidents, and the decade when he ruled (1953–1961) the most prosperous in American, and indeed world, history. His presidency was surrounded by mythology, much of which he deliberately contrived himself. He sought to give the impression that he was a mere constitutional monarch, who delegated decisions to his colleagues and indeed to Congress, and who was anxious to spend the maximum amount of time playing golf. His stratagem worked. His right-wing rival for Republican leadership, Senator Robert Taft, sneered, "I really think he should have been a golf pro." His first biographer claimed that the "unanimous consensus" of "journalists and academics, pundits and prophets, the national community of intellectuals and critics" had been that Eisenhower's conduct of the presidency had been "unskillful and his definition of it inac-

curate . . . [he] elected to leave his nation to fly on automatic pilot." He was seen as well-meaning, intellectually limited, ignorant, inarticulate, often weak and always lazy.

The reality was quite different. . . . Eisenhower worked very much harder than anyone, including close colleagues, supposed. A typical day started at 7:30 AM, by which time he had read *The New York Times, Herald Tribune,* and *Christian Science Monitor,* and finished close to midnight (he often worked afterwards). Many of his appointments (especially those dealing with parts of defense and foreign policy) were deliberately left off of lists given to the press. . . . Long and vital meetings with the State and Defense secretaries, the head of the CIA and other figures, took place unrecorded and in secret, before the formal sessions of the National Security Council. The running of defense and foreign policy, far from being bureaucratic and inflexible, as his critics supposed, in fact took place in accordance with highly efficient staff principles, contrasting strongly with the romantic anarchy of the Kennedy regime which followed. Eisenhower himself was in charge throughout.[16]

While the Gallup polls consistently rated Eisenhower first or second among presidents, polls of academic historians placed him near the bottom of the list of all presidents.[17] Norman Mailer proclaimed that the 1950s was "one of the worst decades in the history of man."[18] Similar to the efforts to discredit presidents Harding and Coolidge in the 1930s, intellectuals and academicians attempted to minimize the record of the Eisenhower Administration. The U.S. intellectual elite claimed that the nation was restless, that "the Eisenhower stock could not have been lower," and "we need to get the nation moving again."[19] Henry Kissinger came to the Nixon Administration from Harvard University with academia's near-contempt for Eisenhower, but found that he "knew more about leadership and about the realities of Washington politics than he had ever imagined when he was teaching political science up at Harvard."[20]

The decade of Eisenhower and the 1950s was one of strong economic growth, with inflation less than 2 percent, a balanced federal budget, no wars, no loss of territory, no Vietnam or Watergate, no trade deficit, no gridlock between the branches of government, no riots, the initiation of the interstate highway system, and the containment of communism. Many typical Americans believe it was the best decade of the century. While the common wisdom among academicians was that Eisenhower was lazy and a lackluster leader ill-suited for the presidency, his papers show he was firmly in command, well-informed, politically sophisticated, and a strategic genius.[21] "Eisenhower's presidency was highly competent, effective, and successful, the most so of any presidency since World War II."[22]

> Eisenhower read a huge volume of official documents and maintained a copious correspondence with high-level friends at home and abroad . . . Kennan . . . wrote that on foreign affairs Eisenhower was a "man of keen political intelligence and penetration. . . . When he spoke of such matters seriously and in a protected official circle, insights of a higher order flashed out time after time through the curious military gobbledygook, in which he was accustomed to expressing and concealing his thoughts." In fact, Eisenhower used gobbledygook, especially at press conferences, to avoid giving answers which plain English could not conceal; he often pretended ignorance for the same reason. Indeed, he was Machiavellian enough to pretend to misunderstand his own translator when dealing with difficult foreigners. Transcripts of his secret conferences show the power and lucidity of his thoughts. . . .
>
> Eisenhower concealed his gifts and activities because he thought it essential that the . . . leadership, which he recognized both America and the world needed, should be exercised by stealth. He had three quite clear principles. The first was to avoid war. Of course if Soviet Russia was bent on destroying the West, resistance must be made, and America must be strong enough to make it. But the occasions of unnecessary war (as he judged Korea) must be avoided by

clarity, firmness, caution and wisdom. In this limited aim he was successful. He ended the Korean conflict. He avoided war with China. He stamped out the Suez war in 1956, and skillfully averted another Middle-Eastern war in 1958. Of Vietnam he said: "I cannot conceive of a greater tragedy for America than to get heavily involved now in an all-out war in any of those regions." Again: "There is going to be no involvement . . . unless it is as a result of the constitutional process that is placed upon Congress to declare it." Congressional authorization; Allied support—those were the two conditions he laid down for American military involvement anywhere, and they were reflected in the Middle East and South-East Asian systems of alliances he added to NATO.[23]

One of the reasons Eisenhower hated war was because he did not believe that "limited" war was a viable concept. In war, as he understood it, the object was to destroy your enemy's power as quickly as possible with all the means at your disposal. That was his . . . guiding principle and it explains why he wound up Korea, to him a "nonsense," as quickly as he could, and why he deplored Eden's absurd Suez expedition in 1956, in which the Prime Minister personally approved the weights of bombs to be dropped on Egyptian targets.[24]

Better than anyone, Eisenhower understood the radical changes brought on by thermonuclear weapons. He abhorred war, more than anything except Nazi Germany. He rejected a preventive strike against the Soviet Union. On five occasions, he opposed using atomic bombs against China and intervention in Asia against the recommendations of virtually all of his policy apparatus.[25] The record of his leadership in the Indochina crisis is particularly instructive, "showing thinking that was hard-headed, rigorous, and informed" and a "remarkable capacity for reality testing" in contrast to the record of Lyndon Johnson in Vietnam, which showed a lack of sustained policy analysis and strategic direction and a remarkable capacity for self-deception.[26]

Eisenhower exhibited decisiveness in the Suez Canal crisis. The French had built the Canal in the nineteenth century. The British purchased a share after the local government went bankrupt. When the U.S. and Britain canceled a planned loan for the Aswan Dam (Congress declined to authorize the funding), Egyptian Prime Minister Nasser retaliated by nationalizing the Canal as a source of revenue to build the dam. The Soviet Union also offered to help fund the dam. The French and the British initiated military action to take back the Suez Canal, colluding with the Israelis to invade Egypt. Eisenhower, trying to avoid the stigma of colonialism and giving the Soviet Union the upper hand, cut off economic aid to Britain, forcing it to capitulate or face financial collapse. Nasser had closed the Canal, jeopardizing European oil supplies and the U.S. refused to fill the gap. The Security Council was circumvented for the first time to avoid a French or British veto, and a UN emergency force was sent to monitor a ceasefire. The American actions spurred the Europeans to create a common market. The vacuum left in the Middle East was filled by the Soviets, who helped pay for the dam, which in turn led to further U.S. involvement to counter the communist threat to Middle East oil.

The U-2 and Francis Gary Powers was Eisenhower's worst hour. The plane was built at the famous Lockheed Skunk Works. A number of engineering obstacles were overcome, several through development of a pressurized suit for the pilot, with the project being completed in only 88 days. The plane could fly at 80,000 feet, had a camera arc of 750 miles, and could reputedly photograph a license plate on a car on the ground. The intelligence gleaned from these flights convinced Eisenhower that the U.S. was far ahead of the Soviet Union militarily. The Soviets were outraged by the U-2 flights, but didn't have the capability to shoot the plane down. Gradually, the pilots became aware they were being tracked and that missiles were probably being shot at them. The president was not made fully aware of these concerns and continued to personally approve requests for additional missions. It is possible Eisenhower's judgment and thinking may not have been as clear after three medical crises—a heart attack in 1955, surgery for Crohn's disease in 1956, and a mild stroke in 1957. Assuming Powers had committed suicide as he was instructed and the plane had disintegrated, it seems that Eisenhower then lied about the U.S involvement and disclaimed responsibility. The Soviets had baited him and sprung the trap—producing Gary Powers and wreckage of the plane, creating an international embarrassment. Nikita Khrushchev, who had tried to be conciliatory with the Americans, felt betrayed and cancelled a planned US—USSR summit conference, a devastating blow to Eisenhower who wanted to reach an accommodation with the Soviets prior to the end of his term.[27] Khrushchev, however, who had served his apprenticeship under Stalin, was tough, cunning, and clever, not about to give Eisenhower another chance at the end of his tenure.

Eisenhower believed that the foundation of military strength was economic strength and that the Soviet goal was more to bankrupt America than to conquer it on the field of battle. Eisenhower thought the military services were trying to perpetuate a "way of life" instead of exerting fiscal restraint. Each service thought its budget was insufficient, but that the other services were receiving adequate funding. In his farewell address he gave a tribute to sound fiscal finance that was lost on his successors: "We cannot mortgage the material assets of our grandchildren without asking the loss also of their political and spiritual heritage. We want democracy to survive for all generations, not become the insolvent phantom of tomorrow."[28]

> It was Eisenhower's secret fear, in the tense atmosphere generated by the Cold War, that the government would fall into the grip of a combination of bellicose senators, over-eager brass hats, and greedy arms-suppliers. In his farewell address, broadcast on January 17 1961, he coined and popularized a new phrase: "In the councils of government, we must guard against the acquisition of influence, whether sought or unsought, by the military-industrial complex." His use of this term has often been misunderstood. Eisenhower was not condemning militarism so much as making an important economic point in a military context. Historians can trace the rise of huge executive power in the United States, accompanied by prodigious spending, through the

pre-World War One years of the Wilson administration, the vast expansion of federal and military power in 1917-1918, the revival of large-scale federal industrial projects during the New Deal, their expansion during World War Two on a gigantic and unprecedented scale, and the way to which the onset of the Cold War made a large-scale, free-spending federal government, linked to an enormous arms industry, and voracious armed forces, a permanent feature of the American system. Eisenhower's . . . principle, reflected in his private diaries and papers, was that the security of freedom throughout the world depended ultimately on the health and strength of the U.S. economy. Given time, the strength of that economy would duplicate itself in Western Europe and Japan—he could see it happening—thus spreading the burden. But the U.S. economy itself could be destroyed by intemperate spending by a greedy, over-large state, generating profligacy and inflation. He said of the military: "They don't know much about fighting inflation. This country could choke itself to death piling up military expenditures just as surely as it can defeat itself by not spending enough for protection." Or again: "There is no defense of any country which busts it own economy."[29]

Eisenhower opposed efforts of the armed forces to achieve clear superiority that would have led to federal deficits and a weaker economy. "He believed that a healthy economy was as critical to national defense as a powerful military."[30]

Every gun that is made, every warship launched, every rocket fired, signifies, in the final sense, a theft from those who hunger and are not fed, those who are cold and not clothed. This world in arms is not spending money alone. It is spending the sweat of its laborers, the genius of its scientists, the hopes of its children. We pay for a single fighter plane with a half-million bushels of wheat. We pay for a single destroyer with new homes that could have housed more than eight thousand people. This is not a way of life at all, in any true sense. Under the cloud of threatening war, it is humanity hanging from a cross of iron.[31]

More than any other leader, Eisenhower spoke out about the cost of the arms race. In 1960, he criticized all of the candidates for president, even Republicans Richard Nixon and Nelson Rockefeller, for proposing deficit spending and purchasing new weapons systems without military justification.[32] Eisenhower used tough rhetoric on the military-industrial complex and to keep America strong economically, but his policies were sometimes half-measures. In the latter part of his second term, America's energy surplus had begun to vanish; its economy weakened considerably.

Eisenhower was equally opposed to reckless spending in the domestic field. He was not opposed to deficit finance as a temporary device to fight recession. In 1958, to overcome such a dip, he ran up a $9.4 billion deficit, the largest so far for the U.S. government in peacetime. But that was an emergency. Normally he ran balanced budgets. What he was most opposed to was a massive, permanent increase in federal commitments. He put holding down inflation before social security because he held that price stability was ultimately the only reliable form of social security. . . . His nightmare was a combination of excessive defense spending and a runaway welfare machine—a destructive conjunction that became reality in the late 1960s. While he was still in charge, federal spending as a percentage of GNP, and with it inflation, was held to a manageable figure, despite all the pressures. . . . By the end of the 1960s this prosperity was radiating widely all over the world, as the pump-priming by U.S. economic aid took effect. The world was more secure and stable too. In 1950-2, the risk of a major war was acute. By the end of the decade a certain stability had been reached, lines drawn, rules worked out, alliances and commitments settled across the globe. Perhaps only Eisenhower himself knew which of those commitments were real, but the Soviets and Chinese had learned that it was safest to assume that they all were. Thus the containment policy had been successfully applied. Militant Marxism-Leninism, which had expanded rapidly in the 1940s in both Europe and Asia, found its impetuous march slowed to a crawl or even halted entirely. These were tremendous achievements.[33]

The importance of Eisenhower's insights on the economy was lost to the next generation of leaders. While the structural budget deficit was essentially zero in his second term, it climbed to 1 percent of the Gross National Product in the 1960s, almost 2 percent in the 1970s, and an incredible 3 percent in the 1980s, thereby, as he said, mortgaging America's future. This deficit spending was attributable to domestic spending. Medicare, Medicaid, food stamps, college loans and dozens of other programs were created, thus increasing U.S. spending on social programs from 22 percent to 56 percent of federal outlays by the middle of the 1990s, while defense spending plummeted from 62 percent to 22 percent. Although Eisenhower opposed large new domestic programs with some limited exceptions such as the interstate highway system, he was no mean-spirited opponent of government assistance. He agreed to an increase in the minimum wage to a dollar an hour, expansion of unemployment compensation, and adding 10 million social security recipients to the rolls and increasing benefits. George Meany, head of the AFL-CIO, exclaimed, "American labor has never had it so good." By not opposing or seeking to dismantle New Deal programs, Eisenhower in effect ratified them and ended the public controversy over whether these programs should continue in existence. With increased mobility uprooting many traditions and white collar jobs exceeding the number of blue collar jobs for the first time, the economy experienced an undercurrent of enormous change in the 1950s. Eisenhower's stable domestic policy enabled America to thrive from these challenges.

Eisenhower worked to end the last vestiges of segregation in the federal government, moved to end segregation on the Washington transit system, got the local phone company to hire African-American telephone operators, and worked to end segregation in public facilities such as restaurants, movie theaters, and hotels. He banned segregation on interstate trains and buses and in terminals. In 1957, a civil rights bill was enacted creating a civil rights commission with broad investigatory powers and authorized to bring voting rights cases, a triumph for both President Eisenhower and Senate Majority Leader Lyndon Johnson.

Eisenhower's refusal, however, to take strong public stands on civil rights and McCarthyism gave solace to segregationists and witch-hunters, some of whom justified their actions by claiming he was secretly on their side. He never, for example, said that he thought segregation was morally wrong or publicly endorsed the Supreme Court's civil rights decisions. During his presidency, Eisenhower experienced disappointments, such as his ineffective Cuba policy leading to Fidel Castro's takeover of that country. Castro was more a revolutionary than a Marxist. By ignoring him and then not accommodating his interests, the United States allowed him to fall into the lap of the Soviet Union.[35]

The Soviet satellite Sputnik shocked America probably more than any event in the second half of the twentieth century, created a public hysteria, and resulted in more spending on the military and education. During the early and middle 1950s, Americans would mock announcements from Moscow about new inventions or discoveries. Almost invariably, it was widely known that someone in the United States had long ago developed or fabricated the touted device or process. In some cases, the so-called inventions were widely used in everyday American life. The Soviet satellite was a crushing setback and almost everyone was seeking a scapegoat

Wernher von Braun, a German immigrant, was the leading expert in the world on rocketry, having developed the V-2, which was the first object to reach outer space and inflicted terror on London in World War II. Hitler had personally supervised the effort and contributed the concept of having a sensitive fuse to trigger the explosion on impact, maximizing the "annihilation" as he termed it. At the end of the war, von Braun was working on a missile that could reach the American East Coast. He and his team of 100 scientists escaped to the American army, because they believed the U.S. the best society to pursue their technological dreams. Stalin was outraged—he had pressed his army to capture the German rocket scientists. The Germans at the time were far ahead of anyone else, with the U.S. a distant third behind the Soviet Union.

Von Braun then led the U.S. effort to put a satellite in space, but his team was generally neglected and under funded. The Pentagon civilian experts put their bets on a Navy rocket and delayed the launch of von Braun's Redstone rocket by several years. Von Braun's team actually put a rocket in space that could have carried a satellite, but he was barred by his superiors from putting such a device on top of the rocket. Initially, Eisenhower didn't believe in putting men in space or in exploration of the moon. The Soviet leadership understood the psychological value of being first in space with a satellite. The U-2 changed Eisenhower's perspective, because he saw the advantage for photo reconnaissance, but his administration was caught off guard by the Soviet launch and was slow to respond, even labeling Sputnik a "useless hunk of iron." Sputnik undermined the Administration's public statements that there was not a missile gap and the U.S. was militarily far ahead of the Soviets. The Navy's rocket, the first American test, blew-up on the launch pad, badly damaging America's credibility. The rocket lifted four feet off the pad, where the engine failed, and the entire missile system toppled and exploded. America became the butt of jokes around the world. Finally, von Braun's Army team was given their chance and made a successful launch.

The National Defense Education Act was passed to provide federal aid for improved teaching in science, mathematics, and foreign languages. After a series of additional Soviet firsts, including the first man to orbit the earth, America leapfrogged the Soviets and put a man on the moon, something no other nation was able to achieve. In hindsight, Sputnik may have been more about the Soviet's ability to leverage rocket technology than inherent technical supremacy. Eisenhower wisely resisted pleas for shelters, more bombers, missiles, and satellites. With his military background, he was the only man with the authority to pull off such pleadings.

Eisenhower's most lasting contribution was the interstate highway system. As early as 1919, he had been in a cross-country tour advocating improved roads, particularly as a means of increasing the army's mobility. In that era, it took 62 days to cross the country on the treacherous highways and primitive U.S. transportation system. Eisenhower proposed today's interstate highway system as part of an effort to improve the defense capability of the country. Perhaps no other government program has had as wide an impact on the nation's economy. Eisenhower justified the expenditure as necessary for public safety, to alleviate congestion, and to enable evacuation in the event of a nuclear attack. In the proposal to build the system he noted: "The amount of concrete poured to form these roadways would build eighty Hoover dams or six sidewalks to the moon. To build them, bulldozers and shovels would move enough dirt and rock to bury all of Connecticut two feet deep. More than any single action of the government since the end of the war, this would change the face of America." Eisenhower was never prone to exaggeration. Upon completion, Eisenhower could have finished the trip that took 62 days in 1919 in just 72 hours, a 95 percent reduction in time.

Presidents Truman and Eisenhower ended the cycle of war in Europe. They developed the policies, organizations, and structures that would eventually lead to the demise of communism, and America's first successful transition after a major conflict. They kept the nation on a steady course after two of its most difficult periods—the Great Depression and World War II. They provided outstanding leadership that could have been a model for future presidents.

12

Broadcasting
and Civil Society

NEWS SATISFIES AN INNATE HUMAN INSTINCT to know what is occurring beyond one's direct experience. Anthropologists, historians, and sociologists report that across the cultural range, people share the same definition of what is news. The desire for news may be more intense in America, because its settlers satisfied strong drives to go beyond everyday experience by their decisions to migrate across the ocean to the North American continent. In his five-and-a-half years as a prisoner of war in Hanoi, John McCain missed receiving the news as much as he missed lack of comfort or food.[1]

The news and press played a critical role in colonial America, exemplified by Benjamin Franklin's printing business. Although there was little opposition to the passage of the sugar duties by the British Parliament, the enactment of the Stamp Act precipitated widespread popular opposition, because it was a tax on the press, on communications, and on public speech—the lifeblood of colonial America. When the British suggested the use of military force to compel compliance, Benjamin Franklin wisely predicted such a force would not work, he said, "Suppose a military force is sent into America. They will find nobody in arms. What are they then to do? They cannot force a man to take stamps who chooses to do without them. They will not find a rebellion; they may indeed make one."

Pamphlets and famous pamphleteers such as Thomas Paine played a crucial role in mobilizing support for the American Revolution. In the early 1800s, pamphlets evolved into sheets or newspapers that were highly partisan and politically charged, engaging in mudslinging, exposés, and political vilification. In the 1830s, Alexis de Tocqueville described the critical role of newspapers in developing public opinion and strengthening civil society:

> When men are no longer united amongst themselves by firm and lasting ties, it is impossible to obtain the co-operation of any great number of them, unless you can persuade every man whose help you require that his private interest obliges him voluntarily to unite his exertions to the exertions of all the others. This can be habitually and conveniently effected only by means of a newspaper: nothing but a newspaper can drop the same thought into a thousand minds at the same moment. . . .

> To suppose that they only serve to protect freedom would be to diminish their importance: they maintain civilization. I shall not deny that, in democratic countries, newspapers frequently lead citizens to launch together into very ill-digested schemes; but if there were no newspapers, there would be no common activity. The evil which they produce is therefore much less than that which they cure. . . .

> Hardly any democratic associations can do without newspapers. There is, consequently, a necessary connection between public associations and newspapers: newspapers make associations, and associations make newspapers; and if it has been correctly advanced, that associations will increase in number as the conditions of men become more equal, it is not less certain that the number of newspapers increases in proportion to that of associations. Thus, it is, in

America, that we find at the same time the greatest numbers of associations and of newspapers.[2]

Martin Van Buren's success in organizing the Albany Regency or Bucktail faction of the Democratic Party was directly related to his utilization of newspapers, handbills, and editorials for public support. By 1848, most political campaigns aimed towards obtaining the support of the more than 600 "party" newspapers across the country. Throughout the 1800s, the theater, the church, and the newspaper were the three institutions "setting out and legitimizing culture."[3] Newspapers played an increasingly vital role in the formulation of public opinion.

The Telegraph Transforms the Newspaper

The telegraph revolutionized the role of newspapers from being predominantly sources of the local news to coverage of national events. The invention of the telegraph was monumental in its effect, the first time in human history the message could now travel over distances faster than a messenger. Newspapers pooled resources setting up the Associated Press to cover news throughout the country for a fee. During the Civil War, the thirst for news was virtually unquenchable, and the news media expanded their operations accordingly.

Differentiation between the press and politics was not clear. Newspapermen frequently ran for national office. In 1872, Horace Greeley, founder of the *New York Tribune,* was the Democratic nominee for president. In 1892, editor of that newspaper, Whitelaw Reid, was the Republican nominee for vice president. In 1936, Frank Knox, publisher of *The Chicago Daily News,* was Alf Landon's running mate. William Randolph Hearst served as a member of Congress and ran unsuccessfully for governor of New York State.

After the Civil War, newspapers continued with expanded coverage, which evolved into a very pro-active form of writing labeled "yellow journalism." Besides being a forum for muckraking and the progressive movement, yellow journalism was probably the leading cause of and contributor to the Spanish-American War. Even with this activism, news coverage was often sporadic. The media widely publicized Samuel Langley's failure to launch his flying machine, but gave little exposure to the Wright Brothers' flights just nine days later. There was little public awareness of the ability to fly until some five years after the flight.

Usually newspapers were editorially conservative and generally supported Republican candidates. Newspaper managers tended to be conservative businessmen who reined in their editors and reporters. During the period of political domination by the Democratic Party in the New Deal and Fair Deal, Henry Luce at Time Inc. viewed himself as an organ of the Republican Party. He openly touted the underdog candidacy of Wendell Willkie. Luce was also a cheerleader for Dwight Eisenhower's presidency, even sabotaging the campaign of his personal friend Bob Taft to help secure Ike the nomination.[4] Luce invented the concept of the weekly news magazine, *Time,* and the weekly photographic magazine, *Life.* By utilizing new printing techniques and glossy paper, he changed the all-print format of magazines to incorporate pictures. With *Life* and *Time* and his leading business magazine, *Fortune,* Luce dominated the magazine market for decades. The twentieth century also saw the rise of *The New York Times, The Wall Street Journal,* and *The Washington Post* as probably the three most influential newspapers in the world.

Syndicated newspaper columnists, such as Walter Lippmann, Joseph Alsop, and Drew Pearson, had a huge impact on public opinion. While presidents came and went, these writers frequently made up America's mind, often playing off each other in a form of pack journalism rather than by objectively analyzing reality. Newspapers swept news stories and advertisements off the page across from the editorials to make room for the opinion columns. Their power and influence was incredible. Lippmann somehow persuaded Soviet leader Nikita Khrushchev to rearrange his schedule to meet an interview request. A request to the U.S. president for an interview was almost invariably accommodated. These columnists were the predecessors to television's "talking heads."

Contemporary broadcast media such as radio and television, which reach huge masses of people, are even more powerful—they are broadcast on the public airwaves, are spoken or visual, and are much more widely available. The average subscriber interacts with a newspaper through the sense of touch—a medium which is at roughly 30 hertz of the electromagnetic spectrum. By contrast, the radio interacts with the sense of hearing which ranges up to 30,000 hertz. Television interacts with the visual senses at up to 30,000,000 hertz (which is shrunk to 6 million hertz for the typical television channel).

Radio

The use of the radio waves caused a revolution in communications. In 1865 James Clark Maxwell had developed a theory of electromagnetic waves, which were observed by Heinrich Hertz in 1888. Marconi used this new knowledge to develop first a wireless telegraph in 1895 and then the radio, using the best devices and technology available for practical applications. By 1901, a signal was transmitted across the Atlantic, although it was only one-way and in Morse code. Reginald Aubrey Fessenden was the first to transmit speech by radio. Previously, voice communication had been by direct contact involving the physical presence of the person speaking. Fessenden would befuddle unsuspecting wireless operators by playing bursts of noise, such as orchestra music and readings of Bible passages. He worked for Thomas Edison, who remarked on the possibility of broadcasting voices: "what do you say are men's chances of jumping over the moon? I think one as likely as the other." John Fleming and Lee De Forest invented the vacuum tube which allowed radio signals to be amplified. De Forest was a reckless inventor, associated with twenty-five bankrupt companies which made and lost fortunes, eventually denouncing radio and broadcasting for polluting the air with crass commercials instead of opera and classical music.

In a bitter patent war over amplification of radio transmission and reception, Edward Armstrong defeated De Forest. This fight went to the Supreme Court twice. The first time, in 1928, Justice Cardozo wrote an opinion that failed to grasp the nature of radio technology and awarded the rights to De Forest. Radio engineers were incensed by the blunder and the Supreme Court eventually reversed itself, but not until 1934. Armstrong sold rights to this technology to both RCA and Westinghouse Corporation, which, in October 1920, started pioneering radio station KDKA in Pittsburgh. By the end of 1922, there were 580 commercial broadcasting stations. Within a decade, radio receivers were installed in well over a majority of American households, a faster deployment than any other major technology in history up until that time. The first consumers had to wear earphones, but soon the loudspeaker was introduced. The sale of millions of radios helped to drive the economic boom of the 1920s; by the end of the decade, production went from virtually zero to five million a year. Instant radio communication had a far-reaching impact on capitalism and on financial markets, reducing the need for inventory and expanding the size and scope of exchanges.

The initial radio signals were crackly, full of static. Armstrong invented frequency modulation or FM radio that made signals crystal clear, a process which took years and thousands of experiments to develop. David Sarnoff and RCA had the right of first refusal to Armstrong's invention. Sarnoff was heavily invested in AM radio and the National Broadcasting Corporation (NBC). In the midst of the Great Depression, Sarnoff didn't want to risk his investment of $75 million in equipment and an embedded consumer base of 40 million radios, and, besides, he wanted his next investment to be in television. Armstrong struck out on his own by selling a good portion of his shares of RCA which he had obtained from the sale of his intellectual property rights in AM. Armstrong had to market the FM technology and convince people of its superiority, then design and build transmission equipment, design and manufacture receivers, and sell all of these in sufficient quantity to get to the tipping point where the better technology could succeed. The Federal Communications Commission (FCC), which was under the thumb of RCA and Sarnoff, delayed the process interminably. RCA refused to manufacture the radio sets, but General Electric did. A new chairman of the FCC saw Sarnoff's duplicity and awarded licenses to Armstrong, but not until 1940, when World War II put the technology on hold. After the war, another new FCC chairman, who subsequently went to work for Sarnoff at a high salary, revoked many of the licenses, obsolescing half a million FM radios and stranding the investment of many of the pioneers in the industry. RCA developed its own system and spent years litigating with Armstrong over the intellectual property rights, until Armstrong's patents expired. By force of these events, Armstrong was driven to commit suicide.[6]

The news media loved President Franklin Roosevelt (FDR), who understood and used the media, conducting over three hundred press conferences in each of his first two terms. His press operations and use of the radio were emulated for decades and became a decisive factor in his popularity. In his first week in office, he began his famous radio fireside chats. FDR's talks resonated with the poor, the downtrodden, the immigrants, and children. He tried to use radio to engage the nation in an informal dialogue, avoiding condescension and providing common sense explanations of the difficult issues that were making people uneasy. FDR used the radio to help create a new sense of national community and a feeling of togetherness missing at least since the beginning of the Depression and perhaps since the Civil War. He exploited the new medium to expand his popularity and spread his message of hope and vision. He built a heroic image of himself as a battler against the Depression and a wartime president fighting the evil Axis.

FDR was considered the first great radio voice, better than professionals in the industry. The broadcast media actually begged him to do more shows, but, to avoid overexposure, he limited his fireside chats to a couple each year. FDR skillfully took reporters behind the scenes, then used his personal rapport to get his viewpoint across, shaping almost every story about his administration. He made the radio his personal instrument of power and changed the balance of politics, diminishing the influence of Congress and the political parties. Most Americans had never seen or heard a president, but they could now hear him in their own living rooms.[7] FDR's use of radio has been underestimated in terms of its impact. Radio was more powerful than any previous medium, and radios had become household items in the 1920s. FDR reached several times more people in one of his radio broadcasts than

Theodore Roosevelt reached with all of his public appearances. The power of the new medium was greatly underestimated even by those who broadcast regularly. Orson Welles came to this realization suddenly when his journalistic hoax, the make-believe broadcast depicting H.G. Wells' *War of the Worlds,* precipitated panic across America. The newspaper headlines the next day summarized the damage: "Radio War Terrorizes U.S."; "Panic Grips Nation as Radio Announces 'Mars Attacks World'."[8]

In the next decade, radio became the most important means of entertainment and threatened magazines for the lead in advertising and merchandising. There was an inherent tension between the print media and the new medium of broadcast radio. Associated Press members voted to cut-off wire service to radio networks to prevent them from broadcasting the news ahead of the newspapers.

FDR resonated well, not only with the new broadcast medium, but with the print journalists as well. He had a knack for explaining complex issues and complicated subjects that delighted the press. FDR benefited tremendously from the indulgence of the press. They applauded after his first press conference. He even had an informal agreement with the press that he would not be photographed in his wheelchair—only two out of 35,000 images made show him in a wheelchair. White House photographers would knock down their colleagues whose lenses captured him wheelchair-bound. When FDR spotted someone taking such a shot, he would motion to the Secret Service who would expose the film.[9] In stark contrast to the criticisms levied by the press against Harding and Coolidge, many of FDR's flaws and inadequacies were never made public until long after his term in office.

In recent decades, radio has become increasingly dominated by conservative talk shows; this is perhaps a reaction or alternative to left wing influence over television news and the print media. Talk radio is interactive, and the positions taken must be defended, unlike television news and newspapers. Talk radio today, however, has a smaller audience than television news programs.

By the 1950s, the use of transistors in radios caused a dramatic decline in price and a cultural revolution. Previously, families would gather together around a large radio set in the living room to listen to the news, music or other programming with parental supervision. Transistor radios were much cheaper and, by comparison, tiny and portable. Their widespread availability and use allowed children to choose their own music and programming without adult presence. If they wished, kids could select broadcasts their parents disliked and would not have permitted into the living room. The introduction of the Walkman and car radios meant children and young adults could listen to programming almost anywhere at anytime. Similarly, transistors and other advances in electronics drove down the cost of record players and tape recorders, enabling the young audience to acquire these devices to listen to their own preferences in music and entertainment. Music, an important component of culture, is used to set moods, for example, romantic, religious, or provocative. The ubiquitous transistor enhanced development of a radical culture in the 1950s and 1960s. Rock-and-roll music espoused youthful rebellion, including sexual freedom and drug use.

Elvis Presley became a phenomenon, with 6 of RCA's top 25 records of all time, sales reaching $75,000 per day. Widespread public protests took place against his suggestive music and performances. Steve Allen invited Elvis to appear and the ratings for his show beat Ed Sullivan's for the first time. Even though he had sworn never to televise Elvis' "vulgar" act, Sullivan signed him for $50,000 for three appearances and praised him on the show as a fine, decent kid.[10]

A well-known management consultant studied 200 years of writing about success, noticing a startling change in American literature. Beginning about the time of the advent of radio and television, the literature and culture becomes increasingly superficial, filled with social image consciousness and quick fixes. By contrast, the literature of the first 150 years emphasized character and integrity as the foundation of success, with Benjamin Franklin's autobiography being representative of our early literature. Derived from the values of the founding fathers, the "Character Ethic" emphasized moral character, religion, frugality, the concept of getting ahead, hard work, industry, honesty, perseverance, sobriety, and punctuality. This ethic stimulated individual ambition, encouraged self-reliance, and fostered self-discipline. The study concluded:

> Shortly after World War I the basic view of success shifted from the Character Ethic to what we might call the Personality Ethic. Success became more a function of personality, of public image, of attitudes and behaviors, skills and techniques, that lubricate the processes of human interaction. This Personality Ethic essentially took two paths: one was human and public relations techniques, and the other was positive mental attitude. . . . Parts of the personality approach were clearly manipulative, even deceptive, encouraging people to use techniques to get other people to like them, or fake interest in the hobbies of others to get out of them what they wanted, or to use the "power look," or to intimidate their way through life.[11]

By the end of the 1800s, the Character Ethic was being challenged from many sources: including Marxism, psychoanalysis, secularism, and New Thought. Out of this challenge, the Personality Ethic became ascendant, encouraging a philosophy of getting along and avoiding arguments and conflict. "Keeping up with the Joneses" came in vogue in the 1920s. Dale Carnegie's *How To Win Friends and Influence People* appeared in 1936 and became an instant bestseller. The Personality Ethic was expressed by a range of different concepts from Norman Vincent Peale's *The Power of Positive Thinking* to astrology, palmistry, and fortunetelling. In this environment, winning at the game of success often meant a loss of human integrity.[12] This radical change in the cultural values was not limited to the general society, but infected politics as well. "Television has made the personality of the candidate central; his quirks, hair, style, skin color, voice tone, and apparent sincerity are as important as his themes and programs."[13] The personality cult became a basis for political power internationally, exemplified by leaders, such as Winston Churchill, Mao Tse-tung, Joseph Stalin, Adolf Hitler, and, of course, FDR.

Radio and television expose personalities. A personality connects with the viewing public via the media. By contrast, character is an attribute that cannot be assessed or determined by a media transmission. Thus, character is a trait that has become downgraded by the modern mass media. Personality is captured easily by the television or radio image, but character is a term derived from ideas, the ideal, or belief in an ideology that cannot be effectively communicated in a broadcast medium. The slickness of the image prevails over the integrity of the character.[14]

Television

The most powerful new media technology was television, invented by a farm boy, Philo Farnsworth, after years of hard work. When funding for his invention ran out early in the Great Depression, Farnsworth and his employees had so much confidence in their technology they worked without pay, developing a cathode-ray tube system to replace the early mechanical scanning systems. The new system had the capacity for five hundred lines, while the old technology had just forty-eight and provided only flickering images. Farnsworth believed television would transform the news by eliminating the distortion of the middlemen acting as reporters and interpreters. He believed television would become a great teaching tool, eliminating illiteracy and heralding an era of world peace. He was probably at least partially right about the latter; the number of people killed in war plunged after television became popular, but his reasoning seems not quite accurate: people did not necessarily become better educated about the need for peace, they became horrified when war scenes were broadcast over the public airwaves into their living rooms. When Farnsworth finally developed the cathode tube, his rival, Vladimir Zworykin, who was funded by RCA, copied it. Farnsworth licensed his technology to Philadelphia Storage Battery (Philco) the leading manufacturer of radios. RCA used its influence to abrogate this contract and worked to stymie other deals. The U.S. Patent Office awarded Farnsworth a patent and rejected Zworykin's application. Farnsworth's technology languished for years as the Great Depression and World War II prevented television from becoming commercialized, but the tactics of RCA caused him to sink into an alcoholic depression from which he miraculously recovered to see his invention succeed.[15]

Daniel Boorstin described the advent of television, one of the most important educational institutions and inventions of the twentieth century:

> Television opened another world. It did not simply multiply the sources of news and entertainment, it actually multiplied experience. At the TV set the viewer could see and hear what was going on with a rounded immediacy. Simultaneity was of the essence. When you took a picture you had to wait to have it developed; when you bought a phonograph record you knew in advance how it would sound. But now on TV you could share the suspense of the event itself. This new category of experience-at-a-distance would transform American life more radically than any other modern invention except the automobile.[16]

In a generation, television infiltrated most aspects of American culture and spread to its farthest geographical reaches, drastically changing lifestyles and experience. Boorstin described in depth the transformational nature of the medium. Television not only democratized learning as did the printing press, it democratized experience. It became the community or national hearth, providing a set of unifying experiences. The experiencing, however, was done alone, with family at home, or with a few friends, not actually in the larger community. While the experience of the objective event was common, the method for viewing it led to a separateness or segregation between individuals and their neighborhood or larger community. The experience was felt and seen not in the public square but in the private home. Missing was the audience intra relationship and the information gained from personally sharing the experience with neighbors (did they applaud, laugh, approve, or criticize?). Television delivered a one-way window to the world, which was controlled by those responsible for the content with television networks deciding what was important. The viewer, of course, still had the option of deciding whether to watch and could "keep an eye on the set" while doing homework, housework, or reading. In an audience, the spectator decides what to focus on, but on television the producer, camera man, or director provides the focus for the viewers.[17]

> By enabling him to be anywhere instantly, by filling his present moment with experience engrossing and overwhelming, television dulled the American's sense of his past, and even somehow separated him from the longer past. If Americans had not been able to accompany the astronauts to the moon they would have had to read about it the next morning in some printed account that was engrossing in retrospect. But on television, Americans witnessed historic events as vivid items of the present. In these ways, television created a time myopia, focusing interest on the exciting, disturbing, inspiring, or catastrophic instantaneous *now*.[18]

The delivery mechanism for television evolved rapidly. At first, all programming originated in the studio. Mobile television cameras enabled taped and then live coverage, mostly of local events. Satellite transmission allowed live coverage of events throughout the globe and enabled cable television to develop a much greater number of programming channels. Video Cassette Recorders enabled viewers to buy movies and programming for their own televisions. Home cameras allowed people to develop their own individualized programming and produce home movies. Each step in this evolution made television increasingly powerful. During the 1960s and 1970s television's influence continued to grow exponentially, as its coverage became global, more events were broadcast live and in real time, and "experts" were used to give commentary on events.

Measuring and determining the far-ranging impact of the new media is both difficult and controversial, and Americans, to date, have not held a full airing or public debate on the transformational impact of television. The news media, naturally enough, has seemed reluctant to discuss matters that might be negative about themselves. Yet, the nation has rapidly evolved from a literary culture to a society where much of its values and information comes from nonliterary forms, such as television, films, and radio.

Americans typically spend three to six hours a day watching television or twenty to forty hours a week. Very little of this viewing comes out of time spent sleeping or working, which comprises about half of a 168 hour week. The twenty or forty hours typically comes out of the other half of the week's schedule, much of which has traditionally been devoted to civil society activities, such as family time, community activities, and religious events. Sunday football games on TV have become substitutes for church socials. Attendance and collections at African-American churches plunge on Sundays when their professional football team is at home. Evening news and television entertainment has replaced neighborhood events and town hall meetings as community events. There has also been a decline in political activity and awareness. Television is arguably one of the major reasons civil society has become weakened. In that connection, we might remember de Tocqueville's warning about the crucial role of news in developing public opinion and strengtherning society.

For many Americans, television became a form of addiction, absorbing the attention of individuals to the exclusion of traditional formative institutions, such as the church, family, and school. Americans were soon spending more hours before television sets than at work or in school.[19] When the TV set was off, the viewer often felt a vacuum or emptiness. By the mid-1950s, most Americans could not recall reading any kind of book in the past year and only one American adult in three hundred read serious books on their own initiative with regularity.[20]

Cultural Change

Television became a powerful force for cultural change. While early in the twentieth century only an occasional door-to-door salesman visited the typical American home, "by the middle of the century a ceaseless stream of the most subtle electronic impulses created by the nation's most richly rewarded hucksters was beamed into this new marketplace, relentlessly selling not just the American dream but an endless series of material products through whose purchase that dream might be more quickly achieved."[21] A product advertised in print or on radio was overpowered by television marketing, which was visual and animated. Even where there were very few sets, sales would sky-rocket. Huge amounts of advertising were shifted to television, partic-ularly from afternoon newspapers and mass-circulation weeklies, many of which failed within a decade. Advertising men became icons.[22] Advertising billings went from $12 million in 1949 to $40 mil-lion the next year and then to $128 million in 1951.

Television affected lives in myriad ways, many of which are only now beginning to be understood. Mass markets for products were cre-ated overnight, as well as great wealth accumulated through the mass marketing. Public airing of controversies and tension often let off steam and enabled American society to assimilate enormous change. Television chronicled American progress. The broadcast media and the press became such important forces in American culture they were referred to as the fourth estate or fourth branch of government. Even the individual who penned the term, Thomas Macauley, said that he

> could not have imagined the prestige of journalists in the twentieth-century United States. They have long since made themselves the tribunes of the people. Their supposed detachment and lack of partisanship, their closeness to the information, their articulateness, and their constant and direct access to the whole citizenry have made them also the counselors of the people. Foreign observers are now aston-ished by the almost constitutional—perhaps we should say supra-constitutional—powers of our Washington press corps.[23]

Television spread the belief everything was becoming global. With television, any event occurring in the world is potentially of inter-est to and can influence public opinion throughout the planet. The national borders and cultures that had kept people apart began to break down. Students began to feel a sense of world community. A movement started in the most affluent country, America, and spread to Europe and Asia; students began to demonstrate against "The Establishment." While some criticism of the conformity of the established order was undoubtedly appropriate, the student movement gradually moved toward militancy, anarchy, and nihilism. The real revolutionaries were not the students, but the new broadcasting technologies. The widespread use of the English language made it possible for international broadcasts by the major networks and CNN and in turn made English the global language. English was not only the language of economic progress, but replaced German as the language of science and French as the language of diplomacy. Television spread American culture globally. Movies and television films broadcast internationally were accompanied by advertising agencies and products advertised by American-owned companies. Throughout the late 1950s and 1960s, foreign earnings from television exploded.

Television began as a device to receive video signals transmitted by fixed broadcast stations within a reach of fifty miles. In most totalitarian countries, broadcasting and its content were controlled or strictly regulated by the state, often with censorship over what the masses could see. In the fifty years after its initial deployment, the number of television sets grew at a faster and faster pace, with over a billion sets being used throughout the world today. America developed a robust cable television industry, providing programming and channels in addition to the traditional broadcasters. Video on Demand (VOD), Video Cassette Recorders (VCRs), and devices, such as TIVO allowed viewers to watch whatever they want whenever they desire. Programming quality was greatly improved by the migration from video tapes to CDs to DVDs. MP3 and other audio formats greatly expanded the availability of and improved the quality of music and other forms of audio for television.

VCRs and satellite-delivered programming radically altered the nature of television. Initially, only cable systems had satellite dishes and only movie theaters had projectors. Increases in chip speed and miniaturization made these devices as small as pizza pies and shoe boxes. Millions of people throughout the globe could pull down signals from satellites or broadcast their own movies, tapes, and eventually DVDs. Both of these technologies were invented in America and commercialized in the 1970s, although VCRs were, for the most part, manufactured abroad by European and Japanese companies. VCRs and satellite-delivered programming meant that fixed broadcasting stations were no longer the only source of signals: programming could originate from anywhere and governments could no longer control content and stop its dissemination. Satellite-delivered programming radically changed journalism and the news business by making news events throughout the world available in real time. Even during the Vietnam War, video footage had to be shipped by airplane to the United States before it could be aired on the news.

Initially, television was viewed predominantly in the family living space. Over time, rapid advances in transistors and improvements in electronics and picture tubes brought down the cost of a television set and most homes had multiple units. Cable television provided dozens of channels of programming, some of which were well outside of the mainstream of American culture, including sexual content and violence. Increasingly, children could view their own programming in a different part of the house and frequently what they were watching was unsupervised by parents. Similar phenomenon occurred with personal computers and cell phones; children now had access to the world of the Internet, as well as direct links to their friends. The impact of these technologies was to short-circuit childhood innocence and to expose children to parts of the culture traditionally off limits. Television went from community-shared events with community standards to atomized individual viewing without ethical standards.

Programming, the availability of the television signal, and the penetration level of television sets are all interconnected, and present what is often referred to as the issue of which comes first the chicken or the egg. Television had the most rapid increase in use of any consumer communications device up until that time. In 1950 alone, for example, the number of sets rose from three to ten million. The broadcasting industry deployed new towers, coaxial cable, and microwave relays to make broadcast signals available throughout the country. At first, programming was lacking and filled in by events, such as Senator Estes Kefauver's organized crime hearings, the first nationally broadcast show covering twenty cities in the East and Midwest during the time period television penetration was reaching critical mass. Besides his televised hearings, Senator Kefauver appeared on the game show *What's My Line?* and narrated episodes of *Crime Syndicated.* In 1952, he won several improbable presidential primary victories, demonstrating the power of television.[24] On January 20, 1949, more people watched President Truman sworn in on television than the total number of viewers who had witnessed all previous presidents taking the oath.

Bill Paley of CBS, Desi Arnaz, and Walter Annenberg changed the entire programming model. Instead of requiring affiliate broadcasting stations to pay for national programming, Paley provided it for free and encouraged the local affiliates to do everything they could to expand their audience. The larger the audience, the more that could be charged for advertising. CBS quickly became the most profitable network. Desi Arnaz married Lucille Ball and created the *I Love Lucy* show. In order to have the show produced from Hollywood instead of the more lucrative New York market, he suggested that it be filmed and in the process established creative rights. Forced to accept a salary cut to make up for the greater expense of filming (all previous shows had been broadcast live), Arnaz more than made up for the reduction with the rights to re-broadcast the show. Walter Annenberg published a weekly magazine listing television programs, *TV Guide,* that became the first universal programming guide and the largest-circulation magazine, which was eventually sold for billions of dollars.[25]

By the early 1950s, individuals were watching as much as four or five hours of television a day, although the programming was fairly staid by today's standards. Time slots were segmented by population: children in the morning, housewives during the daytime, teenagers in the afternoon, adults in the evening, kids on Saturday morning, and families on Sunday night. Television programming was initially a celebration of American suburban family life with shows, such as *Ozzie and Harriet, Leave It to Beaver, The Donna Reed Show,* and *Father Knows Best.* The titles of other programming touted the success of American capitalism, including *Texaco Star Theater, The Colgate Comedy Hour, Goodyear Television Playhouse,* and *General Electric Theater* hosted by Ronald Reagan.[26] Programming began to change as, for example, playwright Rod Serling characterized James Dean as an upset, psyched out angry young man in *Rebel Without A Cause.* Serling was admittedly trying to capitalize on the new youth culture. The rise of the baby boomers brought about the idealization of youth. In the 1950s, over half the population was under 30 years old and at one point half of the U.S. was under twenty-five with 40 percent under seventeen. "There was a postwar mystification of the young, a gradual erosion of confidence in their elders, in the so-called truths, in the whole litany of moral codes. They just didn't believe in them anymore. In television we were more aware of this and more in tune with what was happening. We could portray it immediately too—write a script one week and have it on the air the next."[27] James Dean and Elvis Presley became symbols of the secular, younger generation, embracing alienation and rebellion.

Hollywood was initially a major rival, then a major supplier of programming, and eventually a major owner of the television channels. The city of Hollywood originally banned movie-houses, but ran out of municipal water and was forced to incorporate into Los Angeles County. The movie producers quickly moved in. By 1915 Universal City had been built and a movie a day was being produced. Most of the producers were poor Jewish immigrants from large families, forced to work at an early age, including William Fox of Twentieth Century-Fox, Louis Mayer of Metro-Goldwyn-Mayer, and the Warner Brothers. United Artists (Mary Pickford, Charlie Chaplin, Sam Goldwyn, and Douglas Fairbanks) was also a force in the business. By 1920, 100,000 people were employed in an industry with revenues of $1 billion.[28] Soon, there were more U.S. movie theaters than U.S. banks, twice as many as there were hotels, and three times as many as there were department stores. Censorship and family viewing limited content to the equivalent of PG programming. In the mid-50s, Hollywood producers put hundreds of television films on the air, most of them with multiple episodes, such as *Dragnet, Perry Mason, Superman, Border Patrol, Davy Crockett, Wyatt Earp,* and *Lassie.*

Walt Disney became the best-known movie mogul of all, churning out movies at unprecedented rates. He pioneered a wide variety of marketing tools, such as branding and merchandising. His brother Roy served as the business manager, a sibling partnership rife with strife, but which was one of the more productive in American history. Their first success was Mickey Mouse, but the stress of the Depression caused Walt to have a nervous breakdown. Success with the cartoon *Three Little Pigs* enabled his company to obtain a $1 million line of credit at Bank of America to produce their first full length feature, *Snow White and the Seven Dwarfs,* a smash hit, earning five times its cost when tickets sold for as little as a dime. Disney's litany of successful productions includes Pluto, Goofy and Donald Duck, *Pinocchio,* and *Fantasia,* the latter being produced with the first technology sold by Hewlett-Packard. The war put the company heavily in debt, but Disney again recovered with numerous hits. The brothers tried to secure $10 million for an amusement park, but no bank was willing to finance it. They funded the park by obtaining financing from the ABC television network in return for producing a one-hour weekly show, the first major deal between the archrival broadcasters and movie producers. Both the show and the park were stunning successes. The show was *Davy Crockett,* which became an American icon with a theme song that was a number-one hit for thirteen weeks. The park attracted over a million visitors in the first two months. Walt Disney's last major film was the huge hit *Mary Poppins.* He made plans for his city of the future, Epcot and Disneyworld. Eventually, Disney Corporation purchased the ABC television network and a number of other media properties and became one of the largest entertainment companies in the world.

Disney also became a symbol of the values of small town America and the traditional American morals that came under assault by the new American morality. Walt Disney was an American patriot. He was a firm believer in technology and always kept his company on the cutting edge. In the late 1960s, Disney was pilloried for lack of culture and reliance on optimism and happiness. The political left linked him to McCarthyism and big business. In reality, he was a supporter of Franklin Roosevelt, consistently poked fun at big business and large corporations in his films, and put his faith in the generally optimistic nature of the American people.

By the late 1960s, the complaints about Disney, however, seemed quaint or politically motivated, given the violent and sexual content of most television programming. There has not, however, been any public consensus about what can be done to change programming, in significant part because the broadcast industry has such an important role in the formulation of public opinion. There are five to six incidents of violence per hour on prime-time television and twenty to twenty-five per hour on Saturday morning cartoons. With many American kids spending more time watching television than they do in school, young children on average witness 8,000 television murders and 100,000 other assorted acts of violence before graduation from elementary school. The average young child is exposed to 20,000 commercials a year. Children are exposed to themes that in prior generations they might not have experienced well into adulthood.[29] In the past, most parents made every effort to shield their young children from violence, foul language, and indecent behavior, but today television exposes children to those experiences at an early age.

Television has the power to alter an individual's perception of the world and to change moral behavior and sensibilities through constant repetition and sheer saturation, the principle that governs television advertising and earns the broadcasting industry tens of billions of dollars a year. Sponsors of broadcast advertising clearly believe it works and pay large sums of money to market their products and services.

Prime time and cable programming provide a stream of violence, sexually-oriented materials, and crude language. The Center for Media and Public Affairs found first-run syndicated programs average 37 violent acts per episode.[30] Studies have found that while there is some cathartic effect from watching violence on television, children who watch a lot of violence have a heightened risk of aggressive child and adult behavior, including spousal abuse and violent crimes.

We have seen an explosion in moral pathologies; abused and abandoned children, out-of-wedlock births, abortion on demand, "no-fault" divorce, drug use, violent crime and just plain trashy behavior. What has also largely vanished from the scene—what seems to be gone with the wind—are unwritten rules of decency and civility, social strictures and basic good manners. Part of the explanation is that many people ignored or forgot what almost everybody once knew: namely, that the good requires constant reinforcement and the bad only needs permission. . . .

The cultural anthropologist David Murray compares television to the ancient cathedral. It is the site of our culture where the most powerful forces of imagination are harnessed to produce some of the most effective symbolic devices ever encountered. Those who work in television have a Promethean role and they hold the fire that ignites hearts and minds. They have the power to shape sensibilities. The question we face today is the same question we have faced since the dawn of society: In whose service will the power be used?[31]

Television has a particularly powerful effect on children and teenagers in their formative years. Television violence can cultivate values that favor the use of aggression to resolve conflicts.[32] The teenagers who carried out the Columbine High School massacre said they hoped to kill hundreds in a bloodbath that would have Hollywood fighting over their story.[33] In the twenty-two months following the Columbine shootings, nineteen separate incidents of school violence were patterned after the shootings, ten of them foiled. Perpetrators of these acts usually specifically referenced Columbine as a model or motivation. The copycat efforts occurred notwithstanding a general trend of reduced violence in the public schools.[34] Television coverage of violent crime is so impressionable, many citizens believe crime is increasing even when it is actually declining.

During the period 1950 to 1990 when owning TV sets grew from 15 to 93 percent of American households, the number of murders in the United States increased from 8,000 to over 21,000, doubling on a per capita basis. By the age of eighteen, a typical young viewer witnesses 200,000 acts of violence on television, including tens of thousands of murders. Between 1945 and 1975, homicide rates in the United States and Canada increased by over 90 percent, but declined by 7 percent in South Africa which had no television. Studies of children in remote Canadian and American communities found a significant increase in violent behavior after they began viewing television.

The impact of television on crime and violence is not limited to the criminals and victims. It involves destruction of communities—of the American tradition of society working together to create a better world or better place. With crime rampant, the average American has lost the freedom to walk in the streets, to interact with other people, or to participate fully in civil society. Television has created a vicious cycle. It portrays a violent world. People then fear for their safety and withdraw into their homes where the primary form of entertainment is television. Ratings then go up and more crime and violence is viewed on the news, reinforcing this cycle.

Crime is not the only social problem exacerbated by television. Proponents of restrictive morality are often characterized as prudes. Pre-marital sex, prostitution, and adultery are prominently displayed usually with few or no consequences.[36]

Traditional methods of education relied on repetitive methods of learning to inculcate moral and cultural values. By contrast, contemporary television news and entertainment emphasize the new, the different, and frequently the bizarre. The success of a television channel depends on differentiation, sensation, and ratings.

Perhaps the most ambivalent relationship the media has pursued is that with the civil rights movement. While television coverage was essential to the triumph of the civil rights movement in the 1950s and 1960s, it was resistant to its principles. In 1960, the television networks blacked out African-American speakers at both political party conventions to avoid offending southern stations.[37] The press and media widely criticized Martin Luther King's strategy and tactics, with reporters even testifying against him at trial. When British singer

Petula Clark touched Harry Belafonte's wrist to close out a duet on a 1968 show, the sponsors excised her interracial touch from the broad-cast.[38] Decades later, African Americans were still under-represented on television shows, in media ownership, and as reporters, news direc-tors, and producers. The news media's focus on the social pathologies of the ghetto and African-American communities reinforces many stereotypes. While the media portrays the majority of the poor as being African American and the majority of African Americans as being poor, the vast majority of African Americans are above the poverty line and the majority of poor people are not African American.[39]

Television, more than other media, blurs the lines of distinction between news and opinion. Over a period of centuries, the newspaper developed journalistic standards that gradually separated out news, advertising, and editorials, such as distinct editorial and news pages. Television broadcasting grew explosively overnight—reaching almost all American homes in the decade between the late 1940s and 1950s, providing much less time to consider journalistic boundaries.

Media bias may have had significant impact on the political process. Between 1930 and 1994, when radio and television were in their prime, Republicans controlled the House of Representatives, for just four out of sixty-four years. Except for Dwight Eisenhower, whose military heroism assumed mythic proportions, Republicans could not elect a president in almost forty years.

Numerous studies confirm the bias of the public media. A detailed analysis of the data found that journalists and reporters vote Democratic by 30 to 50 percentage points above the overall electorate. Even in landslide Republican years, 80 to 90 percent of journalists vote Democratic. Many of the most influential reporters and executives enter journalism after service in election campaigns or the government and a substantial majority worked for Democrats.[40] Analysis of the content of the reporting shows that these viewpoints shape news coverage. By a two- or three-to-one margin, newspapers more frequently categorize Republicans as conservatives than Democrats as left-wing. The adjec-tives used to describe conservatives are more negative than those used to describe the left.[41]

This bias has led to a decline in public trust in the media. Except for talk radio and Fox News, which are widely believed to have a conservative bias, most Americans assume that the media has a bias in favor of the left. This bias causes viewers to be cynical about the objectivity of the news. Many Americans are apathetic or distrustful, tuning out political news and having little understanding of public-policy issues. A depressing cycle has resulted: a disparaging press feeds an already negative and apathetic public, which makes the electorate still more cynical and turned off.

The media have resisted efforts to monitor bias. The National News Council was established to address media concentration and the reality that publishers had "power without responsibility." The council sought to help victims who had been "misquoted, libeled, held up to unjustified ridicule, or whose legitimate views have been ignored in a one-sided report." The media just ignored and refused to publish the organization's findings, eventually causing it to fold.[42]

While the public media exhibit a bias, the measure that drives the television business is the size of the audience or how many eyeballs the broadcast network or station attracts: the economics of the business drive the broadcasters to air programming that will maximize their viewership levels. Regardless of the political attitudes of the media employees, they have little control over the programming content. It is driven by audience size. While conservatives often blame Hollywood or the broadcasters for the content of the programming, the reality is that the viewers are largely responsible for what appears on television; viewers watch the programs and drive the ratings.

Television has often been the mouthpiece for the poor, the underprivileged, and citizens without another voice in American society. From this perspective, the media play a crucial counter-balancing and countervailing role in maintaining a pluralist society. At the same time, the media consistently provide negative, if not outright hostile, coverage of business through films, such as "Erin Brockovich", "Jurassic Park," and "Roger and Me." Analysis of a year's programs found businessmen committing a third of the murders on network television.[43]

Television news and programming consistently advocate more

regulation. Network reporters turn to government regulation for solutions to many problems. The news also tends to favor government solutions to social problems, such as welfare and retirement programs. Efforts to reform and streamline these programs are often vilified. In the 1990s, welfare reform legislation was strongly attacked in the public media with many dire predictions about what would happen if it were implemented, almost none of which came true. Class-action lawyers often cooperate with television news producers on so-called investigative television stories tailor-made for lawsuits and the plaintiff bar. In a now infamous incident, NBC even faked an explosion of a gas tank on a General Motors truck.

Television can be manipulated by criminals and terrorists who use the medium to gain national and world-wide attention. September 11 may have been the ultimate media event. Osama Bin Laden and al-Qaeda planned the terrorist attack so that it would have maximum news media impact. As their ratings soared, the news media were big winners, a good fortune almost too indecent to even mention but which was a factor in the networks' decision to temporarily suspend commercial advertising. Coverage of terrorist events, nevertheless, is important for two reasons: an informed and vigilant citizenry is the best defense against terrorism, and the war against terrorism is aimed at the hearts and minds of the public, particularly in the Middle East.

Little public attention was focused on the terrorist threat before September 11. Press attention at the time was focused on Congressman Gary Condit who was connected to a woman who had disappeared, to shark attacks, to Monica Lewinski, and to other relatively insignificant events. Important national issues were ignored or relegated to the back pages. On July 26, 1999, Secretary of Defense William S. Cohen published an op-ed piece in *The Washington Post* warning of the imminence of a terrorist attack against the United States. There was not a single follow-up story on the evening news.[44] Neither Bin Laden nor al Qaeda nor terrorism was an important issue in the 2000 presidential campaign; Congress, the candidates, and the news media paid little attention to these threats.

The fear factor became a critical component of the public fascination. Instead of focusing attention on the international terrorist threat, news coverage became a roadmap of American vulnerabilities. One al-Qaeda memo lamenting slow progress in developing weapons of mass destruction concluded: "We only became aware of them when the enemy drew our attention to them by repeatedly expressing concern that they can be produced simply."[45] The terrorists' pursuit of weapons of mass destruction was based on American public statements about their ready availability and the ease with which they can be produced.

The news media becomes the terrorists' unwitting ally by spreading fear and suspicion and causing Americans to diminish the quality of their lives. Saturation coverage of terrorist attacks breeds false fears and public panic. In the aftermath of 9/11, news reports spread the myth that everything had changed, when in reality very little of importance had changed. America's obsession with the event was the primary way in which America changed. The public media and the terrorists benefit from the heavy coverage of attacks. Terrorists receive enormous amounts of free publicity, while the publishers and broadcasters make money through increased sales, advertisements, and viewers. Two economists, Bruno Frey of the University of Zurich and Dominic Rohner of Cambridge University, found that media coverage causes more attacks and more attacks bring more media coverage.[46] The two trends are interrelated and reinforce one another.

In the Middle East, America has been losing the propaganda and diplomacy battle. For decades, the United States has not managed its message effectively in the region. A culture of hostility against America festered in the decade after the first Persian Gulf War, in large part due to the continued sanctions against Iraq that were perceived as affecting only the Iraqi people and the lack of any resolution of the conflict in Israel and Palestine, the top regional concern of most Arab nations. Bias in the U.S. media has been used as a pretext for one-sided coverage in the Arab media: the Al-Jazeera television network, for example, presents views highly critical of the United States. Post-Cold War budget cuts killed off local broadcasting of Radio Free Afghanistan, which beamed anti-Soviet and pro-democracy news into the country from 1986 to 1993. Instead, the United States had to rely on Voice of

America. After the U.S. defeated Saddam Hussein's army, the only tele-vision on the air was an anti-American station.

In the first weeks of the war in Afghanistan, U.S. news coverage was particularly perplexing, being overwhelmingly negative even though the conflict had just started. The media consensus was that the war was in trouble and the likelihood of overturning the Taliban remote. The Northern Alliance was given little or no chance of defeat-ing the Taliban. The American effort was compared to the war in Vietnam and the Soviet effort in that country in the Cold War. The cov-erage was off-target, as the Americans and the Northern Alliance secured a rapid victory in the war against the Taliban.

Television and Politics

Television revolutionized politics, altering the basis for power from party bosses and cigar-smoked rooms to press conferences and make-up. Prior to television, a candidate would appear before tens of thou-sands of people on a good day, but the evening news put him on the air in front of millions and even tens of millions of people in one night. Media advisors were considered so influential and powerful that their willingness to sign on with a candidate made that individual a con-tender. "Television not only changed the balance of power, it became part of the new balance of power."[47]

The advent of television network news was arguably the most important political event in the second half of the twentieth century. Weekly news magazines were considered major national outlets when they had over a million subscribers, but television news shows could reach well over fifty million people every night. It was and still is a much more powerful, visual medium with people actually seeing and experiencing the events. Coverage, however, is truncated—there is only so much that can be seen and heard in a one or two minute time slot on the evening news, in contrast to a newspaper which has virtually unlimited space. The standard joke was that if the Ten Commandments had been issued in the modern world, the television news would report that, "Moses came down from the mountain with

the Ten Commandments, the two most important of which are . . . "
But the coverage was much more powerful—there is the old adage that
a picture is worth a thousand words. By the end of the 1970s, the three
network news shows attracted 120 million viewers nightly and had no
appreciable competition. The television media gained prestige—by the
late 1960s Walter Cronkite became the most trusted man in America.

The television show *60 Minutes* further revolutionized the news.
Within seven years of its first airing in 1968, it was the most-watched
show on television. "*60 Minutes* pioneered almost every one of the
techniques of television investigative journalism: the carefully re-edit-
ed interview, the surprise 'gotcha' visit to a malefactor's home or office,
the hidden camera, the rejection of any pretense of objectivity. Week
after week, it treated America to the crimes and misdeeds of its two
favorite targets: the Pentagon and big business. . . . By the late 1970s, the
other networks were all desperately producing their own imitations of
'*60 Minutes*' and local television was replicating its techniques."[48]

Television didn't just cover the news, it created the news. Many
demonstrations, riots, and other "pseudo" events would never have
occurred without news coverage. Political, campaign, and legislative
events were scheduled not because of their merit or substance, but
based on whether they could generate media coverage. This radically
changed the traditional function of journalism. Historically, the role of
the reporter had been to observe events, sense what is important, and
file a story. Instead, the media began to produce the events, as candidates, politicians, and legislators based their actions on what the media
wanted to see and hear. This was a revolutionary change that gave the
media enormous political clout. Initially, television covered political
campaigns, but soon became the deciding factor in many congressional and presidential races.

The media focused on campaign tactics, such as fundraising and
candidate personalities rather than issues. Personality became more
important than credentials, experience, or issues. John F. Kennedy's
telegenic image was instrumental in his successful race for president.
Personality and political fundraising replaced policy as the focus of
most political campaigns, whereas party platforms and issues played a

declining role. More and more, it appeared to the viewing public as if the players were just pursuing their personal, selfish interests.

Political parties have been weakened by the modern media. Instead of the conventions and smoke-filled rooms, the presidential primary became the mechanism for selecting presidents. Media coverage itself often affected voter perception. In 1992, the media's relentlessly negative coverage of the economy shaped the voters' assessment of the campaign and played a decisive role in Bill Clinton's defeat of George H.W. Bush.[49] The media disproportionately impact middle of the road or swing voters, because many of them haven't formed an opinion and are more open to what they see and hear in the news.

The intellectual content of campaigns and attention span of voters have lessened. In the nineteenth century political speeches generally lasted two or three hours and dealt with issues in a systematic fashion. With radio, the length of the speech was reduced to an hour and then to half an hour. With television, the length of the speech was reduced to fifteen or twenty minutes, then to a minute for a commercial spot, and subsequently to the now generic thirty-second spot. Presidential conventions have been downgraded from decision forums to a method of electronic-age ratification. President Kennedy used the televised news conference to burnish his own image and to downgrade the importance of events, such as the Bay of Pigs, even increasing his popularity after that loss by effective personal appearances.

The media has encouraged and fostered a public attitude of cynicism toward politics and American institutions. Dwight Eisenhower's campaign was the first to run television spots. David Ogilvy, a well-known media consultant, believed that these spots were a gross abuse of advertising and the television medium. At the same time, Joe McCarthy was manipulating the media to popularize his anti-communist crusade. The main reason for this cynicism may be inherent in the medium. Bad news gets good ratings, but good news doesn't, a phenomenon recognized by Marshall McLuhan. Prior to the 1960s, newspaper reporters and editors were reluctant to run negative stories on a public figure's character, because of libel laws. The Supreme Court extended the libel laws and permitted greater latitude in criticism of public officials, requiring that actual malice be demonstrated to secure a verdict for libel.[50] While the court emphasized the free speech aspect in its decision, it had the unintended consequence of lowering the decorum of political debate. More frequent negative stories about public officials undermined confidence in government and the political system. Even though the 1960s were a decade of growth and opportunity, the major news stories were negative—repression of civil rights demonstrations in the South, near nuclear annihilation in a confrontation with the Soviet Union over Cuba, the war in Vietnam, and the Kennedy Assassination. This coverage had an impact on the national psyche—it was a time when over half of Americans watched the evening news. Over the past few decades, the pattern has remained the same. Contrast the limited coverage of success and progress in America versus the extensive coverage of the bizarre and criminal, such as the O.J Simpson murder trial, the Bobbitt trial, Tonya Harding, John Mark Karr, and the Duke lacrosse rape allegations. The negative coverage extends to gotcha journalism and outright attacks on public officials. Scaremongering is in the media's interest: it drives ratings. Paul Ehrlich appeared on Johnny Carson's *The Tonight Show* twenty-five times in the 1970s. Jimmy Carter bought into and endorsed this pessimism, helping to bring on his demise.[51] The media produces these materials and covers these events because sleaze and crime sell, making news like a national soap opera.

The level of cynicism towards politicians and government coincides with the level of negative coverage in the media.[52] Most media coverage of politics is negative.[53] The Center for Media and Public Affairs found that media coverage is even more negative than campaign ads. As President Clinton was conducting sensitive trade negotiations with the Japanese, this item appeared in *The Washington Post*:

> The Japanese media continue to portray the United States as a dangerous and decadent country, with people like the Menendez brothers, the Bobbitts and Tonya Harding presented as the paradigms of American life.
>
> Last month an episode of the popular Fuji-TV situations comedy "Double Kitchen" portrayed a family trip to

Hawaii. In the course of a five-day vacation, the script had this typical Japanese family being assaulted by a black bell-boy who didn't like his tip, robbed at gunpoint in their hotel room, robbed at knifepoint on the street and arrested by overzealous police on false charges of cocaine possession.[54]

This depiction, the article noted, clashed with the reality of the Japanese evening news where Chrysler's new compact car the Neon was labeled the "Japanese car killer" and the American triumph in semiconductors was broadcast every night on national television. The article concluded by describing a commercial being run nightly by the Japanese national financial newspaper:

> The TV ad purports to be a quiz show on current economics. The first questions is "Which country leads the world in semiconductor sales?" Most of the contestants clearly believe that the correct answer is still Japan. But one contestant—the one who reads the newspaper—bangs his buzzer and shouts out "America!".
>
> "That right!" the host roars. "Now America leads the world!"

The modern news media, being focussed on entertainment and ratings, does not cover progress as well as it covers decay, of course. Iraq, scandal, and local crimes are defined events easily susceptible to coverage, more so than the positive entrepreneurial and technological changes that were such important factors in progress over the last century. This bias not only skews the public's view of current events, it has, in the past few decades, fundamentally altered history and Americans' view of everyday life. As former Senator Barack Obama noted: "In an environment in which a single ill-considered remark can generate more bad publicity than years of ill-considered policies, it should have come as no surprise to me that on Capital Hill jokes get screened, irony became suspect, spontaneity was frowned upon, and passion was considered downright dangerous."[55]

Partly as a result of news cynicism and negative coverage, institutions are more and more remote from the people, leading to indifference, apathy, and alienation from the political process itself. This may be the function of the inherent nature of mass institutions in an industrial society, but the news media does little to counteract the adverse trend. Instead of participating in the community through meetings and gatherings, the typical American has became more isolated from government by viewing it through television alone with family, or with a few friends. Communications are not truly based on personal views and are not interactive—they go in one direction. Most Americans today do not know the policies or the issues as citizens did in colonial times. Cynicism and negativism feed public depression and despair about the future. Carl Bernstein, who became known for his reporting with Bob Woodward for *The Washington Post* on the Watergate scandal, noted:

> Increasingly, the picture of our society as rendered in the media is illusionary and delusionary: disfigured, unreal, out of touch with truth, disconnected from the true context of our lives. It is disfigured by celebrity, by celebrity worship, by gossip, by sensationalism, by denial of our society's real condition and by a social disease that we—the press—are turning into an escape sinkhole.
>
> Over the past 20 years, we have abdicated our primary function—the best obtainable version of the truth—and allowed our agenda and priorities to become bastardized by what I call, "The Triumph of the Idiot Culture" . . .
>
> In this culture of journalistic titillation, we teach our readers and viewers that the trivial is significant, that the lurid and loopy are more important than real news. We do not serve them, we condescend to them, calculating what we think will sell, boost our ratings and our bank accounts.
>
> Finally, there is one other great uncovered story: the media itself. For the story of the American media is also at the heart of our national condition. The reality is that the media are probably the most powerful of all our institutions today and they are squandering their power and ignoring their obligation.[56]

13

Drucker and Deming
make management paramount

By THINKING OF HOW TO BETTER MANAGE BUSINESS, improvements were implemented that swept the free enterprise system and catapulted capitalism into an economic paradigm—W. Edwards Deming (1900–1993) and Peter Drucker (1909–2005) probably had as much positive impact on the twentieth century as any other two individuals. Traditional nominations for great men are usually heads of government, intellectuals, or industry leaders. Drucker and Deming, however, were simply consultants, but their work throughout the second half of the twentieth century radically transformed the corporate world.

In remarks about Peter Drucker, General Electric's Jack Welch noted, "The world knows he was the greatest management thinker of the last century." Drucker believed that few policies remain valid for as long as twenty or thirty years and that most of our assumptions about business, technology, and organization have outlived their time, a belief that reflected Thomas Jefferson's hope that every generation would have the creative energy to renew society. For Drucker, the first management theorists were John D. Rockefeller, J.P. Morgan, and especially Andrew Carnegie. Drucker believed that improved business practices were the success story of the twentieth century and that the industrial revolution of mass production and management was "made in the U.S.A."

American W. Edwards Deming, more than any other single individual, was responsible for transforming Japan's manufacturing sector—from its reputation for being cheap and shoddy—to becoming the leading producer in the world, unmatched for its quality, reliability, and dependability.

Drucker

In seeking to liberate factory work from waste and inefficiency, Frederick Taylor (1856–1915) and his Scientific Management theory had been the original pioneer. His insights made mass production and the assembly-line possible, which in turn led to Drucker's and Deming's productivity revolution.[1] Taylor's philosophy instilled in factory management the concept of always looking for a way of doing something better.

> The most important step toward the "knowledge economy" was, however, scientific management. . . . [Frederick] Taylor for the first time in history, looked at work itself as deserving the attention of an educated man. Before, work had always been taken for granted, especially by the educated. If they ever thought of it, they knew that work had been ordained—by God or by nature—and that the only way to produce more was to work more and work harder. Taylor saw that this was false. The key to producing more was to "work smarter." The key to productivity was knowledge, not sweat.
>
> [S]cientific management . . . has proved to be the most effective idea of this century . . . Wherever it has been applied, it has raised the productivity and with it the earnings of the manual worker, and especially of the laborer, while greatly reducing his physical efforts and his hours of work. It has probably multiplied the laborer's productivity by a factor of one hundred.[2]

When Drucker began his analysis of the corporation, virtually nobody sought to produce managers. Within two decades, almost every private sector organization was focusing on business administration. The success of the American manufacturing industry in World War II drew attention to its management. Drucker became known for introducing "decentralization" as a principle of management. He is credited with moving the vast majority of Fortune 500 companies toward radical decentralization. His model was Alfred Sloan who had begun making General Motors a decentralized company in the 1920s.[3] Drucker viewed the corporation as a human resource, not as a profit generating machine. He believed that the big salaries of top executives poisoned the corporation. Drucker was among the first to emphasize that there is no business without a customer, to set out the basics of competitive strategy; he developed and introduced management by objectives or MBO, and wrote about knowledge workers long before the information revolution. His style was not to provide answers, but to ask questions. When Jack Welch first became chief executive officer of GE, Drucker raised two issues: If you weren't already in a business, would you enter it today? And if the answer is no what are you going to do about it? If you are not number one or two in a business, shouldn't it be overhauled, sold, or closed?

Drucker was born in Austria, attended classes taught by John Maynard Keynes and Joseph Schumpeter. He escaped from Nazi Germany to America. His 1954 book *The Practice of Management* was the first to present the exercise of business management as a coherent whole. By reducing management to basic principles within a discipline, he ensured that the discipline could be taught and widely disseminated. Drucker wrote well over two dozen books and hundreds of articles. In *The Effective Executive* (1966), Drucker contrasted the difference between doing the right thing and getting the right thing done. "One meets or one works." To be effective, an executive must get the right things done. Time management is the key to achieving this goal.[4]

Deming and Drucker spawned an entire industry specializing in new management theories; they greatly increased the popularity of the MBA and attendance at business schools. While their theories were taught across the globe, the best business schools were found in America. Management theories proliferated and covered the breadth of business and corporate activities, including Contingency Theory, Systems Theory, Chaos Theory, Management by Walking Around, The Focused Factory, Just-in-Time Inventory, quality circles, networking and the Productivity Paradox. In modern America, management consultants discuss revolutionary change more than do perhaps any other group of specialists.

Other leaders contributed concepts and ideas to the new changes in management. Vannevar Bush, Franklin Roosevelt's science advisor, developed a pluralist model for government, science, and engineering that provided key roles for industry, the armed forces, and colleges and universities. He separated out research from development, funding basic research for the colleges and universities and encouraging industry to bring the findings and fruits of this effort to market. Basic science was kept separate from engineering, a model that proved extremely successful for the next fifty years. To implement this vision, he conceived of the National Science Foundation (NSF) and the Advanced Research Projects Agency (ARPA), which played key roles in keeping America at the cutting-edges of technology. He founded the Raytheon Corporation and laid the foundation for other Boston firms springing up on Route 128's high technology corridor. A.A. Berle and Gardiner Means described the growing separation between business ownership of a firm and its management, between entrepreneurs and professional managers. The work of other influential thinkers, such as Steven Covey, who wrote the *Seven Habits of Highly Effective People,* and Tom Peters, who wrote *In Search of Excellence* became widely noted.

The twentieth-century management revolution embraced not just changes in factory operation and corporate strategy, but in sales and marketing as well. As early as the 1920s, sales and management books proliferated. Salesmanship met with nothing but condescension from the elite, yielding literary works with scathing criticism of the marketing profession—from Sinclair Lewis' *Babbitt* to Arthur Miller's *Death of a Salesman.*[5] At the same time, American industry spent the century building trademarks such as Coca-Cola, Campbell's soup, and

Kellogg's Cornflakes into the global consciousness, thereby creating billions of dollars of goodwill.

Drucker's and Deming's radical changes were unlike previous innovations, based on information that was portable, fungible, and easily replicable. Any business manager anywhere could apply these improved techniques and methods at almost any time. Unlike advanced equipment or trained workers, management concepts can be used by any number of businesses at the same time. Corporations throughout the world could implement the Drucker and Deming principles. Those competitors or industries that failed to keep abreast did so at risk and could rapidly lose their competitive advantage.

In the larger American culture, however, political will dissipated, being diffused by public attention to Vietnam, by riots in the cities and on campuses, and by television entertainment and marketing gambits. As examples in this chapter illustrate, effective management became the driving force of the private sector, but it did not permeate popular culture as Edison's invention factories had done a century earlier. America's competitive edge began to dull a situation which became less apparent and understandable to the general public.

Leaders of the management revolution were able to build on the principles of the Revolutionary War generation, which transformed the definition of economic growth from "one man's gain is another man's loss" to the concept of limitless opportunity. No other change in colonial America more radically altered human history or was more directly connected to the dominance of the United States in the twentieth century. Economic growth is vital to the success and harmony of a free society. If people believe the economy is expanding, they tend to be more optimistic, happier, and willing to work as a team.

The rate of economic growth has major long-term consequences. During the first millennium of the Christian era, there was basically no economic growth and the level of wealth and income throughout the globe was stagnant: most humans lived in dire poverty and in constant fear of famine. In the era of the Decline of Rome and the Dark Ages, each individual earned only about $400 per year in today's dollars. During the last millennium, economic growth was only a twentieth of a percent between the years 1000 and 1500 and a sixteenth of a percent between the years 1500 and 1820. Annual per capita income reached only about $800 or two dollars a day for the Revolutionary War generation. Since 1820, income has been climbing at well over 1 percent a year per person and has reached over $30,000 annually for an individual living in the United States. As a general rule, higher economic growth has translated into longer and healthier life, greater opportunity, more social tolerance, and more democratic values. Slow or no growth more often than not has resulted in class conflict, prejudice, and totalitarian government. The standard of living has risen even more than reflected in the official statistics. The price of tires has gone up several fold, but they last more than 10 times longer than the old 4-ply cotton-lined tires. The price of light has fallen by 99 percent, but by conventional measures of inflation, lights bulbs and fixtures have increased in cost by well over 100 percent in the past century.[6]

Over long periods of time, small differences in economic growth have translated into huge differentials. Between 1870 and 1990, real growth per individual in the U.S. rose 1.75 percent a year, but if the growth rate had been 1 percentage point lower, the American standard of living today would be roughly on the same level as that of Mexico or Hungary.[7] Small changes in growth rates can have major impacts. If the economy grows at only 2.3 percent instead of 2.5 percent over a period of a decade, federal revenues are hundreds of billions of dollars lower, which forces major spending cuts or results in large additions to the federal deficit.

Productivity is the most crucial factor that affects businesses, the economy, and the standard of living, providing jobs, wages, profits, and national wealth. Productivity is the consequence of incremental and cumulative buildup of knowledge, the source of sustainable growth.[8] It was very difficult to measure until the pioneering work of economist Robert Solow. American annual productivity growth rose steadily from less than a tenth of 1 percent before 1820 to average about 1.5 percent between 1820 and 1890 and then 2.25 percent between 1890 and 1993. During the 1960s, productivity growth rose to 3 percent, falling to only a half a percent in the 1970s before increasing to 1.5 percent in the

1980s. Between the end of the nineteenth century and 1950, other industrial countries fell far behind the U.S., but have been catching up.

For two hundred years, America was the most consistently successful engine of economic growth and prosperity in the world. Notwithstanding the two stock market plunges of the first decade of the new millennium, American wealth has soared—a person who invested $100 in the Dow Jones Industrials in 1900 would be worth over $50 million today. America has enjoyed the crucial components for economic growth: freedom, robust competition, free trade, a spirit of innovation, and a culture which values entrepreneurs. Economic freedom implies not just personal liberty, but personal property rights as well. Countries with the greatest degree of freedom grow at several percentage points faster than those nations with the least amount of freedom. Competition is a cornerstone of economic and entrepreneurial success. It encourages the efficient use of resources and promotes the interests of consumers. Technology, worker skills, financial capital, and economic organization are also critical to economic growth. Technology plays the key role with its importance increasing, accounting for the majority of all economic growth. Whereas worker skills and financial capital can only be used once, technology is based on ideas and knowledge that can be used multiple and almost an infinite number of times concurrently. A software package can cost billions of dollars for the first copy, but almost nothing for subsequent copies that can be produced almost without limitation, all of which can be used simultaneously.[9]

HOUSING AND HOME FURNISHINGS

After World War II, the most important demographic trend was the increase in population of the Baby Boomers, which had far reaching impact on all aspects of American life. At the end of 1945, the Armed Forces were discharging around a million men a month, imposing many kinds of burdens on the employment market, housing, and, in fact, even the courting industry. The housing industry, for example, was not able to build units fast enough and homelessness became a problem. Many families were forced to double up; trailer camps began to spring up. The housing shortage was so dire people were living in huts and abandoned railcars.[10] The powerful housing lobby blocked efforts to fund government housing programs.

William Levitt, however, built the first Levittown and young married couples rushed to pay under $10,000 for a basic four-room home with central heat, refrigeration, electrical range, and washing machine. During World War II, Levitt and his brother had built military housing. By the end of the war, they were so proficient they could build entire airfields in the Pacific. The Levitts broke the construction of a house into twenty-seven different processes and trained teams of workers in each stage. The step-by-step process reduced dependence on highly skilled craft workers and increased the construction speed. Instead of paying hourly wages and overtime, the Levitts paid by piecework, which could be done because they had standardized the process.[11] Restrictive deeds made everything uniform, the predecessor to suburban housing developments. Levittown was, in many respects, the beginning of suburbia with new community schools, churches, shopping centers, and parks.

There was huge pent-up demand. During the Great Depression, housing starts plummeted from over a million per year to less than 100,000 while the marriage and birth rates were increasing. Housing starts rose from their nadir of 100,000 in 1944 to 1.7 million in 1950. Levitt simplified the purchase of the house as well with no down payment and closing costs. The GI Bill provided for Veterans Administration mortgages with guarantees, enabling banks to make loans without any money down. While criticized as cheap and tacky, the Levitt houses were built sturdily and represented a substantial improvement in the quality of life for just about everyone who bought them. Instead of paying rent, many Americans were now building up equity in their homes. This capital could be used to obtain credit such as charge accounts which were previously the province only of the wealthy. American housing continually improved and got bigger.

Following the housing boom of the 1950s and 1960s, companies such as Home Depot and Lowe's created a home improvement market, driving down the costs of renovations and additions and educating the consumer on being a do-it-yourselfer. When Arthur Blank and Bernie Marcus linked up at Handy Dan, they soon found themselves fired, but viewed the adversity as an opportunity and started up Home Depot. The American homeowner and the home improvement stores caused the lawn care industry to explode with expensive lawn mowers, new and specialized forms of fertilizer, and many types of grass seed.

Westinghouse became adept at selling the appliances that went into these houses, using Ronald Reagan and Betty Furness to advertise new products live on television. Betty concluded each commercial with a trademark line. "You can be sure if it's Westinghouse."[12] Many new labor-saving devices became household items. The washing machine replaced scrubbing on a washboard and initially consisted of crude mechanical efforts which involved hand-operating a stick within a box, but Alva Fisher invented an electrical device with blades that lifted the clothes as the cylinder spun. Spin-driers also became household appliances.[13] Single-handled faucets were invented to prevent people from burning their hands. The inventor, Alfred Moen, became one of the world's largest producers of plumbing products. New household devices included: electric coffee percolators, automatic dishwashers, Tupperware, Teflon cookware, electric toothbrushes, VCRs, telephone answering machines, and microwave ovens.

THE AUTOMOBILE AND ENERGY

The household labor-savings devices were tied into the electrical power grid and drove energy consumption, as did many other modern conveniences. Beginning with the take off point for the industrial revolution in 1800, energy use expanded by seventy-five times per capita. During World War II, vast new petroleum factories, pipelines, and refineries were built. After the war, large supplies of oil, coupled with frequent gas wars among filling stations, kept the price low. Between the late 1940s and 1972, America's consumption of oil increased from 6 million to 16 million barrels a day. There were some temporary shortages in 1947–1948, but exploration increased U.S. reserves over 20 percent by 1950.[14] The onset of the Cold War made alternative sources of oil in the Middle East risky, so there was a domestic initiative to develop synthetic fuels as Germany had done in World War II, but the costs seemed far too high with the cheap availability of foreign oil.

Kerr-McGee developed the technology to make offshore oil exploration and rigs possible. More refineries were built in larger sizes. New refining techniques increased the yield of higher value products such as gasoline, diesel, and jet fuel. Tanker fleets were expanded and huge supertankers built. Gasoline stations sprang up throughout the continent. Soon oil surpassed coal as the leading source of energy, helped out by the United Mine Workers who made the coal industry an unreliable supplier by their frequent threats and strikes.[15]

When the war was over, gasoline rationing ended, people threw away their coupon books, as Americans resumed their love affair with the automobile. The automobile industry was transformed: from 26 million registered vehicles at the end of the war to 50 million registered vehicles at the beginning of the 1950s and almost 75 million at the end of the 1950s, with 70 million cars sold in the decade (and roughly 45 million reaching the scrap heap and creating a visual pollution problem). The annual model change in the fall became a national festival of buzz and hoopla. The average size and speed of a car increased rapidly, driving the cost up from $1,270 to $1,822. In the 1950s, General Motors (GM) was the largest corporation in the world, the first ever to gross a billion dollars annually. GM developed higher compression engines such as the V-8, and bigger and faster automobiles like the entirely new Chevrolet. New options included power steering, power brakes, independent front wheel suspension, and air-conditioning.[16] By the end of the 1950s, the Chevrolet was four feet longer and had five times as much horsepower, more than many large trucks. New accessories were added, including multiple carburetors, high-lift valves, stiffer valve springs, bigger manifolds, and strong-sounding mufflers. GM's Charles Kettering, an inventive genius, used this talent to become one of the wealthiest men in America, inventing the starter motor to replace the hand-crank. He also developed high octane gasoline, using it to produce a high-compression engine. His other inventions included a car heater, chrome plating, anti-knock fuel, Freon for refrigerators, improved diesel engines, and a special car paint that reduced the time required to dry from seventeen days to three hours.[17] Between 1970 and the mid-1990s, anti-lock brakes, airbags, power windows, cruise control, windshield wiper delay, remote-control side mirror, power door locks, and air conditioning became standard features in automobiles. Tires were developed that could fix their own flats. Car sound systems outperformed the best home stereos of only a generation ago. Global-positioning systems rendered maps obsolete.

Labor relations remained difficult, but GM tied worker wages to productivity and inflation.[18] The industrial revolution kept reducing the number of laborers required, as the machine continued to substitute for human work. During the Eisenhower Administration, the automobile work force dropped 172,000 employees while the industry turned out a half million more cars a year. Labor's leverage declined as union members were replaced by machines. Instead of a progressive force, labor unions became conservative, fearful of change, and closer to management.[19] New workers joined the service sector and government, which soon had the highest numbers of unionized workers.

The population movement to the suburbs made the car a necessity. Only eight shopping centers existed in America at the end of World War II, but there were 20,000 by the early 1980s, accounting for two-thirds of all retail sales.[20] American shoppers gravitated from neighborhood stores to retail shopping centers to indoor malls. The learner's permit and driver's license became the right of passage for suburban teenagers.

THE SOUTH ADVANCES

The South was revived by advances in drugs, vaccines, air conditioning, and the defense industry. The military became professionalized and the defense budget was institutionalized at much higher levels, which accrued disproportionately to the South which had more military bases, shipyards, and defense contracts. Throughout the nineteenth and early twentieth centuries, disease was the ultimate horror, claiming the lives of more people than any other cause, particularly babies and very young children. Southerners were exposed not just to those diseases prevalent in the north, but many tropical plagues as well. With the discovery of the virus and its treatment with penicillin and other drugs, the South became a much more habitable place and its warmer climate began to attract people rather than repel them. In the early 1970s, aches and pains were treated basically with aspirin, but within a couple of decades there were a plethora of such drugs: Tylenol, Advil, Motrin, Aleve, and Actron. Whereas antacids were formerly the only drugs for heartburn, new remedies included Axid, Pepcid, Tagamet, and Zantac 75.[21] Vaccines eliminated entire categories of people being sick from diseases such as smallpox, yellow fever, polio, and malaria and opened the way for people to move to the southern part of the U.S.

Beginning early in the twentieth century, polio terrorized populated areas every summer. Annual epidemics left thousands of children dead or crippled for life, causing a hysteria reminiscent of medieval plagues. Jonas Salk developed the first effective vaccine against polio and became a national hero. His efforts, the culmination of years of work by researchers across the globe, resulted in a field test of more than one million children, one of the largest clinical experiments in the history of medicine. In 1952, there were more than 55,000 cases, 3,300 of which were fatal. In 1962, there were just 910 cases in total.

Over a period of decades, Will Carrier made several advances in the commercialization of air conditioning, including formulas for regulating air temperature and humidity and a centrifugal refrigeration machine. In the 1920s, movie theaters were the first public places to be air conditioned. The Great Depression and World War II delayed the mass commercialization of this technology. Air conditioning had an impact on post-World War II America rivaled only by the automobile, television, and the computer. It drove migration to the South and West—Nevada's population increased by almost 900 percent in the second half of the twentieth century. Sales of window air conditioning units rose from 75,000 in 1948 to over one million in 1953. Ironically, civil rights legislation, resisted so much by the established southern elites, further encouraged the shift of resources to the South and created an unprecedented regional boom, particularly in cities such as Atlanta, Charlotte, Miami, and Raleigh-Durham.

RETAILING

The retail business was being transformed as fast as any other. Traditional powerhouses such as Montgomery Ward and A&P were forced to exit the market by the end of the century. Korvettes revolutionized the retail markets by pioneering in discount shopping. The company's turnover of its inventory was so rapid it cut costs below competitors, becoming a forerunner of Wal-Mart. Sales went up over 2,500 percent, an unheard of increase.[22] Clarence Saunders invented the concept of the self-service supermarket, founding Piggly Wiggly to implement the idea. Before, customers asked staff behind the counter to hand over whatever was required from shelves behind them. The subsequent development of bar codes by Norman Woodland provided further impetus to implement this concept.[23]

AGRICULTURE AND FOOD PROCESSING

The agriculture and food sector underwent unprecedented change. The percentage of people in farming plunged to well under 10 percent of the population while production increased astronomically. The original hand plow that barely kept families from starvation evolved into the plow drawn by horse or mule that enabled families to eat and sell some surplus to distant city dwellers which in turn evolved to the modern farm tractor and combine which can feed one hundred or more people. In 1800, an American farmer took 344 hours to produce 100 bushels of corn, an effort which required just 147 hours a century later and only three hours by 1980.[24]

The American agricultural sector became the most efficient in the world. Farm labor has been replaced with capital and new technologies. Many agricultural activities are tightly bound to the local farm, including fertilizer and seed sales, animal vets, harvester and tractor sales, and agronomists. While agricultural machinery and chemicals can be manufactured anywhere, these industries are dominated by American companies that are also powerful exporters. The U.S. has more cropland per capita than any nation except Argentina, a better climate, the most educated and best trained farmers, the world's best infrastructure, the leading agricultural research facilities, and the most efficient food processing industry.[25]

Until the 1950s, the vast majority of food in America was prepared at home and eaten in the family kitchen or at the dining room table. Pre-packaged foods became the rage, eliminating many steps in cooking and becoming part of a wave of consumerism. Companies perfected new foods that could be sold out of metal aerosol cans, including more than one hundred million cans of squirtable whipped cream. Standard Packaging specialized in making disposable products such as plastic forks and spoons, bags that can be boiled, and trays that can be cooked, tripling sales in four years to become a hundred million dollar a year company. The company's CEO provoked controversy by proclaiming, "Everything we make is thrown away." Salt coming in small throwaway containers cost seventeen times more than salt sold by the pound; packaging cost ten times more than the contents. The annual cost per person of pre-packaged foods was in the hundreds of dollars.[26]

The McDonald brothers built their first hamburger outlet in San Bernardino, California. They couldn't obtain financing, but as a last resort were able to borrow $5,000 from newly formed Bank of America. Gradually, they refined the painfully slow car-hop process until they were delivering fast food, profiting from workers' increased mobility and the new premium the American consumer placed on time. The McDonalds narrowed their menu to the best-selling items, developed new grills, and eliminated plates and silverware (and dish-washers at the same time). They added two key new items—milkshakes and French fries. The entire process was standardized and automated, like an automobile assembly line.[27] Soon a milkshake mixer salesman, Ray Kroc, discovered their business and took over the franchise. The McDonald brothers were satisfied with their local operation, but Kroc was one of the first to develop the notion of a national franchise—expanding from 2 stores in 1955 to 228 in 1960. Kroc proved a fierce competitor and drove home his principles of quality and service.

Kroc developed systems for training huge numbers of people to facilitate growth, even establishing Hamburger University. McDonald's became a place where people would work their first job. At one point, every sixteenth American began their work career at McDonald's. Prior to the formation of McDonald's, these were called entry level jobs, but they became known derogatorily as hamburger flipping jobs by the dysfunctional counter-culture of the 1960s and 1970s, even though it was work with the world's most successful food company.

Small entrepreneurial businesses changed America's eating habits. Weight Watchers was founded by an overweight housewife to help Americans develop a healthy diet, in the process becoming a billion-dollar-a-year company bought by H.J. Heinz Company. Old Bay Seasoning revolutionized the eating of crabs. Gustav Brunn, his hand-cranked spice-grinder in tow, migrated to the United States with his wife and children, settling in Baltimore. After a brief job at a sausage factory, he went to McCormick & Co. which was interested in his sausage-seasoning experience. His limited English and perhaps his Jewish origins became insurmountable problems and he ended up instead renting a small second-floor space on property now occupied by the Orioles' Camden Yards, starting the Baltimore Spice Company. The location was upstairs from a seafood business and across the street from a fish market that sold crabs, but they were not a popular item. Wholesaler steamers came over to buy spices, raising Brunn's curiosity about what they were buying. He played around with proportions and variations and put together thirteen different ingredients. At first the wholesaler steamers wouldn't buy the new seasoning, but eventually they began buying it in larger and larger quantities until Old Bay Seasoning became synonymous with crabs. McCormick then bought the recipe of the man they had fired many years before.

In a couple of generations, the nation's spending at restaurants doubled to 40 percent of the share of all food.[28] Norman Brinker pioneered in the creation of theme restaurants. He ran Chili's restaurant chain and within the first decade of his leadership sales soared from $30 million to $500 million. He started a restaurant chain called Steak and Ale and grew the brand into a national franchise with over a hundred outlets, creating the first salad bar in a restaurant. Horses were always his first love, but when he was sixty-one a polo pony fell on him,

leaving him in a coma, a fever of 106, and little prospect of every walking out of the hospital. Within a few months he returned to run
Brinker International with restaurants such as Grady's, American Grill,
and On the Border. An estimated six million people have worked in
companies that Brinker founded or ran.

John Styth Pemberton, a druggist, developed the formula for
Coca-Cola and sold it for $282.29 in 1887 to Asa Griggs Chandler, who
in turn sold it for $25 million when the company was shipping over
100 million cases during Prohibition. In the 1980s and early 1990s,
Coke was run by one of the greatest American CEOs, Roberto Goizueta,
a Catholic Cuban immigrant. After a major overhaul of the company
in his first year, the market value of Coca-Cola stock soared from $4
billion to $150 billion during his tenure, transforming the wealth of its
home city, Atlanta. Coke became the most recognized brand in the
world.

Pepsi-Cola was invented by another Southern druggist. In World
War II, the Allied supply chain was kept well stocked with colas in an
effort to drive down alcohol use. Forest Mars created one of the world's
great fortunes out of M&Ms and Milky Way, becoming one of the most
successful American entrepreneurs. Headquartered near the CIA in
suburban Washington, D.C., the Mars Corporation was even more
secretive than the federal agency, but had tens of thousands employees
and revenues in the tens of billions of dollars. Mars' sons also ran the
business and were as highly secretive, bearing and leaving no traces of
identity, even though among the richest individuals in the world. Mars
borrowed production techniques from the steel, concrete, and pharmaceutical industries.[29] Milton Hershey was the first to market the nickel candy bar, making luxury chocolate available to people who were not
rich. He gave away his fortune, setting up a charitable trust to run his
company and to fund the wealthiest orphanage in the world. Hershey
spent years experimenting and produced the Hershey Bar, the Hershey
Almond Bar, and Hershey kisses. He created a utopian community in
which to manufacture his product—Hershey, Pennsylvania. Changes
in food processing have improved America's diet, making fresh fruit,
green vegetables, and fresh meat more readily available. Over the past

couple hundred years, agricultural advances resulted in a several hundred fold improvement in food production.[30]

FINANCIAL SECTOR

The post-World War II era witnessed a transformation of the Wall Street stockmarket. By the mid-nineties, financial services exceeded the manufacturing sector in terms of the proportion of the economy and the market value of its stocks. Merrill Lynch changed the nature of investing by radically altering the brokerage business. In the 1940s, it trained a sales team in all types of securities and the technicalities of the brokerage industry and started a research department to find good values in the stock market. The company initiated a national advertising campaign to solicit members of the general public to become customers of the firm. By the end of the decade, Merrill Lynch was the largest brokerage firm on Wall Street. Other firms copied the model and stock volume exploded over the next five decades—recovering back to the pre-Depression level trading volume of two million shares a day in 1954 and reaching a one day volume of one billion shares five years later. The year 1954 also saw the Dow Jones Industrial Average finally break through its 1929 high, the longest period between highs in the history of the index. The brokerage industry was deregulated in 1975, ending the system of fixed commissions. The price of stock trading plummeted almost overnight and precipitated a wave of consolidation as small firms were unable to compete. Discount brokerage firms drove the price per transaction down to minimal levels and volume increased more than 800 percent over two decades. Charles Schwab pioneered in the use of the Internet and created the largest on-line brokerage firm. The Great Crash was the first billion-share year, but by the turn of the millennium billion-share days were the norm.[31]

In 1951, William Boyles developed the credit card to relieve merchants of the headache of maintaining their own charge accounts, to enable consumers to charge at a wide range of businesses, and to provide financial institutions with profits by charging interest on unpaid balances and fees on the items charged. By the early 1970s, companies such as Visa and MasterCard were international powerhouses. Debit cards were developed as a substitute for cash.[32] In 1968, commercial banks carried only slightly more than $1 billion worth of credit card debt on their books. In the next fifteen years, the debt increased 5000 percent to more than $60 billion.[33] Between 1990 and 2003 the number of people holding credit cards increased by 75 percent, while the amount actually charged soared by 350 percent to $1.5 trillion, up from $338 billion.

General George Doriot founded the first publicly owned venture capital investment company which became a model for the industry that provided the funding for much of the cable television, computer, and biotechnology industries. As the first and only firm of its kind, the company was persistently harassed by the SEC, IRS, and other regulatory investigations, but eventually Doriot prevailed, establishing valuable precedents and a model for future venture capital efforts. The company struggled for years, like most start-up businesses. An investment in Digital Equipment Corporation (DEC) ensured the company's success, but it was forced to liquidate by an antiquated federal regulation barring any venture capital firm from owning anything for more than ten years. During the Carter Administration, federal legislation was necessary to set-up the structure of the venture capital firms that worked so well in the 1980s and 1990s.

Gerry Tsai went to work for Edward Johnson at Fidelity Funds and observed that with the postwar affluence there were many new investors with relatively small amounts of money to invest—in the thousands of dollars. He started up a mutual fund with a quarter of a million dollars and grew it to $200 million just three years later. When he began, there was only $78 million invested in mutual funds, but within thirty years the figure had risen to over $20 billion.[35]

Warren Buffett became one of the great American investors. Beginning in 1951, Buffett generated average annual investment returns in excess of 30 percent. A $1,000 investment in his Berkshire Hathaway company in 1965 was worth $5.5 million thirty years later. In his home town of Omaha, over thirty families had more than $100 million in Berkshire Hathaway holdings. His success is based on the ability to read and interpret financial statements and hold stocks for the long term. With over $100 billion in assets, his firm is largely run on his intuition, without meetings, advisers, procedures, and even very many financial reports. One owner who sold his firm to Buffett for hundreds of millions of dollars remarked, "It was easier to sell my business than to renew my driver's license." His company has seventeen employees and no public relations, human-relations, investor-relations, or legal department. After one of his better managers lost over $300 million on a mining deal he responded, "We all make mistakes" and ended the meeting after ten minutes. The manager confided to a reporter "I would have fired me if I was him."[36] Buffett doesn't use analysts, investment advisers, investment committees, computers, calculators, or cell phones (except when he is on the road).

TRANSPORTATION

In post-World War II era, deregulation, containerization, and the rise of inter-modal transportation (i.e. transport using more than one mode, such as rail and ship or truck and air) made it far cheaper and easier to ship goods around the world. The cost of moving goods declined from almost 8 percent of the world economy in 1980 to 6 percent a quarter of a century later.

Rail passenger services had been the predominant form of personal transportation, but airlines put many railroads out of business. Air travel doubled every few years until it provided fifty times more interstate passenger miles than all forms of transportation before the war. Even during the Great Depression, airline traffic continued to soar with the total number of passengers increasing from 380,000 in 1930 to over one million in 1938.[37] Between 1930 and 2000, the cost of air flight declined 90 percent.[38] The railroad continued to be the preferred transport mechanism for freight. Rate regulation of rail freight crippled the industry for decades, leading to the bankruptcy of the Penn Central railroad. Nationalization was debated, but would have cost taxpayers billions of dollars. Instead, deregulation brought a revival of what was thought of as a rusting, industrial age business.

Unprofitable lines were sold or abandoned, labor costs slashed, and productivity improved by more than 200 percent over 15 years. A bidding war was fought over the old Penn Central. Freight transportation by truck, pipeline, and waterways exploded, rivaling the volume shipped by rail.[39]

A revolution in freight-hauling caused a rapid expansion in international trade and faster economic growth. Container or packet shipping transformed the freight industry. Historically, freight was loaded and unloaded piecemeal into slings by manual labor. For centuries, cargo was shipped in boxes, bales, and crates that were handled piece by piece, a process taking about sixteen days to load and unload a large ocean freighter. Malcolm McLean developed the process of containerization, drastically reducing loading and unloading times and eliminating losses from pilferage and damage. The Interstate Commerce Commission forced him to sell his trucking business in order to be in the ocean shipping industry and the longshoremen refused to load his ships. McLean determined that delivery of beer from Newark to Miami cost $4 a ton the old-fashioned way, but with containers shipping was more than 90 percent cheaper. He developed the logistics for transporting supplies and materials to Vietnam and then brought back Japanese goods on the return voyage when his ships would otherwise have been empty. He eventually sold his company to RJ Reynolds Industries. Unable to work within a large corporation, he started up a company to build supertankers that could handle thousands of containers. Due to falling oil prices, his timing was wrong and he was forced into bankruptcy. Nevertheless, his supertanker concept combined with large container ports is the model widely embraced throughout the world and has brought about a rapid decline in costs.[40]

The container made possible the globalization of world commerce. Factories in distant countries could deliver products across oceans even cheaper than to local manufacturers. Containerization drastically reduced shipping times and expanded port capacity, increasing competition by breaking down the boundaries between different modes of transportation. The container crane made it much easier to load and unload ships without running the risk of capsizing them. Deregulation of the transportation sector was also important, resulting in huge productivity gains. During the 1970s, worldwide container shipping capacity increased by more than 20 percent in a year four times, surging from 2 million tons in 1970 to 10 million in 1980. The top half dozen world container ports were all in Asia, with the two largest being in Hong Kong and Singapore.

The modern container port is a factory on a vast scale. A typical port will unload 10,000 containers and three huge ocean liners a day. Decades of competition and labor negotiations were required before longshoreman would permit these efficient facilities to be built and manned by union workers. Government efforts to set standards for the containers were long-delayed and often failures. The Interstate Commerce Commission took twenty-three years to allow railroads to transport freight in truck trailers.[41]

Companies such as UPS and Fed-Ex that deliver freight fast anywhere in the world have encouraged improvements in supply chain management. Supply shortages can readily be addressed and quickly remedied, allowing just-in-time manufacturing processes to be implemented, significantly improving the profitability of the manufacturing sector.

AIR FLIGHT

The airline industry is another success story. Charles Lindbergh was the first individual to make a solo, non-stop trans-Atlantic flight, becoming the most famous man on the planet literally overnight. He had plenty of competition from a pantheon of flight enthusiasts, such as Admiral Richard Byrd and Igor Sikorsky. His competitors, however, had built complex, sophisticated models, some of which barely got off the ground and crashed. Lindbergh understood the need for simplicity and efficiency in order to carry the sheer weight of the 425 gallons of fuel needed to complete the transatlantic flight. His plane had no front windshield or radio, so it could carry more fuel. Fighting off exhaustion on the thirty-three and a half hour flight, he landed in Paris with four hours of fuel to spare.[42]

Initially, almost all the revenue for the new industry was from mail delivery. C.R. Smith built American Airlines from a collection of mail routes into the largest domestic passenger carrier. Smith convinced Douglas aircraft to build the DC-3, which became the most successful commercial aircraft up until that time. Even prior to World War II, American airlines had developed the capability to go more than 200 miles per hour at altitudes of almost 10,000 feet with Boeing airplanes making the flight from New York to Los Angeles in fifteen hours. Clipper planes traveled across the Pacific Ocean with one or two stops. The American aircraft industry already had the capability to build the world's largest aircraft.[43]

A Supreme Court decision held that airspace is public property. In 1945 two farmers sued because low-flying military aircraft were terrifying their chickens and alleged that airplanes were trespassing on their land. The Supreme Court overturned hundreds of years of property law precedents, believing it had no other choice in the modern world. Commercial air flight was upheld.[44] Indeed, government basically determined the fortunes of the airlines for the first sixty-four years of commercial aviation. Juan Trippe's Pan American Airways, for example, controlled all U.S. overseas flights. In many cases, no other airline had the capital to make the investment to fly to the farthest regions of the globe and the U.S. government needed a strong American presence to protect its interests. Trippe hired Charles Lindbergh to bolster his credentials in Washington and across the globe. For navigational purposes, Pan Am had the largest private radio network in the world. It was the first airline with regularly scheduled flights across the Pacific, stopping in Hawaii, Midway, Wake Island, and Guam. Pan Am had to build the bases, construct hotels for the required overnight stays, and contract with ocean-going vessels to deliver the fuel. In 1947, Pan American inaugurated the first around-the-world regular service. Increasingly frequent international flights reduced American isolation from the rest of the world.

Boeing made its first two airplanes in 1916, which were assembled in a shipyard in Puget Sound and a hangar at a lake in Seattle. Being a strong believer in the quality of his work, Bill Boeing test flew the planes himself, staking his life on it. Boeing built half of the 7,000 B-17 Flying Fortresses in World War II, the other half being produced by other manufacturers according to Boeing plans.

The basis for the great surge in airplane speed, reliability, and range were the investments in air technology during and after World War II. Military aircraft advances spilled over into the civilian sector. Big projects in military aviation required focus and superior management, such as that provided at Lockheed's Skunk Works. At one point, Lockheed's Kelly Johnson was responsible for about a third of the man-made objects in the sky. After World War II, he developed most of the first military jets, the F-104, the C-130, the U-2, and the SR-71. Kelly took over an ailing satellite program which was behind schedule by three years, was 700 percent above budget, and had 1,271 inspectors in just one part of the program. Its successful launch rate was twelve and a half percent. He reduced the number of inspectors from 1,271 to 35, got the project back on schedule, began operating below budget, and increased the successful launch rate.

Frank Whittle of the U.K. patented a gas turbine for jet propulsion in 1930, made a test run in 1937, flew the first jet in 1941, and produced the first jet fighter in 1943. The bureaucratic British Air Ministry delayed his efforts, as did a skeptical National Academy of Sciences. Whittle was favorably impressed by the American enthusiasm for innovation and became an immigrant to the U.S. where he helped the United States become dominant in the manufacture of jet engines.[45]

In 1958, the introduction of the Boeing 707 directly led to a demise of passenger railroad and steamship services. A three-day trip across the continent by rail took only five hours by air and a one-week trip across the Atlantic Ocean by boat was just seven hours by air.[46] Boeing and Pan Am then upped the ante even further, agreeing to put up $2 billion and $550 million respectively to build the Boeing 747, whose passenger economy section alone was longer than the Wright Brothers' first flight. The deal was almost vetoed by President Johnson for putting the two companies at financial risk, but Charles Lindbergh convinced him of its merit. The design and building of the plane was a major undertaking between Boeing, Pan Am, and Pratt and Whitney.

The plane became the symbol of America's technological prowess, improving the productivity of overseas flight by 3.5 times, while reducing air and noise pollution. By 2004, the fleet of 747s totaled 900, having flown over 35 billion miles or 7,400 trips to the moon, carrying half a million people a day.[47] The revolution in world supply and transportation systems enabled Boeing to reduce the time it takes to build a 737 airplane from twenty-eight to eleven days. The company plans to build future generations of planes in just a couple of days with all parts being computer-designed for assembly. The company will use reverse auctions to encourage suppliers to cut prices.[48]

In the 1970s, both airline companies and unions opposed deregulation, but the proposal was passed with the strong support of President Carter. Prices almost immediately began to plummet; Pan American and Eastern airlines went bankrupt, being excessively dependent on government price controls and political determinations of who owned the routes and gates at the airports. In their place, airlines such as American, Delta, and United became ascendant, dependent on hubs and reservation systems. Based on highly sophisticated software, the new reservation systems gave these airlines a huge competitive advantage in steering customers to their flights and in managing their businesses. In particular, highly elaborate algorithms maximized their pricing and profitability. Companies such as IBM and Control Data spent enormous amounts of time and resources developing and deploying such systems, which were ideally suited for hub networks and to attract lucrative business customers. With the advent of the Internet, the paradigm for the entire industry changed. The customer could use the same software and processing power, made available over the Internet, to find the cheapest pricing and best flights. Almost overnight, pricing power went from American, Delta, and United to the consumer, who in turn chose low-cost airlines like Southwest, Air Tran, and Jet Blue. Wall Street quickly grasped the significance of the change, while Delta, American, and United stayed with their outmoded, high-cost, mainframe computer-based systems. For much of the 1990s, the market value of upstart Southwest airlines stock exceeded the market value of the big three airlines combined. Delta and United subsequently filed for bankruptcy.

During World War II, the British invented a radar transmitter known as the cavity magnetron, technology which was given to the United States for use in military applications. Radar is the sending out of a radio-wave pulse that strikes an object such as a ship, plane, or cloud that reflects back to the transmitting station, providing information about distance, composition, and other key attributes of the target. A team of physicists was put to work advancing this technology in a secret lab at MIT. Eventually, ten Nobel Prizes were awarded for the development of this key technology. The U.S. military used this advance to develop stealth technology and precisely guide planes through heavy fog and severe weather during the Berlin airlift. Civilian uses included air-traffic control, the microwave oven, AT&T's long distance microwave network, weather forecasting, and medical scanning devices. Nuclear magnetic resonance used in MRI machines in hospitals led to a revolution in the medical field.

ADVANCED MATERIALS AND CONGLOMERATES

New materials and substances, forerunners of the revolution in nanotechnology, led to important technological advances, creating new industries. Prior to World War II, rubber was derived from trees that were grown naturally in Brazil and Asia. During the war, the threat of having this supply cut off spurred the creation of a substitute so that, by 1945, the production of synthetic rubber surpassed 800,000 tons annually, accounting for 85 percent of all U.S. consumption and providing a major boost to the war effort. Du Pont developed nylon, which would eventually change fashion and fabrics throughout the globe. Nylon, which became the company's most profitable product, was the result of research into polymers, molecules that gave rubber and silk their special properties. In 1938, Du Pont's Roy Plunkett invented Teflon, which was used in cooking ware, bridges, boats, planes, spacesuits, missile nose cones, heat shields, telephone and computer cables, and artificial body parts.[49] In the 1960s, Stephanie Louise Kwolek, a chemist at DuPont, experimented with a variety of strong fibers and discovered liquid polymers, which resulted in the development of

Kevlar used to make bulletproof vests, fiber-optic cable, radial tires, and airplane fuselages.

Magnetic tape made possible the repeating of experience through cameras and tape recorders. The development of the tape recorder made instant replay available to a wide range of sports, news, and broadcast entertainment. Home tape recorders allowed families to repeat their most prized experiences, from birthdays to holiday gatherings. The Polaroid instant camera gave the photographer quick feedback within one minute, then in just two seconds. Repeating these experiences reshaped human consciousness.[50]

Conglomerates were based on the assumption that good managers could improve any business. Between 1950 and 1970, the percentage of firms restricting their business to one industry fell from 70 to 35 percent. The basic assumption of this approach did not work and the resulting failed enterprises contributed to poor economic performance during the 1970s.[51]

Even though conglomerates were out of favor, General Electric (GE) became one of America's premier companies. Jack Welch, one of America's great managers, made GE into the most admired company in the world. Many of his innovative management principles and theories became clichés by the end of his tenure. GE is number one in most of its businesses, usually exiting when falling below number two. The company, whose senior management is half foreign and almost all of whom have worked abroad, developed a wide range of global businesses in fields, such as aircraft engines, finance, power systems, plastics, broadcasting, medical systems, appliances, and lighting. GE's ability to provide customers long-term service and contracts made clients dependent on its support. GE was one of the first major American companies to target foreign markets, such as China, India, and Mexico, and to make more money internationally than domestically.

Deming

The nature of the relationship between Japan and the United States over the past two centuries provides important insights on how to deal with the new Chinese and Asian competitive threat. In the nineteenth and early twentieth centuries, American success was contagious. Japan emulated U.S. practices and tipped the balance of power in Asia. As a result of the American effort to open Japanese markets in the mid-1800s, Japan grew as fast as any European nation, 5 percent or more a year, with a rapidly growing manufacturing sector, a vast rail and telegraph network, a large merchant marine and navy, and a capable military. Japan used its strong economy and military force in wars against China in 1894–1995 and Russia in 1904–1905, and in annexing Korea in 1910. While not a world power, Japan was a regional force in Asia.

For almost a century prior to World War II, Japan focused on manufacturing and industrial growth.[52] In the first half of the twentieth century, it accounted for as much as five percent of the world's industrial production. American occupation of the country after World War II enabled capitalism to flourish, ending the stifling prewar society and liberating Japan's entrepreneurial spirit. Deming began talking to Japan's industrial leaders in 1950. He recalls a meeting, one of his very first lectures in Japan, where about 70 percent of industrial capital of the country was in the room. The Japanese were surprised that someone who just defeated them was willing to teach them the secrets of American business success. Japanese businessmen had been awed by American mass production in World War II that had overwhelmed the Japanese military. They assumed that Deming's methods were why Americans led the world in manufacturing. Deming and the Japanese industrial leadership were able to build a synergism, common language, set of ideas, and new system that became a national standard for Japan. The Japanese had for decades been building the foundation for this economic renaissance. Education, for example, was compulsory and universal, resembling the U.S. model, and teachers were encouraged to teach with an international perspective.

Deming told the Japanese leaders that they could become competitive with Americans in five years by focusing on high-quality products. A Japanese executive wrote that at first, "We really didn't believe him, but in order not to lose face, we did what we were told and it worked."[53] The Japanese became so committed to quality that they would take American books and try to translate the contents them-selves and copy them by hand. Japanese companies were rooted in sci-ence and engineering, whereas American managers were from business or law.

> As much as any man [Deming] gave the Japanese the system that allowed them to maximize their greatest natural strength, their manpower. His system, for quality control provided them with a series of industrial disciplines mathe-matically defined, and with a manner of group participa-tion that fitted well with the traditions of their culture. It was in essence a mathematical means of controlling the level of quality on an industrial line by seeking ever finer manufacturing tolerances.[54]

Deming preached that quality requires a total commitment of management from the top down.

> Deming, who was accustomed to being ignored, real-ized he had touched something formidable. It was like watching some raw, powerful human force trying to assert itself. They were going to succeed, he realized. He could tell that. No one was going to stop these people, because they so earnestly wanted to succeed. They had no other priority. They would make any sacrifice ... Their unity of purpose—the fact that everyone in the country, from top to bottom, had the same goal—was staggering to him.[55]

The contrast with Deming's reception in America was startling.

> It was puzzling. Here was this genius who was becom-ing so famous in Japan, whose every word was so impor-tant, and whose words actually turned into deeds—there was tangible evidence that what he said was true, that statis-tical controls could bring higher quality. Yet he was not famous at all in his own country and seemed excluded from the main business circles. They did not bring this up with him for fear it might embarrass him.[56]

Deming had been raised in Cody, Wyoming, home of Buffalo Bill, and in Powell, where his family lived on the frontier in a tarpaper shack without plumbing or electricity. Sometimes the money he earned doing chores was all the family had. He began his education at the University of Wyoming, taught at the Colorado School of Mines, and received a masters degree from the University of Colorado and a doctorate in physics from Yale. He developed many of his theories while working in the summer at the famous AT&T Hawthorne plant and at Bell Labs with Walter Shewhart who developed statistical control processes.

Deming's philosophy had its roots in Frederick Taylor's Scientific Management theory and at AT&T's famous experiments in quality control at the Hawthorne Plant. Taylor's management theory was prevailing at the time, breaking down the assembly line process into components and assigning workers to the same basic tasks. Deming developed a system that emphasized continuous improvement by the whole organization. Quality checks were not done at the end of the process; they were present at each step in the system. He sought to reduce internal conflicts and to get everyone and every part of the organization moving in the same direction. Deming believed organizations are a product of their interactions, that the entire group needs to be rewarded based on its performance. His emphasis on correcting problems was to find the common or basic causes and to improve the whole system. He had a set of fourteen points aimed at transforming organizations.

During World War II, through Deming's efforts, tens of thousands of engineers, statisticians, and production workers were taught to use statistics and analytical methods to improve the quality of U.S. goods and armaments. After the war, Deming continued to support and teach these concepts, but Americans were not fully committed to quality world-class manufacturing. In the late 1940s, America was producing half of the world's manufactured goods. From 1945 to 1964, American industry was in a seller's market. Most international competitors were in ruins from the war, while American manufacturers were largely removed from the ravages of the conflict. The world was so hungry for American products that U.S. companies didn't need to sell quality goods to make profits.

AMERICAN QUALITY GETS THE BOOT

The U.S. was so far ahead and its competitors so inferior in economic strength and technology the nation didn't even realize it was in a race. American management took its dominance for granted and assumed the rest of the world could not catch up. Corporate leaders were caught up in a self-absorbed culture of conformity. Most of American industry opposed quality standards. American business was actually diminishing product quality through efforts such as planned obsolescence. After World War II, automobile longevity declined by three years even though a much higher percentage of the roads were paved: sales of automobile parts and breakdowns soared year after year. The industry wanted to keep the consumer buying cars, so it had little or no desire to make quality automobiles that would delay purchases. The life expectancy of automobile parts, such as tires, kept declining; automobile mufflers had only a half their former life expectancy. Household appliances were also lower quality, particularly washing machines, refrigerators, and driers. Cheap plastic replaced metal in order to improve styling and to allow the use of more colors. Televisions in the late 1940s were of superior quality to those made in the late 1950s, which often had to be repaired within a few weeks of purchase. The Consumers Union found that only one out of seventeen television models deserved to be check-rated. Between World War II and 1960, the number of product repairman doubled to honor warranties and needed repairs.[57]

During the 1950s, 1960s, and 1970s, corporate CEOs were usually career men whose main function was to be a mediator among the stakeholders, more a caretaker role. They were responsible for reducing conflict and improving the company's image. It was assumed, unfortunately, that American management was superior.

American automobile manufacturers were mismanaged, continuing to bet on large cars in the face of an acute energy shortage. Chrysler was forced to accept a federal bailout to escape bankruptcy. The Big Three auto manufacturers never had to compete hard domestically and had become so encumbered they were organizational elephants on the way to becoming dinosaurs. In the 1960s, worker absenteeism soared, reaching as much as 10 percent on Mondays and

Fridays. Workers would sabotage and vandalize cars by, for example, leaving screws in brake drums, scratching paint, and omitting parts of the assembly line process. Some 63 percent of managers said hourly workers were less conscientious than a decade ago and only 2 percent said they were more conscientious.[58]

U.S. business leaders thought the Japanese were copy-cats and not innovators. Yet, it was the American companies that now lacked the proper instruments or corporate dashboards to measure quality.[59] Labor unions would demand and get pay raises without regard to productivity improvements. The United States Steelworkers strikes, particularly a lengthy one in 1959, opened the door to foreign steel imports, which exceeded 15 million tons by the end of the 1960s. The government did not focus on the international consequences of policies such as antitrust (the Department of Justice seldom lost an antitrust case during the post-World War II period). American affluence led to complacency. American culture was transfixed by television, which focused attention on issues such as Vietnam, civil rights, urban riots, and student protests. The American people instinctively knew something was seriously wrong, coining a phrase they uttered almost daily, "boy, they sure don't make things like they used to." There was no concerted national effort to maintain America's competitive edge nor to ensure its continued world leadership in manufacturing.

TRADING PLACES

Japan started out the post-war period a century behind the United States and in twenty-five years accelerated until it was only a decade behind and had the world's second largest economy.[60] In the early 1950s, virtually no Japanese households owned televisions, washing machines or refrigerators, but only ten years later half of them owned all three, and by 1990 over 90 percent owned them all. Steel production went from under 10 million tons in the early 1950s to almost 100 million tons in only fifteen years. After three decades of double digit economic growth between 1950 and 1980, Japan accounted for 15 percent of the world's production.[61]

There were ample warnings about America's deteriorating position, but no political will to fix the problem. In 1966 Harvard professor Wickham Skinner warned that American industries "appear to be losing ground to foreign competition."[62] That same year Joseph Juran, who worked with Deming to improve manufacturing processes in Japan, predicted: "The Japanese are headed for world quality leadership and will attain it in the next two decades because no one else is moving there at the same pace."[63]

Juran, the son of a Romanian immigrant, was raised in a tarpaper shack in Minnesota. He held sixteen jobs by the time he graduated from college when he was hired by Western Electric at its Hawthorne Works. Juran found quality improvement an easier sell in Japan than the United States. He believed American companies were less interested in quality because they were dominated more by financial men than by operations and production executives. Juran formulated an 80-20 rule, concluding that 80 percent of a company's problems stem from 20 percent of the causes that should be the focus of management attention.

Various reasons or excuses have been propounded for the Japanese success and the American failure, such as: too many U.S. companies were competing for market share, the Japanese used industrial policy to give preferred treatment to certain large domestic firms, or the Japanese had special arrangements through their networks of businesses *(keiretsu)* and gained monopoly profits enabling them to sell at or below cost in foreign markets. The most important reason, however, was simply the Japanese commitment to capitalism, competition, and quality. In those industries where the Japanese prevailed, they had more intense competition than did U.S. industries. They had four times as many steel firms, four times as many automobile manufacturers, and three times as many makers of consumer electronics. American oligopolies such as RCA, Zenith, and General Electric gave up the consumer electronics industry to the more entrepreneurial Japanese. Ineffectively managed, vertically integrated American automobile behemoths gave up market share to the better run, more competitive Japanese automobile industry. In their battle against American producers, the Japanese had at least twelve automobile manufacturers, eight makers of VCRs, thirteen makers of fax machines, and twenty copier manufacturers.[64]

The Japanese government-led industrial policies, however, were largely a failure. Its lead agency, MITI, made investments in the wrong industries, awarded grants to poor technologies or approaches, and contributed to the calcification of domestic industries by its bureaucratic approach. Outlays in biotechnology, hypersonic planes, deep underground construction, superconductivity, textiles, and other areas failed to establish Japan as a world leader in those areas. The *keiretsu* became major obstacles to entrepreneurial and innovative approaches and actually ended up being a drag on the Japanese economy. On the other hand, for certain key manufacturing sectors, the country did develop successful export promotion programs. In the early 1950s, for example, buyers of machine tools were subsidized for half the purchase price. Targeted export industries were awarded large tax breaks and subsidized financing. During the critical period immediately after World War II, imports in these key sectors were banned.[65]

Deming came back to America to teach his management philosophy and methods, but few paid attention. The American automobile industry, however, was in deep trouble, producing shoddy cars inferior to the high quality of the Japanese manufacturers. Seemingly overnight, America and Japan were trading places. Deming appeared on an NBC show about Japanese quality called *If Japan Can, Why Can't We?* A manager at Ford was watching, brought Deming to the company, and the Taurus was the result, soon becoming America's number one selling automobile and Ford made quality job number one.

When an American automobile company was having trouble making transmissions, it tested twelve Japanese transmissions to determine why they weren't having any of the same problems. The engineer reported the measuring equipment was broken. It wasn't; there was simply too little variance to measure. For practical purposes, the transmissions were identical. The Japanese awarded the Deming Prize to its distinguished manufacturers for such advances in quality. The Deming Prize money came from Deming's book royalties, which, while virtually unknown in America, were bestsellers in Japan.

Deming's teachings are not easily summarized, because he focused on the big picture, overhauling the whole organization. He had four basic concepts, which now have been incorporated into many other management philosophies:

1. Business should be customer-driven, focusing on what the customer needs even if he isn't sure exactly what is needed to improve the business. The consumer defines value.
2. Systems, not individuals, must be the focus of quality. People are not the problem, the system is and must be overhauled accordingly.
3. Strategy and getting to the root cause is essential before change can be accomplished and an organization significantly improved.
4. Employees must be empowered and given the key role in changing the organization. Employees will be motivated if they are being listened to.

Deming died disappointed that he was unable to get the attention of American business leaders in the 1950s and 1960s to have them understand the importance of making quality the number one priority.

Two world-class companies built through the application of Deming's principles are Matsushita and Sony. Konosuke Matsushita grew a business from a start-up to $42 billion in annual revenues, creating a household brand—Panasonic. His company had faster revenue growth than American companies run by famous CEOs, such as Henry Ford, Sam Walton, and Ray Kroc. In 1917, he started his first factory at home with his wife, working eighteen hours seven days a week. Matsushita adopted the philosophy that each product had to be 30 percent better and 30 percent cheaper than the competition. Even in the Depression, he made no layoffs, instead assigning his employees to sell excess inventory.

Akio Morita, cofounder of Sony, built a manufacturing empire based on the production of transistor radios, VCRs, satellite dishes, TVs, stereos, CD players, and boom boxes. His initial big product was Japan's first tape recorder after World War II and he quickly followed with the transistor radio and Walkman. Sony grew even faster than Matsushita and became a household name in the west, a symbol of Japanese manufacturing prowess. The Japanese achieved similar feats in automobiles, replacing West Germany as the world's leading exporter in the 1970s and going on to lead the world in production by 1980.

By the early 1970s, the Japanese were incredulous about the backwardness of America's industrial production. Quality control had fallen far behind with expenses for warranty repair at least double and sometimes quadruple for American products. Labor relations were poor and investment in plant and equipment inadequate. By contrast, Japan was surging and challenging the world in manufacturing.

> In the 1980s, Japan surpassed the Soviet Union in economic production. It was the world's largest producer of ships, automobiles, and televisions. It had the largest corporation in the world. It had the largest banks. It had the largest stock market. It was the most successful trader on earth. It was the world's greatest creditor. It was calculated to be the world's richest nation in total assets, domestic and foreign. It became the greatest financial power in the world. . . .

> The United States had possessed all the advantages in resources, population, science and technology, and industrial plant; Japan was one of the poorest countries in the world in oil, coal, iron ore, and the minerals of modern industry, and its population was less than half that of the United States. But Japanese success was ascribed to several factors. Cheap labor was one. Japanese employees and salesmen worked tirelessly and aggressively for wages Americans would not accept. The work ethic gave Japanese an advantage. . . . [T]he Japanese adapted American innovations and turned them into salable products, as the Americans had once raided British and European technology, and eventually the Japanese made their own technological advances. As the world's thriftiest savers, the Japanese invested heavily in their businesses and in research into salable products. They

were not profligate consumers who spent on luxury or for the moment, as Americas were increasingly wont to do. American businessmen faulted Japanese tariffs for the failure of their exports to Japan. . . . Import duties played a part in the restraint of trade, but so did legal agreements and price-fixing. Finally, the Japanese were criticized for their freedom from heavy expenditures for defense because Japan's consti-tution—written under American supervision after the war—forbade the country from establishing a military, and the United Sates was protecting under defense agree-ments.[66]

America never fully recovered from the edge it lost during the 1950s, 1960s, and 1970s. Entire industries, such as consumer electron-ics, apparel, and toys moved overseas. The steel and automobile indus-tries lost substantial market share to international competition. America's share of the world's manufactured goods plummeted from a half to a quarter. American companies, particularly defense firms, developed the technology for the facsimile machine. Not being in the consumer electronics business, Americans didn't understand the mar-ket for the fax. Who would spend over $1,000 for a device hooked up to the phone which would send paper at a $1 per page when a letter at the post office cost only 25 cents? The Japanese looked at consumer uses for the product, particularly the demand for overnight courier services. When the fax machine became popular, not one fax machine for sale in the U.S. was American-made, even though many of the parts were purchased and much of the technology was licensed from U.S. businesses. When the consumer electronics industry moved abroad, it also translated into the loss of much of the manufacturing capability for computers. Within a few years after the development of new com-puter products and technologies, such as mini-computers and PCs, most of that manufacturing shifted abroad. Almost all PCs today are manufactured overseas. Similarly, all the manufacturing of plasma and liquid-crystal display (LCD) panels for high definition television and other communications uses is done abroad.

THE UNITED STATES REBOUNDS AND JAPAN FALTERS

American industry made a comeback. By the 1990s, manufacturing revived and reached levels of output achieved in the 1960s. It was, however, a much lower percentage of the world's total output. In the same decade, investment in the U.S. reached record levels for the post-World War II period. Productivity gains reached levels previously attained only in the 1960s and nineteenth century. By 1994, the United States once again produced more cars than did Japan, although an increasing share of the cars manufactured in America were made by Japanese and other international companies. Americans led in the world in producing new products such as drugs, medical equipment, and commercial jets. It regained its role as the world's largest exporter. Part of the resurgence was due to the adoption of quality methods from Deming and others which contributed to the surge in American productivity.

During the four decades after World War II, the Japanese economy grew at a pace of 5 to 7 percent annually and became the envy of the world. America found itself increasingly unable to compete with the Japanese because of the expense of the Cold War, complacency on the part of American business, and the inability to rein in its welfare programs and government . The excesses of the 1960s forced President Nixon to abandon the Bretton Woods system of fixed exchange rates and to depreciate the dollar. To limit the domestic consequences, he imposed a tariff on imported goods that was not removed until other countries appreciated their currencies by changing how they were pegged to the dollar. Nixon then imposed wage and price controls, which increased inflationary expectations. President Carter tried to talk down the dollar; when combined with an ineffective Federal Reserve Bank (Fed) policy, this action led to rampant inflation in the 1970s. The new Fed Bank Chairman Paul Volcker's successful effort to bring down the rate of inflation with a tight monetary policy created extremely high interest rates that caused the dollar to shoot up and the shock to fall disproportionately on domestic manufacturers, creating a "rust bowl" in the Northeast and Midwest. Japanese manufacturers dominated markets such as consumer electronics and automobiles. The Reagan Administration tried to talk down the dollar, with the

Japanese yen appreciating the most and creating expectations of additional appreciation. These actions destabilized the Japanese financial system. Japan experienced one of the greatest speculative booms in history—with stocks and real estate soaring to unheard of prices. When the bubble burst, the Japanese stock market declined 60 percent and property prices by 80 percent.

Like many other government efforts to manage economies, the American-Japanese attempts to manage trade and currencies did not work. Markets generally outsmart government.[67] As Peter Drucker stated in the early 1990s, even the supposedly sound economic efforts to weaken the dollar to correct the trade imbalance with Japan failed.

> Every time the dollar declines . . . we are told by the experts that "this time" the trade deficit with Japan will surely go away. And every time the dollar declines, the Japanese howl that *endaka*—the high yen—will destroy their industries and drive them into bankruptcy.
>
> U.S. manufacturing exports to Japan have indeed nearly doubled in the past 10 years. But they have increased even faster in countries—some in Europe, others in Latin America—where the dollar's value has actually increased. And despite *endaka,* Japanese manufactured exports to the U.S. have grown just as fast as U.S. manufactured-goods exported to Japan. Therefore, the trade deficit has remained pretty much the same—even widening a bit since the dollar was first devalued. . . .
>
> According to all economic theory this simply could not have happened: The U.S. trade deficit with Japan *must* have disappeared. At least it must have markedly shrunk. And the Washington experts still promise us that, indeed, this *will* happen the next time around, and "inevitably" so. But if for a whole decade the inevitable does not happen, one should stop promising it. In fact, the cheap dollar policy of U.S. governments in the past 10 years has rested on totally wrong assumptions regarding the Japanese economy. Japan, rather than the U.S., is the beneficiary of a cheap dollar. . . .

Japan imports all its industrial raw materials, four-fifths of its fuel and energy, and a little more than one-third of its food. . . . According to economic theory and economic history, commodity prices should have gone up in dollars by the same proportion by which the dollar went down. But they didn't.

On the contrary, during the past 10 years the dollar prices of commodities—whether foods, industrial raw materials or oil—have actually plummeted. In yen, Japan, the world's largest commodity importers, gets an incredible bargain. Feeding its population, running its factories and heating its homes now costs Japan little more than a third of what it had cost it 10 years ago. As an importer, Japan benefits heavily from *endaka*—and so does its standard of living. . . .

A very large and growing part of Japan's exports to the U.S.—may be enough to account for the entire U.S. trade deficit with Japan—comprises parts, supplies and machinery for the plants Japan has built in this country and the companies it has bought here. If Toyota, for instance, builds a plant in Kentucky, most of the machinery and tools it requires will be bought from the people who have supplied Toyota's plants in Japan for years. And the parts for the cars the plant builds will come from the people who supply Toyota in Nagoya.

U.S. manufacturers act exactly the same way when they invest in plants of companies abroad. But the cheap dollar has made it prohibitively expensive for Americans to invest in Japan. In fact, it has forced a shrinking of the U.S. investment base in Japan. . . .

A cheaper yen would, in all likelihood, unleash a flood of American investments in Japan—now the world's number two consumer market—and with it a flood of exports of high-value-added and high-quality-job goods. But it is also quite possible that a higher dollar would bring in substantially larger foreign-exchange earnings from our commodity exports to Japan—the world's largest commodity importer and by far the largest buyer of American food and raw materials exports, such as timber.[68]

The self-serving strategy of the United States could not alter the competitive advantage of the Japanese manufacturers and it triggered a speculative boom and a bust followed by stagnation. Japan may have faced many of the same problems if it had not acquiesced to U.S. demands, but Japan almost certainly would have been better off by opposing the U.S. policies.

In the deflationary 1990s, Japan experienced its worst recession of the post-World War II era, suffering through what became known as the "Japanese Disease." A succession of oil and currency shocks led to a boom-and-bust economy. The rapid drop in land prices and the stock market created a serious banking crisis that was prolonged by cumbersome financial regulations. Interest rates were cut too slowly, and banks refused to write-off nonperforming loans. Excessive regulations and inflexibility impeded recovery; Japanese red tape is even worse than Russia's. Regulations that kept a major portion of land devoted to agriculture, for example, contributed to the speculative boom, but also prevented recovery because many Japanese didn't have the space to build bigger homes or buy consumer goods such as large appliances and second television sets. Businesses refused to downsize; the retail sector remained inflexible; and regulations continued to provide excessive protections to landlords. Large Japanese corporations were impervious to change, antitrust laws, and the obvious business strategy of entering into the new information technology and biotechnology markets. Small Japanese firms escaped to Hawaii where the business climate was much better and healthier without the Japanese regulatory and financial hardships. In Japan, services were heavily regulated with prices high due to lack of competition.

During the American occupation and subsequently, the Japanese adopted a Western-type retirement system. Fear about providing for the world's most rapidly aging population drove savings rates to extremely high levels that quashed economic growth. The culture remained resistant to tapping the productive potential of the elderly, women, and outside ethnic and racial groups. Japanese society experienced a weakening of its work ethic and stubbornly clung to a value system that placed excessive emphasis on homogeneity and conformity. A decline in public spiritedness led to business and political scandals and a languishing of the nation's political will. The capital gains rate was increased to 20 percent and a national sales tax was implemented and then increased. The United States pressured the Japanese government to increase domestic spending through infrastructure investment, creating a "construction-industrial complex." The Japanese then ran up a huge national debt, which was compounded by pension liabilities. The country squandered much of the infrastructure spending on useless projects, such as paving over river beds, tunneling through mountains to nowhere, and building new harbors in dying fishing villages. The final result was that even zero percent loans and hundreds of billions of dollars in pump priming could not revive the economy.

The fallout from the oil and currency shocks and other global changes caused Japan's government to shift gears from promoting export growth industries to protecting inefficient domestic businesses. The retail industry, agriculture, housing and public works sectors had always dragged down Japanese productivity. Deming's quality methods were never applied to these sectors. Protectionism had sheltered these industries and its cartels from competition; Japanese suffered from what is known as a dual economy—an efficient export economy and an inefficient consumer sector. The Japanese had particularly low productivity in retailing, housing, and agriculture sectors that favored the producer over the consumer and brought on economic stagnation.[69] Japanese productivity in food processing was only a third of the United States and continued to lose ground. Textile production was almost as bad.[70] The energy business was similarly noncompetitive. Inefficient land policies made the housing sector even worse. MITI took counterproductive actions to reduce competition. Simultaneously, the efficient exporters were being driven to other countries by high costs and competition, particularly from China. These disparities saddled Japan with low consumer spending and excessively high savings and investment.

By emphasizing the reform of stagnant domestic industries and losing its focus on high growth export sectors, Japan's growth fell from 4 to 2 percent a year during the 1990s. At the lower rate of growth, it was more difficult to pay off debts, find jobs, improve living standards, and create wealth, particularly with so much of the attention and resources being focused on the inefficient sectors. Many public interest groups opposed reforms in these sectors, so they too became stagnant.[71]

The Japanese still dominate industries such as consumer electronics and automobiles. Toyota has become the leading automobile company in the world, outpacing General Motors and Ford. Toyota designs better cars, uses quality processes to get the most out of its suppliers, and offers superior automobiles and customer service. Toyota also skillfully deployed more than $10 billion of its capital in the United States, creating more jobs in America than the entire Japanese economy created in the first five years of the new millennium. The Japanese took advantage of American automobile companies who are hamstrung by enormous health care costs and the complex U.S. tax code. Toyota leveraged it advantages in the American market while the U.S. companies were stuck with its disadvantages and suffered from complacency, poor product decisions, and ineffective management. Decades of government policy intervention failed to alter the basic Japanese competitive advantage over American manufacturers. Japanese competition has, however, forced American industries to transform themselves.[72]

Drucker and Deming created a revolution in management that positively impacted many organizations in the private sector in the U.S. and Japan. These principles and strategies could not overcome the overall lack of competitiveness in the American culture and political system, and the stagnation in the domestic-oriented part of Japan's dual economy. The management revolution succeeded where managers were smart enough to apply its principles.

14

Cyberspace

THE TINY UBIQUITOUS MICROCHIP, derived from the most common of elements, is keystone to the computer-based, contemporary, worldwide, fast-paced, new information technology. This remarkable invention improved data capacity and processing speed by more than a billion-fold in slightly over fifty years. The chip is the most revolutionary invention in human history.

Working at Bell Labs in the late 1940s, William Brattain, William Shockley, and John Bardeen sought to replace the bulky, unreliable, and inefficient vacuum tube, the basis for AT&T's telecommunications network. Initially, its inventors seemed to have no inkling that the microchip could be used in computers. First-generation computers were monstrous devices built around huge racks of vacuum tubes that used high power and generated too much heat. The cumbersome early devices led humorist Dave Barry to observe: "Because of the extremely high cost and phenomenal inaccuracy of early computers, the only customer for them was the federal government."

The Bell Labs team developed the transistor, which had its first major popular application in Sony's transistor radio. The transistor, while similar to the vacuum tube it replaced, was compact and energy efficient. Prior to the transistor, the telephone network had been comprised entirely of analog technology and electromechanical switches.

The transistor and microchip spurred conversion of this huge and cost-ly network to digital technology and to electronic switches that could be placed into units, which were compact, but powerful to operate.

Transistor development was thwarted by the problem of inter-connection and a so-called tyranny of numbers. Circuits could use 10,000, 100,000, or a million transistors and comparable numbers of resistors, diodes, and capacitors. The resulting super-circuits could outperform anything that had been developed before, but all the com-ponents had to be connected in a loop, each component requiring sev-eral or numerous interconnections with other parts of the circuit.[1] It was impossible, however, to wire that many different parts together. The mere labor cost for wiring was greater than the total cost of the components. Even the simplest computer calculation can require thou-sands of transistors, so it was imperative for fast computers to have millions or billions of transistors or components.

In the late 1950s, Jack Kilby developed the first semiconductor or microchip at Texas Instruments. He built on the work of Gordon Teal, who had discovered that silicon was the best substance to use for man-ufacturing transistors. The microchip combined transistors, resistors, capacitors, and distributed capacitors onto a single device, hence the term "integrated circuit." Kilby was able to make all the parts or com-ponents of the circuit out of one material—silicon. Integration elimi-nated much of the interconnection problem and its inherent tyranny of too many numbers. Wiring was no longer needed; the connection could be imprinted on the silicon or printed circuit board, and multi-ple transistors could be put on the same silicon or board. Separately and independently, Robert Noyce also developed an integrated circuit. He improved Kilby's design and developed a process for manufactur-ing chips. The microchip radically altered the electronic manufactur-ing process. Developing the first chip or integrated circuit might cost tens of millions or billions-plus dollars, but any number of copies can be made subsequently for little cost. These transistors and chips are now used in thousands of devices—cell phones, televisions, comput-ers, cameras, CD players, and automobiles and are manufactured by the billions.

Unlike the beginning of the industrial era when Thomas Edison was among the more famous men on the planet, Kilby and Noyce lived in relative anonymity—even though they were responsible for an essential invention of the twentieth century. Kilby, for example, was far better known in Japan than in his own country. Eventually, he was properly recognized by being awarded a Nobel Prize. When he gave the requisite speech in the Scandinavian lecture hall, he was introduced as the man who launched the global digital revolution. Given his modesty and proclivity for avoiding publicity, Kilby opened his speech by declining the accolade saying that it reminded him of the beaver who told the rabbit at the base of the Hoover dam: "No, I didn't build it myself, but it's based on an idea of mine."

From the original microchip, Intel invented the dynamic random-access memory or DRAM chip, but was forced out of that market by efficient Japanese manufacturers. Intel then moved to develop the microprocessor or computer-on-a-chip. Initially, Intel designers expected the need for three separate chips, but inventors at Texas Instruments found a way to reduce all of the functions to one chip. Texas Instruments did not understand the commercial potential and lost its advantage to Intel.[2] The first Intel microprocessor contained 2,300 transistors and packed as much computing power as the original ENIAC mainframe computer, which was as big as a two-car garage. Included in this chip were all of the key components of the personal computer for the next two decades—the working memory (DRAM), the software memory (EPROM), and the basic microprocessor (CPU). Over the next twenty years, more than half of the revenues from the semiconductor industry were from parts and processes invented by Intel. Initially, Intel envisioned selling these chips for traffic lights, cars, and domestic ovens, but not for home computers (which were then nonexistent).

In the middle 1970s, the Japanese used their lead in advanced manufacturing techniques together with their superb mastery of quality processes to surpass the U.S. in the production of computer chips and semiconductors. Japanese success was largely due to Japanese ability to replicate and manufacture American inventions on a mass basis, not, as was the popular impression at the time, on help from government agencies responsible for the nation's industrial policy. Japan, however, failed to keep pace with itself. The next generation of integrated circuits was based not on the capability of producing huge quantities of the same chip design, but rather on new technology and principles developed by computer scientist Carver Mead that used computer-aided engineering and design. His techniques dramatically simplified design methods and opened the way for chips with custom uses. A series of advances based on Mead's efforts, such as the silicon compiler, resulted in chips being designed for specific applications and uses. These advances undermined Japan's strategy of investing in huge fabrication or manufacturing facilities and moved the value-added to the design stage and toward more entrepreneurial firms that could make a variety of chips to incorporate different designs. Application-specific or custom-designed chips can be hundreds of times more efficient than commodity chips. Mead's theories were used also to develop a technique for integrating circuits on the wafers that hold the chips. Previously, engineers had to use expensive and cumbersome wires to hold the chips in place. The design of chip hardware increasingly involved software and reliance on entrepreneurs rather than on corporate conglomerates with bureaucracies. This paradigm shift added to the complexity and entrepreneurial nature of chip manufacturing, favoring America's strengths.

The computer chip is governed by Moore's Law, named after Gordon Moore, a founder of Intel. The power, speed, or productivity of the silicon chip doubles every eighteen months without any corresponding increase in cost or significant increase in size. Doubling something every eighteen months for thirty years increases it by a factor of more than a million times. Over a period of fifty-five years, it increases by a factor of a billion. As chip power continues to double, this number will reach one trillion around 2020. Each integrated microprocessor has the power of the equivalent of a billion of the transistors invented in the early 1950s. A billion transistors is the equivalent of the central processing units of sixteen Cray leading-edge super-computers. This increase in efficiency far exceeds any other invention in history—the printing press by a million fold, the most advanced facto-ry processes by thousands of times, advances such as the steam engine, the wheel, and the automobile by millions of times. Gordon Moore, Carver Mead, Jack Kilby, and other leaders and inventors in the field of microelectronics may be considered true revolutionaries of the twenti-eth century.

The impact of this magnitude of change is overwhelming. The lit-tle greeting cards that play "Happy Birthday" have more computer power than existed on the entire planet before 1950. A home video camera has more power than the original IBM 360 mainframe. The lat-est model automobiles have more computing power than the vehicles that took man to the moon. Most new video game machines have more processing power than a super-computer less than a decade ago. The performance gap between PCs and mainframe computers has become close: a new PC has the processing power of a mainframe or a super computer just a decade ago.

Microchips penetrate countless aspects of daily life with astonish-ing speed. The first applications included calculators, word processors, and a broad range of business applications. The chip plays a major role in the automobile. The consumer electronics industry was trans-formed, as chips became a central part of televisions, kitchen appli-ances, VCRs, CDs, mobile telephones, digital cameras, DVDs, and hun-dreds of everyday items.

J.R. Simplot helped to establish Micron Technology, one of the leading manufacturers of semiconductor products. He made two for-tunes—one out of potato chips and another out of computer chips. He had started out as a potato farmer in Idaho and eventually supplied McDonald's with over half of its potatoes for French fries. He made numerous advances in potato farming—fast sorting, food dehydration (which created potato flakes for the troops in World War II), and freez-ing potatoes that had led to his contract to sell frozen French fries to McDonald's in the 1960s, which made him a billionaire. Subsequently, Simplot became the chief financier and driving force behind Micron, one of the largest computer chip companies. Micron became the only major American manufacturer of DRAM chips—staving off a number of tough Japanese manufacturers in the high-volume, low-margin end of the chip business.

In today's world, the powers of the mind are everywhere ascendant over brute force, because the central thrust of the computer chip revolution is the overthrow of matter. Ascendant nations and corporations are now masters not of land and material resources but of ideas and technologies. While America's national wealth has increased dramatically, the total economic output in volume of materials is the same as fifty or a hundred years ago. The nation's economy, for example, is seven times larger than in Harry Truman's administration, but the input of materials is only modestly higher.[3] Americans are many times richer but produce much less in the way of material or physical goods. A microprocessor, for example, is worth its weight in gold. An individual with a PC can today do the work of dozens or even thousands of minds devoted to routine tasks. In most of today's products, knowledge outstrips the value of materials.

SOFTWARE

Software, which controls and directs a computer's functions, is the second key component of the current information revolution. Software development closely paralleled and was directly related to chip development. The computer chip runs software programs. In a fashion similar to the chip, the first copy of a software program can cost thousands, millions, and, in the case of Windows, billions of dollars, but each additional copy usually costs only a few cents. During software's infancy, America had the largest venture capital market in the world, and it funded development of the software industry. English is the international language of computing and software. By the middle of the 1990s, America was making an estimated three quarters of the packaged software sold worldwide, worth over $100 billion annually.

Intellectual property and patents form the basis for the software industry. In 1980, the Congress granted copyright protection to computer programs, protection that encompasses descriptive-source code and computerized-object code. The Supreme Court held that the use of software could be patented with Justice William Rehnquist observing that patents can "include anything under the sun that is made by man."[4]

Microsoft, founded by Bill Gates, is the largest and most important software company. It overwhelmed traditional computer companies like IBM and DEC that did not believe in the personal computer model or its market. Microsoft started out by selling its software fairly cheaply, trying to get its programming language and operating system into as many PCs and organizations as possible. Microsoft programs became the industry standard and the value of its products skyrocketed with their widespread deployment. Once Microsoft's product became the operating system for the IBM and other PCs, then software companies had to write programs for their systems, except for the small portion of the market with Apple MACs.[5]

Bill Gates and his partners at Microsoft became the dominant firm in the new information industry; they created more wealth than any business in the history of American capitalism. In only two decades, Gates went from working in a college dormitory to commanding the most highly valued company in the world, by building on the successes of the computer chip industry. He and Paul Allen read electronics magazines and gained an understanding of Intel's chips and Moore's law. Gates met his future CEO Steve Ballmer at Harvard University (both got perfect scores on their math SATs) and attended class with future computer industry leaders Scott McNealy and Bill Joy of Sun Microsystems. He left Harvard to develop software for the new computer models. Gates continually upgraded his operating system and programming applications to profit from the incredible improvements in semiconductor technology. He also profited from IBM being hamstrung by an antitrust suit during the nascent period of software development—1969 to 1981.[6] Gates' hold over the PC software industry earned him the enmity of many in the technology field and several antitrust suits. He worked hard, paying himself a low salary and betting on the rise of Microsoft stock. One of his board members would bet his Friday-night dinner companions that Gates would be in his office, usually getting him on the first ring of his cell phone. Gates developed new business models based on "increasing returns" and occasionally took week-long retreats to a hideaway to overview his technology development for the coming year ("Think Week").

The software industry was jump-started by other figures and companies such as Larry Ellison of Oracle, which developed software for businesses and relational databases, handling many of the computer functions for the world's largest companies. Highly regarded for his technological vision, Bill Joy was the chief technologist of Sun Microsystems, best known for its networking software, including Java. Besides these American firms, there were thousands of smaller software companies and hundreds of thousands of individual programmers. One of the next big advances predicted for software is effective computer speech recognition technology that will use complex statistical methods to match voice sound bits with the right words, utilizing increased computer power.

DATA STORAGE

Data storage is the third major component of computer technology. This industry has experienced growth even more explosive than that of the computer chip—it has tripled in power every eighteen months. EMC and other American companies have been the key players in this market. Data storage technology has made it possible for the entire contents of the Library of Congress to be stored on an individual's PC.

COMPUTER COMPANIES

America was where electronic computing started and grew the fastest. The computer chip, software, and data storage are part of the larger computer industry. Throughout the earliest stages of this revolution, America had the highest concentration of PCs, by far the largest total number of PCs, and world class computer companies such as IBM, Dell, Compaq, and DEC.

The word *computer* has been part of the English language for centuries, but the initial major application was for the U.S. Census. Charles

Babbage automated mathematical calculations and Hermann Hollerith automated tabulation and manipulation of the U.S. Census data, reducing the process from several years for the 1880 census to six weeks for the 1890 census, saving the Census Bureau $5 million or ten times more than expected. By 1924, this business became IBM. The first American electronic computer, called the ENIAC, was one of the most complicated electronics devices ever built with 18,000 vacuum tubes, 70,000 resisters, 10,000 capacitors, 6,000 switches, and 1,500 relays filling up a 1,500 square foot room. There was enormous demand for its services, which eventually led to the development of the UNIVAC computer that was introduced with great fanfare. The device was used to predict the outcome of the 1952 elections. The machine indicated a Republican victory, but the operators did not trust the calculation, so the election was announced as too close to call.

When Tom Watson launched IBM in 1924 he took over a collection of business information companies and, using research and marketing, eventually molded the firm into a well-run colossus. During the Depression, he narrowly averted bankruptcy, but then profited handsomely from the Roosevelt Administration's creation of many new government agencies, which all needed his information technology. In the economic slowdown, his competitors couldn't keep up with the technology, nor did they have the product inventory. Basically, IBM ran the Social Security system, which required cross tabulation of the files of 30 million Americans, a Herculean task for that era. IBM's business surged in World War II, manufacturing munitions as well as computational machines that facilitated the federal agencies' efforts to carry out the war and performed the calculations for the atomic bomb. Watson began building computers in World War II and is credited by Peter Drucker with being fifteen years ahead of his time. He took the company from revenues of $1.3 million in 1914 to more than $700 million by the time he retired in 1956.[8] Watson was one of the first individuals to predict the transformation to an information society.

Tom Watson Jr. was left with the task of bringing IBM into the electronic computer age. It was not his father (as is often said), but either Howard Aiken or John Mauchly, who both helped to build the first commercial computers, that predicted four to six computers would serve the entire U.S. commercial market. The son suffered medical depression for six years as he resisted the pressure to work at IBM, but military service in World War II changed his outlook. He built the first IBM mainframe, the 701, which used magnetic-core memory and transistors instead of vacuum tubes. IBM developed a computer system to be used as an early warning system for an air attack (made obsolete by long-range missiles), which became the basis for the first airline reservation system, a mainframe project that took years to develop and that put the company deeply into debt, but revolutionized the airline industry. The company went on to develop the IBM 360, historically the most successful mainframe computer, useful in almost every market. By the time Tom Watson Jr. retired in 1971, the company's revenues were $7 billion annually. But then, IBM went on a wild roller-coaster ride.

> In 1985 IBM had the greatest after-tax profit of any company in the history of the world: $6.58 billion. It bestrode the computer market like a colossus. But only seven years later, it had the greatest corporate loss in history up to that time: $5 billion. And the colossus of computing was a company owned by a supernerd Harvard dropout named Bill Gates, who hadn't even been born when IBM built its first computer.
>
> How could so profound a reversal of fortune happen to so powerful a company in so short a time? Simple. In those seven years the computer world changed completely, but IBM didn't change at all.[9]

The company recruited a new chief executive officer from American Express, Louis Gerstner. In one of the great turnarounds in the history of American capitalism, he soon had IBM back into the top position in the computer industry.

Hewlett Packard (HP) is perhaps the most legendary of all high-technology companies. Because of the location of HP, Dave Packard and Bill Hewlett concomitantly launched "Silicon Valley," habitat of many digital technology companies. With a capital investment of $538,

Hewlett and Packard established a business that subsequently employed more than 100,000 people and had revenues in the tens of billions of dollars. Phi Beta Kappa from Stanford University, Packard was a hulking athlete who played football and basketball. After graduation, in just one day on the factory line as an engineer with General Electric in Schenectady, he drastically reduced the company's failure rate for vacuum tubes. He returned to Palo Alto and with Bill Hewlett started HP in 1939 in a garage. The first success was an audio oscillator device to test sound equipment bought by Walt Disney for the film *Fantasia.* After World War II the company expanded rapidly with Hewlett concentrating on the engineering and Packard on management and administration. Sales totaled over a half million in 1947, $30 million in 1958, and $30 billion in the mid-1990s.

Developing the system that became known as the HP way, the company became an international manufacturer of measurement and computation products for industry, science, medicine, and education. The company scored numerous successes in computers, chips, and calculators. Initially HP struggled against Japanese competition in the market for computer printers, but soon it leapfrogged them: in the mid-80s, Japan controlled 80 percent of the market, but by the mid-90s HP's share had soared to 60 percent of what had become a $20 billion a year industry. HP pioneered inkjet technology and developed the business equation that became the template for the printer market— keep the price of the printer low and make profits on the cartridges, preferable to sending out a repairman whenever the quality of the printing degraded.[10] After purchasing Compaq, HP led the world in manufacturing PCs. The company pioneered in profit-sharing, stock purchases, and flex-time. With a liberal work culture, the company was consistently listed among the "best-run companies" and "best places to work" in America.

Another world-renowned American computer company is Apple, which came about because Steve Jobs befriended Steve Wozniak (an HP employee at the time), who designed the first Apple computer and built it in his garage. More than anyone else, Jobs popularized the personal computer, making it available to the mass market. After selling

600 PCs to hobby stores, Jobs' second-generation PCs sold 130,000 in only three years. Soon after taking the company public, the market value of Apple had become greater than that of Ford Motor Company. Jobs hired a CEO from Pepsi, John Sculley, who subsequently forced Jobs out of the Apple Company. Jobs then founded a new PC business, Next, which was bought by Apple. Steve soon reclaimed his role at the company. Napster exploded on the scene, permitting students and hackers to download music for free (and illegally). Jobs introduced the iPOD, which soon dominated the consumer electronics market and allowed songs to be downloaded for 99 cents. Jobs then entered the billion-unit-a year mobile phone industry. His company consistently ranks first among the world's most innovative firms; its consumer-friendly reputation is based on products combining advanced technology with simplicity and ease of use.

Most other aspects of the computer industry have been led by U.S. firms and inventors. Computer and corporate networking has been dominated by EDS, IBM, and Cisco. Reynold Johnson of IBM, who originally developed a machine to score multiple-choice tests by reading pencil marks on an answer sheet, invented a disk drive to store data. Douglas Engelbart developed the mouse, on-screen "windows," and "groupware." George Heilmeier at RCA invented the liquid crystal display. Daniel Bricklin developed the spread sheet popularized by Lotus. DEC outflanked IBM by developing the mini-computer and growing revenues 30 percent a year for nineteen straight years, reached $7.6 billion in annual sales. It missed the PC revolution and was forced to sell out to Compaq.

Although the U.S. was well ahead in almost every aspect of computer technology by the mid-1990s, there was one disturbing trend—a rapidly expanding share of the manufacturing was moving abroad. The tendency to move production offshore followed the pattern of the consumer electronics industry in the previous three decades. By the end of the 1990s, despite the fact some microprocessors were still made in the U.S., the vast majority of PC products were being manufactured abroad—disk drives in Japan and China, power supplies and magnesium casings in China, memory chips in South Korea, Taiwan and

Germany, liquid-crystal displays in South Korea, Taiwan, Japan, and China, and graphics processors in Taiwan.

THE INTERNET

Another great phenomenon of the early stages of the information revolution was developed in America by a Department of Defense research agency—the Internet, which almost overnight became the worldwide network for computers in the mid-1990s. To prevent it from being vulnerable to a nuclear attack, the Internet was designed as a distributed network with no central hub and with a limitless number of nodes and grids that provided alternative routes in the event that parts of the network were wiped out. Originally, it was built as a high speed data network for universities and research institutions, but soon was embraced by the mass market. An electronic mail system was designed along with the now famous protocols such as TCP/IP, HTTP, URL, and HTML to make the network interoperable and provide a worldwide transport standard. At the beginning of the 1990s, hardly anybody had e-mail. Within a few short years, e-mail had become a vital communications mechanism for the majority of Americans as well as for many citizens throughout the globe. Other communications tools, such as instant messaging, were also widely deployed. American companies, such as Cisco and UUNET/MCI, made the plumbing for and developed the network that transported Internet traffic.

Actually, the Internet was not a separate network, but part of the traditional telecommunications system, utilizing infrastructure already in place. The incremental increase in communications and information was transported over this network, which basically had been deregulated, whereas the traditional system remained subject to a wide legacy of traditional regulations and taxes; without these, the cost of communication over the Internet was low and in some cases, even free. Even Bill Gates misjudged the initial impact of the Internet, then issued an urgent message to his employees comparing its rise to the advent of the PC.

Timothy Berners-Lee, a London-born mathematician, invented

the World Wide Web (the "Web"), turned down patenting rights, and fought to keep the network open. Netscape, an American company, developed the Web "browser" that enabled pages on the Web to be retrieved and displayed on any computer.

> August 9, 1995, will go down in history as the day the dot-com boom was born. What set it off was the initial public offer of Netscape, a tiny, two-year-old software maker in Silicon Valley that had almost no revenues and not a penny of profits. Netscape was actually giving most of its product away. Yet its browser software had fueled an explosion in Internet use, helping turn what had started as a U.S.-government-funded online sandbox for scientists and engineers into the digital thoroughfare for the world. The day Netscape stock began to trade, it rocketed from $28 a share to $71, astonishing investors from Silicon Valley to Wall Street.[11]

The browser used modems that were already part of most PCs and allowed users to access and browse the Web and "to go surfing." At the same time, a program came out with built-in Internet support, Windows 95.[12] Prior to the browser, there were a number of proprietary, incompatible, protocols or standards being used on the Web. The browser encouraged Internet users to utilize the HTML language and documents that were moved by HTTP protocol, making the Internet interoperable and compatible. In turn, this capability drove digitization—making information digital so it could be sent anywhere on the Internet. These advances led to an explosion in information dissemination, faster innovation, and the dot-com bubble.

The Internet spawned industries that were totally new, most founded by American companies. Amazon.com, a Seattle company, pioneered and led in e-commerce, an industry with countless entrants including almost every major corporation in the world. E-Bay popularized interactive, on-line auctions and stimulated business-to-business and business-to-consumer e-commerce. Hundreds of thousands of people earn a living by buying and selling on the E-Bay site. PayPal aided e-commerce by enabling anyone with an e-mail address to send money to anyone else with an e-mail address, becoming a form of Internet money. Google has organized the seemingly infinite amount of information on the Web through its famous search engine which uses mathematical formulas to order the data. The company's revenues are soaring as a result of its ability to target advertising. Google searches now make the most intimate details of an individual's life available to anyone who desires to do a search, an incentive for everyone to live cleanly, honestly, and intelligently. Social networking sites such as Facebook and MySpace chart new forms of social relationships.

The Internet facilitated the development of open-source software. The free, open-source model has become the greatest threat to Microsoft, as many of the best programmers in the world voluntarily contribute their talents to the development of this software. Its Linux operating system is free and available worldwide.

The Internet continues its rapid evolution, with "blogging," POD Casting, and new forms of file sharing and instant messaging being invented and distributed continuously. Whole new industries are being created to influence activities, events, and information on the Web.

FIBER OPTIC CABLES

Fiber optics also experienced explosive growth. Under the leadership of House Speaker Newt Gingrich, Congress passed the Telecommunications Act of 1996 which greatly facilitated the deployment of fiber. First, it allowed traditional telecommunications providers, such as local and long-distance telephone companies, to get into each other's businesses and build long-distance fiber lines. Second, it protected the Internet from traditional, heavy telecommunications regulation and under President Clinton the FCC embraced this policy. Enough undersea fiber cable was laid to go around the world over a dozen times. Hundreds of thousands of miles of fiber was laid over railroad lines and along roads. Some of the more advanced fiber optic lines had enough capacity to carry almost all of the earth's phone traffic at one time. For the last half of the 1990s, improvements in fiber capacity were exploding at twice the rate of chip speed. Fiber capacity increased about 1,000 fold in a few years. This rapid expansion was based on the assumption that Internet traffic was doubling every hundred days, multiplying tenfold every year. The Internet did reach these rates of expansion in 1995 and 1996 when it was converting from an academic network to a network for the masses, but it fell far short of this growth rate in subsequent years, although it still grew at a rapid pace. The result was a fiber glut and a price crash, which reached 65 percent annually over two years with long-distance phone calls plummeting from around $1 to a few cents a minute. Innovation outpaced the market, and many companies went bankrupt as a result. This fiber investment has remained in the ground available for use, continuing to foster expanded use of the Internet.

Expansion in coaxial cable capacity and then fiber optic cables drastically changed the long-distance industry until the cost of distance dropped to essentially nothing. The number of overseas calls increased from 1 million in 1950 to 23 million in 1970, to 200 million in 1980, to over 6 billion in 2001. Outright fraud at MCI also contributed to the price crash and expansion of calls. As fiber optic capacity for Internet traffic expanded rapidly, it became a transport mechanism for audio and video. Napster and MP3 devices radically changed the music industry and created a huge controversy over the legality of file sharing and the downloading of popular music. Video, which required much more capacity and involved the transport of vastly greater numbers of digital bits, initially strained the capacity of transport over the Internet. As video capability was built into more computers and as chips became fast enough to process the data streams needed for video transport, a whole new real-time world was created. People who were familiar with the real-time news available through cable television were ready adopters to real-time video over the Internet.

These advances across a broad area of electronics are the first of three stages or components of cyberspace exploration, the new technology frontier. The other two are biotechnology or medicine, and advanced materials or nanotechnology. Not all technologies fit neatly into these three baskets, but the three areas are likely to be the critical components of future technology.

XEROX

Xeroxing is an example of a technology with an impact that was greatly underestimated and which has had a major facilitating effect across all disciplines. In the 1930s, Chester Carlson developed a process called xerography that he patented in 1940. Carlson's process was based on physics rather than chemistry, which was at the time the basis for paper copying and an integral part of Kodak's business. Thomas Edison had invented the mimeograph machine. In 1940, there were 500,000 mimeograph machines in use. The Photostat was at the time a state-of-the-art process. These offset duplicating processes produced high-quality copies in high-volume. Over the ensuing decade, more than twenty major corporations rejected Xeroxing, and it took thirteen years to perfect a commercial machine by 1960. Haloid, a small Kodak competitor, seized on the technology and converted itself into Xerox. This electrophotography process was described as dry printing or xerography, taken from the Greek *xeros* (meaning *dry*) and *graphien* (meaning *writing*), or Xerox for short. It was a full two decades after the invention before Xerox sold its first copiers, making it possible to distribute information to small groups, a critical factor in encouraging innovation. Three management studies all agreed that there was little or no market for the Xerox machine. Initially, the company projected a demand of only a few thousand for its first model, but actually produced close to 200,000. One year after the first copier was sold, 50 million paper copies a month were being made. Today, billions of copies a month are being run. The Xerox machine dramatically changed the office environment from one where only copies of an original could be run, to a place where copies could be easily made of copies. The Xerox machine is a basic underpinning of innovation and tool for facilitating the dissemination of information to small groups, provided, of course, the innovators don't drown in a blizzard of paper.

Xerox pioneered in almost every aspect of the computer business—the personal computer, the laser printer, windowing software, the mouse, and numerous other peripherals. It capitalized,however, on none of these advances, because of a lack of leadership and effective management.

BIOTECHNOLOGY AND MEDICAL ADVANCES

The rapid, incredible changes taking place in the fields of medicine, biology, and biotechnology constitute a second stage of the contemporary information revolution. James Watson and Francis Crick won Nobel Prizes for discovering DNA. Robert Jarvik pioneered in the artificial heart, one of the first widely publicized manifestations of the biotechnology advances that overcame major obstacles such as rejection by the body and excess heat generation. A dynamic and powerful partnership between the federal government and the private sector has been responsible for America leading the world in health and medical practices. The National Institutes of Health and other federal health research agencies have led the way in basic research, assisted by huge increases in federal funding and America's broad base of medical knowledge in the private sector and at colleges and universities. U.S. pharmaceutical companies, biotechnology companies, and the medical industry lead the world in applied research. These companies have experienced strong returns on their investment as a result of a climate that provides incentives for research and development. This second stage of the information revolution is in its beginning stages, but it will be possible eventually to measure and sort out important events, trends, and technologies.

The growth of biotechnology and medical knowledge is intertwined with the revolution described above in the electronics field. The brain and the microchip, for example, work similarly and the neuron and transistor share an underlying physics. Computer viruses have similarities to human viruses and similar principles are being used to control both. Computer companies such as IBM have studied the brain and neuron to improve computer design. Super fast computers are being used to map the human genome, to model the human protein, to develop advanced neurosurgery techniques, and to determine which chemicals to experiment with to create new pharmaceuticals. DNA chips have revolutionized biological research, playing a critical role in sequencing the human genome by measuring the activity of genes and identifying variations in people's genetic composition. These chips, configured in microarrays, were used to identify the SARS virus, and can be used to determine how individuals metabolize commonly prescribed drugs to determine the most appropriate drug and dose for each patient.

America has played a pioneering role in medical advances and innovation. During World War II, Britain was unable to produce penicillin on a massive scale, and American drug companies stepped in to provide enough to supply the Allied troops. Americans worked to develop and improve insulin—the first effective treatment for juvenile-onset diabetes, which previously had been almost universally fatal. America's role in this sector covers: cancer chemotherapy, vaccines for polio, eradication of smallpox, leading pharmaceutical advances, improvements in public sanitation, the availability of a wide range of antibiotics, X-rays, CT scans, MRI imaging, and medical devices for open-heart surgery.

The modern biotechnology industry was founded by Genentech and Robert Swanson and Herbert Boyer. At the time, founding a company of this nature was out of fashion—venture capitalists wanted to fund electronics companies and scientists in the 1970s didn't want to work for business. Professors were fired or denied tenure for expressing an interest in commercial activities. Swanson and Boyer each invested $500 to start the company. After repeated failures, the company almost folded. A crucial turning point was a Supreme Court ruling that living organisms are patentable.[13] Prior to this decision, without clear patent protection, much advanced biological research was done secretly. The patent process compels publication of the methods and means for a patentable product and opens it up. Another important event was the Bayh-Dole Act of 1980 that allowed universities to keep title to their inventions made under federally funded research programs. On October 14 of that year, Genentech went forward with its Initial Public Offering or IPO. The company created the first version of stock options for employees. A graduate student who had been paid in stock for summer work suddenly found himself a millionaire. Many Genentech employees left the company and founded the next generation of biotechnology companies, playing key roles in creating the new industry. The company produced synthetic human insulin, the first genetically engineered drug, created because there was a growing shortfall of animal insulin. The company was also a leader in producing synthetic human growth hormone. Genentech thrived on the excitement of working to develop ways of keeping people alive.

Since the time that Genentech started up, thousands of biotech companies have been founded and billions of dollars have been invested. New drugs have been developed to treat heart attacks and breast cancer.[14] Yet, given the level of investment, the results have been disappointing. Many strategies have had promise, but few have worked out. The industry, however, is still in its nascent stages and there have been some successes with cancer and AIDS.

The human genome project, popularly known as gene mapping, became biology's holy grail. Initially projected to take twenty years, it was completed in only twelve years. This massive effort was undertaken and completed by an odd consortium of entities, including the federal government, nonprofit organizations, and entrepreneurial biotechnology start-up companies. A critical component for speeding completion of the work was the marriage of computers with biotechnology instruments to speed processing of the data. Some of the most powerful computers in the world were used to decipher and sequence the human genes. By deciphering fragments of genes rather than entire genes, the process was speeded up.

Even though many connections between genes and human disorders have been made, there has been very little accomplished in the way of cures, which was the original promise of the project. Celera Genomics produced a map of the 30,000 genes that control human biology—only 300 of which don't have counterparts in mice.

DNA and the human genome project have generated a number of spin-offs. Gene hunters have tracked down the genetic origin of disorders such as Down's syndrome, cystic fibrosis, and muscular dystrophy. An important result of this project has been the use of the data to determine human evolution, confirming that man originated in Africa, most likely with a single African Eve. DNA fingerprinting has proven invaluable in crime-solving, determining paternity, and establishing the identity of war victims and other deceased individuals. It has been particularly effective in exonerating a number of criminals serving long terms for crimes they did not commit. Scientists are poised to create new life forms by the use of synthetic DNA, blurring the lines between the artificial and biological. This entire effort raises the ethical issue as to what extent human genes can be modified in ways that affect man's basic humanity. One goal is to produce cells that make hydrogen or other fuels.

Neuroscience is another area that opens up both huge opportunities and ethical issues. The industry's discoveries about how the brain functions have changed the modern perspective on education and learning. During human fetal development, most brain cells are created and assigned general jobs. About half of the brain cells die by the twentieth week of fetal life. Most brain development occurs in the womb and immediately after birth, when an enormous number of connections or synapses are made between brain cells. Interaction with the environment determines which synapses are strengthened and which are lost or pruned—about twenty billion a day. Nature's robust process is to start with many alternatives and winnow down to a few. The brain goes through crucial periods in which it must have certain kinds of stimulation to develop powers such as vision, language, and reasoning. These discoveries emphasize the importance of early childhood development. Neuroscience and Buddhism have shown how thinking and the environment can alter and grow the mind, changing the brain even in late adulthood.[15] The brain can use the outside world to shape itself. Neuroscientists are also developing new therapies to relieve pain, improve reasoning ability, and increase memory. Research in this field has been greatly facilitated by the development of machines for measuring brain activity, particularly MRI imaging.

NANOTECHNOLOGY AND ADVANCED MATERIALS

A third stage of the Information Revolution will probably be nanotechnology, the art of manipulating materials on an atomic or molecular scale to build microscopic devices. Theorizing that tiny things could be used to build much bigger things and manufacturing could be molecular, Richard Feynman won the Nobel Prize for his work in this field. Actual nanotechnology operates by manipulating individual atoms to form desired structures in a molecular universe viewable through an electron microscope. A nanometer is one-billionth of a meter—about a dozen times the diameter of an atom. Carbon nanotubes were one of the first advances in this field. They are 100 hundred times stronger than steel and their discovery won the Nobel Prize. Nanotechnology is in such an infant, formative stage that the technologies and the long-term impact are largely undefined.

William Gibson visualized these phenomena when he coined the term "cyberspace" for his novel *Neuromancer*. In 1984, Gibson antici-pated the interrelated concepts of the microchip—computers, data storage, software, biotechnology, and the Internet—in describing our entry into the information revolution.

Information Technology:
Roots, Impact, and Implications

Fundamental to today's astonishingly instantaneous transfer, recep-tion, and use of information are, first, America's highly progressive tra-dition and, second, its history of pace-setting leadership in technology. America's progressive tradition and its history of technological leader-ship has been a foundation for today's astonishing information trans-fer, reception, and use. America's progress may be visualized as waves of change: the Revolutionary Era, Jefferson's democratic revolution, the agrarian revolution, Jackson's egalitarian revolution, and the indus-trial revolution. Today, we are experiencing a new global revolution based on the American model of freedom, democracy, and the free enterprise system. These forces that originated in America are now spreading throughout the world, especially in the information sector. Almost the entire world has access to technologies that could not have been imagined a generation ago.

American mastery of technology and innovation was the essen-tial catalyst of the economic engine that, by the twentieth century, had made the United States the largest economy on earth. Early Americans overcame the huge British edge in textiles and steam engines, largely by stealing the technology, but also by deploying it more widely, and managing their plentiful and fertile agricultural land to lead the world in cotton production. In the early industrial age, America used its ingenuity and bountiful natural resources to dominate energy production and manufacture of steel, rubber, plastics, aluminum, etc. American industry extended this lead by developing improved manufacturing processes and producing from these materials automobiles, trucks, radios, chemicals, airplanes, and countless high-quality products—and more of them—than anyone else on the planet. Its agricultural and manufacturing base gave the United States an economic advantage at the start of today's worldwide information age.

According to some historians, at the time of their Revolution the typical American needed to know only as much as is contained in today's *New York Times* Sunday edition. Americans currently face an environment where human knowledge doubles almost every generation and in some fields doubles every few years. This phenomenon is the information revolution as we have described it, sometimes referred to as the Third Wave. Alvin and Heidi Toffler developed this concept and described it as a huge change that ripples through an entire society.[16] They said it is like watching a wave come across a lake; the change ripples from individual—to family—to neighborhood—to business— to government—to the society at large: an unstoppable wave of change.

The First Wave of change, about 10,000 years ago, was from hunting-gathering to farming or agriculture. With hunter-gatherers, there were tens of thousands of people chasing and hunting food. Then they learned how to plant food so they could stay in the same place. With extra time from being able to consume farm goods, people began writing, inventing, and creating the ingredients of modern civilization. This transformation required political and social organizations to develop, as well as tax systems to support monarchs, armies, and governments.

The founding fathers played a major role in transforming the American economy from an agricultural to an industrial age, which has been called the Second Wave of change. This revolution was rooted in the science and the principles of Sir Isaac Newton, whose world was mechanical, with clearly delineated causes and effects and universal laws. Key catalysts in this transformation were Gutenberg's invention of printing with moveable type in 1455 and Martin Luther's Protestant Reformation in 1517. These events were precursor to the industrial revolution that reached full stride about three hundred years later in the 1800s.

The Third Wave is America's very recent conversion from the product-manufacturing technology of its industrial age to the computer-based technology of the information age.[17] Newton's theories had their limitations, particularly in understanding whole systems and their properties and characteristics. Albert Einstein, by quantum physics and the theory of relativity tried to explain these systems and the universe, which precipitated a different way of looking at the world and which eventually led to the new information technology.

In most aspects of the Third Wave's first phase—including computers, integrated circuits, software, the Internet, and data storage—America led the world. This lead, however, has been threatened by many of the advancing technologies of the second phase, particularly in areas such as mobile technology and broadband. The language of information technology is English, giving America a built-in advantage. Yet, there are forecasts and projections that Chinese could supplant English as the leading language of the Internet. The world is probably at the beginning of this Third Wave of change and thus an early lead may rapidly evaporate in a field undergoing such rapid transformation. At the beginning of the industrial revolution, for example, Great Britain led the world only to relinquish its edge to the United States.

The information-age economy will likely be dramatically different from industrial-age economy, in fact, it may even become similar to the agricultural-age economy. In some respects, the industrial age was an anomalous era of centralized institutions, hierarchical structures, massive organizations, and big government bureaus. The information age may very well propel us back to the basic format of the agricultural era: decentralized institutions, flat organizational structures, customized processes and products, a focus on family and community life, and small entrepreneurial firms and governments.

In many respects, the Third Wave and the rapid changes of the past few decades, have been the most radical since the American Revolution. Communism has imploded, socialism has been discredited, and political power in America has shifted to the West and the Sunbelt. In the computer industry, there has been a vast improvement in productivity—integrated circuits have increased in power by approximately a billion-fold in slightly over fifty years. Powerful memory technology enables the entire Library of Congress to be placed on a desktop computer and revolutionary changes in fiber optics potentially allow every voice phone call in the world to be placed on a single fiber strand. Productivity improvements in manufacturing are causing jobs to disappear, just as jobs declined rapidly in the agricultural era during the transformation to the industrial age. Enormous changes are also occurring in attitudes towards family, religion, relationships, the environment, and globalization.

America dominated the beginning stages of the information revolution. The genesis of this superiority was innovation, the distinguishing characteristic of American civilization. American success has not rested on invention only, but on the practical application of technology. Thomas Edison's major contribution was not invention of the light bulb; it was development of the electrical grid that eventually illuminated businesses and homes across America. The scientist develops knowledge and theories; the inventor develops solutions; the innovator applies solutions to everyday life. Science without invention and invention without innovation are, in some respects, fruitless. It is the practical application of technology or innovation that is the key.[18] The innovator applies the fruits of science and invention to daily life and benefits the society at large. Rapid dissemination of innovation throughout society is the key component of economic growth.

The pinnacle of American dominance of information technology was the 1990s; its foundation had been laid over the previous two centuries. America had the best transportation infrastructure—via air, ground, and water—that facilitated travel and shipping that thus greased the wheels of the information revolution. America also had the world's best communication systems—via telephone, postal service, cable television, and broadcasting. A culture of innovation permeated the society. The U.S. led the world both in developing and using technology. The technology boom captured the American imagination. The latest advance, merger, or stock market records were front-page stories and the lead story on the evening news virtually every day. These events permeated the culture. Corporate CEOs and technology entrepreneurs were idolized and the focus of national attention. The interest in and preoccupation with information capability served as a vision and organizing principle for American society. The political culture was dominated by figures who were intensely focused on and went to great lengths to promote technology. The broad-based popular commitment to information technology lent a national unity of purpose to the culture.

IMPACT BEYOND THE TECHNOLOGY SECTOR

America's technological preeminence has implications far beyond the technology sector—arguably it has had a broader impact on other areas. Even as early as 1991, business expenditures for information technology such as computers and telecommunications equipment exceeded all other capital expenses for U.S. corporations. A typical car has dozens of computers to regulate functions such as fuel mixture, timing, ignition, suspension, engine diagnostics, emissions, seat positions, and instrument panels. The company in America with the greatest technological impact, with even more impact than Microsoft, may very well be Wal-Mart.

J.C. Penney taught Sam Walton how to sell retail during the Depression, and after World War II Walton started his own business. He developed a winning formula—big stores in small towns with low prices and an emphasis on people ("Our people make the difference"). He borrowed the hypermarket concept from Europe: almost everything a shopper could imagine was under one roof. Walton may have been the most important entrepreneur of the twentieth century. A penny-pincher, he made traveling executives sleep up to eight in a room, drove an old pick-up truck, and flew economy class, believing that every dollar misspent came out of customers' and stockholders' pockets. He left a fortune of over $20 billion. One hundred shares of Wal-Mart stock purchased in the company's first year, would have gone through nine splits and been worth over $10 million 30 years later.

With well over a million employees and several million other people whose jobs depend on the company, Wal-Mart is the largest private sector employer in the world. The company has revolutionized American retailing, with customers spending tens of millions of dollars in its stores every hour, 24 hours a day, almost every day of the year. Walton improved the retail industry's distribution system by shifting the value added from the point of production to the point of sale. These value-added services included advertising, marketing, information, transportation, inventory management, sales service, and billing. Computers, transportation systems, and communications technologies were used to effectively manage these functions on a big scale over huge distances. Wal-Mart shares information with its suppliers to help them plan production, viewing them as an extension of the company. These relationships greatly improve profitability by speeding deliveries so that the product is sold before it must be paid for, far faster than other retailers. Computerized inventory control and a sophisticated supply network make this possible. The company's computer system is the second most powerful in the world after the Pentagon's. Its vast data base, larger than any except that of the federal government, provides a treasury of information used for improving sales (e.g., pairing bananas with cereal and flashlights with Halloween costumes). The company also uses data to encourage purchases of higher margin products. It knows more about many of its products than even the manufacturers.

Wal-Mart did more than transform retailing, it shook up the entire world of wholesaling when it set up its own distribution centers. Together these changes have been credited with half of the annual productivity growth in America between 1995 and 1999.[19] Wal-Mart has the world's premier supply chain management system; it includes a massive network of distribution centers with miles of conveyor belts that keep control of all its inventories, informing suppliers when to provide additional goods. One major computer manufacturer sold 400,000 computers to 4,000 stores in one peak day during the Christmas season.[20] Wal-Mart has point of sale terminals linked by satellite to its huge computer and data system. The company has radio frequency identification chips that transmit the whereabouts of products at all times and help to regulate remaining inventory, storage temperature, expiration date, and other critical information as well as provide an additional source of data. By monitoring weather forecasts, for example, Wal-Mart projects demand for its products, such as more water and soda drinks during heat waves.

The company is powerful enough to drive entire markets. Companies locate their plants and operations based on where Wal-Mart needs them. The deodorant industry jettisoned its paper boxes because Wal-Mart insisted, in order to save the customer a nickel per sale. Wal-Mart uses its massive leverage to dictate prices and terms to suppliers, which sometimes forces manufacturing offshore.

Although Wal-Mart has been criticized for low pay, poor employee relations, and smothering small-family enterprises, the company has played a major role in keeping inflation down. For the more than $250 billion in goods sold annually by Wal-Mart stores, it accounts for 60 percent of American sales of those products and 7 to 8 percent of total consumer spending. Some economists estimate Wal-Mart has brought consumers savings of 10 to 20 percent and lowered the consumer price index by as much as a cumulative 3 percent or well over $1,000 annually per household, significantly improving living standards.[21] Wal-Mart brings products to the poor and middle classes that formerly only were available to the rich; salmon, for example, formerly available for $15 or $20 a pound, can be bought for a fraction of the cost. Each Wal-Mart creates a small number of additional jobs, but also substitutes about 100 to 200 jobs at Wal-Mart locations for the jobs that are lost at local stores which go out of business.[22]

The explosion in the power of the computer chip and rapid advances in software have enabled American companies to open up new markets for such products as cellular phones and wireless devices. In the 1940s, researchers at Bell Labs proposed radio telephones that could use the same frequencies again and again. A geographical area would be divided into separate "'cells", each one served by its own low-power transmitter. The capacity of a cellular system could then be increased almost indefinitely by shrinking cells and increasing their total number. Cellular telephony required highly sophisticated transmitters and receivers and coordination among cells to "hand-off" calls and coordinate frequencies, but this technology did not exist until the advent of the computer chip and microelectronics. The estimate of the number of users worldwide by the year 2000 was less than a million. The actual number of subscribers ended up being well over one hundred million and rose into the billions of users within a few years. The Federal Communications Commission (FCC) delay in allocating spectrum for cellular systems cost the U.S. economy heavily and significantly impaired U.S. competitiveness—the Europeans borrowed U.S. technology and got a head start.

The phenomenal, unexpected growth in cell phone use was made possible by rapid advances in computer chip technology, which drastically reduced the cost of handsets and vastly improved the use of the spectrum or air frequencies. This explosive growth in turn led to the development of new technologies such as blackberries and other wireless devices. Whole new markets opened up, particularly for the one-half of the globe that had never made a phone call, including the most remote places in the world. These technologies in turn brought productivity improvements and new wealth to these impoverished areas. An extra 10 mobile phones for each 100 people in a developing country can lead to an extra half a percentage point of growth in the economy, substituting for travel and allowing price data to be distributed more quickly and easily. A whole range of new services become available—such as making payments for all types of goods and services through the use of the cell phone. This in effect creates a new banking system for people who never have used bank accounts and rarely even have currency.

Wireless devices are likely to assume many, if not all, of the functions of a PC while being approximately the size of a wallet, as all the benefits of the computing world are extended to wireless communications. Two waves of change are likely to occur. First, functions of the PC will gravitate into the mobile phone or wireless device. Over 2.5 billion cell phones are already in use and more than one million are being added every day. Besides the revolution generated by the computer chip, more effective use of the spectrum is driving this change. Spectrum efficiency has already vastly improved as much as a trillion-fold.[23] Chips already incorporate crystals, copper coils, and vacuum tubes and are now incorporating features such as music downloading, text messaging, and voice communication. Secondly, tiny wireless devices can be embedded in a wide range of objects from televisions to cars to industrial machinery to human beings and will communicate from their placements with an outside network. Vending machines might be an ideal application for this technology for tracking inventory in each machine, particularly when the machines can accept payment by mobile phone, as many of them do in Japan and Europe. Vehicle-fleet management is another ideal application. Many cars have satellite navigation devices. Cars could contact emergency services automatically if an accident occurs. Monitoring devices at manufacturing and refinery plants can predict when machinery is about to break down and can drastically improve efficiency. New technology is being developed to power these devices through electromagnetic fields, magnetic resonance, or sensors which harvest energy from the environment.

Other incredible advances are being made with satellite technology. Satellite photography, for example, enables anyone with a computer to explore the farthest reaches of the planet—even reading the license plate numbers on cars. The Global Positioning System or GPS may be the greatest advance in navigation since the compass or sextant. GPS greatly advanced navigation beyond earlier systems such as Loran and has been widely deployed on cars, trucks, boats, and airplanes. Twenty-four satellites circle the globe twice a day and receivers decode a signal from four of these satellites that calculates a position based on the different times and distances to the satellites, accurate to within a few feet. The technology has spawned a multibillion-dollar industry with applications from sailboats to golf carts to the blind. The U.S. military services use these devices on cruise missiles, precision-guided bombs, and other munitions.[24] Satellites also deliver radio with a national footprint for use in cars and home receivers that carry national and segmented programming.

The impact of the new information technology in electronics has been far-reaching. Computer chips changed the face of almost every aspect of the electronics industry—television, radio, cable, and satellite. New technologies abound—VOD, DVD, broadband, MP3, and podcasting. Nolan Bushnell is often regarded as the founder of the video game business. He invented and patented Pong and founded Atari, the first company to exploit the concept. The game industry evolved into three leading companies with game platforms—Sega, Sony, and Nintendo—that were eventually joined by Microsoft.[25]

The digital economy and information revolution are moving at an increasingly rapid pace. The digital economy runs on real time and rapid decision-making processes. Product lifecycles have plummeted until they have reached months then weeks and, in the case of security, days and even hours.

Computer technology has thus altered the American economy and the business sector in fundamental ways. Economic forecasting and resulting monetary and fiscal policy was at one time little better than systematic guesswork. During the 1980s and 1990s, a much broader array of economic data became available. Computer software and advances in computing power enhanced the ability of economists, the Federal Reserve Bank, and the legislative and executive branches of government to use this data to monitor the health of the economy and proactively determine economic policy. Sophisticated models that captured decades of data and a wealth of current market information provided national economic policy makers with far better tools than were available previously. Using devices as powerful as supercomputers, economic policymakers have the ability to project the impact of various policy options, giving them unprecedented control over the economy. Confidence in their ability to steer the economy contributed to the increased value of stocks and other assets in the 1980s and 1990s.

Similarly, the Internet gives the consumer potentially more control over expenditures. It allows price comparisons for all sorts of goods from automobiles to computers to clothes, for example. It can eliminate wasteful practices, such as enabling the purchase of a single song instead of an entire CD. Consumers no longer must pay for prints of photo images they don't want—they can eliminate marginal photographs immediately through use of a digital camera. They can manage income and expenditures online and eventually determine economic policy at the individual or family level.

On society's level, information technology provides enormous opportunities for e-government, such as delivery of services over the web to meet the needs of citizens (e.g., driver license renewal), coordination across government agencies through use of an intranet, improving purchasing through solicitations over the Internet, and making government more transparent and accountable to the individual citizen. The Pentagon uses sophisticated simulations to make war games closer to real-life conditions. Electronic sensors can monitor everything going on in a battlefield area. Command and control computer systems process the data and develop options for military action. This information can be shipped throughout the world and military actions or strategy can be directed from anywhere in real time. Advanced technology in defense programs has served as the precursor for civilian technologies such as the Internet and GPS.

AMERICA'S REVOLUTIONARY VALUES RE-EMERGE

In the industrial age, America's distinctive form of individualism became suppressed by the growth of bureaucratic organizations and by mass production. Computers, however, have undermined the hierarchical structure of the industrial workplace. Information technology has made sweeping changes at work, as it boosted productivity. Many factories are now as dependent on computers as industrial machines. Computers and the Internet have sparked a knowledge explosion, as new ideas are worked on and developed by people throughout the world simultaneously and information is disseminated instantaneously. Today's information age is encouraging individualism and expand-ing personal freedom. The ubiquitous and omnipresent computer chip has opened a new frontier of almost limitless opportunity for every-one. Computers, telecommunications, and the Internet have advanced the cause of freedom, democracy, liberty, and free enterprise across the globe.

15

Lessons on Change

RIP VAN WINKLE lived in a village in the Catskills, then under the reign of King George III. After a game of nine pins and a keg of beer, he falls into a deep sleep one autumn afternoon. He emerges from slumber, not knowing whether he slept through a single night or perhaps longer.

Rip's story is often trivialized and misunderstood, because modern Americans assume that, as a matter of course, anyone who goes to sleep for twenty years will awake having missed out on amazing changes. But Washington Irving was describing sheer 1796 wonderment at America's sudden transformation—almost as if a bolt of lightning had struck—a degree of change like no other in mankind's slow pace through generations, centuries, and even millennia.

Upon re-entering his village, one of the first changes Rip sees is that the portrait of King George III has been replaced by one of a different title—General Washington (who had within a few years had become as indispensable to his country as would be a king). Anyone observing history before the American Revolution would see little connection between what was happening to Rip and the year by which the American Revolution had plunked mankind into the modern world. Irving, however, notes that "the very character of the people seemed changed. There was a busy, bustling, disputatious tone about it, instead of the accustomed phlegm and drowsy tranquility." Rip's old lifestyle has vanished, swept away by the Revolution that had taken place and the American Constitution that had been produced during the twenty years Rip had slept. Activism now rules the public square. Men are "haranguing vehemently about rights of citizens—election—members of congress—liberty—Bunker's hill—heroes of seventy-six—and other words that were a perfect Babylonish jargon to the bewildered Van Winkle." Rip is astonished:

> I'm not myself—I'm somebody else—that's me yon-der—no that's somebody else, got into my shoes—I was myself last night, but I fell asleep on the mountain, and they've changed my gun, and everything's changed, and I'm changed, and I can't tell what's my name or who I am!

Rip has not only slept twenty years, he has missed the seminal experience of America becoming a nation.

> The disorientation is funny, the comic tension lying in the contrast between Rip's old-world indolent ways and the vigorous public mores of a post-Revolution village. But a serious issue underlies the humor. Irving singles out 1776 to 1796 as the absent years, making Rip's return represent not just one individual's experience, but a nation's experience, illuminating just how much things have changed for every-one. If Irving chose 1755 to 1775, the changes would have been all local, the person and place alone, not the very *char-acter* of things. Rips sojourn would have no political or civic meaning, just a private one. The selected time frame, then, highlights the advent of democracy itself, and what it does to people deep down. Irving dramatizes the transformation by throwing a simple-minded colonial denizen of a remote village into the newly formed United States at its most polit-ical moment, Election Day. How better to illuminate the civic burdens thrust upon the people?
>
> Thus the amusing tale of a twenty-year sleep becomes a parable of civic life. Rip's vertigo discloses the taxing

responsibilities of American citizenship. Before, the villagers were subjects. Now they are political agents, voters, and they tell Rip that he, too, is "now a free citizen of the United States." Rip used to dwell wholly within the immediate circumstances of his life, all in the present, but the times now demand that he attend to faraway affairs, and to remember formative events of the past ("heroes of seventy-six" etc.). Before, villagers found an old newspaper and debated public matters months after they had played out, but now they participate directly in those outcomes. In fact, one of his old cronies sits in Congress, an elevation Rip cannot even imagine. The public square is no longer a place for idle talk and an afternoon smoke, the people relating on common, natural interests. They gather beneath a political sign, the American flag, not a giant swaying shade tree, and the discourse divides them into partisans.[1]

While the new paradigm of Rip's era was tenuous and problematic, from a modern day perspective the rapid rate and depth of human progress over the past two centuries validates the success of the revolutionary generation, who created one of the greatest civilizations in human history. In particular, leaders such as Benjamin Franklin and Thomas Paine leveraged printing-press technology, which played a crucial role in all of the major changes of the era: the Age of the Enlightenment, global exploration, the scientific revolution, the movements sweeping Europe such as the Reformation, and the rise of new civilizations and the fall of played-out cultures with backing from partisans who wanted independence from the Old World. The founding fathers overthrew customs, habits, and traditions that had gone unaltered and mostly unchallenged for centuries.

Historically, Americans have been able to dig deep when it really mattered—bringing the cannons from Ticonderoga two-hundred miles in the deep of winter to route the British from Boston, crossing the Delaware in the bitter cold of winter to defeat the British at Trenton and Princeton, bringing an end to the War with the brilliant Yorktown campaign, eking out a resolution to the War of 1812, saving the British and French from German domination in World War I, securing the greatest military victory in history over the Japanese and Germans in World War II, and winning the Cold War without firing a shot.

Colonial Americans were informed pioneers who, even though confronted with the grim reality of struggling for subsistence, had extensive knowledge about their politics, culture, and politicians. Their awareness that the decline and fall of Rome had ended with invasion by the barbarians provided an important impetus for warding off the Indians. The presidents of the founding fathers' generation were great leaders on three levels: they were visionaries, they comforted the nation, and they could execute. These presidents understood the importance of a lean, effective government. The colonial economy valued work whereas the European economy emphasized idleness as an aristocratic privilege. Women were elevated in their roles. America developed the concept of economic growth, which values growing the pie instead of dividing the pie.

Thomas Jefferson, one of the most effective revolutionary leaders in American history, embraced democracy, equality, immigration, renewal for each generation, and tiny government, but he lost his way when he imposed an instrument of expansive government, an economic embargo. In the nineteenth century, Americans achieved rapid change through civil society. The temperance movement, for example, brought a drastic reduction in liquor consumption in stark contrast to government-imposed Prohibition, which failed a century later.

John Marshall played a crucial role in defining the new nation's legal, corporate, and financial structure, which set the stage for the country's rapid technological change and economic progress in the nineteenth century. The methods of production changed more in a few decades than in the previous two thousand years. Vastly improved transportation networks enabled the movement of much greater amounts of agricultural goods to market and drastically reduced the time needed to move them.

The inability of the American political system to deal with the issue of slavery revealed flaws in the nation's system of governance. Between the establishment of the American republic and the Civil War, the South had disproportionate representation in each branch of the government. This dominance and a series of weak candidates for president resulted in little real national debate over the critical issue of slavery. Reaction against the slave power led to the election of Abraham Lincoln and a revival of the revolution to secure civil rights. Lincoln skillfully navigated America through its most difficult period, the Civil War. Reconstruction laws were on the verge of instituting equality for African Americans, but they were superseded by court decisions and Jim Crow laws that left African Americans in the South in only slightly better position than under slavery. America had the political will to carry out revolution after revolution in other areas, but it failed to consummate the fight for equal rights for slaves.

The North's superior technological and industrial strength were decisive in determining the outcome of the Civil War. Almost all inventors and industrialists were from the North. Militarily, the North had the vast majority of armaments and virtually all the ship production; in fact, shipbuilding made possible the naval blockade that was a decisive factor in winning the war. The North's maritime advantage was also crucial to winning the War in the west. President Lincoln used the North's much more effective communications systems, particularly telegraph, to mobilize public opinion.

In the industrial age, Thomas Edison and his colleagues upgraded people's daily lives more profoundly than any changes mankind had witnessed, even over periods of thousands of years. Edison was granted over 1,000 patents, and his inventions accounted for the livelihood of over 10 million Americans. Edison developed the entire concept of the electrical grid and power system, giving human activities great flexibility and productivity. In the 1920s, productivity increased at several times the previous rate and manufacturing doubled, electricity being responsible for half this improvement. Edison's success was built on a culture that valued manufacturing, entrepreneurship, and innovation, and an agricultural sector that provided a foundation for industrialism. The automobile assembly line, for example, was based on the production lines used in the meatpacking business. The transportation advances used for bringing agricultural goods to market served the same purpose for industrial commodities. Trains that brought agricultural products to the cities often returned with manufactured goods. The industrial revolution became a major focus of American life.

In the 1930s, government policies in general prolonged the Great Depression. Banking and securities legislation and suspension of the gold standard addressed the crucial issues raised by the stock market crash and the overly-restrictive monetary supply. The New Deal, however, went far beyond these financial issues and instituted a whole new concept of the role of government, systematizing interest-group politics and making government accountable to special interests as well as to individuals. A vast expansion of the public sector was accompanied by a soak-the-rich-tax initiative that when enacted actually worsened the effects of the Great Depression. Over the next six decades, common wisdom sustained the concept that it was capitalism and not ineffective government policies that were responsible for the Depression.

The news media helped to overcome the isolationism that delayed U.S. entry into World War II against the Axis powers. American technological and manufacturing prowess was largely responsible for the Allied victory. World War II was a great triumph for America and the war changed the nation more than any other event, with the exception of the Civil War. Presidents Truman and Eisenhower developed the policies, organizations, and structures that would enable the United States to assume the leadership role it had failed to seize in the aftermath of World War I. The Truman-Eisenhower initiatives eventually led to the demise of communist governments in Europe.

The broadcast media became a powerful and dominating force, weakening civil society and fundamentally altering political will. Radio was the basis of and responsible for much of Franklin Roosevelt's power and success. In its latter stages, radio became the vehicle for the spread of a counter-culture, particularly rock-and-roll music. Television provided the nation with a set of common experiences, but reduced time spent on community events, civic and religious associations, and the family. Television mystified youth and eroded confidence in the elderly and their wisdom.

Television became the most powerful communications medium

in history, helping to bring about the end of communism, spreading the sense of globalization, being a powerful force for education and cultural change, and revolutionizing politics by altering the basis for power. Television propagated a culture of sex and violence. The news media, perhaps without intent, has nevertheless encouraged and fostered a public attitude of cynicism toward politics and American institutions. The broadcast media heightens public fears and anxieties over events such as 9/11 and the global financial crisis. The strong role of broadcasting in the formulation of public opinion prevents public consensus from emerging over what to do about programming content.

In the last 50 years, broadcasting has fundamentally altered the political culture. Politicians' personalities became more important than their character or their position on political issues. The new media focuses on current news, which is government solutions to problems rather than our former reliance on civil society. During the ascendancy of radio, a vast array of government programs was initiated under the New Deal. During the ascendancy of television, the Great Society and War on Poverty also greatly expanded the role of government. Television network news was arguably the most important political event of the second half of the twentieth century, reaching tens of millions of people instantaneously. Television altered the basis for the news by not just covering it, but also formatting it to be entertaining and occasionally even creating it.

Peter Drucker and W. Edwards Deming led new directions in business management that swept through free enterprise system and catapulted capitalism into the economic paradigm that ruled the world. The automobile, the agricultural sector, food business, the transportation sector, housing, medicine, and the health industry were transformed by these new management principles. Japan embraced the U.S. capitalist model, and Deming's quality values transformed Japan into a fierce competitor. American affluence fed industrial complacency, and the United States lost its lead in manufacturing. The Japanese continue to maintain a leading edge in many sectors of manufacturing.

At the time of the American Revolution the typical American needed to know only a limited amount of information. Today,

Americans face an environment where human knowledge doubles almost every generation and in some fields doubles every few years, placing a premium on learning and an informed citizenry.

The 1990s was the pinnacle of American technological dominance of the information revolution; the U.S. led the world both in developing and using every aspect of information technology. The keystone of this revolution has been the ubiquitous microchip or computer chip—a remarkable invention that has improved its own capabilities and productivity by more than one billion fold in slightly over fifty years. Software is the second key component of the information revolution and Bill Gates founded Microsoft, the dominant firm that created more wealth than any other business in the history of American capitalism.

Information technology brought about profound change in people's lives. The impact of the magnitude of change is overwhelming. The little greeting cards that play "Happy Birthday" have more computer power than existed on the entire planet before 1950. A home video camera has more power than the original IBM 360 mainframe. The latest model automobiles have more computing power than the vehicles that took man to the moon.

The Internet is another great phenomenon of the early stages of electronic communications. Developed by a Department of Defense research agency, the Internet almost overnight became the worldwide network for computers. Biotechnology and nanotechnology are probably the next stages of the information revolution.

CONCLUSION

Until recently, Americans—the people who settled the New World—continued their determination to continually improve their everyday lives. This determnation resulted in eight revolutions: the original American revolution, Jefferson's democracy, Jackson's egalitarianism, the agrarian revolution, the industrial revolution, the radical transformation in business management, public change brought about by new broadcasting technology, and the information revolution. These revolutions and the culture they thrived on brought about unprecedented change and progress for the entire human race and made America civilization a world icon.

Unfortunately, the modern mass media cover warfare much better than they cover the spirit of innovation and entrepreneurialism that drove American success for over two centuries. The news media are far more suited to covering government programs that address social problems than they are uncovering difficult everyday work of raising families, participating in community and in civic associations, and doing the hard work of actually solving problems through the work of civil society.

Thus diverted into passivity by media culture, Americans have lost their focus on solving problems We have thrown off the taxing responsibilities of American civilization. In the past, the United States worked best when the culture focused on innovation and solving problems through individual responsibility, strong families, and vibrant community associations. In 1927, when the *Literary Digest* raised the issue of whether there was a dearth of great men, only three Americans were named most often to refute the charge and all of them were innovators—Thomas Edison, Orville Wright, and Henry Ford.[2] What would a list of great men look like today?

The world now faces a global financial meltdown. The lessons to be learned from studying American history hold the key to solving this problem. More than ever before, Americans agree the country is on the wrong track. The next volume of *Political Will* analyses what went wrong and what can be done to get back on track.

Like Rip van Winkle's village before the advent of democracy, we, the American people, have become subjects of the entertainment world. Like Rip, we need to wake up. Modern politicians and candidates seek to seize the mantle of change. Because they shared a civic determination to solve social problems through civil society, and because they shared with their public a commitment to hard work and innovation, America's founding fathers were and still are the masters when it comes to instituting profound change.

Notes

PREFACE

1 Philip Howard, T*he Death of Common Sense*, New York, Random House, 1994, p. 50.

2 Gordon Wood, *The Radicalism of the American Revolution*, New York, Vantage, pp. 4–5.

CHAPTER 2

1 George Otto Trevelyan, *The American Revolution*, New York, Longmans, Green, 1905, p. 113.

2 Joseph Ellis, *His Excellency*, New York, Alfred A. Knopf, 2004, p. 190.

3 William Shakespeare, *Hamlet*, Act II, Scene II.

4 Walter Mead, *Special Providence*, Washington, D.C., Council on Foreign Relations, 2001.

5 Thomas Fleming and David McCullough, *What If?* New York, Berkley Books, pp. 155–199.

6 Paul Johnson, *A History of the American People*, New York, HarperCollins, 2000, p. 128.

7 Jack Welch, "Five Questions to Ask," *The Wall Street Journal*, October 28, 2004.

8 Gary Wills, *Inventing America*, New York, Houghton Mifflin, 2002.

9 Ellis, *His Excellency*, p. xiv.

10 Harvey Kaye, *Thomas Paine*, New York, Hill and Wang, 2005, pp. 1–7.

11 Walter Isaacson, *Benjamin Franklin: An American Life*, Thorndike Press, 2003.

12 Samuel Eliot Morison, Henry Steel Commager, and William Leuchtenburg, *The Growth of the American Republic*, New York, Oxford University Press, 1980, p. 179.

13 Welch.

14 Ellis, *His Excellency*, p. 111.

15 Gordon S. Wood, *The American Revolution*, New York, The Modern Library, 2002, p. 84.

16 Welch.

17 Ellis, *His Excellency*, p. 74.

18 Bernard Bailyn, *To Begin the World Anew*, New York, Alfred Knopf, 2003, p. 133.

19 Johnson, pp. 181, 218.

20 Ron Chernow, *Alexander Hamilton*, New York, Penguin Press, 2004, p. 26.

21 William Randall, *Alexander Hamilton*, New York, HarperCollins, 2003, pp. 116–118.

22 David McCullough, *John Adams*, New York, Simon & Schuster, 2001, pp. 140–141.

23 Richard Ferrie, *The World Turned Upside Down*, New York, Holiday House, 1999.

24 Morison, Commager, and Leuchtenburg, p. 201.

25 Wood, *The American Revolution*, p. 88.

26 Joseph Ellis, *American Creation*, New York, Alfred A. Knopf, 2004, pp. 4–5.

27 Ellis, *His Excellency*, p. 73.

28 Bernard Bailyn, *The Ideological Origins of the American Revolution*, Cambridge, Mass., Belknap Press, 1967, pp. 182–183.

29 Willard Stern Randall, *Thomas Jefferson: A Life*, New York, Henry Holt, 1993, p. 285.

30 Forest McDonald, *Recovering the Past*, Lawrence, University Press of Kansas, pp. 183–184.

31 Randall, *Alexander Hamilton*, p. 327.

32 Joseph Ellis, *American Creation*, p. 100.

33 Bailyn, *To Begin the World Anew*, pp. 107, 112–113.

34 Garry Wills, *James Madison*, New York, Times Books, 2002, p. 37.

35 Stanley Elkins and Eric McKittrick, *The Age of Federalism*, New York, Oxford University Press, 1993, pp. 634–661.

36 Joseph Ellis, *American Sphinx*, New York, Vintage Press, 1996, p. 242.

37 Ellis, *His Excellency*, p. 198.

38 McCullough, *John Adams*, p. 415.

39 Gordon Wood, *Revolutionary Characters*, New York, Penguin Press, 2006, pp. 59, 60.

40 Wood, *Revolutionary Characters*, p. 63.

41 Chernow, p. 481.

42 Wood, *Revolutionary Characters*, p. 129, 132.

43 Robert Remini, *The House*, New York HarperCollins, 2006, pp. 3, 43.

44 Ellis, *His Excellency*, p. 190.

45 Ellis, *His Excellency*, p. 271.

46 Chernow, p. 266.

47 John Steele Gordon, *Hamilton's Blessing*, New York, Walker, 1997, p. 4.

48 John Steele Gordon, "Our Debt to Hamilton," *The Wall Street Journal*, March 12, 1997.

49 John Steele Gordon, *An Empire of Wealth*, New York, HarperCollins, 2004, p. 75.

50 Chernow, pp. 347, 349.

51 Elkins and McKittrick, p. 375.

52 Ellis, *His Excellency*, p. 279.

53 James Douglas Grant, *John Adams: Party of One*, New York, Farrar, Straus & Giroux, 2005.

54 McCullough, *John Adams*, p. 556.

55 Grant, p. 450.

56 Ralph Adams Brown, *The Presidency of John Adams*, Lawrence, University Press of Kansas, 1975, p. 197.

CHAPTER 3

1 Gordon S. Wood, *The Radicalism of the American Revolution*, New York, Vantage, p. 3.

2 Wood, *The Radicalism of the American Revolution*, pp. 4–7.

3 Robert Friedel, *A Culture of Improvement*, Cambridge, Mass., MIT Press, 2007, pp. 116–117.

4 Richard Tarnas, *The Passion of the Western Mind*, New York, Ballantine Books, 1991, p. 282.

5 Bernard Bailyn, *To Begin the World Anew*, New York, Alfred Knopf, 2003, p. 30.

6 Letter to Peter Collinson, May 9, 1753.

7 Arthur Schlesinger, *The Cycles of American History*, Boston, Houghton Mifflin, 1986, p. 6.

8 Jerry Muller, *Adam Smith in His Times and Ours*, New York, Free Press, 1993, pp. 120, 136.

9 Tarnas, p. 159.

10 Peter Drucker, "The Rise, Fall and Return of Pluralism," *The Wall Street Journal*, June 1, 1999.

11 Alan Macfarlane, *The Riddle of the Modern World*, New York, St. Martin's Press, 2000, p. 278.

12 Jared Diamond, *Guns, Germs and Steel*, New York, W.W. Norton, 1999, pp. 79–81, 91, 197, 358–361.

13 Michael Barone, *Our First Revolution*, New York, Crown Publishers, 2007.

14 John Marshall, *The Life of George Washington*, Philadelphia, C.P. Wayne, 1804, v. 1, pp. 471–472.

15 Charles and Mary Beard, *The Basic History of the United States*, New York, Doubleday, 1944, pp. 18–19.

16 Daniel Boorstin, *The Americans: The Colonial Experience*, New York, Random House, 1958, pp. 5, 18.

17 Mark Noll, *America's God*, New York, Oxford Press, 2002, p. 4.

18 Letter from John Adams to Hezekiah Niles, 1818.

19 Noll, p. 54.

20 Paul Johnson, *A History of the American People*, New York, HarperCollins, 2000, p. 117.

21 Gordon Wood, *Rising Glory of America, 1760–1820*, New York, George Braziller, 1971, p. 9.

22 Wood, *The Radicalism of the American*

Revolution, pp. 12, 19.

23 Wood, *The Radicalism of the American Revolution*, p. 32.

24 Boorstin, *The Americans: The Colonial Experience*, p. 351.

25 John Steele Gordon, *An Empire of Wealth*, New York, HarperCollins, 2004, p. 26.

26 Wood, *The Radicalism of the American Revolution*, p. 248.

27 Beard, p. 116.

28 Willard Stern Randall, *Thomas Jefferson: A Life*, New York, Henry Holt, 1993, p. 361.

29 Daniel Boorstin, "I Am Optimistic About America," *Parade Magazine*, July 10, 1994, p. 4.

30 James Q. Wilson, *The Moral Sense*, New York, The Free Press, 1993, p. 15.

31 David Brion Davis, *Slavery and Human Progress*, New York, Oxford Press, 1984, p. 81.

32 Wood, *The Radicalism of the American Revolution*, p. 186.

33 Barnard Lewis, *The Middle East*, New York, Scribner, 1995, pp. 174-177.

34 Joseph Ellis, *American Creation*, New York, Alfred A. Knopf, 2007, p. 35.

35 William Bennett, *America: The Last Best Hope*, Nashville, Thomas Nelson, 2006, p. 197.

36 Davis.

37 Wood, *The Radicalism of the American Revolution*, p. 61.

38 Bernard Bailyn, *The Ideological Origins of the American Revolution*, Cambridge, Mass., The Belknap Press, 1967.

39 Beard, pp. 64, 67.

40 Forest McDonald, *Recovering the Past*, Lawrence, University Press of Kansas, pp. 172–175.

41 Webster as quoted in Boorstin, *The Americans: The Colonial Experience*, p. 287.

42 Boortsin, *The Americans: The Colonial Experience*, p. 150.

CHAPTER 4

1 Bernard Bailyn, *To Begin the World Anew*, New York, Alfred Knopf, 2003, p. 41.

2 Gordon Wood, *The Radicalism of the American Revolution*, New York, Alfred Knopf, 1992, pp. 230, 232.

3 Wood, p. 234.

4 Wood, pp. 366–369.

5 Mark Noll, *America's God*, New York, Oxford Press, 2002, pp. 166, 233–235.

6 Alexis de Tocqueville, *Democracy in America*, New American Library, 1956, pp. 144–145, 48.

7 Tocqueville, *Democracy in America*, p. 1.

8 Max Lerner, *America as a Civilization*, New York, Simon & Schuster, 1962, p. 232.

9 Alan Macfarlane, *The Riddle of the Modern World*, New York, St. Martin's Press, 2000, pp. 181, 182, 186–187.

10 Wood, p. 234.

11 Tocqueville, *Democracy in America*, II, p. 711.

12 Joyce Appleby, *Thomas Jefferson*, New York, Times Books, 2002, p. 51.

13 Alexis de Tocqueville, *Journey to America*, p. 183.

14 Wood, pp. 306–307.

15 Alexis de Tocqueville, *Letters*, 1831.

16 Charles Taylor, *A Secular Age*, Cambridge, Mass., Harvard Press. 2007, pp. 186–189.

17 Richard Brookhiser, "Alexander the Great," *The Wall Street Journal*, June 30, 2005.

18 Alvin Felzenberg, *The Leaders We Deserved*, New York, Basic Books, 2008, pp. 116–119.

19 Bailyn, p. 33.

20 Wood, pp. 328–329.

21 Tocqueville, *Democracy in America*, p. 198.

22 Wood, p. 329.

23 James Q. Wilson, *On Character*, Washington D.C., AEI Press, 1991, pp. 29–30.

24 Paul Boller, *Presidential Campaigns*, New York, Oxford Press, 2004, p. 11.

25 Joseph Ellis, *American Sphinx*, New York, Vintage, 1996, p. 247.

26 Joseph Ellis, *His Excellency George Washington*, New York, Alfred Knopf, 2004, p. 252.

27 Felzenberg, p. 87.

28 Irving Brant, *James Madison*, Indianapolis, Bobbs-Merrill, 1961, pp. 407, 419.

29 Whig President William Henry Harrison died after only one month in office, and his successor, John Tyler, acted more as a Democrat than a Whig.

CHAPTER 5

1 Jon Meachem, *American Lion,* New York, Random House, 2008, p. xx.
2 Robert Remini, *Henry Clay,* New York, W.W. Norton, 1991, p. 250.
3 Robert Remini, *The Revolutionary Age of Andrew Jackson,* New York, Harpers Row, 1976, pp. 80–82.
4 Sean Wilentz, *The Rise of American Democracy,* New York, W.W. Norton, 2005, p. xix.
5 Meachem, p. 139.
6 Robert Remini, *Daniel Webster,* New York, W.W. Norton, 1997, p. 461.
7 Meachem, pp. 140–141.
8 Arthur Schlesinger, *The Age of Jackson,* Boston, Little Brown, 1945, p. 119.
9 Remini, *The Revolutionary Age of Andrew Jackson,* p. 397.
10 Richard Hofstadtler, *The American Political Tradition,* New York, Alfred Knopf, 1970, p. 209.
11 Pierre Berton, *The Invasion of Canada: 1812–1813,* Toronto, Penguin Books, 1980, p. 254.
12 John Marshall, *The Life of George Washington,* Philadelphia, C.P. Wayne, 1804.
13 John Steele Gordon, *An Empire of Wealth,* New York, HarperCollins, 2004, pp. 180–184.
14 Meacham, p. 356.

CHAPTER 6

1 Oliver Ellsworth wrote the Judiciary Act of 1789, which organized the federal courts and has been the subject of only minor changes over two centuries. The judiciary was originally by far the weakest and least effective branch of government. The court system was continually hampered by personnel turnover, lack of space and clerical support, and no mechanism for reporting its decisions. Nominations to the Supreme Court were almost routinely declined, because judges had to spend much of their time on circuit court duties riding on horseback as much as 10,000 miles a year. John Jay who served as Chief Justice and turned down re-appointment, said the court lacked "energy, weight, and dignity" as well as "public confidence and respect." Jay resigned to run for governor of New York. The second Chief Justice, John Rutledge, resigned before confirmation to become a member of the South Carolina Supreme Court, and the third, Oliver Ellsworth, resigned to take a diplomatic post.
2. William Sterne Randall, *Alexander Hamilton,* New York, HarperCollins, 2003, p. 246.
3 Jean Edward Smith, *John Marshall: Definer of a Nation,* New York, Henry Holt, 1998, p. 323.
4 See *Marbury v. Madison,* 5 U.S. 137 (1803) and *Fletcher v. Peck,* 10 U.S. 87 (1810).
5 John Steele Gordon, *An Empire of Wealth,* New York, HarperCollins, 2004, pp. 114–120.
6 Smith, pp. 146-147. See *Dartmouth College v. Woodward 17* U.S. 518 (1819) and *Bracken v. College of William and Mary* (3Call, 73) 252.
7 Smith, p. 1.
8 Charles and Mary Beard, *The Basic History of the United States,* New York, Doubleday, 1944, p. 195.
9 George Melloan, "The Central Economic Lesson of This Century," *The Wall Street Journal,* December 28, 1999.
10 Gordon, *An Empire of Wealth,* p. 97.
11 Jerry Muller, *Adam Smith in His Times and Ours,* New York, Free Press, 1993, pp. 2, 140.
12 Adam Smith, *Wealth of Nations,* London, Dent, 1904, Book One, p. 11.
13 Robert Friedel, *A Culture of Improvement,* Cambridge, Mass., MIT Press, 2007, pp. 211–234.
14 Stephen Yafa, *Big Cotton,* Viking Press, 2000, pp. 50–68.
15 Gordon, *An Empire of Wealth,* p. 85.
16 Paul Johnson, *A History of the American People,* New York, HarperCollins, 2000, p. 308.

17 Yafa, pp. 70–100.

18 Gordon, *An Empire of Wealth*, pp. 171, 173.

19 Daniel Boorstin, *The National Experience*, New York, Random House, 1965 pp. 10–15.

20 Walter McDougall, *Throes of Democracy*, New York, HarperCollins, 2007, p. 130.

21 Eric Jay Dolin, *Leviathan*, New York, W.W. Norton, 2007, pp. 205–206.

22 Gordon, *An Empire of Wealth*, pp. 100–101, 104.

23 Gordon, *An Empire of Wealth*, pp. 100–110.

24 John Steele Gordon, *The Great Game*, New York Simon & Schuster, 1999, pp. 56–57.

25 McDougall, p. 146.

26 Jared Diamond, *Guns, Germs and Steel*, New York, W.W. Norton, 1999, pp.

244–245.

27 Harold Evans, *They Made America*, New York, Little Brown, 2004, pp. 19.

28 Evans, pp. 36–41, 43–45.

29 Gordon, *An Empire of Wealth*, pp. 142-145. See *Gibbons v. Ogden* 22 U.S. 1(1824).

30 Larry Schweikart and Michael Allen, *A Patriots History of the United States*, New York, Sentinel, 2007, p. 191.

31 Gordon Wood, *Revolutionary Characters*, New York, Penguin Press, 2006, p. 26, 271.

32 Wood, p. 326.

33 Robert Fogel, *The Fourth Great Awakening*, University of Chicago Press, 2000, p. 58.

34 Gordon, *An Empire of Wealth*, p. 166.

35 McDougall, p. 153.

CHAPTER 7

1 Doris Kearns Goodwin, *Team of Rivals*, New York, Simon & Schuster, 2005. p. 545.

2 Lewis Lehrman, "Listen to Mr. Lincoln," *The Wall Street Journal*, February 12, 1996.

3 Allen Nevins, *The Emergence of Lincoln*, New York, Charles Scribner, 1950, p. 156.

4 Oswald Garrison Villard, *John Brown*, Boston, Houghton Mifflin, 1910, p. 560.

5 Robert Remini, *Daniel Webster*, New York, W.W. Norton, 1997, p. 184.

6 Mark Noll, *America's God*, New York, Oxford Press, 2002, pp. 216–217, 386.

7 Noll, p. 392.

8 Don Fehrenbacher, *The Dred Scott Case*, New York, Oxford Press, 1978, p. 36.

9 Anne Farrow, Joel Ling, and Jennifer Frank, *Complicity*, New York, Ballantine, 2005, pp. 139–153.

10 Alexis de Tocqueville, *Democracy in America*, New York, Harper & Row, 1969, v. 1, p. 342.

11 Don Fehrenbacher, "Why the War Came," in Geoffrey Ward, *The American Civil War*, New York, Alfred Knopf, 1990, p. 85.

12 Michael Holt, *American Whig Party*, New York Oxford Press, 1999, p. 89.

13 Jules Witcover, *Party of the People*, New York, Random House, 2003, p. 153.

14 Goodwin, p. 9.

15 David Brion Davis, *Inhuman Bondage*, Oxford, Oxford Press, 2006, p. 290.

16 H.W. Crocker III, *Robert E. Lee on Leadership*, New York, Three Rivers Press, 2000, p. 22.

17 David Herbert Donald, *Lincoln*, London, Jonathan Cape, 1995, pp. 176–177.

18 Donald, p. 224.

19 John Steele Gordon, *An Empire of Wealth*, New York, HarperCollins, 2004, p. 186.

20 Burke Davis, *Our Incredible Civil War*, New York, Holt Rinehart and Winston, pp. 28–29.

21 C. Vann Woodward, "What the War Made Us," in Geoffrey Ward, *The American Civil War*, New York, Alfred A. Knopf, 1990, p. xvi.

22 Shelby Foote, "Men of War: An Interview with Shelby Foote," in Ward, p. 264.

23 Donald, p. 337.

24 Allen Guelzo, *Abraham Lincoln: Redeemer President*, Grand Rapids, Michigan, William Erdmans Publishing, 1999, pp. 173–174.

25 Roy B. Basler, ed., *The Collected Works of Abraham Lincoln*, New Brunswick, New Jersey, Rutgers Press, 1953–1955, vol. 1, pp. 5–6.

26 Donald Phillips, *Lincoln on Leadership*, New York, Warner Books, 1992, pp. 21, 140–141.

27 George Will, "Interstate Ribbons of Progress," *The Washington Post*, July 9, 2006.

28 Paul Johnson, *A History of the American*

People, New York, HarperCollins, p. 458.

29 Allan Nevins, *Ordeal of the Union,* New York, Charles Scribner, 1947, p. 248.

30 Tom Wheeler, *Mr. Lincoln's T-Mails,* New York, HarperCollins, pp. xvi, 3–7, 17, 20.

31 Wheeler, pp. 93–95, 123.

32 Gordon, *An Empire of Wealth,* pp. 193–194.

33 Gordon, *An Empire of Wealth,* pp. 195, 199.

34 Goodwin, p. xvi.

35 Jeffrey Hummel, *Emancipating Slaves, Enslaving Free Men,* Chicago, Open Court Publishing House, 1996, pp. 142–143, 256.

36 Gordon, *An Empire of Wealth,* p. 202.

37 Allan Nevins, *The War for the Union,* New York, Charles Scribner's, 1960, pp. 65–70.

38 Robert Friedel, *A Culture of Improvement,* Cambridge, Mass., MIT Press, 2007, p. 376.

39 Bruce Catton, *This Hallowed Ground,* New York, Doubleday, 1955, p. 305.

40 Everett Carll Ladd, "The American Ideology" in Jeffery Eisenach and Albert Stephen Hanser, *Renewing American Civilization,* New York, McGraw-Hill, pp. 141–142.

41 Alonzo McDonald, "Foreword," in D. Elton Trueblood, *Abraham Lincoln: The Spiritual Growth of a Public Man,* Washington, D.C., The Trinity Forum, p. 7; Elton Trueblood, pp. 13–32.

42 Johnson, p. 482.

43 Bruce Catton, *A Stillness at Appomattox,* Garden City, New York, Doubleday, 1955, p. 367.

44 Catton, *This Hallowed Ground,* p. 138.

45 Peter F. Drucker, *The Effective Executive,* New York, HarperCollins, pp. 72–73.

46 Johnson, p. 478.

47 Catton, *A Stillness at Appomattox,* pp. 236–253.

48 Catton, *This Hallowed Ground,* p. 373.

49 James M. McPherson, "Why the War Came," in Ward, p. 352.

50 James M. McPherson in Ward, p. 352.

51 Hummel, p. 290.

52 Noll, p. 434.

53 Donald, p. 576.

54 Guelzo, p. 452.

55 Goodwin, pp. 748.

56 John Steele Gordon, *The Great Game,* New York, Simon & Schuster, 1999, p. 91.

57 C. Vann Woodward, "What the War Made Us," in Ward, p. 400.

58 Roger Ransom, *Conflict and Compromise,* Cambridge Press, 1989, pp. 218, 227, 241–242.

59 Michael Zak, *Back to Basics for the Republican Party,* Gaithersburg, Md., Signature Printing, 2003, pp. 90, 100–101, 112.

60 Douglas Blackmon, *Slavery By Another Name,* New York, Doubleday, 2008, p. 2.

61 Blackmon.

62 Blackmon, p. 364.

63 Robert Remini, *The House,* New York HarperCollins, 2006, p. 195.

64 Frank Scaturro, *President Grant Reconsidered,* New York, Madison Books, 1999, p. 10.

65 Peter Kolchin, *American Slavery,* New York, Hill and Wang, 2003, p. 230.

66 Kenneth Joust, *The Supreme Court A to Z,* Washington, D.C., Congressional Quarterly, 2003, p. 477; Frank Scaturro, *The Supreme Court's Retreat From Reconstruction,* Westport, Conn., Greenwood Press, 2000.

67 Peter Irons, *Jim Crow's Children,* New York, Penguin Boos, 2002, p. 28; *Plessy v. Ferguson,* 163 U.S. 536 (1896).

68 Harold Evans, *The American Century,* New York, Alfred A Knopf, 2000, pp. 34–35.

69 Juan Williams, *Eyes on the Prize,* New York Penguin, 1987, p. 10.

70 Kolchin, p. 236.

CHAPTER 8

1 Edison scholar Paul Israel quoted in Harold Evans, *They Made America,* New York, Little Brown, 2004, p. 166.

2 Evans, *They Made America,* pp. 165–166.

3 John Steele Gordon, *An Empire of Wealth,* New York HarperCollins, 2004, pp. 302–303.

4 Paul Johnson, *A History of the American*

People, New York, HarperCollins, 2000, p. 689.

5 Bob Davis and David Wessel, "A Dawn of Electricity, Feuds and Hype," *The Wall Street Journal,* April 6, 1998.

6 Gordon, *An Empire of Wealth,* pp. 307–308; Paul David quoted in Davis and Wessel.

7 Daniel Boorstin, *The Americans: The Democratic Experience,* Cardinal Books, p. 1.

8 Evans, *They Made America,* pp. 137, 153.

9 Walter McDougall, *Throes of Democracy,* New York, HarperCollins, 2007, p. 134.

10 Max Lerner, *America as a Civilization,* New York, Simon & Schuster, 1962, p. 216.

11 Roger Ransom, *Conflict and Compromise,* New York, Cambridge Press, 1989, p. 264.

12 Paul Kennedy, *The Rise and Fall of the Great Powers,* London, Fontana, 1990, p. 149.

13 Johnson, p. 531.

14 Peter Drucker, "The Rise, Fall and Return of Pluralism," *The Wall Street Journal,* June 1, 1999.

15 Johnson, p. 532.

16 Gordon, *An Empire of Wealth,* p. 259.

17 Johnson, p. 560.

18 Gordon, *An Empire of Wealth,* pp. 231–232.

19 John Steele Gordon, *Hamilton's Blessing,* New York Walker, 1997, pp. 99–100.

20 Johnson, p. 595.

21 Boorstin, pp. 320–329.

22 Gordon, *An Empire of Wealth,* pp. 172–176.

23 Johnson, p. 530.

24 Robert Friedel, *A Culture of Improvement,* Cambridge, Mass., MIT Press, 2007, p. 435.

25 Boorstin, pp. 340–345.

26 David Reynolds, *Waking Giant,* New York, HarperCollins, 2008, p. 344.

27 Gordon, *An Empire of Wealth,* pp. 153–158.

28 Johnson, p. 580.

29 Gordon, *An Empire of Wealth,* pp. 158–161.

30 Evans, *They Made America,* p. 12.

31 Seth Shulman, *The Telephone Gambit,* New York, Newton, 2008.

32 Jeffrey Frieden, *Global Capitalism,* New York, W.W. Norton, 2006, p. 5.

33 Edmund Morris, *Theodore Rex,* New York Random House, 2001, p. 273.

34 David McCullough, *The Path Between Two Seas,* New York, Simon & Schuster, 1977,

35 Friedel, p. 417.

36 Rinker Buck, *If We Had Wings,* New York, Crown Publishers, 2001, pp. 6–7.

37 George F. Will, "Soothing Assumptions," *The Washington Post,* June 27, 1996, p. A 29.

38 Recently historians, such as Seth Shulman have argued that Glenn Curtiss did not receive the credit he was warranted for his role in developing the airplane and flying technology.

39 Stephen Ambrose, *Nothing Like It in the World,* New York, Simon & Schuster, 2000, p. 377.

40 Johnson, p. 531, 533.

41 Gordon, *An Empire of Wealth,* pp. 217–218.

42 William Bennett, *America: The Last Best Hope,* Nashville, Thomas Nelson, 2006, p. 435; Ambrose, p. 377.

43 Ambrose, p. 222.

44 Ambrose, p. 253, 178.

45 John Gordon Steele, *The Great Game,* New York, Simon & Schuster, 1999, p. 99.

46 Gordon, *An Empire of Wealth,* pp. 210–216.

47 Gordon, *The Great Game,* p. 152.

48 Gordon, *An Empire of Wealth,* pp. 234–235.

49 Jean Strouse, *Morgan,* New York, Perennial, 2000, pp. 314–315.

50 Daniel Yergin, *The Prize,* New York, Simon & Schuster, 1991, p. 24.

51 Yergin, pp. 26–28.

52 Gordon, *An Empire of Wealth,* pp. 254–255.

53 Ron Chernow, *Titan,* New York, Random House, 1998, p. 177

54 Chernow, p. 249.

55 Allan Nevins, *John D. Rockefeller,* New York, Charles Scribner, 1953, vol. 2, p. 87; quoted in Chernow, p. 232.

56 Johnson, p. 603.

57 Yergin, pp. 178–179, 218–219.

58 Johnson, p. 532.

59 Gordon, *An Empire of Wealth,* pp. 242–249.

60 Johnson, p. 552.

61 Charles Slack, *Noble Obsession,* New York, Hyperion. 2002.

62 Henry Adams, *The Education of Henry Adams,* Boston, 1918, pp. iii, xxxiv.

63 Friedel, pp. 470–471.

64 Gordon *An Empire of Wealth,* pp. 297–298.

65 Harold Evans, *The American Century*, New York, Alfred Knopf, 1998, pp. 112–113.

66 Gordon, *An Empire of Wealth*, pp. 289–299.

67 Gordon, *An Empire of Wealth*, pp. 309–310.

68 Gordon, *An Empire of Wealth*, pp. 299–300.

69 Yergin, pp. 208–211.

70 Joel Garreau, *The Edge City*, New York, Doubleday, pp. 106–109.

71 Yergin, pp. 208–209.

72 "The First Hundred Years," *The Economist*, January 13, 1996.

73 Boorstin, p. 82.

CHAPTER 9

1 Edmund Morris, *The Rise of Theodore Roosevelt*, New York, Modern Library, 2001.

2 Mark Sullivan, *Our Times*, New York Charles Scribner, 1926, vol. 1, p. 137.

3 Brink Lindsey, *The Age of Abundance*, New York, HarperCollins, 2007, pp. 28–29.

4 Morris, *The Rise of Theodore Roosevelt*, pp. 400–436.

5 Marilyn Yalom, *A History of the Wife*, New York, HarperCollins, 2001, p. 190.

6 Max Lerner, *America as a Civilization*, New York, Simon & Schuster, 1962, pp. 274–278.

7 Ron Chernow, *The House of Morgan*, New York, Simon & Schuster, 1990, p. 81.

8 Lewis Gould, *The Presidency of Theodore Roosevelt*, Lawrence, University of Kansas, 1991, pp. 27–28.

9 Jean Strouse, *Morgan*, New York, Perennial, 2000, pp. 440–441.

10 Chernow, *Titan*, pp. 458, 534.

11 Strouse, pp. 302–303, 316.

12 Chernow, *Titan*, p. 568.

13 Daniel Yergin, *The Prize*, New York, Simon & Schuster, 1991, pp. 108–113.

14 Chernow, *Titan*, p. 559.

15 Josiah Bunting, *Ulysses S. Grant*, New York, Times Books, 2004.

16 Frank Scaturro, *President Grant Reconsidered*, New York, Madison Books, 1999, pp. 49–50.

17 David McCullough, *The Path Between the Seas*, New York, Simon & Schuster, 1977, pp. 26–27.

18 Scaturro, pp. 30, 32–33.

19 John Steele Gordon, *The Great Game*, New York, Simon & Schuster, pp. 129–134.

20 Quoted to William Riordan, reporter for *New York Evening Post*.

21 Roby Morris, *Fraud of the Century*, New York, Simon & Schuster, 2003, pp. 100–101.

22 Gordon, *The Great Game*, pp. 109–126.

23 John Steele Gordon, *An Empire of Wealth*, New York, HarperCollins, 2004, p. 264.

24 Gordon, *An Empire of Wealth*, pp. 266–269; Strouse, pp. 348–349.

25 John Steele Gordon, "History Repeats," *The Wall Street Journal*, October 7, 1998.

26 Gordon, *An Empire of Wealth*, pp. 278–279.

27 Marvin Olasky, *The American Leadership Tradition*, New York, The Free Press, 1999, p. 156.

28 Olasky, p. 157.

29 H.W. Brands, *The Reckless Decade*, Chicago University Press, 1995, pp. 262–265.

30 Brands, *The Reckless Decade*, p. 307.

31 Eileen Shields-West, *The World Almanac of Presidential Campaigns*, New York, World Almanac, 1992, pp. 92–134.

32 Neal Boortz and John Linder, *The Fair Tax Book*, New York, HarperCollins, 2005, pp. 15–16.

33 Robert Hormats, *The Price of Liberty*, New York, Times Books, 2007, p. 107; Paul Johnson, *A History of the American People*, New York, HarperCollins, 2000, p. 646.

34 Peter Jay, *The Wealth of Man*, New York, Public Affairs, 2000, pp. 217–220.

35 Henry Kissinger, *Diplomacy*, New York, Simon & Schuster, pp. 46–47.

36 Johnson, *A History of the American People*, p. 648.

37 Robert Kagan, "Liberalism and American Foreign Policy," edited by Hilton Kramer and Roger Kimball, *The Betrayal of Liberalism*, Chicago, Ivan Dee, 1999, pp. 176, 184.

38 Alvin Felzenberg, *The Leaders We Deserved*, New York, Basic Books, 2008, pp. 64–65.

39 Paul Johnson, *Modern Times*, New York, Harper Row, 1983, p. 35.

40 Gordon, *An Empire of Wealth*, pp. 295–296.

41 Johnson, *Modern Times,* p. 216.

42 John Steele Gordon, *Hamilton's Blessing,* New York, Walker, 1997, pp. 108–111.

43 Michael Barone, *Our Country: The Shaping of America from Roosevelt to Reagan,* New York, The Free Press, pp. 31–32.

44 Johnson, *Modern Times,* pp. 224–227.

45 Johnson, *Modern Times,* pp. 215–217.

46 David Greenberg, *Calvin Coolidge,* New York, Times Book, 2006, p. 55.

47 Johnson, *Modern Times,* pp. 218–223.

48 Robert Sobel, Coolidge: *An American Enigma,* Washington, Regnery, 1998, p. 393.

49 Jeffrey Frieden, *Global Capitalism,* New York, W.W. Norton, 2006, pp. 140–145.

50 Felzenberg, pp. 207–207.

51 Johnson, *Modern Times,* pp. 218–228

52 Greenberg, pp. 7, 101.

53 Robert McElvaine, *The Great Depression,* New York, Three Rivers Press, 1993, pp. 38–39.

54 Sobel.

55 David Brinkley, *Washington Goes to War,* Thorndike Press, 1988, p. 13.

56 Andrew Roberts, *A History of the English Speaking Peoples,* New York, Harper-Collins, 2006, pp. 37, 65.

57 Robert Friedel, *A Culture of Improvement,* Cambridge, Mass., MIT Press, 2007, p. 498.

CHAPTER 10

1 Cynthia Crossen, "Before the Depression, Economic Indicators Forecast Rosy Future," *The Wall Street Journal,* August 6, 2003.

2 Milton and Rose Friedman, *Free to Choose,* New York, Avon, 1979, pp. 62–63.

3 Alan Reynolds, "What Do We Know About the Great Crash?" *National Review,* November 9, 1999.

4 John Steele Gordon, *The Great Game,* New York, Simon & Schuster, 1999, p. 225.

5 John Steele Gordon, *An Empire of Wealth,* New York, HarperCollins, 2004, pp. 321–326.

6 Alvin Felzenberg, *The Leaders We Deserve,* New York, Basic Books, 2008, p. 155.

7 Gordon, *An Empire of Wealth,* pp. 318, 320–322.

8 Ben Bernanke, *The Great Depression,* Princeton Press, 2000, p. 153.

9 Andrew Roberts, *A History of the English Speaking Peoples,* New York, Harper-Collins, 2006, pp. 201–202.

10 Gordon, *An Empire of Wealth,* pp. 323–325.

11 Paul Johnson, *Modern Times,* New York, Harper Row, 1983, p. 244, 245.

12 Robert McElvaine, *The Great Depression,* New York, Three Rivers Press, 1993, p. 70.

13 Amity Shlaes, *The Forgotten Man,* New York, HarperCollins, 2007, pp. 148–149.

14 Robert Remini, *The House,* New York, HarperCollins, 2006, p. 307.

15 Felzenberg, p. 154.

16 William Manchester, *The Glory and the Dream,* New York, Bantom Books, 1984, pp. 12–15.

17 Gordon, *An Empire of Wealth,* p. 328.

18 Manchester, pp. 40-41.

19 Doris Kearns Goodwin, *No Ordinary Time,* New York, Simon & Schuster, 1944, p. 608.

20 Richard Hofstadtler, *The American Political Tradition,* New York, Alfred Knopf, 1970, p. 312.

21 Michael Barone, *Our Country,* New York, The Free Press, p. 54.

22 Bernanke, p. 8.

23 Robert J. Samuelson, *The Good Life and Its Discontents,* New York, Times Books, 1995, p. 94.

24 Hofstadtler, p. 312.

25 Goodwin, p. 190.

26 Manchester, p. 80.

27 Gordon, *An Empire of Wealth,* p. 337.

28 Amity Shlaes, "The Real Deal," *The Wall Street Journal,* June 25, 2007.

29 Arthur Schlesinger, *The Age of Roosevelt,* Boston, Houghton Mifflin, 1958, vol. 2, p. 60.

30 Tim Egan, *The Worst Hard Time,* Boston, Houghton Mifflin Company, 2006; George Will, "When the Skies Filled With Dust," *The Washington Post,* April 29, 2007, p. B07.

31 Johnson, *Modern Times,* pp. 157–161.

32 John Steele Gordon, *Hamilton's Blessing,* New York, Walker Publishing, 1997, p. 124.

33 Allen Meltzer, *A History of the Federal Reserve,* University of Chicago Press. 2003, p. 389.

34 Herbert Stein and Murray Foss, *The New Illustrated Guide to the American Economy,* American Enterprise Institute, 1995, p. 175; Meltzer, p. 271.

35 Felzenberg, p. 155.

36 Meltzer, pp. 9–11, 280.

37 Ron Coase, "The Federal Communications Commission," *The Journal of Law and Economics,* October 1959, pp. 1–40.

38 Douglas Irwin, *Free Trade Under Fire,* Princeton Press, 2002, p. 153.

39 Angus Maddison, "Monitoring the World Economy 1820–1992," Paris, OECD, 1995, p. 68.

40 Stephen Ambrose, *Nothing Like It In the World.* New York, Simon & Schuster, 2000, pp. 149–158.

41 Taylor Branch, *At Canaan's Edge,* New York, Simon & Schuster, 2006, pp. 341–342.

42 Carl Wittke, *We Who Built America,* New York, Prentice Hall, p. 487, 524–531.

43 James Loewen, *Lies My Teacher Told Me,* New York, Simon & Schuster, 1995 p. 164.

44 Ann Hagedorn, *Savage Peace,* New York, Simon & Schuster, 2007, pp. 112, 198, 377.

45 Rodney Stark, *For the Glory of God,* Princeton University Press, 2003, p. 346.

46 Manchester, pp. 130–131, 152–163, 388-389.

47 Alvin Hansen, quoted in Alan Brinkley, "The New Deal and the Idea of the State," in *The Rise and Fall of the New Deal Order, 1930-1980,* edited by Steve Fraser and Gary Gerstle, Princeton, Princeton University Press, 1989, p. 85.

48 Samuelson, *The Good Life and Its Discontents,* p. 24.

49 Dwight D. Eisenhower, *Crusade in Europe,* New York, Doubleday, 1948, p. 2.

50 Manchester, pp. 189, 216–217.

51 Henry Kissinger, *Diplomacy,* New York, Simon & Schuster, pp. 392–393.

52 Robert Hormats, *The Price of Liberty,* New York, Times Books, 2007, p. 134.

53 Paul Johnson, *A History of the American People,* New York, HarperCollins, 2000, p. 779.

54 Gordon, *An Empire of Wealth,* pp. 358–359.

55 Michael Barone, *Hard America Soft America,* New York, Random House, 2004, p. 31.

56 Roberts, p. 300.

57 Gordon, *An Empire of Wealth,* p. 353.

58 Manchester, p. 296; Robert Samuelson, "War and Remembrance," *The Washington Post,* January 12, 1994.

59 Larry Schweikart and Michael Allen, *A Patriot's History of the United States,* New York, Sentinel, 2004, p. 600.

60 Doris Kearns Goodwin, *No Ordinary Time,* New York Simon & Schuster, 1944, p. 608

61 Rinker Buck, *If We Had Wings,* New York, Crown Publishers, 2001, p. 22.

62 Daniel Yergin, *The Prize,* New York, Simon & Schuster, 1991, p. 382.

63 Joseph Schumpeter, *Capitalism, Socialism and Democracy,* New York, 1942.

64 Robert Friedel, *A Culture of Improvement,* Cambridge, Mass., MIT Press, 2007, p. 474.

65 Richard Overy, *How the Allies Won.* New York, W.W. Norton, 1996.

66 Johnson, *Modern Times,* pp. 400–401.

67 Barone, pp. 152–153.

68 Johnson *Modern Times,* p. 402.

69 Donald White, *The American Century,* New Haven, Conn., Yale Press, 1996, p. 192.

70 Alfred Sloan, *My Years With General Motors,* N. Y., Doubleday, 1963, pp. 232–233, 444–445.

71 Samuelson, T*he Good Life and Its Discontents,* p. 29.

72 Yergin, pp. 347, 357–363.

73 Goodwin, p. 510.

74 Roberts, p. 344.

75 Eisenhower, p. 202, 203.

76 Johnson, *Modern Times,* pp. 400–403.

77 Ira Flatow, *They All Laughed,* New York, HarperCollins, 1992, pp. 168–186, 192–196.

78 Yergin, pp. 376–377.

79 Daniel Boorstin, *The Democratic Experience,* New York, Random House, 1973, p. 584.

80 Friedel, p. 369.

81 Manchester, pp. 210–216.

82 Manchester, pp. 311–314, 337.

83 Manchester, pp. 268–269; George Will, "Breaking a Sinister Silence", *The Washington Post,* February 19, 1998, p. A17.

84 Johnson, *A History of the American People,* p. 801.

85 David McCullough, Truman, New York, Simon & Schuster, 1992, p. 424.

86 Bruce Lee, "Why Truman Bombed Hiroshima," *The Wall Street Journal,* May 5, 1995.

87 Roberts, p. 377.

88 Peter Drucker, *The Effective Executive,* New York, HarperCollins, 1966, pp. 89–91.

89 Stephen Ambrose, *Eisenhower,* New York, Simon & Schuster, 1990, p. 201–203.

90 Manchester, p. 359.

91 McElvaine, pp. 114, 326.

92 Hofstadtler, p. 311.

93 Manchester, p. 365.

94 White, p. 43.

95 Haynes Johnson, "What it Meant for America," *The Washington Post,* July 26, 1995, p. H6.

CHAPTER 11

1 Donald White, *The American Century,* New Haven, Conn., Yale Press, 1996, pp. 50–51, 57.

2 John Steele Gordon, *An Empire of Wealth,* New York, HarperCollins, 2004, p. 362.

3 These wars included the Crusades (eleventh through thirteenth centuries), the Hundred Years' War (1337–1453), Habsburg-Valois Wars (1522–1559), the French Wars of Religion (1562–1598), Eighty Years War (1568–1648), Thirty Years' War (1618-1648), English Civil War (1642–1651), Great Northern War (1700–1721), War of Spanish Succession (1701–1713), War of the Quadruple Alliance (1717–1720), War of Austrian Succession (1740–1748), Seven Years War (1755–1763), French Revolution (1789–1799), Napoleonic Wars (1792–1815), Polish-Russian War (1830–1831), Crimean War (1853–1856), Austria-Prussian War (1866), Franco-Prussian War (1870–1871), Spanish Civil War (1936–1939), World War I (1914–1918), and World War II (1939–1945).

4 John Lewis Gaddis, *The Cold War,* New York, Penguin Press, 2005, p. 15.

5 Jeffrey Frieden, *Global Capitalism,* New York, W.W. Norton, 2006, p. 289.

6 Frieden, pp. 259, 279.

7 Harold Evans, *The American Century,* New York, Alfred A. Knopf, 2000, p. 410.

8 White, p. 204.

9 Jung Chang and Jon Halliday, *Mao,* New York, Alfred A Knopf, 2006, pp. 296–297.

10 Robert Remini, *The House,* New York, HarperCollins, 2006, p. 354.

11 Gordon, pp. 378–380.

12 Chang and Halliday, pp. 358–359.

13 Dwight Eisenhower, *Mandate for Change,* New York, Doubleday, 1963, p. 114.

14 Alvin Felzenberg, *The Leaders We Deserve,* New York, Basic Books, 2008, pp. 132–133.

15 Ted Morgan, *Reds,* New York, Random House, 2003, p. 374.

16 Paul Johnson, *Modern Times,* New York, Harper Row, 1983, pp. 461.

17 Gunter Bischof and Stephen Ambrose in *Introduction to Eisenhower: A Centenary Assessment,* Baton Rouge, Louisiana State University Press, 1995, p. 4.

18 Lance Morrow, "Dreaming of the Eisenhower Years," *Time,* July 28, 1980, p. 33.

19 David Halberstam, *The Best and the Brightest,* New York, Ballantine Books, 1992, p. 39.

20 Stephen Ambrose, *Eisenhower,* New York, Simon & Schuster, 1990, pp. 575–576.

21 Fred Greenstein, *The Hidden-Hand Presidency,* New York, 1982.

22 David Stebenne, "Dwight D. Eisenhower," Alan Brinkley and Davis Dyer," *The Reader's Companion to the American Presidency,* Boston, Houghton Mifflin, 2003, p. 403.

23 Johnson, *Modern Times,* p. 462.

24 Paul Johnson, *A History of the American People,* New York, HarperCollins, pp. 831–832.

25 Ambrose, *Eisenhower,* p. 379.

26 Fred Greenstein, in Ambrose, *Eisenhower: A Centenary Assessment,* p. 62.

27 Halberstam, pp. 704–711.

28 Robert Hormats, *The Price of Liberty*, New York, Times Books, 2007, pp. 193–206.

29 Johnson, *A History of the American People*, p. 832

30 Bischof and Ambrose, *Eisenhower: A Centenary Assessment*, p. 253.

31 Eisenhower Paper: cited in ·Ambrose, *Eisenhower: A Centenary Assessment*, p. 252.

32 Taylor Branch, *Parting the Waters*, New York, Simon & Schuster, 1988, p. 322.

33 Johnson, *A History of the American People*, pp. 832–833.

34 Ambrose, Eisenhower, p. 386.

35 Colin Powell, *My American Journey*, New York Random House, 1999, p. 369.

CHAPTER 12

1 Bill Kovach and Tom Rosenstiel, *The Elements of Journalism*, New York, Three Rivers Press, 2001, pp. 9–10; John McCain, *Faith of My Fathers*, New York, Random House, 1999, p. 221.

2 Alexis de Tocqueville, *Democracy in America*, book 2, chapter 2, pp. 202–203.

3 Allen Guelzo, *Abraham Lincoln: Redeemer President*, Grand Rapids, Michigan, William Erdmans, 1999, p. 315.

4 David Halberstam, *The Powers That Be*, New York, Alfred A. Knopf, 1979, pp. 45–93.

5 Harold Evans, *They Made America*, New York, Little Brown, 2004, p. 216.

6 Evans, pp. 228–233.

7 Halberstam, *The Powers That Be*, pp. 9, 13–15.

8 William Manchester, *The Glory and the Dream*, New York, Bantom Books, 1975, pp. 190–195.

9 Charles Krauthammer, "FDR in a Wheelchair? No," *The Washington Post*, June 14, 1996.

10 David Halberstam, *The Fifties*, New York, Fawcett Columbine, 1993, p. 478.

11 Steven Covey, *The Seven Habits of Highly Effective People*, Free Press, 1989.

12 Richard Huber, *The American Idea of Success*, New York, Pushcart, 1987.

13 Theodore White, *America in Search of Itself*, New York, Harper Row, 1982, p. 167.

14 Daniel Boorstin, *The Image*, New York, Atheneum, 1962, pp. 195–205.

15 Evans, pp. 334–341.

16 Daniel Boorstin, *The Democratic Experience*, New York, Random House, 1973, pp. 392–393.

17 Boorstin, *The Democratic Experience*, pp. 392–397.

18 Boorstin, *The Democratic Experience*, p. 395.

19 Manchester, p. 586.

20 Vance Packard, *The Waste Makers*, New York, David McKay, 1960, p. 324.

21 Halberstam, *The Powers That Be*, p. 23.

22 Halberstam, *The Fifties*, p. 501.

23 Boorstin, *The Image*, p. 16.

24 Donald Ritchie, *Reporting From Washington*, Oxford University Press, 2005, pp. 188–189.

25 John Steele Gordon, *The Business of America*, New York, Walker, 2001, pp. 62–63, 241–243.

26 Brink Lindsey, *The Age of Abundance*, New York, HarperCollins, 2007, pp. 75, 83.

27 Serling quoted in Halberstam, *The Fifties*, p. 482.

28 Paul Johnson, *A History of the American People*, New York, HarperCollins, pp. 691–693.

29 Stanley Rothman, "Rise and Decline of Mass Culture," *Society*, July/August 1993. pp. 29–35.

30 Senator Joe Lieberman, "Crude, Rude, and Lewd," Democratic Leadership Council, *Blueprint*, Fall 2000.

31 William J. Bennett, "Television's Destructive Power," *The Washington Post*, February 29, 1996.

32 "APA Study Concludes TV Doesn't Portray Americans as They Really Are," *Communications Daily*, February 26, 1992.

33 "Columbine Killers Had Dreams of Fame," *The Atlanta Journal Constitution*, December 13, 1999.

34 Malcolm Gladwell, *The Tipping Point*, New York, Little Brown, 2006, pp. 266–267.

35 Robert Lichter, Linda Lichter, and Stanley Rothman, *Prime Time: How TV Portrays American Culture,* Washington D.C., Regnery Publishing, 1994, p. 416.

36 Lichter et. al, pp. 404–405.

37 Taylor Branch, *Parting the Waters,* New York Touchstone Books, p. 323.

38 Taylor Branch, *At Canaan's Edge,* New York, Simon & Schuster, 2008, p. 691.

39 Stephan and Abigail Thernstrom, *America in Black and White,* New York, Simon & Schuster, 1997, pp. 233–235.

40 Dom Bonafedem "Crossing Over," *National Journal,* January 14, 1989, p. 102; Richard Harwood, "Tainted Journalists," *The Washington Post,* December 4, 1988, p. L6.

41 David W. Brady and Jonathan Ma, "Spot the Difference," *The Wall Street Journal,* November 12, 2003.

42 Alice Schroeder, The Snowball, New York, Banton Books, 2008, p. 379.

43 Burton Yale Pines, *Out of Focus,* Washington D.C. Regnery Publishing, p. 240.

44 Richard Cohen, "The Terrorism Story—And How We Blew It," *The Washington Post,* October 4, 2001.

45 "Al-Qaida computer rich find for U.S.," *The Washington Post,* January 1, 2002.

46 Richard Morin, "What's Black and White and Red All Over," *The Washington Post,* June 15, 2006, p. A02.

47 Halberstam, *The Powers That Be,* p. 384.

48 David Frum, *How We Got Here,* New York, Basic Books, 2000, p. 36.

49 Marc Hetherington, "The Media's Role informing Voters' National Economic Evaluations in 1992", *American Journal of Political Science,* May 1996, pp. 372–395.

50 See *New York Times v. Sullivan,* 376 U.S. 254 (1964).

51 Frum, p. 161.

52 Richard Harwood, "The Messenger Shouldn't Bear All the Blame," *The Washington Post,* February 5, 1996.

53 "TV Coverage of Politics Negative," *Campaigns and Elections,* June 1996, p. 50.

54 T.R. Reid, "'Rising Sun' Meets 'Rising Sam'," *The Washington Post,* February 10, 1994, p. A1.

55 Barack Obama, *The Audacity of Hope,* New York Crown, 2006, p. 123.

56 Carl Bernstein, "Mending America's Fault Lines," *The Atlanta Constitution,* June 19, 1994.

CHAPTER 13

1 Jack Beatty, *The World According to Peter Drucker,* New York, Free Press, 1998, p. 117.

2 Peter Drucker, *The Age of Discontinuity,* New York, Harper & Row, 1969, p. 271.

3 Beatty, p. 56.

4 Beatty, pp. 124–125.

5 Andrew Roberts, *A History of the English Speaking Peoples,* New York, Harper-Collins, 2006, p. 167.

6 W. Michael Cox and Richard Alm, *Myths of Rich and Poor,* New York, Basic Books, 1999, p. 20.

7 Robert Barro, "21st Century Capitalism," *Business Week,* November 1994, p. 18.

8 Alan Greenspan, *The Age of Turbulence,* New York, Penguin Press, 2007, p. 467.

9 Some estimates conclude that 55–60 percent of economic growth is related to new knowledge and technology; 25–30 percent to education and training; and 15 percent to capital. Other estimates place more importance on capital. Nobel Laureate Robert Solow analyzed America's economic record from 1909 to 1949 and traced seven-eighths of growth to technological progress and improvements in the skills of workers. Edward Denison reached similar conclusions analyzing the postwar era of strong growth: for the period 1948–1973 technological progress accounted for the largest portion of the nation's 3.8 percent annual growth in GDP.

10 Robert Halberstam, *The Fifties,* New York, Fawcett Columbine, 1993, p. 139.

11 Halberstam, *The Fifties,* pp. 132–134.

12 Halberstam, *The Fifties,* pp. 498–499.

13 Stephen Van Dulken, *Inventing the 20th Century,* New York, University Press, 2000, p. 26.

14 Daniel Yergin, *The Prize,* New York, Simon & Schuster, 1991, p. 409.

15 Yergin, pp. 542–543.

16 Halberstam, *The Fifties*, p. 495.

17 David Halberstam, *The Reckoning*, New York, William Morrow, 1986, pp. 322–323.

18 Halberstam, *The Fifties*, pp. 115–117.

19 William Manchester, *The Glory and the Dream*, New York, Bantam Books, 1975, p. 1091.

20 Yergin, p. 551.

21 Cox and Alm, p. 31.

22 Halberstam, *The Fifties*, pp. 152–154.

23 Van Dulken, pp. 50, 108.

24 Bob Davis and David Wessel, *Prosperity*, New York, Random House, 1998, p. 9.

25 Thomas J. Duesterberg, "The Coming Boom in American Agriculture," Indianapolis, Hudson Institute, 1994.

26 Vance Packard, *The Waste Makers*, New York, Penguin, 1963, pp. 44–45.

27 Halberstam, *The Fifties*, pp. 156–159.

28 Cox and Alm, p. 63.

29 Joel Glenn Brenner, *The Emperors of Chocolate*, New York, Random House, 1999, p. 156.

30 Peter Jay, *The Wealth of Man*, New York, Public Affairs, 2000, p. 290.

31 John Steele Gordon, *The Great Game*, New York, Simon & Schuster, 1999, p. 393.

32 John Steele Gordon, *An Empire of Wealth*, New York, HarperCollins, 2004, pp. 366–367.

33 David Frum, *How We Got Here*, New York, Basic Books, 2000, p. 185.

34 Harold Evans, *They Made America*, New York, Little Brown, 2004, pp. 302–307.

35 Halberstam, *The Reckoning*, pp. 229–232.

36 Susan Pulliam and Karen Richardson, "Warren Buffett, Unplugged," *The Wall Street Journal*, November 12–13, 2005.

37 Thomas McCraw, *Prophets of Regulation*, Cambridge, Mass., Harvard Press, 1984, p. 259.

38 Jeffrey Frieden, *Global Capitalism*, New York, W.W. Norton, 2006, p. 439.

39 Theodore Caplow, Louis Hicks, Ben J. Wattenberg, *The First Measured Century*, Washington, D.C., AEI Press, 2001.

40 Evans, *They Made America*, pp. 381–383.

41 Marc Levinson, *The Box*, Princeton University Press, 2006, pp. 153–154, 233, 273.

42 Rinker Buck, *If We Had Wings*, New York, Crown Publishers, 2001, pp. 14–15.

43 Roberts, p. 283.

44 Larry Lessig, *Free Culture*, New York, The Penguin Press, 2004, p. 2.

45 Harold Evans, *American Century*, New York Alfred A. Knopf, 2000, p. 11.

46 Gordon, *An Empire of Wealth*, pp. 402–403.

47 Evans, *They Made America*, pp. 285–300.

48 Thomas Friedman, *The World is Flat*, New York, Farrar, Straus and Giroux, 2005, pp. 196–197.

49 Ira Flatow, *They All Laughed*, New York, HarperCollins, 1992, pp. 135–146.

50 Daniel Boorstin, *The Democratic Experience*, New York, Random House, 1973, pp. 386–389.

51 Robert J. Samuelson, *The Good Life and Its Discontents*, New York, Times Books, 1995, pp. 76–77.

52 George Lodge, *The New American Ideology*, New York, Alfred Knopf, 1980, p. 255.

53 Halberstam, *The Reckoning*, p. 316.

54 Halberstam, *The Reckoning*, p. 312.

55 Halberstam, *The Reckoning*, p. 317.

56 Halberstam, *The Reckoning*, p. 318.

57 Packard, pp. 93–94, 98–99. 103, 108–109, 128.

58 Frum, p. 21.

59 Joseph Juran, "Made in U.S.A.: A Renaissance in Quality," in *Manufacturing Renaissance*, edited by Gary Pisano and Robert Hayes, Cambridge, Mass., Harvard Business School Press, p. 194.

60 Frieden, p. 280.

61 Joseph Nye, *The Paradox of American Power*, New York, Oxford Press, 2002, p. 23.

62 Pisano and Hayes, p. xv.

63 Juran, p. 193.

64 George Gilder, *Microcosm*, New York, Simon & Schuster,, pp. 340–341.

65 Richard Katz, *Japan, The System That Soured*, Armonk, New York, M.E. Sharpe, 1998, p. 154.

66 Donald White, *The American Century*, New Haven, Yale Press, 1996, p. 400, 410.

67 See Andrew Dick, *Industrial Policy and Semiconductors: Missing the Target*, AEI, 1995 for an extensive analysis of the failures of government efforts to manage trade.

68 Peter Drucker, "A Weak Dollar Strengthens Japan," *The Wall Street Journal,* November 22, 1994.

69 William Lewis, *The Power of Productivity,* University of Chicago Press, 2004, p. 25.

70 Katz, p. 32.

71 Katz, p. 14.

72 Martin Kenney and Richard Florida, *Beyond Mass Production,* Cambridge, Mass., Oxford Press, 1993.

CHAPTER 14

1 T. R. Reid, *The Chip,* New York, Random House, 2001, pp. 3–18.

2 George Gilder, *Microcosm,* New York, Simon and Schuster, pp. 101–102.

3 Alan Greenspan, *The Age of Turbulence,* New York, Penguin Press, 2007, p. 493.

4 *Diamond v. Dehr* 450 U.S. 175 (1981).

5 Bill Gates, *The Road Ahead,* New York, Viking, 1995, pp. 44–63.

6 David Warsh, *Knowledge and the Wealth of Nations,* New York, W.W. Norton, p. 347.

7 Robert Friedel, *A Culture of Improvement,* Cambridge, Mass., MIT Press, 2007, p. 508.

8 Harold Evans, *They Made America,* New York, Little Brown, 2004, pp. 356–366.

9 John Steele Gordon, *The Business of America,* New York, Walker, 2001, p. 191.

10 Michael Malone, *Bill & Dave,* New York, Portfolio, 2007, p. 329.

11 Greenspan, p. 164.

12 Tom Friedman, *The World is Flat,* New York, Farrar, Straus and Giroux, 2005, pp. 56–57.

13 *Diamond v. Chakrabarty* 447 U.S. 303 (1980).

14 Frederick Dorey, "The Man Who Invented the Biotech Industry," *The Wall Street Journal,* December 14, 1999; Evans, pp. 420–431.

15 Sharon Begley, *Train Your Mind,* New York, Ballantine Books, 2007.

16 See their books, *Future Shock, The Third Wave, and War and Anti-War.*

17 The Tofflers' system is not unique or without parallels in history and philosophy. For example, Adam Smith had four stages— hunter-gatherer, pastoralist, settled agriculturist and commercial society.

18 Evans, pp. 11–14.

19 William Lewis, *The Power of Productivity,* University of Chicago, 2004.

20 Friedman, p. 129.

21 Robert Samuelson, "Wal-Mart as Red Herring," *The Washington Post,* August 30, 2006, p. A 19.

22 Charles Fishman, *The Wal-Mart Effect,* New York, Penguin, 2006, pp. 1–2, 143–145.

23 "Marconi's Brainwave," *The Economist,* April 28, 2007, p. 4.

24 Chalmers Johnson, *Nemesis,* New York, Metropolitan Books, 2006, p. 233.

25 Stephen Van Dulken, *Inventing the 20th Century,* New York University Press, 2000, p. 208.

CHAPTER 15

1 Mark Bauerlein, *The Dumbest Generation,* New York, Penguin, 2008, pp. 208–209.

2 Jonah Goldberg, *Liberal Fascism,* New York, Doubleday, 2007, p. 27.

Index

Acknowledgements

WRITING A BOOK IS A MAJOR UNDERTAKING and would not be possible without the assistance of many other people, particularly when it embraces a theme as complex and laden with controversial issues as is American history.

Carol Lawson spent months of her time wordsmithing the entire text. She played a vital role by making the author's dense prose amenable to understanding by the general public.

Bob Meyers provided cogent insights on just about every aspect of the book, undertaking the difficult task of making sense of the manuscript during some of its early stages.

Wickham Skinner spent long hours ploughing through some of the almost indecipherable early drafts of the chapters relating to business and the economy.

Alice Skinner provided useful analysis on family and civil society.

Stuart Shotwell was able to provide a good critique on the Civil War and other parts of the manuscript.

Bill Frenzel somehow managed to wage through one of the first versions of this book and give me important encouragement.

Frank Scaturra provided me with invaluable insight about the publishing world and the era of Ulysses S. Grant.

Elsbeth and Schuyler Loughrey provided their father with sufficient forbearance to complete the project, which has encompassed forty years of the author's life.

Susanna Lawson Buschman produced the beautifully designed book that you hold in your hands today.

My wife, Phoebe, went through all of the struggles her husband endured to produce *Political Will*, a journey which would not have been possible without her strong support.